CW01430574

THE TRIAL OF THE KAISER

THE TRIAL
OF THE KAISER

WILLIAM A. SCHABAS

OXFORD
UNIVERSITY PRESS

OXFORD
UNIVERSITY PRESS

Great Clarendon Street, Oxford, ox2 6dp
United Kingdom

Oxford University Press is a department of the University of Oxford.
It furthers the University's objective of excellence in research, scholarship,
and education by publishing worldwide. Oxford is a registered trade mark of
Oxford University Press in the UK and in certain other countries

Published in the United States of America by Oxford University Press
198 Madison Avenue, New York, NY 10016, United States of America

British Library Cataloguing in Publication Data
Data available

Library of Congress Control Number: 2018950871

ISBN 978-0-19-883385-7

Printed and bound by
CPI Group (UK) Ltd, Croydon, CR0 4YY

To Cherif

Preface

I think it was from Cherif Bassiouni that I initially learned about the failed efforts to prosecute international crimes following the First World War. Cherif, who passed away in September 2017, was the gentle patriarch of international criminal law for more than a generation. When I attended law school in the early 1980s, the rather modest collection of writings on international criminal law in the university library consisted almost exclusively of his work. Cherif was always extremely conscious of the historical dimension. He often began his lectures with references to the trial of the Kaiser that was imposed by Article 227 of the Treaty of Versailles. It represented the first call, at least in the modern era, for an international criminal court.

My work to try to deepen our knowledge of these early efforts at international justice began before Cherif took ill. He inquired frequently about the progress of my research. It was a great pleasure to inform him of discoveries in the various archives that might affect and even alter conventional assessments of the plans for a trial of Kaiser Wilhelm II. One day, some months after Cherif was diagnosed with his final illness, a courier arrived at my office in London with a thick file of research materials. Cherif had sent me the collection of documents that he had used to write an article on the subject that was published in 2002 in the *Denver Journal of International Law and Policy*.[1] Only days before he passed away, Cherif gave me some precious books from his own library dealing with the atrocities perpetrated in the First World War. I had already planned to dedicate this book to him. I wanted it to be a surprise. Now I regret that I never told him.

Besides Cherif, many other individuals provided me with assistance during the course of this project. Several Leiden University law students helped me to find and review published and unpublished materials in the Dutch language: Wout Apeldoorn, Lena Ellen Becker, Vasco van den Berg, Joey Bos, Cindy Buys, Misha Jans, David Koeller, Barbara van der Kroon, Ruben Libgott, Miloe van Nieuwmegen, and Lisanne Willemsen. Professor Michael A. Newton of Vanderbilt University pointed the way to the Tennessee archival materials on the Luke Lea caper to kidnap Wilhelm II. Jeremy Akin, a law student at the University of Georgia, visited archives and libraries in the United States and England on my behalf. Dr Aurora Rasi did the same in Italy. Dr Joe Powderly accompanied me on a field visit to Doorn, and he read a draft of the manuscript. Dr Harry Rhea shared research materials with me that he had assembled from archives in the United States for his own doctoral thesis, which is now published.[2] I am especially grateful to Professor André Klip, who is himself an expert on this subject and who most helpfully reviewed the entire manuscript.

John Louth and Matthew Cotton of Oxford University Press offered invaluable advice about the form the manuscript would take. John's guidance in finishing the project was quite decisive and I am immensely grateful to him. Merel Alstein saw the project through to completion. Penelope Soteriou carefully studied the manuscript, proposed countless corrections and improvements, and focused my attention whenever I was distracted by matters of less importance.

I thank you all.

William A. Schabas
London and Paris, 8 May 2018

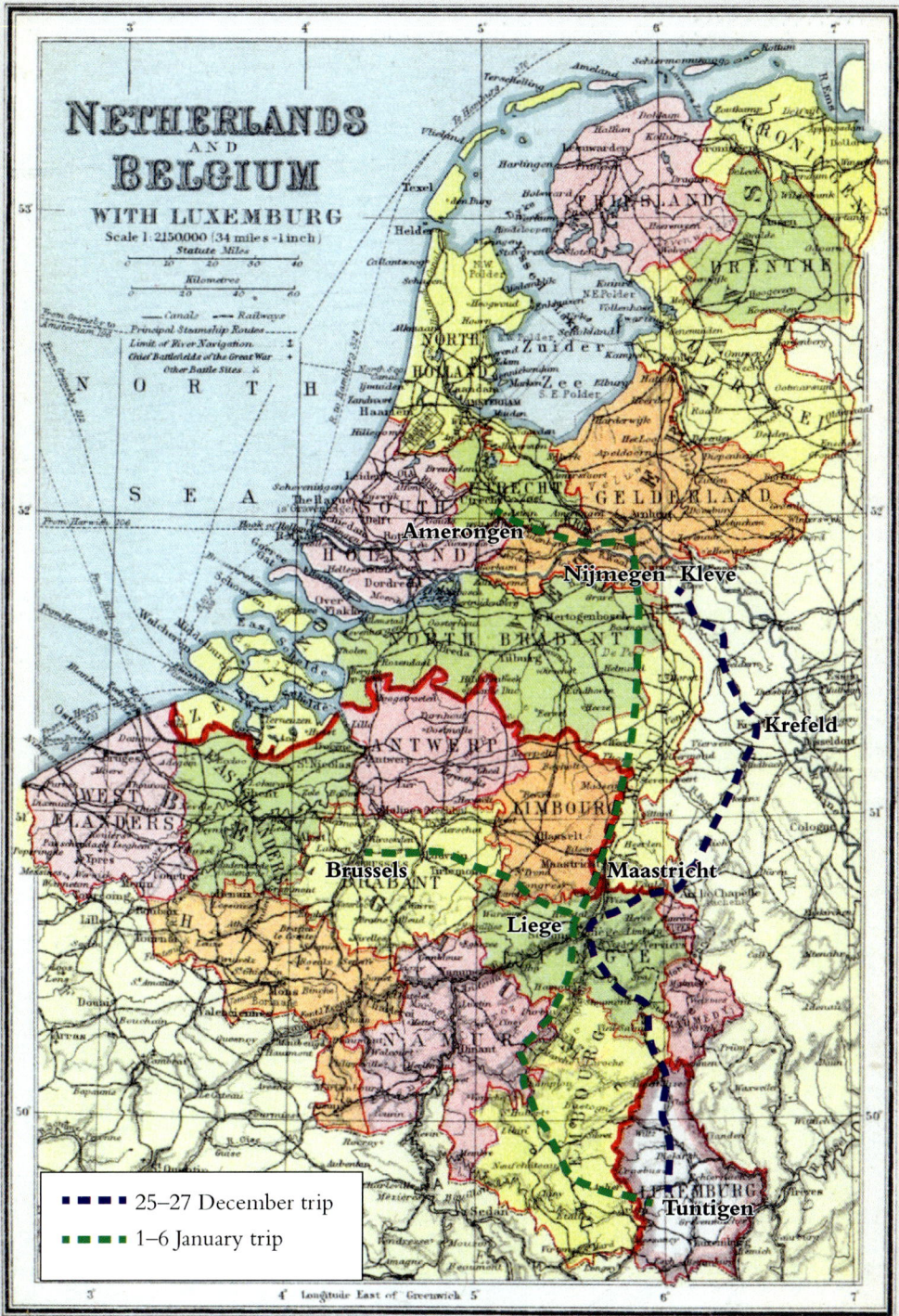

NETHERLANDS
AND
BELGIUM
WITH LUXEMBURG
Scale 1:2150000 (34 miles = 1 inch)
Statute Miles

NORTH SEA

Amerongen

Nijmegen Kleve

Krefeld

Brussels

Maastricht

Liege

Tuntigen

- - - 25–27 December trip
- - - 1–6 January trip

George Philip & Son. Ld

Map of Belgium, Luxembourg, and the Netherlands with routes taken by Luke Lea and his accomplices.

Col. Luke Lea, the former Senator who organised the attempt to kidnap Kaiser Wilhelm II.

Courtesy of the Tennessee State Library & Archives

Bust of the Kaiser with his final home, Huis Doorn, in the background.

Photo by William A. Schabas

The Kaiser's office at Huis Doorn, showing the saddle chair on which he liked to work.

Photo by William A. Schabas

Portrait of Kaiser Wilhelm at his summer home, the Achilleon, in Corfu.

Photo by William A. Schabas

A carriage from the Imperial train that took the Kaiser to the Netherlands, now in the Deutsche Technikmuseum in Berlin.
Photo by William A. Schabas

The Kaiser pacing the platform at Eijsden train station on 10 November 1918.
L'album de la guerre 1914–1919, 1926 (L'Illustration)

Cartoon from Punch.

Punch, 21 January 1920. The Internet Archive

Wilhelm II and Count Bentinck crossing the moat at Amerongen Castle.

U.S. National Archives and Records Administration

Contents

I

The Power of the Beaten Path

It is often said that international criminal justice began with the great Nuremberg trial of 1945 and 1946. In his opening address, American Prosecutor Robert H. Jackson spoke of how four great nations, flushed with victory, had stayed the hand of vengeance. International justice prospered for several more years. There was another international tribunal in Tokyo. Several thematic trials, of doctors, lawyers, generals, businessmen, and bureaucrats, were held in the Nuremberg courtroom where the great trial of the twenty-odd Nazi leaders had taken place. However, attempts within the United Nations to establish a permanent international criminal court soon stalled. They did not revive until the modern period in the final decade of the last century. But this familiar narrative of the beginnings of international justice is incomplete. The first chapter is missing.

In his post-trial report to President Harry Truman, Robert Jackson invoked the words of Benjamin N. Cardozo: 'The power of the precedent is the power of the beaten path.'[1] Jackson told the President that '[o]ne of the chief obstacles to this trial was the lack of a beaten path'.[2] Robert Jackson's role in beating the path cannot be gainsaid. But he did not set out on entirely unexplored land. Two and a half decades earlier, others had scouted the terrain, identifying welcoming contours and sometimes making prescient choices at forks in the road. They had also mapped some of the unfordable streams, the precipices, and the *culs-de-sac*, leaving blazes and waymarks to show the trails to be avoided as well as the way forward. Jackson's celebrated and richly deserved contribution to justice at Nuremberg owes a debt to the early pioneers and explorers of his figurative path.

Although there are a few examples of medieval trials with international dimensions, international criminal justice as we know it really originated during the final years of what Eric Hobsbawm called 'the long nineteenth century'. Central to these developments, which began within weeks of the outbreak of the First World War and concluded less than a decade later, were attempts to prosecute Kaiser Wilhelm II. Much effort was devoted at the legal and diplomatic levels to organising a trial of the German Emperor, who had abandoned his homeland and abdicated in November 1918. Article 227 of the Treaty of Versailles defined the formal charge, described the international tribunal, and called for his surrender. However, the trial of the Kaiser never took place. Other provisions of the Treaty of Versailles provided for prosecution of German officers, including those with the highest ranks like Hindenburg and Ludendorff. In the end, only a few trials of relatively minor military figures were conducted reluctantly by German courts as partial implementation of the treaty. The 'big fish' were never brought to book. This inchoate phase in the history of international justice left the half-formed trail, muddy and soon rather overgrown, that Robert Jackson and others transformed into a proper 'beaten' path in 1945 and 1946.

With the exception of the Charter of the United Nations, the Treaty of Versailles, adopted on 28 June 1919, was the most important international convention of the twentieth century. It was part of a complex package of treaties concluded during the great law-making exercise known as the Paris Peace Conference. Some of these confirmed the terms of peace with the vanquished; others provided for the creation of new States such as Poland, Czechoslovakia, and Yugoslavia. A huge range of issues was addressed in this orgy of international legislating. Germany's colonies were redistributed among the victors. It was an ugly, avaricious process disguised with the benign label of 'mandates' and the deceitful claim of implementing 'a sacred trust of civilisation' intended to benefit 'peoples not yet able to stand by themselves under the strenuous conditions of the modern world'.[3] New international bodies, principally the League of Nations and the International Labour Organization, were set up. Special measures and mechanisms to protect national, ethnic, racial, and religious minorities were enacted, forerunners of the more comprehensive international scheme of human rights developed in the post-Second World War period. Arrangements for railways, shipping, and a multitude of other issues were addressed. Alongside the many progressive features stood the unbearable harshness of the Treaty of Versailles for vanquished Germany. It is blamed for sowing the seeds of the Second World War.

Five of the treaties adopted at the Paris Peace Conference contained clauses providing for criminal prosecution of members of the armies of the defeated.[4] In a sense, this was an innovation, as such rules had not figured in earlier peace treaties. But there was nothing new or controversial in the principle by which prisoners in the custody of a party to a conflict could be punished for war crimes perpetrated during the conflict. The main purpose of the treaty provisions was to compel the defeated countries to surrender suspects for trial, and to cooperate in providing documents and conducting investigations. Trials were to take place before military tribunals of the victorious powers or, exceptionally, before joint tribunals of two or more countries. The treaty with Germany contained a special clause that was unique and unprecedented. Article 227 of the Treaty of Versailles stated that the former Emperor of Germany, Wilhelm II of Hohenzollern, was to be tried by an international criminal tribunal for a 'supreme crime against international morality and the sanctity of treaties'. The trial was to be held before a 'special tribunal' composed of judges from what were labelled the 'Principal Allied and Associated Powers': Britain, France, the United States, Italy, and Japan.

The international tribunal described in Article 227 is the atavistic forerunner of the International Criminal Court and of the various modern-day temporary or ad hoc tribunals, as well as of the Nuremberg and Tokyo international military tribunals. The vaguely framed charges in Article 227 nevertheless form the embryo of the 'core crimes'—genocide, crimes against humanity, war crimes, and the crime of aggression—that are prosecuted by today's international courts and tribunals, as well as those set up during the post-Second World War phase. Moreover, the notion that Heads of State may be threatened with criminal prosecution before an international tribunal for atrocities perpetrated while they were in office is today well accepted. Several have been charged, some have stood trial, and at least a few have gone to jail for lengthy terms: Rwanda's Prime Minister Jean Kambanda, Liberia's President Charles Taylor, Slobodan Milošević of Serbia and Radovan Karadžić of the Bosnian Serbs, Côte d'Ivoire's Laurent Gbagbo, Muammar Ghaddafi of Libya, Omar Al Bashir of Sudan, Chad's Hissène Habré, and Augusto Pinochet of Chile.

When it was suggested that the German Emperor be brought to trial for starting the First World War, there were no precedents, no examples of others who had met such a fate. British lawmakers looked to the case of Napoleon, a century earlier. Then their forerunners had called for a trial, but only before a French court. In 1815, it was unimaginable that the courts of another country might try France's former Emperor, and even more unthinkable that an international tribunal could be established for the task. And with what crime might Napoleon have been charged? In 1815, the only one the British lawyers could think of was treason against his own country. But the French had no taste for such a trial. Ultimately, exile to St Helena, by decree and without trial, was the best that British justice could propose.

Several factors explain the failure to implement Article 227 of the treaty and to hold the trial of the Kaiser. Although agreed to by the many Allied and Associated Powers that were parties to the treaty, only France and Britain showed any real enthusiasm for the idea, and even their leaders were divided on the subject. The charge itself remained a mystery. The words had been crafted rather casually by the US Secretary of State Robert Lansing, who was himself opposed to any trial. Lansing never thought he was drafting a legal instrument or treaty provision. Woodrow Wilson borrowed some of Lansing's words and fashioned the enigmatic text one evening. The following morning, the American President insisted that the other leaders sign the draft article. They complied without debate or real discussion. The Peace Conference was at a decisive point and it looked as if the talks might collapse. Wilson, who was in frail health, both physical and mental, had been threatening to return to the United States. Wilson's clauses on criminal penalties and the trial of the Kaiser were among the last to be accepted by the German negotiators.

Once the Treaty of Versailles had been signed on 28 June 1919, the British proceeded to organise the trial as if 'supreme crime against international morality and the sanctity of treaties' meant responsibility for initiating the First World War, breaching the neutrality of Belgium and Luxembourg, and violating the laws of armed conflict while it was underway by such acts as unrestricted submarine warfare. Royal families and monarchists throughout Europe closed ranks to protect the deposed Emperor. There was even some low-key resistance from the King of England, who shared a grandmother with the German Emperor. In the final days of the war, the Kaiser had obtained sanctuary in the Netherlands, possibly after being invited by the Dutch Queen. The country's governing elite was thick with pro-German elements, including the all-important Foreign Minister. Holland had remained neutral during the war. The Dutch bristled at bullying from the British and the French and refused to surrender the accused. At one point, rogue American soldiers led by a former Senator undertook a bizarre attempt to kidnap the German Emperor in the Dutch castle where he had been billeted, hoping to bring their prize to Paris as a gift to President Wilson.

The trial of the Kaiser is more than a good story. It marks the first international debates about perplexing issues of international law that retain their salience. For two months, in February and March 1919, the Commission on the Responsibility of the Authors of the War and on Enforcement of Penalties (set up by the plenary Peace Conference) debated the shape of prosecutions, including the special problems posed by the trial of Kaiser Wilhelm II. They could not agree, ultimately producing a majority Report accompanied by dissenting opinions from the American and Japanese delegations. The Report, together with the minutes of the debates within the Commission and its three Sub-Commissions, provides precious insights into the international law-making process, manifesting both recognition of the law as it stood at the time and visions of how it ought to be, and the direction in which it should be reformed and developed. Several of the world's leading international lawyers contributed to this process. A number of riddles stand out. Some of them, a century later, remain unsolved.

The first riddle concerns the immunity of a Head of State from prosecution. The issue was much debated during the Paris Peace Conference. Although the Americans and the Japanese went along with their European allies in agreeing to hold the trial, they never really accepted the claim that the victors were entitled to put the Emperor on trial without Germany's consent. That helps to explain why Article 227 is in the Treaty of Versailles. German acceptance of the trial of their former Emperor was a *sine qua non* for prosecution by the Allies. That Germany agreed to a trial of its former Emperor by signing and ratifying the Treaty of Versailles considerably weakens the claim that Article 227 represents a watershed in international law as far as the immunity of the Head of State is concerned.

The issue of Head of State immunity remains a live one to the modern day. In 1998, British judges ruled that the former President of Chile, Augusto Pinochet, could not claim immunity before their courts when charged with the international crime of torture.[5] For a few years, *Pinochet* was a radical precedent. According to the judgment, nobody was above the law as far as liability for international crimes was concerned, even a Head of State. But the influential ruling of the British courts was implicitly overruled four years later by an even more prestigious tribunal, the International Court of Justice. It held that a sitting or former Head of State could not be brought to trial before the courts of any country but his or her own. In effect, said the judges, one country cannot stand in judgment of another. However, the International Court of Justice acknowledged that a Head of State might also be tried by 'certain international criminal tribunals'.[6] In 2017, a special rapporteur of the International Law Commission proposed that the rule be revised, and that

trial be permitted before foreign courts of a former Head of State charged
with genocide, crimes against humanity, and war crimes. But the members
of the Commission were seriously divided on the subject, many refusing to
reverse the precedent of the International Court.[7]

At the International Criminal Court, a similar debate has swirled around
the President of Sudan, Omar Al Bashir. In 2009, a Pre-Trial Chamber of the
Court issued an arrest warrant against him for crimes against humanity and
war crimes. Two years later, it condemned Malawi for failing to arrest Bashir
while he was on an official visit. The Court referred to the 1919 debates at
the Paris Peace Conference, selectively citing one paragraph in the Report of
the Commission on the Responsibilities as evidence that the notion of immunity had already been rejected then.[8] Subsequently, a single judge of the
Court produced a more detailed analysis of the Peace Conference proceedings, reaching the same conclusion. He wrote that Article 227 of the Treaty
of Versailles 'marked the first step towards the development of a customary
international law norm that rejects official position immunity—even for
Heads of State—before international criminal courts'.[9] But most judges of
the International Criminal Court seem to have rejected the theory that there
is a rule of customary law lifting the immunity of a Head of State. Instead, they
have taken the view that when the Security Council assigned the situation
in Sudan to the International Criminal Court, its resolution implicitly lifted
the immunity of President Bashir.[10] That claim has little evidence to support
it, beyond sheer conjecture, as another judge of the Court has pointed out.[11]
The reception given to Bashir in their capitals by two permanent members of
the Security Council, Russia and China, makes it hard to conclude that when
they voted as permanent members of the Security Council they ever meant
to lift his immunity. It is useful to know more about what happened in 1919
in order to address this legal riddle.

The second riddle concerns the crime of aggression. The discussions at
the Paris Peace Conference manifested differences of opinion about whether
waging a war of aggression was a crime under international law or, for that
matter, whether it was even contrary to international law. A recent book, *The
Internationalists*, by Oona Hathaway and Scott Shapiro, traces the development
of the prohibition of aggressive war focusing on the adoption of the Kellogg–
Briand Pact in 1928.[12] But the real start of this debate was in 1919 as delegates
to the Paris Peace Conference considered at some length whether Wilhelm II
could be brought to justice for having started the war. The proceedings in the
Commission on Responsibilities provided the first international forum for

debate about the illegality of aggressive war. Regardless of the legal issue, there was, of course, an important factual matter. Did the Germans start the war? But assuming that was the case—the French and the British had few doubts about the matter—whether this amounted to a breach of international law, not to mention one that was punishable as a crime, remained an open question. Prominent experts in London and Paris told their governments that the legal prohibition of aggressive war had crystallised. The Americans and the Dutch were not convinced, although both said they would be happy to see international law evolve in such a direction.

That international law prohibits the waging of aggressive war is no longer in doubt. The Kellogg–Briand Pact of 1928 confirmed that this was the direction taken by international law.[13] The issue was firmly resolved after the Second World War by the Charter of the United Nations. German and Japanese leaders were convicted by the Nuremberg and Tokyo international military tribunals for the waging of aggressive war under the heading 'crimes against peace', as well as war crimes and crimes against humanity conducted in the course of the war. Judges of the International Military Tribunal labelled aggression 'the supreme international crime differing only from other war crimes in that it contains within itself the accumulated evil of the whole'.[14] Although there have been many trials since then for war crimes and crimes against humanity, the crime of waging aggressive war has had a more uncertain career, putting its 'supreme' status in doubt. The first of the modern international courts, the International Criminal Tribunal for the former Yugoslavia and the International Criminal Tribunal for Rwanda, set up by the United Nations Security Council in the early 1990s, were not even given jurisdiction over the crime of aggression.

When the Rome Statute of the International Criminal Court was adopted, in 1998, delegates to the Diplomatic Conference could not agree on how to formulate the crime of aggression. Some were even indifferent about its inclusion in the Rome Statute at all. Eventually, rather feeble amendments to the Rome Statute incorporating the crime of aggression were adopted at the Kampala Review Conference in 2010.[15] They were further weakened when the hesitant final step in activating the Court's jurisdiction over aggression was taken, in December 2017.[16] The restrictive jurisdictional formula for the crime of aggression contrasts dramatically with that for the other core crimes of genocide, crimes against humanity, and war crimes. Whereas in principle the Statute applies to crimes committed on the territory of a State Party regardless of the nationality of the offender, an exception is made for the crime of aggression. Moreover, it cannot be prosecuted at all if committed by a country that has not joined the Court. Thus, despite apparent unanimity on the issue of the illegality of the use of force to settle international disputes dating to 1945, the threat that individuals will be brought to justice by an international tribunal remains empty. Impunity for launching a war of aggression thrives, just as it did in 1919.

Retroactive prosecution is another riddle. Given that in 1919 there had never previously been any prosecution at the international level nor any codification of international crimes, any attempt to bring the Kaiser to justice confronted the objection that this was the retroactive application of criminal law. Such a practice was prohibited by many national constitutions, but there was no international legal standard. That would have to wait until the adoption of the Universal Declaration of Human Rights in 1948. Article 11(2) of the Declaration affirmed that no one could be convicted of a crime 'on account of any act or omission which did not constitute a penal offence, under national or international law, at the time when it was committed'.[17] But even in 1919, concerns about the perceived unfairness of a trial for crimes that had not been codified when they were committed greatly concerned international lawyers. It was one of the objections raised by the Dutch in refusing to extradite, as well as by the Americans in withholding consent with the majority conclusions at the Peace Conference.

The problem might appear to be resolved at the International Criminal Court. It cannot deal with crimes perpetrated before the entry into force of the Rome Statute in 2002.[18] This seems to have very largely neutralised any objection by defendants on the grounds of retroactivity. Yet the issue recurs constantly at temporary or ad hoc tribunals and, probably even more important, before national courts. International human rights institutions insist upon various forms of accountability for past abuses. It is a component of the doctrine of transitional justice as well as a so-called procedural obligation imposed upon States as part of their respect for the right to life and the prohibition of torture. For example, several cases before the European Court of Human Rights have concerned efforts by States in Central and Eastern Europe to prosecute acts perpetrated in the 1940s and 1950s using definitions of crimes that were only adopted in the 1990s. Sometimes the Court has endorsed the convictions,[19] sometimes it has reproved them.[20]

Criminal prosecution of even older offences, such as enforced disappearances in fascist Spain or genocide in the Ottoman Empire, is quite unlikely if not impossible because there may be no potential defendants left alive. Yet the characterisation of the acts using the language of international criminal law remains an important issue at the political level. In other words, even if there is no possibility of a criminal trial, is it appropriate to condemn atrocities perpetrated in the early decades of the twentieth century using the labels genocide, crimes against humanity, war crimes, and aggression?

The debates in 1919 also make useful contributions to other issues of international criminal law. Although no international criminal court was established, there was considerable discussion not only about the desirability of setting one up, but also about its composition and procedure. The issue of extradition, or surrender, of the Kaiser also posed important problems. Ultimately, of course, when the Dutch refused to give him up, the Allies quite quickly abandoned their efforts. They might well have explored other options, such as trial *in absentia*. Perhaps they would have succeeded in persuading the Netherlands to host the trial, thereby dodging the extradition issue entirely. As the months wore on, they were increasingly ambivalent. For many, Dutch refusal brought not only humiliation, but also relief.

Finally, and outside the strictly judicial sphere, the political factors cannot be overlooked. The thirst for justice seemed to vary from one country to another, and it also waned as time went by. Without greater unanimity, it was unreasonable to expect the trial to go ahead. The Dutch seemed to sense this. Their determination to refuse surrender of the Kaiser became firmer with each signal from London, Paris, Washington, and Rome that a 'Napoleonic solution', that is, exile in a remote place, would be a satisfactory substitute for trial and judgment. This left a stain on the image as a home for international justice now cultivated by the Netherlands.

After initially resisting the British and French demands for justice, President Woodrow Wilson agreed to compromise. Article 227 of the Treaty of Versailles, calling for the establishment of a 'special tribunal' with judges from five different countries, was the result. As things turned out, the call was premature. The plan to try the Kaiser and to establish an international tribunal may have been an inauspicious beginning, but it was hardly the end of a failed idea.

2

'Hang the Kaiser'

Kaiser Bill, we are coming,
With our army over sea.
And you forgot our motto.
Which is, 'Do not tread on me.'
It's a job we never started,
But we'll finish Germany;
And we'll hang you, Kaiser William.
On the highest linden tree.[1]

Hostilities on the Western Front began in the first days of August 1914. A speedy victory over France required German forces to avoid fortifications on the border between the two countries and instead to pass through neutral Belgium and Luxembourg on their way to Paris. When he addressed the Reichstag on 4 August, Chancellor Bethmann-Hollweg conceded that Germany had violated international law, promising to repair the wrong once victory was assured.[2] Speaking to the British Ambassador that evening, Bethmann-Hollweg notoriously described the 1839 treaty protecting Belgian neutrality as 'a scrap of paper' for which 'Great Britain was going to make war on a kindred nation who desired nothing better than to be friends with her'.[3] When Foreign Minister Edward Grey addressed the House of Commons on 3 August, he stressed the profound British strategic interest in a neutral Belgium rather than the sanctity of an international treaty. Grey cited Gladstone who, at the time of the Franco-Prussian War of 1870, said Britain had 'an interest in the independence of Belgium which is wider than that which we may have in the literal operation of the guarantee'.[4]

Within days of the German attack, great brutality by the invaders, described as 'violations of the laws and customs of war', was being reported. On

The Trial of the Kaiser. William A. Schabas. © William A. Schabas, 2018. Published 2018 by Oxford University Press.

7 August 1914, the Belgian Minister of Justice announced the establishment of a commission charged with gathering evidence of enemy violations of 'the law of nations and the duties of humanity'. A series of reports was published in the months that followed.[5] In France, on 23 September 1914, the ministers of the interior and of war established a commission of inquiry. Chaired by Georges Payelle, a senior judge, it issued twelve detailed reports on German atrocities over the course of the war, addressing a range of issues, including the use of gas and other prohibited means of warfare, such as dum-dum bullets.[6] In early December 1914, Britain set up the Committee on Alleged German Outrages, chaired by Viscount James Bryce. Its report, published in May 1915, documented a range of violations in occupied Belgium, including massacres of the civilian population, looting, wanton destruction of property, rape of women and girls, the use of human shields, and abuse of prisoners. It concluded that 'in the conduct of the war generally innocent civilians, both men and women, were murdered in large numbers, women violated, and children murdered'. Moreover, 'looting, house burning, and the wanton destruction of property were ordered and countenanced by the officers of the German army'. The Commission said that 'the rules and usages of war were frequently broken'.[7] After the war, there was considerable scepticism about the validity of the reports of atrocities, particularly during the 1920s and 1930s, when it was suggested that these were exaggerations of Allied propagandists. But more recently, historians have tended to attribute considerable credence to the allegations and to judge those who made them, like Bryce, as persons of integrity.[8]

English public opinion was further galvanised when nurse Edith Cavell was convicted of treason by German courts for assisting Allied soldiers to escape from occupied Belgium. She was executed by firing squad on 12 October 1915. A huge monument to Nurse Cavell, bearing the inscription 'Humanity', sits at the foot of London's Charing Cross Road, across from the National Portrait Gallery. Shortly after her death, Charles Fryatt, the skipper of an English merchant steamship trading with the Dutch and frequently crossing the North Sea, was sentenced to death by a German court-martial for ramming a submarine. Fryatt was executed by firing squad on 27 July 1916. His execution, like that of Nurse Cavell, was often invoked as an act requiring criminal punishment of the Germans who were responsible.[9]

During the early days and months of the First World War, captured enemy combatants were tried for various violations of the laws and customs of war. For example, on 5 October 1914, the newspaper *Écho de Paris* reported that two German soldiers had been tried by French courts and sentenced to death for pillage.[10] On 26 January 1915, Karl Vogelgesang was sentenced to death for pillage and arson committed in Belgium.[11] *Le Temps* published a call for war crimes trials by a French prosecutor.[12] Initially, the British treated the crews of German submarines as war criminals who were to be tried for breaching international law. When Germany retaliated, by putting captured officers in military detention barracks, Britain changed its policy with respect to sub-mariners. By mid-1916, both sides in the conflict had come to understand the vulnerability of their own prisoners, and the danger of escalating reprisals. Reciprocity in staying criminal prosecution while the war was underway no doubt saved the lives of many prisoners of war. Eventually, the practice of deferring prosecutions was codified to some extent in the first Geneva Convention on prisoners of war, but that would have to wait until 1929.[13]

Had the Germans won the war, they might well have insisted on charging French and British leaders, and perhaps even King George V, with provoking the conflict. German thinking on this point became evident when Romania surrendered to Germany and Austria in May 1918. Military leaders in Berlin wanted to try Romania's monarch, King Ferdinand, and the country's polit-ical leaders. The charge would have been launching war against Austria and Germany in 1916, in violation of an international agreement. The onerous Treaty of Bucharest accepted by Romania reserved the right of Germany and Austria to detain those prisoners who were suspected of violating the laws and customs of war. In the Reichstag, an independent socialist deputy warned the government that punishment of Romanian war criminals might provide a justification to the Allied Powers for doing the same thing. Most Germans were not worried because of their confidence in a favourable out-come of the war.[14]

During 1916, the French and the British discussed various measures to deal with German war crimes. In France, proposals for an international court for the repression of war crimes were warmly received by the central committee of the *Ligue pour la défense des droits de l'homme et du citoyen*.[15] In England, Hugh Bellot, one of the country's prominent international lawyers,[16] wrote that 'the Hague Court, if instituted, might be invested with an original jurisdiction for the trial and punishment of offenders brought before it either during the war or upon its conclusion, or both'.[17] The French Government prepared two draft agreements, one for a court in which all of the Allies would participate, the other for a court to be established only by Britain and France. These are the first known drafts of an international criminal court statute at the offi-cial or governmental level. Trial was to be by a jury composed of nationals of the participating countries. The tribunal would exercise jurisdiction over 'ordering, allowing to be ordered or perpetrating on land or sea, crimes, killings, murders and assaults of any kind against the life and security of persons in violation of the laws and customs of war on land or sea'. The tribunal would be able to function in the absence of the accused, the surrender of those judged *in absentia* being a condition of any peace agreement.[18]

That the German Emperor himself might be punished for leading his country, and the continent, into war, and that he could be held personally accountable for various outrages attributable to German combatants, was an idea that surfaced only occasionally. An unsigned article in the *Edinburgh Review*, published in October 1914, described the invasion of Belgium not as an 'act of war', but as a 'criminal act', insisting that 'the nations of the world must devise means to bring the authors of such act to trial and punishment'.[19] But at sessions of the French General Society of Prisons in 1915 and 1916, where there was 'a very good debate' about prosecuting war crimes committed by Germans before French courts, 'the question of the responsibility of the German Emperor was barely touched'.[20]

When a German submarine torpedoed the ocean liner *RMS Lusitania* off the south coast of Ireland on 7 May 1915, taking the lives of more than 1,000 civilian passengers, there were calls to hold the German Emperor personally responsible for the atrocity. Lord Robert Cecil, a future Nobel Peace Prize laureate, told a meeting at Chelsea Town Hall that 'for the terrible outrages, the wholesale breaches of every law and custom of civilised warfare which the Germans had committed, the people who were responsible were the German rulers, the Emperor and those who were closely advising him, and it was upon them if possible that our punishment and wrath should fall'.[21] A coroner's jury in Kinsale, Ireland, near where the *RMS Lusitania* went down, delivered a verdict stating that 'this appalling crime was contrary to international law and the conventions of all civilised nations, and we therefore charge to [sic] officers of the said submarine and the Emperor and Government of Germany, under whose orders they acted, with the crime of wilful and wholesale murder before the tribunal of the civilised world'.[22]

Prime Minister Asquith's response to the sinking of the *RMS Lusitania*, which seemed to indicate that perpetrators who acted under orders were immune to punishment, was criticised as being 'too vague' and 'quite ineffective as a preventive measure'.[23] 'If each offender can plead as an excuse the order of his immediate superior officer we arrive at last at the German Government or the Kaiser', wrote Hugh Bellot. But Bellot did not seem to think that prosecuting the Kaiser was feasible either. 'To indict a Government is as futile as to indict a nation, and even a Hague Tribunal would hesitate to create another St. Charles the Martyr in the person of William the Second.'[24]

As the war drew to a close, in the final months of 1918, policy-makers in Britain and France increased their attention to the prosecution of war crimes. Initially, however, Kaiser Wilhelm did not figure in the discussions. Angered by new reports of German atrocities as the armies retreated in north-eastern France, the French approached the British with a request for 'a solemn declaration on the part of the Allies, having as its object the *punishment* of, and *reparation* for, these crimes'.[25] But the British did not endorse the French proposal. The Imperial War Cabinet agreed to express 'the warmest sympathy with the French Government', but thought 'suggestions as to actual method should be more precise'.[26] As an alternative, Foreign Minister Balfour suggested that Britain threaten Germany with reprisals, specifically the aerial bombing of several German towns, a measure he said would 'produce the maximum of terror'.[27] The French went ahead on their own, informing Germany that organisers as well as perpetrators of crimes should be held accountable, morally, penally, and materially, regardless of their position. 'Acts so contrary to international law and to the very principle of all human civilisation shall not go unpunished', France insisted.[28] When Foreign Minister Stéphane Pichon reported on the government's position in the Senate on 15 October, he received a firm endorsement.[29]

On 30 September 1918, Britain's most senior lawyers, Attorney General Frederick E. Smith (later Lord Birkenhead) and Solicitor General Gordon Hewart, who were known as the Law Officers of the Crown, urged Prime Minister Lloyd George to set up a 'strong Committee of Jurists and others' to consider how to prosecute German war criminals. Smith and Hewart noted that a French Committee was 'working with similar aims'.[30] Smith, who had built his reputation prosecuting the Irish nationalist Roger Casement in 1916, was already on record as a strong advocate of criminal trials. Speaking to the New York State Bar Association in January 1918, Smith contended that war crimes prosecutions would do more to preserve peace than establishment of a League of Nations, an institution for which he had no enthusiasm.[31] At a meeting in Liverpool on 18 September 1918, Smith said he had given 'close attention to the subject of international law, and I will tell you plainly that there is in international law abundant warrant for the punishment, both in their persons and in their purses, of proved and identified criminals'.[32]

The British Set Up a Committee

Early in November, several days before the armistice, but at a time when the outcome of the conflict was no longer in any doubt, acting under the authority of the War Cabinet, Attorney General Smith appointed a Committee of Enquiry into Breaches of the Law of War. The Committee was chaired by Sir John Macdonnell, who was then King's Remembrancer, a senior judicial post of ancient origin. The Vice-Chairman was J. H. Morgan, a military lawyer. A number of distinguished jurists were named to sit on the Committee, including Frederick Pollock, a prominent barrister who would later be instructed to prepare the case against the Kaiser for trial. Hugh Bellot and J. E. G. de Montmorency served as secretaries of the Committee. The Committee was assigned to inquire into and report upon the facts with respect to 'breaches of the laws and customs of war, affecting members of the British armed forces or other British subjects, committed by the forces of the German Empire and their allies on land, on sea, and in the air during the present war'. This was to include assessing the degree of responsibility of German military officials, 'including the German General Staff, or other highly placed individuals'. There was no explicit reference to the German Emperor himself. The Committee was also to consider issues concerning the creation of an appropriate tribunal for such offences.[33] Sub-Committees were established to deal with offences on land, at sea, and in the air. A fourth Sub-Committee was to address legal matters. It was chaired by Professor J. H. Morgan and included Sir Frederick Pollock, who had earlier served on the Bryce Committee.

The Attorney General addressed the Committee at its first meeting, on 6 November 1919. 'It is certain that in the events that have taken place in the last four and a half years many great crimes against International Law have been committed', said Smith. 'This conclusion is not very vigorously disputed even in Germany today. The very origin of the War, the violation of Belgium, will for all time, I think, be remembered in the pages of history as one of the greatest crimes against civilisation.'[34] The task of the Committee, he said, was 'fixing and assigning responsibility for specific breaches of International Law in its many branches and departments of the War'. He gave as an example abuses of prisoners of war.[35] Kaiser Wilhelm II was not mentioned.

Prime Minister Lloyd George was questioned at a meeting of the Imperial War Cabinet about Allied plans for prosecution. The Imperial War Cabinet consisted not only of senior British ministers, but also representatives of the Dominions: Canada, Australia, New Zealand, South Africa, and Newfoundland, as well as India. Lloyd George said that criminal justice had figured in discussions with the Allies about the terms of an armistice, but that the matter had been 'left over until the peace conference'.[36] Indeed, the issue had not been addressed in discussions of war aims and terms of armistice in recent meetings of the Cabinet. Of course, the fate of the Kaiser himself was an inevitable concern, but it is not apparent that the possibility of prosecution was as yet taken seriously. On 11 November, after the armistice had been signed, British leaders celebrated with an 'intimate dinner' at 10 Downing Street. Sir Henry Wilson, who was Chief of the Imperial General Staff, recalled that: 'Lloyd George wants to shoot the Kaiser. F.E. [Smith] agrees. Winston does not.'[37] We do not know at what stage of the evening's revelry this discussion occurred, but it is likely that drink had been taken previously.

On 14 November, Parliament was dissolved and an election was called. The electorate had expanded hugely compared with the previous Parliamentary elections, in 1910. There were now three times as many eligible voters, more than 21 million, compared with fewer than 8 million for the previous ballot. New legislation ensured the vote to most women over the age of 30 and all men over the age of 21. For those who had served in the war, the voting age was lowered to 19. The terms of peace with Germany did not initially feature in what became known as the 'khaki election', where issues of social policy and Irish independence were at the heart of the preliminary campaigning. Early in the campaign, Lloyd George spoke cautiously of punishing Germany and its leaders: 'We must not allow any sense of revenge, any spirit of greed, and grasping desire to over-rule the fundamentals of justice', he said. As the campaign reached its paroxysm in early December, Lloyd George issued his 'Final Manifesto of Six Points', two of which were 'Trial of the Kaiser' and 'Punishment of those responsible for atrocities'. This was soon transformed into the more brutal slogan 'Hang the Kaiser', although Lloyd George claimed that these were not his words. He had only called for prosecution, not execution.[38]

Many years later, Vittorio Emanuele Orlando, Italy's Prime Minister in 1918 and 1919, described the thirst for justice that emerged in Britain in the aftermath of the war and that he witnessed first-hand in London. There was 'a state of anger and grudge that exploded immediately after the armistice' and that 'worsened specifically between the middle and end of November 1918, by when tens of thousands of British officers and soldiers who had been prisoners of war in Germany returned to London, to tell of their privations, their sufferings, the roughness of their treatment, the "tortures" (this was the word used) they had been subjected to'. Orlando said that the rising popular anger within Britain fuelled the election campaign, whose flames were fanned by Lloyd George and others. 'It looked politically astute to take advantage of that state of mind, but it was an error to be paid for bitterly', wrote Orlando.[39]

Lloyd George and Smith ensured there were political initiatives to correspond with their electoral programme. By the time of the electoral triumph, on 14 December 1918, important decisions about whether to try the Kaiser, the charges he would face, and the tribunal before which he would appear had already been made. The plan had been endorsed by the Imperial War Cabinet, by the country's leading lawyers, and by the leaders of the two main European allies, France and Italy.

Clemenceau Wants Justice

Britain and France first discussed prosecuting the Kaiser at a meeting in Paris immediately following the armistice. Georges Clemenceau, the French Prime Minister, told George Curzon, a member of the Imperial War Cabinet, of his openness to trial of the Kaiser 'as an act of international justice, of world retribution'. Clemenceau's views had probably been informed by a memorandum of two law professors at the University of Paris, Ferdinand Larnaude and Albert Geouffre de Lapradelle. In a lengthy analysis, the academics concluded that any legal obstacles to a trial of the former German Emperor could be overcome.[40] The memorandum was prepared at the request of the Cabinet, but it is not clear whether it was commissioned and submitted prior to the armistice. Clemenceau was pushing on an open door, easily convincing Curzon that a trial of the Kaiser 'would be one of the most imposing events in history and that the conception was well worthy of being pursued'.[41]

The discussion extended to the form a tribunal for the Kaiser might take. Clemenceau contemplated an international court whose judges would not only be drawn from the Allied powers involved in the war, but also from neutral countries. The issue of obtaining custody of the Kaiser also arose. A few days earlier, Wilhelm II had crossed the border into the Netherlands, which had remained neutral during the war, and it was not apparent that he would be willingly surrendered by his Dutch hosts. Clemenceau considered the possibility of a trial at which the Kaiser would not be present. This was nothing exceptional under French law, where *in absentia* proceedings are a frequent occurrence if custody of the accused cannot be obtained. He thought there would be no problem serving an indictment on the Kaiser in the Netherlands.[42]

After the meeting, Curzon wrote to Lloyd George to report about the encounter. He urged the Prime Minister to support the proposal of 'an international tribunal of jurists of the highest eminence (they might or might not include neutrals, probably Yes)'. He said he did not know enough about international law to predict whether the Netherlands would surrender its guest. But he said that was not very important and seemed to endorse Clemenceau's idea of a trial *in absentia*. With a sentence of 'outlawry from the principal countries of the world, it would be a punishment signal, crushing, unheard of in history', wrote Curzon.[43] He credited Clemenceau with the origin of the proposal to try the Kaiser, but also made clear that he had been convinced of its wisdom. Curzon warned Lloyd George that public opinion would resisting letting 'this arch-criminal escape by a final act of cowardice'. He said that the 'supreme and colossal nature of his crime seems to call for some supreme and unprecedented condemnation'. Curzon thought execution and even imprisonment were not really necessary. That was because 'continued life, an inglorious and ignoble exile, under the weight of such a sentence as has never before been given in the history of mankind, would be a penance worse than death'.[44]

Lloyd George replied to Curzon that the matter was worthy of consideration by the Imperial War Cabinet. Writing in the late 1930s, Lloyd George insisted that the idea of trying the Kaiser had been a personal initiative of Curzon. He suggested that this had never been discussed or even considered at the official level within Britain until Curzon's discussion with Clemenceau.[45] The likelihood, then, is that the trial of Kaiser Wilhelm was really a French initiative, developed by French academics and embraced by Clemenceau, who then persuaded Curzon during their *tête-à-tête* following the armistice. It might seem that Lloyd George was trying to distance himself from the plan to hold a trial by attributing it to Curzon, but later in the same account Lloyd George admitted that he was himself an enthusiastic supporter. Maurice Hankey, the Cabinet Secretary, even suggested that Curzon was 'not in a very vindictive spirit' and that it was Lloyd George 'who felt strongly on the subject' and 'took it up with great vigour'.[46]

By July 1919, Curzon's ardour for a trial cooled somewhat, possibly because he had been influenced by King George V. At this point, Lloyd George reminded Curzon how he had been the initiator of the whole idea. The two men were not particularly close on a personal level, but they were often allied politically. In early 1919, with Foreign Secretary Balfour busy in Paris at the Peace Conference, Curzon was made Deputy Foreign Secretary and, later that same year, Foreign Secretary. He held the position until 1924, but was then passed over for Prime Minister. Lloyd George was not the only one to have doubts about Curzon's abilities. Churchill wrote of Curzon's career: 'The morning had been golden; the noontide was bronze; and the evening lead.'[47] Referring to Curzon as the first to propose trial of Kaiser Wilhelm at the official level, Churchill invoked the 'piquant conjunction' of Oscar Wilde, referring to an English country gentleman galloping after a fox: 'The inexpressible in pursuit of the uneatable.'[48] Curzon's personal traits have been described as 'coldness, arrogance, and pomposity'.[49]

The Imperial War Cabinet took up the matter of trial of the Kaiser at its meeting of 20 November 1918. Curzon reported on his encounter with Clemenceau the previous week. According to Curzon, Clemenceau had explained that the French experts 'had not studied this question from the international law point of view, but, undoubtedly public opinion in France was strongly in favour of the trial of the ex-Kaiser'.[50] This may have been Clemenceau's misunderstanding, or Curzon's, or possibly both, because in their opinion Larnaude and de Lapradelle relied most heavily on international law to make the case. 'A way must be found to permit all the acts of which [Wilhelm II] has been guilty, because he ordered them as an Emperor and King and War Lord, to be adduced', it said. 'International law can supply this way; the facts charged against William II are international crimes; he must be tried before an international tribunal.'[51]

'We know the war was started by the Kaiser, and we have reason to believe that all the cruelty, the iniquities, and the horrors that have been perpetrated, if not directly inspired by him, have been countenanced and in no way discouraged by him', Curzon told the Imperial War Cabinet. 'In my view the Kaiser is the arch-Criminal of the world, and just as in any other sphere of life when you get hold of a criminal you bring him to justice, so I do not see, because he is an Emperor and living in exile in another country, why he should be saved from the punishment which is his due.' Curzon insisted that any action to get hold of the Kaiser would best be taken immediately, before the Peace Conference, when the German Emperor could still be considered a prisoner of war. 'If you postponed it till after the Peace Conference you might not get him at all', he warned.[52]

Curzon thought that were Wilhelm to be tried and convicted, 'it might be difficult to proceed as far as an execution, but, if found guilty, the ex-Kaiser could be treated as a universal outlaw, so that there would be no land on which he could set his foot. Moreover, this act of justice, taken by means of representatives of all the Allies and neutral countries, would be the first step in calling into being a League of Nations.' Curzon said he had been assured by the Attorney General that the Committee studying the issue of war crimes prosecutions had not yet considered the question of indicting the Kaiser. However, the Attorney told him that 'many of the members were in favour of that course, and would put before the War Cabinet proposals for the constitution of a tribunal for this purpose'.[53]

Lloyd George immediately endorsed what he described as 'Clemenceau's proposal', although, he said, 'with reservations'. In fact, he had none. Lloyd George felt it unnecessary 'to lay down any limit of punishment. If the ex-Kaiser were guilty, he was guilty of a capital offence, for by his action he had recklessly put to death several millions'. Lloyd George said that '[r]ulers who plunged the civilised world into war must be made to pay the penalty'. It was not 'sufficient punishment to this man that he should get away with twenty millions of money, as I see is stated, to Holland or Corfu, or wherever he goes. I think he ought to stand his trial. With regard to the question of international law, well, we are making international law, and all we can claim is that international law should be based on justice.' Like Curzon, Lloyd George invoked the League of Nations, which was still quite embryonic, noting that it was composed of diplomats and statesmen, but that 'this ought to be a judicial tribunal which should be set up by the Allies. Germany ought to be invited to join it, and I have no doubt she will send men, in her present state, who will judge the ex-Kaiser very impartially. There is a sense of justice in the world which will not be satisfied as long as this man is at large.' Lloyd George insisted the Netherlands be warned that it would not be admitted to the League of Nations if it refused to surrender Wilhelm II.[54]

Lloyd George's enthusiasm for Clemenceau's proposal was not initially shared by his Cabinet colleagues. 'It is not possible to indict a man for making war', said William 'Billy' Hughes, the Australian Prime Minister. 'But it is an indisputable fact that the ex-Kaiser has committed many crimes against international law, and for these he could be arraigned.' This was indeed the heart of the issue that would be debated for the next eighteen months: should the Kaiser be prosecuted for the crime of starting the war, or for crimes committed in the conduct of the war, or both? Robert Borden, Canada's Prime

Minister, took a different view, saying the Kaiser could only be tried, if at all, for 'his crime against humanity in willing and preparing a war'. Borden said that the only appropriate place would be an international tribunal. He also described as futile an attempt to conduct a trial while the Kaiser was in the sanctuary of a neutral country. 'It is important to consider whether we can ensure his delivery by the Dutch Government to the Allies', said Borden. 'It is worthwhile thinking what we should have done with him if he had surrendered to the British, as Napoleon did. Reference to the Attorney General's Committee of Enquiry should be as broad as possible. The exact phrasing can be left to the Prime Minister and to Lord Reading. They should consider the constitutional powers of the Kaiser as to declaring war.'[55]

Churchill was also hesitant. He seemed to have a soft spot for the Kaiser. Writing more than a decade later in *Colliers* magazine, when he was himself in the political wilderness, Churchill accused Lloyd George of pushing for trial 'to gratify the passions of victorious crowds. He would have redraped this poor bedraggled fugitive in the sombre robes of more than mortal guilt and of superhuman responsibility and led him forth to a scaffold of vicarious expiation.'[56] Churchill was less inclined to such hyperbole in Cabinet meetings. 'It will be difficult to say that the ex-Kaiser's guilt is greater than that of many of his advisers, or greater than that of the Parliament of the nation which supported him in making war', he cautioned the Cabinet at the 20 November 1918 meeting. 'It might be that after an indictment has been laid against the ex-Kaiser it would be found that it could not be sustained. A serious impasse would be created. The question should be looked at very carefully before the Government commits itself to any decision.'[57] Churchill cited these words in *The World Crisis*, where he expressed concern that hanging the Kaiser 'was the best way to restore at once his dignity and his dynasty'.[58]

Lord Reading, Ambassador to the United States at the time, had mixed views. 'The Government should know exactly what it proposes to do, and whether it is feasible to prosecute the ex-Kaiser at all', he told the War Cabinet. 'Legal opinion should be taken as to the charges on which he could be indicted, the procedure that should be followed, and the possibility of his being handed over by the Government of Holland for trial.' Arthur Balfour, the Secretary of State for Foreign Affairs, thought the Crown Prince should also be tried. 'It will be difficult to prove that the son is anything but subordinate to the father', he said. 'And there are other cases of men who have committed the greatest cruelties. I have in mind the Turkish leaders, Talat Pasha and Enver

Pasha. It is my hope that the Imperial War Cabinet can take up these cases at a future date.'[59]

'I truly regret any hesitation here with regard to trying the ex-Kaiser for high treason against humanity', said Lloyd George as the discussion concluded. 'This case is entirely different from that of Napoleon, who not only showed great talent and power, but himself fought with his own troops. The ex-Kaiser is a man of no strength of character, who has shown himself to be a coward who ran away at the first hint of trouble.'[60] The Cabinet agreed to ask the Law Officers of the Crown to examine the question of charging the former Emperor, as well as the former Crown Prince, 'for the crime against humanity of having caused the war' and 'for offences, by one or both, against international law during the war', with the purpose of 'bringing home to one or both the responsibility for the acts charged'. They were also 'to consider the constitution of a tribunal to try the charges framed' and, together with the Foreign Office, 'the practicability of inducing the Dutch Government to hand over the ex-Emperor and the Crown Prince to such a tribunal for trial'.[61]

3

Kaiserdämmerung

The House of Hohenzollern can be traced back almost a millennium, to the Swabian Alps in what is today southern Germany. The dynasty arose in the area around the town of Hechingen during the eleventh century, taking its name from Hohenzollern Castle. Religion split the Hohenzollern family into two branches. The Franconian or Protestant side established itself much further north, taking the titles of Margrave of Brandenburg and Duke of Prussia. With the creation of the German Empire in 1871, Wilhelm I of Hohenzollern was crowned as the imperial monarch and King of Prussia. He held the post until his death in 1888 when, after the brief reign of Frederick III, he was succeeded by his grandson, Wilhelm II. Born in 1859, Wilhelm II had blood ties with many royal families in Europe. His mother, Victoria, was the eldest daughter of Queen Victoria of England. Consequently, he was the nephew of Edward VII, the English King from 1901 to 1911, and first cousin to his successor, George V, who occupied the throne throughout the First World War and until his death in 1936. There was a more distant family tie with Queen Wilhelmina of the Netherlands. The aunt of Kaiser Wilhelm's great-great-grandfather, Friedrich Wilhelm III, had married Wilhelm V van Oranje Nassau, and was thus an ancestor of the Dutch monarch.

By mid-1918, Germany's defeat had become increasingly certain. Prussian militarism obtained a respite during 1917 when revolutionary Russia withdrew from the conflict. American entry into the war had helped to seal Berlin's fate. A bold offensive in March 1918 that bolstered German hopes of victory was followed by important Allied military achievements on the Western Front in August and September. Austria-Hungary recognised the impending defeat on the Western Front and contacted the Allies in an effort to make a separate peace. When Bulgaria accepted an armistice on 30 September 1918, followed a few days later by the abdication of its monarch,

The Trial of the Kaiser. William A. Schabas. © William A. Schabas, 2018. Published 2018 by Oxford University Press.

the Germans finally understood that the end was near. They approached
United States President Woodrow Wilson in the hope of arranging an armistice. Later in the month, the German military contemplated a last, desperate
battle. But when the admirals tried to provoke a final assault on the British
fleet, the sailors refused, extinguishing fires in the boilers of their ships so that
they would be unable to sail. Councils of workers, sailors, and soldiers started
to form, as they had in Russia a year earlier.[1]

Kaiser Wilhelm II left his palace in the suburbs of the German capital in
late October 1918, travelling in the elegance of his royal train to the Belgian
resort town of Spa, close to the border between the two countries. There,
the German military had located its Supreme Headquarters on the Western
Front. Wilhelm established his royal household at the Château de la Fraineuse
in Spa, working there during the day. But he took his meals and spent the
night on the train, where he was more comfortable.

The German Emperor was being urged to abdicate, something President
Wilson had already implied was a condition for any armistice. When the
Minister of the Interior travelled to Spa to propose this in person, Wilhelm
replied that he wouldn't dream of abdicating. 'I too have sworn my oath and
will keep it', he said. 'I won't dream of quitting my throne on account of a
few hundred Jews or 1,000 workers—you go and tell that to your masters in
Berlin.'[2] Wilhelm insisted that Bolshevism was sweeping Germany. A strong
hand was required to protect the country from chaos, a challenge that only
the Hohenzollern dynasty could meet.

Revolution spread in Germany. The states that made up the country were
ruled by hereditary monarchs. By the night of 7–8 November, beginning
with the House of Wittelsbach in Bavaria, most of these royal houses were
overthrown. A general strike and mass demonstrations were planned in
Berlin. The Social Democrats, then the majority in Parliament, called upon
the Kaiser to abdicate immediately. Early on 9 November, the Supreme Army
Command held a conclave of commanders in order to assess the loyalty of the
troops, and their willingness to march on Berlin and restore the regime. Most
were not in a revolutionary mood. Tired and exhausted, they hoped the war
would end and they could return home. There would be little appetite for any
action directed against other Germans.

Wilhelm refused to recognise that the old order was doomed, that he
had been abandoned by his myrmidons. He also had a grossly unrealistic
assessment of Germany's military position. Years later, he continued to insist that in November 1918 the Germans were only months from victory.

He blamed General Ludendorff's misjudgement, saying 'it was he who lost his nerve in Spa to such an extent that in an audience with me he urgently demanded that we offer an armistice as well as introduce a changed form of government with a new chancellor! And that immediately!' This, Wilhelm believed, was enough to 'set the stone of revolution rolling' and cost him his throne.[3]

But Wilhelm also had other culprits to blame for German defeat. Writing to his most trusted general, August von Mackensen, he said the Germans had inflicted upon themselves the 'deepest, most disgusting shame ever perpetrated by a people in history'. In a characteristically anti-Semitic outburst, he said the Germans had been egged on and misled 'by the tribe of Juda whom they hated'. Wilhelm said no German should ever 'rest until these parasites have been destroyed and exterminated from German soil! This poisonous mushroom on the German oak-tree!'[4]

Late in the morning of 9 November 1918, Wilhelm finally conceded. Return to Germany was out of the question because he could no longer count on the support of the army. Word reached Spa that revolutionary troops were on their way from Berlin. The Kaiser and his entourage were all too aware of what had recently befallen the Russian royal family at the hands of revolutionaries. The Kaiser summoned his generals, who were lodged at the Hotel Britannique. The Crown Council met in the cold garden house, at the rear of the Château de la Fraineuse. Wilhelm stood by the wood fire, the only source of heat in the room, leaning on the chimney, shivering. General Paul von Hindenburg, a veteran of the Franco-Prussian War, then well into his seventies, was struck dumb with emotion and wept openly. It fell to General Wilhelm Groener to confront the Kaiser with the grim reality: 'Sire, you no longer have an army. The army will march home in peace and order under its leaders and commanding generals, but not under the command of Your Majesty, for it no longer stands behind Your Majesty.'[5]

The Kaiser reacted with fury. 'I demand a written statement of this opinion', he shouted at Groener. 'I will have an announcement in black and white from all the generals commanding that the army is no longer behind its Supreme War Lord. Have they not sworn it to me in their military oath?' 'In the present situation, sire, the oath is mere fiction', the General replied. Then a message arrived from the Commandant of Berlin: 'All troops deserted—completely out of hand.'[6]

Wilhelm adjourned the meeting. He went to the garden, behind the Château. He considered a partial abdication whereby he would retain the title of King of Prussia, but would no longer be Emperor of Germany. More bad news arrived from Berlin. The hope of those who urged abdication was that it might save the monarchy. But an announcement by Prince Max from the Reichstag balcony that the Kaiser had abdicated failed to calm the protests. Spartacists had seized the imperial palace and proclaimed a Soviet republic.[7]

Hindenburg, Groener, and the other generals returned to the Château. 'You no longer have a War Lord', the Kaiser barked at Groener. General Groener later described the situation: 'The Kaiser said nothing, just looked—looked from one to the other, with an expression first of amazement, then piteous appeal, and then—just a curious wondering vagueness. He said nothing, and we took him—just as if he were a little child—and sent him to Holland.'[8]

Left alone by the generals, the Kaiser continued to reflect on his options. He moved to the imperial train, with his luggage, to ready himself for flight. He reserved his decision until the following morning. 'I have no desire to be hanged by some strangers', he told one of his confidantes. 'Who would have thought it would come to this. The German people are a pack of bastards.'

Early in the morning of 10 November 1919, a Sunday, well before the sun had risen, the Kaiser left Spa on his royal train. It was an elegant assemblage of ten carriages in white and gold livery, staffed by footmen, butlers, chefs, and other servants, and an entourage of officials and advisers. He did not say fare-well to his generals, or even write them a note. He left a letter for the Crown Prince, who was to follow him to the Netherlands a day later:

> Dear Boy, Since the Field Marshall can no longer guarantee my security here, and since he also will no longer take the responsibility for the loyalty of the troops, I have decided, after severe inward struggle, to leave the collapsed army. Berlin is totally lost in the hands of the Socialists, and two governments have already been formed there, one by Ebert as Reich's Chancellor, and another at the same time by the Independents. I recommend that you remain at your post and hold the troops together until they start the march back home. As God wills auf Wiedersehen. General von Marschall will keep you informed. Your stricken father, Wilhelm.[9]

The train headed northwest in the direction of Liège, a major rail hub where it could join the main line towards Maastricht in the southern tip of the Netherlands. But out of concern that his own mutinous troops might attack the train, when he had travelled only a few kilometres from Spa, at La Reid, the Kaiser decided to disembark and continue the journey to the Dutch border by car. Two vehicles were commandeered, their im-perial insignia removed. Wilhelm then made his way with a small group, leaving the bulk of his staff to proceed by train. It took about an hour to make the 45-kilometre trip to Eijsden, on the border between Belgium and Holland, where Limburg Province dangles from the southeast corner of the Netherlands.[10]

The German authorities warned the Dutch of his arrival. The previous day, in the early evening, when it seemed the Kaiser had made up his mind to seek asylum in Holland, the Foreign Ministry's representative in Spa sent telegrams to German representatives in Brussels and The Hague announcing the plans. Friedrich Rosen, the German Ambassador in the Dutch capital, only received the message early the following morning, after Wilhelm had already reached the border. In the middle of the night, Rosen also received a telegram from another German official saying 'we will cross border' in the morning, referring to the official telegram sent the previous evening. But Rosen chose to await the formal message before making any moves.[11]

In Brussels, Baron von der Lancken, the German Governor, notified the Dutch Head of Mission, Maurits van Vollenhoven, that the Kaiser would take the Liège–Maastricht route and arrive in the Netherlands late that night or early the following day. Von der Lancken asked Van Vollenhoven to inform Dutch border officials to facilitate the Kaiser crossing into the Netherlands. Van Vollenhoven claimed he was the first Dutchman to know of the Kaiser's plans. There was no secure telegram communication. With Von der Lancken's agreement, Van Vollenhoven dispatched envoys to The Hague and to Maastricht to communicate the intentions of the Kaiser. Travelling by motorcycle, they did not arrive before the Kaiser had reached the border.[12]

Crossing the Border

The Kaiser and his entourage arrived at the frontier in their motorcars before 7 am, when it was still dark. He was dressed in a Prussian general's coat, grey with red cuffs and no decorations. The Kaiser carried a cane. The group passed the Belgian post of Moelingen and proceeded to the Dutch border, at Eijsden, where there was a railway station on the line from Liège to Maastricht. At the time, the station actually straddled the border, with one end of the platform in the Netherlands and the other in Belgium. One of the officers accompanying Wilhelm demanded that the border guard allow them to enter.

'Impossible.'

'But I demand that we shall pass. The German Emperor himself is here, and he must be allowed to continue his journey into Holland. You can safely do this, your Government is fully acquainted.'

A second German officer stepped up to the Dutch guard, who by then had been joined by a colleague. 'I wish to pass at once. You surely recognise me. I am the German Emperor.'

'I see you are the Kaiser', said the Dutch guard. 'But my orders are to allow none to pass.'

'Who gave you those orders', said the Kaiser.

'My captain. He is still asleep, in the guardroom.'

'Call him instantly. Say that the German Emperor is here and must pass through the barrier.'

'Very well', said the guard. 'But first I must lock the gates.' He proceeded to do so, leaving the Kaiser inside Belgian territory. Soon the captain arrived. The Kaiser repeated his demand, only to be told that the Dutch officials would require instructions from The Hague before admitting him.

'That will take some time', said the Kaiser. 'I cannot stand here in the road. Take me to some place where I can wait.'

The Dutch captain told the Kaiser that he would allow him to cross the border and enter the Netherlands, but that he must give his word to return to Belgium immediately if requested to do so. The captain agreed to ask the station-master's permission for the Kaiser to wait on the platform. Then 59 years old, never before in his life had Wilhelm been given orders by an army captain or a railway attendant. But he promptly made the requested undertaking to the Dutch officer. The captain went to talk to the station-master and only then returned to unlock the gates.[13]

Winston Churchill, who had known him at the height of his glory, wrote of the Kaiser's debacle: 'A broken man sits hunched in a railway carriage, hour after hour, at a Dutch frontier station awaiting permission to escape as a refugee from the execration of a people whose armies he has led through measureless sacrifices to measureless defeat, and whose conquests and treasures he has squandered.'[14]

Workers from a nearby Belgian factory ran to catch sight of the celebrated visitor, hooting and shouting. 'À bas Guillaume, assassin', one of them called out. The Kaiser sought sanctuary in the station-master's office. The official coldly pointed to a sign forbidding entry of unauthorised persons. Someone on the platform offered him a cigarette, which he accepted, but this only provoked anger in the crowd. Wilhelm was 'visibly surprised and terrified'. Later in the morning, the station was closed to the public. Wilhelm paced back and forth on the platform until his imperial train arrived from Liège, providing him with a bit of sanctuary and protection.[15]

Several hours passed while the Dutch Cabinet and the Queen debated the matter. Because this was a Sunday, the Dutch telephone system only functioned for a limited number of hours. The Prime Minister, Charles Ruijs de Beerenbrouck, and the staunchly pro-German Foreign Minister, Herman Adriaan van Karnebeek, sought a place to house the Kaiser and his entourage. Queen Wilhelmina offered one of her castles, but this was rejected by the Cabinet. Van Karnebeek unsuccessfully communicated with several Dutch aristocrats in search of a host. Early in the afternoon, the Queen's commissioner for Utrecht province, Count Lijnden van Sandenburg, telephoned Godard van Aldenburg-Bentinck at his castle in Amerongen. Bentinck was enjoying a cigar in the library when a servant interrupted to say there was a telephone call from The Hague. 'The German Emperor has crossed the frontier. Will you take him in, also his suite of about thirty persons, for a few days until a suitable lodging can be found for him?'[16]

The Bentincks were resident in the Netherlands, but they were considered to be German nobility of a relatively high rank. Count Bentinck was a hereditary knight of the Prussian branch of the Knights of St John of Jerusalem, the *Johanniter Orden*, of which the Kaiser was the head. Bentinck had taken a vow to help a brother Knight 'in adversity and distress'. The Kaiser had never met Bentinck, but some years before the war he had visited his older brother, whose castle was in nearby Middachten. When told of his proposed host, the Kaiser said: 'Who is this Bentinck? I don't think I know him.' Bentinck was initially unenthusiastic about welcoming the Kaiser, but he agreed to convene a family council. Three hours later, there was another call from The Hague. No other arrangements were possible. Bentinck was told the Kaiser would stay 'for three days only'. The Count explained that he was without coal, a consequence of wartime, and was short of servants. He was promised that the government would send him a truckload of coal that evening.[17] Dutch officials accompanied by the German Ambassador drove to Eijsden. They informed Wilhelm that the Cabinet had unanimously agreed that he could stay with Bentinck for three days and then a definitive residence would be assigned. The Kaiser also received a telegram from Queen Wilhelmina granting him asylum in the Netherlands.

Was the Kaiser Invited to the Netherlands?

It is not entirely clear how much warning, if any, the Dutch had of the arrival of Kaiser Wilhelm on their territory. The German socialist politician Philipp Scheidemann claimed in his memoir that the English King, George V, had arranged the Kaiser's exile,[18] but there is no evidence of this and Scheidemann would hardly have been in a position to know anything.[19] Plausible claims have been made over the years that the Kaiser was actually invited to the Netherlands by Queen Wilhelmina.[20] German historian Martin Kohlrausch thinks it likely that there was some prior agreement with the Dutch Queen, who acted out of a sense of 'dynastic solidarity' and possibly a concern that Wilhelm could meet the same fate as the Romanovs.[21] Another scholar points to a message dated 5 November 1918 from Kaiser Wilhelm complimenting Dutch adherence to neutrality that the German Emperor specifically requested be passed to Queen Wilhelmina as evidence that flight to the Netherlands was already being contemplated.[22]

It is beyond dispute that the Queen's equerry, General Joannes Benedictus van Heutsz, had been in Spa during the days immediately prior to the Kaiser's flight and had actually met the German Emperor. A distinguished imperialist of the old school, Van Heutsz was hailed as the 'pacifier of Aceh' for his effective suppression of anti-colonial rebellion in the Dutch East Indies. Born in 1851, Van Heutsz would have been about 68 years old when he undertook a mysterious mission to the headquarters of the German general staff in the final days of the war. By his own account, in mid-September 1918 the German Headquarters had invited Van Heutsz to visit the Western Front. Perhaps it was nothing more than a courtesy extended to a distinguished retired general in a neighbouring country. Van Heutsz replied that as the Queen's *adjudant-generaal*, he would require her consent.

Van Heutsz claimed that on 30 October 1918 he received an official invitation on behalf of the German Emperor himself, who by then had already arrived in Belgium. The following week, on 5 November, Van Heutsz travelled to German military headquarters in Spa. Van Heutsz insisted that his visit 'had a strictly military character'. The highlight of the trip, it seems, was a luncheon with the Kaiser. It took place on 8 November and not, as the Dutch newspaper *De Telegraaf* had stated, on 9 November. Van Heutsz insisted that there was no mention whatsoever of any intent by the Kaiser to seek asylum in the Netherlands. The same evening, Van Heutsz dined with General von

Hindenburg. It was Hindenburg who told the Kaiser the following evening that preparations were being made for his flight to Holland.[23] Van Heutsz returned to the Netherlands on 9 November. He expressed disappointment at not being able to visit a German submarine base at Zeebrugge during his tour of the military installations because of developments that had not been foreseen when the visit was first planned. He claimed surprise upon arriving in Maastricht to learn of the Kaiser's plans to abdicate.

The visit to Spa by Van Heutsz first attracted the attention of the *Petit Journal*, one of the major French newspapers. On 23 November, it reported that Van Heutsz had travelled to Spa to negotiate the details of the Kaiser's flight. The proof, said the *Petit Journal*, was the Kaiser's surprise upon arriving at the border when the Dutch guards claimed they had not been forewarned.[24] Several days later, the Dutch Minister of Foreign Affairs attempted to assure the French Ambassador that there had been no prior agreement about an offer of asylum to the Kaiser, although he did not explicitly deny the possibility that Van Heutsz might have discussed the matter with Wilhelm.[25] An article in *De Telegraaf* of 10 December prompted a statement by the Prime Minister in the *Tweede Kamer* or lower house:

> Of course, the government would have preferred the Kaiser to have chosen a different place of residence than the Netherlands. Important: Sunday the tenth of November the government came to know that the Kaiser entered Dutch territory earlier that morning. The fact had already occurred. The government did not know that the Kaiser was planning on fleeing to the Netherlands and was surprised by his arrival. All stories and assumptions regarding the government knowing he would arrive are not true. The government did not itself, nor through any third party (the name of general Heutsz is often mentioned) undertake any action to invite the Kaiser. After his abdication the Kaiser could not be held as a prisoner of war [as he arrived as a private person, not as a military commander]. The Kaiser called upon the right to be a guest [*gastrecht*], which thousands of aliens before him had enjoyed without distinction of class or social standing.

The Dutch Government understood immediately that many countries would not appreciate its courteous welcome to the Kaiser, said Ruijs de Beerenbrouck. Nevertheless, refusal would go against 'the age old tradition of hospitality'.[26]

After the speech, Foreign Minister Van Karnebeek met with the British Ambassador, Walter Townley, and impressed upon him the message that the Dutch had not been apprised of the Kaiser's arrival. Townley reported to the Foreign Office that Van Karnebeek had described in detail being 'herded out of bed by his cook in the early morning', then telephoning Queen Wilhelmina with the news. He immediately went to the Palace where he found Her Majesty to be 'much depressed'.[27] He provided similar explanations to the other ambassadors.[28] On 14 December, in London, the Dutch Ambassador, Reneke de Marees van Swinderen, paid a call on the British Foreign Minister to make the same points.[29]

There is a message addressed to Foreign Secretary Arthur Balfour in the files of the Foreign Office from a representative of the Belgian embassy in London, presumably the ambassador. It encloses a letter dated 3 December from the Collège des bourgmestres et echevins de la Ville de Spa signed by 'Bn de Crawhez' and addressed to Général Delobbe. The letter describes the visit of a British officer to the Villa Pompéia, in Spa, on 27 November. The caretaker of the building, Duguet Delges, *rentier*, made the following statement: 'Voici, Messieurs, the room where the Dutch General stayed who came to get the Kaiser when he abdicated.' A minute in the file says '[t]he General in question was no doubt Van Heutsz'.[30]

The British, French, and Americans were all suspicious of the pro-German tendencies of both the Dutch Queen herself and her government. In a letter to Foreign Minister Balfour, the French Ambassador, de Fleuriau, cited the attitude to the Kaiser as evidence of *'des dispositions germanophiles en Hollande'*.[31] The French Ambassador to the Netherlands was instructed to inform the Dutch Government that its 'pro-German sympathies and actions have not passed unnoticed by the French Government'.[32] The Belgian Minister in The Hague seemed satisfied with the explanations given by the Dutch, dismissing the Van Heutsz visit as an unfortunate coincidence, *'une fâcheuse coincidence'*.[33] But despite the official denials, doubts persisted about the real purpose of the Van Heutsz mission. The American Ambassador, John W. Garrett, reported that '[t]he question of whether or not the Kaiser was invited directly or indirectly by the Dutch Government to seek refuge on Netherlands soil is still unsettled, and the statement of the Ministers in reply to questions on the point have been most equivocal'.[34]

'How is it possible that the Kaiser just walked in without our government knowing?' asked the Communist deputy Van Ravensteijn in the *Tweede Kamer* on 11 December 1918.[35] There is even some evidence that the Prime Minister himself thought he had not been told the full story. He was suspicious of the explanations provided by Van Heutsz and endorsed by Van Karnebeek.[36] The Dutch Ambassador to France thought much harm had been done to the country by its failure to deny the Van Heutsz story immediately.[37] He reported that only a few French newspapers had published the government's official explanation.[38]

It may well be the case that Van Heutsz went to organise the Kaiser's flight at the behest of the Royal Court, without the approval or authorisation of government officials, or at least some of them. Van Karnebeek's inquiry appears to have consisted of obtaining the account from Van Heutsz and nothing further. Can it be credible that in the twilight of the German Empire, the *Götterdämmerung* of the House of Hohenzollern, with Berlin in flames, Kaiser Wilhelm took the time to dine with a retired Dutch general engaged in a bit of military tourism? That Van Heutsz denied any discussion about the Kaiser's plans to flee to the Netherlands is hardly surprising, but nor is it at all convincing. Surely Van Heutsz and the Kaiser talked about more than the autumn weather. Moreover, it seems reckless for the Kaiser to have made the trip to the Dutch border without any prior indication as to whether he would be welcome. Had the Dutch authorities denied him entry to the country, he would have had few remaining options. Summary execution might have awaited him in Germany, at the hands of a revolution spiralling in unforeseen directions. On 9 November 1918, the whole world was speculating about the fate of Kaiser Wilhelm. It would not have taken much imagination by the Dutch authorities to foresee a visit, given that their border was the nearest. Would they not, at the very least, have planned for such a contingency? There is certainly evidence that by the end of October they were anticipating his abdication.[39]

From Eijsden to Amerongen

Angry protests followed the Kaiser as the imperial train made its way to nearby Maastricht, and then on to Nijmegen and Arnhem, stopping finally in Maarn, close to Utrecht and about half an hour's drive from Amerongen. The Kaiser left his train. In heavy rain, he was greeted on the platform by his host Count Bentinck. While waiting for Bentinck's car to depart the station at Maarn, the Kaiser conversed with the Count, 'gesticulating freely and affecting an almost exaggerated nonchalance. Indeed, the whole time from his alighting from the train he had talked vivaciously to those accompanying him to the car.'[40] The British Ambassador, Walter Townley, reported to London that there were very few spectators at Maarn. The crowd was 'entirely composed of local residents, yokels and reporters', although the ex-Emperor's arrival had been advertised in all of the surrounding villages earlier that day. 'There was nothing of an ovation beyond a very faint cheer of welcome raised on his arrival by Count Bentinck's retainers among whom some booing was audible. To the cheers German Emperor responded by saluting although with some hesitation as though not quite sure how to interpret this demonstration', Townley explained in his telegram of 12 November. The 'special correspondent' of *The Times* reported that Wilhelm 'had grown a little stouter than he used to be'.[41] But there was no *Times* correspondent on the station platform. The journalist had been given the story by Lady Susan Townley, the wife of the British Ambassador. Lady Susan was the 'emissary' described, using the masculine pronoun, by Ambassador Townley in his report to the Foreign Office.[42] A few days later, Townley wrote to Charles Hardinge, the Permanent Under-Secretary, suggesting that the 'day's outing' of Lady Susan, where she allegedly stumbled upon the German monarch, was entirely her own initiative.[43] 'I think this rather "thin"', minuted Eric Drummond in the Foreign Office file. Townley was reprimanded by Foreign Minister Balfour for this bit of deceit, described as 'a serious indiscretion on the part of Lady Susan'. He resigned the posting, his last, shortly afterwards.[44] King George V was reported to be 'infuriated' when he heard reports that Lady Susan 'had jeered at the Kaiser as he arrived from Germany to begin his exile'.[45]

In February 1919, an opposition Member of Parliament questioned the Foreign Minister whether he was aware that Townley's wife 'was a member of the committee which received the ex-Kaiser on his arrival in Holland; and what action, if any, he proposes to take in the matter'. Bureaucrats in the Foreign Office connived to provide an evasive answer. Cecil Harmsworth, the Under-Secretary of State, claimed that Lady Susan 'happened to be motoring in the neighbourhood', a flagrant misrepresentation. 'No committee, official or otherwise, was appointed to receive the ex-Kaiser on his arrival in Holland, and Lady Susan Townley was not, therefore, a member of any such committee', he added. When asked if Ambassador Townley had tendered his resignation, Harmsworth answered: 'I do not understand that to be a fact.'[46]

In her own memoir, Lady Susan described the Kaiser upon his arrival at Maarn:

> He looked very white, white-haired and white-faced, when he stepped out of the train and walked past me to the motor-car, talking to Count Godard. But his gait was firm, and his nonchalance, whether natural or assumed, perfect. He was *crane*, as the French would say! Count Godard, or more probably the Governor of the Province, who was a noted pro-Boche, had tried to organise

a welcoming demonstration by planting a few boys in the branches of the surrounding trees with orders to cheer the fallen monarch. He automatically lifted his hand to respond to this welcome, but it fell back, the gesture unfinished, as a low, prolonged booing drowned the faint cheer.[47]

The Kaiser took a seat in Bentinck's car for the short drive to Amerongen Castle. The Governor of Utrecht province was also present, as was General Onnen, who was responsible for the internment of officers. In the car, the Kaiser told General Onnen that 'he thought he might be very useful to Queen of Holland, with whom he had family ties, after the war'.[48] Upon arriving at Amerongen, the Kaiser promptly asked his host for 'a cup of real good English tea'.[49]

After agreeing to the Queen's request to provide three days' lodgings as an emergency measure when other doors in Holland were closed, Bentinck found himself playing host to Wilhelm for about eighteen months. The Kaiser was no ordinary house guest. Count Bentinck had to scramble in order to find accommodation for the ex-Emperor's substantial entourage. Bentinck leased the two guest houses in Amerongen and located emergency housing elsewhere as well. Wilhelm himself stayed in the castle.

Surrounded by a double moat, it overlooked the Nederrijn or Nether Rhine, a branch of the great river that has such an important place in German mythology. Amerongen Castle was built in the late eighteenth century on the site of a medieval fortress destroyed by the French in 1673. Wilhelm slept in a bed that had once been used by Louis XIV of France. His bedroom provided a superb view of the river. Although he was comfortable enough in the castle in terms of material surroundings, any contact with the outside world was monitored. His telephone calls and correspondence were subject to censorship. He could not leave Amerongen Castle without a Dutch escort. Gendarmes were posted at the gatehouse to keep the curious away, but also to monitor the movements of Wilhelm.

It was not as if the Kaiser had arrived in the Netherlands with only the shirt on his back. The British Ambassador reported to London that the Kaiser was said to have taken £30 million with him. General Onnen, who accompanied Wilhelm to Amerongen, thought this quite possible, and remarked how the Kaiser had not only an immense quantity of luggage, but also that he was concerned that certain cases be handled only in the presence of his retainers.[50] Within days of the Kaiser's flight, large sums of money were being transferred from Germany to his accounts in the Netherlands: 652,000 marks were deposited in the Von der Heydt'schen Bank in Amsterdam in November 1918 alone, and another 8 million marks in January 1919. Over the first year of exile in the Netherlands, the transfers totalled 66 million marks. This was enough for him to live in style, although the Dutch insisted that the size of the royal entourage be reduced in scale to a few dozen servants and attendants. Wilhelm also received money from the German Government, although the amounts were not very large. In March 1919, British Military Intelligence intercepted a letter from the German Foreign Office to its consulate in Maastricht about a transfer of 2,044 florins from the Deutsche Bank in Berlin as reimbursement for an advance to the ex-Kaiser's court. The letter said that in the future, 3,000 florins would be provided monthly without it being necessary for the consulate to make a request. The amount, equivalent to about €15,000 today, was deemed not sufficiently important to warrant a protest, although technically the payments were in violation of the armistice agreement.[51]

The royal train that had accompanied him was well equipped. Although many of the furnishings were the Kaiser's personal property, the train itself as well as many of its fittings belonged to a Germany railway company, the Preussische-Hessensche Staatseisenbahn. A few days after the Kaiser disembarked at Maarn, the imperial train was moved to Rotterdam. It sat on a siding for several weeks, where it was burgled and vandalised. The train was returned to the German railway authorities in February 1919, but only after it had been repaired.[52] Seventy years later, the German model railway firm Märklin produced an HO gauge version of the Kaiser's train for hobbyists and collectors. Exhibited in a Berlin transport museum until the end of the Second World War, the car with the Kaiser's bedroom was used for several years by the Soviet military and then parked in Dresden until after German reunification. It was partially restored and returned to Berlin, where it is on display at the Deutsches Technikmuseum.

Rumours of political intrigue swirled. There were concerns that Wilhelm was planning a return to Germany, and to power. In mid-December, Friedrich Rosen, the German Ambassador, circulated a statement to foreign diplomats:

> I am in a position to [make] the following statement of acts about the veracity and exactness of which I do not entertain the slightest doubt. The former German emperor has no political relations whatsoever with Germany. Indeed, he possesses hardly any means of communication with Germany at all. The only correspondence that takes place consists in very short family news forwarded to his children through the German Foreign Office, and even these are few and far between. On his arrival in Holland—and twice since—the former Emperor has expressed to me his very clear opinion that there are no

chances whatever of his regaining the throne of Prussia or of Germany. He does not in any way entertain such a desire. His religious conviction leads him to believe firmly that what has occurred to him is a decree of Providence, the ultimate object of which he cannot understand, but which it is his duty to submit to in Christian humility. He has daily expressed similar views to the gentlemen of his entourage. Among the gentleman who accompanied the former Emperor to Holland there were three whose influence might be considered as doubtful: General Oberst von Plessen, Oberst Leutnant von Motlke and Admiral Graf Platen. These gentlemen have some time ago been removed from the Emperor's suite and have gone back to Germany. Those remaining with the Emperor at Amerongen have no tendency whatever to lend themselves to any political intrigue.[53]

Reports circulated that the Kaiser had suffered a breakdown. Foreign Minister Van Karnebeek expressed concern that Wilhelm was suicidal. It would not have been the first time the Emperor had buckled under strain. It seems this happened several times during the war.

Over the final weeks of 1918, Wilhelm refused to leave his rooms in Amerongen Castle, even to take meals. At the end of December, the *Telegraaf* reported that the Kaiser had been 'very seriously ill' due to influenza, and that his condition appeared serious enough to require surgical attention. He was attended by Professor Lanz, a Swiss doctor based in Antwerp, who visited him frequently, but who confirmed that he was 'progressing favourably'.[54] Lanz was said to be 'a specialist in mental cases', according to Ambassador Garrett, 'though publicly it is announced that the imperial patient is suffering from the Spanish grippe'. Garrett described him as '[t]he lonely guest at Amerongen', reporting that from all accounts the Kaiser was 'developing marked neural derangement and appears to be in desperate physical conditions; he has given away to acute fits of depression', although acknowledging that '[m]ost of these tales are doubtless gross exaggerations'.[55]

Whether stories of the Kaiser's mental instability were contrived by his entourage in order to forestall Dutch requests that he leave is a matter of speculation. Illness might also provide a pretext to remove Wilhelm from Amerongen in order to obtain treatment, and this could facilitate an escape. Wilhelm was also very worried about a kidnap attempt and even an assassination. He kept a loaded pistol at hand. His paranoia proved to be not entirely without foundation. This became apparent in the first days of the new year.

4

Making the Case
in International Law

The plan to prosecute the Kaiser had been hatched at the meeting between Clemenceau and Curzon a day or two after the armistice. Neither Clemenceau nor Curzon were lawyers, but in support of his proposal Clemenceau invoked a report by two French law professors, Ferdinand Larnaude and Albert de Lapradelle. Meeting on 20 November 1918, the Imperial War Cabinet heard Curzon's account of the meeting with Clemenceau followed by an enthusiastic endorsement from Lloyd George. The Prime Minister had practised law for many years, as a solicitor in Wales and later in London, but he had no expertise in international law. There were some great legal minds in the Cabinet, notably Lord Reading, who was initially somewhat sceptical about trying the Kaiser. The Cabinet session concluded with a request to Attorney General F. E. Smith for a legal opinion. Smith turned to the Committee of Enquiry that had been established earlier in the month.

'In regard to the proceedings against the ex-Kaiser, the Committee are of opinion that little aid can be derived from precedents', it reported.[1] The French law professors cited by Clemenceau were of similar mind. 'A new international law has arisen', wrote Larnaude and de Lapradelle.[2] But in fact, they were not on entirely uncharted territory. There was a precedent. Just over a century earlier, at the conclusion of the last great European war, the British had dispatched the fallen French Emperor by imprisoning him on a lonely and desolate island in the middle of the Atlantic Ocean. The Napoleonic precedent would be regularly alluded to as the fate of Kaiser Wilhelm was being debated. Hugh Bellot, Secretary of the Sub-Committee on Law of the British Committee of Enquiry, prepared a study on Napoleon's treatment

The Trial of the Kaiser. William A. Schabas. © William A. Schabas, 2018. Published 2018 by Oxford University Press.

that was published in the Second Interim Report[3] and, somewhat later, in an academic law journal.[4] The Sub-Committee explicitly distinguished the case of Wilhelm II from that of Napoleon, who was not charged with violating the laws and customs of war. 'His offence, if any, was that he was a rebel to the lawful French Government or that he had violated the arrangement agreed to by him in 1814', said the Sub-Committee.[5]

That Napoleon might have been judged by an international criminal tribunal for violations of international law was something that never crossed the minds of the authorities in 1815. The Prussians had hoped to capture Napoleon following his defeat at Waterloo on 18 June 1815. Their plan was for summary execution, premised on the claim that Napoleon had been 'outlawed' by the Congress of Vienna. The Duke of Wellington disputed such an interpretation and opposed any attempt at assassination.[6] Wellington said that were Napoleon to be captured, he was to be treated as a prisoner of war pending any further determination by the Allies. If apprehended by the French authorities, they might well punish him under the laws of France, for rebellion or treason. But the French authorities did not seem keen on this, and there was general agreement that it was better if Napoleon did not remain in his homeland, where he still had a considerable following. Napoleon fled Paris and made his way to Rochefort, on the Atlantic coast. It was thought he would try to escape to America, where he might obtain asylum. A British squadron waited outside the harbour, planning to arrest him. Then, to considerable surprise, Napoleon surrendered. He boarded the *HMS Bellerophon* and was taken to Plymouth.

The British obtained the agreement of the other members of the anti-French coalition to keep Napoleon in their custody. They could not release him, but they were free to determine the place of detention. Malta, St Helena, and the Cape of Good Hope were among the options. The Prime Minister, Lord Liverpool, wrote to the Foreign Secretary, Lord Castlereagh, insisting that the prisoner not remain in Britain where '[v]ery nice legal questions might arise upon the subject, which would be particularly embarrassing'.[7] Napoleon protested the decision that he be sent to St Helena, but the British were inflexible.

At the heart of the 'nice legal questions' was the absence of any provision in English law allowing permanent detention without trial. Today, Napoleon would challenge the threat of indefinite deprivation of liberty without charge by invoking Article 5 of the European Convention on Human Rights, first in English courts and, if unsuccessful there, in Strasbourg at the European Court of Human Rights. But even in 1815, Liverpool and Castlereagh anticipated an application by the little corporal for a writ of *habeas corpus*, with an uncertain outcome. Like Clemenceau, Curzon, and Lloyd George in 1919, they had to concoct a legal theory to support their essentially political determination. In 1815, there was as yet no treaty of peace with France. British Government lawyers said this meant they could detain Napoleon as a prisoner of war, but only temporarily.

Napoleon had been a party to the 1814 peace agreement with Austria, Russia, Prussia, and Britain. Thereby, he abdicated the throne, but retained the title of Emperor and was given the island of Elba as a kind of principality. When he left Elba and returned to France, the theory went, he had made himself an outlaw. Meeting in Vienna, the 'Powers' issued a declaration that by breaking the 1814 agreement and returning to France Napoleon had deprived himself of the protection of the law and confirmed that he could never agree to peace. It said he had placed himself '*hors des relations civiles et sociales et que, comme ennemi et perturbateur du repos du monde, il s'est livré à la vindicte publique*'.[8] The theory was more or less the same as the one invoked by the United States Government to justify detaining 'unlawful combatants' indefinitely at the Guantanamo base in Cuba.[9] Castlereagh embraced the argument. Napoleon could be held forever without charge as a prisoner of war because he had unleashed a war that would never end.[10] But in case the approach did not withstand judicial scrutiny, Castlereagh had Parliament enact legislation securing the legality of Napoleon's banishment.[11] The preamble to the law made it clear that Napoleon's detention had little or nothing to do with criminal punishment or accountability: 'Whereas it is necessary for the Preservation of the Tranquillity of Europe, and for the general Safety, that Napoleon Buonaparte should be detained and kept in Custody as is hereinafter provided ...'.[12]

Eventually, after efforts to obtain custody of the Kaiser met with Dutch intransigence, the British and the French revived the notion of a Napoleonic solution. Even after their ardour for punishment had weakened, they remained concerned about the Kaiser's political role in post-war Germany, just as their predecessors had worried about Napoleon. Abandoning insistence on trial, they proposed a compromise whereby the Kaiser would be exiled to a distant colony of the Netherlands rather than remain in his comfortable castle an hour's drive from the border with Germany. Because the Kaiser had a form of asylum, the Dutch could lawfully dictate where on their territory he was to live. However, they could not prevent him leaving if he wished to do so.[13]

The Legal Experts

One of France's eminent international lawyers, writing in 1915, was quite dismissive about claims that the Kaiser was subject to criminal penalties. Writing in the *Journal du droit international*, known then and now to French international lawyers as the 'Clunet', he cited an article in the *Edinburgh Review* describing the violation of Belgian neutrality as an international crime.[14] For Louis Renault, this might be 'the law of the future, a future that I will not see'. As for the present, the law did not allow prosecution of the Emperor. He noted the 'precedent' of the coroner's jury in Kinsale, Ireland, charging the Kaiser with breaches of international law.[15] Renault said this was '*une simple manifestation, une satisfaction donnée à l'opinion publique*', and not a credible criminal accusation in a legal sense.[16] Renault, who had received the Nobel Peace Prize in 1907, died in 1918 and therefore did not participate in the postwar debates.

The 'French jurists' to whom Clemenceau referred in his meeting with Curzon were prepared to be more creative. Ferdinand Larnaude was dean of the Faculty of Law of the University of Paris, a position he had held since 1913. Larnaude was described as a 'radical Republican'. His colleague, Albert Geouffre de Lapradelle, was professor of international law at the same university. It is not known for how long the two academics had been at work on their study or when it was commissioned by the French Cabinet. There are no preliminary publications authored by them or by their collaborators to suggest that their study of the issue of trying the Kaiser was at all protracted. Larnaude did not mention the Kaiser in a speech he delivered on 13 September 1918 calling for prosecution of German war criminals.[17] Whether they had provided Clemenceau with a written opinion before he met Curzon or whether this came later is also unclear. A French newspaper suggests Clemenceau sought their opinion on 21 November,[18] but this is obviously inconsistent with his comments to Curzon.

Clemenceau again referred to the opinion of Larnaude and de Lapradelle in his speech at the first Plenary of the Paris Conference, in January 1918, promising that it would be distributed to all delegates. 'Also in England, and surely in America, there have been works on this subject', he added.[19] The study of the French academics appeared in English under the title 'Inquiry into the Penal Liabilities of Emperor William II' as an annex to the minutes of the Commission on Responsibilities.[20] The first version of the work was published by the French War Ministry dated 1918.[21] It was reproduced in the French *Journal Officiel* of 19 January 1919 and in a prominent French law journal.[22] The report of the French jurists was even discussed in the international press.[23]

The Committee of Enquiry appointed by Attorney General Smith at the beginning of November had already constituted itself into four subcommittees when the War Cabinet asked Smith to examine the Kaiser issue. On 6 November 1919, Smith had cautioned the Committee that it could not usefully consider the matter of responsibility for the origin of the war, as this raised 'questions of policy' that needed to be dealt with 'by Councils in which all the Allies will be represented'.[24] Two weeks later, after the War Cabinet meeting, he changed his instructions, assigning the Sub-Committee on Law to provide a report on trial of the Kaiser. He expanded the Sub-Committee's membership somewhat, which is why it is called the Special Sub-Committee. Five questions were asked of the Special Sub-Committee: Whether it is desirable to take proceedings against the Kaiser? What should be the nature and constitution of the tribunal for the trial of the German Kaiser? What should be the chief heads of the charges to be preferred against him? What should be the law to be applied by the tribunal? What should be its procedure?[25] Without waiting for its conclusions to be considered by the plenary Committee, it was to report as quickly as possible to Attorney General Smith. Some weeks later, a member of the Committee, Frederick Pollock, in a letter to Oliver Wendell Holmes, described the work of the Committee as being to '[e]xpand "Hang the Kaiser" in rational terms'.[26]

The Special Sub-Committee delivered its Report within a week, on 28 November 1918.[27] The next day, Hugh Bellot produced a draft report for the Sub-Committee on Law. Thus, there were two reports, one from the Special Sub-Committee dated 28 November and the other from the Sub-Committee on Law dated 29 November. Both documents were delivered to Maurice Hankey, the Secretary of the War Cabinet, on 1 December. Bellot's draft Interim Report was circulated to the members of the War Cabinet, but with the proviso that it had not yet been approved by the plenary Committee. It was being circulated 'as a contribution towards the discussion of the question of the attitude of the Allies towards the ex-Kaiser'.[28] Only later in December were the Interim Recommendations of the Committee of Enquiry formally approved and circulated.[29] The Interim Recommendations did not mention trial of the Kaiser, and only alluded to criminal responsibility for starting the war and violating the neutrality of Belgium and Luxembourg, noting that

if it were decided to prosecute persons responsible for these acts, then specific provision would be required in the treaty of peace.[30] This comment was
not further explained, but it would suggest that the Committee considered
treaty authorisation to be necessary because Germany's consent would be
required. On 7 January 1919, the Committee adopted a lengthier section entitled 'Reasons for Recommendations', in which issues relating to the Kaiser
were addressed.[31] All of these materials were published together in the First
Interim Report of the Committee dated 13 January 1919.

The report of the Special Sub-Committee on Law of 28 November provided a favourable and very succinct answer to the question of the desirability of proceedings against the Kaiser. It was an issue involving a question
of policy, the Committee acknowledged, 'but in view of the grave charges
which might be preferred and established against the Kaiser, the vindica-
tion of the principles of International Law, which he has violated, would be
incomplete were he not brought to trial'. The Special Sub-Committee also
noted that trial of other offenders could be seriously prejudiced 'if they could
plead the superior orders of a sovereign against whom no steps had been
taken'.[32] The Interim Report of the Committee of Enquiry was slightly less
unequivocal, stating that '[t]he opinion of the majority of the members of the
Committee on the whole' favoured trial.[33]

'Grave Charges', Including Starting the War

Experts from both Britain and France concurred in dividing the types of
charges that might be made against the Kaiser into three categories: waging
a war of aggression, violating the treaties of neutrality, and unlawful conduct
during the conflict. In one sense, the most straightforward and uncontroversial charges consisted of violations of the laws and customs of war. The
Report explained that there was ample precedent for the prosecution of
enemy combatants for such crimes if they were taken prisoner. The Special
Sub-Committee provided an enumeration of distinct war crimes that included 'Illegal Methods of Submarine Warfare', 'Promiscuous Bombardment
from the Air of Undefended Towns and Villages', 'Murder of Hostages', and
the 'Execution of Edith Cavell and Captain Fryatt'.[34] Similarly, the French
report described as war crimes:

> The use of forbidden arms, the poisoning of air or of water, the ill-treatment
> of prisoners, the arrest and massacre of hostages, the destruction of towns

and ships, even of hospital ships, the violation of family life by means of *déportations en masse* of peaceful inhabitants and deliberate violations of the honour of young girls, the submarine torpedoing of ships loaded with women and children, the bombarding of cities, sometimes undefended, by aeroplane or by long-range guns, with no other object than to terrorise an inoffensive population.[35]

Attributing such crimes to the supreme commander who was not in fact the physical perpetrator seemed a more difficult legal proposition. The British Special Sub-Committee had a simple, although not particularly elegant, solution to the problem. The Kaiser would be punishable for all such violations of the laws and customs of war perpetrated by German forces because, by virtue of the German Constitution, he was at the very top of the military hierarchy. 'Such being his constitutional position, both in theory and in practice, for all acts ordered or approved by him during the war, whether by explicit order or approval shown by long course of conduct, he is, it is suggested, responsible', said the Special Sub-Committee.[36]

The French jurists took the challenge of proving the Kaiser's complicity somewhat more seriously. 'His will commanded; his hand did not execute. He was not the principal party to the crime', they wrote. 'But there is no accessory without a principal. Consequently, there can be no prosecution of the Emperor without a prosecution of officers or soldiers.'[37] This was probably not an accurate statement of French law at the time. It is always possible to prosecute an accomplice or accessory even in the absence of the physical perpetrator, who may avoid trial for a variety of reasons, including his or her own death or some personal feature such as youth or insanity. Nevertheless, the French experts were correct to see a genuine problem in attributing guilt merely because an individual was the supreme commander. There may have been some criminal policy decisions that were taken at the highest level of the German command structure, such as aspects of submarine warfare, but holding Wilhelm responsible for an isolated rape or murder committed by a rogue soldier in Belgium or north-eastern France was incompatible with basic principles of criminal law. Even if the Kaiser could be held responsible 'in a narrow field and in a limited number of particular cases', the French jurists suggested this would only trivialise things. They said he was responsible 'in numberless cases', and that 'his guilt, if it is to be properly established, must be presented once and for all by bringing together the whole series of acts with which he is charged'.[38]

The other two categories of crime being considered for prosecution did not raise similar problems of attribution. If Germany had committed aggression, that is, the launching of an unlawful war, and violated Belgian neutrality, then surely the Kaiser belonged to a very small inner circle of those who had taken the fateful decisions. But there were other problems with these charges. The first was determining that they were violations of international law. Only then would the issue of personal responsibility for such acts arise. It was self-evident that breaching a treaty was a violation of international law, but far less certain that this could be said of launching a war of aggression. Moreover, even if these were violations of international law, it did not follow that individuals could be prosecuted as criminals for their part in the decision-making.

International law was in flux. Until the outbreak of the First World War, war was considered an instrument of national policy, a means of settling disputes when other methods were unsuccessful. This had changed irrevocably by the time of the Second World War. At its conclusion, the International Military Tribunal had little hesitation in condemning Nazi leaders for crimes against peace, that is, for the launching of a war of aggression. Ruling on a defence challenge that contended the charge of crimes against peace amounted to retroactive application of criminal law,[39] the tribunal pointed to the Kellogg-Briand Pact of 1928 to show that aggressive war had been condemned by international law long before Hitler invaded Poland.[40] At the governmental level, the first indications of this dramatic shift in international law can be found in the debates about prosecuting Kaiser Wilhelm II. The French jurists wrote: 'But the old conception of war as a simple process of political coercion is no longer adequate in face of the military proceedings of the German Empire, which have placed upon it the heaviest responsibilities, not only political but legal.' Larnaude and de Lapradelle pointed to declarations of President Wilson as evidence of the existence of this 'new international law'.[41]

The French jurists wrote:

> By the side of these great principles there must exist another, implied in the idea that there is between nations as between individuals a true regime of right, namely, the principle of the responsibility, not only political but legal, of the people who go to war in order to steal from a neighbouring State some provinces against the will of their populations and because they either wish to secure the wealth these provinces contain or to ruin their industries and their commerce; and who, in order to reach this result, adopt as war measures

practices which have no relation to the military necessities of the struggle, but are inspired only by this 'illicit ambition', such, for example, as the abstraction of industrial and even agricultural tools, the systematic flooding of mines, the complete destruction of masonry or concrete installations in factories, the devastation of whole regions by fire, by the razing of houses, and by the cutting down of fruit trees.[42]

The French jurists concluded that the Kaiser should be prosecuted for 'premeditating aggression, and the not less monstrous crime of the violation of Treaties'.[43]

The British Special Sub-Committee was of the same mind. Its Report invoked 'the opinion of the civilised world', describing provoking or bringing about 'an aggressive and unjust war' as 'a great crime against humanity and in breach of International Law' attributable to the Kaiser in conjunction with his ministers and military advisers. The Sub-Committee said that '[o]ne of the main objects of bringing him to trial would be defeated if foremost among the charges to be made against him was not that of having long planned and deliberately instigated an aggressive and unjust war'.[44] Several weeks later, the First Interim Report of the plenary Committee described the case of the Kaiser as 'unique', explaining that '[w]hile there is no exact precedent for punishment, there is also no exact precedent in modern times for a series of crimes brought about by a group of men of whom the ex-Kaiser was one'.[45]

The Special Sub-Committee was divided on whether to prosecute the Kaiser for launching an aggressive war, and only decided in favour by a vote of four to three. But it seems the differences were more about practical matters than the legality of the charge. The Sub-Committee noted concerns that such a charge would require an examination of the pre-war political situation, the controversies that preceded the outbreak of the conflict, 'and, indeed, the entire political history of Europe for some years before that date'. The Sub-Committee warned of the difficulty in limiting the scope of such an inquiry and said this would distract attention from other serious charges.[46]

Another difficulty in establishing the Kaiser's responsibility could be determining his authority under the German Constitution. However, the Sub-Committee observed that a sovereign's conduct might be constitutionally correct, yet nevertheless amount to a violation of international law. The Special Sub-Committee also concluded that it was 'unquestionable' that the Kaiser be prosecuted for acts perpetrated in violation of the neutrality treaties with Belgium and Luxembourg, and for 'the series of

violations, numerous and varied, of the laws and customs of war committed on land, at sea and from the air, by the military, naval and aviation
forces of Germany'.[47]

At more or less the same time as the Committee of Enquiry was com-
pleting its first interim report, in mid-December 1918, there was another significant English contribution to the preparation of international prosecution.
James Headlam Morley, an intelligence analyst in the British Foreign Office,
produced an internal memorandum on post-war trials, including that of the
Kaiser. Unlike the members of the Committee, who were all senior and very
distinguished lawyers, some of them reputed for expertise in international
law, Headlam Morley was a historian by training. He had been invited to
join the propaganda department of the Foreign Office at the outbreak of the
war where he produced, as part of his official functions, a book entitled *The
History of Twelve Days*.[48] It was an account of the outbreak of the war based
upon official government publications. The December 1918 memorandum
does not suggest whether or not Headlam Morley was asked to prepare the
study, or by whom, or whether it was a personal initiative. There is a minute
on the Foreign Office file describing the paper as '[a] memo full of sound
sense', but it is followed by another saying '[i]t must not, however, be taken as
representing a FO view'.

Basing a criminal charge on 'the fact that the policy of a country has been
so directed as to result to war, even if it could be shown that this result was
deliberately brought about, is of course something absolutely new', wrote
Headlam Morley. He explained that international relations had, until then,
been premised on 'the assumption that war was under certain circumstances
the legal and natural method of settling an international issue'. Nevertheless,
alongside such a legal and diplomatic recognition of the legitimacy of resort to force, 'there had undoubtedly before the war arisen a feeling which
was generally gaining in strength that war should, if possible, be avoided'.
Headlam Morley thought 'that the common feeling of the world would have
expressed general reprobation for any statesman who deliberately chose war
if it could be avoided'.

He distinguished between the use of force in self-defence, which would of
course be quite legitimate, and resort to war in order to extend power or to
annex territory. Headlam Morley wrote:

> Going back to the period before the outbreak of the war, we may say that
> there was a general body of feeling which recognised the criminality of a war
> deliberately undertaken for purposes of aggression when it could have been

avoided, sufficient to justify the assertion that the man or party who adopted this method would be looked on morally as criminal. The moral crime is of course quite different from a legal crime. It is common to all that there is no Court existing which has power to try the German Emperor on this charge nor is there any kind of precedent for it.

He said that a trial for launching aggressive war, 'though it would not be in accordance with legal precedent, would not be a lawless act, but a precedent on which law in the future could be established'.

Headlam Morley's objection was not so much with the legitimacy of prosecuting the crime of starting the war than with the strength of the actual case against the Kaiser. 'That we can prove folly, incompetence, recklessness, against the Emperor is undoubted; can more be proven?' Headlam Morley's judgment was no doubt well informed, as there were few who had studied the documentary materials surrounding the outbreak of the war as much as he had. He said that if such evidence existed, it would be in the possession of the Germans. Better, thought Headlam Morley, that the matter be viewed as one to be left to the Germans, who could try their former Emperor for leading them into war on the basis of their own materials.[49]

Larnaude and de Lapradelle reasoned that the new international law meant a State could be held responsible for violating the law of nations. Yet Germany's liability as a State could only be civil or financial, explained the French academics. The final responsibility, they concluded, 'must rest and can rest only upon individuals. The personal responsibility for the criminal acts rests upon all German statesmen, civilian and military leaders, and first and foremost upon William II.'[50] In order to reach their conclusion, Larnaude and de Lapradelle undertook a peroration on the German Emperor's position within the State and his very personal role in governmental decisions, especially those of a military nature. They concluded their analysis by listing the crimes Wilhelm had committed, insisting that these were all crimes against international law: 'a war conceived in injustice, the violation of the neutrality of Belgium and Luxembourg, the violation of the established rules of international custom and of the Hague Conventions'.[51] The tone was self-assured, but never before in scholarly legal writing had such things been said.

The French jurists were more concerned than their British counterparts about the legality of charges that might appear contrary to the maxim *nullum crimen sine lege*, that is, the prohibition of retroactive punishments. Perhaps they had more scruples on this point because the rule was enshrined in Article 8 of the *Déclaration des droits de l'homme et du citoyen*, adopted by the French National Assembly in 1789. For the British, who had no written constitution, the prohibition of retroactive punishment was nothing more than an interpretative presumption, capable of being overridden by legislation, and not a peremptory norm. The issue presented itself not only for the new crimes of waging aggressive war and violating treaties, but also for violations of the laws and customs of war. Even if The Hague conventions set out legal rules that German soldiers had violated, they did not specify any punishment. 'The failure of these Conventions to mention the consequences of their violation by their signatories does not mean that it was desired to leave them free of penalty', said Larnaude and de Lapradelle.[52] Here, they compared international criminal law with domestic criminal law, where 'a very high degree of codification' has been attained. International law, on the other hand, was 'still in a large measure in a formative state … [T]he law is evolved by way of a reaction to the deed, and the penalty is based only upon the conscience of the judge who himself appears only to save the criminal from vengeance.'[53]

Finally, there was the issue of the immunity of a Head of State from prosecution by courts of a State other than his or her own. Both the French and the British had in past centuries indulged in trying and punishing their own monarchs, but they had never prosecuted one from a foreign country. The French experts considered it to be a rule of international law that national courts could not judge a foreign sovereign for an offence against 'ordinary law'. Even if the Emperor might be tried for 'a crime not committed in the exercise of his functions', prosecution was not possible to the extent that the punishable act related to his official role. 'If the immunity ceased to apply to the ex-Emperor in respect of his personal crimes, it still extends to official crimes, acts of a foreign Government, of which, as a matter of course, the courts have always refused to take cognizance.'[54]

The British Committee of Enquiry was less inclined to acknowledge the immunity of the Kaiser. Under the sub-heading 'Alleged Immunity of the ex-Kaiser', the First Interim Report noted that the question 'has rarely been discussed in modern times' and has been only a matter of 'academic interest'. This may have been another way of acknowledging that no State had ever attempted to prosecute the Head of State of another country. The British Committee viewed this otherwise, contending that 'no modern usage establishing such immunity appears to exist'. The Committee distinguished the situation of a Head of State visiting another country at its invitation and that of one who invades or occupies. In the latter case, it said 'there seems to be no authority'.[55] John Macdonnell, the chairman of the Committee, wrote a separate note on the question, developing the summary discussion of the point in the main report. He canvassed the writings of international law publicists, finding some support for immunity, but questioning the validity of the reasoning of the writers favourable to it. 'The result of an examination of the authorities, if such can be said to exist, would seem to be that there is no rule or usage exempting from criminal jurisdiction foreign sovereigns who have invaded the territory of another sovereign', he concluded.[56]

Although it was not circulated publicly, American international lawyers also prepared an opinion that addressed the immunity issue. The authors, David Hunter Miller and James Brown Scott, were members of the American delegation to the Paris Peace Conference. They wrote that under the 'system of law' in force in July and August 1914:

> ... a Chief of State was not internationally responsible for the political act of his Government, even in a case when that Government was internationally responsible for its own political act, as Germany and Austria-Hungary were and are responsible for the invasion of Belgium in violation of a solemn treaty and of the rules of international law. Consequently, no international penal responsibility existed or now exists for those acts then committed, and the creation at this time of such penal responsibility for such past acts would be extra-legal from the viewpoint of international law; would be contrary to the spirit both of international law and of the municipal law of civilised States and under whatever forms it might be clothed would, in reality, be a political and not a legal creation. Therefore, the authors of the war cannot be considered as penally responsible for its commencement.

They explained that their legal conclusions did not limit the authority of the Allies 'to administer political punishment upon those whom they may regard as having been responsible for the disturbance of the world's peace, and to prevent a recurrence'.[57]

Modern international law authorities, notably the International Court of Justice ruling in 2002,[58] confirm the correctness of the French opinion. Macdonnell summarily dismissed authorities that did not accord with his own preference. His opinion suited Curzon and Lloyd George, but it was not very convincing.

'A Greater Stage': Establishing
an International Criminal Court

Both the British and the French experts were favourable to the establishment of an international tribunal for the purpose of trying the Kaiser. The
French experts thought their own law to be inadequate for most of what
was being attributed to the Kaiser, although they were more positive about
the British and American courts. According to Larnaude and de Lapradelle,
'the Emperor can be tried by our military tribunals for certain war crimes,
and more than that he can be tried, without limitation whatsoever, by the
courts-martial of the principal armies who are acting in conjunction with
ours'.[59] But the British Committee was not as positive about English law.
'[N]o English Court, administering the ordinary criminal law, would have
jurisdiction to try an enemy alien in respect of any, or all events of the great
majority, of the offences in question', it said.[60]

Even if the national legal framework had been deemed sufficient, there was
a strong feeling that the scale of the alleged crimes and the historic nature of
the proceedings required an international body. The French experts said that
'a higher court, more resounding discussion and a greater stage' was required.
'[T]he "question of William II" would be considered from too narrow a point
of view and dwarfed, if it were reduced to the proportions of a case before
a criminal court or a military tribunal.' Only an international court could
'proclaim the solemn and purifying legal consequences which the public
conscience requires'.[61] The British Special Sub-Committee proposed trial
of the Kaiser by 'an International Tribunal, free from national bias, the decisions of which would possess unquestionable authority, which would speak
in the name of the conscience of the world, which would help to re-establish
and strengthen International Law'. It said this would provide a deterrent and
warning to highly placed officials.[62] The plenary Committee pointed to 'the
greater moral weight attached to the opinions and acts' of an international
tribunal, including 'the fact that it would be the mouthpiece of the united
voice of the Associated Governments upon the questions involved'.[63]

Expert advice provided to the American delegation by George Finch was
not so positive. Finch acknowledged that an international tribunal would
'no doubt lend greater solemnity and prestige to the proceedings', but he
felt it 'would probably be open to certain objections of a practical nature'.

Although Finch thought a 'joint tribunal' with judges of more than one nationality was possible, this would only be acceptable to the extent that the
country of such judges could claim to be directly victimised by the alleged
crime. For example, he said, it would not be acceptable for American judges
to sit on a joint tribunal dealing with acts perpetrated before the United
States had entered the war. 'It is believed that on the whole it would be more
in accordance with previous practice, less open to objection from the accused
and of greater facility in operation to constitute separate tribunals for each
nation or each group of nations whose armies were actually united in campaign', wrote Finch.[64] This became the American position during subsequent
negotiations. Defended by Robert Lansing and James Brown Scott, this was
one of the issues that split the Commission on Responsibilities.

In its quite summary report, the Special Sub-Committee did not go into
any detail about the composition of the proposed international tribunal. It
made two observations. First, while all States might be interested in the proceedings and decisions of such a tribunal, they were 'not all equally so', and
'certain States may justly claim a larger share of representation in the composition of the Tribunal'. Second, judges from neutral countries should not
be invited to participate. The Special Sub-Committee's concern was 'that
in all probability, having regard to the ethnical, economic and geographical
character of certain of the neutral States, their representatives might not be
free from pressure or apprehension of pressure'.[65] This was a curious remark,
the message apparently being that neutrals are less likely to be neutral than
non-neutrals!

The plenary Committee of Enquiry devoted more attention to the matter,
pointing to problems about the size and scale of such an institution. Because
it was contemplating an international tribunal that would prosecute many
accused persons and not just the Kaiser, the British thought that the 'chief'
Allied States and the United States should appoint six members, four of them
with judicial or legal experience and two with military expertise. Other
Allied States, that is, those not deserving of the adjective 'chief', might also be
able to appoint one or perhaps more members to the tribunal.[66]

The French jurists stopped short of prescribing the structure and organisation of the proposed tribunal, noting only that it would not be difficult to find
qualified judges from the supreme courts of the Allied nations who would be
'true representatives of justice in the loftiest sense'.[67] They briefly considered
leaving it to the League of Nations, whose creation was being promoted and

that would soon exist, to set up the tribunal and determine the procedure and the system of penalties applicable to international crimes. This had been proposed by one of their colleagues at the Law Faculty of the University of Paris, Professor Emile Garçon. Larnaude and de Lapradelle agreed that the League of Nations would 'doubtless organise and create tribunals before which the States and their Governments will appear', but said it was not possible 'to postpone the immediate trial which the public conscience so insistently demands'.[68] Like the British, they rejected the participation of neutral States who, by failing to protest against violations of international law had 'cut themselves off from all settlements concerning the war. They must not be admitted to "the criminal liquidation" of the conflict.'[69] The British Committee proposed that the international tribunal apply 'the principles of the Law of Nations as they result from the usages established among civilised peoples, from the laws of humanity and the dictates of the public conscience', a formulation derived from the preamble of the Hague Conventions on the laws and customs of war of 1899 and 1907, as well as 'the regulations contained in the Hague Conventions and Declarations and the Geneva Conventions so far as the same or any of them may be applicable'.[70] The preambular reference to the Hague Conventions is commonly known as the Martens clause, after the Russian diplomat who proposed that it be inserted as a residual provision, applicable '[u]ntil a more complete code of the laws of war has been issued ... in cases not included in the Regulations adopted by them'.

The Special Sub-Committee discussed the procedure to be followed, taking into account the differences in approach of the inquisitorial system of the French and the adversarial system of the English and the Americans. 'It is suggested that neither should be strictly adhered to', said the Sub-Committee. 'The procedure ought to be as simple as possible, consistently with justice to the accused.'[71] Several fair trial rights were set out, including proceedings that were 'public and mainly oral', a right to counsel, and the possibility of examining and cross-examining witnesses. To this the plenary Committee added the right to be notified of the charges in writing 'a reasonable time' before trial, and to receive a reasoned judgment.[72] The British experts acknowledged the impossibility of applying English rules of evidence to proceedings where the majority of the judges would be unfamiliar with them.[73]

The French jurists essentially ignored the question of procedure. 'What procedure will the tribunal follow?' they asked. 'It will decide that point itself.'[74] Although they seemed opposed to *in absentia* trial, Larnaude and de

Lapradelle insisted that, present or not present, the Kaiser had to be put on trial. They said that the judgment of the 'High Court of International Criminal Justice', established for that purpose, 'must have the universal validity of *res judicata*. This will mean the life or death of international law; the future of the League of Nations hangs in the balance. The Allied and Associated belligerents will cast the die'.[75]

5

Britain, France, and Italy Agree to Try the Kaiser

Trial of the Kaiser had emerged as a burning issue at a time when an immense number of complex policy matters relating to the aftermath of the war and the peace settlement with Germany confronted Britain's leaders. Barely two weeks had passed since Clemenceau had mooted the idea. Welcomed by Curzon and embraced by Lloyd George, the proposed trial had now taken centre stage. Lloyd George opened the Imperial War Cabinet meeting of 28 November 1918 saying an early decision was required as to action regarding the Kaiser. Clemenceau was expected in London in a few days and the British Prime Minister wanted 'to be fortified in any discussions on the subject to the views of the Imperial War Cabinet'. Lloyd George said that he knew the French Government was strongly in favour of prosecution. Referring to the decision taken by the Cabinet the previous week to seek an opinion from the Law Officers of the Crown, Lloyd George revealed that 'a very powerful legal Committee' had now come to 'a unanimous decision'.[1]

Attorney General F. E. Smith presented the report of the Committee that had been set up barely a week earlier. Writing of the meeting two decades later, Lloyd George said that he had rarely seen an assembly of Ministers 'so enthralled by the exposition of a case'. Cabinet speeches were traditionally brief, rarely more than five minutes, wrote Lloyd George. But on 28 November 1918, at a moment when time was exceedingly precious, Smith kept his audience entranced for the best part of an hour. He spoke without notes. It was 'a masterly performance', Lloyd George observed, and it seemingly won over the doubters of the previous week. He wrote of the 'limpid clarity of the statement, the unerring choice of the apt word, the mellowness of a voice which had a great range but was subdued to the proportions and

The Trial of the Kaiser. William A. Schabas. © William A. Schabas, 2018. Published 2018 by Oxford University Press.

the quality of the audience'. Lloyd George said that Smith had held every member of the Cabinet, 'representing as they did between them the greatest Empire on earth, in complete bondage to the sway of one of the finest intellects and one of the most perfect speakers ever contributed by the British Bar to politics'.[2] Not everyone was a fan. A year later, the American Secretary of State Robert Lansing, in a letter to President Woodrow Wilson, described Smith as someone 'whose vanity is beyond measure' and who 'has imagined himself the central figure in the prosecution of the Kaiser'.[3]

There were two diametrically opposite courses, Smith told the War Cabinet: to grant immunity to the Kaiser or to punish him. 'It was difficult to see how we could justify the first course, as the ex-Kaiser had been the supreme authority in Germany, and the public statements made by him during the war would appear fully to warrant his trial', he said. What was an even more serious charge, in his opinion, was that the ex-Kaiser had, during the war, 'made a daring challenge to international law'. Smith thought submarine commanders should be prosecuted, but 'he did not see how this could be done if the "All Highest" were granted immunity'.[4]

Smith said that the Committee had unanimously concluded that the ex-Kaiser ought to be punished, either by way of trial or à la Napoleon. According to Smith, the Committee inclined to the first of those courses. But he added a note of equivocation, indicating that he personally did not rule out a Napoleonic solution. 'That course may be recommended by powerful argument and I do not myself exclude it, Prime Minister', he said.

However, there were obvious advantages to holding a trial. 'It is, of course, very desirable that we should be able to say that this man received fair play, and that he has had a fair trial, but grave difficulties beset this course in its complete application', said Smith. He questioned how the Court might be composed, and whether neutrals and even Germans might sit as judges. Smith warned that the advantage of the judicial route over the Napoleonic approach would be lost if the tribunal were seen to be unfair. However, he inclined to the view that the judges come only from Allied countries. 'Grave judges should be appointed but we should, as it seems to me at present, take the risk of saying that in this quarrel we, the Allies, taking our stand upon the universally admitted principles of the moral law, take our own standards of right and commit the trial of them to our own tribunals', said Smith. Time did not permit him to develop the arguments, he explained, but he wanted it put on record that he was aware that there were 'formidable arguments' supporting the opposite view.

Smith cited a speech by Edmund Burke during the celebrated impeachment trial of Warren Hastings in the late eighteenth century. Burke had contended that the supreme head of a nation must be held responsible, in certain circumstances, for the actions of the nation. Smith told the War Cabinet that were the Kaiser to avoid some form of accountability, 'common people will say everywhere that he has escaped because he is an emperor. In my judgment, they will be right. They will say that august influence has been exerted to save him'. He thought it necessary 'for all time to teach the lesson that failure is not the only risk which a man possessing at the moment in any country despotic powers, and taking the awful decision between Peace and War, has to fear'. For the future, he wanted rulers with the authority to decide on matters of war and peace to know that they were gambling with their own personal safety.

Smith turned to the problem of obtaining custody over the Kaiser. He observed that the French were already of the view that he could be extradited from the Netherlands. 'Holland must, in effect, give him up', he thought. The Allies would have powerful arguments for surrender. Smith considered that the 'internal condition of Holland seems to me to be such that it would be very difficult for her to reject arguments of the kind indicated'. He also considered the possibility of the Kaiser returning to Germany. He thought this unlikely because 'taking of unnecessary risks has not up to the present been a distinguishing feature of his career'. Smith could not rule out the possibility that the Germans themselves might wish to deal with the Kaiser.

'The great question', said Smith, was to determine the offences for which the Kaiser might be charged. He briefly set out three categories. The first was responsibility for the origin of the war, said Smith. The Sub-Committee had been favourable to such a charge, but only by a thin majority of four to three.[5] Smith made it clear that he sided with the minority.

> Well Sir, I can only say, without giving a decision, that the trial of such a charge would involve infinite disputation. We do not wish to be confronted by a meticulous examination of the history of European politics of the last twenty years. It is very easy to see that no German advocate of the ex-Kaiser would find it difficult to enlarge the area of discussion from the question of the origin of the war to a close discussion of the military significance of the Russian strategic railways. The view that I have at present, is that it would not be wise to add so general a charge, but this provisional view might easily be modified if new and decisive documents were produced.
>
> The second charge was responsibility for the invasion of Belgium 'in breach of International Law and for all the consequent criminal acts which took place'. That is an absolutely clear issue and upon it I do not think that any honest

tribunal could hesitate. The third was responsibility for unrestricted submarine warfare. I wish to press most strongly upon my colleagues certain fundamental considerations in regard to submarine warfare, as it has been carried on since the incident of the *Lusitania*. Since then, thousands of women and children, in our clear and expressed view, have been brutally murdered. I am dealing with the case where a ship is torpedoed carrying no munitions of war, but which it is known must or may be carrying women and children, and where it is equally known that such passengers had no possible means of escape and I do not in this connection deal with the vile cases of assassination when helpless boats, vainly attempting to escape, have been fired on and destroyed ... It is surely vital that if ever there is another war, whether in ten or fifteen years, or however distant it may be, those responsible on both sides for the conduct of that war should be made to feel that unrestricted submarine warfare has been so branded with the punitive censure of the whole civilised world that it has definitely passed into the category of international crime.

There was little to add. A rather perfunctory discussion followed.

'The only thing that occurs to me is that it might create difficulty with America; that is all', said Lord Reading.

'America must paddle her own canoe', answered Lloyd George. 'We have responsibilities in the matter greater than hers. Our sufferings have been much greater.'

The Canadian Prime Minister, Robert Borden, had seemed favourable to a trial at the 20 November meeting of the Imperial War Cabinet. Now, he was rather more equivocal. He thought that 'if judgment of some kind is to be passed upon the ex-Kaiser, that it could be done more effectively by a resolution of the Peace Conference than by any trial. I am not quite sure that that would not be the best way.' In his memoirs, Borden said that the Attorney General had made 'a powerful argument in favour of proceeding against the Kaiser', but 'I did not concur'.[6]

Bonar Law had chosen to conceal his lack of enthusiasm for the idea. Only the previous day, he had shouted at the Prime Minister: 'George, if you take my advice you will not touch it! If you do, believe me, you will always regret it.'[7] In the Cabinet meeting he was more subdued, attempting to summarise what seemed a consensus: 'Then I understand the decision of the Cabinet is that, so far as we have the power, we intend to punish the ex-Kaiser.'

'As the person responsible for these offences against international law and against humanity', replied Lloyd George.

The minutes record that the Imperial War Cabinet adopted the Committee's report and agreed that, 'so far as the British Government have the power, the ex-Kaiser should be held personally responsible for his crimes against international law'.[8] It does not, however, seem that the report of the Special Sub-Committee delivered to the Attorney prior to the Cabinet meeting and published in January as part of the First Interim Report of the Committee of Enquiry[9] was actually produced at the 28 November Cabinet meeting. What, then, did it mean to say that the Cabinet had adopted the Report of the Committee?[10]

The following day, Lloyd George addressed a campaign rally in Newcastle-on-Tyne. The Prime Minister told the meeting that there were 'two un-doubted offences against the law of nations' for which the Kaiser should be tried. 'There is, first of all, the great crime against humanity involved in de-liberately planning and plotting a great war, which has caused indescribable suffering to millions of people.'[11] The second was the invasion of Belgium. But of course, that is not what Smith argued before the War Cabinet. Is that what the War Cabinet agreed to when it adopted the Report of the Special Sub-Committee? After the vote of thanks, Lloyd George said he had over-looked mentioning that 'some of the greatest jurists in this country' had in-vestigated the issue of the Kaiser's responsibility for the invasion of Belgium and the conduct of the war. 'They have investigated it, and have come finally to the conclusion quite unanimously that in their judgment the Kaiser was guilty of an indictable offence for which he ought to be held responsible.' In his memoirs, Lloyd George tried to downplay his enthusiasm for trying the Kaiser. He wrote that prior to 9 December he had made no public reference to the Report of the Special Sub-Committee and Smith's presentation in the War Cabinet, but that was obviously not an accurate recollection.[12]

The Allies Meet, But Without the Americans

On or about 15 November, Clemenceau proposed to Lloyd George a pre-liminary meeting pending the arrival in Europe of President Wilson. Lloyd George agreed, but insisted it be in London, where he was preoccupied with the election campaign. Lloyd George also invited the Italian Prime Minister, Vittorio Orlando, and Woodrow Wilson's personal representative in Paris, Colonel Edward House, who answered that he was ill and could not attend.[13] Clemenceau assured House 'that the meeting was of no importance whatever and that he thought that [Lloyd] George had asked him to come over simply for electioneering purposes'. Clemenceau gave House 'his solemn word of honour that he would discuss no question of any importance with [Lloyd] George'.[14]

Orlando described being welcomed upon arrival at London's Charing Cross station on 1 December 'by a Prince representing the King and by all the members of the Cabinet, from Lloyd George to Bonar Law, to Balfour, Austin Chamberlain and Lords Curzon and Milner'. As the visitors 'passed through the streets of the immense metropolis amid the cheers of enthusiastic crowds it was that cry for vengeance that seemed to outweigh all others'.

Acknowledging *The Times* as the newspaper that 'best represents the phlegm that the English see as a form of their national dignity', Orlando referred to the editorial view: '*Vox populi* is not always *Vox Dei*; but in general it is, on the great questions of good and evil. There is no doubt that the voice of the people is demanding the punishment of the ex-Emperor of Germany.'[15] Clemenceau's right-hand man, General Jean Jules Henri Mordacq, described the climate in London: 'As if an order had gone out to do so, virtually everyone asked me if, in France, we had decided to put Kaiser Wilhelm on trial, adding that in England, there was virtual unanimity, from the workers and farmers to the King, on this issue.' The English public thought that failure to bring to justice the man most responsible for the war 'would be a real crime against God and humanity'.[16]

The leaders of the three European allies assembled on 2 December in the Cabinet Room at 10 Downing Street. Clemenceau, Marshal Foch, and Generals Weygand and Mordacq represented France. Italy's delegation was composed of Prime Minister Orlando, Secretary of State Sidney Sonnino, and the *Chef du cabinet*, Luigi Aldrovandi. Lloyd George, Balfour, Bonar Law, Maurice Hankey, and General Henry Wilson were the British representatives. After dealing with preparations for the Peace Conference and the issue of reparations, the leaders turned to the Kaiser. Lloyd George circulated Smith's presentation to the Imperial War Cabinet and the Report of the Special Sub-Committee, drawing attention to the latter's suggestion that an international tribunal be set up composed of the chief Allied States and the United States of America. He then referred to the opinion of the British Law Officers, saying that they had proposed the Kaiser be tried on the following charges: '1. His responsibility for the invasion of Belgium in breach of international law, and for all consequent criminal acts which took place; 2. His responsibility in the matter of unrestricted submarine warfare; 3. Offences in the category of the execution of Captain Fryatt.'[17] Although the majority of the Special Sub-Committee had given its agreement to a charge of launching an aggressive war, the minority view expressed by Attorney General Smith at the 28 November War Cabinet meeting seemed to have prevailed. Had the participants in the Downing Street meeting on 2 December studied the British documents attentively, they might have noticed the distinction, and openly debated the charge of aggressive war.

'[I]t would show an immense progress if we could punish the man who was guilty of a great historic crime like the declaration of war in August, 1914', said Clemenceau. He stated that he supported the British proposal 'energet-ically', but without drawing attention to controversy about the aggressive war issue. Clemenceau also referred to accomplices, noting that the Crown Prince would be at the top of the list. He thought some of the 'great soldiers, who had merely obeyed orders' should escape prosecution. For Clemenceau, 'if we could get seven or eight persons, and make them responsible before an international tribunal, this would be an enormous progress for humanity. The ex-Kaiser was the person really responsible for the war.' Clemenceau was not interested in camp commanders who had ill-treated prisoners. For them, a court martial was all that was required. The French Prime Minister wanted only the former Kaiser to be brought to justice, adding that this would be enough to satisfy the public. 'They will feel that justice will in future be done in the case of Kaisers and Kings just as much as in the case of common men. If this could be achieved, it would be a magnificant advance and a moral revolution.'[18]

The Italian representatives were divided in their views. Sonnino, the Secretary of State, questioned whether a trial might make the ex-Kaiser a 'patriotic martyr'. He also asked whether it was right to prosecute the leaders of a country for the acts of that country, when the nation as a whole was re-sponsible. 'A nation usually gets the Government it deserves', said Sonnino. 'Was not St Helena useful to the Bonapartists? The Answer was "Yes". And the regime of Napoleon III had been the result.'[19] Orlando, on the other hand, was on the same page as Lloyd George and Clemenceau, describing trial of the Kaiser as 'a great question of universal conscience of mankind. It was a matter of universal sentiment which touched the highest moral laws.' Orlando said that the idea that nations were responsible for the faults of their governments might have been persuasive in the past. This was not the case of 'mere blunders, but with crimes, and the ex-Kaiser ought to pay like other criminals. The ex-Kaiser, for example, had decorated, personally, captains of submarines which had come straight back from perpetrating murder.'[20] Orlando turned to the method of bringing the Kaiser to justice.

He described it as 'a question of detail'. One plan, he said, would be to have a declaration by the Allied governments pronouncing the ex-Kaiser to be a criminal. 'As to the idea that the ex-Kaiser might be regarded as a martyr, he personally did not believe that he ever would be. Anyhow, we could not calculate for centuries ahead, and we had to deal with a very strong sentiment in all countries at the present time', said Orlando.[21]

Lloyd George asked whether a political condemnation of the Kaiser would be sufficient. An actual trial was 'much the more striking'. Clemenceau agreed, saying he stood for trial. The Italians were less certain.

'The question of the constitution of the Court presents almost insurmountable difficulties', said Orlando.

'And what if Holland declines to give up the ex-Kaiser, basing herself on her tradition of liberal views', said Sonnino.

Lloyd George answered: 'Holland would then be put outside the League of Nations.' Clemenceau added: 'There would be no question of Holland standing against the opinion of all the Allied powers.'

Balfour said it meant nothing to say Holland would not be admitted to the League of Nations, as the organisation did not yet exist. According to Balfour, 'extreme measures' might be needed to convince the Dutch to surrender the Kaiser. Imposition of a blockade was one method. 'No doubt that would bring Holland to terms, but before taking such high-handed action we must be sure of the co-operation of America', he said.[22] Lloyd George added his agreement, pointing out that every European country would depend upon the Allies for food for some time to come. His plan was not to send any supplies to the Dutch until they surrendered the Kaiser.[23]

Balfour returned to the example of Napoleon. Exile and internment was 'a clear and simple course' that could be effected by administrative action, but it would lose the advantage of a trial. On the other hand, a disadvantage of trial would be the perceived need to involve neutral countries. It might also be delayed and prolonged, and this 'would weary the whole world'. Balfour referred to the impeachment of Warren Hastings, as Attorney General Smith had done at the War Cabinet meeting of the previous week. He expressed concern that trial might involve airing German arguments about the causes of the war. 'There would be all the arguments of lawyers, which would draw attention off the fact that this man was the ringleader in the greatest crime against the human race on which the eyes of the whole world ought to be fixed', concluded Balfour.[24]

Clemenceau did not want neutral States to participate in the international tribunal. 'They had no right to it, they had not intervened in the war, and had undergone no sacrifice. The right of constituting the Court belonged to those who had made sacrifices. The Allies had secured this right by their immense losses in men and sacrifices of all kinds.'[25]

'But if there are no neutrals on the Tribunal', answered Balfour, 'will this not take away from it all appearances of impartiality? If the Allies set up the Court themselves, where would be the moral effect before the world?' Clemenceau said that all justice was relative. It would not be possible to prevent judicial impartiality being challenged. But when a crime took place on a scale so unprecedented in history, Clemenceau thought 'France, Great Britain, Italy, and the United States must place themselves high enough to take the responsibility for dealing with it'. Supporting Clemenceau, Lloyd George added: 'Every judge tried an offence against the society of which he was a member. The same would be applicable in the present case.'[26]

The meeting of the three Allies concluded that 'the ex-Kaiser and his principal accomplices should be brought to trial before an International Court'. Lloyd George asked whether they should await the Peace Conference before demanding the surrender of the former Emperor or, assuming the United States concurred, would they try to proceed and obtain custody immediately? Clemenceau, perhaps recalling his promise to Colonel House, preferred to postpone the matter until Wilson's arrival in Europe. Lloyd George persisted, however, and it was agreed that he would seek the views of the American President.[27]

The three leaders also decided to make an immediate demand to the Netherlands for rendition of the Kaiser, but once again, only if President Wilson was in agreement.[28] When they reconvened in the afternoon, Lloyd George presented the meeting with a draft telegram to be sent to President Wilson. After some minor amendments from Balfour and Reading, who were also in attendance, agreement was reached on the following text:

> At a Conference of the Governments of France, Great Britain, and Italy, held in London this morning, the three Governments agreed to recommend that a demand ought to be presented to Holland for the surrender of the person of the ex-Kaiser for trial by an international court, to be appointed by the Allies, on the charge of being the criminal mainly responsible for the War and the breaches of international law by the forces of Germany by land, sea, and air.
>
> During its deliberations the Conference had before it the opinion of a Committee of nine of the most eminent jurists of the British Isles, who

recommended unanimously that the ex-Kaiser and his principal accomplices should be brought to trial before a court consisting of nominees of the principal nations victorious in the war.

In coming to the conclusion set forth above, the Conference were influenced by the following principal considerations:

(a) That justice requires that the ex-Kaiser and his principal accomplices who designed and caused the war with its malignant purpose, or who were responsible for the incalculable sufferings inflicted upon the human race during the war, should be brought to trial and punished for their crimes.

(b) That the certainty of inevitable personal punishment for crimes against humanity and international right will be a very important security against future attempts to make war wrongfully or to violate international law, and is a necessary stage in the development of the authority of a League of Nations.

(c) That it will be impossible to bring to justice lesser criminals, such as those who have oppressed the French, Belgians, and other peoples, committed murder on the high seas, and maltreated prisoners of war, if the arch-criminal, who for thirty years has proclaimed himself the sole arbiter of German policy, and has been so in fact, escapes condign punishment.

(d) That the court by which the question of responsibility for the war and its grosser barbarities should be determined ought to be appointed by those nations who have played a principal part in winning the war, and have thereby shown their understanding of what freedom means and their readiness to make unlimited sacrifices in its behalf.

(This clause is intended to relate only to the composition of the court which will deal with crimes committed in connection with the late war, and is not intended to prejudice the question of the composition of international courts under a League of Nations.)

The Conference hopes that the Government of the United States will share its views and co-operate with the Allies in the presentation to Holland of a demand for the surrender of the person of the ex-Kaiser and of the Crown Prince for trial before an international court to be appointed by the Allies.[29]

Consensus in the War Cabinet

After reaching unanimity with the leaders of France and Italy, but before they had left London, Lloyd George convened the Imperial War Cabinet, where there was somewhat less of a consensus. He presented the Cabinet members with the minutes and conclusions of the previous day's Conference, including the telegram that was to be sent to President Wilson. Lloyd George pointed out that 'there had been a certain amount of discussion' as to whether the Kaiser 'should be treated summarily, as was done in the case of Napoleon, or whether a State trial should be held'. Lloyd George noted that Clemenceau had been strongly in favour of a State trial, 'as he considered it would be very much more impressive'. Answering a question from Lord Reading, Lloyd George confirmed that the Conference the previous day definitely favoured a State trial. '[T]here was no question about it', he said, 'and that if we wished to propose any other course we must ask our Allies if they would agree.'[30]

Borden of Canada said he was still not convinced of the wisdom of a trial for the Kaiser. 'A trial before such a tribunal might become impressive in more senses than one if it were dragged out for many months or even for years, with the attendant opportunity for the ex-Kaiser to exercise his well-known art of posing and intriguing', he said. Borden thought 'the public opinion of the world and the justice of the case would be better satisfied if the ex-Kaiser were dealt with by resolution of the Peace Conference'. He said the sentence of a tribunal established by the enemies of the Kaiser 'would not rank higher in point of fairness or justice than a sentence by the Peace Conference upon facts which were known and admitted'. Lloyd George invited Borden to make his point when the Cabinet was joined by the French and Italian representatives. Chamberlain encouraged Borden, 'as he thought that a good many people held the view that a State trial would give the ex-Kaiser's friends too much opportunity for exalting him'.[31]

Lord Reading questioned Lloyd George about the nature of the proposed court. He expressed a preference for an 'International Court' as opposed to a 'Judicial Court'.[32] Lloyd George recalled that this issue had arisen the previous day when the draft telegram was being discussed. Reading had made the same point then, and the change had been agreed to,[33] as Lloyd George explained to the War Cabinet. Borden challenged the accuracy of the term 'International Court' if it was only to be composed of nominees of the victors.[34]

The Australian Prime Minister, 'Billy' Hughes, said that if the issue was dealt with by a resolution of the Peace Conference, the Kaiser would not be able to defend himself. Borden replied that in any case the Kaiser's defence would be purely formal. Hughes did not like the idea of an International Court, in case one did not get a conviction. He said such a result would be 'dreadful', and not worth the risk. 'It was in the interest of mankind that he should die', said Hughes. He was not convinced that international law was then clear enough to sustain trial and conviction.[35]

'The case which could be made against the ex-Kaiser was one such as the world had never known, and the charges could only be brought out properly before an International Tribunal', said Lloyd George. Nothing could be more impressive, he thought, and even if the tribunal sat for months, 'this would only be a very small matter compared with the fact that it was going to initiate the principle that the rulers of the future would be held personally responsible for their acts if through any fault of theirs blood and treasure were wasted by nations going to war'. Lloyd George described trial of the Kaiser as 'a tremendous innovation'. He harkened back to Napoleon's fate, explaining that 'it never entered into the heads of our ancestors that he should be treated as a criminal'. But that was now the plan for Kaiser Wilhelm. 'It would be un-dignified to get a person such as the ex-Kaiser or the ex-Crown Prince out of the way by means of a resolution of the Peace Conference', he insisted.[36]

Winston Churchill said that although initially hesitant, he was now 'in-clined to agree' with Lloyd George that an international tribunal was the way to deal with the Kaiser. Curzon described Lloyd George's arguments for trial before an international tribunal to be 'very powerful, in fact, overwhelming'.[37] Borden remained sceptical, but seemed prepared to compromise. He said that if there were to be a trial, then it should be premised upon 'definite and per-manent principle' and 'should be expressed as to include all persons respon-sible for forcing upon the world an unjust and aggressive war'. Borden urged that the tribunal be established on 'a permanent basis, so that all rulers and advisers of rulers in the future might know the penalty for any such action as that undertaken by the German autocracy in 1914'.[38] Although initially opposed to the idea, Borden may quite inadvertently have earned the distinc-tion of being the first to propose a permanent international criminal court. Lloyd George said he agreed with Borden's proposal.

After about an hour, the French and Italian leaders joined the meeting of the Imperial War Cabinet. The Kaiser issue was only discussed briefly. Despite the invitation of Lloyd George in the Cabinet meeting, Borden did not raise any objection or propose that the Kaiser be condemned by resolution of the Peace Conference rather than by judgment of an international court. Only Clemenceau intervened, to say that in his opinion, the question of the Kaiser 'should remain open until an official talk could take place between all the Governments concerned'.[39]

The message was sent to President Wilson that evening.[40] The British Ambassador in Paris communicated the contents of the telegram to Colonel House. 'Colonel House told me that views in this telegram coincided entirely with his own. He has already expressed them to the President of the United States and though he cannot remember exactly what the latter replied he is sure that he expressed no dissent', Grahame reported to the Foreign Office.[41] House sought Wilson's agreement on a number of points that had been decided at the December conference, but the trial of the Kaiser was not one of them. He said the decision should be deferred until the President's arrival in Europe.[42] The memoirs of Lloyd George record that President Wilson 'intimated' that he was in agreement with the decision of the Allies.[43] But when Wilson set sail for Paris on the evening of 3 December, he had been informed of the decision at the London meeting and made it quite clear that he was not prepared to provide an endorsement. On 4 December, the British mission to Washington reported that the telegram had been communicated to the President and the Secretary of State, who preferred to reserve their position until Wilson arrived in Paris.[44] The Under Secretary of State, Frank L. Polk, expressed Wilson's position more dramatically. He wrote that he had spoken to the President, who said that 'under no circumstances was he prepared to commit himself at this time. The question of the punishment of the German Kaiser could be taken up when he reached France.'[45] Meanwhile, Wilson told journalists who were on board the ship with him, somewhere between New York City and Cherbourg, that he was not 'wholly convinced that the Kaiser was personally responsible for the war or the prosecution of it ... The Kaiser was probably a victim of circumstance and environment. In a case of this sort you can't with certainty put your finger on the guilty party'.[46]

6

The Dutch Are Divided

Prior to the First World War, the Dutch economy had been dependent upon commerce with colonies in the East Indies and on agricultural exports, as well as trade from Germany that passed through Rotterdam, located at the mouth of the Rhine. The port of Rotterdam was the main transit point for German goods. German business at Rotterdam dropped dramatically with the outbreak of the war. Trade with the Dutch colonies also declined steadily during the four years of the conflict. By 1918, Rotterdam's volume of business was less than 10 per cent of what it had been in 1913. Holland continued to sell its own agricultural produce. Cereals, fodder, and fertilizer came from the Allies, while coal, iron, and potash were of German origin. When the United States entered the war, there was less tolerance by the Allies of any trade with Germany. The Dutch resisted, fearing perhaps that if they starved Germany the consequence would be invasion, but also aware that the Allies would never provide them with the goods they needed from German trade.[1]

Germany no doubt benefited considerably, in an economic sense, from Dutch neutrality. It also sheltered parts of the German border from attack. The Germans had contemplated violating Dutch neutrality as well as Belgian neutrality in order to attack France. They would have marched through the southern province of Limburg, using the country's railways as part of their mobilisation. They thought better of it, however, and dropped the plan. The minor tactical advantage that a violation of Dutch sovereign territory might offer was outweighed by the political cost. On 2 August 1914, as Germany was breaching the neutrality of Belgium, to which it was committed by treaty, pouring its troops through Belgium at points that were very close to the border with the Netherlands, it confirmed that it would respect Dutch neutrality. The British soon followed with their own declaration of respect for Dutch neutrality.

For the Dutch, maintaining neutrality during the war involved a delicate balance between the Germans and the British.[2] In February 1917, German submarines sank seven Dutch merchant ships, probably on the quite reasonable belief that they had been involved in trade with England. Then the Dutch delayed the return of two German submarines that had been damaged within their own territorial waters. In March 1918, the United States and Britain requisitioned all Dutch ships that were then in their ports. They claimed to be acting under the right of *angary*, which entitled the belligerent in an armed conflict to seize and to use for the purposes of war, or to prevent the enemy from so doing, property on the territory of the belligerent, even that belonging to a neutral State or its citizens. The Dutch were humiliated, but had few options.

The situation eased somewhat when the war ended. In late November 1918, the Allies agreed to facilitate the import of limited amounts of wheat, rice, oils, fats, fertilizers, and maize, but this was conditional on restricting Dutch exports to Germany. The Netherlands never really recovered its special position as the *entrepôt* of Europe. The war brought the collapse of several European empires. The Dutch, neutral and with colonial possessions that were important but of modest proportions compared to the British and the French, managed to survive the turmoil. But henceforth they remained largely dependent on a friendly and constructive relationship with the Powers that had won the war.

Neutrality is an international law concept used to describe States that do not take sides in an armed conflict involving other States.[3] By the twenty-first century, it had become largely irrelevant in international law. Several important European States remained neutral during the First World War, including Denmark, Luxembourg, Sweden, Switzerland, and Spain. One way to secure neutrality was by treaty. Belgian neutrality was guaranteed in this way. Pursuant to the Treaty of London, adopted in 1839, Britain, Austria, France, the German Confederation (led by Prussia), Russia, and the Netherlands agreed to respect Belgian neutrality in the event of a conflict. The 1839 treaty was originally intended as a barrier to French aggression. Violation of the Belgian neutrality treaty by Germany at the beginning of August 1914 provoked the entry of Britain in the conflict. It was also described as an international crime perpetrated by Germany's leaders, including the Kaiser.

Dutch neutrality was not guaranteed by a treaty to which other States were parties, unlike the case of Belgium and Luxembourg. Nor was it mandated constitutionally, as in the case of Switzerland. Rather, Dutch neutrality was government policy. The Dutch maintained an army to ensure that their neutrality was respected, although it would probably have been no match for the much more powerful armed forces of its neighbours, had they chosen to attack. In 1940, the Dutch surrendered within five or six days of German aggression.

The Convention on the Rights and Duties of Neutral Powers and Persons in Case of War on Land, adopted at the 1907 Hague Conference, declared the territory of a neutral State to be inviolable.[4] Neutral States were required to remain completely impartial, to deny assistance of any kind to belligerents, and to intern soldiers belonging to parties to the conflict should they enter their territory. During the First World War, the Dutch interned soldiers from Britain, Belgium, and Germany, and took other measures to preserve their neutral status. Nevertheless, the Hague Convention only applied, under the general participation (*si omnes*) clause, if it had been ratified by all parties to the conflict.[5] Because Serbia had not ratified the Convention, it was not applicable to the First World War. Despite this obstacle, some argued that the Hague Convention's provisions could be invoked as a codification of customary international law.

Had Wilhelm Abdicated?

Wilhelm's legal status upon his arrival in the Netherlands was a matter of some dispute. He had not in fact abdicated. Abdication cannot be imposed by others. It can only be done with the consent of the abdicator. Wilhelm was therefore still the Emperor of Germany and the King of Prussia when he arrived in the Netherlands. On 9 November, the German Chancellor had taken it upon himself to announce the Kaiser's abdication. He had tried desperately and without success to communicate with Wilhelm by telephone in order to obtain his accord. Prince Max of Baden agreed to an official announcement that the Kaiser had abdicated. But, by then, Germany was no longer a monarchy. Philipp Scheidemann, leader of the Social Democrats, stood on the balcony of the Reichstag and proclaimed the German Republic.

As an officer in the armed forces of a belligerent, the Kaiser ought to have been interned. This was how the Dutch had treated German, Belgian, and British soldiers who found themselves in Holland. It was an important requirement of neutrality. On 10 November, the day the Kaiser arrived in Holland, the British Ambassador immediately told Foreign Minister Van Karnebeek that the Kaiser and his suite were 'subjects for internment by the Netherlands government'.[6] The following day, Townley asked Van Karnebeek to provide him with a list of those who had accompanied the Kaiser. He noted that under the armistice, the Germans were to release all Allied prisoners, but that there was no comparable rule with respect to German prisoners. Townley said that '[u]nder these circumstances it is clear that my government will maintain their captor rights over German prisoners of war now interned in Holland', the implication being that the Dutch would be required to surrender the Kaiser and his entourage.[7] The French Government announced that because Wilhelm had abdicated from the throne, he could not invoke any particular privilege, and should therefore be interned on the grounds that he was the leader of Germany's armed forces.[8] But on 11 November, the Dutch Cabinet decided 'to treat the German Kaiser entirely as a private person and provisionally to let him reside at the castle of Amerongen under the responsibility of the Queen's commissioner in Utrecht'.[9]

In the lower house of the Estates General, known as the Second Chamber or *Tweede Kamer*, Jan Schaper of the Social Democratic Workers Party questioned the government about its application of the asylum law to the Kaiser. 'If there is a risk to our country because of this man—who is partly responsible for the death of 20 million men in the prime of their life—he cannot become an uninvited reason for us to run into international trouble', he said.[10] The following day, Schaper returned to the issue, insisting on the danger the Kaiser's stay in the country could provoke. 'I fear that Wilhelm and the place of his stay can become a centre for counter revolution in Germany', said Schaper.[11] His objections were echoed by Willem van Ravesteijn, of the Dutch Communist Party, who demanded expulsion of the Kaiser without delay. 'In my opinion we are housing a monster', he said. Van Ravesteijn charged that Wilhelm was not an ordinary deserter and he said the German people had a right to try him. He expressed concern that the new German Government would attempt to seize him by force. Ravesteijn also anticipated that the Allies would ask the Dutch Government not to provide Wilhelm with asylum.[12]

But there was an important pro-German constituency in the Netherlands, and Wilhelm had friends and supporters in the *Tweede Kamer*. On 19 November 1918, a deputy of the Anti-Revolutionary Party referred to demands from the foreign press to extradite or at least expel the Kaiser. Jan Gerrit Scheurer said that the Netherlands could not extradite the Kaiser, 'nor hand him over to his enemies, neither on request of the foreign press nor on request of Mr. Schaper. I trust our government to act as a neutral country in guaranteeing justice'. He said the Kaiser was entitled to enjoy Dutch hospitality, just as other aliens were during the war.[13] Charles de Wijkerslooth de Weerdesteyn, of the ruling Roman Catholic Party, explained that Wilhelm had abdicated both as the Kaiser and as the military commander, entitling him to enjoy the normal rules governing refugees in the Netherlands. De Wijkerslooth de Weerdesteyn said Dutch law stipulated that a refugee could only be expelled if he was a danger to public safety. Moreover, he continued, the *Marechaussee*, or Specialist Police, had the authority to assign a certain place of residence to a foreigner who constitutes a threat to public safety. De Wijkerslooth de Weerdesteyn noted that extradition of asylum seekers on grounds of political crimes was explicitly prohibited and, furthermore, that there had been no request to extradite the Kaiser.[14]

Charles Ruijs de Beerenbrouck, who was both the Prime Minister and Minister of the Interior, replied that the Kaiser was residing in Amerongen at the request of the Dutch Government. The Prime Minister insisted that during the war, 'hundreds of thousands of foreigners have found refuge and repose in the Netherlands. Because of his former position there was no reason to make in advance any exception against this man who, as a foreigner, came to your frontier and requested admission'. Ruijs de Beerenbrouck told the *Tweede Kamer* that the government would remain on guard lest there be any abuse. He added that national interests might demand 'that the exigencies of the case should outweigh humanitarian considerations and historical traditions'. He said the government had no reason to think that countries whose citizens, 'without distinction of rank, have so often found asylum in Holland, will refuse to respect our traditions and forget the instances in which they themselves have given hospitality to fallen sovereigns'.[15]

Townley reported to London on the Prime Minister's remarks the following day. The Foreign Office file contains a minute from 'L.C.': 'A disingenuous statement. The Dutch government did not *ask* anyone to afford hospitality to the other refugees.' It is followed by a minute from 'R. G.': 'I scarcely see that the Dutch govt. could have acted otherwise than as they have done.' Finally, Balfour himself wrote: 'No, poor Dutch!'[16]

A summary of the Prime Minister's remarks in the *Tweede Kamer* was sent by Foreign Minister Van Karnebeek to the Dutch embassy in Washington, together with instructions to contradict 'wild rumours circulating in the foreign press'. He instructed Dutch diplomats to spread the news that the Kaiser had been assigned a fixed place of residence and that he had not once left the grounds of Amerongen Castle. He insisted that there was no difference in the asylum being offered to the Kaiser and that provided to other refugees over the years. 'The offering of asylum is a trait deeply rooted in the spirit and tolerance of the Dutch people, and in the course of our history refugees of humble and of high position, as well as princes, have benefited from it', wrote Van Karnebeek.[17]

Wilhelm himself did not formally abdicate until late in the month of November, after his wife had joined him at Amerongen. She travelled from Potsdam by special train, accompanied only by a single lady-in-waiting, Countess Keller. The Kaiserin's request to bring a staff of eleven was refused by the Dutch Government. The Dutch minister in Berlin saw her off at the station.[18] The train flew a red flag while it was inside Germany, signifying the new political order in Berlin.[19] The Kaiserin was accompanied throughout the journey to Amerongen by a representative of the German mission in The Hague, who had brought with him the abdication document for signature by her husband. Ambassador Rosen had already advised the Dutch Government that the Kaiser would abdicate '*Um alle möglichen Zweifel oder Missdeutungen zu zerstreuen*', to dispel all doubts and misinterpretations.[20] It seems this was Wilhelm's *quid pro quo* if he wanted his wife to join him.

> Hereby for all time I resign the rights to the crown of Prussia and rights to the German Imperial crown connected with this. At the same time I release all officials of the German Empire and Prussia as well as all officers now commissioned officers and men of the navy and Prussian army and the federal contingents from the oath of allegiance which they have made to me as their Kaiser, king and commander-in-chief. I expect of them that they will assist those who are now possessed of actual power until the new institution of the German empire and protecting the German people against the threatened danger of anarchy, famine and foreign domination.[21]

Wilhelm dutifully affixed his signature on 28 November 1918. In the *Tweede Kamer*, Jan Schaper said he hoped the Kaiser had enough of a sense of honour that he would not jeopardise the Netherlands by remaining in the country.

'He has always been late—even with abdicating—but I hope he will not be late this time and leave this country on grounds of honour ... I hope a warning and a request on his honour will do the job.'[22] Ernst Heldring, a very prominent Dutch business and political figure, wrote in his diary that 'the only salvation lies in the departure of the Emperor'.[23]

The Dutch Cabinet met on 6 December 1918 and decided to ask Friedrich Rosen to persuade the Kaiser to return to Germany, ideally within a few days. But when telephoned by Van Karnebeek, Rosen refused to do this.[24] The Utrecht governor, Van Sandenburg, told the Kaiser of the Cabinet's request after church services on 8 December 1918. A visibly distressed Wilhelm apparently agreed, indicating he did not want to cause problems for Holland.[25]

His staff made material preparations for clandestine flight, including obtaining a false passport from the German mission in The Hague, and various elements of disguise. The Kaiser put on eyeglasses and grew a white beard, something he retained for the rest of his life. He reduced the size of his iconic moustache. The embassy also made a car available should a fast departure be necessary. There was talk that the Kaiser might find refuge somewhere in Scandinavia, but nothing concrete materialised. Suggestions for a place of permanent exile included Corfu, where the Kaiser had spent many summers pursuing his avocation of archaeology, and where he owned a castle, the Achilleon. Algeria, St Helena, Argentina, Chile, and Switzerland were also considered. The Dutch Government hinted that Wilhelm move to Zeeland, a province on the North Sea. The former Emperor declined, and the Dutch did not insist.[26]

In the meantime, Queen Wilhelmina invited George V to visit the Netherlands. In a telegram to Balfour, Ambassador Townley wrote: '[W]ith late German Emperor an honoured guest in the country and various other questions pending on account, of which attitude of Netherlands government is severely criticised in foreign press, the moment appears to me singularly ill-chosen for a Royal visit.' On the file in the Foreign Office, 'L. O.' minuted that 'the idea of H.M. and the Queen visiting Holland, while the ex-Emperor is in that country, cannot for a moment be entertained'. 'R. G.' described it as 'a preposterous idea' that would be 'most unpopular in this country, indeed it can scarcely take place, until some time after the ex-Emperor has left Holland'.[27] The English King invoked 'state business' when he declined the invitation, but Queen Wilhelmina persisted, asking him to indicate when he might be able to make the trip. 'You will be the first to understand my and my people's feelings as to the attacks directed against the Netherlands by a certain press in some countries', she said, adding that she had learned from her own Ambassador to London 'that the present press campaign does not express the views of responsible quarters in England'.[28] A further reply was drafted for King George stating that it was impossible for him to set any date, given 'features in the situation, which would render a visit on my part to the Netherlands at the present time open to very serious misinterpretation both in your country and in mine; (and it might be added in the world at large)'.[29]

Dutch Lawyers Provide Advice

On 9 December 1918, three international law specialists, Bernard Cornelis Johannes Loder, Antonius Struyken, and Albert Edward Bles, provided Van Karnebeek, with a lengthy legal opinion. They began by emphasising the importance of the Kaiser's status when he entered the Netherlands. If he was still a German military commander, they felt he should not have been allowed to cross the border or, if he did, he should have been treated as a prisoner of war. However, given the unequivocal act of abdication of 28 November, they concluded that there was no longer any issue, and that now the Kaiser was clearly a private person.

The legal experts referred to a 1904 treaty (the *Vestigingsverdrag*) with Germany conferring on nationals of both countries the right to settle temporarily in the other country, although this privilege could be denied in the interests of public order and national security. Dutch legislation also allowed the government to expel foreign nationals if they were a threat to public order. The legal experts considered that the Dutch Government had the authority to deny the Kaiser entry and to remove him from the country. Furthermore, the government could also impose a place of residence on a foreign national who constituted a threat to public order, health, or morals. There were no particular obligations under international law, the experts said, to the extent that the Netherlands had been neutral in the war. They said that the issue of immunities did not arise because the Kaiser had abdicated and was a private citizen, like any other.

They also said that the Netherlands was free to extradite him. As a military commander during the war, they felt he could be held accountable for the actions of his troops. This would provide a basis for extradition, they believed. Extradition to Germany and Italy would be a simple matter, regardless of where the crimes took place, because this was governed by existing treaties.

Nor would it be a problem with respect to France and Belgium for acts committed on their territories. As for other scenarios, they reserved their opinion.

If the crimes imputed to the Kaiser were to be deemed political offences, extradition might well be unlawful, they said. Dutch extradition law did not prohibit extradition for political offences, but the rule against such extradition had been observed consistently and was deemed part of the common law of the civilised world. The experts considered that acts of war could not be treated as political crimes. Therefore, there was no obstacle to extradition of the Kaiser for acts by his troops, committed under his orders, that were contrary to the law of nations. The experts referred to evolving international law in the context of the global conflict, with the emergency of a supra-State entity. It was not unthinkable, the experts suggested, that the Kaiser be tried by an international judicial organ. Indeed, they considered that the seriousness of the crimes likely to be imputed to the Kaiser warranted a trial before such an international body rather than in Germany or one of the countries with which it had been at war.

The conclusions of the three experts were very supportive of Dutch action directed at the Kaiser. They said the government could terminate his stay in the Netherlands and that it could extradite him. Moreover, as a part of the international community, the Netherlands would be in no position to block proceedings before an international court of justice.[30]

On 10 December, Prime Minister Ruijs de Beerenbrouck delivered a lengthy statement in the lower house of the Estates General. After describing how the Kaiser's arrival had taken the government by surprise, he insisted upon the ex-Emperor's status as a guest according to Holland's tradition of hospitality. 'All efforts to link the Dutch tolerance regarding the Kaiser's presence on Dutch territory with a non-neutral stance have to be disregarded. Any other Head of State would have had the same treatment', he said. Ruijs de Beerenbrouck declared that the Dutch Government considered the Kaiser's stay in Holland to be only temporary. He said that if the visit was prolonged, guarantees would be required 'to secure that the Kaiser's presence will not be a reason for internal unrest'. The Prime Minister turned to 'the mood abroad'. He said 'the possibility that at a certain moment the Government will be confronted with a formal request for extradition is not excluded'. This would be addressed on the basis of existing laws. Ruijs de Beerenbrouck also said it was possible that foreign governments would call for a meeting to decide on the Kaiser's definitive place of residence. He said the government 'would allow such a meeting, provided that it can take part of such a meeting, allowing the decision to be in accordance with the honour and dignity of our country'.[31]

Marchant, of the Leftist Liberal Party, said he was happy with the government's handling of the matter and did not understand the foreign disapproval.[32] Schaper, the Social Democrat, was supportive.[33] Alexander de Savornin Lohman, of the Christian Historical Union, also agreed with the government's position. He explained that accepting the Kaiser was not 'a friendly favour', but rather application of the country's asylum law, an 'ancient body of law' that could not be disregarded. 'Some people are stating that the Netherlands is acting without regard of the opinion in the surrounding nations', he said. 'There is, however, just one opinion we have to respect: justice.'[34]

The Communist Party, on the other hand, thought the government had not properly judged the attitude of the Allies. Van Ravensteijn said he had heard that the Kaiser had first sounded out Switzerland as a place of refuge, but it refused him entry. He thought it would have been a 'smart move' for the Netherlands to have done the same. Now that the Kaiser was inside the country, Van Ravensteijn thought he should be sent back to Germany rather than extradited to the Allies. The Communist Party considered that the German people had the right to try the Kaiser, he said. 'We are not dealing with a neutral person, but with a war criminal! A man who in foreign countries is considered to be responsible for unleashing a world war and who should be tried.[35]

Reporting to London on the Prime Minister's statement, Ambassador Townley said that the 'Netherlands Government would not be disinclined to consider a different place of residence for ex-German Emperor if Foreign Governments were to propose one'.[36] A year later, the Dutch Government reminded the British and the French that in December 1918 the Prime Minister had invited their proposal and that they had not replied.[37]

A further public explanation of the government position came from the Foreign Minister in response to a parliamentary question. Senator David van Embden asked if the government understood that the stay of the Emperor 'is a source of continued irritation to the feelings of almost all the world towards this nation, and is thus causing inestimable moral injury to the Netherlands'.[38] The answer, from the Ministers of Justice and Foreign Affairs, admitted that they were 'aware that wrong judgments of the line of conduct adopted by the Government in this matter have occurred under the influence of inaccurate representations abroad'. The claim was repeated that the Kaiser had already abdicated when he reached the border. He had confronted the Dutch Government 'with a *fait accompli* as there had been no warning of his coming, of any nature'. The Ministers said that after abdication, there could be no question of internment, but that the choice of residence could not be left to the Kaiser. Should extradition be demanded, the reply of the Netherlands 'would depend upon the law and circumstances'. The Ministers also confirmed that there had been no commission to determine the Kaiser's legal situation. They acknowledged that confidential advice had been obtained from several lawyers.[39]

Ambassador Garrett reported to Washington that Van Karnebeek seemed to realise the danger the Kaiser's presence might pose for Holland. Garrett said that the Dutch 'feared that a demand might be made by the United States and the Allies calling for such action or couched in such terms as to threaten the honour of Holland and make it difficult to concede the demand, however much the Dutch might be inclined to meet it favourably'.[40] The Dutch Government was anxious to maintain close relations with the Americans. Woodrow Wilson had been invited to make a State visit to the Netherlands while in Europe attending the Peace Conference. Queen Wilhelmina gave a favourable reading of the American President's equivocal answer. She summoned Ambassador Garrett for a meeting in order to press the invitation. He was provided with a proposed programme for the visit that included various receptions, a gala dinner, and visits to Leiden University and the Peace Palace in The Hague. Alas, the presence of the Kaiser on Dutch territory complicated things. Newspaper accounts were dismissive of the importance of the issue, pointing to the very great contrast in the way the President was to be treated and the very lukewarm reception given to the Kaiser. Garrett was suspicious, finding that the comparison between the two 'was expressed so negatively as to convey the impression that should the President accept the Queen's invitation, America would thereby lose her moral right to protest at the Kaiser's presence in Holland'.[41]

Reporting to Washington at the end of 1918, the American Ambassador said it was difficult to assess the precise attitude of the Dutch people to the Kaiser's presence in their country. He noted that the newspapers were initially very insistent in claiming this was an exercise in Dutch hospitality, but that 'there has of late been apparent an undertone of irritation at his presence which is seemingly gaining in extent. The rumours are persistent despite denials that it has been unofficially hinted to him that the Government would be relieved of embarrassment were he voluntarily to leave Holland.'[42]

But the Kaiser never left, voluntarily or involuntarily. He remained in the Netherlands until his death more than twenty years later. Over the coming year and especially following the formal demand for surrender by the Allies, in January 1920, the Dutch polished their arguments against rendition. In particular, they developed the claim that trial by the Allies had a whiff of unfairness because the charges did not correspond to crimes that were recognised at the time of their commission, or that they were simply formulated too vaguely. As for the Allies, especially Britain and France, they never refined their own legal contentions or adequately answered the arguments of the Dutch. Their demands rarely went beyond mere bullying, such as threats to exclude the Netherlands from the League of Nations or imposition of various forms of restrictions on trade and other commercial activity.

7

Aborted Kidnap

In 1960, Israeli agents kidnapped a leading Nazi, one of the many who had evaded prosecution by the post-Second World War tribunals. His name had been mentioned occasionally at Nuremberg,[1] but he was not high enough on the list of wanted criminals to make the shortlist for the International Military Tribunal. Eventually, Adolf Eichmann made his way to Argentina, where he joined a netherworld of nostalgic remnants of the Third Reich. Israeli agents abducted him, secretly spiriting him in an El Al plane destined for Tel Aviv. When he appeared before the judges in Jerusalem, Eichmann argued that prosecution was blocked because of the illegality of his arrest. The court dismissed the argument with a Latin expression, *mala captus bene detentus*, literally, wrongly captured but properly detained.[2] Since then, similar issues have arisen occasionally before international criminal tribunals, as well as before national courts.[3] Law enforcement agents are often involved, but sometimes such abductions are the work of freelance bounty hunters.

Forty-one years before Eichmann's kidnap in Buenos Aires, in early January 1919, a small group of American soldiers posted in Europe and acting without any official authority crossed into the Netherlands from Belgium with a view to bringing Kaiser Wilhelm to justice. Nothing suggests that in kidnapping Eichmann the Israelis were inspired by the Americans in 1919. The Americans, on the other hand, may have taken the idea from 'Fighting' Fred Funston, a general in the US Army who, posing as a prisoner, managed to capture rebel leader Emilio Aguinaldo in the Philippines, in 1901.[4]

Luke Lea, the ringleader of the mission to kidnap the Kaiser, attributed his ardour to an encounter with a member of the British royal family. In June 1918, after disembarking in England on its way to the trenches of northern France, the 55th Field Artillery Brigade of the American Expeditionary Force paraded before Prince Arthur, the Duke of Connaught. When tea was served,

Colonel Lea, as a senior officer in the Brigade, was seated near the Duke. The seventh child of Queen Victoria, the Duke of Connaught boasted that he was the uncle of both King George V of England and Kaiser Wilhelm II. Blood is thicker than water was his message. Connaught made no distinction in terms of loyalty to his two powerful nephews. Testifying before the army inquiry into his aborted trip to Amerongen and his effort to abduct the Kaiser, Lea referred to the Duke's statements that day as confirmation that 'powerful influences' were protecting the Kaiser. He said he felt the war would not be completely successful if the German Emperor went unpunished.[5] In his account of the episode, Lea wrote:

> Why should those not responsible for the war and against whom we had waged war—the German people—be killed, wounded and imprisoned, and the only person against who we had really waged war, the Kaiser, escape punishment, not ever being brought to trial but permitted to live in luxurious pomp and glory with all of his fabulous fortune untouched?[6]

Another explanation of Lea's motivation, nourished by accounts of one of his accomplices, presents the whole business as resembling a prank by hyperactive college students addled with drink. In the United States, Lea was quite a militant prohibitionist. It did not follow that when in Europe he was also an abstainer. If he had been studying the election of December 1918, Lea might have appreciated the determination of the British, perhaps with the exception of a few bluebloods, to bring the Kaiser to book. He could not have known that it was their American cousins, mainly the resolute and unyielding Secretary of State, Robert Lansing, coupled with the lukewarm but opportunistic President Wilson, who obstructed the efforts at prosecution.

After nearly three years of neutrality during the First World War, the United States entered the conflict in early April 1917. Its participation was provoked when Germany adopted unrestricted submarine attacks on American merchant and passenger vessels as well as by an intercepted message from the Foreign Ministry in Berlin to Mexico offering assistance in efforts to recover territory annexed by the United States the previous century. Washington mobilised more than 4 million soldiers. Combat as well as disease resulted in 100,000 deaths of American servicemen. By early 1918, about 10,000 American doughboys were arriving in Europe every day, helping to seal the fate of Kaiser Wilhelm's armies.

The 55th Field Artillery Brigade was made up mainly of National Guardsman from Tennessee and the neighbouring Carolinas. Colonel Luke Lea commanded the 114th Field Artillery, a regiment within the 55th Field

Artillery Brigade. The 55th sustained its final casualties from German artillery only minutes before the armistice took effect at 11 am on 11 November 1918. It had distinguished itself fighting to take the Saint-Mihiel salient, a bulge in the line near Verdun that the Germans had held since the start of the war and that posed a continuing threat to Paris.[7]

Born and raised at Lealand, his family's 1,000-acre farm near Nashville, Tennessee, Luke Lea studied law at Columbia University where he edited the *Columbia Law Review*, graduating in 1903. Four years later, Lea established *The Tennessean*, to this day Nashville's major newspaper. He successfully ran for election to the US Senate in 1911. Lea was then 31 years old, the youngest member of the sixty-second Congress. As his six-year term concluded, defeat in the Democratic Party primary meant he could not stand for re-election. The United States had just entered the war. Lea turned his sights to Europe, raising a volunteer regiment that headed overseas in mid-1918. After the armistice, Lea and his troops were based in Tuntingen (now Tutange), Luxembourg.[8]

The Magnificent Seven

Lea's plan began to take shape just prior to Christmas 1918. He started to assemble his 'magnificent seven' from the ranks of the 114th. Captain Leland Stanford ('Larry') MacPhail, commander of Battery B, was a close associate from Tennessee. Like Lea, MacPhail was somewhat of a boy wonder. By the age of 25, he was running a department store in Nashville. Captain Thomas P. Henderson, commander of Battery F, a lifelong friend of Lea, was a lawyer and an activist in the Democratic Party. First lieutenant Ellsworth Brown was a signals officer, recruited so that he could assess the means Wilhelm was using to communicate with Germany. Three sergeants completed the team: Marmaduke Clokey, Owen Johnson, and Dan Reilly. One was a skilled mechanic.

MacPhail described paying a visit to Lea just before Christmas. Lea was billeted with a French priest. MacPhail found the two of them drinking wine and studying some detailed maps.

'Where did you get the maps, Luke', asked MacPhail.

'Why, I disremember', Lea replied. ('I knew damn well where he got them', MacPhail recalled two decades later. 'He got them from the French War Office.')

'I've been considering a little project and I'd be mighty pleased if you'd join me', said Lea. 'I was thinking of motoring up to Holland and kidnapping the Kaiser.'[9]

Lea's idea was to catch the Kaiser by surprise in Amerongen, spirit him across the Dutch border, and deliver him to the Paris Peace Conference 'as a Christmas present'. Lea's 'Plan B' was to collect information about the Kaiser's situation and circumstances, including the extent of his contacts with German monarchists. This would be provided to the American negotiating team in Paris so as to assist in the efforts to obtain custody of the Kaiser from the Dutch.

The first of two trips to the Netherlands was little more than a 'recce', a reconnaissance mission. Late in the afternoon on 24 December, after searching for maps of the Netherlands, Henderson, MacPhail, and Lea motored north from Tuntingen.[10] Lea was a colonel with more than enough authority to take a short leave during the holiday season together with his band of brothers. They were accompanied by Reilly and Clokey, as well as an interpreter. The Americans drove through Luxembourg, crossing into Belgium near Troisvierges. By the time they reached Liège, where they stopped for the night, it was already 25 December. The following morning, they purchased a Baedeker guide to Germany and a roadmap of Belgium. They made for what was then the German border at Eupen. Then they continued north within Germany, skirting the frontier with the Netherlands, remaining within a 10-kilometre zone on the right bank of the Rhine occupied by the victorious Allied Powers in accordance with Article V of the armistice. They took their Christmas dinner in Krefeld, close to Dusseldorf, before pushing further north.[11]

At the border town of Kleve, Lea met a Dutch businessman who provided information about Kaiser Wilhelm. He told Lea that the Kaiser had no servants guarding or taking care of him, but said there was a bodyguard of Dutch soldiers because there had been an attempt on the ex-Emperor's life. The businessman was trying to get papers for entry to Belgium. Lea agreed to help in exchange for assistance entering the Netherlands. But Dutch border officials refused the Americans, saying they required passports. The party turned around for the long drive back to Luxembourg.[12]

On New Year's Day, Lea presented Brigadier General Oliver L. Spaulding, the commander of the 55th, with a request for a four-day leave on behalf of himself and his officers. This included permission to visit a neutral country, a requirement imposed by army regulations. When Spaulding questioned

Lea about the reasons, he answered: 'Nowhere forbidden by orders of GHQ. I don't want to tell you where. I do not want you to be responsible for this trip.' Spaulding answered: 'It's the damnest order of leave I have ever read. But it violates no special or general order, so I'll sign it.'[13] Lea later testified before the army inquiry that he had told General Spaulding that he 'did not wish to take the usual leave to Nice, but to visit as many different countries as I could, provided I did not violate any GHQ orders, and to secure information there as to the actual conditions obtaining. I did not specifically mention Holland.'[14]

Lea later claimed that the others in his team knew nothing of his plan to kidnap the Kaiser or even to visit Amerongen. In fact, before the army disciplinary inquiry into the mission, Lea suggested that he had not even contemplated visiting the Kaiser. The whole idea came to him after entering Holland a few days later, he lied. But in an interview with *The New Yorker* in 1941, Larry MacPhail confessed that all of them were in on the plot from the beginning. 'We'll nab the old gentleman, fellows, and we'll turn him over to the United States Government', said Lea in his briefing at the outset of the trip. 'They'll be legally obliged to string him up.'[15]

They group set out from Tuntingen on the afternoon of 1 January 1919. The party, all in uniform and armed with pistols, travelled in one of the Brigade's staff cars, a Winton Six limousine. 'The Winton furnished variety', wrote Lea in his memoir, with characteristic sarcasm. 'It always needed repairs, but never twice in the same place until a complete cycle of repairs had been passed.'[16] Predictably, the Winton broke down soon after they had crossed the border into Belgium, the first of many mechanical problems encountered by the group. The car was fixed late in the day, but broke down again near Arlon, just inside Belgium. They had travelled perhaps 10 kilometres that day. Lea decided to send for another vehicle. An army supply truck drove Marmaduke Clokey back to the base in Luxembourg. He obtained an eight-cylinder Cadillac from the 115th Field Artillery. The Cadillac motor company supplied about 2,000 such vehicles to the American Expeditionary Forces. It was the standard staff car for officers.

Clokey rejoined the group early on 2 January. He was accompanied by the Cadillac's driver, Egbert Hail, who then became the eighth recruit to the mission and the only member of the group who was not from Tennessee. By then, the others had managed to repair the Winton. They proceeded north to Liège, where they spent the night and purchased fuel for the vehicles. The Americans turned west towards Louvain and then drove on to Brussels.

Help from the American Ambassador

Lea didn't think Ambassador Brand Whitlock remembered him, although the two had met in Washington before the war. Whitlock had been active in Democratic Party politics in his native Ohio and served as mayor of Toledo. While in the Senate, Lea had voted to confirm Whitlock's appointment as Ambassador to Belgium. Whitlock remained in Brussels until April 1917, when the United States entered the war against Germany. He fulfilled important functions, including intervening with the German occupiers in an attempt to block the execution of the English nurse, Edith Cavell, in 1915.[17]

Lea told Whitlock that he was on leave and that 'on account of my service in the Senate I was very interested in the international situation and was very anxious to go into Holland and obtain first-hand and direct information in regard to certain questions that interested me'. Lea said that in answer to the Ambassador's question about his precise destination, 'I told him as much over Holland as I could go within the time. I did not mention Amerongen as a destination.' Nor, apparently, did he indicate any specific interest in the situation of Kaiser Wilhelm II.[18]

Ambassador Whitlock described the visit in his diary:

> Colonel Luke Lea of the 11th Field Artillery, until recently Senator from Tennessee, called; a big, handsome fellow, a great friend of W.J. Bryan's. He said that he was on leave; is now stationed in the Grand Duchy—with several of his officers—for the purpose of visiting Belgium and Holland. I told him that he could not enter Holland in uniform unless he wished to be interned until the end of the peace negotiations, whereupon he said he and they had civilian clothing at Liège—'Leege', as he pronounced it. I said that if he went as a civilian I would give him passports, but I tried to dissuade him from going at all. But he was insistent, persistent, and I sent Swift with him to see [Dutch embassy official] Van Vollenhoven as to their rules …
>
> Lea interesting, big, broad white teeth showing in an open smile, broad, cheerful, good-natured countenance, handsome in uniform. Told stories and talked of Bryan. He said—what was rather pathetic—that some time ago Bryan told him that he was 'reading up' on European history, as undoubtedly he would be one of the peace commissioners.[19]

The Americans had passport photos made, taking turns wearing Lea's overcoat as it was the cleanest and most presentable. On his passport application, Lea described the purpose of his travels as 'journalistic investigation'. He pointed out that he was the owner of two newspapers and that in civilian life he was a 'publisher or journalist'. The others wrote: 'accompanying Colonel Lea'. The passport identified him as 'Senator Luke Lea'. When Lea objected that this might be deemed misleading, the consular clerk answered that he had no more blank forms and that in any event 'once a Senator, always a Senator'. The passport also stated that the mission to Holland was 'official business'. Lea told the consular officer that this was not what his application had claimed. The clerk answered that it was all right 'for it to go in that form and better for it to'.[20] While they waited for the passports to be issued, the Americans made a visit to the Waterloo battlefield, on the outskirts of Brussels.

Whitlock invited the Americans to join him for a previously scheduled dinner with the Dutch Head of Mission. Maurice van Vollenhoven, seemingly impressed by the interest the American 'Senator' was showing in his country, and perhaps hoping that a warm Dutch welcome might help persuade the American President to make a much-coveted official visit to the Netherlands, offered Lea a *laissez-passer* if he would attend at the Embassy the next morning. Such a document would facilitate crossing the border, as well as permit Lea and his companions to travel in uniform. Whitlock encouraged Lea to stay in Brussels until the following day, it being well worth the wait to get the official blessing of the Dutch authorities.[21] The Americans spent the night at the Grand Hotel Central, on the Place de la Bourse. Early the next day, Lea was accompanied to the Dutch Mission by an American diplomat. The *laissez-passer* described Lea as being on official business for the American Government and authorised him as well as his team to wear their uniforms while in the Netherlands.[22] Van Vollenhoven assured him it would open all doors for them in the Netherlands. He said its issuance had been authorised by The Hague.

With a passport in his pocket describing him as a Senator of the United States who was on 'official business', and a *laissez-passer* issued by the Dutch mission in Brussels authorising travel in uniform, Lea and his group returned to Liège, picking up the Winton along the way. A snowstorm had made the roads to the north impassable, and they spent the night in the Belgian city. Finally, on the morning of 5 January, they reached the Dutch border near Maastricht, not far from where the Kaiser himself had crossed not quite two months earlier.

'No American officers are wanted or permitted in Holland', said the border guard to the seven uniformed men. Lea brandished the *laissez-passer*. 'No trick of Houdini's ever created the astonishment my producing Her Majesty's laissez passer did', recalled Lea in his memoir. 'Brusqueness, gruffness and rudeness gave place immediately to courtesy and consideration.' The guard promptly saluted and waved them through.[23] They proceeded north to Nijmegen, where one of the cars broke down in the public square. While it was being repaired, the Americans stopped at the Hotel de Kroon. There they encountered a Dutch teenager with a smattering of English who claimed to know the way to Amerongen. Constant Boetter, whom the Americans nicknamed 'Hans', was hired as a guide and interpreter.

Late in the afternoon, they reached the Waal River, a distributary branch of the Rhine. The bridge had been washed away and crossing had to be made by ferry. They were no more than a half-hour's drive from Amerongen. Lea unsuccessfully tried to convince the ferry operator to wait for them on their return. He felt this was a serious logistical problem. Lea calculated that were they to succeed in abducting Wilhelm, a hasty return to Belgium would then be difficult as they would inevitably be stalled at the river. In his memoir of the escapade, Lea wrote that '[t]he inability to cross immediately the river at [word missing] made it impossible to take the Kaiser out of Holland at that time without his consent', a sentence that incidentally provides ample confirmation that he was attempting a kidnap and nothing less. 'Capture at the river while waiting on the Amerongen side of the river for the ferry, or on the ferry, would have been inevitable.'[24] Lea contemplated abandoning the entire mission, then changed his mind, and his strategy. He now hoped to reason with Wilhelm and persuade him to surrender peacefully. Lea would use his political skills to convince the Kaiser that trial in Paris was a better option than uncertain exile in Amerongen.

At 8.30 in the evening on 5 January, the American soldiers arrived at Amerongen. Their pistols were concealed under the seats of the cars. They were given direction by a townsman on the way to Bentinck's castle. A sentry awaited them at the entrance to the grounds. Lea thought him to be 'unmistakably' a German soldier because of his military bearing, although the guard wore a Dutch uniform. Lea shone his flashlight not on the sentry, but on himself, so as to indicate his Sam Browne belt, 'the insignia of the rank of an officer in all armies'. Lea had studied German at university and had some recent practice interrogating prisoners of war. He used the language to call the sentry to attention. The guard dutifully obliged, clicking his heels, and saluted. To the astonishment of the other Americans, in his workable German Lea successfully ordered the obedient sentry to take them to the castle. However, they were not escorted to the castle proper, but to the lodge of the manager of the estate. While Lieutenant Brown and the non-commissioned officers waited with the vehicles, Lea, Henderson, and MacPhail, accompanied by 'Hans' the interpreter, entered the lodge.[25]

Kaiser Wilhelm, Count Godard Bentinck, and his family and guests were just finishing dinner when a servant interrupted them to announce the arrival of a party of American officers on an official visit to see the former Emperor. Carlos Bentinck, one of the Count's sons, in full dinner dress, a tailcoat and white tie, went to meet the Americans. Carlos Bentinck was a Dutch diplomat, recently 'posted' by the Foreign Ministry to Amerongen in order to help his father manage the distinguished houseguest. Throughout the encounters that evening, Bentinck sought to deal with the matter in such a way as to avoid conflict or provocation. He described Lea as a man of 'large stature' who introduced himself as 'Colonel Senator Luke Lea'.[26] The young Dutch interpreter swooned, awestruck by this encounter with nobility. Lea had him taken back to one of the cars.[27] Lea himself was rather less impressed. He thought the young Count Bentinck affected mannerisms of the Kaiser, noting his upturned moustache.

The Dutch aristocrat spoke to them in English. Lea introduced himself and the other American officers. He said they had come to meet the Kaiser, but that they would only explain the real purpose of the visit to the former Emperor himself. According to Lea, Bentinck appeared disturbed and excited. The young Count excused himself and returned to consult with the Kaiser.

Champagne and Cigars

While they were waiting for Bentinck to return, a butler offered the Americans water to drink and cigars. Lea speculated that Bentinck was sensitive to American attitudes about alcoholic drinks and didn't want to cause offence by serving liquor. When Henderson complained about the water, the butler fetched a bottle of champagne. Upon his return, Bentinck informed Lea that 'His August Majesty' was only prepared to meet with the American party if they first declared the purpose of their visit. He also told them that they could not enter the castle itself without the permission of the Governor of Utrecht. They were joined at this point by the mayor or *burgemeester* of Amerongen, Rudolf Everhard Willem van Weede, who was also dining with the Kaiser. To a few remarks in Lea's rudimentary German, Van Weede responded in 'beautiful, fluent, Bostonian English'. 'Colonel Lea, I am sure we will progress more rapidly speaking in English', he said in a patronising tone. 'I am a graduate of Harvard University.' In his unpublished memoir, deposited in the Tennessee State Archives, Lea described the local Dutch official:

> If anyone wants a mental picture of the *burgemeester* he can easily draw one by tracing the outlines of a typical rich man's son with a $20,000 a year income to spend at Harvard, clad in a racoon coat, seated in a Locomobile, witnessing 'Fair Harvard' being defeated in a football game by a rough and rugged eleven from a fresh water college.[28]

Bentinck and Van Weede insisted that Lea provide a more elaborate explanation of the purpose of the visit than the very vague 'journalistic investigations' indicated on the passport. Lea persisted in his position that he would only tell this to the Kaiser in person. The suspicious *burgemeester* asked Lea if it was customary in the United States for a journalist seeking an interview with a prominent official to arrive unannounced on a Sunday evening. Lea feebly explained that he knew of many such instances, and that the party would have been at Amerongen much earlier in the day had it not been for an automobile accident.[29]

Lea produced the *laissez-passer* that had been issued in Brussels. Carlos Bentinck later told a representative of the American embassy that when Lea brandished the *laissez-passer*, he said: 'This will explain.'[30] At the inquiry following the visit, Lea contended that he knew nothing of the contents of the *laissez-passer*, which was written in Dutch, an explanation the Judge Advocate General accepted. But in his memoir, Lea claimed he produced the document in order to give 'an official colour to our presence'. The *laissez-passer* made an immediate impression, 'even upon the blasé Bentinck and the Harvardised burgomaster', Lea recalled.

The two Dutchmen questioned Lea about the meaning of the term 'journalistic investigation'. Was it a military technical term, or were the Americans newspaper reporters, they asked. Were they acting for the military intelligence of the United States Army? Bentinck and Van Weede left the Americans alone again. While they were gone, Lea and his colleagues inspected the room, noting its elegant and impeccable furnishings, as well as stationery, writing implements, and ashtrays bearing the German Emperor's crest.[31] Bentinck and Van Weede reported to the Kaiser that a party of American officers had come on an official mission to see him 'for no good purpose'. Wilhelm said he would not be able to see them without knowing the exact authority with which they came.[32]

Bentinck and Van Weede returned to the Americans. The *burgemeester* spoke, his manner 'a cross between Hohenzollern Highness and Harvard High Hat':

> His Imperial Majesty did not appreciate ordinary soldiers, not even one of the rank of a Colonel, seeking an audience with him save in response to an invitation. Such an act was never countenanced in court circles. It was simply incomprehensible.
>
> His August Majesty, however, after conferring with [a General whose name escaped the Americans], has graciously condescended to give an audience to your group of American officers on the conditions he has named. His August Majesty is aware that Americans are impulsive creatures and often perform even official duties in unconventional and unexpected manner.
>
> His Majesty has been unwilling to refuse to meet you and your officers lest you be here officially. His Majesty has done me the honour to instruct me to say that if you, Colonel Lea, will make the statement on your word of honour as an American officer that you are here as a representative of President Wilson, or of General Pershing, or even of Colonel House, he will grant you a brief audience. Otherwise His Majesty will decline to grant any audience to any uninvited persons no matter in what form they seek it.[33]

Lea later wrote that he was willing to go to any length 'within the bounds of truth' to see the Kaiser, but that he was 'of course unwilling to make a false statement'. To Bentinck and Van Weede he acknowledged that he was not a representative of President Wilson, of General Pershing, or 'even Colonel House'. The Kaiser had called his bluff. Lea had played upon his status as a former Senator, a man with connections in Washington including a personal relationship with Colonel House, who was President Wilson's right-hand man. But he was forced to concede that he was not any sort of official representative, and that the visit was made while he was on leave and on his personal account.[34]

Count Bentinck told Lea that he might obtain authority for the interview by telephoning to Utrecht, but Lea asked him not to do so. Bentinck and the *burgemeester* had a cordial and rather lengthy chat with the Americans.[35] The Americans had the impression that the Dutch were stalling for time. Sergeant Owen Johnson, who had remained outside, spotted one of the Dutchmen in dinner dress, probably the *burgemeester*, issuing orders, rifles, and ammunition to four soldiers and a policeman stationed near the American vehicles. Elsworth Brown warned the American officers that a rather large contingent of Dutch soldiers had assembled. Machine guns and floodlights were being positioned on the castle walls. The Dutch authorities were concerned that the small party of Americans, visibly unarmed, might be accompanied by a much larger force.

Lea made one final effort, and in doing so revealed the real purpose of the mission. He asked that the Kaiser be told that the Americans would provide him with safe conduct and drive him to Paris. According to Lea, even if convicted the Kaiser would probably not suffer any great punishment, other than the exile of a brave man who had remained loyal to his own people. According to Lea's memoir, the Kaiser refused the offer.[36]

By this point, Lea and his party had been at Amerongen for about two hours. The time had come to beat a retreat. Returning to their vehicles, they found themselves surrounded by two companies of Dutch soldiers. Lea later described them as having 'all the appearance of German soldiers dressed in policemen's uniforms', but this was a fantasy.[37] The scene was now illuminated by two large searchlights. The eight American soldiers, with sidearms concealed under the seats of the vehicles, were no match for the well-armed Dutch forces even if they had wanted to exchange fire.

A large crowd of Dutch civilians had also gathered, attracted by the excitement in what was otherwise a rather tranquil dorp. Many of them had just attended a moving picture show and were on their way home. Some of them openly manifested sympathy with the Americans. One of them spoke to the chauffeur, Marmaduke Clokey: 'Well, you came for the old boy, did you? You might as well get the old … He has to leave the village. He might as well go tonight or tomorrow.' Another asked one of the American lieutenants if they were there to arrest the 'damn crazy German Kaiser'. Someone shouted, in English, 'did you get the old son-of-a-bitch?'[38]

The situation had the potential to spin quickly out of control. 'We knew vacillation or hesitation on our part might provoke either attack or detention', Lea wrote in his memoir. He awakened Hail and Clokey, who had fallen asleep in the Cadillac. Henderson brought the men from the Winton. Lea gave orders about the retreat. He and MacPhail would sit in the back of the Cadillac, with Hail and Clokey in the front. Henderson and the other Americans, along with the Dutch interpreter, were to take the Winton.

'We did not request the soldiers to move but as the cars glided forward, they fell back on either side and formed an armed passageway for us', Lea wrote. The Americans quickly passed through the town of Amerongen, but were soon stopped at the river because the ferryman was on the other side. Nervous about being arrested, Lea ordered the party to travel to the border by separate routes. In the Winton, Lea headed to Maastricht and then into Belgium, dropping 'Hans' Boetter in Nijmegen along the way. The Cadillac, with MacPhail, Johnson, and Hail aboard, crossed at Kleve into Germany.[39]

A Souvenir Ashtray

As the Americans were leaving Amerongen Castle, MacPhail helped himself to a souvenir. He pocketed a bronze ashtray adorned with a pipe-smoking dog that bore the monogram 'W.I.', presumably meaning 'Wilhelm Imperator'. As they departed, a servant reported the theft. The Dutch police moved into action, not for attempted kidnap, but for petty larceny. Amerongen's chief of police called ahead to Arnhem in an effort to catch the thieves, but the Americans had already passed through the town. A few days later, Van Weede told a representative of the American embassy that one of the cars was stopped and searched at the border crossing, near Maastricht (another report places the search at Nijmegen), but that nothing was found. The American accounts do not mention this happening. In any case, the ashtray was in the Winton and seems to have crossed into Germany without incident.[40]

Wilhelm was apparently amused about the pilfered ashtray.[41] Carlos Bentinck told an investigator from the American embassy that he regretted that so much importance had been given to the matter. Even *burgemeester* Van Weede, who had initially called upon the local police to pursue the issue, thought the theft of the ashtray to be rather trivial. Indeed, that was his assessment of the entire visit from the American delegation. 'You know what I think it is, I think it is a bet', he told the embassy official in his Harvard English. 'Somebody told them they couldn't do it and they bet that they could see the Kaiser.'[42]

Dutch newspapers, including the *Handelsblad*, reported that the Americans numbered twelve and were armed with rifles, that the vehicles were armoured, and that they 'gave that they were sent by the American Minister at The Hague to speak with the ex-Emperor'. It said they were arrested and taken to the *burgemeester*. The local stringer who was responsible for this information confessed a few days later that the version he filed had been considerably embroidered.

Upon learning of the events, apparently through the newspapers, the American Ambassador to the Netherlands telephoned the Dutch Foreign

Minister. He reported to Washington that it was unnecessary to tell Van Karnebeek that he knew nothing of the events at Amerongen. He said that 'no one who might have taken part in them had any connection with the American Legation at The Hague or with me'.[43] Captain Goelet, one of Colonel Davis's aides, went to Brussels and informed Brand Whitlock, the American Ambassador. Whitlock wrote in his diary:

Very simple! Senator Luke Lea of Tennessee and his joy-riding party, hunting souvenirs, wished to see the Kaiser—though why I can't imagine. Sent a telegram and letter to The Hague saying that in any event, the visit and the uniforms had been authorised by the Dutch Government through its representative here. What nuisances the traveling souvenir-hunting Americans are! Now for hell a-popping![44]

Brand Whitlock sent Garrett a telegram:

[O]nly Americans recently going to Holland from here have comprised the party of United States Senator Luke Lea from Tennessee, Colonel of the 114th Field Artillery. He came to the Legation last Tuesday [2 January] saying he was on leave for the purpose of visiting Belgium and Holland. I told him that he could not enter Holland in uniform. He said that they would send for their civilian clothes and on Saturday [5 January] he applied for emergency passports. The Dutch Legation here gave Senator Lea a pass to enter Holland and I now learn that the Dutch Minister here indorsed the pass with permission for them to go in uniform. In the future, before visaing any passports for Holland, I shall telegraph you and ask if you desire the bearers to enter the country and I should be obliged if you will do the same in the case of Americans who wish to visit Belgium.[45]

Whitlock wrote to Garrett confirming his telegram and adding that he had given emergency passports to Senator Lea and three officers, Elsworth Brown, Leland S. MacPhail, and Thomas P. Henderson, as well as to two military chauffeurs.[46]

Embassy officials interviewed Count Bentinck, Van Weede, and several other eyewitnesses.[47] Garrett reported to Washington that the account of the raid had been greatly exaggerated by the editor of the local paper, the *Amerongen Courant*, who also happened to be a stringer for the major Dutch newspapers. 'It is evident from the way the newspapers have been handled since Wednesday that Dutch officials desire to keep this affair from going any further, and it is to [be] hoped that they will not take any further steps about it', wrote Ambassador Garrett.[48] The Dutch were anxious that nothing interfere with their efforts to receive a State visit from President Wilson. The ambassador urged the War Department and General Pershing to take the appropriate steps 'to prevent a recurrence of such a disgraceful episode'.[49]

Lea returned to his command in Luxembourg. He informed General Spaulding of the trip and what the Americans had learned. Lea asked Spaulding's authorisation to travel to Paris and report personally to Colonel House. He said he also knew President Wilson personally, but thought it improper to report to him directly except 'through channels', given that the President was also commander-in-chief of the army. Spaulding told Lea that he should write to Colonel House. If Colonel House wanted a personal briefing, then Lea would have to make a specific request to travel to Paris. General Spaulding indicated that the letter to House should be quite summary, something that Lea said he interpreted as a sign that the mails should not be trusted and that it was better to report the information in person. Lea immediately wrote to House. There was no reply. But Lea found a pretext to travel to Paris on other business, and attempted to contact House personally. He was told that House was ill and could see nobody.[50]

In reality, there was little to report. Brown had found some radio equipment, but Lea's suspicion that the Kaiser was being protected by German soldiers was unfounded. He also explained that 'the ruling class of Holland' was 'extremely proud of having the Kaiser as a visitor'. He spoke of anti-American sentiment, driven by anger at requisition of Dutch ships and concern that the United States would back Belgium's territorial designs on Limburg, a matter that was being debated at the Peace Conference. '[I]t will not surrender the Kaiser without at least using his presence as a trading basis for the protection of its present territorial integrity', he thought. Of course, it is quite impossible that Lea could have obtained any evidence to support this observation based upon his very brief conversations with Count Bentinck.[51]

Lea was ordered to Chaumont, the headquarters of the American Expeditionary Force, where he was subjected to a formal army inquiry headed by Inspector General J. C. Johnson. Lea argued that his visit was 'harmless', to the extent that it involved visiting a man who was no longer a Head of State and only a private citizen and that the American forces allowed officers to engage in journalistic activities. If, on the other hand, the Kaiser was actually holding court and scheming with regard to military activities inside Germany, then the mission was 'helpful' and 'of sufficient value to the Government to transcend other phases of the trip'. Years later, Lea and his associates would boast about an effort to kidnap the Kaiser, but testifying before the army inquiry he was evasive and downright dishonest: 'The exact purpose of the trip is hard to define as it depended largely upon different circumstances that would develop from time to time. It was my intention to use each opportunity to accomplish the best results for the Government but under no circumstances to violate the laws or neutrality of Holland.'[52]

In order to protect his accomplices, he testified that none of them had been informed of the purpose of the mission until they reached Amerongen, without explaining why he would be secretive about an activity that was either 'harmless' or 'helpful', and the compliant investigators did not push the point. He told the inquiry that the group was travelling to Utrecht and then on to The Hague, but that he changed plans in Nijmegen because of continuing mechanical problems with the vehicles. The Dutch teenager volunteered the information that if they travelled to Utrecht they would pass by the castle where the Kaiser was detained. Lea suggested that it was only then that the idea occurred to him to pay a visit to Amerongen. MacPhail backed up the story of Lea's sudden change of plans, explaining how through sheer serendipity they learned that Kaiser Wilhelm might be in the vicinity.

The main accusation against Lea was using a government car for personal purposes while on leave. He insisted on making a rather lengthy second submission to the inquiry dealing specifically with this charge. He used lawyerly language, talking about principles of interpretation and construction of legislation. Lea contended that 'necessity created a custom' by which officers could use official vehicles for unofficial trips. He argued this was necessary for their mental well-being, and that travelling by train was not a satisfactory alternative. 'I do not believe there is a single officer in the A.E.F. who will state under oath that he has never used his car except upon official business', Lea to the inquiry. 'The line of demarcation between official and unofficial business is very slight.' This statement was hardly consistent with Lea's claims to have insisted before Count Bentinck and the *burgemeester* of Amerongen that his trip was entirely unofficial.

Lea was informed by a general that the Kaiser intended to press charges claiming that 'a party of American officers, headed by one Senator Colonel Luke Lea, had appeared uninvited at the castle of his host, Count Bentinck, and had made him nervous'. The general said, however, that were Lea to be court-martialled for the offence, his accusor would be compelled to testify in person. It was unlikely that the Kaiser would agree to come to Paris to pursue the case. Lea spoke sarcastically about the 'dreadful charge' of upsetting the Kaiser, saying 'it had been the ambition of every American soldier to make the Kaiser "nervous"'. He told the general he would plead guilty to the charge and serve any sentence imposed upon him, and that 'after the sentence was completed I would go on the Vaudeville stage at $1,000 a week, as the only soldier who had been proved to have made the Kaiser "nervous", and give half my weekly pay cheque' to the brigadier. The investigating officer questioned Lea about the theft of the Kaiser's ashtray. 'I did not see any article of property taken while I was at Amerongen', he claimed, adding, 'I did not know of my own knowledge that any was taken'. But he continued: 'I have heard some conversation in regard to it, which is purely hearsay.'[53]

MacPhail was also summoned to Chaumont. Before testifying, he chatted with Lea over lunch. MacPhail asked Lea to represent him as his lawyer. Later in the day, Lea was again questioned by the investigator about the issue. He answered: 'Mr Inspector General, if you had asked me that question this morning I would have necessarily been forced to answer it.' Lea said that over lunch, he had been retained as counsel to Captain MacPhail. 'MacPhail has told me all the facts of the incident, and I cannot answer your question as it is all privileged being between lawyer and client.' When MacPhail was called to testify, Lea interrupted: 'Your reply, Captain MacPhail, is that "on advice of counsel I decline to answer".'[54]

Advocate General W. A. Bethel reported to General Pershing that 'although this officer has committed a very grave indiscretion', there was 'little likelihood of conviction of a serious military offence'. Bethel said that there 'is practically no conflict in the narration of facts by any of the witnesses',[55] but that is only because he only spoke to Lea and his accomplices, and they had obviously coordinated their versions. He could not have said this if he had consulted the account from the American Embassy investigators in The Hague. Bethel described Lea as being 'perfectly honest, but, nevertheless, mistaken', a rather generous description of his deceitful and incomplete account of the events. According to Bethel:

> If Colonel Lea, before his departure, had formed a secret design to go to Amerongen Castle in Holland for any purpose with reference to the Kaiser, his failure to disclose such intention to his Commanding Officer when obtaining leave, and to the American and Dutch Ministers in Brussels when obtaining passports, would have been equivalent to active deception. So also, if Colonel Lea had represented himself as an official emissary of the American Government or as undertaking the trip upon official business, or if he had connived at such representations by other persons, he would have practiced a gross and inexcusable deception. In either case he would have been guilty of an offence which should be tried by court-martial. I am not only morally

certain that a charge of deception cannot be proved but I feel that in justice to Colonel Lea I should say also that I think he was innocent of all intent to deceive in these matters.

He informed General Pershing that 'there is no evidence whatever that Colonel Lea had any intention even to go into Holland when asking for his leave of absence, or any intention to stop at Amerongen in asking for his passports'.[56]

Yet Lea's account was riddled with inconsistencies, and it was clear from his own evidence that he had misrepresented himself, encouraging the impression that he was on an official mission by insisting upon travelling in uniform. Bethel either ignored or was not aware of the earlier leave of absence at Christmas, for which official authorisation was also obtained, when Lea unsuccessfully attempted to enter the Netherlands. This would be compelling evidence that he intended to go to the Netherlands when he sought leave from General Spaulding a second time. In his report, Bethel also transmitted the view of the Dutch authorities that the matter not go any further. The Inspector General had recommended that Lea be court-martialled for trying to communicate with the enemy. Bethel acknowledged that Lea was probably guilty of such an offence. But he thought it 'undignified for the Government of the United States' to try Lea for what was nothing more than a manifestation of 'poor judgment'. His attempt to visit the Kaiser was described as 'premeditated but for an hour or two'. He thought a reprimand to be as effective a punishment as a court-martial trial.

Lea was actually praised for his candour, but the Amerongen mission was described as 'amazingly indiscreet'. The Adjutant-General told Lea:

As an officer of the American Army you had no right whatsoever to present yourself at the chateau of the ex-Emperor without the authority of the President of the United States first obtained. Furthermore, it should have been apparent to you that the meaning and purpose of your visit might well have been misunderstood, as indeed it was in some quarters, and might have entailed the most disastrous consequences, both political and military.[57]

The Secretary of the Army subsequently confirmed that no other action would be taken.[58]

Lea spent six weeks in Chaumont while the inquiry ran its course. When it finished, in late March 1919, he returned to the 114th Field Artillery and was reunited with MacPhail and Henderson. They sailed home from St Nazaire on the *USS Finland*. The exploit had not been a secret, but Lea's personal role only came to public attention upon his return at the end of March. 'Ex-Senator Lea Attempted to Kidnap the Ex-Kaiser', said a banner headline on page 1 of the *Washington Times* of 1 April 1919.

Some months later, Lea had lunch with General Robert Bullard, who had commanded one of the armies in France. 'What did John Pershing say to you about your trip to see the Kaiser?' asked Bullard. Lea referred to the official report, which described it as 'amazingly indiscreet', but said he had never discussed the matter informally with 'Black Jack' Pershing. 'Well, I'll tell you what John Pershing really thought about the trip', said Bullard. 'John Pershing said to me, "Bullard, I'm a poor man, but I'd have given a year's pay to have been able to have taken Lea's trip into Holland, and to have entered the Castle of Count Bentinct without an invitation."'[59]

MacPhail never returned the stolen ashtray, which adorned the study of his Bel Air, Maryland home for many years. He had a very public career as part owner and general manager of several major league baseball teams, including the Cincinnati Reds and the Brooklyn Dodgers. Lea resumed his political and business activities in Tennessee. By the end of the 1920s, he had built a significant publishing empire, but it did not withstand the strains of the Great Depression. Lea was found guilty of bank fraud in North Carolina and given a lengthy prison sentence. An independent audit showed him to have been wrongfully convicted. He received a full pardon.

8

The Commission
on Responsibilities

For six months in 1919, in the words of Margaret MacMillan, 'Paris was the capital of the world'.[1] The Paris Peace Conference of 1919—there was another Paris Peace Conference in 1946—was convened by the 'Great Powers': the United States, the United Kingdom, France, Italy, and Japan. They invited the 'Lesser Powers', more politely called the other 'Allied and Associated Powers', consisting of smaller or less mighty countries that had nevertheless contributed to the victory. Belgium, Greece, Montenegro, Serbia, Portugal, and Romania were included, as well as four self-governing dominions of the British Empire (Canada, Australia, New Zealand, and South Africa) and India. Several South American states that had broken off relations with Germany also participated, along with Siam. In total, twenty-nine countries were represented.

Not only the belligerents and their allies, who had been directly affected by the war, but essentially all who were concerned with the political, economic, and cultural architecture of the post-war world were drawn to Paris for the Conference. Kurdish, Armenian, and Jewish activists, to mention only a few, lobbied for national aspirations. Non-governmental organisations—although the term was not then in general use—campaigned for their own particular issues. Small States sent top diplomats in order to ensure that special interests were not overlooked. Although the Conference itself was very much a man's world, feminists lobbied on the periphery of the meetings to advance their concerns, including calls to ensure that post-war criminal prosecutions focused on the rape and enforced prostitution of girls and women in some of the territories occupied during the war in Belgium, parts of northeast France, eastern Europe, and Asia minor.[2]

The Trial of the Kaiser. William A. Schabas. © William A. Schabas, 2018. Published 2018 by Oxford University Press.

The Conference lasted for twelve months, but the biggest part of its work was completed by June when the Treaty of Versailles governing the peace with Germany was finalised. Several treaties with other belligerents were also concluded at the Conference. The post-war negotiations continued well into 1920 under the auspices of what was called the Conference of Ambassadors. The Treaty of Sèvres, with Turkey, was only completed in August 1920.

Both the British and President Woodrow Wilson's key adviser, Colonel Edward House, were concerned that Paris would not offer the serenity required for the negotiations. They favoured Geneva, in neutral Switzerland. But Georges Clemenceau insisted that France was the primary victim and the scene of the war's worst battles, and for that reason alone it deserved to host the negotiations. Wilson, who sailed to France on the *USS George Washington* in early December, was enamoured with the City of Light. Who could blame him? The French made him comfortable in an elegant *hôtel particulier* that was owned by the heirs of Joachim Murat, one of Napoleon's most trusted generals.

Attention was paid to symbolism. The first session of the Conference took place on 18 January 1919. On the same day, forty-eight years earlier, the Kaiser's grandfather, Wilhelm I, had been proclaimed Emperor of Germany in the Hall of Mirrors at the nearby Palace of Versailles. The peace negotiations with Germany concluded slightly more than five months later, on 28 June 1919, the fifth anniversary of the assassination of Archduke Franz Ferdinand in Sarajevo. The signing of the treaty with Germany took place that day in the Hall of Mirrors at the Palace of Versailles.

The Paris Peace Conference redrew the borders of Europe, Africa, and the Middle East. It agreed on establishment of the League of Nations and the International Labour Organization. The colonial empire of Germany and the remnants of Ottoman rule in Asia Minor were carved up and distributed as spoils to the victors. Woodrow Wilson had proclaimed a right of self-determination, although its geographic scope was essentially limited to Europe. The Paris Peace Conference was also the crucible for what became, decades later, the international human rights legal framework. Provisions in the treaties adopted at Paris by which new States like Poland, Czechoslovakia, and Yugoslavia were established set out guarantees of fundamental rights, including protection of minorities from discrimination. For example, Article 1 of the treaty establishing the Polish State, known as the 'little treaty of Versailles', declares: 'Poland undertakes to assure full and complete protection of life and liberty to all inhabitants of Poland without distinction of birth, nationality, language, race or religion.'[3] It is the ancestor of provisions in the Universal Declaration of Human Rights, adopted by the General Assembly of the United Nations, in Paris, almost exactly three decades later.[4]

International criminal justice also took its first hesitant steps at the Paris Peace Conference. The organisation, composition, and procedure of an international criminal court was debated, along with substantive legal issues, including the definitions of international crimes, modes of liability and participation in criminal acts, defences such as superior orders, and the immunities of certain senior officials and Heads of State. Discussions were directed at delivering criminal punishment to Germans, Austrians, Bulgarians, and Turks both for starting the war and for conducting it in a brutal and inhumane manner. Never before had attention been given to post-war criminal prosecution of individual perpetrators.

These developments in the fields of human rights and international criminal justice were still quite embryonic. The provisions on equality, non-discrimination, and the right to life in the treaties establishing new States were not extended to what was later called the 'third world', nor did they apply to the victorious Allied powers and the vast territories they controlled throughout the world. Inclusion in the Covenant of the League of Nations of a Japanese-sponsored provision condemning racial discrimination was vetoed by President Wilson.[5] Moreover, the initiatives directed at international criminal justice never really bore much fruit. Within weeks of the signature of the Treaty of Versailles, the British Cabinet decided to confine the prosecutions to 'a few of the clearest and most flagrant cases who can be numbered in tens rather than in hundreds'.[6] Only a handful of war crimes cases were ever brought to trial. By agreement with the Allies, and in spite of the provisions of the Treaty of Versailles, the proceedings took place before German courts. Those convicted were rather minor German war criminals and the sentences were quite derisory.[7] Perceptive observers could have understood these frail efforts to promote human rights and international justice as humble beginnings of a system destined for greater things. Others might have dismissed them as half-hearted but ultimately failed experiments directed at naïve projects that were incompatible with human nature and the imperatives of self-interested States.

The leaders of the delegations of each of the four 'Powers' were charismatic statesmen: Woodrow Wilson, the President of the United States; David Lloyd George, Prime Minister of the United Kingdom, but also representing the British Empire's dominions; Georges Clemenceau, Prime Minister of France; and Vittorio Orlando, Prime Minister of Italy. A century earlier, they would all have been titled noblemen, but times had changed. None of the four claimed any aristocratic heritage. Each had been elected to high office by popular vote. Although included among the 'Powers', Japan played a secondary role and did not send a Head of State or Government to Paris.

On 12 January, President Wilson and his Secretary of State, Robert Lansing, together with the Prime Ministers and Foreign Ministers of Britain, France, and Italy, met as the 'Supreme War Council' in the rooms of the French Foreign Minister, Stéphane Pichon, at the Quai d'Orsay in Paris. They were accompanied by their military advisers. In the course of the meeting, as the discussion turned from questions relating to the armistice and other military matters to the negotiation of the peace treaties, the Supreme War Council agreed to adjourn and to reconvene immediately as the 'Supreme Council' of the Peace Conference. The meeting itself was then described by the minutes as a 'Conversation'.[8] An agenda item provided for establishment of Commissions and Committees, one of which was to deal with 'Penalties for crimes committed during the War'. Eleven 'general principles' were listed, including '[r]esponsibility of the authors of the war' and the '[s]olemn repudiation of all infringements of the law of nations and of principles of humanity'. These were said to be based upon President Wilson's speeches of 27 September 1918 and 8 January 1919, and the Allied reply of 5 November 1918.[9] Issues of criminal responsibility had not appeared in the armistice of 11 November 1918.

The 'Conversations' continued for several days. At the 'Conversation' of 17 January, where the agenda of the opening session of the Preliminary Peace Conference was fixed, Lloyd George proposed that 'Punishment of those guilty of offences against the Law of Nations' be included.[10] This was agreed, but with the title 'Penalties against crimes committed during the war', a somewhat narrower proposition that did not necessarily allude to international law. The minutes record French Foreign Minister Stéphane Pichon insisting that it be 'noticed that Mr Lloyd George's proposal regarding penalties against crimes committed during the war was included'.[11]

Establishing the Commission on Responsibilities

The first formal session of the Preliminary Peace Conference convened at the Ministry of Foreign Affairs in Paris on 18 January 1919 under the presidency of Raymond Poincaré, the President of the French Republic. In addition to the five 'Powers', representatives of Belgium, Bolivia, Brazil, China, Cuba, Ecuador, Greece, Peru, Portugal, Romania, Serbia, and Siam were in attendance. Three new States, the Hedjaz (subsequently a region in Saudi Arabia), Poland, and the Czecho-Slovak Republic, were also present. Delegates of several other States had yet to reach Paris. After the formalities, Poincaré relinquished the chair to the French Prime Minister, Georges Clemenceau. On Woodrow Wilson's proposal, Clemenceau was then elected President of the Preliminary Peace Conference.[12]

In his brief remarks, Clemenceau focused attention on the punishment of war criminals. He invited delegates to prepare memoranda on the responsibility of the authors of the war and the penalty for the crimes committed during the war. He insisted upon the urgency of determining the responsibility of the authors of the war. 'I have no need to explain the reason. If we wish to establish law in the world, we can from this day on, because we are the victors, punish violations of law. We demand the punishment of the authors of the abominable crimes committed during the war', Clemenceau said. 'If this Conference claims to represent the rights of justice, one of the first things we have to do is to see that justice is satisfied by proper reparation, and the fixing of responsibilities. The same applies to the responsibility for the many crimes committed against the law of nations during the war.' Clemenceau drew attention to the memorandum prepared late in 1918 by two French law professors, Ferdinand Larnaude and Albert Geouffre de Lapradelle, entitled 'Inquiry into the Penal Liabilities of Emperor William II'. He promised that it would be distributed to the delegates by the Secretariat-General.[13]

In order to prepare the final peace negotiations, and as a prelude to the main discussions within the 'Council of Four' which only began late in March, several thematic Commissions were established. The Commissions dealt with such matters as the League of Nations, reparation for war damage, labour legislation, and international control of ports, waterways, and railways. One of them concerned 'responsibilities'. At the second plenary session of the

Conference, held on 25 January, Lloyd George presented a draft resolution setting out the mandate of a commission to deal with the issue of responsibilities and penalties.

> *Relative to the Responsibility of the Authors of the War and the Enforcement of Penalties*
> That a commission, composed of two representatives apiece from the five Great Powers and five representatives to be elected by the other Powers, be appointed to inquire into and report upon the following:
> 1. The responsibility of the authors of the war.
> 2. The facts as to breaches of the laws and customs of war committed by the forces of the German Empire and their Allies, on land, on sea and in the air during the present war.
> 3. The degree of responsibility for these offenses attaching to particular members of the enemy forces, including members of the General Staffs and other individuals, however highly placed.
> 4. The constitution and procedure of a tribunal appropriate to the trial of these offenses.
> 5. Any other matters cognate or ancillary to the above which may arise in the course of the inquiry and which the commission finds it useful and relevant to take into consideration.[14]

On the request of Sidney Sonnino, the Italian representative, there was a minor change to the final words of paragraph 3. He had objected to the term 'highly placed individuals' in the draft because he felt responsibility should not be confined in this way. The broader formulation, 'other individuals, however highly placed', was adopted.[15] The resolution did not mention Kaiser Wilhelm by name. But when the Commission began its work, much of the debate revolved around the issues related to prosecution of the former Emperor. The Commission on Responsibilities, as it became known, was the forum for the first serious multilateral negotiations about criminal prosecution for offences related to the conduct of armed conflict, and for its initiation.[16] Its full name was the 'Commission on the Responsibility of the Authors of the War and on the Enforcement of Penalties', a formulation derived from the title of the 25 January resolution.

Many of the 'Allied and Associated Powers' protested that the proceedings were dominated by the 'Great Powers'. They insisted upon more substantial representation on the Commissions. Clemenceau was not entirely unsympathetic to the enlargement of the Commissions. He felt that 'to please the public' smaller States should be given things to do. He said that although the 'Powers' would have been entitled to decide all matters themselves, in light of the contributions and sacrifices they had made, they had generously decided to enlarge the discussions, in the spirit of the idea of a League of Nations.[17]

On 27 January, representatives of countries with 'special interests' met at the French Foreign Office to appoint their delegates to the Commission on Responsibilities and the other commissions established by the Conference. Belgium requested that it be given a seat on the Commission on Responsibilities.[18] 'Who could deny that we have an absolute right to be represented on the Commission, when our country was the first to be invaded, the first to be submerged by invasion, when her neutrality was violated in spite of the treaty signed by the enemy, and when some of the most abominable crimes with which the enemy can be reproached were committed on our soil, as also on Serbian soil?', said Paul Hymans, the Belgian Foreign Minister. Because Belgium was the principal victim of Germany, at least on the Western Front, it would have been expected to play a prominent role in prosecutions. But beyond contributing a member to the Commission on Responsibilities, its involvement was quite marginal. This is explained by the hegemony of the 'Powers', who did not leave much space for participation by smaller countries. But Belgium did not seek out opportunities for greater engagement. In particular, there was considerable political opposition within Belgium to prosecution of the Kaiser.

The Greek President, Eleftherios Venizelos, also demanded that his country have a representative on the Commission dealing with responsibilities. 'Concerning the responsibility of the authors of the war, I will demand that Greece be given also one representative, considering the fact that we have to deplore the loss of three or four hundred thousand men in the Ottoman Empire and that it should present before the Commission first, and before the Conference, afterward, our point of view more specially on this question', said Venizelos.[19] In addition to Belgium and Greece, the 'special interests' meeting designated Serbia, Romania, and Poland to participate in the Commission alongside the 'Great Powers'.[20] Each of the five smaller States was entitled to designate one member of the Commission, while the five larger States were entitled to two.

Many of the fifteen members of the Commission already knew each other, or at the very least knew of each other. Several of them belonged to the global elite of the international law fraternity. Over the years, these specialists in international law had attended the same international conferences and academic gatherings. The Commission's membership included three members of the prestigious *Institut de droit international* and three editors of major international law journals. Three delegates to the Commission, from Belgium and Japan, went on to serve as judges of the Permanent Court of International Justice, established in 1921. Until January 1919, most of the professional work of these experts had been devoted to fine tuning an existing and somewhat static legal system. Suddenly, they were tasked with inventing an entirely new scheme of law, including the creation of institutions to administer it. Their work had the potential to transform international law. They were given only a few weeks in order to accomplish this task.

Foremost among them was Robert Lansing, an American lawyer, saturnine and inflexible. Before entering public service, Lansing had been legal counsel in several international arbitrations. These were trials applying international law, but they were held before temporary or ad hoc tribunals that were set up on a case-by-case basis, as no permanent international court yet existed. They were not criminal trials. In 1914, President Woodrow Wilson appointed Lansing as Legal Advisor to the State Department, in effect the country's senior international lawyer. Subsequently, Wilson named Lansing as his Secretary of State. But Lansing was present in Paris as only one of four American Commissioners and not as the country's chief diplomat, a position that Wilson retained himself for the purposes of the peace negotiations. Lansing was assisted on the Commission by James Brown Scott, a Canadian-born academic lawyer. Scott had participated in the United States delegation to the 1907 Hague Conference. He was editor of the *American Journal of International Law* and a highly regarded publicist.[21]

The British Empire delegation was led by Sir Gordon Hewart, the Attorney General, although he did not attend regularly or participate in most of the meetings. Hewart had just been appointed as the senior Law Officer of the Crown in the British Government, replacing F. E. Smith after he was renamed Lord Birkenhead and appointed as Britain's Lord Chancellor or Minister of Justice. The second position on the British delegation was filled by two alternate members, Sir Ernest Pollock, the Solicitor General, and William F. Massey, the Prime Minister of New Zealand. Both Hewart and Pollock were very distinguished lawyers, although with no particular renown in the realm of international law. Massey, born in Ireland, a loyal Orangeman and a farmer by vocation, was a very able and very conservative politician. He never showed any particular deference to the expert international lawyers who surrounded him. In some sense, he served as the conscience of the Commission. Clemenceau wrote of Massey's '*éloquente bienveillance du rustique*

discours', saying a favourite taunt was to ask him up until what age he practised cannibalism. Massey would reply: 'At least I cooked them, whereas you
ate them raw.'[22]

André Tardieu, then a Minister in Clemenceau's cabinet and a close ally of
the Prime Minister, led the French delegation. Tardieu had begun his career
as a diplomat, but switched to journalism, serving as foreign affairs editor of
the newspaper *Le Temps*.[23] Accompanying Tardieu was Ferdinand Larnaude,
the Dean of the Faculty of Law of the University of Paris and co-author of
the French report on prosecuting Kaiser Wilhelm that Clemenceau had circulated to all of the delegations at the Conference. Larnaude's co-author and
academic colleague, Albert de Lapradelle, was named Secretary-General of
the Commission. Italy's delegation consisted of Vittorio Scialoja and Giuseppe
Brambilla. Scialoja was a law professor and member of the Italian Senate.
The Japanese representatives, Mineichirō Adachi and Harukazu Nagaoka,
were diplomats and international lawyers. Both later served as judges of the
Permanent Court of International Justice. Japan showed little interest in the
issues before the Commission, made only incidental contributions to the debates, and dissented on the conclusions.

The other States were only entitled to have one member on the
Commission. Belgium was represented by Edouard Rolin-Jaequemyns. His
father, Gustave, had been a pioneer in the field of public international law
and one of the founders of the *Institut de droit international*. Edouard had
served as rapporteur of the commission on the laws and customs of war at the
1899 Hague Conference.[24] Greece sent its foreign minister, Nicolaos Politis,
an eminent professor of law with appointments at both the University of
Paris and the University of Aix, in southern France.[25] Serbia's representative,
Slobodan Jovanovitch, was a professor of international law at the University
of Belgrade. Romania was represented by a government jurisconsult, M. S.
Rosental. Poland appointed two alternates, Konstanty Skirmunt and Leon
Lubienski, both of them members of the Polish National Committee. Neither
made any significant contribution to the debates.

English and French were the working languages of the Commission, as
they were of the Peace Conference. Some members of the Commission
appear to have been fairly fluent in both of the official languages. André
Tardieu, James Brown Scott, Ernest Pollock, and Edouard Rolin-
Jaequemyns intervened in both English and French. At one meeting,
Pollock explained that he chose to speak in French 'out of respect and
admiration for France, and for the great service she has rendered in the

interest of right and justice, and also to show my thanks for the welcome she has given us in her beautiful capital'.[26]

Various sets of minutes of the proceedings of the Commission and its three Sub-Commissions are found in the national archives of France, Britain, and the United States. Official minutes were taken and subsequently approved. They were published in French by the French Government.[27] A printed English-language version of the minutes of the Commission, but not those of the Sub-Commissions, for which no publisher is indicated, also exists.[28] The American archives contain draft minutes with handwritten corrections as well as a final typewritten version, in English, but these are more of a transcript than minutes or summary records and do not correspond to what was published. There are at least two versions of the minutes in both English and French for each meeting of the Commission and its Sub-Commissions, and often more. Sometimes sets of minutes are identified as being prepared by the British, but as a general rule they do not indicate their source. Italian minutes of some of the meetings are also deposited in the American archives. These different sets of minutes resemble each other in a general sense, in that they describe the same meetings, but they are far from consistent or identical. Some of them are virtual transcripts, while others are more summary in nature. The most complete would appear to be the French stenographic transcript prepared by the Secretariat of the Conference and available, in part, in the British National Archives.[29] The French stenographic notes were eventually published in a volume edited by Albert de Lapradelle, the secretary of the Commission, although they are not entirely complete.[30] In the English minutes, the remarks of those who spoke French are reproduced based upon what was said by the interpreters. The same is true of the French minutes and of the stenographic notes. The translations do not always correspond to the original language versions. Sometimes, without explanation, English-language translations of entire speeches of francophone participants are simply left out altogether or are rather brutally summarised.[31]

Organising the Work of the Commission

The Commission on Responsibilities assembled for its first session on 3 February 1919 at the French Ministry of the Interior on Place Beauvau. André Tardieu evoked the magnitude of death and destruction in his introductory remarks. 'How could we deny that before any question of peace can arise, justice should punish the authors of the aggression which has caused the deaths of so many million men?' he said. 'How could we be deaf to the call which comes to us from the tombs of our dead for the punishment of the guilty and also for the protection of humanity against the repetition of the crime?'[32] Most if not all members of the Commission would have been touched quite directly by the conflict, with relatives and friends numbering among the dead, missing, and disabled. For them, delivering justice to those responsible for the war and for atrocities committed during the war was more than an academic exercise.

On Tardieu's proposal, the senior American member of the Commission, Robert Lansing, was elected chairman unopposed. Initially, the work of the Commission was divided among three smaller Sub-Commissions. Tardieu thought there should be two Sub-Commissions, one dealing with the facts and the other with the law. The Belgian representative, Rolin-Jaequemyns, convinced the Commission to divide the legal problems between two Sub-Commissions, one for the origins of the war and the other for the violations of the laws of war committed during the conflict.[33] The mandates of the three Sub-Commissions were finalised at the second meeting of the Commission, on 7 February 1919. Sub-Commission I, also called the 'Sub-Commission on Criminal Acts', was charged with discovering and collecting evidence necessary 'to establish the facts relating to culpable conduct which (1) brought about the world war or accompanied its inception; (2) took place in the course of hostilities'. Sub-Commission II, the 'Sub-Commission on the Responsibility for the War', and Sub-Commission III, 'Sub-Commission on Responsibility for Violations of the Laws and Customs of War', were to address the legal issues.[34] The structure was ill conceived. The first Sub-Commission could not properly determine the 'criminal acts' until the second and third Sub-Commissions had established the legal framework. If Sub-Commission I were to conclude that 'culpable conduct' had occurred, this could usurp the function of the other bodies who were required to determine what a culpable act might consist of. The Commission decided that the three Sub-Commissions would work simultaneously '[i]n view of the fact that a number of obviously culpable acts have been sufficiently established to permit of their immediate consideration, subject to the final and definite confirmation of the facts'.[35] Much time and energy was consumed in quarrels about the relationship between the various Sub-Commissions and their respective responsibilities.

Upon Ernest Pollock's request, the second and third Sub-Commissions held their first meeting together, but the session was unproductive and did little more than agree upon dates for future meetings.[36]

Early reports on the work of the Commission and its Sub-Commissions were rather positive. On 7 February 1919, Ernest Pollock wrote to Prime Minister Lloyd George, stating that 'there is general accord among members of the Commission', although 'their deliberations will take some time'. Pollock, quite accurately, thought that the British were somewhat ahead of the other countries in considering the issues involved in establishment of the international tribunal.[37] He pointed to a difference of opinion concerning a proposal to use the armistice, which was due for renewal, as a means to ensure detention of suspected war criminals. 'Mr Lansing, our President, and his colleague alone voted against it', Pollock told the Prime Minister.[38] But this was a marginal issue and the Commission did not give it further consideration.

Irreconcilable differences soon became apparent, with the British and French on one side and the Americans on the other. The smaller delegations tended to side with the British and the French, with the exception of Belgium, which was less predictable. Most of the disputes took place in Sub-Commission III, where Lansing and Pollock squared off in debates about fundamental issues, including whether the Kaiser could be found guilty of acts committed by his subordinates, even those in which he had no direct involvement. The Americans didn't want to try the Kaiser at all. Pollock reported to Foreign Minister Balfour's personal secretary that although the French, the Belgians, and the British were anxious to try the Kaiser. The Americans, on the other hand, feared it would lead to execution. This would 'make a national martyr of William II and prepare for the Restoration of this dynasty in the same way that Macauley suggested the execution of Charles I had led to the Restoration in England'.[39]

The Americans were also opposed to the creation of an international tribunal, something Pollock considered essential if the Kaiser were to be brought to trial. Pollock told members of the Commission that the demand of 'those in authority' in London 'that we shall set up a tribunal to try the Kaiser is insistent, and urgent, and I can't possibly neglect it'.[40]

On 1 March, Maurice Hankey provided Lloyd George with a progress report. Hankey was now the deputy secretary of the Conference, formally the assistant to Paul Dutasta, although it is said that the Englishman 'took over most of the work'.[41] Hankey described 'good progress', with an agreement on an international court for some charges. He did not draw the Prime Minister's attention to the decision against prosecution for starting the war. 'My impression is that this Commission will by March 8th give us sufficient material for preliminaries of peace with Germany', he wrote.[42] In fact, it would take three more weeks. Hankey's letter did not reflect the sharp division, although Lloyd George was already aware of trouble brewing.

Only once did Robert Lansing brief the other leading members of his national delegation, who met regularly as the 'American Commissioners'. On 5 March 1919, he complained to his colleagues that the British had sought the establishment of an international tribunal, or as Lansing described it, one 'on which all the different nations concerned should be represented', with authority to try individuals, including the ex-Kaiser. The British were 'displeased' by the American objection to such a scheme, said Lansing, and expressed this by withdrawing their support for an American proposal on military commissions. Lansing retaliated by threatening to withdraw the American member of the Drafting Committee.[43] The other delegates, including the French, had 'attempted to smooth matters over' and find a compromise. Lansing told his colleagues that he thought the British were 'not very sincere' about trying the Kaiser and 'merely felt they had to urge this measure because of a political pledge'.[44] That was perhaps true for some of them, but Lansing surely underestimated the determination of Prime Minister Lloyd George.

At one point in mid-March 1919, Lansing wrote to the Under Secretary of State, Frank L. Polk, claiming that President Wilson 'approved entirely of my attitude' and that 'he is even more radically opposed than I am to that folly'.[45] In reality, Wilson did not share Lansing's intransigence. In early April, the President readily abandoned the objections and reached a compromise with the other leaders. Indeed, it seems that there was little on which Lansing and Wilson concurred, despite Lansing's positive impression. Eventually, Wilson asked Lansing to resign to 'afford me an opportunity to select someone whose mind would more willingly go along with mine'. Lansing demurred: 'Ever since January 1919, I have been conscious of the fact that you no longer were disposed to welcome my advice in matters pertaining to the negotiations in Paris, to our foreign service, or to international affairs in general.'[46]

The Differences Become Public

The Sub-Commissions completed their work on 8 March 1919. In the course of four sessions during the second week of March, the plenary Commission debated the three Sub-Commission Reports. Differences that had emerged within the Sub-Commissions became more acute in the plenary sessions. After acknowledging an inability to reach consensus, the Commission adjourned for a week. Rolin-Jaequemyns, Ernest Pollock, and Mariano d'Amelio, one of the Italian representatives, were designated as a Drafting Committee. They submitted a draft Report on 24 March 1919.[47] Several more sessions of the Commission were necessary before the final Report was adopted at the end of March.

Although its deliberations were in principle confidential, the difficulties within the Commission soon became public. As early as 27 February, *Le Temps* reported that there were two opposing approaches, one calling for the Kaiser to be tried before an international court for starting the war, for violating Belgian neutrality, and for violations of the laws and customs of war during the conflict. The second was to confine prosecution of the Kaiser to violations of existing law, such as the sinking of *RMS Lusitania*, and to do this before a national court. The League of Nations would be left to impose a moral condemnation.[48] On 14 March, after an encounter in the Supreme Council and with the temperature rising within the Commission, *Le Temps* again discussed the tensions, this time pointing to the Americans as opposing the establishment of an international tribunal.[49] Larnaude spoke of the press coverage in the Commission's meeting that day. He said it was impossible to suspect any of its members for the leak, but offered no alternative theory as to how the newspaper had obtained its information. Several members of the Commission expressed agreement with Larnaude, but none volunteered any explanation. Larnaude did not seem to be aware that a tale of dissention in the Commission, highlighting conflict between the Americans and the French, had been published in the *New York Times* two days before the account in the French press.[50] This might have pointed him to the source of the leak. Rosental of Romania suggested that a request be made to the French Government's censor that publication of reports that were not official be prohibited, but this was not taken up by any of the other members.[51]

Difficulties within the Commission on Responsibilities came to the attention of the Supreme Council of the Paris Peace Conference on 12 March

1919. The issue was the fate of Emperor Karl of Austria. Lloyd George informed the Council that the Austrian Government was planning legislation
to banish the former Emperor. The British Prime Minister informed the
Council that the Austrian Emperor was not to be held responsible for the war.
'The whole responsibility rested with his uncle, Francis Joseph. Furthermore,
when the Emperor Charles had ascended the throne, he had done his best
though rather clumsily, to bring about peace. In view of the present situation
in Austria, he would suggest that the Swiss Government be given the desired guarantee so as to avoid the occurrence of an awful tragedy', said Lloyd
George. The concern was that the Austrian royal family might be subject to a
violent attack if it remained in the country. Balfour suggested making a temporary assurance that there would be no proceedings against Karl pending a
formal determination by the Commission on Responsibilities.[52]

Lansing, who represented the United States at the Council in the absence
of President Wilson, reported that the Commission on Responsibilities 'had
not attempted to draw up a list of criminals, because the Sub-Committee
[sic], dealing with the responsibility for the war, had decided that no one
could be tried under that particular head. That is to say, the Sub-Committee
[sic] had come to the conclusion that the accused could not be brought before any legal tribunal, since they were only guilty of a moral responsibility.'
Lansing continued: 'The great difficulty lies in the fact that the Committee
[sic] on Responsibilities had reached the conclusion that the late rulers of
the various enemy States could not be held responsible for making the war;
but they could be held liable for the violations of the customs and laws of
war, which had taken place through their failure to prevent or to put a stop
to such occurrences. The Committee [sic] held that the Emperor of Austria
could also be made responsible for the latter acts.'[53] The meeting agreed to
authorise the British Government to ask the Swiss Government to give hospitality to the Imperial Family, 'a guarantee being given, if so required by the
Swiss Government, that no difficulties would be raised'.[54]

A day later, Lansing referred to this exchange in a meeting of the
Commission on Responsibilities, implying that the British position was inconsistent. In the Supreme Council, the British were saying that Emperor
Karl could go free because he had not been responsible for starting the war,
whereas in the Commission they were insisting that the Kaiser could be prosecuted for violations of the laws and customs of war even if the act of starting
the war could not be considered an international crime. There was nobody at
the meeting to challenge Lansing's account. He was the only member of the

Commission to have been present in the Supreme Council when the fate of the Austrian Emperor was discussed.[55]

Hankey provided Lloyd George with a copy of Lansing's remarks in the Commission, commenting: 'Personally, I cannot trace much connection between Mr Lansing's version of what you said yesterday and the original.'[56] Lloyd George replied to Hankey that he was 'amazed' by the account of Lansing's speech.'As you know it does not in the remotest degree represent the attitude which I took at yesterday's Council Meeting in reference to the Emperor Karl', he said. Lloyd George explained how he had distinguished the role of the Austrian Emperor, noting that he was not responsible at all for the initiation of the war, that he tried to end it upon assuming the throne, and that he did not really control the direction of the war.'Not one of these three conditions would be applicable to the case of the Kaiser.'[57] Lloyd George asked that William Massey, the alternate member of the British delegation, set the record straight at the next meeting of the Commission.'It was very wrong of Lansing to mislead the Committee', said Lloyd George.[58]

At the 15 March session of the Commission, William Massey politely but firmly charged Lansing with distorting both the views of Lloyd George and the tone of the debate within the Supreme Council. He told the Commission that Lloyd George had studied the minutes of the fourth meeting of the Commission and that 'he had come to the conclusion that what Mr. Lansing had said had unintentionally conveyed a wrong impression, and he asked me to go through and read what he did say at the Council of Ten. This of course is in strict confidence.'[59] Massey read portions of the minutes of the Supreme Council to make his point. Lansing replied that he 'intended in no way to convey another impression than the portions that have been read from the minutes by Mr. Massey. I would say that I distinctly said, as I recall my remarks, that Mr Lloyd George thought he could not be held responsible, for the war, but that Mr Lloyd George failed to say that he could not be held responsible for the breaches of the laws and customs of war, and that there was a danger of his being extradited for those offences if the present policy was followed, which was included in the report supported by the British Delegates included in this Commission'. Massey again took the floor with a final word on the issue: 'I would like to add to what has been said, and speak for Mr Lloyd George as well as for myself, that if any wrong impression has been created— any incorrect or inaccurate impression—by the remarks of Mr Lansing, it was simply unintentional on his part.'[60]

Lansing of the United States and Pollock of the United Kingdom were both steeped in the same common law traditions. They were also political representatives of two closely aligned countries, with many common interests. Their views should have been more in harmony than they were. Yet their differences could not be resolved. Lansing proved to be a very strict positivist, unwilling to seize the opportunity for progressive development of international law. On the other hand, Pollock was unembarrassed about the idea that new legal rules would be established at the Peace Conference and then enforced retroactively. 'Law is not something incapable of development', Pollock said at the seventh meeting of the Commission on Responsibilities. 'The law in France, in the days of Louis XIV, is not the same as it is today. The law in the British Empire is not the same as it was in the days of Henry VIII. And we regard the occasion of the Peace Conference—with its association of, I think I am right in saying, something like fifteen or sixteen countries—as an opportunity when those countries, in accord with the traditions and principles of law, may bring up to date the duties which now arise from the settled opinion of civilised States.'[61]

Speaking directly to Lansing, who was by then openly declaring that he would dissent from the conclusions of the Commission, Pollock said: 'I am not the least disconcerted by the statement or by the suggestion that unless a case is within the municipal law, or justiciable by some particular tribunal at the present day, it is not justiciable by the settled opinion of these fourteen, fifteen or sixteen States which are now engaged at the Peace Conference. And hence, if it is said to be an advancement of the law, I am glad to hear it. It is in accordance with the principles of law. But we believe, for the peace of the world, it is right we should bring to trial those who are responsible for such unconscionable breaches of the principles of humanity which have been committed. That, I believe, is the root difference between your views, Sir, and mine.'[62]

'I must confess that I am a little surprised at your remarks', replied Lansing. 'I never conceived your position to be part of the general jurisprudence of England—the ancient jurisprudence upon which my country has modelled its law and practice—that there is any provision by which a criminal can be brought to justice when there is no penal statute by which to punish him.'

Lansing insisted that the United States was favourable to prosecution of 'direct violations of the laws of war'. Referring to the responsibility for starting the war, he stated, 'only moral sanctions apply. Beyond that, I do not see how we can go.'

'The American representatives on this Commission agree that the United States ought not to put itself in a position that if a case arises which relates to a moral wrong and if it comes before a tribunal, such as is proposed, and the tribunal has no authority to punish, the necessary finding would be that there is no legal warrant to pass on the case and that, therefore, the party is not guilty', Lansing declared. 'I am unwilling to put the Government of the United States in that position, because I believe that the ex-Kaiser, and others, are guilty of a great moral wrong against the world. To try them is to admit doubt as to their guilt. To try them may even offer the opportunity of escaping from a verdict of guilty.'[63]

'We Have Failed'

'We have failed. Frankly, we have failed', said Lansing during the seventh plenary session of the Commission, on 17 March 1919. 'It is not a failure from lack of desire, or lack of effort. It is simply that our views no more mingle than oil and water, and I consider, therefore, that the wise course to pursue is for the Commission, at the present time, to vote, and that the United States dissent and file a minority report.'[64] When Lansing announced his refusal to endorse the majority report, the other delegates rescinded many of the compromise formulations that they had so carefully crafted over the previous weeks. This had only been done, they said, in the hopes of reaching consensus. But if there was no consensus, they preferred to return to their original positions. Ultimately, the Commission on Responsibilities remained too divided, the central points in dispute being the creation of an international tribunal and the immunity of the Kaiser.

The Drafting Committee presented its Report to the Commission on 24 March 1919. The draft Report comprised five chapters, entitled 'Responsibility of the Authors of the War', 'Violations of the Laws and Customs of War', 'Degree of Responsibility', 'Constitution and Procedure of Appropriate Tribunal', and 'Cognate Matters'. Each of the five chapters corresponded to one of the paragraphs in the terms of reference of the Commission adopted at the Preliminary Peace Conference. The Commission concluded that the Kaiser should be brought to trial on charges of responsibility for violations of the laws and customs of war and the laws of humanity, but that those responsible for starting the war should not be prosecuted. Instead, it recommended that in the future penal sanctions should be provided for such violations of international law.[65]

As promised, Lansing and Scott authored a detailed memorandum of 're-servations' to the Report adopted by the majority at the eleventh meeting of the Commission, on 31 March 1919. Like the Americans, the Japanese delegates did not endorse the final report, submitting short dissenting reasons that in general echoed the more substantial dissent of Lansing and Scott. The American dissenting opinion was about the same length as the report itself. The memorandum of reservations was confused and repetitive in places, perhaps because Lansing and Scott each wrote a portion. The memorandum began by declaring that the American members of the Commission were 'as earnestly desirous as the other members of the Commission that those persons responsible for causing the Great War and those responsible for violations of the laws and customs of war should be punished for their crimes, moral and legal'.[66]

The American reservations are dated 4 April 1919, which was when Lansing sent them to President Wilson for his approval. There is some confusion about the date because Wilson had referred to the American reservations two days earlier, on 2 April 1919, in the Council of Four. He mentioned that the American representatives had 'signed a minority report'.[67] But it seems that on 3 April, the Secretariat of the Conference pressed Lansing for the text so that they could publish the report together with its annexes, including the American memorandum. Lansing wrote to Wilson on 4 April saying that he could not do this without the President's consent.

At the core of the disagreement was the plan to try the Kaiser. The American memorandum lamented the 'inconsistency' of the majority of the Commission, explaining that it was 'due in large measure to a determination to punish certain persons high in authority, particularly the heads of enemy states, even though Heads of States were not hitherto legally responsible for the atrocious acts committed by subordinate authorities'.[68] Accordingly, members of the Commission appeared determined to prosecute the Kaiser. They had insisted 'that the jurisdiction of the high tribunal whose constitution they recommended should include the Heads of States, and they therefore inserted a provision to this effect in express words in the clause dealing with the jurisdiction of the tribunal'.[69] Lansing and Scott said they had assumed an 'ungracious task' in opposing their colleagues 'when they believed as sincerely and as profoundly as any other member that the particular Heads of States in question were morally guilty, even if they were not punishable before an international tribunal, such as the one proposed'.[70]

Sending the final report to Lloyd George, but not the reservations as they had not yet been finalised, Pollock minimised the extent of the disagreements. He said that 'the Japanese regard their Mikado as a God' and could not therefore accept a phrase in the report declaring that Heads of States could be punished by the 'High Tribunal'. He explained that this was also at the heart of the American disagreement, because 'they were reluctant to create the possibility of their President ever being incriminated'. He said that the Americans had some other objections as well, but that he anticipated 'they will endeavour to prove that their divergence is as little as possible, as I believe that they are somewhat afraid of adverse public criticism upon their reservations'.[71] Pollock also told the Prime Minister that he had prepared a note dealing with the disagreements of the United States. It said that despite the American objections, there was 'a large measure of agreement'.[72] Pollock's conciliatory text appeared in the draft report, but was elided from the final version at the insistence of Lansing.[73]

Preparatory works, often spoken of in English with the French term *travaux préparatoires*, are recognised sources for the purposes of interpreting treaty provisions.[74] A comparable body of materials to that of the Commission on Responsibilities exists for the preparation of the Nuremberg trial[75] and for the International Criminal Tribunal for the former Yugoslavia.[76] The documentation on the drafting of the Rome Statute of the International Criminal Court is very substantial.[77] The proceedings of the Commission on Responsibilities have their own particular fascination, especially because of their pioneering nature. But there is an important difference between the documentary record of the creation of these subsequent generations of international criminal justice institutions and the Report adopted by the Commission on Responsibilities (together with the dissenting opinions). They were virtually ignored by those who actually drafted Article 227 of the Treaty of Versailles.

The Report of the Commission was destined for the Supreme Council. It had mutated into the 'Council of Four' by the time the Commission's Report was completed at the end of March. Draft clauses were proposed in the Commission's Report that Wilson, Lloyd George, Clemenceau, and Orlando were invited to cut and paste into the treaty with the Germans. Lloyd George did not accept the views of his own legal experts, who were opposed to trial of the Kaiser for starting the war, and Wilson rejected the firm position of his main deputy, Secretary of State Lansing, who rejected a trial altogether. In a few days, the Council of Four achieved the consensus that had eluded the Commission on Responsibilities for nearly two months.

Consequently, the Report of the Commission on Responsibilities is of little use for purposes of interpreting Article 227. There is a disconnect between the work of the Commission in February and March 1919 and that of the Council of Four in April and May. There is no real evidence that the four leaders who negotiated Article 227 had even read the Report of the Commission. Nevertheless, in modern scholarly writing on the development of international criminal law, the stillborn Report of the Commission generally receives considerably more attention than the debates within the Council of Four. This is probably due to the stature of several members of the Commission on Responsibilities within the international legal community. It may also be explained by the relative accessibility of the Report of the Commission, which was published in the *American Journal of International Law*. The actual debates in the Commission and its Sub-Commissions are rarely referred to by legal scholars and virtually never cited by historians. The situation is rather different for the Council of Four, where the materials seem well known to historians, but quite unfamiliar to legal academics.

To the present day, the Commission's relatively succinct Report is sometimes referred to as evidence of an emerging international consensus on matters such as immunity of Heads of State, definitions of war crimes, and responsibility for aggression.[78] For example, judges at the International Criminal Court have cited the Commission's Report to support arguments that Heads of State have no immunity before international tribunals.[79] This is surely overstating things, given the importance of the dissenting views and the total neglect of the Report by the real lawmakers, the Council of Four. The Report of the Commission is often greatly misunderstood. For example, Ricardo Alfaro, a special rapporteur of the International Law Commission, writing in 1949, summarised the work of the Commission on Responsibilities:

> Long and interesting debates took place in which no agreement was reached among the victorious powers on the subject of establishing the proposed tribunal for the exercise of an international jurisdiction of a general character. There was agreement, however, on the point that the German Kaiser should be arraigned as responsible for the war and its horrors, and such agreement was embodied in Article 227 of the Treaty of Versailles ...[80]

Alfaro's Report is often cited as an authority on the history of international criminal law. Yet its account of the Commission on Responsibilities is quite inaccurate. There was no agreement in the Commission about any of the major legal issues. The suggestion that the Report influenced the content of Article 227 is unconvincing. The debates paint a picture of profound controversy within the Commission, not one of emerging consensus.

Because the Commission was the first significant international negotiation with respect to international criminal prosecution, it provides a window into the debates at the time. Nevertheless, it is difficult to invoke the Commission's work and its proceedings as evidence of specific legal development because there was so much discord among the members. The Report of the Commission and the proceedings of its meetings tell us much about the dynamics of creation. They provide fascinating insight into international law-making. But they offer little real clarity about the state of the law in 1919.

9

Prosecuting Crimes against Peace

The Peace Conference charged the Commission on Responsibilities with reporting on '[t]he responsibility of the authors of the war' and 'breaches of the laws and customs of war'. Neither of these crimes, or categories of crimes, had previously been defined in a treaty or some other generally recognised international text. Historically, the definition of crimes, as well as the establishment of mechanisms for their repression, was reserved to governments, not international organisations. Determining which courts and which authority would exercise jurisdiction over any specific wrongful act was a straightforward exercise for which the main criteria were the location of the crime and the nationality or allegiance of the offender. The notion that there were international crimes seems to have originated at the time of the emergence of nation States, in the seventeenth century. It was also associated with the growth of global trade. Not surprisingly, piracy was the first crime to be recognised as one of international concern.

Pirates were *hostes humani generis*, that is, enemies of mankind. The concept is traced to Cicero.[1] They belonged to no State. Their crimes were often perpetrated on the high seas, beyond the reach of national jurisdictions. To meet their menace, rules developed whereby all States could exercise criminal jurisdiction over pirates. During the eighteenth and nineteenth centuries, the concept expanded to deal with other threats that were international or transnational in nature, including the slave trade, trafficking in persons (sometimes called the 'white slave trade'), the international drug trade, and other crimes against protected interests with an international dimension. Rules governing prosecution of these international crimes were, in some cases, set out in treaties. The focus of this early generation of international crimes was on crimes against the authority and the prerogatives of States, in particular acts that challenged their commercial and political interests. According to Antonio Cassese, piracy and the other offences of this period are not true international crimes because they do not protect 'values considered important by the whole international community'.[2] M. Cherif Bassiouni described the category as 'international delicts' and 'international infractions', suggesting they are secondary in nature, as opposed to 'international crimes', which sit at the apex of the hierarchy.[3]

True international crimes, according to today's scholars, consist of genocide, crimes against humanity, war crimes, and the crime of aggression. These are the four categories of crimes subject to prosecution by the International Criminal Court. The preamble to the Rome Statute of the International Criminal Court describes them as 'crimes of concern to the international community as a whole'. Some other crimes, such as torture, enforced disappearance, slavery, and apartheid, are also often encompassed within the rubric of international crimes. Efforts to deal with this more contemporary generation of international crime can be traced as far back as the First World War. The debates within the Commission on Responsibilities provide important insights and understandings about the genesis of international crimes.

Germany's Role in Starting the War

Chapter I of the Report of the Commission on Responsibilities is entitled 'Responsibility of the Authors of the War'. It sets out the classic narrative about how Germany and Austria had provoked the war.[4] The Sarajevo assassination was described as 'a pretext to initiate war' exploited by both Austria and Germany. A 'decisive consultation' took place on 5 July 1914 at which Austria and Germany developed a plan to submit an ultimatum to Serbia, although the bellicose agenda was subsequently disguised when the Kaiser went for a Baltic Sea cruise. The Entente Powers, the Report explained, consistently maintained a conciliatory posture, but their efforts were ignored or rebuffed by Germany and Austria. Chapter I is amply referenced with footnotes to various volumes of documents, known by the colour of their covers. These were published by governments with a view to vindicating their own conduct during the July Crisis. France produced a Yellow Book, Serbia a Blue

Book, Austria-Hungary a Red Book, Russia an Orange Book, and so on.[5] France, Belgium, and Britain also prepared reports dealing with atrocities and other violations of the laws of war perpetrated by German forces.[6] Although the American delegates dissented from the Report, they did not dispute the conclusion of the Commission that Germany was responsible for initiating a war of aggression. In fact, their dissenting memorandum adds fuel to the case, invoking incriminating documents that are not referred to in the Report itself. Noting the rejection of attempts at conciliation in late July 1914, the American memorandum describes Germany as being 'flushed with the hope of certain victory and of the fruits of conquest' and 'determined to force the war'. Germany's acts, including violation of the neutrality of Belgium and Luxembourg, 'should be condemned in no uncertain terms', and their per-petrators 'held up to the execration of mankind', says the American memo-randum.[7] 'The documents tell the whole story. They need neither explanation nor comment', wrote James Brown Scott in his account of the negotiations, published in the early 1920s. According to Scott, they confirmed that Germany aided and abetted Austria-Hungary in going to war.[8]

The draft of Chapter I of the final Report of the Commission originated in Sub-Commission I. Also known as the 'Sub-Commission on Criminal Acts', it was charged with establishing the acts that brought about the war or accompanied its inception. Several States made submissions to the Sub-Commission addressing the acts that led to the war.[9] It held three very un-productive and rather perfunctory meetings. Its members squabbled about how to classify the material and other mundane matters.[10] By the time of the third meeting, on 24 February 1919, the unrealistic nature of its assign-ment had become apparent. The Sub-Commission decided to devolve its task to a three-member Drafting Committee, comprising representatives from France, Britain, and Greece, a measure it ought to have taken at its very first session. Ten days later, the Drafting Committee produced a narrative report about the war, including an explanation of its origins, followed by annexes in tabular form listing specific war crimes with precise references to the relevant government report.[11] The actual compilation of the material was largely the work of Captain R. Masson and Dr Coleman Phillipson. Masson was identi-fied as an alternate member of the French delegation. Phillipson, an academic lawyer, was the author of perhaps what was then the most comprehensive compilation of war crimes committed during the war, based largely upon the official reports published by the Belgians and the French.[12]

The first part of the draft spoke to the causes of the great conflict. Although insisting its work was not yet completed, the Drafting Committee explained that a number of facts enabled it to conclude that:

> Austria-Hungary plotted with Germany in order to render a conflict with Serbia unavoidable; that Germany supported the Austrian policy, fully conscious of the consequences it would entail, and defeated all attempts on the part of the Entente Powers to bring about a peaceful settlement of the question at issue; that Turkey connived at and approved of the proceedings of the Central Powers, and prepared for her ultimate participation in the war by placing her land and sea forces under German leadership; that Bulgaria, whilst carrying on negotiations with the Entente Powers, had entered into a secret understanding with Germany, which culminated in a treacherous attack on Serbia; and ... that the neutrality of Belgium and Luxembourg was deliberately and flagrantly violated.[13]

An annex, consisting of fewer than three pages, summarised the case against Germany, supported by citations and references. It began with the words: 'The following facts appear sufficiently well established ...'. Much shorter discussions of the responsibility of Turkey and Bulgaria followed.[14] 'Many months before the crisis of 1914 the German emperor had ceased to be pacific', began the annex. It was followed by a reference to a remark attributed to the Kaiser: 'War with France is inevitable, it must come to that someday or other.' It also charged the Emperor with approving of Austria-Hungary's ultimatum to Serbia, stating that on 1 August 1914 the Kaiser had addressed a telegram to the King of England telling him that '[t]he troops on my frontier have, at this moment, been stopped'.[15]

Other than a few rather pedantic corrections, the Sub-Commission accepted the draft Report.[16] This was agreed without a vote.[17] Complementary information from Romania, Greece, and Japan was added subsequently. As far as Wilhelm's personal involvement was concerned, the Report from Sub-Commission I was quite underwhelming. The Sub-Commission's Report received a withering critique from James Headlam Morley, a member of the British delegation to the Conference. Insisting that he did not question German responsibility for the war, Headlam Morley felt the authorities relied upon by the Sub-Commission to be superficial and ambiguous.[18]

Sub-Commission I's Report was quickly approved by the plenary Commission at its third meeting.[19] The text was then revised by the three-member Drafting Committee.[20] The most damning reference to the Kaiser in Sub-Commission I's Report, about the inevitability of war, was replaced with a footnote to the Belgian Yellow Book and an aggressive comment attributed not to Wilhelm but to General von Moltke.[21] When he presented the draft Report to the eighth meeting of the Commission, Rolin-Jaequemyns explained 'that it would perhaps be preferable, in order to keep on sound ground, not to lay down in advance a presumption of guilt in respect of any person which applies to the point of suppressing any special mention of chiefs of States or even the ex-Kaiser'.[22]

When the narrative portion of the draft was discussed, Robert Lansing challenged the statement that Wilhelm had 'ceased to be pacific'. 'I doubt if he was pacific before 1913', said the American Secretary of State. 'He may have pretended to be. I think we must give some proof that he posed as a champion of peace if we make a statement like that. I am not criticising the fact that in November 1913 he was for war.'[23] Lansing's point was well accepted by Pollock and Larnaude. 'It is quite true, I dare say that in earlier history, if we went back to it, we should find that the Kaiser was not pacific at an earlier date', said Pollock. Rolin-Jaequemyns agreed to replace the phrase with 'no longer posed as the champion of peace'.[24]

The draft Report also addressed the involvement of Turkey and Bulgaria. It said that the Young Turk Government 'had been meditating revenge since the Balkan wars' and counted on Germany to do this, handing over command of its military to a German general only a few months before the outbreak of the war. As for Germany, the Report said it hoped, 'by means of Turkey, to raise the whole of Islam against the Entente Powers'. A scheme that included staged frontier incidents proved 'Bulgaria had long premeditated war against Serbia, and perfidiously brought it about'.[25] Lansing was again critical, urging the Commission to be 'very careful' with its allegations. He referred to the statement about Germany attempting to incite Muslim unrest. 'I quite agree with the fact, but where is the proof?' asked Lansing.[26] Pollock explained that the language was derived from the report of Sub-Commission I, but conceded that Lansing had a point.[27]

'Isn't it a fact that in a famous speech the Kaiser said the Mohammedans could always count on his protection and assistance, that he was their friend?' asked William Massey of the British delegation. German foreign policy under the Kaiser had always been sensitive to the Muslim world. The hope was to exploit resentment at French and British imperialism in the Middle East, North Africa, and beyond.

'Quite right. It was in Jerusalem, in 1910, I think. At that time, he was "pacific"', answered Lansing, with more than a soupçon of sarcasm.[28]

'Mr Lansing is revealing diplomatic secrets', countered Pollock.[29]

Was Aggression an International Crime?

That Germany and Austria were responsible for starting the war was a conclusion reached by the Commission quite easily. The more interesting debate was about whether starting the war might be considered an international crime for which individuals could be tried before a court of law and punished if found guilty. This issue was initially addressed by Sub-Commission II, where discussion focused on a British memorandum. The British did not object as such to treating the launching of a war of aggression as an international crime. However, they were opposed to prosecuting the Kaiser for such an act. Their memorandum pointed out that any inquiry into responsibility for the war, if it was to be thorough, would necessitate examining events that had occurred over many years in various countries. This would raise difficult and complex problems that were 'more fitly investigated by historians and statesmen, than by a tribunal appropriate to the trial of offenders against the laws and customs of war'. The memorandum warned that were a tribunal to be established for the prosecution of war crimes, it 'might hardly be a good Court to discuss and deal decisively with such a subject as the authorship of the war'.[30] Pollock did not mention that German defendants, including the Kaiser, might relish the opportunity to litigate the contribution of Britain and France to the pre-war arms race.

The French strongly disagreed, presenting the Sub-Commission with their own memorandum on the subject. 'The League of Nations, founded January 25, 1919, considers, in accord with the universal conscience, that a war of aggression is a crime', it began. 'The crime constituted by the aggression of 1914 should be the object, not only of reparation, but of penalties.' In its final pages, the memorandum turned to the issue of individual responsibilities, and in particular that of Kaiser Wilhelm:

> Heavy guilt, then, weighs upon Germany; but it is impossible to arraign an entire country at the bar of justice. Even admitting—and it is not our purpose to examine this matter here—that the majority of the German people wished and approved these crimes, this people had leaders and among

these leaders a supreme chief. It is this responsible head that we must seek, for modern law knows no irresponsible authority, even at the summit of hierarchies.

In England as in France the courts are overwhelmed with complaints emanating from private persons against William II; instinctively in the eyes of the peoples he is the responsible person. Are they right?

Was it really credible to think the Kaiser was not responsible for instigating the war, asked the French text. 'He is uncontestably the highest authority; and where the highest authority is the highest responsibility must be found', it said. 'William II is guilty of having premeditated the war and responsible for the violation of treaties.' The French memorandum did not provide any direct evidence of Wilhelm's personal involvement, basing its case essentially on a presumption that, as Head of State, and in light of the constitutional structure of Germany, he bore ultimate responsibility.[31]

At the second meeting of Sub-Commission II, Ernest Pollock spoke directly to the criminal liability of the Kaiser. 'If we are to bring the responsibility for having provoked the war, which we all know was wickedly done by the Germans, into the court or the tribunal', he said, 'we should undoubtedly have to examine a good deal of the foreign policies of a number of European countries for a considerable time before the war. Well, now, it would be easy for us to keep in mind that a moral responsibility lies upon the authors of the war, but it is quite a different question whether, having regard to the limits of any tribunal, it is possible to bring any such criminal responsibility against the authors of the war before an actual court.' Pollock insisted that he was not abandoning the idea of a trial of Kaiser Wilhelm. However, he said, 'we shall have an overwhelming case upon the facts proving the outrages against the laws of war against the Germans, and if we succeed before the tribunal in establishing that, would it not be better to leave large questions of politics which would involve a very long inquiry aside?'[32]

Replying to Pollock, Ferdinand Larnaude focused upon the importance of bringing the German people to recognise their own responsibility for the war. He said that they still believed that they were the victims of the Entente. '[I]f a tribunal succeeded in establishing from indisputable and undeniable and irrefutable proofs, that the responsibility for the war lies within the German Empire, perhaps, then we might get a conviction amongst the German people that they are responsible …'.[33]

'I think we had better keep more closely to the reference entrusted to us, rather than look forward to the day when every German will hold up his hands and say, "After all, it was really William who created the war"', answered Pollock.[34] James Brown Scott, standing in for Robert Lansing, and on this occasion choosing to speak in French, argued that the responsibility for provoking the war was a moral rather than a legal issue.[35] The distinction between 'moral' and 'legal' responsibility was one that the Americans would return to again and again. After more comments by both Larnaude and Rolin-Jaequemyns, Scott ventured a summary of the discussion. 'I think, therefore, that we ought to report that we do not advise that the Kaiser should be charged before the tribunal criminally, as having provoked the war, and the acts which have taken place at its beginning', he said.[36] Scott said confidently that the Kaiser's guilt could be established 'for the crime he has committed in Belgium, and on the sea, and elsewhere', explaining that he was 'not prepared to spend much time over the questions of what are—what I might call "political responsibilities", because we can catch him absolutely on his brutality. If we can handle him on one thing, I don't care much about giving him twelve months for another.'[37]

Sub-Commission II's Report reprised in large part the text of a second British memorandum dated 17 February 1919.[38] It relied upon practical rather than legal objections to support its decision recommending that prosecutions not be undertaken for provoking the war.[39] The Report of Sub-Commission II was adopted by the plenary Commission following only brief discussion.[40]

The draft Report of the Commission, prepared by the three rapporteurs and submitted to the eighth meeting of the Commission, changed the focus and relied upon a legal argument. According to the draft Report:

> ... premeditation of a war of aggression, treacherously dissimulated under a peaceful pretence then suddenly declared under false pretexts, is conduct which the public conscience reproves and which history condemns, but by reason of the purely optional character of the Institutions at The Hague for the maintenance of peace (International Commission of Enquiry, Mediation and Arbitration) a war of aggression may not be considered as an act directly contrary to positive law, or one which can be successfully brought before a tribunal such as the Commission is authorised to consider under its terms of reference.[41]

The draft Report also reproduced the paragraph from Sub-Commission II's Report about the practical objections to prosecution for provoking the war. This was left unchanged in the final report of the Commission.[42]

'Can you not at least nuance what you have said, and not suggest that war is as legitimate when it is premeditated as when it is in self defence?' protested Larnaude during discussion of the relevant paragraphs at the ninth meeting of the Commission. 'I acknowledge that on this issue, positive international law does not distinguish between legitimate wars and illegitimate wars. But there is something so new about this war that compels international law to evolve on this issue.'[43]

Robert Lansing, who had by now made clear that he would not sign the Report, was increasingly fractious on the point. 'Gentlemen, it seems to me that we shouldn't stagger at the truth the way we are doing', he said. 'That is the truth that is stated in that paragraph. I would object seriously to a new doctrine which has been lately advocated by a very few men should be set up to counteract the standing policy of the world. Because that is a correct declaration there as to what the truth is in regard to war at the present time.'[44]

'Then we ought to keep the paragraph', said Ernest Pollock. 'It is quite right in saying that a war of aggression may not be considered as an act directly contrary to positive law. That is a statement that is perfectly sound. Then let us leave the paragraph. We can't gain anything by suppressing it.'[45]

'I think I should add one thing', said Lansing. 'I am quite in accord with the sentiment of thinking men of today that a war of aggression—I do not care whether it is treacherously dissimulated under a peaceful pretence or not—but a war of aggression ought to be declared an international crime. But it is not now. It has not been so declared. Therefore I think this statement is perfectly applicable.'[46]

The Report of Sub-Commission I had also contained a short section on violations in north-eastern France. The rapporteurs of the Commission broadened this to 'Violations of Territory', adding the example of a raid upon Serbia by Bulgaria. The Report specified that these acts violated international law because they were perpetrated before the declaration of war.[47] Lansing and Pollock felt this section weakened the entire Report. The French said they would be sorry to see the removal of any reference to the measures taken by their country at the beginning of August 1914, 'which she alone in history has ever taken … decid[ing] that her troops should withdraw 10 kilometres from the frontier'. The Commission agreed to remove the third section, but to incorporate some of the language about the French conduct and the German incursions elsewhere in the report.[48]

Neutrality of Belgium and Luxembourg

Actual hostilities in the war began on 29 July 1914 with the shelling of Serbia, including the city of Belgrade, by Austrian forces. Austria had declared war on Serbia the previous day. The contention that this was a breach of international law as it stood at the time was not developed and the Commission did not concern itself with the matter, except to the extent that Germany and Austria were alleged to have exploited the Sarajevo assassination as a pretext to launch an aggressive war. In a memorandum submitted to the Commission, Serbia's representative, Slobodan Jovanovitch, wrote that '[s]uch an attempt formed after premeditation by a Great Power against the independence of a smaller State deserves condemnation from the point of view of international law, which has proclaimed the equality of all States'.[49] In contrast, Germany's invasion of Belgium and Luxembourg on the Western Front during the first days of August 1914 was widely denounced for violating international law. Treaties adopted during the nineteenth century guaranteed the neutrality of Belgium and Luxembourg. These had been subscribed to by Germany or by its predecessor, Prussia. Ironically, the purpose, at the time, was to contain France, not Germany.

In addition to studying 'acts which provoked the war', Sub-Commission I of the Commission on Responsibilities was also charged with examining 'acts which accompanied the outbreak of the war'. This was generally understood to mean the invasion of Belgium and Luxembourg. The Report adopted by Sub-Commission I summarily outlined the applicable treaties, refuting the German allegation that France had itself violated the neutrality of Belgium and Luxembourg. The Sub-Commission's one-line summary was hardly controversial. '[T]he neutrality of Belgium and Luxembourg was deliberately and flagrantly violated.'[50] Several incursions into French territory by Germany in the first days of August were also described briefly.[51]

Sub-Commission I cited the notorious admission by Bethmann-Hollweg on 4 August 1914. Reporting to the Reichstag that day, the German Chancellor admitted German responsibility for violating the neutrality of the two countries. 'Necessity knows no law', he said, acknowledging that the occupation of Belgium and Luxembourg was a breach of international law. 'We have been obliged to refuse to pay attention to the justifiable protests of Belgium and Luxembourg', Bethmann-Hollweg told the German legislators. 'The wrong—I speak openly—the wrong we are thereby committing we will try to make good as soon as our military aims have been attained.'[52] At one point during the war, Germany even offered to compensate Belgium. It proposed to do this by purchasing the Belgian Congo at a price well in excess of its real market value!

The rapporteurs of the plenary Commission considerably elaborated upon these elements of Sub-Commission I's Report, in particular with respect to Belgium. Sub-Commission I's Report did not invoke the fifth 1907 Hague Convention on neutrality. The draft Report of the Commission added a reference, noting that the Hague Convention described the territory of all neutral States, regardless of whether there was a specific treaty, as 'inviolable'.[53] Germany was a party to the 1907 Hague Convention, although the draft Report did not mention this. The unclear and incomplete discussion of the Convention manifested conflicting views about its legal status.

Lansing pointed out that Serbia was not a party to the 1907 Hague Convention on neutrality. 'Therefore it did not apply in this war', he said.[54] Technically, Lansing's position was quite accurate. The *si omnes* clause in the various Hague Conventions of 1907 required that all participants in a conflict be parties to the treaties.[55] But there was a way to address this. The Hague Convention on neutrality could be presented as a codification of international custom, making it irrelevant whether it had been ratified by Serbia and, for that matter, Germany or any other State. 'Even if Germany did not guarantee the neutrality of Belgium, the fact that she had violated this neutrality should be first of all considered as contrary to the law of nations', insisted Vittorio Scialoja, the representative of Italy.[56] Larnaude and Rolin-Jaequemyns concurred. It was agreed to retain a reference to the Hague Convention.[57] The final Report contains the following phrase: 'That Convention was declaratory of the law of nations ...'.[58] This confirmed the application of the principles it set out regardless of whether the Convention governed the conduct of Germany during the First World War in a technical legal sense.

Other members of the Commission believed that the neutrality treaties concerning Belgium and Luxembourg offered a more solid legal basis. '[I]t was in violation of these specific treaties of neutrality with those two countries that the great crime of Germany was committed', said Lansing.[59] Pollock agreed with Lansing: Germany's acceptance of the Belgian Treaty in 1839 and the Luxembourg Treaty in 1867 'hold her formally bound whatever the convention at the Hague may have stated', he said, 'and I am inclined to think that you had better stand on the guaranteed neutrality rather than make any reference to the Hague Convention'.[60] But when

William Massey proposed that the conclusions explicitly describe Prussia as a guarantor party, Lansing was hesitant. It was Prussia, not Germany, that had ratified the neutrality conventions with Belgium and Luxembourg. Germany did not yet exist when those treaties were finalised. 'I would avoid that because there has always been the question raised as to how far Prussia's treaty liability has bound the entire German Empire. Our view has been that it does cover the entire German Empire, but why raise the question?' commented Lansing.[61]

Even if Germany had violated the neutrality of the two States, this did not mean that its leaders, including the Kaiser, could be charged with a criminal offence. 'Invasion of Belgium and Luxembourg in breach of Treaties' figured at the top of a list of crimes for which the Kaiser might be brought to trial, according to a British memorandum circulated on 13 February 1919.[62] It was not entirely clear whether the British thought that violating the treaties themselves constituted a crime. 'The ex-Kaiser's responsibility for acts done or sanctioned by him in his military and naval capacity after the invasion of Belgium, in breach of the treaties of 1831 and 1839 and of Luxembourg in breach of the treaty of 1867, and for the series of violations numerous and varied of the laws and customs of war committed on land, at sea and from the air, by the military, naval and air forces of Germany, is unquestionable', said the accompanying commentary.[63] This might imply that the real crime was not the violation of the treaty, but rather the acts that followed.

At the second meeting of Sub-Commission II, Ernest Pollock presented a new British memorandum that asked whether States rather than individuals were to be blamed when international agreements were breached. Pollock's memorandum offered an explanation:

> So many highly placed individuals and perhaps constitutional advisers of the ex-Kaiser must have concurred in the proposal that the German Empire should refuse to recognise its duties under the Treaties guaranteeing the neutrality of Luxembourg and of Belgium that there is, in our opinion, not a little difficulty in establishing penal responsibility upon the Sovereign head of the State for conduct which was in essence national, and a matter of State policy, rather than one of individual will.

The memorandum concluded that although 'the breaches of the above treaties should be reported to the Peace Conference as involving grave moral responsibility against the ex-Kaiser, we are of the opinion that no criminal charge should be made against him personally in respect to them'. The moral responsibility, it said, would 'be of value in estimating the criminal charges which will be brought and established against him for breaches of the laws and customs of war in the course of the hostilities'.[64]

Ferdinand Larnaude objected strenuously, distinguishing between the issue of inciting the war, about which he had reluctantly accepted the British position that criminal prosecution should not be undertaken, and that of the violation of the neutrality of Belgium and Luxembourg. 'The truth is that a new law of nations has been born, and that the birth of this new order of things is showing to the authors of the war themselves that they have made necessary the creation of this new law of nations by the very crimes they have committed', he said. Larnaude spoke of 'une sorte de renaissance de droit naturel', a revival of natural law, in recent years. 'Therefore, we cannot very well admit that there should be no sanction—that there should be no punishment for such crimes, and that it should not be possible to bring these authors before a tribunal.'[65]

Pollock thought he had been misunderstood by Larnaude. 'The point is this: Before any tribunal that is set up, can Wilhelm Hohenzollern be found guilty personally, and in his own proper person, of the breaches of the treaty with Belgium, and with Luxembourg?' said the British Solicitor General. 'The defence would be that it was an act by the state as a whole, and the—and get away from saying that Wilhelm Hohenzollern, and no one else, is guilty of that crime.' Pollock contrasted this with submarine warfare, where he said the case against the Kaiser would be 'quite easy' to establish.[66] 'Because I think he would have a much better defence in the one case, and an easier defence to put forward than he would in the other', replied Pollock. '[A]s we have the choice of a great number of charges, I should bring the charge for a grave matter, and one which can be the most easily established. If you have got a prisoner, and have got such a number of charges against him, you always select the best case.'[67]

'International law in its present state, does not admit, as you say, of penal sanctions, and I regret it', conceded Larnaude. 'I hope there will be a new law of nations after the labours of the Peace Conference, and that one of the first things the Peace Conference will be asked to decide will be that there shall be, in the future, chastisement for such offences—violations of treaties, etc., as have taken place in this war. I regret that it is not possible to do more for the time being …'.[68] Larnaude indicated that he was willing to go along with the recommendation that the Kaiser not be prosecuted. However, he wanted the

Report to condemn the violation of the treaties and to make clear that such violations cannot occur again. Pollock agreed to reformulate the draft.

At the third meeting of Sub-Commission II, Pollock presented a revised version of the paragraphs of his memorandum dealing with the neutrality of Belgium and Luxembourg. Stronger language had been added to describe the breaches of the neutrality treaties.[69] But Larnaude was dissatisfied and returned to his earlier position supporting criminal prosecution of the Kaiser for violating the treaties. 'We have the greatest interest in getting at the Kaiser ... We must come back to the idea of personal responsibility', he said.[70] What troubled Larnaude above all was the assertion that individuals were not responsible for acts of States. Paragraphs in Pollock's original draft, cited above, suggested there could be no international criminal responsibility for the violation of treaties.[71] When Rolin-Jaequemyns proposed that the troublesome paragraphs be removed, Larnaude gave his consent to the draft Report. He rallied to the conclusion that there should be no trial of the Kaiser for violating the neutrality treaties. Sub-Commission II agreed that it had finished its work, leaving Pollock and Rolin-Jaequemyns to revise the text and then submit it to the Commission.[72]

At the end of February 1919, Pollock informed Balfour that a Sub-Commission of the Commission had abandoned the notion of prosecution of the Kaiser for starting the war. 'Any court charged with investigation into such a matter would find itself investigating events that happened a number of years before the war in different European countries, the issues would probably become confused, and would not present an opportunity for clear-cut decisions such as are desirable in a court appropriate for the trial of offences against the laws of war', wrote Pollock. 'You are aware no doubt of the strong feeling in Great Britain that the ex-Kaiser must himself be charged for the outrages which, if he did not instigate, he certainly condoned and failed to control', he continued. 'This view is shared very strongly by France, Serbia, Belgium, Romania and indeed I think I may say by all countries, except the United States.' Pollock said he hoped that the United States would at the very least remain complacent and allow the tribunal proposal to proceed. 'My own view is that we can make a very good case against the ex-Kaiser, certainly for brutalities committed upon the sea.'[73]

Balfour transmitted Pollock's views to Philip Kerr, the private secretary of the Prime Minister. Kerr sent the letter on to Lloyd George, commenting that, 'personally, I think it would be a great pity, if they are going to try the Kaiser at all, that he should not be tried on the major count of being the person principally responsible for launching the war on Europe. If there are technical reasons against a public trial on this count I would prefer that the Peace Conference should on its own responsibility declare the Kaiser a criminal, stating its reasons in a solemn document and determine the punishment, e.g., imprisonment for life, which it thinks he deserves. It seems to me that to try him on technical breaches of the laws of war and not on the fundamental issue would be worse than to leave him alone altogether. Perhaps you would see the Attorney General on the subject before he leaves for Paris at the end of this week'.[74]

The following day, Kerr met with Pollock and communicated what he said he understood to be the views of Lloyd George. He told Pollock that he was certain it would ultimately be impossible for Lansing or any other American to resist bringing the Kaiser to trial. 'Neither he nor anybody else could afford to stand out as protecting the Kaiser against fair trial while bringing his subordinates to action', reported Kerr to Lloyd George.[75] These exchanges within the British Government probably explain why Sub-Commission II held an additional meeting, convened at the request of Pollock and Gordon Hewart, the Attorney General, who had returned to Paris at the beginning of March. The British proposed adding a paragraph to the Report on which agreement had been already reached at the previous session. Hewart justified this saying that since the 20 February meeting the Report of Sub-Commission I, on punishable acts, had become available. He did not specify the nature of any new information that would justify reconsidering the Report of Sub-Commission II. Indeed, the reference to the Report of Sub-Commission I appears to have been a mere pretext to allow the British to make the change that they wanted. The British proposal read:

> We desire to add a reference to the report of Sub-Commission I upon culpable and criminal acts, and in particular to Annex 'A' to that report dealing with (1) Acts which provoked the world war and (2) Acts which accompanied the outbreak of the world war.
>
> It may well be that the Peace Conference, notwithstanding the technical and practical difficulties which we have mentioned, may think it right in a matter so unprecedented to adopt special measures and even to create special machinery, in order to deal with the authors of such acts, and to exhibit in an unmistakable way the condemnation in which they are held.[76]

Predictably, Larnaude welcomed the apparent toughening of the British position. He seized the opportunity to ask for further amendment of the Report in order to underscore the charge that the breach of neutrality was not only a 'moral' issue, but a legal one as well. He also endorsed the notion of 'special machinery', recognising that it 'might not be a tribunal properly speaking'.[77]

Rolin-Jaequemyns suggested that the Sub-Commission's work might be complicated by issues of translation. He said that the word 'condemnation' in the final words of the amendment had been rendered in French as '*horreur*'. The Belgians noted that the text had been drafted in English and that what was meant by 'condemnation' was 'a protest against juridical facts'. He was interrupted by the interpreter who asked if the word 'condemnation' was used 'in its moral sense or in its juridical character', to which Rolin-Jaequemyns replied 'in the fullest meaning of the term'. Pollock joined in immediately: 'Yes, "to condemn" in the sense that he was to be found guilty of crimes which all the world has recognised as crimes and in which he would be placed in the position of receiving the execration of the world.'[78]

The Commission considered the Report of Sub-Commission II at its third meeting. Larnaude was not satisfied with French version of the final phrase adopted at the last meeting of the Sub-Commission. The words 'and to exhibit in an unmistakable way the condemnation in which they are held' had been rendered in French as '*et pour proclamer d'une manière indiscutable la condemnation solonnelle dont ils sont l'objet*'.[79] Larnaude was not only concerned about the alignment of the versions in the two languages. He also wanted the Report to encourage the Peace Conference to go beyond mere 'moral condemnation'.[80] After some discussion, it was agreed to strike the entire phrase.[81]

The draft Report of the Commission reflected shifting views with respect to the violation of neutrality of Belgium and Luxembourg. The relevant section began by insisting on the point that Larnaude had been making from the start of the discussions: 'the violation of the neutrality of Luxembourg and Belgium by one of the guarantor Powers requires a legal sanction, because with regard to both there existed a duty not only political or moral, but legal'. When the provision was discussed at the ninth meeting of the Commission, Robert Lansing said 'I object to that absolutely'. Larnaude noted that the comment was 'quite in conformity' with the American representative's opinion.[82]

A new argument that had not been made by Sub-Commission II was developed. According to the rapporteurs, the violation of international law constituted 'an aggravation of the attack upon the independence of States which is the fundamental principle of international right', a point that was not very far from arguing that a war of aggression constituted a breach of international law. Repeating its conclusion that no criminal prosecution could be made 'against the responsible authorities or individuals (and notably the ex-Kaiser)', the draft Report said 'the gravity of these gross outrages upon the law of nations and of international good faith is such that the Commission thinks they should be the subject of a formal condemnation'. The concluding paragraph used the language developed in the British proposal at the final meeting of the Sub-Commission:

> On the whole case, including both the acts which brought about the war and those which accompanied its inception, particularly the violation of the neutrality of Belgium and Luxembourg, the Commission is of opinion that it is a matter for the Peace Conference to consider whether it might not be right, in a matter so unprecedented, to adopt special measures, and even to create a special organ, in order to deal as they deserve with the authors of such criminal acts.[83]

The paragraph referring to 'condemnation' that had been so carefully negotiated disappeared, to Pollock's dismay.[84] He insisted that the new text, drafted by the rapporteurs, should be dropped and replaced with that of Sub-Commission II's Report, even if the consequence would be a reservation by the Americans.[85] Delegates complained that there was an inherent contradiction in declaring that no criminal charge should be made against the Kaiser for violating the neutrality treaties, yet calling upon the Peace Conference to create 'special machinery'. Pollock described this as a 'reservation', allowing the Peace Conference 'if they think right' to 'do something more. That was the intention and we discussed this for four hours', he said, referring to the final meeting of the Sub-Commission.[86]

The section was significantly revised in the final version of the Report. There is no evidence in the records of this being debated again or any formal decision being taken. The controversial phrase about a 'formal condemnation by the Conference' appeared in the text in italics. The Report confirmed that 'no criminal charge can be made against the responsible authorities or individuals (and notably the ex-Kaiser) on the special head of these breaches of neutrality'. The second paragraph of the numbered conclusions addressed the issue:

> 2. On the special head of the breaches of the neutrality of Luxembourg and Belgium, the gravity of these outrages upon the principles of the law of nations and upon international good faith is such that they would be made the subject of a formal condemnation by the Conference.

Two other paragraphs dealt with both categories relating to the outbreak of the war, provoking the war, and violation of neutrality:

> On the whole case, including both the acts which brought about the war and those which accompanied its inception, particularly the violation of the neutrality of Belgium and Luxembourg, it is a matter for the Peace Conference to consider whether it might not be right, in a matter so unprecedented, to adopt special measures, and even to create a special organ in order to deal as they deserve with the authors of such acts.

Moreover, '[i]t is desirable that for the future penal sanctions should be provided for such grave outrages against the elementary principles of international law'.[87]

The final *voeu* of the Commission was fulfilled more than a quarter of a century later when the London Conference included 'crimes against peace' within the subject-matter jurisdiction of the International Military Tribunal. They were defined as 'planning, preparation, initiation or waging of a war of aggression, or a war in violation of international treaties, agreements or assurances, or participation in a common plan or conspiracy for the accomplishment of any of the foregoing'.[88] The definition covered both of the categories debated in Paris in February and March 1919. Issuing its judgment on 30 September 1946, the tribunal described crimes against peace as 'the supreme international crime differing only from other war crimes in that it contains within itself the accumulated evil of the whole'.[89] But these penal sanctions only applied to the aggressors in the Second World War. The world was to wait another half century before more general provision was made for launching an aggressive war. In 1998, the crime of aggression was listed in the jurisdiction of the International Criminal Court, where it was described as being among 'the most serious crimes of concern to the international community as a whole'.[90] Yet the work was still incomplete. The crime itself was fully defined in 2010.[91] The jurisdiction of the Court over the 'supreme' crime of aggression was only activated in 2018, and even then, in an emasculated fashion.[92] A century after the call to condemn those who launch aggressive war, the task that was launched at the Paris Peace Conference remains unfinished business of international law.

10

International Law and War Crimes

Having concluded very early in its work that starting the war and breaching the neutrality of Belgium and Luxembourg should not be dealt with as criminal offences, the only remaining option for the Commission on Responsibilities, if the Kaiser were to be brought to justice, was to charge him with war crimes in the strict sense. These were violations of the laws applicable to the conduct of hostilities rather than to the origin of the war or the violation of treaties. They also governed the treatment of civilian non-combatants in an occupied territory. Some of these laws were of quite ancient origin. Evidence of what has been called a 'warrior's code' can be found in the writings of Thucydides and Euripides, for example. Technological development has dictated constant revision of the laws and customs of war. The First World War presented new challenges, including aerial and submarine warfare, and the use of poison gas.

The expression 'laws and customs of war' is taken from the eponymous Hague Conventions of 1899 and 1907, although it was used earlier in the nineteenth century.[1] Adopted on 29 July 1899, the second Hague Convention 'with respect to the laws and customs of war on land' sets out a number of specific rules concerning the conduct of hostilities, prisoners of war, and the treatment of civilian non-combatants in an occupied territory. The pre-ambular Martens clause states that:

> Until a more complete code of the laws of war is issued, the High Contracting Parties think it right to declare that in cases not included in the Regulations adopted by them, populations and belligerents remain under the protection and empire of the principles of international law, as they result from the usages

The Trial of the Kaiser. William A. Schabas. © William A. Schabas, 2018. Published 2018 by Oxford University Press.

established between civilised nations, from the laws of humanity, and the requirements of the public conscience.

The same words are reprised in the 1907 Convention, which builds upon the 1899 text, but provides slightly more refined and elaborate provisions. The formulations in the two Hague Conventions were used as a basis for identifying violations of the laws and customs of war by the 1913 Commission of Inquiry into the Balkan Wars.[2]

One of the tasks that the Preliminary Peace Conference assigned the Commission on Responsibilities was to inquire into and report upon '[t]he facts as to breaches of the laws and customs of war committed by the forces of the German Empire and their Allies, on land, on sea and in the air during the present war'.[3] The Commission mandated Sub-Commission I to inquire into 'culpable conduct which ... [t]ook place in the conduct of hostilities'. Sub-Commission III, on the other hand, was assigned to examine 'responsibility for violations of the laws and customs of war', its duty being 'to consider whether on the facts established by the Sub-Commission on criminal acts in relation to conduct which took place in the course of hostilities, prosecutions can be instituted'.[4] The findings of both of these bodies contributed to the discussion of war crimes in the final Report of the Commission.

War Crimes and Other Atrocities

Chapter II of the Report of the Commission on Responsibilities is entitled 'Violations of the Laws and Customs of War'. The first paragraph invokes the sources of evidence, including the reports on war crimes of the Bryce Commission[5] and the French Commission chaired by Georges Payelle.[6] The Commission also referred to several other sources, including numerous publications of the Belgian Government, as well as submissions by Greece, Serbia, Romania, Poland, and the Armenian delegation. It proposed a list of thirty-two distinct offences, beginning with 'murders and massacres; systematic terrorism', 'putting hostages to death', 'torture of civilians', 'deliberate starvation of civilians', 'rape', and 'abduction of girls and women for the purpose of enforced prostitution', and ending with 'employment of prisoners of war on unauthorised works', 'misuse of flags of truce', and 'poisoning of wells'. The Report specifies that the offences enumerated 'are not regarded as complete and exhaustive; to these such additions can from time to time be made as may seem necessary'.[7]

The entire Commission Report itself consists of fewer than twenty published pages. There is also an annex of more than thirty pages entitled 'Summary of Examples of Offences against the Laws and Customs of War and the Laws of Humanity'. The annex is in tabular form. For each of thirty-two categories of war crimes, the annex provides examples, grouped by country and accompanied by references.

'Murders and massacres; systematic terrorism' is the first of the categories. Several such incidents reported from Belgium are attributed to German troops, based upon information in the reports of the Belgian Commission of Inquiry and the Grey Book: a group of 450 men shot in front of the church in Tamines on 22 August 1914, 500 inhabitants massacred in Andenne and Seilles on 20 to 21 August, and 606 victims of massacre in Dinant during August 1914. In Liège, on 22 August 1914, a proclamation was issued by a German general to the municipal authorities: 'It was with my consent that the Commanding General ordered the whole place [Andenne] to be burnt down and that about 100 persons were shot.'[8] France produced a report from the national Commission of Enquiry on the use of human shields in Néry, a village barely 50 kilometres from central Paris, on 1 September 1914: 'At a sugar works the Germans took the manager and his family, as well as all the employees, and made them march parallel to them during the three hours that the engagement lasted, to protect themselves against flanking fire, which resulted in casualties among the exposed persons.'[9] Massacres of Armenians 'by the Turks systematically organised with German complicity' appear under the same heading. The Report states that more than 200,000 victims were 'assassinated, burned alive or drowned'. Sources of this information include the Armenian memorandum addressed to the conference, the report by Viscount Bryce, '[v]arious documents in the possession of the British Government', and 'Notes of a German traveller in Turkey during 1915 (Published by the Swiss Committee for the relief of the Armenians)'.[10] The Polish Delegation's memorandum is cited as evidence of shooting of several hundred inhabitants of Kalisz by 'German military authorities' in 1914 and '[t]ens of thousands of civilians hanged' in 1914 and 1915, 'especially during retreat of Austrian armies'.[11]

Under the heading 'Rape', the Report refers to acts of German troops in August 1914 in three Belgian municipalities, Louvain, Korbeek-Lo, and

Nimy. For Greece, it lists multiple cases of rape of women and girls in eastern Macedonia, carried out from 1916 to 1918 and attributed to 'Bulgarian authorities'. The list also mentions a large number of Greek victims of rape in Ayvalık (Aivali) and Goumisi, Asia Minor, in 1915, attributable to Turkish officials. The Report states that in many Serbian villages few women were spared from rape at the hands of officers and policemen, but also by ordinary soldiers. Women were abused in the presence of their daughters and vice versa. Often, victims were beaten before the rape and subsequently mutilated. Bulgarian soldiers with venereal diseases were ordered to rape girls. A woman was 'given up to officer's dog' by Bulgarian soldiers. There is a general allegation of rape perpetrated by Austrian soldiers against Serb women.[12]

The Report documents a number of sinkings of hospital ships by submarines, including the famous case of the *HMS Llandovery Castle*. 'Was carrying all the proper marks and lights but was torpedoed without warning [by a German submarine]. 234 lives lost out of 258 persons carried', according to the Report.[13] Sailing from Halifax to Liverpool, it was sunk by U–86 off the southern coast of Ireland in June 1918. Survivors were murdered so that there would be no witnesses. Two senior officers on the U-boat were tried and convicted at Leipzig in 1921 after unsuccessfully invoking a defence of superior orders.[14]

Other categories of war crime include such issues as property dedicated to cultural, educational, and religious purposes. From France, there were reports of destruction of burial places in Carlepont, Roiglise, and Manancourt. Serbia alleged destruction of schools, monasteries, and churches. In Macedonia, there was evidence of the demolition of historic monuments, ancient inscriptions, obliteration of portraits of sovereigns and saints, and damage to public gardens, fountains, and tombstones.[15] The Report refers to shots fired by German troops on men wearing Red Cross badges at Beauvechain, Belgium, on 19 August 1914. It also cites the French Commission about stretcher-bearers being allowed onto a battlefield at La Neuville in order to attend to the dead and wounded, only to be fired upon by German troops.[16] There are also several references to the use of explosive and expanding bullets. The Belgian Commission of Inquiry is authority for prohibited weapons being used by German troops in August and September 1914, in Werchter, Lubbeck, Ninove, and Alost. Such bullets were found in the possession of German troops of the 7th Infantry Regiment in Bixshoote, Belgium. The Report describes an order by German General Headquarters to German soldiers that they were to get rid of any such bullets if captured.[17]

Summarising the evidence, the Commission Report says that despite 'the explicit regulations, of established customs, and the clear dictates of humanity, Germany and her allies have piled outrage upon outrage'. The cases listed in Annex I were mentioned only by way of example.

> Violations of the rights of combatants, of the rights of civilians, and of the rights of both, are multiplied in this list of the most cruel practices which primitive barbarism, aided by all the resources of modern sciences, could devise for the execution of a system of terrorism carefully planned and carried out to the end.[18]

Codifying International War Crimes

Although Sub-Commission I gave some consideration to the definition of war crimes, this was officially the task of Sub-Commission III. Some of its members were hesitant about their authority to actually establish the law and sought authority for their work in national law. Rolin-Jaequemyns of Belgium proposed that in the absence of any codified international law setting out both crimes and their punishments, the law of Germany should be the authority.[19] Robert Lansing, who chaired Sub-Commission III, thought the way to proceed was to 'collect the rules of warfare as issued at various times, and particularly prior to this great war, that were in force in Great Britain, in Germany, in Austria, in France, and in the United States'.[20] Nevertheless, Lansing recognised that the task of the Commission was to determine the rules of international law and not merely to assess the domestic law in force in the belligerent countries. 'Of course, there is no absolute international law in regard to laws and customs of war', said Lansing. 'That is my view, that there is no *absolute* law that has been enacted. We are more or less bound by the general principles of international law for the reason that at the very instant war was declared there were certain belligerents that were not signatories to the Hague Convention. That swept the Hague Conventions aside as absolute law and left them merely as guides to the conscience of the world as to what international law was.'[21]

The list in the Report of thirty-two distinct war crimes is one of the more enduring contributions of the Commission on Responsibilities to the development of the laws and customs of war. Although there had been earlier attempts at codification of laws relating to armed conflict, including the two Hague conventions, this was the very first compilation of violations deemed to be punishable under international law. Decades later, when experts met in London to map out the prosecution of Nazi war crimes, the enumeration prepared by the Commission provided a starting point.[22] It was invoked as authority in post-Second World War trials.[23] It was also incorporated into national war crimes legislation.[24] Elements derived from the Commission's list have appeared more recently in provisions of the Statute of the International Criminal Tribunal for the former Yugoslavia and the International Criminal Court.

The list of war crimes can be traced to a number of submissions made to the Commission. The British presented the Commission with categories of violations of the laws and customs of war that were based upon the work of the Committee of Enquiry, published in January 1919.[25] Two lists are found in a memorandum dated 13 February 1919. The first of the two was intended for prosecutions of German military personnel in general, whereas the second was destined specifically for the trial of the Kaiser. Both contain a charge of '[s]ystematic terrorism in Belgium and France', whereas the list for the Kaiser also includes a charge of '[i]nvasion of Belgium and Luxembourg in breach of treaties', as well as '[w]rongful execution of Edith Cavell and Captain Fryatt'.[26] A third list is in a memorandum dated 21 February 1919 that was submitted to Sub-Commission III.[27] The language in the different lists is inconsistent. For example, the second list speaks of '[d]eliberate bombardment of hospitals from the air', while the third one refers to 'indiscriminate bombardment from the air' and 'wilful and reckless bombardment of hospitals'.

The French delegation also prepared detailed compilations of war crimes. A memorandum dated 17 February 1919 that was considered by Sub-Commission I provides a list of war crimes together with references to their source in international treaties and examples drawn from the Payelle reports. It includes ill-treatment of the wounded, prisoners, and medical personnel; use of asphyxiating gas, exploding bullets, and mines; destruction of property; attacks on undefended places and on cultural objects; pillage and confiscation; use of human shields; forced labour and deportations; and submarine warfare. Under the heading 'Honour', the French memorandum deals with rapes and other attacks on civilians.[28] The French submitted another list of war crimes grouped in two general categories, crimes committed '*dans le combat*', that is, in the course of hostilities, and those directed '*contre la population pacifique*', that is, against civilian non-combatants. Some forty-eight distinct types of war crime were identified.[29] France also submitted a document on submarine warfare.[30]

Belgium's report begins by insisting that the first breach of international law perpetrated by Germany was the invasion itself, which violated the neutrality treaty. '*La conduit de la guerre fut digne de ses origines*', said Belgium, proceeding to list a large number of violations of the laws and customs of war. These were divided into acts '*aux cours des operations de guerre*' and those during the occupation of the country. The first category, on the conduct of hostilities, includes abuse of the flag and emblems of the Red Cross, treachery, employment of prohibited weapons such as dum-dum bullets and flame throwers, abusive treatment and detention of medical personnel, use of human shields, and torpedoing without warning of fishing boats and commercial vessels. The second category focuses on the forced labour and deportations imposed upon Belgian civilians. A detailed annex enumerates the allegations of war crimes by region and municipality.[31]

Submissions by other governments also indicate the scope of war crimes under international law. For example, Italy used the following headings for Austrian war crimes: treatment of wounded and sick, bad treatment of prisoners, violation of the obligation to give quarter, use of forbidden arms and ammunition such as expanding or explosive bullets and asphyxiating gas, treacherous ruses—making use of the enemy flag, bombardment of undefended places, air attacks, pillage and confiscation, destruction of private property and educational and charitable institutions, forced labour, and the deportation of civilians.[32] Serbia's submission includes the following headings: violations of the 1907 Hague Convention in the treatment of belligerents; massacre of the civilian population; torture; rape; internment; requisitions; pillage; forced labour; and denationalisation.[33] The Greek report lists murder, pillage, rape, theft, kidnapping, famine, and deportation, accompanied by a detailed annex of specific violations.[34] Mineichirō Adachi of Japan produced a list of Japanese vessels sunk by enemy submarines without warning.[35] The Romanian representative, M. S. Rosental, reported on 'devastation of places devoted to teaching purposes, robberies of historical documents, robberies committed in private homes, the distribution of millions of spurious bank notes'. In Romania, when cattle were seized the peasants were given worthless pieces of paper in payment.[36] The Polish report concentrates on violations in the course of enemy occupation. It refers to denationalisation and massacre of civilians.[37]

Several of the submissions make reference to treaty law as authority for the identification of specific war crimes. In addition to the 1907 Hague Convention, the Italian report cites the 1906 Geneva Convention[38] and the

1868 St Petersburg Declaration[39] as legal sources. The French report refers to the 1899 Hague Declaration on expanding bullets.[40] A British memorandum[41] invokes the ninth Hague Convention of 1907 dealing with naval bombardment[42] and the tenth Hague Convention of 1907 forbidding the destruction of hospital ships.[43]

Lansing made his own contribution in the form of a 'Memorandum on the Principles which should determine Inhuman and Improper Acts of War'. It is a quite brutal defence of military necessity as a justification for acts of war. Lansing began with the proposition that '[s]laying and maiming men in accordance with generally accepted rules of war are from their nature cruel and contrary to the modern conception of humanity'. He insisted that '[t]he principle underlying the accepted rules of war is the necessity of exercising physical force to protect national safety, or to maintain national rights'. Therefore, concluded Lansing, in determining the criminality of an act, the relevant factors are 'the wantonness or malice of the perpetrator, the needlessness of the act from a military point of view, the perpetration of a justifiable act in a needlessly harsh and cruel manner, and the improper motive which inspired it'.[44]

The American Secretary of State had never been inclined to a particularly humanitarian standard of military conduct. In 1915, after the sinking of the *RMS Lusitania*, Colonel House described Lansing as manifesting 'one curious state of mind. He believes that almost any form of atrocity is permissible provided a nation's safety is involved.'[45] While America was still neutral, Lansing corresponded regularly with President Wilson about whether to protest violations of the laws and customs of war committed during the European conflict.[46] In its Report, Sub-Commission III politely acknowledged Lansing's submission as 'a useful and interesting memorandum'.[47] The minutes of the Sub-Commission do not record any discussion of the document. Lansing's paper on principles was annexed to the American dissenting memorandum.[48]

The list in the Report of Sub-Commission I comprises thirty-one distinct crimes, but they are not organised by subject.[49] Sub-Commission I did not identify the sources for the list in its Report, nor do the minutes record any debate either in the Sub-Commission or in the plenary Commission.[50] Sub-Commission III's list is divided into three categories, reflecting the approach taken in the French submission: violations affecting civilians, violations affecting combatants, and violations affecting both civilians and combatants.[51] Most of the specific war crimes listed in the Report of Sub-Commission III include a reference to a specific provision in the 1907 Hague Convention. There is much overlap in the Reports of the two Sub-Commissions, although the terminology is not entirely consistent. For example, Sub-Commission I spoke of 'rape' and 'abduction of girls and women for the purposes of enforced prostitution', whereas Sub-Commission III referred to 'honour of women'.

Sub-Commission III's Report also considers the 'Principles underlying the Laws and Customs of War' in some detail. It declares that it was 'unnecessary to examine or rely in detail upon Conventions drawn up at The Hague or elsewhere'. These conventions were 'in the main declaratory of principles' that were expressed 'to serve as general rules of conduct for the belligerents in their mutual relations, and in their relations with the inhabitants of invaded territories'. The Report cites the Martens clause. It also invokes a statement by the German delegate to the 1907 Hague Conference:

> Military acts are not solely governed by stipulations of international law. There are other factors. Conscience, good sense, and the sense of duty imposed by the principles of humanity will be the surest guides for the conduct of sailors and will constitute the most effective guarantee against abuses. The officers of the German Navy, I loudly proclaim it, will always fulfil in the strictest fashion, the duties which emanate from the unwritten law of humanity and civilisation.[52]

The Drafting Committee appears to have adopted the list in the Report of Sub-Commission I, making only a few small changes. It added one category of offence from the list in the Report of Sub-Committee III: 'Employment of prisoners of war on unauthorised works.'[53] Several crimes in Sub-Committee III's list are not included in the final Report, such as use of civilians as shields, bombardment from the air, propagation of disease, and employing delayed action bombs. In the plenary Commission, Ferdinand Larnaude complained that the Drafting Committee text did not adequately address 'terrorism'. He pointed out that the list of crimes prepared by Sub-Commission III began with the crime of '[s]ystematic terrorism'.[54] It was clear that the Drafting Committee had considered the Sub-Commission III list, which mentions '[m]urders and massacres' after '[s]ystematic terrorism', whereas Sub-Commission I's list begins with '[m]assacre of civilians' and makes no mention of terrorism. The Drafting Committee version starts with '[m]urders and massacres', but drops the reference to '[s]ystematic terrorism'. The revised text, incorporated in the final Report of the Commission, begins with '[m]urders and massacres; systematic terrorism'.

In the final Report, the Commission omitted any discussion of the principles underlying the identification of the laws and customs of war. It did not refer to provisions of the Hague Conventions, or other sources such as the St Petersburg Declaration on prohibited weapons, as a basis for listing specific acts as violations of the laws and customs of war. A lone reference to the 'laws of war and of humanity as indicated by the Hague Conventions of 1899 and 1907' in the draft Report[55] was deleted.

Laws of Humanity

There is no reference to 'laws of humanity' in the title of Chapter II of the Report of the Commission. However, the first paragraph of the Chapter concludes that there is 'abundant evidence of outrages of every description committed on land, at sea, and in the air, against the laws and customs of war and of the laws of humanity'.[56] The Chapter then presents the list of war crimes, discussed above. Chapter IV of the Report also refers to '[v]iolations of the laws and customs of war and the laws of humanity'.[57] The Preliminary Peace Conference had assigned the Commission to report on '[t]he facts as to breaches of the laws and customs of war'. The phrase 'laws of humanity' was added by the Commission, although there is no explanation of the term in the Report. Its inclusion was a matter of great controversy, provoking one of the significant objections in the American dissent.

The expression 'laws of humanity' originates in the Martens clause, one of the preambular paragraphs of the Hague Conventions dealing with the laws and customs of war. A British memorandum provides the first references to 'violations of the laws and customs of war and the laws of humanity' in the work of the Commission on Responsibilities. On one occasion, it speaks of 'the principles of International Law and the laws of humanity'. The memorandum also refers to 'offences not only against the laws of war, but also against the laws of humanity', implying a distinction between the two concepts.[58] The term 'laws of humanity' is also found in the Interim Report of the British Committee of Enquiry.[59]

War crimes are described in Sub-Commission I's Report under the heading 'Offences against the Laws and Customs of War and the Principles of Humanity'[60] ('*Infractions aux lois et coutumes de la guerre et aux principes de l'humanité*').[61] The first paragraph of Part II of the Report refers to the 'fundamental principles of humanity'[62] (*des principes d'humanité fondamentaux*).[63] The concluding paragraph says that '[t]he war was carried out by the Central Empires together with their Allies, Turkey and Bulgaria, by barbarous or illegitimate methods in violation of the established laws and customs of war and the elementary principles of humanity'[64] (*des principes élémentaires d'humanité*).[65] Sub-Commission III's Report does not refer explicitly to the laws of humanity in tandem with the laws and customs of war. However, it cites the Martens clause of the Hague Conventions, with its reference to 'laws of humanity'. In addition, it speaks of outrages that are 'contrary to the principles of the laws and customs of war, whether declared in any Conventions or not, but certainly being dictated by the public conscience of civilised humanity'.[66] Ernest Pollock first raised the issue in Sub-Commission III: 'If we are going to lay down what the laws are we mustn't forget that the Hague Convention itself uses in laying down the law the words "the principles of humanity".'[67]

The Drafting Committee of the plenary Commission employed the formulation 'laws of war and humanity'[68] (*violations des lois de la guerre et de l'humanité*)[69] in the first paragraph of Chapter II and spoke of 'laws and customs of war and the principles of humanity'[70] (*lois et coutumes de la guerre et des principes de l'humanité*)[71] at the beginning of Chapter IV. When Chapter II was discussed in the plenary Commission, Robert Lansing asked that the reference to 'humanity' be deleted from the phrase 'against the laws of war and of humanity as indicated by the Hague Conventions of 1899 and 1907'.[72] Larnaude objected: 'We have always put "laws and customs of war and humanity" everywhere'.[73] The French transcript has him saying '*Il n'est pas possible de supprimer ce mot. Nous l'avons toujours maintenu*.'[74] According to the published English minutes, 'Mr Larnaude said it was not possible to suppress the reference to the laws of humanity, which occurred many times in the Report.'[75] Lansing answered: 'I know you have and I'm going to reserve on this.'[76]

Pollock explained his own understanding of the expression. 'I think the "laws of war" include those of humanity', he said. '[I]t is important to call attention to the wide range of the meaning of these words "laws of war". I want to keep the words "laws of humanity" and if Mr Lansing is unable to accept them and wishes to make a reservation on that point, then perhaps he could cede to the rest of us the right to put them in subject to his reservation.' Larnaude concurred with Pollock: 'As I understand the American concerns, adding the word 'humanity' may extend to acts that are not violations of the laws and customs of war. The French delegation only wants to strengthen the mention of the laws and customs of war, not to make a distinct, special charge that will not be a violation of the laws and customs of war.' Pollock and Larnaude insisted that public opinion would better understand the reference to 'humanity' than the more technical term 'laws and customs of war'. Pollock stated:

> People who are not lawyers want to see that we have not overlooked anything, that we have not taken too narrow a view of the laws. When we know that the laws of war include the laws of humanity, that is a very good reason for putting it in, in order to show these persons who are not lawyers precisely what we mean.[77]

But Lansing continued to insist that the mandate of the Commission was confined to 'laws and customs of war'. If the phrase 'laws of humanity' added anything, then the Commission was exceeding its jurisdiction. 'All war is inhuman and we cannot make it humane by any method and therefore every act of war is a violation of humanity', said Lansing. Lansing referred to the memorandum that he had submitted to Sub-Commission III on elements of war crimes.[78] 'I am not willing to subscribe to anything which charges that a violation of that conception of humanity which is general to all nations is a matter of guilt. I believe that the laws and customs of war lay down certain acts which are wanton, needless, without military value, as being inhuman. In other words, where human suffering is needlessly caused, that is inhuman in the views of the laws and customs of war. But any destruction of human life, any wanton outrage, any suffering that is caused results from a violation of humanity. I cannot, therefore, subscribe to an extension of guilt to the general phrase "and humanity" because that would include legitimate acts of war.'[79]

'Now we are all agreed, because I want to follow Mr Lansing's reasoning as far as I can', said Pollock. 'We are all agreed that the laws and customs of war include the laws of humanity. Outrages which are committed ...'

'Might I just interrupt you? What do you mean by "laws of humanity"?' said Lansing.

'The laws which are to be conformed to by the persons who are endeavouring in the course of war, to avoid as far as possible human sufferings. That is what I mean. Now we all agree that the laws of humanity in the sense in which I phrase it are included in the laws and customs of war. This paragraph is distinctive. It says this: that there are a large number of facts which have been brought before us, and it says this: that these various memoranda supply abundant evidence of outrages … I think it would be quite wrong in a report which will fall into the hands of persons not expert in law to leave out the words "and humanity" because it is proposed on that side of the laws and customs of war that we find the greatest evidence of outrages.'[80]

The Belgian Rolin-Jaequemyns had initially seemed somewhat ambivalent in this debate between Lansing, Pollock, and Larnaude, but he now came down clearly in favour of the British and French position. 'We should weaken the reasoning if we posed on the one side the laws and customs of war and on the other side the laws and customs of humanity. The essential principle recognised by the Hague Convention is that what is contrary to the laws and customs of war is contrary to the laws of humanity inasmuch as it inflicts unnecessary suffering.'[81]

Lansing brought the meeting to a conclusion. The argument that the Report has to go before the people of the world did not appeal to him, he said. 'I do not think we should allow the view as to what public opinion will be to enter into the drafting of our report. I might add that even if public opinion is to be considered, the list of crimes on the following page makes absolutely non-essential the word "humanity".'[82]

The issue returned to the agenda the following day because of further references to the term in the draft Report. The American Secretary of State again insisted that the reference to 'humanity' be removed. The British Solicitor General responded: 'Well, that is the whole question, sir. I am very sorry, but we have held on to "the principles of humanity" in the previous page. I must ask that we adhere to them here. And, sir, in accordance with the principles of humanity, I bet to ask you, sir, that we do not debate it again.'

'That's quite right, except that "the principles of humanity" do not appear in the other', said Lansing.

'We could be content with the words—with the word "laws" instead of "principles".'

'I am not content with the word "humanity" …'

'We have spoken of the laws of humanity, we don't need to use the word "principles", "laws" will do, won't it?'

'*Je préfère en effet le mot "lois"*', said Larnaude.

Lansing, who was in the chair, declared that the matter should not be discussed further.[83]

The Americans addressed the 'laws of humanity' issue in their memorandum of reservations. Explaining that the mandate of the Commission was
to examine violations of the 'laws and customs of war', Lansing and Scott
challenged the addition by the majority of the term 'principles of humanity'.
'The laws and customs of war are a standard certain, to be found in books of
authority and in the practice of nations. The laws and principles of humanity
vary with the individual, which, if for no other reason, should exclude them
from consideration in a court of justice, especially one charged with the administration of criminal law.'[84] The American delegates said that 'an act could
not be a crime in the legal sense of the word, unless it were made so by law,
and that the commission of an act declared to be a crime by law could not be
punished unless the law prescribed the penalty to be inflicted'. The memorandum cited a United States Supreme Court decision of 1812 holding that
'the legislative authority of the Union must first make an act a crime, affix
a punishment to it, and declare the court that shall have jurisdiction of the
offence'. They said that '[w]hat is true of the American States must be true of
this looser union which we call the Society of Nations'.[85]

Today, this word evokes the notion of 'crimes against humanity', which is a
distinct category of international crime first applied in the trial of the major
war criminals at Nuremberg in 1945 and 1946. Crimes against humanity
consist of various forms of attacks and persecutions directed at 'any civilian
population'. The concept was devised in order to address atrocities that did
not fit within the classic notion of war crimes, essentially those committed
against a country's own population. When the United Nations War Crimes
Commission began studying the scope of post-Second World War prosecutions, in 1944, the British Government argued that attempting to address Nazi
treatment of minorities within Germany 'raises serious difficulties'.[86] The
representatives of Britain, France, the United States, and the Soviet Union,
meeting in London in 1945 to draft the Charter of the International Military
Tribunal, were concerned that a broad definition of crimes against humanity
might apply to their own conduct. The American negotiator, Robert Jackson,
told the meeting that a restrictive approach to the concept was required because '[w]e have some regrettable circumstances at times in our own country
in which minorities are unfairly treated'.[87] They agreed upon a definition that
encompassed those Nazi atrocities that could be linked to the war. The term
itself, 'crimes against humanity', was the inspired last-minute contribution
of Hersch Lauterpacht.[88] It was another fifty years before crimes against humanity applied unequivocally to acts perpetrated in peacetime.[89]

The authors of the history of the United Nations War Crimes Commission, published in 1948, viewed the references to 'laws of humanity' and 'principles of humanity' in the Report of the Commission on Responsibilities as a direct ancestor of the notion of 'crimes against humanity' codified at Nuremberg and interpreted by the International Military Tribunal. 'Thus, in 1919 we find, for the first time, the specific juxtaposition of these two types of offences', they said. The 1948 study goes on to say that it is 'not known whether the 1919 Commission, in using the term "crimes against the laws of humanity", had in mind offenses which were not covered by the other expression "violation of the laws and customs of war"'.[90] This is a misreading of the debates in 1919. To be fair to those writing in 1948, the transcripts of the sessions of the Commission and the Sub-Commissions may not then have been available. The transcripts make it quite clear that Larnaude and Pollock meant no more than a clarification for a non-specialist public. There was no serious suggestion in their remarks that acts other than classic war crimes, whose victims were enemy combatants or civilians in an occupied territory, had been contemplated.

But what did the members of the Commission mean by 'laws of humanity' in 1919? They certainly attached considerable significance to the term. Its inclusion prompted one of the major objections from the United States. It would have been a simple thing to remove the words in order to buy peace with the Americans if the concept of 'laws of humanity' was only rhetorical and not substantive. Nevertheless, the comments by both Larnaude and Pollock in the Commission clearly indicate that they did not intend any notion going beyond war crimes as such. Had this been their intention, there would have been some manifestation in the list of punishable crimes, and in the annex, where the acts charged against the Germans are listed.

In 1918 and 1919, the term 'crime against humanity' was used not infrequently. But it had no rigorous definition, nor was it generally employed in a context that resembled the meaning it would take on at Nuremberg. For example, in the Imperial War Cabinet, Prime Minister Robert Borden of Canada spoke of Kaiser Wilhelm's 'crime against humanity in willing and preparing a war'.[91] The Cabinet itself requested the Law Officers of the Crown to examine the question of charging the Kaiser 'for the crime against humanity of having caused the war'.[92] The Special Sub-Committee referred to instigating aggressive and unjust war as 'a great crime against humanity'.[93] In campaign speeches, Prime Minister Lloyd George spoke of 'the great crime against humanity involved in deliberately planning and plotting a great war'.[94] When Britain, France, and Italy agreed to prosecute the Kaiser in early December 1918, they adopted a text affirming that 'the certainty of inevitable personal punishment for crimes against humanity and international right will be a very important security against future attempts to make war wrongfully or to violate international law'.[95] But at Nuremberg, provoking a war of aggression was labelled 'crimes against peace', not 'crimes against humanity'.

However, that is not to say that the possibility of an extension of international law to atrocities perpetrated by a country against its own population was not being considered at the time of the First World War. In May 1915, Britain, France, and Russia sent a declaration to the Government of the Ottoman Empire referring to recent reports of massacres of the Armenian population, an important minority living for centuries within its own borders. The three Powers denounced 'these new crimes of Turkey against humanity and civilisation'. An early draft of their declaration spoke of crimes against 'Christianity and civilisation'.[96] The British Ambassador to Paris thought it wise to remove the word 'Christianity'.[97] After this was agreed, the French proposed it be replaced with the word 'humanity'.[98] But the change came too late for the British, who had already issued the statement, which had been published in *The Times*.[99] The French version spoke of '*nouveaux crimes contre l'humanité et civilisation*'. It was communicated to the Ottoman Government by the American Ambassador in Constantinople, acting at the request of the French Government.[100]

At the second meeting of the Commission on Responsibilities, when the concept of laws and customs of war was first discussed, the Greek representative, Nicolaos Politis, argued for a broad approach to the mandate in order to deal with 'reprehensible acts' and not only 'those which the penal laws characterise as criminal and punish as such. I think we all agree that the expression should be understood in a general sense'. By way of illustration, he referred to the massacres of the Armenians perpetrated by the Ottoman Turkish regime. Politis explained that the acts of the Turks 'technically do not fall within any provision of the Penal Code, and it is evident within the conscience of every civilised man that there is something in this a great deal more serious than the mere acts themselves that made up their programme'. Politis described such acts as being in violation of 'what one might call human or moral law'.[101] Unfortunately, Politis did not attend the eighth and ninth meetings of the Commission when the 'laws of humanity' issue was discussed.

When the penalty provisions of the treaty between the Allies and Turkey were being discussed, in 1920, the initial draft called for them to be adapted from the treaties that had already been finalised with Austria, Hungary, and Bulgaria.[102] But when this was discussed by the Allied Council, George Curzon, who was then the British Foreign Minister, said those clauses 'were not sufficiently wide, and would not, in the case of Turkey, cover the massacre of the Armenians'.[103] According to correspondence from Jules Cambon, a 'Commission on Responsibility' was convened. The following clause was drafted: 'The Turkish Government undertakes to hand over to the Allied Powers the persons considered to be responsible for the massacres committed during the continuance of the state of war on territory which formed part of the Turkish Empire on August 1, 1914.'[104] It became Article 230 of the Treaty of Sèvres, an instrument that was signed but never ratified by the Turkish Government, and pursuant to which no prosecutions ever took place.

Lansing's conservative views on the 'laws of humanity' issue as well as on the criminality of aggressive war haunted the United States during the negotiations of post-Second World War prosecutions. When André Gros warned that the German defendants would invoke Lansing's views,[105] the American negotiator, Robert Jackson, replied: 'I must say that sentiment in the United States and the better world opinion have greatly changed since Mr. James Brown Scott and Secretary Lansing announced their views as to criminal responsibility for the first World War. I have no expectation that any rule we could formulate would avoid the criticism of some scholars of international law, for a good many of them since 1918—in language that was used about others—have learned nothing and have forgotten nothing. But I don't think we can take the 1918 view on matters of war and peace.'[106]

More than any other country, the United States position on the definition of international crimes has been a patchwork of deep-seated hesitation and progressive aspirations. Robert Jackson was enthusiastic about prosecuting German atrocities perpetrated against other Germans, yet anxious that a broad approach might rebound against his own government, with its sorry record on racial discrimination. Many decades later, when the International Criminal Court was being created, the United States favoured a great enlargement of the historic definitions both of war crimes and crimes against humanity.[107] Nevertheless, although prepared to see others prosecuted for such crimes, the United States has remained nervous about the potential international mechanisms of accountability that may apply to its own conduct.

Lansing's anxieties about the scope of international crimes, indeed his doubts of their very existence in the case of offences relating to acts that provoked the war, were not confined to the United States. To varying degrees, the representatives of Belgium, Italy, and Japan also expressed concerns. The definitions of the crimes were only one aspect of the debate, admittedly one of more than historic interest because of the importance of establishing the existence of international crimes for future prosecutions. Evidence that international crimes were recognised in 1919 provides a benchmark to address questions about retroactive prosecution. Defining crimes was only one part of the Commission's tasks. The other was institutional. The Commission also considered whether to establish an international criminal court where such international crimes might be charged.

II

An International
Criminal Court

Establishment of an international criminal tribunal had been discussed since the end of the war, and even before.[1] In November 1918, following the armistice, when Clemenceau and Curzon first mooted the prosecution of Wilhelm II, the French Prime Minister spoke of the need for trial before an international court.[2] He was probably reflecting the views of the French experts, Larnaude and de Lapradelle, whose legal opinion argued that because the facts charged against the Kaiser were international crimes, trial before an international tribunal was required.[3] They had insisted that such a prosecution required 'a greater stage', something that only an international tribunal could provide.[4] When Sub-Commission III of the Commission on Responsibilities directed its attention to the subject of the 'tribunal appropriate' for trial of Wilhelm II, Ernest Pollock, the British representative, said that 'nothing but an international tribunal of commanding power, force, and weight would have the moral position before the world to execute the justice which the entire world demands'.[5]

'Constitution and Procedure of an Appropriate Tribunal' is the title of Chapter IV of the Report of the Commission on Responsibilities. This formulation was drawn from the initial resolution of the plenary Peace Conference setting up the Commission on Responsibilities. It referred to '[t]he constitution and procedure of a tribunal appropriate to the trial of these offenses'.[6] Yet none of the three Sub-Commissions was given formal responsibility to address the 'appropriate tribunal' issue. The logic for this was probably reflected in an American memorandum, where the identification of criminal acts was viewed as a 'preliminary' issue. Only if the Commission concluded that crimes had been committed would the issue of the appropriate tribunal require consideration.[7]

The Americans were strenuously opposed to the proposed international criminal court. Although it was not circulated officially, a legal opinion prepared within the United States delegation to the Conference expressed doubts about establishing an international tribunal.[8] Robert Lansing, the American Secretary of State, insisted that the only basis of jurisdiction over specific violations of the laws and customs of war was the nationality of the victim or the place where the crime was committed. Where an offence affected nationals of more than one State, Lansing said the tribunals of those countries that were concerned could unite in the form of a joint commission or joint tribunal. However, he could not see how the United States could participate in a trial concerning crimes of which its own nationals were not victims. Because the United States had only entered the war in 1917, this would affect many possible crimes that might be charged against the Kaiser. 'As the basis of jurisdiction is the nationality of the person affected by the act, the United States would be under great embarrassment to sit upon a tribunal which considers offences committed before it entered the war', said Lansing.[9]

Differences about the wisdom of creating an international tribunal surfaced during the second meeting of the Commission.[10] Ernest Pollock had proposed that renewal of the armistice, which was scheduled for 17 February 1919, be made conditional on an obligation for the Germans to cooperate with prosecutions both in delivering documents and surrendering suspects. Pollock's proposal seemed to assume the establishment of an international tribunal.[11] Lansing was opposed and no action was taken. Subsequently, on a suggestion from the French delegate, Ferdinand Larnaude, Sub-Commissions II and III held their first meeting jointly. Larnaude thought it important that they coordinate their work so as to avoid the two Sub-Commissions making different recommendations about creation of an international tribunal.[12] But the joint meeting was unproductive. When Sub-Commission II met alone, it promptly agreed not to pursue trial of the Kaiser for starting the war and violating the neutrality of Belgium and Luxembourg,[13] thereby obviating the need for any consideration of the tribunal issue. That left Sub-Commission III as the forum for debates about the nature of the 'tribunal appropriate'.

Efforts at Compromise

Faced with American opposition to an international tribunal, the British and French devised a compromise in the form of a multi-national tribunal, composed of national courts from different countries.[14] Reflecting this search for agreement, the initial draft Report of Sub-Commission III spoke of a 'Grand Tribunal' before which the most important cases might be brought. Detailed provisions on the composition and operation of the tribunal, based upon a British memorandum,[15] were included in the draft Report.[16] But Lansing was inflexible. The British and French withdrew their offer of some middle ground, returning to a call for a fully international court. The only element of the attempted compromise with Lansing that remained was the name. Lansing had suggested that the term 'joint high tribunal' replace 'grand tribunal'. 'We don't want to call it "international", which conveys the idea of a full international tribunal', he noted. Larnaude thought 'high tribunal' would do; the French draft used the term '*haut tribunal*'.[17]

In a search for some formula acceptable to the Americans, the delegates from Greece and Italy thought that a State might participate in the international tribunal, but with the discretion to withdraw from a particular case. They hoped that this would address Lansing's concerns about an American judge sitting in cases involving facts that arose when the country was still neutral. Inspired by these initiatives, Larnaude suggested that a State might decide not to participate in the international tribunal for acts committed prior to its entry into the war, an idea that seemed to appeal to Lansing.[18] Accordingly, a clause to this effect was added to a revised draft of the Report of the Sub-Commission.

When the Report of Sub-Commission III was presented to the plenary Commission, the Americans introduced a new challenge to the proposed international tribunal. Lansing wanted to replace the entire section of the Report concerning the 'high tribunal' with a recommendation that the Peace Conference set up an 'International Commission of Inquiry'. This was an idea that had also been advanced informally by the Germans as early as December 1918.[19] According to Lansing's draft amendment:

> … instead of attempting to hale the ex-Kaiser before a Court of Justice for which there is no precedent in the accepted Law of Nations, an International Commission of Inquiry be instituted to investigate and to report upon the

extent of the responsibility of the ex-Kaiser from the political, legal, and moral point of view for the acts of the German Authorities civil and military in violation of the laws and customs of war committed during the course of the war from the first day of August 1914 to the 11th day of November 1918.

The Commission of Inquiry would be composed of representatives of the United States, the British Empire, France, Italy, and Japan, and of one representative of each of the other countries at war with Germany.[20]

There was quite predictable fury from several members of the Commission, including William Massey, who headed the British delegation in Pollock's absence. Lansing's principal rationale for the Commission of Inquiry was the immunity of the Kaiser from criminal prosecution. For this reason, the immunity issue was the focus of the reactions to his proposal. Larnaude, in particular, delivered a lengthy and emotional tirade against the American position.[21] The following day, Lansing revised his proposal so as to allow two representatives of the 'Great Powers' and one each from Belgium, Greece, Portugal, Romania, and Serbia to participate in the Commission of Inquiry.[22] Lansing also changed his tune about the relationship between the Commission of Inquiry and the international tribunal. Under his amended proposal, he explained, 'a commission of this sort, with power to examine the archives of the Governments, would be an assistance to the tribunal we are going to create. This is not a substitution for the tribunal, but it is to assist the tribunal insofar as it is able to collect evidence.'[23] It was only a tactical retreat for Lansing. He had shifted his energies from challenging the creation of the tribunal to the separate but related issue of the immunity from prosecution of Kaiser Wilhelm. Larnaude said that there would be no objection to the Commission of Inquiry provided it did not interfere with the high tribunal.[24]

There was little further discussion by the Commission on Responsibilities about the composition and activity of the tribunal. The Drafting Committee text[25] was adopted with virtually no discussion.[26] Aside from a few stylistic modifications, it was unchanged in the final Report of the Commission. The Commission's Report said that creation of a 'high tribunal' was 'essential'. It proposed that it be composed of three persons from each of the United States, the British Empire, France, Italy, and Japan, and one from each of Belgium, Greece, Poland, Portugal, Romania, Serbia, and Czechoslovakia. They were to be selected by each country from among members of their national courts or tribunals, civil or military. However, the important power of selecting cases for trial was reserved to a Prosecuting Commission composed of five members, one appointed from each of the major powers. The high tribunal would take precedence over national courts, the latter being blocked from proceeding with a case that was being tried at the international level. The law to be applied by the tribunal was 'the principles of the law of nations as they result from the usages established among civilised peoples, from the laws of humanity and from the dictates of public conscience'. These words were taken from the Martens clause in the preamble of the 1899 and 1907 Hague Conventions on the laws and customs of war. The tribunal would be empowered to sentence persons found guilty to punishments for such offences that were already prescribed at a court represented on the tribunal or the country of the convicted person. The tribunal was to determine its own procedure.[27]

'To the unprecedented proposal of creating an international criminal tribunal ... the American members refused to give their assent', said the dissenting memorandum. Robert Lansing and James Brown Scott described their disagreement on the tribunal issue as 'fundamental' and 'radical'. They accepted two propositions of the Commission: that a belligerent had the right to try those taken prisoner or within its power for war crimes, and that it was also entitled to set up military or civilian tribunals for this purpose. They supported reliance on 'the machinery at hand, which had been tried and found competent, with a law and a procedure framed and therefore known in advance', rather than 'an international tribunal with a criminal jurisdiction for which there is no precedent, precept, practice or procedure'. To the extent that international cooperation was necessary because a punishable act affected more than one country, the Americans said that a tribunal could be formed of the countries affected by uniting the national commissions or courts.[28]

That the proposed international tribunal was 'unprecedented' was hardly a compelling argument. Woodrow Wilson's 'fourteen points' had many components that might be called 'unprecedented'. Moreover, the proponents of an international criminal court would have willingly conceded that they were breaking new ground. For them, this was, as Victor Hugo said, an idea whose time had come. Other than a reluctance to innovate, Lansing and Scott did not provide any real explanation for their opposition to the 'high tribunal'. Their complaints were not directed to the idea of an international tribunal, but to two issues that were associated with the proposal in the Report of the Commission. 'It was frankly stated that the purpose was to bring before this tribunal the ex-Kaiser of Germany, and that the jurisdiction of the tribunals must be broad enough to include him even if he had not directly ordered the violations', said the dissenting memorandum. In other words, they were opposed both to trial of the Kaiser and to 'the doctrine of negative criminality' in order to establish his guilt.

Immunity of the Head of State

'[I]n the hierarchy of persons in authority there is no reason why rank, however exalted, should in any circumstances protect the holder of it from responsibility when that responsibility has been established before a properly constituted tribunal', begins Chapter III of the Report of the Commission on Responsibilities. To dispel any doubt, the Report says that this responsibility 'extends even to the case of Heads of States'. By way of explanation, it notes that '[a]n argument has been raised to the contrary based upon the alleged immunity, and in particular the alleged inviolability, of a Sovereign of a State'. According to the Commission, 'even if, in some countries, a Sovereign is exempt from being prosecuted in a national court of his own country the position from an international point of view is quite different'.[29]

The argument had indeed been raised by the dissenting members of the Commission. James Brown Scott, in his account of the Paris negotiations, wrote that:

> ... contrary to the recommendations of the commission on responsibilities, although in thorough accord with the views of the American members of that commission, a sovereign or chief executive of a state was not to be sued for violation of the laws and customs of war. At present such a person is exempt under international law—the law made or consented to by all nations. He is immune from suit in any court, national or international ... In the future the sovereign or chief executive may, by agreement of the nations, be triable for crime or offense by an international tribunal. It cannot be done now.[30]

The issue of sovereign immunity was addressed by both the French and the British legal experts in the opinions prepared in late 1918. The French legal experts, Larnaude and de Lapradelle, understood that immunity barred a prosecution of Kaiser Wilhelm before the courts of a foreign country. For this reason, they emphasised the importance of establishing an international tribunal.[31] The British Committee of Inquiry took a more extreme view, concluding that 'no modern usage establishing such immunity appears to exist'.[32]

The British memorandum of 13 February 1919, which was largely based upon the work of the Committee of Inquiry, referred to the issue in its discussion of prosecuting the Kaiser for starting the war. It said that '[t]he question of the immunity of a Sovereign from the jurisdiction of a foreign Criminal Court has rarely been discussed in modern times, and never in circumstances similar to those in which it is suggested that it might be raised today'.[33] The British presented this as an element of uncertainty. But their discussion concluded by stating that there was ample evidence to prosecute the Kaiser for violations of the laws and customs of war, and that this was 'desirable'. Moreover, said the British memorandum, 'the trial of other offenders might be seriously prejudiced if they attempted and were able to plead the superior orders of a Sovereign against whom no steps had been taken or were being taken'.[34]

Robert Lansing raised the immunity issue in his proposed amendment to the Report of Sub-Commission III, when he sought to replace the proposed international tribunal with a Commission of Inquiry. He based the argument for a Commission on the alleged immunity of the Kaiser: 'In view of the official and personal influences which the ex-Kaiser possessed and exercised upon the course and conduct of the war, and in view of the immunity from suit and prosecution which a Monarch and Chief of State enjoys according to the municipal law of every civilised country and also according to the Common Law of Nations, and last because of this immunity from judicial process the ex-Kaiser escapes the condemnation which his misdeeds require …'[35]

William Massey, speaking on behalf of the British Empire, challenged Lansing. 'I have heard it said that a king or Head of State is above the law', said Massey. 'I believe the idea arose from the fact that the king has very often to sign acts of parliament and statutes which are placed before him (by his ministers, or perhaps through his ministers) by his parliament. In those respects I believe he is above the law; the people who are responsible are the representatives of the people—they are responsible to the people—ministers are undoubtedly responsible to the people, but so far as criminal acts are concerned, and I look back upon the precedents of British history, one British king was alleged to have broken the law: he was tried by a court specially appointed for the purpose, found guilty and was executed. I am merely stating a fact, I am not expressing my own opinion as to whether he should have been executed.'[36] Massey was referring to the trial of Charles I in 1649.[37]

Lansing answered that '[w]hen a people confide to a monarch the exercise of sovereignty he acts as their agent and he is only responsible to them'. Lansing reiterated that he was speaking 'from the purely legal point of view and not the moral point of view because from the moral point of view he is responsible to mankind, whoever he is'. Taking up Massey's example of Charles I, Lansing said: 'What followed? His son was restored to be monarch of England. Napoleon was practically punished—exiled; there was a restoration in his case. Louis XVI was executed—his family was restored to the throne of France. Mary, Queen of Scots, is the only case that I know of within modern times—or what might be called modern times—where a foreign sovereign has been executed, and her son was the ruler of England ... I might add that the judges, if I recall it, of Charles I were executed for having performed the justice to which Mr Massey referred.' However, Lansing's argument was one of policy, not law.[38]

Larnaude's incandescent anger radiates from the pages of the transcripts. He noted that it had already been agreed, 'under the gentle pressure exercised by the Delegate of the United States so as to be able to reach an agreement', not to expressly name the ex-Kaiser. The next step, it seemed, was to remove any reference at all to a Head of State. Here, Larnaude was referring to a paragraph in the Report of Sub-Commission III dealing with the authority of the proposed international tribunal. It was to try 'all authorities, civil or military, belonging to enemy countries, however high their position may have been, without distinction of rank, including the Heads of State'.[39]

'But what the French Delegation cannot accept is that the *right* should be abandoned: that is not possible even when questions of right should lead us to contemplate decisions which may carry with them possible penalty of death for certain people, even before such eventualities we should not give way, and should make sure that law and right should be upheld by kings.'[40] The French academic argued that the Americans confused the responsibility of a sovereign to his or her own people, a matter subject to national law, and that of a sovereign with respect to other States, something governed by international law. 'If you suppress the responsibility of the Emperor, how will it be possible to reach others, such as soldiers, officers, staff officers or even ministers? Again, everything crumbles to the ground and the whole building goes overboard. If we reach such results we should run counter to all we have said here. We should not allow the Kaiser to be a sort of scapegoat, taking the sins of the responsibility for the war upon himself and then escape. We must seek responsibility everywhere and if you exclude the responsibility of the Kaiser, all his accomplices will be cleared and they will escape all the responsibility established, so that the position itself and public opinion which demands that punishment shall be meted out, all this will disappear.'[41]

The meeting ended abruptly. The debate resumed the following day. Nicolaos Politis of Greece took the lead in challenging the American position. He said that any immunity granted to Heads of State under internal law was a matter 'of only practical expediency'. Politis explained that there were fewer obstacles when an international tribunal was established. He insisted upon an important point, one that was rarely articulated during the debates: Germany was going to agree to the trial of the Kaiser by ratifying the treaty, in effect waiving any claim to immunity. '[A] country cannot bring for trial before a national tribunal a foreign potentate—a foreign sovereign. But here this is another question, and we have not to go against a rule of international practice', said Politis. 'What we have to do is to establish an international machinery, with the consent which may have to be imposed—with the consent of the countries over which reigned the person ...' Politis then turned to the policy issues, responding to the fears expressed by Lansing that a prosecution of the Kaiser might result in restoration of the Hohenzollern dynasty. According to Politis, an international trial would serve to prevent such an eventuality. In yet another attempt to placate Lansing, Politis suggested replacing the words 'Heads of States included' with 'against all persons or authorities, civil or military'.[42]

Larnaude was not impressed. '[T]here is an opinion on the part of the members of the commission that the phrase—the sentence referring to the Heads of States should go out. It may be said it is unnecessary. Very well, possibly it is. But if it is unnecessary, it won't do any harm by allowing it to remain. It is quite unusual to insert a paragraph which appears unnecessary because it makes a position clear, and, as I said, I hold very strong opinions. I don't want to repeat anything I said yesterday about the responsibility of the Heads of States, but I look upon it in this way: The higher a man's position is, the more serious his responsibility, and if he commits a crime, as the head of a State, it is a more serious crime than one of his inferiors.'[43]

The Commission only rarely decided matters by voting, but it did so on the troublesome clause at its fifth meeting, on 14 March 1919. After considerable procedural wrangling, the phrase '[a]gainst all authorities or personages, civil or military, belonging to enemy countries, however high their position may have been, without distinction of rank' was put to a vote. It was adopted by nine votes in favour, with James Brown Scott of the United States abstaining.[44] Lansing, who had gone to the train station to meet President Wilson, was not present. When Massey asked the chairman for the opportunity to justify including the phrase 'Heads of State', he was told that the vote had already been taken and that such a proposal was out of order. Larnaude explained, 'expressly and firmly', with the agreement of the chairman, that 'it is understood by everybody here that the fact of excluding the words "Heads of States" does not at all mean, in the event of the omission, that the Heads of States should not be prosecuted. On the contrary, the wording makes it clear that the Heads of States should be brought to trial'.

'Is that going on record?' asked Massey. 'Yes, it is', answered Politis, who was in the chair. 'Then that will satisfy me', answered Massey.[45]

At its seventh meeting, the Head of State issue returned. Ernest Pollock, who had been in London for most of the week, had missed the debate on this point. He proposed no formal amendment, but he wanted instructions to be given the Drafting Committee: 'When the "*Comité de rédaction*" brings up its report, we could not allow the words in paragraph "C" to remain as "authorities or persons", or "personalities", or whatever it is', he said. 'We must include these words, "including Heads of States".' Referring to the phrase 'authorities or persons' in the text adopted by the Commission, Pollock said the word 'personalities' was to be construed with reference to the word 'authorities'.

'Now, a sovereign or Head of a State is not an authority. He is the person who confers authority in the person who exercise it', continued Pollock. 'And to leave out these words "Heads of States" in the case where there is no difficulty in using that word is, to my mind, placing myself and my distinguished colleagues in a position in which they might be derided in all countries, and by all lawyers. And on that ground, at the right time, even if it is necessary to put in a separate memorandum to the Peace Conference, I shall ask at the appropriate time to indicate what we mean by these words, and that it does include "Heads of States". And I beg my colleagues around the table—all of them distinguished jurists—to look around, to look into the word, and see whether or not if jurists in every country would not say to them: "What do you mean? If you meant Heads of States, you ought to have had the courage to say it. There was no need to use cryptic or difficult language on so simple a point." And when we know what the apt phrase is, as lawyers, it behoves us to say it, because I am afraid, after having had the opportunity of looking at this matter for a week, there is danger of not doing full justice to our knowledge of law, and I shall ask my colleagues around the table, at the appropriate time, on the report of the "*Comité de rédaction*", either on a separate memorandum, to put in some document which we shall make it perfectly clear what I mean, and which shall be understood throughout the British Empire, where I am quite certain they would call upon lawyers to have the courage to express their opinions, and to write their opinions in clear and intelligible language.'[46]

Larnaude repeated what Pollock already knew, that when it was agreed not to use the term 'Heads of States', it was on the condition that the minutes record their inclusion in the provision. 'This was consistent with ordinary rules of legislative drafting by which laws should be general and impersonal', said Larnaude. 'But I am nevertheless in agreement with the Solicitor-General, Sir Ernest Pollock, in admitting that it would be dangerous to rely upon the word "authority" alone.'[47]

The Drafting Committee restored the words 'Heads of State' to the controversial paragraph (c) in Chapter IV, on Pollock's insistence.[48] Chapter III of the draft Report consisted of only two short paragraphs. It included the following sentence: 'The Commission does not admit that the Head of a State is, as such, disqualified *de jure* from being held responsible, if he is responsible *de facto*.'[49] The Drafting Committee was itself divided on the matter. When the chair of the committee, Rolin-Jaequemyns, introduced the draft Report, he indicated his own discomfort with the reference to Heads of State. '[I]t might be better, following healthy traditions, not to declare in advance any presumption of guilt with respect to anyone, and this means removing all special reference to Heads of State and even the ex-Kaiser', he said.[50] But there was little discussion of the issue in the plenary Commission. The Japanese representative asked the chairman to clarify whether the words 'Heads of State' remained in the paragraph. Pollock confirmed that they did. Scialoja of Italy said he would follow the almost unanimous view of the Commission, but declared that he preferred the text of Rolin-Jaequemyns, where the reference to 'Heads of State' was omitted.[51] The Commission insisted that the Drafting Committee make another effort.[52]

The Drafting Committee's revision of Chapter III was presented to the tenth meeting of the Commission, on 27 March 1919. It had been very substantially rewritten and 'fattened up' as the Commission had requested. The new text focused on the Head of State issue. Lansing had left the meeting because of other responsibilities. Ernest Pollock, who could not have disagreed more with the American on this issue, replaced him in the chair. The Americans had made it clear they would never agree with the majority of the

Commission. The various concessions that had been made to Lansing in the course of the negotiations were rescinded. The final text not only retained the reference to 'Heads of States'—it also mentioned the Kaiser by name:

> In these circumstances, the Commission desires to state expressly that in the hierarchy of persons in authority, there is no reason why rank, however exalted, should in any circumstances protect the holder of it from responsibility when that responsibility has been established before a properly constituted Tribunal. This extends even to the case of Heads of States. An argument has been raised to the contrary based upon the principle of the irresponsibility of a Sovereign of a State. But this principle, where it is recognised, is one of practical expediency in municipal law, and is not fundamental. Granted, however, that a Sovereign is exempt from being prosecuted in a national Court of his own country, the position from an international point of view is quite different.
>
> We have later on in our Report proposed the establishment of a High Tribunal composed of judges drawn from many nations, and included the possibility of the trial before that Tribunal of a former Head of a State with the consent of that State itself secured by articles ini the Treaty of Peace. If the immunity of a Sovereign is claimed to extend beyond the limits above stated, it would involve laying down the principle that the greatest outrages against the laws and customs of war and the laws of humanity, if proved against him, could in no circumstances be punished. Such a conclusion would shock the conscience of civilised mankind.
>
> In view of the grave charges which may be preferred against—to take one case—the ex-Kaiser, the vindication of the laws and customs of war and the laws of humanity which have been violated would be incomplete if he were not brought to trial and if other offenders less highly placed were punished. Moreover the trial of the other offenders might be seriously prejudiced if they attempted and were able to plead the superior orders of a Sovereign against whom no steps had been or were being taken.
>
> There is little doubt that the ex-Kaiser and others in high authority were cognisant of and could at least have mitigated the barbarities committed during the course of the war. A word from them would have brought about a different method in the action of their subordinates on land, at sea and in the air.
>
> We desire to say that civil and miltiary authorities cannot be relieved from responsibility by the mere fact that a higher authority might have been convicted of the same offence. It will be for the Court to decide whether a plea of superior orders is sufficient to acquit the person charged from resopnsibility.

Conclusion

> There exist weighty charges against a number of enemy individuals. For reasons on which it is unnecessary to insist it would be premature to publish their names, but these are at the disposal of the members of the Commission suggested in the second Conclusion followiing Chapter II.[53]

Larnaude objected to reference to specific individuals. He said it was un-necessary to indicate that the Commission could provide names of potential suspects. 'The conclusion should be abstract and impersonal, like the rest of Chapter III', he said. Rolin-Jaequemyns offered an explanation, as one of the rapporteurs, but said he had no objection to the concerns of France. Rosental of Romania observed that the draft referred only to the Kaiser, and he thought it ought also to mention the former king of Bulgaria. 'We only put in the ex-Kaiser as he is only taken as an example', explained Pollock. 'We might put in, you know, some Turkish authorities or the Sultan, but it is much better to take a single example than it is to go through a whole number of persons that might be included anywhere.'[54]

'Negative Criminality'

There was much controversy within the Commission on Responsibilities about how to establish Kaiser Wilhelm's liability for crimes perpetrated by German combatants. The French memorandum to the Commission de-scribed the German Army as 'the most disciplined in the world', claiming 'there is only one law, the will of the Emperor'. It asked how it could be that the Emperor would not have been thoroughly informed of atrocities perpet-rated by his troops. The memorandum noted that well-publicised events like the sinking of the RMS Lusitania were surely known to Wilhelm. Because similar acts continued, 'it was by his order or at least with his consent'.[55] The British memorandum said that:

> Whatever view may be advanced as to the ex-Kaiser's responsibility as author of the war, there is little room for doubt that at any time he could at least have mitigated the barbarities committed during the course of it. A word from him would have brought about a different method in the actions of his officers both on land and on sea and in the air. But he deliberately sanctioned and carried out a policy of terrorism and ruthless unrestricted warfare. He openly chose Attila as his model and inspired the spirit of this Hun into those who were under his command.[56]

The Commission confronted this issue as it considered paragraph (c) of Chapter IV. It is part of a list of four categories of offenders, labelled (a), (b), (c), and (d), for whom prosecution by an international tribunal is contemplated. This was the same provision that provoked disputes about Head of State im-munity. In the final Report of the Commission, paragraph (c) targets persons in authority 'who ordered, or, with knowledge thereof and with power to intervene, abstained from preventing or taking measures to prevent, putting an end to or repressing, violations of the laws or customs of war'.[57] The provision has its origins in the draft report of Sub-Commission III, where there is a four-paragraph enumeration similar to the one in the final Report of the Commission. Paragraph (c) in the draft describes the jurisdiction of the international tribunal as extending to 'the ex-Kaiser himself, in so far as he ordered or abstained from controlling and mitigating the barbarities committed in many widely separated areas and in many countries'.[58] There was no debate in the Sub-Commission about paragraph (c) of the initial draft. When a new version was prepared, the paragraph was changed and reference to the Kaiser removed: 'Against all authorities, civil or military, however high their position may have been, without distinction of rank, including the Heads of States, who ordered, or abstained from preventing, putting an end to, or repressing, barbarities or acts of violence.'[59] Larnaude later described deletion of the explicit mention of the Kaiser as a 'compromise'.[60]

But the provision, even as amended, was still anathema to the Americans. In a sense, the 'compromise' was even worse, because in principle it extended to other Heads of State. According to Lansing, under this provision 'the President of the United States, or the King of England might be tried for having failed to prevent certain of their soldiers from performing barbarous or atrocious acts'. He said he was not prepared to sign up to such a position. Lansing said he could agree to a text that referred to authorities 'who ordered, or openly gave assent to barbarities or acts of violence they could have prevented'.[61]

'I don't think that the danger in which the President of the United States might find himself is one that really is an argument in which we need to dwell upon', replied Pollock. 'If the President of the United States had been in any way guilty or responsible for the acts which we attribute to William II, I believe the United States would be perhaps the most insistent that the President guilty with such blood upon him should be brought to trial, and the mere fact that he happened to be the President of the United States would not protect him from the execration of those persons who elected him to that high and responsible position. In other words, a criminal or a guilty person who is responsible for what happened in the course of the war, be he the President of the United States, or be he the King of England, or the King of any other country, deserves and should receive, not only from the United States, but from every other country, the condemnation which he ought to receive.'[62]

Pollock attempted to explain the importance of the words 'abstaining from preventing'. He said that 'a person in high authority, or a sovereign of a State might himself be shocked by suddenly finding that outrages and excesses had been committed by persons—by soldiers or sailors who wore his uniform. But once they have been brought to his knowledge, and once he is apprised of the fact that his uniform has been disgraced, the responsibility then lies upon him. If he does not take measures within his power of preventing further and future excesses and outrages, and therefore, if you are trying, we will say the ex-Kaiser, you may put him in what we call in England two charges, or two counts; the one that he allowed; the other that he did not prevent. For the first you would have to show that he either ordered or assented to an order being given under which excesses were first authorised; and under the second you would have to show that if he had knowledge of what had been done, and he took no steps, such as were within his power, of preventing subsequent similar acts being repeated.'[63]

Rolin-Jaequemyns of Belgium warned that incriminating acts of 'mere abstention' might lead to high officials, such as governors and generals, taking shelter successfully behind the Kaiser, contending 'that he is the only guilty man, because he exercised his passive authority, and did not prevent those acts ... On the other hand, if we don't include this passive charge, as it were, in the first part, the fact of including directly and explicitly the Heads of States offers less inconvenience. If we leave out the passive abstention, the fact of mentioning explicitly Heads of States does not open—does not offer as many inconveniences.'[64] Other members of the Sub-Commission did not see the same danger or difficulty.

Lansing said there was no point in debating the point further. 'My friend, the Solicitor General, states that he cannot sign a report with this item "C" left out. I cannot sign a report for the United States with item "C" reading as it does. I would therefore suggest as the only possible solution, to make this report as it is drafted, and with a reservation on the part of the United States submitting an amended article.'[65] On Lansing's suggestion, the final words in the sentence, 'barbarities or acts of violence', were changed to 'violations of the laws and customs of war' in order to respect the Commission's terms of reference.[66]

When the Report of Sub-Commission III was discussed in the plenary Commission, Lansing's hesitations about liability for abstention met with supporters. Adachi of Japan had told the Sub-Commission he initially had been in full accord with the clause, but that he would like to reserve his

assent in light of Lansing's 'weighty arguments'.[67] When the Commission
met, Adachi endorsed the American position, as did Rolin-Jaequemyns of
Belgium.[68] Politis proposed an amendment to paragraph (c) removing liability by abstention, 'to meet the wishes of the representative of Belgium',
and confining liability of authorities to acts that they had ordered.[69] Massey
valiantly tried to argue for retaining the reference to abstention, invoking
English law to support the principle that 'a master is responsible for the acts
of his servant. According to that rule, an officer is responsible for the acts of
his servant, if he does nothing to prevent the commission of crimes, if he has
knowledge of it, if he knows that atrocities are being committed.'[70] The reference by the New Zealand farmer was well intended but ill-informed, and
the lawyers in the room knew it. The vicarious liability of the master only
applies to civil claims, not criminal prosecution. The Commission took a vote
on paragraph (c) in its consideration of the report of Sub-Commission II. An
attempt to remove the phrase about liability by abstention was rejected and
the text in the Sub-Commission's Report, with some minor modifications,
was adopted by eight votes in favour, with James Brown Scott voting against
and Mineichirō Adachi abstaining.[71]

The draft Report made no changes to the text. It now spoke of 'authorities, civil or military ... who ordered, or abstained from preventing, putting
an end to or repressing, violations of the laws or customs of war, provided
that no abstention shall constitute a defence for the actual perpetrators'.[72]
Pollock asked Lansing if he might find it acceptable were the words 'with
knowledge thereof' or 'with knowledge thereof, and power to intervene'
inserted before 'who ordered'. This expressed what was only implied in the
text as adopted by Sub-Commission III, said Pollock. 'I had no idea of con-
victing a person who had no knowledge, or who had no power to intervene,
and if we put in those few words, I feel sure that the proposition may be
adopted.' Larnaude observed that the new clause, 'if it is inserted, does away
with what has been called passive or negative complicity'. Lansing, who was
in no mood to compromise, said '[i]t is now what might be called "criminal
negligence"'. Indifferent to Lansing's attitude, the Commission decided to
include Pollock's proposed amendment.[73]

The Americans considered the issue in their dissenting opinion. As they
saw it, the problem concerned punishment not for crimes where the accused
was the direct perpetrator, which was a matter of no dispute, but rather for
crimes committed by others and for which there was no proof that the accused knew of their commission or, knowing they would be committed,

could have prevented them. In such cases, said the memorandum, 'neither knowledge of commission nor ability to prevent is alone sufficient. The duty or obligation to act is essential.' The American delegates noted that the Commission had softened its position somewhat in the final Report. The memorandum described the final text of the Commission as 'much less objectionable' and suggested that it might be acceptable.[74]

12

The Council of Virgins

❝ Open covenants of peace, openly arrived at, after which there shall be no private international understandings of any kind but diplomacy shall proceed always frankly and in the public view.' This was the first of the 'fourteen points' set out by President Woodrow Wilson in January 1918. Presented to the United States Congress as a statement of American war aims, it became a reference point throughout the negotiations. The Paris Peace Conference might initially appear to have complied fully with the transparency promised by Wilson. The elaborate and complex treaties produced by the Paris Peace Conference required the engagement of a huge number of diplomats, politicians, and lawyers, not to mention specialists in geography, economics, geology, and other scientific fields. Journalists reported daily on the state of the negotiations. The issues were debated in national parliaments.

But at its core, the decision-making was the work of a tiny conclave of immensely powerful men, accompanied by a few of their most trusted advisers, meeting in private. In the first weeks of the Paris Peace Conference, the main decisions were taken in the 'Supreme Council', sometimes called the 'Council of Ten'. It was composed of five Heads of State or government: Woodrow Wilson of the United States, Georges Clemenceau of France, David Lloyd George of Britain, Vittorio Orlando of Italy, and Saïonzi Kinmochi of Japan. To this were added a Secretary of State or Foreign Minister: Robert Lansing, Stéphane Pichon, Arthur Balfour, Sydney Sonnino, and Makino Nobuaki, respectively.

The meetings of the Council of Ten were often enlarged by the presence of advisers. They became cumbersome to convene and leaks of information were difficult to prevent. Lloyd George was rumoured to prefer meeting with Wilson *tête-à-tête*, which meant without Lansing. The American Secretary of State had been his country's voice until the return of Wilson to Paris in

The Trial of the Kaiser. William A. Schabas. © William A. Schabas, 2018. Published 2018 by Oxford University Press.

mid-March 1919. Shortly thereafter, the 'Council of Five', consisting only of Heads of State or government, began to meet. The five foreign ministers met separately. Because Japan's interests were relatively narrow, it did not attend all of the meetings. The 'Council of Four' was the result. It took most of the important decisions, including those concerning the trial of the Kaiser.

The Council of Four was unofficially described as the 'Conseil des dieux' or 'Council of the gods'. It was also referred to as the 'Conseil des vièrges' or 'Council of virgins'. The companion body of foreign ministers was known as 'les demi-vièrges' or 'half-virgins'. The inspiration was a popular French novel, entitled *Les demi-vièrges*, by Marcel Prévost, published in 1894. It was premised on the preposterous idea that Heads of State had virgin minds. Many of those who suffered as a result of the decisions of the Council, and not only the Germans because of the harsh terms of the treaty, but also the Armenians, the Kurds, and the Arabs, whose hopes were buried, would have found the metaphor inappropriate. What they experienced was better described in terms that imply the opposite of virginity.

Generally, the Council met in the rooms of one of its members, usually those of Woodrow Wilson at 11 Place des États-Unis. Official transcripts were not kept, and the proceedings were meant to be confidential and to remain so. The British secretary, Maurice Hankey, prepared minutes of some but not all of the meetings. These eventually became available in archives and were published in the 1940s in the *Foreign Relations of the United States* series dealing with the Paris Peace Conference. Something closer to a verbatim transcript was made by the gifted bilingual amanuensis of the Conference, Paul Mantoux. His notes were first published in French in 1955,[1] and some years later in an English translation.[2] Of the four, only Orlando was not fluent in English. To his dismay, it became the working language of the Council.[3] Thus, the English version of the notes of Mantoux have been translated twice, from English to French and then back. Clemenceau, who had lived in New York for several years, was fluent in English. The minutes do not indicate the language that he spoke during the meetings. Records were also kept by the Italian secretary, Luigi Aldrovandi Marescotti. They have been published in the original Italian as well as in French and German.[4]

The Council of Four held an initial and rather brief discussion about prosecution of the Kaiser on 1 April 1919. Woodrow Wilson pointed to the example of Charles I, the English king who was judged and beheaded in 1649, recalling that execution made the 'despicable character and the greatest liar in history' into a martyr and a subject of poetry. Wilson must have had in mind Andrew Marvell's 'An Horatian Ode upon Cromwell's Return from Ireland'.[5] Wilson thought the same applied to Mary Stuart, another unsavoury monarch to face the scaffold.

'She was a very seductive woman', said Lloyd George, who thought this might explain the attention of poets. As well as plotting assassination, Mary, Queen of Scots, wrote some verse herself. She was tried and then executed for planning the murder of Elizabeth I.

Wilson pointed to Napoleon, who 'admittedly by different methods, like the German Emperor tried to impose his domination upon the world', only to be surrounded by legend because of his internment in St Helena.

'The Napoleonic legend was not due to St Helena alone', answered Lloyd George. 'I would like to see punished the man responsible for the greatest crime in history.'

'He is universally reviled. Isn't that the worst punishment for such a man?', said Wilson.[6]

This was mere foreplay. But Wilson's enigmatic remarks provided confirmation that the American opposition to trial of the Kaiser in the Commission on Responsibilities was supported at the highest level.

There was a more substantial discussion of the issue late in the afternoon the following day. Lloyd George referred to the Report of the Commission on Responsibilities, expressing his dissatisfaction with its recommendation against prosecution of those responsible for initiating the war. 'My view is that if we could hold criminally accountable the great personalities who inflicted such a scourge, indeed the greatest one of all, this might reduce the danger of war in the future.' On the other hand, Lloyd George continued, responsibility was admitted for breaches of treaties resulting in the deaths of millions. Similarly, there were no doubts about atrocities perpetrated during the course of the war. He spoke of 'a range of atrocities whose perpetration was ordered, kidnapping of girls for forced prostitution, the destruction of vessels on the high seas by submarines, abandoning crews in lifeboats hundreds of kilometres from land. We will require that in the treaty's text the enemy recognises our right to judge these crimes and pledges to surrender the guilty. We must also have the right to insist that all relevant documents be produced by Germany. Finally, the Commission proposes the establishment of a court of justice where all countries engaged in the war, be they big or small, will be represented.'

Referring to the American dissent with the majority report of the Commission on Responsibilities, Wilson noted that abandoning the plan to prosecute those responsible for initiating the war brought the two sides closer. Had Wilson been more familiar with the Report, he would have understood that the majority had recommended against prosecuting the Kaiser and others for starting the war.

Lloyd George observed that Japan objected to the admission of the Kaiser's responsibility. 'The Mikado is a god who cannot be held responsible', he said by way of explanation. He hurled a provocative comment at the American President. 'They tell me that the Americans are also opposed to establishing a precedent that might be held against the President of the United States.'

'That's not true', said President Wilson. 'It is Congress that declares war in the United States. But I concede that even if the President does not have legal liability, he is responsible because he advises upon going to war, as I did. During the Spanish–American War, President McKinley was opposed. Congress decided to go ahead in spite of his advice.'

Wilson pointed out the difficulty in establishing the Kaiser's personal responsibility. 'In all likelihood, it is very substantial. However, there are some accounts that have him reluctantly signing orders reluctantly and telling his advisors: "You are going to regret this."'

'Our only objective is to punish those responsible, whoever they may be', answered Lloyd George.

'I would ask that you do not link the American objection to that of the Japanese which, from our standpoint, rests on a ridiculous premise', said Wilson.

'The Japanese principle is the English principle—that the King can commit no crime', answered Lloyd George. 'If the problem of the origins of the war should arise in England, Mr. Asquith would be responsible, not King George. The German Emperor's situation is quite different because he had direct executive power.'

'I question whether we have the right to set up a tribunal made up only of the belligerents. The parties to the dispute would also be the judges', Wilson continued.

'In my view, England and the United States should not be seen as injured parties', said Lloyd George. 'We both made war for justice.'

Wilson was unpersuaded. 'Suppose that, sometime in the future, one country was victorious over another that had attacked it in a violation of international law. Would it alone be able to judge those guilty of crimes against international law of which it had been the victim?'

'Not at all', answered Lloyd George. 'Then the League of Nations would intervene in accordance with fundamental rules that we will have laid down. In the present case, it is not Belgium or France that will judge the offenders. If we want the League of Nations to have a chance to succeed, it must offer more than mere lip service. It must be able to punish crimes against international law. The violation of treaties is precisely the sort of crime in which the League of Nations has a direct interest.'

'Let me think about it', said Wilson. 'Until the present day, responsibility for international crimes has always been a collective responsibility. It is not right to make such an act a crime retroactively, to make an act of this type a personal crime after it has been committed. Undoubtedly some of the crimes that have been committed are punishable by the countries that are concerned. But these are not crimes for which there existed an international tribunal at the time of their commission. It would be accepted to declare that in the future if such crimes are committed during an international conflict they may be punished by an international court, thereby replacing collective responsibility with individual responsibility. But you cannot do this until the principle has been recognised.'

Lloyd George responded: 'In wartime, belligerents have always had the right to punish violations of the laws of war summarily. We didn't contest this when it was done by our enemies, except when they applied it erroneously, such as in the case Captain Fryatt. We can say that there will be no peace until the perpetrators have been surrendered to us. That is what Austria said to Serbia in 1914, when she charged her with a crime for which she was not guilty.'

'Suppose the Austrian version of the crime of Sarajevo had been true', Wilson asked. 'The entire world would have agreed that Austria could demand that the culprits be tried by Serbian courts. If we could get Germany to agree to judge the culprits, I would withdraw my objections. I want to avoid leaving historians with any sympathy for Germany. I want Germany consigned to the execration of history. Nothing should be done to allow it to be said we went beyond our rights, in a just cause. We must avoid letting history reproach us for rendering justice before the crime was recognised.'

'My opinion is that our weakness may also be condemned by history', answered Lloyd George. 'We would have an absolute right to obtain punishment for these crimes if we had custody of the offenders. These are crimes for which no equivalent can be found in the Napoleonic wars, or for that matter in any war of the past two centuries. Napoleon was punished because his ambition wreaked havoc on the world, but not for having committed international crimes such as those we blame on the Germans.'

'I recently reread documents of the 1870 conflict. It strikes me that German conduct then resembles that of which we accuse them today', said Wilson. He was referring to the Franco-Prussian war. As German troops advanced on Paris, the French encouraged popular resistance, to which the Germans reacted with great harshness.

Clemenceau, who thus far had remained silent, seemed roused to participate by the references to Napoleon as well as to the war between France and Germany half a century earlier, of which he had personal memories. 'It's not the same', he told Wilson. 'They were brutal in 1870, but we could not charge them with crimes that had been ordered from above. During that war and in its aftermath, there was nothing like the hatred of the German soldier that we see today.'

'These were crimes that were ordered', added Lloyd George. 'Submarine warfare is one of the most striking examples. I would even say it is not worth making peace if such crimes are to go unpunished. Moreover, I see no difficulty in having the League of Nations establish the tribunal.'

'Unless we wait a long time before holding a trial, judgment will be issued in an atmosphere of passion', said Wilson. 'I am personally furious every time I read the documents about the atrocities that were committed, and I avoid making decisions under such circumstances. I try to judge according to reason.'

Lloyd George did not agree. 'Actually, the terrible stories that we have been hearing for the past five years have exhausted our capacity for indignation. In fifty years, we will judge more severely than today.'

'You may find me to be insensitive', answered Wilson. 'I try to resist emotion.'

'Nothing is done without emotion', Clemenceau said. 'Wasn't Jesus Christ driven by passion when he chased the moneychangers from the temple?'

Lloyd George returned to the issue of retroactivity of prosecution, reacting to the objections of Wilson. 'I see a great disadvantage in solemnly declaring: "We affirm the principle and will deal with these terrible things in the future." We will not be taken seriously.'

And Clemenceau, always ready with an aphorism, added: 'The first tribunal must have been summary and brutal, yet it was the beginning of something great.'

'If Europe had had common sanctions at its disposal, it could have kept the peace', said Lloyd George. 'If we want the League of Nations to have such power in the future, it must show from the start that it can punish crime.'

Wilson closed the day's discussion: 'I agree with you about the crimes that have been committed. But we have to act in such a way that we can live with our own consciences.'[7]

An Ailing Wilson Changes His Mind

Woodrow Wilson suffered from a number of chronic health problems. He was certainly not at his best during the sessions of 1 and 2 April. On 3 April, he recorded a temperature of 39.5 degrees as well as 'profuse diarrhoea'.[8] Wilson remained quite sick for several more days.[9] His physician described him as being stricken with influenza.[10] Lloyd George thought that Wilson might have had a small stroke. The President did not attend the 4 April meeting of the Council. On 5 April, he insisted that the Council session take place in the sitting room next to his bedroom. During the first week of April, there were important developments in Wilson's political posture. It is tempting to link these to his precarious state of health. One writer, Edwin A. Weinstein, considered that Wilson was in a state of euphoria brought on by encephalitis, due to his attack of influenza on 3 April. According to Weinstein, '[p]robably the most startling political expression of the changes in Wilson's behaviour was the reversal of his attitudes on German war guilt and the trial of the ex-Kaiser'.[11] Herbert Hoover stated that prior to his illness Wilson had been 'incisive, quick to grasp essentials, unhesitating in his conclusions, and willing to listen to advice. Afterward, he "groped for ideas".'[12]

While he was ailing, Wilson ordered that his ship, the *USS George Washington*, be taken out of dry-dock and moved to Brest, ready for him to return to the United States. American diplomats made a point of explaining that this was not related to the medical issues, but rather his dissatisfaction with the lack of progress. His departure from the Peace Conference would be devastating.

The other leaders understood that the President had become frustrated with the pace of negotiations. Perhaps they became less intransigent, more inclined to compromise with Wilson and the Americans. But the President's gesture may only have been a bluff. Ultimately, it was Wilson who budged on the war crimes issue, agreeing to the international tribunal opposed by Lansing, and to prosecution of the Kaiser.

Lansing wrote to Wilson on 4 April, when his illness was at its worst. He apologised for disturbing the President, but he insisted that 'the matter is one of high policy and I think that it should have your entire approval before it is filed'. Lansing was referring to the American memorandum, the lengthy dissenting opinion that was to accompany the majority report of the Commission on Responsibilities. The Secretary of State recalled that he had set out the position that the United States had taken during a meeting of the American Commissioners at which Wilson had been present 'some days ago'. The minutes of the American Commissioners record only one session in which Lansing spoke about penalties, and that was at a time when Wilson was in the United States. Lansing informed Wilson that he had maintained this policy to the end. He wrote:

> The British and French were simply determined that the Kaiser should be tried by a high tribunal, the former because of promises on the hustings, the latter because the French members of the Commission had previously written a monograph in favour of his trial and punishment (done, I am informed, at Clemenceau's instigation).

Judging by letters and newspapers, Lansing said he felt that popular sentiment in the United States was sympathetic to judicial trial and punishment of the Kaiser. 'There is a general clamour for vengeance and for physical punishment regardless of legal right or the fundamental principles of jurisprudence', he explained to the President. Lansing felt that the memorandum of the United States was likely to 'excite in America and elsewhere severe criticism', but he said that to support the trial would amount to advocating 'international "Lynch law"'.[13]

Wilson's reply to Lansing's letter of 4 April, if one was made, has not been found. Four days later, on 8 April, Lansing wrote again to Wilson saying he had given 'very careful consideration to the proposal to bring the ex-Kaiser to some sort of trial for violation of the neutrality of Belgium'. It would seem that Wilson had instructed him to find a compromise that might satisfy Clemenceau and Lloyd George. But perhaps Wilson was also persuaded by

Lansing's incautious reference to public opinion in the United States, a matter that may have troubled Wilson more than it did Lansing.

It appears strange that these two men were debating these matters through letters. But the relationship between the President and the Secretary of State seems to have been quite dysfunctional. Wilson and Lansing did not meet in person very frequently. In December, when they sailed together to France, they spent no more than an hour together throughout the entire voyage. 'I had learned from experience that Mr. Wilson preferred to have matters for his decision presented in writing rather than by word of mouth', Lansing wrote in his memoir of the Peace Conference.[14] He said that Wilson, who was himself legally trained and who briefly practised law, did not value the advice of lawyers except on strictly legal questions. 'He considers their objections and criticisms on other subjects to be based on mere technicalities and their judgments to be warped by an undue regard for precedent. This prejudice against the legal profession in general was exhibited on more than one occasion during our sojourn at Paris.' Lansing thought Wilson 'chafed under the restraints' imposed by law. 'It was a thankless task to question a proposed course of action on the ground of illegality, because he appeared to be irritated by such an obstacle to his will and to transfer his irritation against the law to the one who raised it as an objection.'[15]

Lansing's wife told the President's social secretary, Edith Benham, that the Secretary of State 'knows nothing of anything that is going on, that he is left out of everything and the French and British just leave him alone because they know this'. She said she had begged her husband to tell President Wilson 'that he is of no use and can he return and take up his duties as Secretary of State'.[16] On 8 April 1919, Edith Benham wrote in her diary that 'the [President] Heartily dislikes Mr. [Lansing] and I am sorry to say he seems to show it in rather a petty way'.[17] Another Wilson confidante, Ray Stannard Baker, also witnessed Lansing's unhappiness. In his diary Baker wrote that:

> [Lansing] feels strongly that the other American Commissioners have not been properly consulted by the President & are required to bear the odium of a treaty they had no real part in making. They have not only not been consulted but often they have not been informed as to what was going on. Oftentimes I have known far better the real inside proceedings than any of the Commissioners & have repeatedly told Lansing and White (but only occasionally House, who has been much closer to the President than the others) what was going on in the Council of Four.[18]

Lansing's letter of 8 April contained expressions that were to reappear in the Treaty of Versailles. He reiterated his opposition to a trial of the Kaiser, but seemed receptive to Wilson's desire for compromise. Favouring the Napoleonic solution of political denunciation, Lansing wrote to the President that he had given 'very careful consideration to the proposal to bring the ex-Kaiser to some sort of trial for violation of the neutrality of Belgium'. He said that 'the offence is one which cannot be described as a violation of criminal law and, therefore, the offender is not subject to condemnation by a judicial tribunal'. Nevertheless, Germany's conduct was also 'so utterly violative of international morality and the sanctity of treaties that it may be a wise policy to demand that the culpability of the ex-Kaiser, the one most responsible for this heinous act of the German armies, should be determined by an extraordinary tribunal with authority to decide an appropriate punishment as an example for the future and as a menace to those who would by committing a similar act plunge the world into war'. Lansing said the offence 'should be recognised as a political one and not one to which legal criminality attaches'. He described the extraordinary tribunal to be 'of political origin though adopting a procedure similar to judicial tribunals', with the authority to impose a punishment 'as a political measure'. Lansing explained that Napoleon had been exiled by the political power 'as a matter of high international policy', and that '[t]he difference in this case should be that a form of trial intervenes to determine the extent of culpability in order that the extraordinary tribunal, the agent of the political power, should not impose a penalty without full and accurate knowledge'.

Lansing advised Wilson that his proposal provided a way to meet the views of Lloyd George and Clemenceau, although he insisted that 'in the event that an extraordinary tribunal is decided upon it should be made clear beyond question that the constitution, authority and decision are political and not legal, and that high international policy requires that an offense like the invasion of Belgian neutrality cannot be passed over without registering in the most solemn and effective way the condemnation of the nations'. Lansing said that his personal hope was that the idea of a trial would be dropped. He sensed that Wilson was prepared for another outcome, however, and concluded with his hope that the President could 'impress the provisions with a political and not a legal character, since that will avoid criticisms which I think we would find very difficult to meet'.[19]

Agreement to Try the Kaiser

The issue returned to the agenda of the Council of Four on 8 April. The previous evening, Lloyd George's personal secretary, Philip Kerr, had called upon Colonel House to inform him that the war crimes issue would be discussed at 11 o'clock the following morning. House said he did not wish to attend the meeting and had asked the President to send Robert Lansing instead 'in his place and in mine'. When Lloyd George heard he would be debating the issue of prosecutions with the Secretary of State and not Wilson himself, he told Kerr to change the agenda. If Wilson were able to attend in the afternoon session, Lloyd George proposed, they could discuss the trial of the Kaiser then.[20]

Wilson, Clemenceau, Lloyd George, and Orlando met at 3 pm on 8 April. According to his personal physician, Wilson was still 'a little wobbly'.[21] The session was held at Lloyd George's residence on the Rue Nitot. The street is now known as the Rue de l'Amiral-d'Estaing. It was only a short walk from Wilson's rooms. These meetings of the Council of Four, that of 8 April, and the one that preceded it the previous week, were absolutely unique in the history of international criminal justice. Never before, or after, have the leaders of the world's most powerful nations devoted so much time to a debate about criminal law and individual responsibility. None of the four who met in Paris in April could be described as an international lawyer, although three of them, Lloyd George, Orlando, and Wilson, had studied law. Only Orlando had a claim to be a legal professional. In any event, there were no experts in international criminal law on whom to call. The four 'virgins' were on virgin territory.

Wilson suggested that they discuss the report of the Commission on Responsibilities, 'article by article'. 'It would be better to approach the matter more broadly, distinguishing clearly between two categories of punishable acts', said Lloyd George. 'First, criminal acts as such; second, those that were ordered in violation of international law. For example, the submarines were ordered to commit what amounted to piracy. Two hundred years ago, pirate ships didn't sink vessels without warning or abandon crews to their fate.'

'I think you agree with me that those whose acts are purely negative, such as an officer who could have prevented a criminal act by refusing to obey an order and did not do so, is guilty of a crime from a moral but not a legal point of view', said Wilson.

'Let us start with submarines', Lloyd George replied. 'By all established laws, their activity cannot be described as anything but piracy. We would have had the right, under the laws of war, to shoot all enemy sailors who took part in submarine warfare. But we thought they were merely obeying orders. We opted to take them prisoner and wait to punish those who gave the criminal orders. Those who ordered the submarine campaign are obviously guilty. This does exculpate certain crimes such as those of submarine commanders ordered that shipwrecked crews be fired upon.'

If they could have attended the meeting, the legal experts who had laboured for nearly two months in the Commission on Responsibilities would have been appalled at the amateurishness of the discussion. Lloyd George seemed mildly obsessed with piracy, a quite irrelevant matter that had understandably never been considered by the Commission. He was dead wrong when he thought it was permissible to shoot submariners taken prisoner. Wilson's comment was equally uninformed. A subordinate who followed a manifestly unlawful order was not excused from criminal liability, although guilty 'from a moral point of view', whatever that expression might mean. Even German courts said as much in war crimes trials of German sailors.[22]

'There is a general responsibility on men like Admiral Tirpitz', said Wilson, referring to the commander of the German Navy, 'as well as those who carried out the crimes, such as the officers who gave the inhumane orders that you referred to'.

'Basically, everyone who perpetrated a criminal act is guilty', Lloyd George insisted. 'The same applies to ill-treatment of prisoners. If an order came from Berlin, the man who gave it should be punished. But given the uneven treatment of prisoners in different camps, I think that more often the responsibility falls on the head of the military district or of the camp.'

Wilson alluded to the dissenting views of Robert Lansing in the Commission on Responsibilities. 'Mr Lansing doesn't disagree with his colleagues concerning criminal acts in the strict sense. What he finds difficult is knowing how they should be judged and by what law. Shall a tribunal be established that will apply its own laws, selecting them from among national legislation? Mr Lansing says there are courts-martial in each country where crimes of this type are prosecuted. Might we combine these courts-martial into an international court-martial, where French, English, Belgians, Italians, and so on would sit. The tribunal would apply laws in force either where the crime took place or in the victim's country of origin. It will be difficult to catch the true culprits because it is so easy to destroy proof that orders were given. I fear that we won't have the evidence.'

'A perpetrator is responsible unless he can show the order from his commander', said Lloyd George. 'The violation of treaties is more difficult. It is a crime against international law. The 1839 Treaty created a league of four nations to guarantee Belgian neutrality. The man who broke the agreement, thereby causing the unspeakable sufferings of the whole world, is the worst of criminals. There are two ways to treat him. His internment can be ordered, by political means, as the Allies did with Napoleon in 1815, or he can be put on trial. I don't care which method we adopt as long as he is punished and placed where he can do no more harm. At the same time, we must prevent intrigues that might enable him to return to power and also make an example of him. As I said, whether we send him to the Falkland Islands or to Devil's Island or somewhere else does not really matter to me.'

'A solemn judgment will make the greatest impression', said Clemenceau.

'What I want to do is to disgrace the Kaiser and avoid encouraging any sympathy for him', explained Wilson. 'If you refuse to try him for starting the war, that is to say as being responsible for the decision that led to the invasion of Belgium, in accordance with the Commission's conclusions, then you only prosecute him for the method that he used to implement his policy of violence. Unfortunately, there are many precedents in past wars.'

'Not so', interrupted Lloyd George. 'There is no equivalent to the invasion of Belgium in the 1870 War or in recent wars between Japan and Russia, or between the United States and Spain. Those were open conflicts that were resolved by a call to arms, but without breaching an international treaty by those who were themselves its guarantors.'

'The German Emperor must be put on trial', said Clemenceau solemnly. 'In the case of Belgium, violation of the law was so flagrant that the public conscience will not be satisfied unless it is treated as a crime.'

'It is indeed a crime', agreed Wilson, 'but one for which no punishment has been provided because there is no legal precedent. We are here today creating the system of the League of Nations. From it will emerge new rules and principles of international law. But today we have to create the principle and the penalty.'

'The violation of a treaty brings a sanction against the country that is responsible', replied Clemenceau. 'But if one man is responsible for what that country did, will we be satisfied knowing that three or four million Germans were killed and then allow the offender to go free?'

'Suppose that in peacetime, the Kaiser, acting alone, had crossed the Belgian border with a rifle and had fired on the inhabitants. The first Belgian policemen on the spot would have had the right to arrest him and to have him hanged. Should he go unpunished because instead of doing this himself, he sent a million men into Belgium?', asked Lloyd George.

'The people would never understand this', agreed Clemenceau.

'It would probably not be understood in the United States either', said Wilson. 'But I can only do what I think to be right, regardless of whether public feeling corresponds to the judgment of my conscience.'

'That countries go to war may be justified', Lloyd George continued. 'But unprovoked aggression, where there is no complaint against the nation attacked, merely because it was convenient to cross its territory, and despite a solemn commitment that was treated like a scrap of paper, is unquestionably a crime.'

Wilson replied: 'I am seeking the sternest lesson. This is an unspeakable crime. But we will not lower ourselves to the level of the criminal by abandoning principles of law. We have not spared him from universal contempt. We may also be entitled to take political precautions against a political threat. But we shouldn't enhance the criminal by bringing him before the highest tribunal we can think of. Public opinion will be the worst punishment.'

'Don't be so sure', said Clemenceau.

'I too have my doubts about this', added Lloyd George. 'No sovereign was worse than James II. We chased him out and replaced him with a Dutchman. In exile, James II became a symbol of legitimacy, and his partisans later sought to create unrest in England. William II was the greatest salesman in Germany and in the world. We recall his speeches on the merchant marine and everything he did to develop his country economically. Industrialists and businessmen in Germany are going to miss him. They will think: "Under his rule, Germany was powerful and wealthy." Who knows what feelings and what acts might follow? What we do must be a lesson for kings and for all those who are responsible for government.'

'What do you propose?' Wilson asked Lloyd George. This was the turning point. Faced with the insistence of the British Prime Minister and of Clemenceau, the American President was signalling his willingness to soften his position.

'I would bring him to trial solely for breaching the 1839 Treaty', answered Lloyd George. 'The tribunal would hear witnesses who would set out how the treaty was violated. They would recall the atrocities committed in Dinant, in Louvain. And then I would say to the Court: "Render judgment!"' The British Prime Minister's remarks were contradictory. He began by stating that prosecution should be confined to violation of the neutrality treaty, but then proceeded to speak of prosecuting atrocities.

'How would such a tribunal be constituted?' asked Wilson.

'Members must be chosen from the highest courts of our various countries—from the French, Belgian, and Italian courts of cassation, from the English Court of Appeal, and from the American Supreme Court. I think Belgium should be the public prosecutor. We only came to Belgium to defend the law, and I can assure you that judges from our courts will be absolutely impartial. They are men of high conscience, without any responsibility to Parliament or before public opinion.'

'This tribunal would be too large if each great power had three representatives', observed Wilson.

'It should be limited to the great powers. Each should have one judge', said Clemenceau. 'Belgium could play the role of public prosecutor.'

'Then I would add Serbia', said Wilson. 'Another question is whether the verdict would need to be unanimous.'

'In England, the jury must decide unanimously.'

'In France, the jury renders its verdict by majority.'

'In Italy, also', said Orlando.

'In all international transactions, the rule is to require unanimity', said Wilson.

'Think about the effect that would be produced by the acquittal of the Emperor of Germany by one vote against four. I wouldn't completely trust our Japanese friends', said Lloyd George. 'It would have a very bad effect in Europe were we to give Japan the right to acquit the Kaiser.'

'It seems to me that we have agreed on the broad lines of this question', said Wilson. 'I would like to hear Mr Orlando's opinion.' Orlando had not yet participated in the debate, which had been monopolised by the two native speakers of English, a language he did not understand.

'I named two delegates to the Commission on Responsibilities', explained Orlando. 'One was a law professor at the University of Rome, the other a counsellor to our Court of Cassation. Both are esteemed legal experts. I left them completely free. They agreed with the conclusions of the majority, with which I concur. But if I must express my personal opinion, I don't think we have to hold trials. I repeat that I defer to my legal experts, which is why I have not participated in the discussion. But from my stand-point, crime is essentially a violation of the domestic law of each entity, of the duty of the subject towards his sovereign. Creating a different prece-dent is a serious matter.'

'I don't disagree that practical necessity forces us to create new law', con-tinued Orlando. 'But we should be wary of the consequences of violating es-tablished principles. We could find ourselves faced with difficulties which we won't know how to resolve because we are no longer sure of our principles. The Italian government supports the Commission's conclusions. But you asked my personal opinion, and I have given it.'

'I asked Signor Orlando to answer us as a lawyer', said Wilson. 'We have distinguished between two quite different situations. The first is violation of the laws of war, with penalties provided when those guilty of such acts are captured in the course of hostilities. For such crimes, I proposed establishing a military tribunal. It would apply known rules, principles and procedure. The second question concerns the responsibility of Heads of State, and the Kaiser in particular. Here we are venturing onto uncharted territory. But what does Signor Orlando think about the first point?'

Orlando replied: 'I listened to Mr Lloyd George's observation about submarine crews: "We had the right to hang them as pirates." According to the laws of war, that would have been justified. But are we entitled to apply in peacetime a law that assumes a state of war and ongoing hostilities? Furthermore, it will be very difficult to determine responsibility. A general who takes prisoners on the battlefield may be able to obtain their orders, if they are carrying any. But we are no longer at war. Will we be able to trace such orders to their origin?

'We are entitled to insist that the Germans themselves judge those who are guilty of certain crimes. But I cannot conceive of an international court es-tablished in peacetime that can invoke principles from wartime. As for Heads of State, it seems to me that there would be less hypocrisy were the peace treaty to impose punishment, on whatever grounds you wish. But I do not understand how we can arraign them before a tribunal. Until now, Heads of State have been viewed as representatives of collectivities. In fact, the col-lectivity is the perpetrator. The people who pay for them. And in the case of Germany, the people and the sovereign are quite united. If we want to punish as an individual a man who was acting as the instrument of the collectivity, we are establishing an entirely new principle.'

'We have some examples: Louis XVI in France, Charles I in England', interjected Clemenceau.

'In both cases, the issue was domestic', answered Orlando. 'At the international level, there is no precedent for what you are trying to do.'

'Was there a precedent when men were given freedom for the first time?' Clemenceau replied. 'Everyone must assume his own responsibility and I assume mine. I don't understand Signor Orlando's argument. He asks if we can apply the laws of war in peacetime? For me, there is one law above all others: that of responsibility. Civilisation is the organisation of human responsibilities. Monsieur Orlando says: "Yes, within each nation." I say: "At the international level." I say this along with President Wilson who, by establishing the foundations of the League of Nations, has had the honour of transferring fundamental principles of domestic law into international law.

'What we want to do today is essential if we want to see international law established', continued Clemenceau. 'None of us doubts that Wilhelm II was responsible for the war. I agree with Signor Orlando about the solidarity of the German people with the Emperor. However, one man gave the orders, while the others followed them. We are told that it is better not to convict him, and to send him into exile where he will face universal scorn. That is one possibility, but it would not be the one I prefer. We now have the perfect opportunity to take the principle of responsibility, which is at the basis of national law, and transpose it into international law.

'There is no precedent? There never is a precedent. What is a precedent? I'll tell you. Men act for good or evil. From the good they do, we create a precedent. From the evil, criminals—be they individuals or Heads of State—create the precedent by their crimes. We have no precedent? Well, that is our best argument. In recent generations was there any precedent for the atrocities perpetrated by the Germans during the present war? For the systematic destruction of wealth so as to eliminate competition, for the torture of prisoners, for submarine piracy, for the horrific treatment of women in occupied territories? To these precedents, we reply with the precedent of justice.

'Our judges, who will convene at the tribunal we propose to create, will be familiar with applying different laws. We will ask them to join their consciences with the perspective of equity. We shall assemble the greatest judges in England, France, America, and Italy. We shall tell them: "Seek within you the principles upon which you must rely in order to judge the greatest crime of history." If necessary, I can resign myself to a solution that I do not favour. But I beg the Heads of State to consider that, if they follow my advice, they will share in the glory of something unprecedented—I readily acknowledge—by establishing international justice. Until the present, it has existed only in books. Finally, we will make it a reality', concluded Clemenceau.

'A practical question arises. We have no legal means to compel Holland to surrender the Kaiser', said Wilson.

'No. But we can tell Holland that should she refuse, she won't be admitted into the League of Nations', answered Lloyd George.

'Referring to crimes by individuals', continued President Wilson, 'Signor Orlando warned us of applying wartime principles during peacetime. As a lawyer, what does he think the peace treaty can impose upon Germany? Can we extend, so to speak, the procedure of wartime to the period following the war?'

Before Orlando could answer Wilson's question, Clemenceau interjected: 'It would be too easy for the criminals if peace cancelled out responsibility. For those who have suffered over these five years, nothing would sow more hatred than an amnesty for the criminals.'

Lloyd George added: 'As far as we are concerned, we have the right to consider that the war will not be over as long as the enemy hasn't handed over the guilty. Along with the question of reparation, this is one of the greatest concerns of English public opinion. We could not sign a peace treaty that left this unresolved.'

'Ideas are becoming clearer about this', said Wilson. 'Nevertheless, please allow me not to take a final decision until I have spoken with Mr Lansing, who has special expertise in the area of international law.'

'In England, we have brought together six or seven of our greatest authorities on matters of international law, including Sir Frederick Pollock', said Lloyd George. 'They concluded unanimously to charge the Kaiser, and all of those who committed crimes against international law. The British government bases its opinion on the conclusions of these legal experts.' This was an exaggerated account of the alleged consensus of the English experts.

Orlando had the last word. He had shifted his view, possibly persuaded by Clemenceau's passionate eloquence. He made one of the very rare references in the discussions of the Council of Four to the Report of the Commission. Perhaps he was the only one of the four virgins who had read it. 'I must add that after having read the Commission's report, I discussed the conclusions with the Italian delegates. We had a serious, even stormy, discussion. They stuck to their position and I didn't want to impose mine upon them. In my opinion, the only principle which justifies our action is Monsieur

Clemenceau's. I accept Monsieur Clemenceau's views, because they raise us above the legal technicalities. It is history that is taking place. It is no longer law. If we consult the codes, we will have great difficulty in finding there what we seek. If we only speak of international morality, it is different. I still insist that Italy has as much to say on this subject of crimes committed as the other Allied nations. The number of Italian ships sunk by submarine on the high seas constitutes a higher proportion of our merchant fleet than losses of the English merchant marine. One hundred thousand Italians died in the enemy's prisoner-of-war camps, victims of ill-treatment.'[23]

That night, Colonel House wrote in his diary that: 'The President yielded more than I thought he would, but not more I think than the occasion required. We had a long talk over the telephone about it tonight.'[24] Wilson had told his colleagues that he wanted to talk this over with Lansing, but the two men rarely 'talked' and there is no record of them having done so during the evening of 8 April, following the conclusion of the afternoon meeting of the Council of Four. Whether Lansing's letter of 8 April was written and delivered to Wilson before or after that day's meeting of the Council is unknown. Probably Wilson had already decided that he would seek compromise with Lloyd George and Clemenceau before the Council met on 8 April, and with that in mind had requested Lansing's views, set out in his letter. It is unlikely that Wilson would have returned from the meeting, and only then commissioned an opinion from Lansing, who would have promptly prepared a thoughtful and detailed letter, all in a matter of a few hours.

Apparently acting on his own, after his chat with House that evening, Wilson prepared two draft clauses for the treaty with Germany. He borrowed some expressions from Lansing's letter, although Lansing could never have intended that his words be used as terms in an international legal agreement. The first clause dealt with prosecution of war criminals in general and specified that they would be tried by national military tribunals 'in the usual way'. This was relatively uncontroversial. Only if the crime was committed against nationals of more than one country would a joint military tribunal be established. Trial of the Kaiser was the subject of Wilson's second paragraph:

> Request to be made of Holland to deliver the ex-Kaiser into the hands of the Allied and Associated Powers for trial before a special tribunal, that tribunal to consist of five judges one of such judges to be appointed by each of the five Powers here named; namely, the United States of America, Great Britain, France, Italy and Japan; the offence for which it is proposed to try him not to be described as a violation of criminal law but as a supreme offence against

international morality and the sanctity of treaties. The punishment to be determined upon is left to the tribunal selected, which is expected to be guided
by the highest motives of international policy with a view to vindicating the
solemn obligations of international undertakings and the validity of international morality.[25]

This text, crafted by President Wilson himself, but inspired by phrases in
Lansing's letter, is the direct ancestor of Article 227 of the Treaty of Versailles.
Lansing is the author of the expressions 'international morality', 'the sanctity
of treaties', and 'high international policy' that Wilson cut and pasted into
his draft. Moreover, the words 'not to be described as a violation of criminal law' reflect the caveat upon which Lansing had insisted in his letter. The
President himself added the clause about demanding the surrender of the
Kaiser. Wilson, too, devised the idea of a 'special tribunal' comprised of five
judges, one each appointed by the five 'Powers', drawing upon the remarks of
Lloyd George at the meeting earlier that day. Wilson seemed to have dropped
his own idea about a role for Serbia as well as the suggestion of Lloyd George
that Belgium provide the prosecutor. The issue of unanimity of the judgment
was not addressed.

The following morning, Wilson stayed in bed until 10 o'clock. The Council
meeting convened an hour later.[26] Wilson read aloud his two draft articles
dealing with prosecutions. 'I remind you of the objections which were made
by the Japanese delegation. But I do not think they are really in conflict with
this text', he said. In reality, Wilson was ignoring the Japanese objections, just
as he had ignored those of Lansing.

'At the heart of the Japanese objections, although they have not said this
as such, is the idea of divine right. It is a notion that Europe has abandoned
forever', said Lloyd George.

'In any case, the Japanese representatives must join in our decision.
Shouldn't they be summoned?', asked Wilson.

Lloyd George cannot but have been thrilled by his success. Nevertheless,
he thought it better to wait for the Japanese 'in order to present them at the
same time with all questions of a general nature in which Japan is interested'. Lloyd George made some rather lengthy remarks on the theme of war
crimes prosecution. They indicate that he was focused on violations of the
laws and customs of war and not on responsibility for starting the war or for
the violation of neutrality. The previous day, Lloyd George had told Wilson
that he thought prosecution should be confined to the invasion of Belgium.
On 9 April, he took a much broader view. It is clear from his remarks that

he thought the scope of 'international morality and the sanctity of treaties' went well beyond the violation of Belgian neutrality. None of the other three leaders challenged Lloyd George's understanding.

'I think that what the President proposes will cover all of the violations of international law that we want to punish', said the British Prime Minister. 'It will be easy for us to prove that these crimes are not mere reprisals against our actions, as the Germans contended, nor are they permitted as new methods of war. Concerning poisonous gas, for example, I can provide documentary evidence that during the Crimean War the British government rejected a proposal to use sulphurous gas. The proposal was made again at the beginning of the war of 1914 by Mr. Winston Churchill but it was rejected once again as contrary to principles that we were not prepared to abandon. The Germans have no right to say that they introduced a new weapon with an invention that we would be sorry not to have made before them; we had the invention, and we refused to use it ourselves.'[27]

During the afternoon session of 9 April, Wilson insisted that the other three leaders actually sign the text. Wilson first passed the paper to Clemenceau. When the French Prime Minister had signed, Wilson gave it to Lloyd George, and to Orlando, and then he affixed his own signature.[28] Japan signed subsequently. The document bore the title 'Outline Suggested with regard to Responsibility and Punishment'.[29] Wilson handed the paper to Maurice Hankey, instructing him to give it to the Drafting Committee so that the formal clauses of the treaty could be prepared. Hankey told Wilson that the original should be left with the Secretary-General of the Conference for retention in the official archives. A sentence was added specifying that if the victims of a given crime were nationals of only one of the belligerents, the trial would take place before that country's military tribunals.[30]

Wilson was rather pleased with himself. He seemed to think it was the others who had given ground, whereas in fact it was the American view that had softened. Following the afternoon session, he went for a drive with his personal physician, Cary Grayson. 'We made progress today, not through match of wits, but simply through my hammering and forcing them to decisions', he told the doctor. Wilson referred to his threat to return to America. 'It appears to me that the *George Washington* incident has had a beneficial effect on the French. They wanted to know when I was going back and I told them in plain language that the results would be the determining factor.'[31]

That evening, Wilson wrote to Lansing to inform him of the developments. 'Here is the formula which I drew up about criminal responsibility.

I have a copy of it signed by all of the four conferees, and I have undertaken to see Baron Makino about it. I sincerely hope that this concludes a very difficult business.'[32] The letter helps to confirm the conclusion that Wilson did not consult Lansing after the meeting of 8 April and before preparing the draft clauses, despite telling his colleagues on the Council of Four that he wished to do this. Had Wilson and Lansing conferred about the solution during the evening of 8 April and agreed upon the compromise text, the President's letter to Lansing the following day would surely have been phrased differently.

Lansing put a brave face on what may have seemed a great personal humiliation, given the opposition to any trial of the Kaiser that he had stubbornly maintained throughout the sessions of the Commission on Responsibilities. But perhaps, like Wilson, he viewed as a triumph what appeared to be a retreat. Although the text adopted by the Council of Four spoke of trial and used judicial language, in substance it had affinities with the Commission of Inquiry proposed by Lansing at the third meeting of the Commission on Responsibilities. Lansing replied to Wilson that the text was 'very satisfactory' given 'the point of view of the position we took on the Commission [of Responsibilities]'. Lansing continued: 'Impressing the proposed action in relation to the ex-Kaiser with the character of international policy rather than an application of legal justice corresponds in my judgment with the proper attitude which should be taken.' Lansing congratulated Wilson on reaching agreement with the others, '[k]nowing the temper and settled purpose' they had adopted.[33]

The first of the two paragraphs presented no difficulty and could easily be incorporated into treaty provisions, Lansing thought. It provided the basis for Articles 228 to 230 of the treaty, governing prosecution of war criminals other than the Kaiser. However, the second paragraph of the Wilson formula, dealing with the trial of the Kaiser, left Lansing in a quandary, he said. It imposed no obligations on Germany itself. This was not quite right, because by accepting the clause Germany could be said to have consented to the trial, a not insignificant point given the possible objection based upon the alleged immunity of the Kaiser. Lansing's main concern was the constitution of a special tribunal, as this would require agreement with the other Powers and, possibly, approval from the other Allied governments. Lansing added that because the provision imposed obligations upon the United States, such as naming a judge and sharing responsibility for the action of the tribunal, consent from the Senate would be necessary.[34]

The Belgians rebuffed the proposal that they be assigned the role of prosecutor before the special tribunal. On 16 April 1919, Clemenceau told the
Council of Four that he thought this had been agreed with Paul Hymans, the
Belgian Foreign Minister, but that the Prime Minister, Léon Delacroix, would
not consent.[35] Because it was a monarchy, some Belgians considered it improper for the country to be involved in prosecuting the Kaiser, Clemenceau
reported. In his memoirs, Hymans indicated his own personal disagreement
with trial of the Kaiser, claiming he had sent Rolin-Jaequemyns to inform
Dutasta, the Secretary of the Conference, that Belgium was opposed. He said
he had explained to Dutasta the reasons for objecting: it would make a martyr
of the Kaiser and violation of a treaty was not a crime for which individuals
could be punished. Referring to newspaper accounts that Belgium would
demand Wilhelm's extradition, he said that this would complicate relations
with the Netherlands.[36] Belgium's reluctance to participate was not an insurmountable obstacle, thought Wilson. 'We have already said that the German
Emperor is to be tried for violating Belgian neutrality. If Belgium doesn't
want to be the prosecutor, we will still reserve the right to call her as a witness.
I do not think she will refuse to appear.' Wilson pointed out that in the draft,
Belgium had not specifically been assigned responsibility for the prosecution,
although the issue had been addressed during the deliberations.[37]

Lloyd George had to manage the leaders of Canada, Australia, New
Zealand, South Africa, Newfoundland, and India. They all met regularly with
British officials and were, in one form or another, using the Peace Conference
in order to assert ambitions for autonomy within what was still being called
the British Empire. Lloyd George reported to the British Empire delegation
on the developments in the Council of Four at its meeting of 11 April 1919.
Present were Robert Borden of Canada, Billy Hughes of Australia, Louis
Botha of South Africa, and William F. Massey of New Zealand. Massey had
been an active member of the British Empire delegation in the Commission
on Responsibilities, taking the lead when Ernest Pollock was absent.
According to the British Prime Minister, 'President Wilson had come round
to the view of his colleagues on this point' despite American hostility to
the idea of an international tribunal and prosecution of the Kaiser. Lloyd
George described how Wilson had himself drafted the provision, agreeing
on the establishment of an international tribunal. Lloyd George explained
that Wilson had insisted there be only one representative of each of the five
Great Powers rather than the larger court contemplated by the Commission,
effectively scotching any hope of a judge from one of the dominions. He said

that Holland would be asked to hand over the Kaiser, who would be tried 'for breaches of international morality, rather than for his responsibility for the outbreak of the war'.[38]

Several days later, Lloyd George circulated the text adopted by the Council of Four to members of the British Empire delegation. Massey replied that the agreement to have five judges was 'probably sufficient', although he pointed out that 'at least one of the Powers referred to has expressed its hesitation and scruples about the possible consequences which might follow a prosecution of Heads of Enemy States for breaches of the laws and customs of war before a "tribunal constituted by the opposite party".' Was he speaking of Japan or of the United States? Massey said he was puzzled by the charge of 'a supreme offence against international morality and the sanctity of treaties', which was not described as one under criminal law. A man without legal training, Massey might be forgiven for his bewilderment, but experienced lawyers were just as perplexed. Massey told Lloyd George he was not aware whether a penalty or only an admonition could result. He insisted that 'most people are convinced that such a proceeding will not do justice to the millions who have suffered miseries from the crimes committed during the war period, nor will it give satisfaction to the citizens of the Allied countries … The position, as I look upon it, is simply this—either the ex-Kaiser is responsible for, and guilty of, the offences attributed to him, or he is not; and it is for a competent and properly appointed tribunal to decide'. Only a genuinely criminal trial capable of imposing punishment would be acceptable, wrote Massey. 'If guilty, it will be for the tribunal to fix the punishment. If not guilty, he must be allowed to go free, but all side issues should be avoided. Our aim should be to see that justice should be administered without fear or favour.'[39]

13

Finalising the Treaty
of Versailles

Wilson's 'Outline' provided the guidance, but it was the task of the Drafting Committee of the Conference to transpose his words into treaty language. The Drafting Committee was made up of James Brown Scott for the United States, Cecil B. Hurst for Britain, Henri Fromageot for France, Arturo Ricci-Busatti for Italy, and Harukazu Nagaoka for Japan. It reformulated the two-paragraph text of the Council of Five into four articles. The second paragraph of the Outline, concerning trial of the Kaiser, emerged as a four-paragraph provision:

> The Allied and Associated Powers publicly arraign William II of Hohenzollern, formerly German Emperor, not for an offence against criminal law, but for a supreme offence against international morality and the sanctity of treaties.
>
> A special tribunal will be constituted to try the accused, thereby assuring him the guarantees essential to the right of defence. It will be composed of four judges, one appointed by each of the following five powers: namely, the United States of America, Great Britain, France, Italy and Japan.
>
> In its decision the tribunal will be guided by the highest principles of international policy, with a view to vindicating the solemn obligations of international undertakings and the validity of international morality. It will be its duty to fix the punishment which it considers should be imposed.
>
> The Allied and Associated Powers will address a request to the Government of the Netherlands for the surrender to them of the ex-Emperor in order that he may be put on trial.[1]

The only substantive difference with the text formulated by Wilson and signed by the other four leaders was the addition of the reference to assuring to the Kaiser 'the guarantees essential to the right of defence'. The Drafting Committee delivered the text on 26 April. It was placed on the agenda of the

The Trial of the Kaiser. William A. Schabas. © William A. Schabas, 2018. Published 2018 by Oxford University Press.

fifth plenary session of the Paris Peace Conference, set to meet during the afternoon of 28 April 1919. The draft clauses were published in the French and English press,[2] and a day later the Department of State released them in the United States. This was not the proper way to proceed because the draft clauses needed to be confirmed first by the Council of Five as a faithful expression of its instructions.

The British Empire delegation convened on the morning of 28 April 1919. There was a note of urgency because of the scheduled Plenary session, where it was expected that the draft articles would be discussed. George Barnes, a senior member of the British Government delegation and a Member of Parliament, said the draft provisions on penalties required further discussion by the British Empire delegation. He was in favour of punishing the Kaiser, but it was 'a strong order to ask Germany to give up without specification a large number of her nationals to the mercy of the Allies'. General Louis Botha, the South African Prime Minister, expressed regret that the matter had been left so long without being discussed. Botha may well have felt aggrieved because of his government's experience with the British in the aftermath of the Boer War. The other South African delegate, General Jan Christian Smuts, turned to the clauses concerning the Kaiser, describing them as 'embarrassing'. He pointed out their incompatibility with the recommendation of the Commission on Responsibilities, which had opposed trial of the Kaiser. Smuts was mistaken, because the Commission had supported trial of the former Emperor for violations of the laws and customs of war. 'The members of the Commission were eminent jurists and it would make the Conference ridiculous to publish their report and at the same time to approve measures directly contrary to their opinion', said Smuts.

William Massey told the British Empire delegation meeting that 'in view of certain differences among the members, the whole matter had been referred, with their report, to the Council of Four, who had sought to adjust the differences by the measures indicated in the proposed articles'. He said he felt strongly that the Kaiser should be punished. He was afraid that 'the proposed articles in effect meant letting the ex-Emperor off'. The Australian Prime Minister, William M. Hughes, said he objected to the words 'not for an offence against criminal law'. He also criticised the draft articles for vagueness and inconsistency. 'They started out to vindicate "international morality" and then dropped to "international policy"', he charged. 'We would never get a conviction under them. They would make us ridiculous and cover us with confusion.'[3]

Robert Borden, the Canadian Prime Minister who presided over the British Empire delegation meeting of 28 April, later communicated the mood of discontent to Lloyd George, who had not attended. Borden insisted it would be extremely undesirable for the question of responsibilities to be discussed at the Plenary Conference, despite being on the agenda. Lloyd George explained that the item had been put there without his knowledge. Borden then made the same point to Wilson and Clemenceau, who agreed with Lloyd George that the issue should not be considered at the meeting that afternoon.[4]

Lloyd George, Clemenceau, and Pichon met with Wilson on 1 May to consider the text prepared by the Drafting Committee. With respect to Article 1, concerning the Kaiser, Lloyd George said attention had been drawn to the words 'not for an offence against criminal law but ...'. He said it had been pointed out that the draft might be construed as an admission by the Allied and Associated Powers that the German Emperor had not committed offences against criminal law. He proposed the omission of the phrase. Wilson promptly agreed. Maurice Hankey was instructed to communicate the modification to the Secretary-General for the information of the Drafting Committee.[5]

One of Wilson's biographers noted that in agreeing with Lloyd George, the American President 'violated all the principles for which he had earlier fought so long and hard and that he gave away the victory that he had won in the protocol on responsibilities that the Council of Four had approved on April 9, 1919'. The writer thought it possible that 'Wilson was in a daze and did not know what was going on at this meeting'.[6]

Writing much later about the drafting of Article 227, James Brown Scott claimed 'the American commission rendered a service to the world at large in standing as a rock against the trial of the Kaiser for a legal offence'.[7] Scott wrote that charging the Kaiser solely with an offence against international morality and the sanctity of treaties, and declaring that the judgment would be guided by the highest motives of international policy, amounted to 'an admission that law, in the legal sense of the word, did not exist for either offence, or that its violation was not a crime in the sense of criminal law'.[8] But Scott's contention stumbles upon Wilson's agreement to drop the reference to criminal law. Some rock!

Besides removing the phrase about criminal law, there were two other slight changes to the draft. The Drafting Committee text had referred to four judges, not five. Lloyd George pointed out that this was mere inadvertence because the five powers were named.[9] In the third paragraph, the word 'principles' was replaced with 'motives'.

> The Allied and Associated Powers publicly arraign William II of Hohenzollern, formerly German Emperor for a supreme offence against international morality and the sanctity of treaties.
>
> A special tribunal will be constituted to try the accused, thereby assuring him the guarantees essential to the right of defence. It will be composed of five judges, one appointed by each of the following five powers: namely, the United States of America, Great Britain, France, Italy and Japan.
>
> In its decision the tribunal will be guided by the highest motives of international policy, with a view to vindicating the solemn obligations of international undertakings and the validity of international morality. It will be its duty to fix the punishment which it considers should be imposed.
>
> The Allied and Associated Powers will address a request to the Government of the Netherlands for the surrender to them of the ex-Emperor in order that he may be put on trial.[10]

This was the final text of Article 227.

The trial of the Kaiser returned to the agenda of the Plenary of the Peace Conference on 6 May 1919. The Conference met in Plenary session on only eight occasions. The work of this body, which all of the 'smaller' countries attended, was often quite perfunctory because the main decisions were taken elsewhere, in the intimacy of the Council of Four. Robert Lansing described the Plenary as a 'farce', where the delegates were 'called together to listen, not to criticise or object ... It was medieval rather than modern; despotic rather than democratic.'[11]

There was great anticipation because the German delegation was expected in Paris the following day. The delegate for Honduras, Policarpo Bonilla, was the only person to ask to speak on the penalty provisions of the draft treaty. His short intervention consisted of drawing the attention of the participants to a declaration, labelled a *voeu* or 'wish', issued by his government on 23 April on the issue of the punishment of Kaiser Wilhelm.

> Written legislation of all civilised countries confirms the uncontested principle of natural law that no person shall be judged or punished other than for an offence that has previously been defined expressly and made punishable by law.
>
> The delegation of the country that I have the honour to represent considers the judgment of Wilhelm II of Hohenzollern, former Emperor of Germany, charged pursuant to article 1 of the draft under discussion, as inoperative. There is really no law or international precedent that permits this. A Head of State is only accountable before his own people, who may only

judge and convict him pursuant to legislation that has been duly adopted. In the present case, it would be more logical to judge and convict the German people who followed, joined and tolerated the acts of their rulers, but such conviction can only be effective in accordance with the form that the conference has chosen to follow: imposing upon the German people an indemnity or reparation for all harm caused by an unjust war that it allowed itself to participate in.

Consequently, we believe that there is also no right to demand that the Government of the Netherlands extradite the former German Emperor; and, knowing that there does not exist an applicable extradition treaty between one or several of the Allied and Associated Powers, we consider that the Netherlands cannot perform what is being asked of it without breaching its own laws.[12]

The declaration also criticised the draft provisions aimed at trials of German nationals for violations of the laws and customs of war. It said they were flawed, and that the proper course would be to insert clauses in the treaty requiring Germany to judge its own nationals. Somewhat provocatively, but justifiably, the declaration of Honduras also said that if the purpose was to 'guarantee the rights of humanity and pay homage to absolutely justice', a 'stunning precedent' would be created by including within the treaty a clause of reciprocity, 'stipulating the obligation for the Allied and Associated Governments to bring to justice and punish offences against the laws and customs of war and the laws of their own countries, however few these might be, that were perpetrated by their own nationals'. This is one of the very rare occasions during the entire post-war period when the victors considered whether they too might have perpetrated crimes under international law. Bonilla concluded by acknowledging that his remarks might not please everyone, but that he was confident his view would prevail when spirits became calmer and that in any event it would be welcomed by 'the impartial historian who is to judge the events of today in the future'.[13]

It is not impossible that Robert Lansing and James Brown Scott had a hand in Bonilla's attack on the provisions governing the trial of the Kaiser. Prior to presenting the statement, the Honduran diplomat had sent a copy to the head of the Latin American Desk at the US State Department for his 'esteemed opinion'.[14] That Honduras would solicit the blessing of the US Government for such a statement is unsurprising, given its subservient relationship with Washington at the time. But this is the only evidence of any collusion.

'Tense and Concentrated Hatred'

In mid-April, the German Government was invited to send a delegation to Paris. The Germans were instructed to appear at Versailles on the evening of 25 April in order to receive the text of the preliminaries of the treaty, as drawn up by the Allied and Associated Powers, which was a summary or *précis* of the provisions. On 21 April, Germany responded positively to the invitation. However, its delegation only left Berlin for Paris on 28 April, arriving the following evening. The Germans were lodged at the Hôtel des Réservoirs in Versailles. Now a government building, in its heyday the hotel had hosted Emile Zola, Marcel Proust, and other eminent personalities. The German delegation was headed by Count Ulrich Brockdorff-Rantzau, a seasoned diplomat. Among his achievements was organising the sealed train by which Vladimir Lenin returned to revolutionary Russia from exile in Switzerland in April 1917. Brockdorff-Rantzau was the first Foreign Minister of the Weimar Republic.

On 7 May, at the Plenary Session of the Conference, 'in an atmosphere of tense and concentrated hatred',[15] Clemenceau presented the draft peace treaty accompanied by the official summary to the German delegation. Brockdorff-Rantzau chose to remain seated while Clemenceau spoke, the first but certainly not the last German to manifest bitterness about the terms of the Treaty of Versailles. Speaking to the Conference, Brockdorff-Rantzau admitted a degree of German responsibility for the war, but said: 'We energetically deny that Germany and its people, who were convinced that they fought a war of defence, were alone guilty.' As for wrongs committed during the conduct of the war, 'Germany is not the only guilty one. Every European nation knows of deeds and of people whom their own countrymen remember only with regret.' Brockdorff-Rantzau turned to the terrible suffering within Germany since the armistice, a consequence of Allied interdiction of imports of food and other essentials. He spoke of 'hundreds of thousands of non-combatants who have perished since the 11th of November by reason of the blockade', saying they had been 'killed with cold deliberation after our adversaries had conquered and victory had been assured them. Think of that when you speak of guilt and of punishment.' He concluded that 'guilt of all participants can be fixed only by an impartial inquiry, by a neutral commission before whom all the leading actors of the tragedy may be heard, and to whom all archives will be opened'.[16]

The Germans were instructed to provide their reply within fifteen days, although the deadline was extended subsequently. On 13 May 1919, Brockdorff-Rantzau wrote to the Conference declaring that the German delegates did not share the view about the origin of the war. They did not consider that the former German Government was the party which was solely or chiefly to blame for the war.[17] He asked to be provided with a copy of the report of the Commission on Responsibilities. The request was considered in a joint session of the Commission on Responsibilities and the Commission on Reparations.[18] A draft reply was prepared.[19] The Council of Four decided, on 20 May 1919, that Clemenceau should inform the Germans that the Commission's report was a 'document of an internal character' that could not be transmitted to 'an outsider'.[20] That the Commission was divided on the issues was quite notorious. This had been reported in the press. The report of the Commission had apparently been published in an American newspaper.[21] But the Report would not have been of much assistance to the Germans because the relationship between the provisions in the treaty, especially Article 227, was tenuous at best.

Count Brockdorff-Rantzau replied to Clemenceau on 24 May 1919. He started by conceding German responsibility for the invasion of Belgium, 'as the German armies had only reached the French territories by the violation of Belgium's neutrality. It was for this aggression that the German Government admitted Germany to be responsible: it did not admit Germany's alleged responsibility for the origin of the war or for the merely incidental fact that the formal declaration of war had emanated from Germany'. He protested the refusal to provide the German delegation with a copy of the report of the Commission on Responsibilities: 'The German nation never having assumed the responsibility for the origin of the war, has a right to demand that it be informed by its opponents for what reason and on what evidence these conditions of Peace are based on Germany being to blame for all damages and all sufferings of this war. It cannot therefore consent to be put off with the remark that the data on the question of responsibility collected by the Allied and Associated Governments through a special Commission are documents concerning those governments alone. This, a question of life and death for the German nation, must be discussed in all publicity; methods of secret diplomacy are here out of place.'[22]

On 29 May, Count Brockdorff-Rantzau presented Germany's formal reply to the draft treaty. The remarks on the penalty provisions were prepared by a distinguished panel that included the eminent sociologist Max

Weber. Weber had dabbled in politics, although without great achievement. In 1918, he joined the Heidelberg workers' council. He later helped to draft the Constitution of the Weimar Republic. Weber supported the controversial provision on emergency powers that proved to be the Republic's undoing, in 1933. The German expert panel on the penalty clauses in the treaty also included a prominent international lawyer, Albrecht Mendelssohn Bartholdy, grandson of the great composer, as well as historian Hans Delbrück and diplomat Max Montgelas. With its numerous annexes, the German reply on penalties comprised more than 200 pages.

The German reply said that prosecution of the Kaiser was not founded 'upon any legal basis'. It insisted that 'international law in force provides punishment as a sanction for commandments and prohibitions; no law of any of the interested powers threatens with punishment the violation of the international law of morality or the breach of treaties'. The German document noted that there was 'no criminal tribunal competent to decide the impeachment in question'. For this reason, the drafters of the treaty 'had to create a criminal law with retroactive powers, as exceptional law, to form the basis of judgment'. Moreover, it affirmed that Germany could not allow a German to be put before 'a foreign special tribunal, to be convicted on the basis of an exceptional law promulgated by foreign powers solely against him, on the principles not of right, but of politics, and to be punished for an action which was not punishable at the time it was committed'. The German reply also addressed the provisions governing trials for violations of the laws and customs of war, covered by Articles 228, 229, and 230. It said that Germany could not agree to surrender suspects for trial because its Criminal Code prohibited extradition of German nationals. It went on to challenge the very basis of prosecution of war crimes which it said was a matter reserved to the responsibility of a State, not an individual:

> In the opinion of the German Delegation, one of the noblest objects of the conclusion of peace is to appease passions which mutual reproach for the violation of international law has aroused, by satisfying the offended sense of justice in all cases where an injustice has actually been committed. This end cannot be attained if, as the draft requires, the demand for the atonement of a wrong committed is, for political purposes, accompanied by the branding and proscription of the opponent, or, if, by giving the role of judge to the victor, might is put in the place of right. If a violation of the law is to be atoned for, the proceedings themselves must be legal. Under the law of nations in force at present, only the state, as bearer of the international obligation, is responsible for acts in violation of the laws and customs of war. If satisfaction is to be given

by the punishment of guilty individuals, the injured state itself may not convict; it can only demand the punishment of the state responsible for the guilty
person. Germany has never refused, and once more declares her readiness to
see to it that violations of international law are punished with the full severity
of the law, and that all accusations, from whichever party they come, are examined impartially.

The German delegation said that it was prepared to let an international tribunal rule on whether or not individuals could be punished for violations
of the laws and customs of war, but on the condition of participation by representatives of neutral States. Were the conclusion to be positive, Germany
would then agree to an international tribunal where all violations, committed by both sides, could be judged. Moreover, Germany would also have
an equal share in the constitution of the tribunal. Its jurisdiction would be
restricted to matters of international law, with punishment left to the national courts.

Instead of prosecution, the Germans proposed that the peace agreement
contain an amnesty. '[W]rongs committed by the nationals of both parties, the
necessity for which resulted from the circumstances of the war, should, so far
as the general feeling for justice allows it, be consigned to oblivion upon the
conclusion of peace.' It said that amnesty had been agreed to in many previous peace treaties as a means to 'contribute towards a reconciliation of the
peoples'. Therefore,

> ... each Power should grant the nationals of the other party immunity for all
> criminal acts committed by them in the course of the war to the benefit of their
> own country, or for contravention of the special laws enacted to the detriment of
> enemy aliens; such acts as infringe the laws and customs of war must be excepted.
> Further, certain acts which were committed before the conclusion of peace by
> the inhabitants of a territory occupied by the enemy should be included in the
> amnesty. The unusual circumstances prevailing during a military or conventional
> occupation will often give cause of a political or military behaviour which gen-
> erally loses its significance with the return of the former authorities, and may
> then remain unpunished without injury to the sense of justice.[23]

Replying to Germany

A reply to the German delegation was prepared by a body named the
'Committee on Responsibilities'. This was something new, not provided

for by any decisions of the plenary Peace Conference. It consisted of five members, one from each of the 'Great Powers': Ernest Pollock, who chaired the Committee, James Brown Scott, Ferdinand Larnaude, Gustave Tosti, and Sakutaro Tachi. All had served as delegates or alternates on the Commission on Responsibilities. There was no place for representatives of the smaller countries. The Committee's conclusions were set out in a memorandum dated 7 June. The Committee opposed any concessions to the Germans on the issue of penalties. Its report did not attempt to justify the legal basis of Article 227, saying it was sufficient to say it represented 'a minimum of what is demanded in respect of the violations of international morality, the sanctity of treaties and the most essential rules of justice'. The Committee explained that 'special and exceptional measures have been contemplated arising from the acts with which the German ex-Emperor is charged and the entirely new circumstances under which such acts took place'.

The Committee attempted to interpret Article 227 of the treaty. 'It is important to understand Article 227 aright and it is essential to explain the method of arraignment set up thereby against the German ex-Emperor, otherwise the meaning and import of the Article might be distorted from its true sense', wrote the Committee. It insisted that the 'public arraignment' of the Kaiser 'has not a juridical character as regards its substance, but only in its form'. The justification, said the Committee, was that by giving judicial forms and judicial procedure, and setting up a regularly constituted tribunal, the judgment would not only be 'a most solemn one', but would also ensure 'guarantees to the accused'. Such a judicial procedure would provide 'in the accused's favour a guarantee such as has not hitherto been known to international law; it is in order to ensure him the most complete rights and liberty as regards his defence that the Allied and Associated Powers have consented to set up this procedure'.

This is the closest we come to any attempt at construing the abstruse text of Article 227 by any of those who were involved in its drafting, albeit rather marginally. James Brown Scott was a member of the Drafting Committee of the Conference that had transformed Wilson's text into treaty language. But the members of the Committee on Responsibilities, including James Brown Scott, had not been privy to the discussions in the Council of Four when the basis of Article 227 was adopted. They knew little or nothing of the comments by Lloyd George about the scope of Article 227, made public only decades later. Members of the Committee could not do much more than speculate about the intentions of those who were at the origin of the text. The comments on the rights and freedoms of the Kaiser were cut from whole cloth by the five experts. That issue was far from the minds of the four leaders in early May when they cooked up the scheme. The phrase 'thereby assuring him the guarantees essential to the right of defence' in the second paragraph of Article 227 was only added by the Drafting Committee. The memorandum of the Committee on Responsibilities is the first reference to the Kaiser's fair trial rights as a rationale for Article 227.[24]

On 12 June, the Council of Four discussed a draft reply to the Germans prepared by Phillip Kerr, the personal secretary of Lloyd George.[25] Kerr described the war itself as 'the greatest crime against humanity and the freedom of peoples that any nation, calling itself civilised, has ever consciously committed'. His note focused not on Germany's responsibility for starting the war, but on an issue that the German reply did not really consider at all, 'the savage and inhuman manner in which it was conducted'. Kerr cited 'a series of promiscuous shootings and burnings with the sole object of terrifying the inhabitants into submission by the very frightfulness of their action'. He accused Germany of being the first to use poison gas (Britain, France, and the United States also used various poisonous gases during the war), 'notwithstanding the appalling suffering it entailed'. He also mentioned the long-distance shelling of towns and submarine warfare, described as a 'piratical challenge to international law'.

'Justice, therefore, is the only possible basis for the settlement of the accounts of this terrible war', Kerr's note continued. 'Justice is what the German Delegation asks for and says that Germany had been promised. Justice is what Germany shall have. But it must be justice for all. There must be justice for the dead and wounded and for those who have been orphaned and bereaved that Europe might be freed from Prussian despotism … There must be justice for those millions whose homes and land, ships and property German savagery has spoliated and destroyed.'[26]

Clemenceau said he liked Kerr's document 'well enough as a magazine article', but thought that it was not vigorous enough. Wilson too was hesitant. If Kerr's text was only used 'to reassure our own people that the Germans were not believed', Wilson thought it might be sufficient. The result of the discussion was inconclusive. Even Lloyd George conceded that the summary nature of Kerr's reply was a shortcoming. Something more elaborate would be required if the Germans refused to sign and Allied military action became necessary. Then 'it might be necessary to stir up public opinion again to a certain extent', said Wilson.[27] Later that day, the Council agreed that Kerr's memorandum would make up part of the materials for the answer to the Germans. Kerr was designated as the English member of a five-member committee charged with finalising the reply.[28]

On 16 June, the Allied and Associated Powers delivered their response, consisting of a covering letter and a detailed discussion of the contentious provisions. The covering letter consolidated but also condensed the text prepared by Kerr and the memorandum of the Committee on Responsibilities. It spoke of establishing a deterrent for those who might follow the example of Germany, an idea that had not been present in the earlier drafts. Previous peace settlements had been 'singularly inadequate in preventing the renewal of war', said the letter. The treaty with Germany was to be a break with the past.

> As regards the German contention that a trial of the accused by tribunals appointed by the Allied and Associated Powers would be a one-sided and inequitable proceeding, the Allied and Associated Powers consider that it is impossible to entrust the trial of those directly responsible for offences against humanity and international right to their accomplices in their crimes. Almost the whole world has banded itself together in order to bring to nought the German plan of conquest and dominion. The tribunals they will establish will therefore represent the deliberate judgment of the greater part of the civilised world. The Allied and Associated Powers are prepared to stand by the verdict of history as to the impartiality and justice with which the accused will be tried.

The first version of the paragraph contained, as its penultimate sentence, the words: 'They cannot entertain the proposal to admit to the tribunal the representatives of countries which have taken no part in the war.' The Council decided that it was better to delete the sentence. The covering letter concluded: 'The Allied and Associated Powers must make it clear that this letter and the memorandum attached constitute their last word.'[29]

Robert Lansing cited the Allied reply in a speech to the American Bar Association in Boston, in September 1919. Lansing insisted that Article 227 reflected the vision of the American reservations to the report of the Commission on Responsibilities. 'Manifestly the tribunal thus created is not a court of legal justice, but rather an instrument of political power', he said. Lansing explained that Article 227 'was in accordance with the suggestion made in the American memorandum that there might be a political sanction but no judicial sanction for the offences of having caused the war and violated the neutrality of Belgium and Luxemburg'.[30]

On 21 June, the Conference was rocked by news from Orkney, in the northern reaches of Scotland. Following the armistice of 11 November 1918, the
German fleet had been impounded at Scapa Flow, a deep-water British naval
base. The vessels continued to be manned by German sailors, many of them
in a revolutionary mood. The French, in particular, hoped to claim some of
the warships as a reparation payment. Early in the morning of 21 June, the
German admiral in charge ordered the sailors to scuttle the vessels. Seacocks,
valves, and pipes were opened. The ships slowly filled with water. The once
mighty German Navy sunk to the seabed. More than fifty of the seventy-four
German ships at Scapa Flow were damaged in this way, many of them beyond
repair. The scuttling of the fleet was not strictly prohibited by the armistice,
but there was a sense that it showed bad faith and was contrary to general
principles governing armistices.[31] The events at Scapa Flow brought an end
to any goodwill from which the German delegation at Versailles might have
benefitted.

The same day, the German delegation answered the Allied reply: 'The
Government of the German Republic is ready to sign the Treaty of Peace
without, however, recognising thereby that the German people was the author of the war and without undertaking any responsibility for delivering
persons in accordance with Articles 227 to 230 of the Treaty of Peace.'[32] In
more detailed comments, the Germans said it was impossible to reconcile the
penalty clauses, Articles 227 to 230, with their 'dignity and honour'. Germany
also objected to the 'war guilt clause', Article 231, by which the State assumed responsibility for the loss and damage resulting from 'the aggression of
Germany and her allies'. Article 231 was the first provision in the part of the
treaty dealing with reparations. Finally, Germany also protested the loss of all
of its colonies.[33]

Although the German reply mentioned Article 227 expressly, the fate of
the ex-Kaiser was hardly a priority. In any case, his fortunes lay with the
Dutch Government more than with Germany. Many Germans were relieved
to see the end of Wilhelm, his family, and royalty in general. The real pre-
occupation of the German negotiators was an unconditional undertaking to
surrender their military and political leaders whose numbers had not been
set and whose identities had not been determined. The treaty gave the Allies a
blank cheque and, potentially, the authority to imprison much of the German
elite. Ultimately, none of the penalty provisions of the treaty on which the
German negotiators dug in their heels proved to be a serious threat. When
the time came to arrest and surrender suspects for trial pursuant to Articles

228, 229, and 230, Germany offered modest resistance and the Allies buckled, agreeing that only a handful of second-level officers be brought to justice before German courts.

Wilson's physician brought him the German reply when he awoke on the morning of 22 June. The President read the note, then said to Dr Grayson: 'Germany does not want to accept responsibility for the war alone. We do not charge Germany alone. It is Germany and her allies.'[34] That afternoon, the Council of Four met to discuss the final German reply. Wilson read a draft note affirming that there was no exception or reservation possible. It was agreed to summon a meeting of the full Council for 9 pm and to submit the draft reply for its consideration.[35] The Council agreed on the text. It was signed by Clemenceau and dispatched to Versailles. The Council also decided that the reply should be published in newspapers the following day.[36]

The strain of the treaty provoked the collapse of the German Government, led by Philipp Heinrich Scheidemann since February 1919. He resigned with the rest of the cabinet as a protest against the harsh terms imposed by the obdurate Allies. Gustav Adolf Bauer replaced him as *Reichsministerpräsident*. One of Bauer's first acts was to bid the Supreme Council for a forty-eight-hour extension. This was refused. Alluding to the Scapa Flow incident, Wilson said that 'if he was assured that he was dealing with honourable men, or even ordinary men, he would be willing to give not forty-eight, but twenty-four, hours. However, he shared Mr Lloyd George's suspicions to the full, and did not trust the Germans.'[37]

The Allied armies made preparations to resume the war should Germany not accept the treaty. Rumours circulated that the Kaiser might be returning to Germany to lead a revived militarism. Late in the afternoon of 22 June, Balfour reported on a dispatch from the Weimar Government to the German delegation in Versailles that said Germany had agreed to sign, 'the Allies having decided to employ the most extreme violence to force Germany to accept terms without material importance, but which tend to besmirch the honour of Germany, and since the German people no longer have the means to defend themselves'.[38] The news arrived as the Council of Four was planning the signing ceremony, then scheduled for the afternoon of the following day.[39] At 5.40 pm, the Secretary of the Conference entered the room with the official note from the Germans announcing their unconditional acceptance of the treaty. 'Orders were given for guns to be fired. No further discussion took place.'[40]

The treaty was formally signed on 28 June, five years to the day from the assassination in Sarajevo. The symbolic venue was the Hall of Mirrors at the Palace of Versailles, in the western suburbs of Paris, where the German Empire had been proclaimed not quite half a century earlier. For many, the mood was one of relief and celebration. It concluded months of tense negotiation, not so much with the Germans, who for most of the time were bystanders at best, but among the Allies themselves as they defined the new borders of Europe, creating new States from the remnants of old empires and distributing Germany's modest colonial possessions among themselves. But there was also much anxiety, rooted in concern that the harshness of the terms had engendered an inherently unstable peace. In the weeks and months that followed, the young Adolf Hitler was radicalised. He spent the summer obsessively studying the provisions of the Treaty of Versailles. By October, as he later described in *Mein Kampf*, he was haranguing the growing crowds of his young movement about the disastrous peace agreement accepted by Germany's leaders.

14

Implementing Article 227

The final paragraph of Article 227 commits the Allied and Associated Powers to 'address a request to the Government of the Netherlands for the surrender to them of the ex-Emperor in order that he may be put on trial'. That the Netherlands would readily consent to surrender the Kaiser was an early assumption of the Allies. In his famous presentation to the Imperial War Cabinet in November 1918, Attorney General F. E. Smith had said he thought it 'unnecessary to ask whether in law we can extradite him because it seems to me that Holland must, in effect, give him up'.[1] Over the months that followed, others expressed similar thoughts. The Allies were intoxicated with victory and may have assumed that their overwhelming military and economic power meant they could dictate terms not only to Germany, but even to neutrals.

Dutch interests at the Paris Peace Conference were overseen by Joost van Hamel, a Dutch parliamentarian and law professor at the University of Amsterdam. In early May, the Americans sought him out for an indication of the attitude that the Netherlands might take to the request to surrender the Kaiser. Van Hamel cited the 'awkward position', a 'legal and moral dilemma', that the provision in the draft treaty with Germany had created for Holland. Insisting he was speaking in his personal capacity, Van Hamel explained that the former Kaiser was in the Netherlands as a fugitive, 'an uninvited foreigner'. He said no ordinary case for extradition existed as the Kaiser had not been charged with a criminal offence. Van Hamel referred to the Dutch tradition of providing asylum to fugitives. At the same time, he acknowledged that justification might be found in principles of international justice and morals. He said the Netherlands could depart from existing extradition law on the condition that trial be based on 'well-defined charges of a condemnable breach of the precepts of law amongst nations'. Van Hamel thought that the Conference ought to address the summons to the Kaiser himself rather than to the Dutch Government.[2]

On 19 June 1919, George Curzon discussed the issue with the Dutch Ambassador to London, Reneke de Marees van Swinderen. Curzon found that the Netherlands was 'ill informed as to the final conclusions which had been arrived at in Paris on the subject'. He reported that the Dutch envoy 'sought information from me as to whether the trial was to be persisted in, what form it was likely to take, and whether a demand for the surrender of the Kaiser would be made to his own government'. At this point, the final paragraph of Article 227 declaring that the Allies were to request the Kaiser's surrender from the Dutch Government had been in existence, and fairly widely circulated in Paris, at least, for nearly two months! Curzon confessed to being taken a bit by surprise, as he had not expected to discuss the matter.

Curzon impressed upon the Dutch Ambassador that the trial should be held 'not so much for the purpose of condemning or punishing the accused if found guilty, as for the purpose of showing the world in a manner which none could contest, and which would remain both a warning and a precedent to the end of time, that crimes of so heinous a character could not pass unnoticed, however exalted the station of the individual who had been guilt of perpetrating them'. When Van Swinderen asked what the sentence might be, Curzon answered that this was 'a matter of relatively minor significance compared with the fact that a sentence of condemnation had been passed'. In his note on the meeting, which was circulated to the Cabinet, Curzon wrote that he 'looked upon the moral deterrent of such action as far more important than the execution of vengeance upon the guilty'.

The Dutch Ambassador objected to the fairness of a tribunal composed exclusively of the Kaiser's enemies. Curzon answered that there was no validity to such charges. 'How, indeed, could a tribunal be composed which did not consist of the enemies of the Kaiser!', he said. 'Was it conceivable that a tribunal should be set up with judges from the smaller neutral States who had taken no part in the war? Such a proposal was out of the question.' Curzon contended that the Kaiser would actually get a fairer hearing from his enemies, because his friends 'would be impelled by every consideration of honour and expediency to show that they were not affected by their friendship, [whereas] his enemies, on the other hand would be more likely to seek some excuse for demonstrating that they were not actuated by motives of wrath or vengeance, but desired to be scrupulously just and fair.'

Ambassador Van Swinderen was 'very anxious' to know what the nature of the demand presented by the Allies might be. Curzon declined to provide him with details, but he advised the Dutch Government against 'making a fuss about the matter or putting technical obstacles in the way'. He urged it to meet the request of the Powers 'with as much compliance and as little disturbance as they could. What object could there be in endeavouring to protect a monarch who had not been invited to take refuge in their country who had forced himself upon their hospitality whose presence could not fail to be very irksome both to the Dutch Government and the Dutch people.'

Any attempt to shield the Kaiser 'would be open to very grave misrepresentation at the hands of both the present and succeeding generations'.

The Dutch Ambassador suggested that the Kaiser himself might offer to appear before the tribunal without any demand being made for his surrender. He offered no explanation as to why he entertained such a possibility. Perhaps this was only his own intuition. Possibly, however, the idea was being discussed within the Dutch Government and even with the Kaiser himself. Curzon did not react to the point.[3]

At one of the final meetings of the Council of Four, on 25 June, Wilson raised the matter with his colleagues. 'Holland is morally obliged to surrender the Kaiser, but I wish to make it as easy for her as possible', said the American President. He was concerned that the request be framed in such a way as to relieve Holland of an appearance that it had breached hospitality. 'We have no means to compel Holland to give us satisfaction', he cautioned.

'I believe we can find some', said Lloyd George. One of the levers that the British considered was denying membership in the League of Nations to the Netherlands. Lloyd George was less sensitive than Wilson about Dutch *amour propre*. He insisted that the Allies could not afford to allow Holland to stand in the way of Wilhelm's prosecution. Clemenceau said he would be surprised if Holland objected. 'Shouldn't we address the Dutch as soon as possible?', asked Clemenceau. 'We can't do it before the treaty goes into effect', answered Wilson.[4]

Signature of the treaty, which took place a few days later, did not mean that the Treaty of Versailles had been brought 'into effect'. The subsequent stage of ratification would also be required, as Wilson was to be painfully reminded upon his return to the United States. In fact, the treaty did not enter into force for another six and a half months, in early 1920. The Council of Four entrusted Robert Lansing, the American Secretary of State and the chairman of the Commission on Responsibilities, with drafting a request to be sent to the Dutch Government. With his usual efficiency, Lansing had a text ready for the Council of Four the following morning.[5] Explaining his draft in a covering letter to President Wilson, Lansing said it was advisable to recall that all of the treaty's signatories, including Germany, were in agreement. No details about the charges against the ex-Emperor were provided aside from the text of Article 227 itself. In his letter, Lansing told Wilson that the draft note 'stated and most clear that the offence is moral', but it did not in fact do this. Lansing did not specify the time and place of delivery, explaining to the President that it was better to leave these indefinite for the time being. He thought it might be appropriate to suggest delivery within one month of deposit of ratifications. Lansing suggested that the Kaiser might be surrendered to the country where the trial was to take place. He indicated that this could be England, which had already expressed its eagerness to host the proceedings.[6]

On 26 June, the Council accepted Lansing's text. Lloyd George described it as a 'very able document'.[7] The Japanese representative, Baron Makino, reserved his assent until he had studied the text more closely. Hankey circulated the letter adopted by the Council, but with the proviso that there was no question of sending it at present. The letter would be used when the time came to implement Article 227, Hankey explained.[8] In January 1920, when the treaty entered into force and the time had come to ask the Dutch to surrender the Kaiser, neither Lloyd George nor Clemenceau could even recall Lansing's letter having been discussed or accepted. Possibly that is because on 26 June their minds were focused on an unfolding crisis, one generated by the tension and uncertainty surrounding signing of the treaty, but based entirely upon rumours that proved to be unfounded.

Flight of the Crown Prince

On 26 June 1919, two days before the signing of the Treaty of Versailles, reports reached Paris from the British Military Mission in Berlin that the German Crown Prince, Friedrich Wilhelm Victor August Ernst of Hohenzollern, had left his place of internment in the northwest of Holland and was driving east, 'destination unknown', accompanied by his staff officers.[9] Like his father, the Crown Prince, then 37 years old, had also fled to the Netherlands in early November 1918. Wilhelm junior stayed briefly at Hillenraadt Castle, adjacent to the German border, until the Dutch cabinet dispatched him to Wieringen, then a remote island in the northwest of the country (land reclamation has since joined Wieringen to the mainland). Crown Prince Wilhelm was housed in an abandoned parsonage—he described it as 'bare and desolate'—without electricity or plumbing.

For a few days, the rumour about the flight of the Crown Prince nourished suggestions that the Kaiser too might be planning a return to Germany. Curzon thought that the Allies needed to warn the Dutch against 'any similar attempt on the part of ex-Emperor coupled with intimation that they will be held responsible for any failure to produce him when request for his surrender is made'.[10] The British Ambassador, Walter Townley, who then had only a few days left in his posting to The Hague, was instructed to ask the Dutch Government whether the Crown Prince's departure had been arranged or approved by them.[11] As one of his final acts, Townley met with the Queen of the Netherlands, the Prime Minister, and the Minister for Foreign Affairs. He reported to London that he had 'impressed upon them the gravity of Holland's responsibility' and that the two ministers 'repeatedly emphasised that they have not the smallest reason to anticipate that German Emperor proposes to leave the country'.[12]

Lloyd George conveyed the news to his colleagues in the Council of Four on 26 June. Noting that the Kaiser's son was accompanied by a staff officer, Lloyd George said that 'nothing good can come of this ... I am told that he is not as stupid as he looks and that he can be quite devious.' The British Prime Minister insisted that the Allies tell the Dutch they were not to let the Kaiser cross the border, even though '[f]rom the strictly legal standpoint, he has the right to go to where he wants'.[13]

At Clemenceau's suggestion, Arthur Balfour prepared a note for the Dutch Government. It was harsh in tone and would prove to be a colossal miscalculation. Balfour's text angered the Dutch, damaging relations with them and strengthening the hand of those who wanted to resist Allied appeals to surrender Wilhelm. After invoking the 'interests of Peace', the note said the Allies had heard 'with great surprise that the titular Crown Prince, who is a German combatant officer of high rank, has been permitted in violation of the laws of war to escape from the neutral country in which he was interned'. Assuming the truth of the reports, the message said that the Allies 'trust[ed] that no similar breach of international obligation will be permitted in the far more important case of the ex-Kaiser'. Within a few days, it became clear that the entire story about the flight of the Crown Prince was a fabrication. The erroneous allegation was removed from the Allied note in a 'modification' distributed by the Secretariat-General of the Peace Conference.[14]

The note went on to describe the Kaiser as 'the potentate whom all the world outside Germany deems guilty of bringing on the great war, and of pursuing it by methods of deliberate barbarism'. Noting that the Kaiser would be formally arraigned by the Treaty of Peace, which was about to be signed, it said 'he still represents the military party whose influence has ruined his country and brought infinite suffering on the human race. His escape would threaten the peace so hardly achieved and even not now finally secured.' Allowing the Kaiser to escape would be 'an international crime, which could not be forgiven those who have contributed to it by their carelessness or their connivance'. In conclusion, the note said that should the Dutch Government consider that safe custody of the Kaiser was too onerous an obligation, 'the Allied and Associated Governments are willing to undertake the duty and so relieve a neutral State of a thankless task which it never sought but which it is under a grave obligation to carry out'.[15] Lloyd George, Clemenceau, and Wilson agreed with Balfour's draft.

'I think the letter should be published', Clemenceau told his colleagues.

'Yes, but not before the Dutch Government has had time to take its precautionary measures', said Lloyd George. 'The Kaiser doesn't have to be warned before it. I propose that publication take place only on Saturday.' The Council of Four agreed that the telegram should appear in the morning newspapers of Sunday 29 June.[16] As President of the Conference, Clemenceau personally addressed the telegram to the Dutch Government on 27 June. It was delivered by the French *chargé d'affaires* in The Hague who remarked to a colleague at the time that 'it appeared to contain a threat'.[17]

'Incredible' was the reaction of the Dutch Ambassador to London. On the one hand, the Netherlands was being reproached for harbouring the Kaiser and the Crown Prince, he protested. Now it was to be blamed for letting them depart. Van Swinderen said that both of the German royals were forbidden by the Dutch from leaving their assigned residence. But he said no precaution had been taken to prevent them leaving the Netherlands if they so wished. Moreover, the Dutch Government 'would be glad to be rid of them'.[18]

Arnold Robertson, now the British *chargé d'affaires* following the departure of Walter Townley, complained to the Foreign Office that the presentation of 'so serious a communication being made in writing' put him in an 'extremely embarrassing position'. He said that the verbal warnings given by Townley 'appear sufficiently to have met the case for the moment, and are much less likely to irritate and prejudice the Netherlands Government than Notes of tenor of that sent in by my French colleague which are likely to defeat their own object'. Robertson said that neither the Dutch Government nor the Dutch press or people 'are by any means convinced that whole responsibility for war rests on shoulders of Germany and her former Emperor, nor are they convinced that atrocities and violations of international law were only committed by one side. German propaganda has done its work.'

'Economic considerations and fact that Germany is Holland's "Hinterland" naturally incline Dutch to interested if not convinced leniency towards her Eastern neighbour', continued Robertson. 'Further, Dutch have strong and obstinate views of their own on international law to the letter of which they are inclined to adhere. It is also important to remember that position of Monarchy is by no means secure in this country and in some circles here surrender of a former Sovereign would be regarded as a dangerous precedent, likely to diminish prestige of Monarchy generally. Finally, there is in Holland a strong feeling against surrendering a man to be tried by his accuser. I do not think that Netherlands Government have yet made up their minds as to exact status of their unwelcome guests, or as to what power they have to hold them or to hand them over. Negotiations will be difficult and delicate but I do not despair as to success if we take line of persuasion and avoid Notes that savour of hectoring in the German manner, which will only harden the hearts of the Netherlands Government and incline them still further to adhere to letter of law as they interpret it. Much is being said and written here about a "Peace of violence" and I venture to think it will be your view that we should avoid all appearance of "Bullying Dutch" who are after all a "Small Nation".'[19]

The Dutch reply to the Clemenceau letter observed that the communication was 'only based on rumours', describing it as 'an admonition to a neutral and friendly Government which has painfully surprised Royal Government'. The Dutch insisted that not only were they 'conscious of their international obligations; they are also conscious of not having failed to fulfil them'.[20] Nevertheless, heightened security was imposed at Amerongen. The Kaiser made it clear to the Dutch Government that he had no plans to leave.[21]

The Crown Prince remained in Wieringen for several more years, spending his time learning how to forge horseshoes. He returned to Germany in 1923, on the symbolic date of 9 November, the day the Kaiser had fled to Holland. This apparently angered his father. Back in Germany, the Crown Prince associated himself with extreme right-wing causes, despite a promise when he returned that he would not engage in politics. He supported Hitler until he realised that the Nazis had no interest in restoring the monarchy. Captured by the French at the end of the Second World War, he was briefly detained on the basis of war crimes charges outstanding from the time of the First World War, although these were not pursued. Wilhelm junior died in 1951.

The Kaiser's Doppelgänger

A creative approach about how to proceed, advanced by some German monarchists, was for the Kaiser to surrender voluntarily. This would strengthen his prestige, provide him with a platform to advance his own views on the origins of the war, and help to resolve the more contentious parts of the treaty. However, when Wilhelm received letters from his supporters in Germany urging such a course, he reacted with anger and trepidation. He said he would never assent to an earthly court.[22]

Another option was for other German leaders to come forward and accept responsibility for the war. On 28 June, the date when the treaty was signed, a curious note arrived from Theodor von Bethmann-Hollweg. He had been Germany's Chancellor at the time of the outbreak of the war. Bethmann-Hollweg was ousted during a Reichstag revolt in mid-1917. Like so many prominent personalities of the time, Bethmann-Hollweg had lost one of his sons in combat. Bethmann-Hollweg's letter 'beg[ged] leave to request the Governments of the Allied and Associated Powers to direct against my person the procedure which they propose to initiate against the Emperor'. Bethmann-Hollweg offered himself as the Kaiser's *alter ego*. 'In accordance with the constitutional laws of Germany, it is I who, in my capacity of former Chancellor of the Empire, bear the exclusive responsibility for political acts of the Emperor during my tenure of office', he wrote.[23]

'I confess that I chuckled', wrote Hankey when he saw the letter, 'for I had always insisted that the proposal to try the Kaiser was an outrage'.[24] Immediately after the conclusion of the signing ceremony of the Treaty of Versailles, on 28 June, the Council met in the Senate Chamber of the Versailles Palace to discuss Bethmann-Hollweg's peculiar proposal. Clemenceau,

Wilson, Lloyd George, Sonnino, and Makino were all present. Clemenceau read aloud the note, which was in French. Mantoux translated it into English.

'It is the best thing he has ever done', quipped Wilson.

'He was never one of the worst', said Lloyd George.

Clemenceau asked if the Council should reply. He thought that they should say the matter would be put before the high tribunal once it had been established. 'No, it concerns the indictment which is something that arises before the tribunal is established', said Lloyd George.

'Bethmann-Hollweg is undoubtedly on the list of those who should be charged', observed Clemenceau. He was referring to the list of Germans charged with war crimes pursuant to Articles 228, 229, and 230 of the treaty.

Wilson disagreed. 'He doesn't belong to either of the two categories of those we intend to put on trial. On the one hand, the Kaiser is charged with breaching Belgian neutrality. On the other hand are those who have violated the laws of war. Neither count applies to Bethmann-Hollweg. He relies on a literal reading of the Imperial constitution.'

'His position would be right if invoked by an English minister. Lord Grey, not the King, was responsible for the activities of our Foreign Office when the war began', said Lloyd George.

'Unfortunately for that argument', replied Wilson, 'we know how the German constitution operated.'

'The German Emperor often said that he was the master and all was subject to his will', said Clemenceau.

'We can write that we respect Herr Bethmann-Hollweg's intentions, but that we reject his interpretation of the German constitution. I've studied that constitution very closely and I know it well', said Wilson.

The taciturn Japanese representative, Nobuaki Makino, asked if the Chancellor was not responsible for the sovereign under the German Constitution.

'That is not my recollection', answered Wilson.

The Council decided that the Commission on Responsibilities should be asked to draft a reply to Bethmann-Hollweg's letter. It wanted 'the spirit in which the offer was made' to be recognised, but said it could not accept Bethmann-Hollweg's interpretation of the German Constitution.[25] It was not entirely clear to whom the Council had addressed its request for a draft reply. The American delegation raised the issue in a memorandum circulated to the other four Allied Powers. The Americans noted that the Council had indicated the 'Commission on Responsibilities' was to draft the reply to Bethmann-Hollweg. But in the mind of the American delegates, that body had concluded its work with the submission of its report in March. In June, the Council had established a smaller 'Committee on Responsibilities' comprised of a member from each of the five 'Powers'. The Committee prepared the reply to the German observations on the penalty clauses of the treaty. But it, too, according to Cecil Hurst of the British Foreign Office, had ceased to exist by the end of June.[26] The American delegates pointed out that the report of the original Commission on Responsibilities had not been adopted by the Council and that the body did not therefore enjoy the Council's confidence. The Americans recommended that the smaller Committee on Responsibilities, to be chaired by Robert Lansing, prepare the reply to Bethmann-Hollweg. The American memorandum said the answer to Bethmann-Hollweg could be found in Article 227 of the treaty, which contemplated the Kaiser alone:

> His former Chancellor can neither appear before this tribunal as defendant nor determine the guilt or innocence of his erstwhile master. While the proposal of the ex-Imperial Chancellor is highly creditable to him as a man and former servant of the late Emperor, Herr von Bethmann-Hollweg should as a jurist, recognise that his proposal is inconsistent with the terms of the Treaty under which the Ex-Emperor's liability 'for a supreme offence against international morality and the sanctity of treaties' is to be tried and determined.[27]

A draft reply was adopted by the Committee on Responsibilities. Referring to the provisions of the Treaty of Versailles, it insisted that there could be no question of any modification. Article 227 was applicable to the Kaiser alone, while all others were subject to Article 228. 'The ex-German Emperor, by virtue of the right of defence reserved and guaranteed to him by Article 227, has the right to avail himself before the Special Tribunal of the objections and exceptions in form and substance, in law and in fact which can be invoked in his behalf', the reply stated. It concluded by declaring that were the Powers to substitute their views, they would be exceeding their responsibility and, in effect, usurping the role of the special tribunal described in Article 227. Only it had the authority to determine the responsibility and culpability of Wilhelm for a supreme offence against international morality and the sanctity of treaties.[28] The 'Heads of Delegations', the body that replaced the Council of Five following conclusion of the Treaty of Versailles, decided that no reply should be sent to Bethmann-Hollweg.[29] In the months that followed, Bethmann-Hollweg was suspected of being at the centre of monarchist intrigues. He withdrew from politics and wrote his memoirs, dying of pneumonia on 1 January 1921.

Others also stepped forward. Unlike Bethmann-Hollweg, who played a central role in the July crisis and thus in the outbreak of the war, these volunteers had no connection with the acts for which Wilhelm might be punished. For example, in August 1919, several hundred women in Silesia addressed an appeal 'to the Britisch [sic] Government', offering to take the place of the Kaiser. 'Extraordinary are the workings of the German mind', minuted a Foreign Office functionary.[30] On 5 August 1919, the German representative in Paris, Von Lersner, wrote to Clemenceau in his capacity as president of the Peace Conference:

> By order of my Government and in accordance with a wish expressed by General von Falkenhayn I have the honour to report to you the General's declaration that, as Chief of the General Staff of the Field Forces for the period between 14th September 1914 and 29th August 1916, he was responsible for the arrangements made by the German High Command and therefore all the decisions and orders of the Ex-Emperor connected with the conduct of the war.[31]

An odd statement, it didn't exactly exculpate the Kaiser. It might even have been useful evidence for the prosecution.

Fulfilling 'the natural duty of son and officer', the Kaiser's second son, Prince Eitel Friedrich, also offered to stand in.[32] In February 1920, the Crown Prince presented himself as a sacrificial lamb, not as a substitute for his father, but rather in place of the military and political leaders that the Allies were seeking to prosecute under Articles 228, 229, and 230 of the Treaty of Versailles. He wrote directly to King George V: 'As former heir to the throne of my German Fatherland I am willing to offer myself on behalf of my compatriots in this fateful hour.' The Crown Prince said that if a sacrifice was required, 'let them take me instead of the nine hundred Germans whose only fault was that they served their Fatherland in war'.[33] King George seems to have ignored the letter.

15

Readying the Case for Trial

For nearly six months, the Commission on Responsibilities followed by the Council of Four had assumed that post-war justice was to be delivered by an international tribunal, variously described as a 'high tribunal' and a 'special tribunal'. Article 227 of the Treaty of Versailles provided that this tribunal would be composed of five judges, one from each of the 'Powers'. The Commission on Responsibilities had set out some general guidelines for its procedure and organisation. But until late June 1919, there is no evidence of any consideration being given to the place of trial.

'I'm not sure where it is going to be held', said Clemenceau at the 25 June 1919 meeting of the Council of Four.

'It certainly can't be held in a neutral country', said Lloyd George. 'I think the trial has to be held either in England or in America. Memories of the invasion are still too fresh in France or Belgium and there is still too much anger.'

'What is the thinking in America?', Clemenceau asked Wilson.

'The Americans wouldn't like to host the trial', Wilson responded. He also said that the trial should not take place 'in any great city'.

'It would probably be best to hold the trial in England. Do we agree?', asked Lloyd George.

The transcript prepared by Mantoux indicates that there was 'Assent' to the proposal that the trial be held in England.[1] Hankey's minutes record that Clemenceau wished to consult his colleagues on the subject and would reply the following day.[2] According to the Hankey minutes of the following day's meeting, Clemenceau again asked for more time before agreeing to trial of the Kaiser in England.[3] Hankey later reported that on 2 July he received a telephone call from Clemenceau's office informing him that the French Prime Minister had accepted trial in England.[4]

The Trial of the Kaiser. William A. Schabas. © William A. Schabas, 2018. Published 2018 by Oxford University Press.

On 3 July, Lloyd George addressed the House of Commons, presenting legislation for the implementation of the Treaty of Versailles. He spoke of the trial of the Kaiser, telling the parliamentarians that '[t]he allied countries have decided quite unanimously that the tribunal shall be an Inter-Allied one, and that it shall sit in London for the trial of the person supremely responsible for this War'. Saying that it had been decided to have an 'Inter-Allied' tribunal was unsurprising; this was in the treaty. But it was the first time that London had been mentioned as the venue for the trial.[5] 'Then the Kaiser looks like getting to London after all', quipped Arthur Hayday MP, to general laughter.

The following day, the *Daily Mail*, a newspaper not always reputed for the scrupulous accuracy of its journalism, provided a detailed account of plans for the trial in London. It reported that the British Government had received assurances from the Dutch that they would surrender Wilhelm. The Kaiser was to be imprisoned in the Tower of London. The *Daily Mail* said that the death penalty would not be sought, but that if found guilty the Kaiser would be banished for life to some remote island.[6] The *Daily Mail*'s account was then picked up by newspapers in other countries. According to the *New York Times*, Lord Sumner would be the presiding judge. It identified Douglass White, then Chief Justice of the United States Supreme Court, as the 'logical choice of the American Government' to fill their position on the bench. Gordon Hewart, England's Solicitor General, would lead for the prosecution.[7] The State Department was reported to be taken by surprise at the announcement of trial in London, although its officials acknowledged an agreement might well have been reached by the Council of Four without them knowing.[8]

Lloyd George had overstepped himself slightly, perhaps inadvertently, in declaring that the trial was to be held in London. He later told the War Cabinet that he had misspoken and that he had meant to say England.[9] The agreement in the Council of Four was for trial in England, with no particular location specified. President Wilson's remark that it not be held in a major city seemed to rule out London.

This issue sparked the attention of someone with a special interest in the fate of Wilhelm, but who had been keeping a low profile: his first cousin, King George V. The two were grandsons of Queen Victoria. As children, George and Wilhelm had played together, but their relations as monarchs had been frosty for many years, consistent with national foreign policies. In 1917, the name of the English royal house was changed from Saxe-Coburg and Gotha to Windsor so as to play down its German ancestry. In November 1918, the King wrote about the Kaiser in his diary: 'Has utterly ruined his country and himself. I look upon him as the greatest criminal known for having plunged the world into this ghastly war which has lasted over four years and three months with all its misery.'[10] There is some evidence that King George disapproved of the War Cabinet decision in November 1918 to push for trial of the Kaiser.[11]

According to Hankey, Lloyd George's declaration in Parliament on 3 July provoked 'a violent tirade ... on and off for half an hour' by his cousin.[12] King George told Lloyd George that he had not been previously informed that the trial was to be held in London. It is not known how the Prime Minister responded. The King pursued the matter, verifying the minutes of the Council of Four and learning of the decision to hold the trial in England. On the King's instructions, his private secretary, Lord Stamfordham, wrote to one of Lloyd George's aides that 'the King now thinks that the Prime Minister will understand His Majesty's feelings of surprise on learning for the first time, from the Prime Minister's speech delivered in the House of Commons on the 3rd instant, of the momentous decision arrived at the night before in Paris'.[13] This prompted a letter of explanation from Maurice Hankey to the King's private secretary. 'I blame myself that the matter is not more fully dealt with in the minutes', he said. Hankey respectfully challenged the King's claim that he had been taken by surprise. He noted that nobody present at the Council of Four sessions could have any doubt that the trial would take place in England, subject only to Clemenceau obtaining the consent of his colleagues. He noted that once Wilson had ruled out trial in the United States, there were no other candidates. He wrote:

> Is it not a reasonable inference from this that by the 26th his trial in England was clearly contemplated, unless Monsieur Clemenceau continued to withhold his assent? What actually occurred was that the proposal was made that the Kaiser should be tried in England, and there was no dissent. It was later in the meeting that Monsieur Clemenceau harked back to it and asked that his final decision might be reserved still longer ... The two Minutes taken together make it perfectly clear that the Council were on the eve of such a decision, and that, if any exception was taken to it by those who had access to the Minutes, there was no time to lose.[14]

The King was still not satisfied with the explanation. Stamfordham replied to Hankey:

> The Minutes give no reason for Monsieur Clemenceau's refusal to agree with his colleagues and his last words on the 25th were to ask for more time before he could give his final assent to the trial of the Kaiser, not in *London*, but

even in England. This apparently was not given until July 2nd. Throughout the discussions as recorded the question of *London* was never mooted, though President Wilson deprecate the trial taking place in any great city. I can only reiterate that the King feel aggrieved that the decision that the trial should be held in London, a decision of such supreme general importance and one so especially affecting His Majesty personally, was not communicated to him in some way otherwise than through the medium of the Press.[15]

Hankey replied that the Prime Minister was now 'inclined to agree that London would not be the best place and informally has been discussing various other possibilities in England'. Hankey also conceded that London was not specifically mentioned in the minutes of the Council of Four, and that Wilson had opposed the idea of holding the trial in a big city. He apologised for not directly informing the King when Clemenceau confirmed his agreement, although why he would have done this is puzzling. Hankey did not normally notify the King directly of such details.[16]

Others provide clues to the King's sensitivity about trial in London. The Bishop of Chelmsford wrote to Stamfordham:

I am profoundly distressed—no other words express what I feel—concerning the trial of the Kaiser in London. It is more than a blunder. It is a crime. For once I agree with John Bull. It can do no good—will place the Royal Family in a most difficult position and do intolerable harm. It cannot help but unsettle men. I most earnestly hope that even now the trial may take place elsewhere.[17]

F. G. Bowles wrote to the King to say that trial of the Kaiser in London 'would be full of mischief and would certainly have very grave and unexpected results'.[18]

Lloyd George and Curzon Quarrel

Alongside the tension with King George, a related dispute was brewing between Lloyd George and Curzon, the acting Foreign Secretary, who seemed to have 'back-pedalled in panic and alarm'.[19] Curzon was 'the exaggerated product of an ancient lineage' who 'stood for everything that Lloyd George's radical soul rejected'.[20] Curzon told Lloyd George that he had never contemplated, and was indeed 'staggered at, the idea of the trial taking place in England ... we may be on the verge of committing a great mistake'. Curzon thought the Kaiser would have 'a fairer trial from us than from other people', but he warned that

... outside this country it will be said and thought that those whom the German Emperor hated most and did his best to injure have insisted on seizing him and executing the final act of vengeance. There will thus spring up an idea, if he is brought here, that he will not receive fair play; and, if he is condemned and sentenced here, that he has not had it.[21]

Curzon was well aware of the sensitivities of King George V. He had already written to the King to say that he was in entire agreement with the monarch's position.[22] Curzon asked Lloyd George if he did not think there was 'a certain refinement of severity' involved in bringing the Kaiser 'to the country the most famous Sovereign of which was his Grandmother; where his Mother was born; and from which she was married; where he has constantly stayed as a Royal Guest; and where his Cousin is at the present moment on the Throne?'

This was a rhetorical question—Curzon knew the answer. He said it was putting the King 'in a very delicate and invidious position if his near relative however great his crimes, is to be tried almost within sight of the Palace where the King lives and where the culprit has so often stayed?' Curzon warned Lloyd George of the social impact of what could well be a rather prolonged trial: 'It is really almost inconceivable that he should be placed in a spot where, day after day, through a period extending very likely over many months, he will have to be brought backwards and forwards to the Court of Justice amid the jeers and insults of the crowd.' He predicted such an arrangement 'would begin by being disgraceful and end, after it had lasted a long time and the public had become indifferent would end by being ridiculous'.

Curzon discussed some of the options for a trial venue, other than the Royal Courts of Justice, located on The Strand in the heart of London's judicial precinct. One alternative might be the Royal Gallery of the House of Lords. Curzon acerbically suggested that the Kaiser might 'be lodged in the apartments which the Lord Chancellor has been prevented by the Commons from occupying because he insisted on a bath'. But he says they don't want him in Westminster, 'in close proximity to our every day proceedings'. What about Hampton Court, one of the royal palaces in west London, then as now a major tourist attraction? 'But a place of holiday resort, where thousands of people would be hanging about every day is hardly a suitable "*mise en scène*" for such a trial', said Curzon. He predicted the Kaiser, if brought to England for trial, would make 'a sustained and prolonged defence'. He would summon to his side his sons, his ex-Ministers, his Generals, his friends, and try 'to overwhelm the Court with evidence as to his innocence and irresponsibility. He will endeavour to break down the proceedings by every form of delay.' Curzon predicted that leading German personalities, like former Chancellor Bethmann-Hollweg, and Generals Hindenburg and Ludendorff, would have to be accommodated. He continued:

> If he be pronounced guilty, and sentence be passed upon him, and it is left to us to carry it out, shall not we in the eyes both of Germany and the rest of the world have to bear the entire responsibility, now and in History? Never mind that the court is international, the verdict will be regarded as having been inspired, just as in all probability it will have to be executed, by ourselves. Would it be possible ever again to make friends with Germany after that? Would not it be a root of bitterness which would last till the end of time? If, on the other hand, he is acquitted or an inconclusive verdict is reached, upon us will fall the blame and ridicule of the fiasco; and the effects of our military triumph will be largely dissipated by this bathos. I do not, of course, know the arguments which prevailed upon the Council of Four to decide in favour of England. I expect that the other countries represented were only too anxious not to shoulder the responsibility themselves. France and Belgium, I can well imagine, might be considered unsuitable places. Italy is too remote, and the Italians are not to be trusted.

Curzon put forward an intriguing idea, one that had not previously been considered. Hold the trial in the Netherlands. He asked:

> But why should Holland be debarred? Is it altogether impossible that the Kaiser should be tried at The Hague? The trial and verdict will surely be independent of the particular locality in which the former will be held, and the judges are as likely to deliver a fair and reasonable finding in one country as they are in another. On the other hand, we would escape all the difficulties, or some at any rate of them, in respect of the contemplated demand of surrender to be addressed to the Dutch Government, and their possible refusal. The Kaiser is already in Holland. It might be easier for them to transfer him from one part of the country to another without raising the question of his leaving Holland. That would also lessen the difficulty as to his witnesses, if he summoned them, reaching the place of trial. It would be much simpler for them to cross a land frontier into Holland than to be brought across the sea to our own shore. I assume that Holland must have been considered and ruled out for some reason that I do not know, but at least the point seems worthy of consideration.

Curzon said he had chatted briefly with Lord Alfred Milner, the Colonial Secretary, and with Winston Churchill. 'I find that their views coincide with mine', he said. 'I believe that the view of the Foreign Office is well-nigh unanimous in the direction which I have described.'[23]

An irritated Lloyd George replied to Curzon the following day. The Prime Minister sensed that Curzon's objections to trial in England betrayed a lack of resolve about the trial itself. Lloyd George suspected the influence of the King. He wrote:

> The arguments you advance in your letter against trying the Kaiser in England I had already heard from The King—every one of them. I therefore assume it was the result of a conversation which you had with H.M. I can hardly, however, believe that it was his suggestion that the Cabinet should be invited to throw over its principal delegate at the Peace Conference in an important decision which he had taken on their behalf and which he had already announced to the House of Commons.
>
> All the reasons which you assign are really arguments against trying the Kaiser at all. You tell me that Churchill and Milner agreed with you. Of course they did; they were firmly opposed to a trial. They are, therefore, quite consistent in their attitude. You, on the other hand, took the initiative in proposing his trial.

He recalled Curzon's enthusiasm at the War Cabinet meeting in November 1918 immediately following the armistice.

> The proposal you made was ultimately adopted by the Cabinet, pressed on their behalf on our Allies, and ultimately adopted by them after a full investigation by a very able Commission representing the leading Allies, including Belgium. To go back on it now would indeed be not only to make the representatives of this country at the Paris Peace Conference look silly, but to make Britain, France, Belgium and all the other Allies look extremely foolish. Even the Americans agreed, the present report, which was ultimately incorporated in the Peace Treaty, having been actually drafted by President Wilson himself, so that there was perfect unanimity in the decisions.
>
> As to whether it should be London or elsewhere, he must be tried somewhere or not at all. You agree that France, Belgium, and Italy are impossible. America, of course, would be out of the question. You now suggest Holland. What right have we to assume that Holland would care to have a foreign tribunal set up in its country to try and sentence an ex-Monarch of a foreign State. We could not compel Holland to lend its courts for that purpose.
>
> There is a good deal of force in the objection urged by the King to a trial taking place in the capital, for, as he pointed out, the Kaiser would have to be driven every day to the Courts and back to his place of internment. That does not apply to Hampton Court. The tripper argument has no force. If the Kaiser were interned at Hampton Court, of course, we could not allow trippers within the grounds. He could be confined to one part of the building, tried in another, the whole of the grounds would be available for him, and the public would only have to put up with the inconvenience—an inconvenience,

by the way, which they accepted without a murmur during the War—that Hampton Court would not be available to sightseers, during the short period when the trial was proceeding.

As for the presence of Generals and Statesmen who wish to testify on behalf of the Kaiser, there is plenty of room for them all in that huge building. In any event, many more of these Generals and Officers will have to come over in connection with trials in respect of breaches of the laws of war, unless it is also proposed that the trial of the executioners of Captain Fryatt, the authors of the submarine war, and the torturers of the prisoners, should also take place in Holland. Is it conceivable that Holland would lend herself for the purpose of such wholesale trials? Or is it proposed that we should change our mind about these trials as well? Is it suggested that we should abandon these prosecutions and let these ruffians go merely because there is a society objection to the trial of the Kaiser? Supposing sentence of death were passed on some of the second-rate villains, will the execution take place on British soil? The Dutch will not look at the proposal. German officers and German officers testifying on British soil is therefore an inevitable consequence of punishment for war crimes.

I took the action which was the natural sequence of decisions arrived at deliberately after long reflection and discussion by the Cabinet, and I do not like the idea of running away from them at the first difficulties that present themselves. I had enough of that with Irish conscription, which I very reluctantly agreed to under great pressure, but was the last, according to the best of my recollection, to abandon.[24]

Curzon denied that there was any complicity between himself and the King in developing the case against trial in London and, perhaps, in England and, perhaps, at all. If his arguments were similar to those of the King, 'it can only be because the same considerations occurred independently to our two minds', he wrote. He said he had never suggested that the Cabinet 'should throw over' Lloyd George, but at the same time confirmed that he had asked that 'the Cabinet should be allowed an opportunity … to discuss the matter before action is finally taken'. Curzon's objection to some of the rather authoritarian law-making of the Council of Four was probably echoed by similar discontent among senior officials in the other governments. It seems clear enough that when Lloyd George volunteered England as the place of trial, there had been no consultation within the British Government about this. The same can be said when he indicated London as the venue in his speech in Parliament on 3 July 1919. To underscore the objection, Curzon's reply affirmed that 'in none of our discussions was the idea ever suggested that the trial of the Kaiser should take place in this country'. When Lloyd George announced the trial was to take place in England, 'the intimation caused as much surprise to other people as it did to me', said Curzon. He also denied changing his mind about the policy of holding a trial, although he indicated that his view was no longer as unequivocal as it had been previously. Curzon acknowledged that there was no way to compel Holland to host the trial, but then the same could be said about surrendering the Kaiser. He thought that there was no harm in asking. 'It would be easier for Holland to acquiesce in the assembling at The Hague—a Capital specially dedicated to international purposes—of a tribunal to try the ex-Emperor, than to agree to surrender his person for deportation and trial elsewhere', wrote Curzon.[25]

Other options were considered by the War Cabinet on 23 July, including the Channel Islands and Dover.[26] Curzon expressed a preference for the Channel Islands. While crossing from France to England with Maurice Hankey, Lloyd George had pointed at Dover Castle, saying 'That's the place for the Kaiser's trial'.[27] Lloyd George's intuition that the King was opposed to the trial itself, and that the mood in Britain was shifting away from prosecution, finds confirmation in the silence on the venue issue over the months that followed. Had the British Government been determined to host the trial, serious preparations would have been expected. Twenty-six years later, when the victorious Allies agreed to try the Nazi leaders, it took them days, not weeks or months, to agree upon where the trial would be held. Work began immediately to ready the Nuremberg courtroom and the detention centre, and to deal with other issues of the infrastructure of such an undertaking. In January 1920, the Treaty of Versailles entered into force and the Allies immediately addressed their request for surrender of the Kaiser. But had the Dutch cooperated, and delivered the former Emperor forthwith, the British would have been quite unprepared. No arrangements had been made for his place of detention and nothing had been planned for the place of trial.

Preparing the Prosecution

The physical arrangements for the trial were not the only thing that was neglected. It is difficult to explain what were at best only half-hearted efforts to prepare the case for prosecution. It is as if the Allies believed the vagueness of Article 227 meant that only summary proof of guilt was required. Perhaps the Allies were confident that evidence of breaches of the laws and customs of war had already been exhaustively assembled during the course of the war by the various commissions of inquiry. This material had been collated by the Commission on Responsibilities. As for violation of the neutrality of Belgium and Luxembourg, Germany had already admitted this. All that remained was to draw the legal conclusions. Finally, if the Kaiser was to be prosecuted for starting the war, the evidence would take the form of documents that were all in the public domain, together with the published memoirs of the participations.

The first indication that thought was being given to the practical legal challenges of prosecution is a minute to a file in the British archives dated 30 June 1919 dealing with an individual case. Cecil B. Hurst, the Principal Legal Adviser to the Foreign Office, sought authorisation to contact the Solicitor General with a view to preparing a scheme for the prosecutions that were mandated by the Treaty of Versailles.[28] Hurst later served as a judge at the Permanent Court of International Justice and was its president from 1934 to 1936. During the Second World War, he was the first chairman of the United Nations War Crimes Commission. Charles Hardinge, the Permanent Under-Secretary, authorised him to proceed and, in mid-July 1919, Hurst drafted a detailed memorandum about implementation of the penalty clauses of the Treaty of Versailles. On trial of the Kaiser, he said that the first step in the enforcement of Article 227 would be establishing an inter-allied organisation in London. Its responsibility would be 'fixing definitely the charges' and collecting evidence that would substantiate such charges. Hurst said that practical arrangements for housing the Kaiser and details about where the trial would be held need not concern the inter-allied organisation. These would be handled by the British Government. There is a minute to the file indicating that Lord Balfour reacted positively to Hurst's memorandum, but that he thought the matter had to go to the War Cabinet.[29]

The Hurst memorandum is the only evidence of any thought being given by any of the four Powers to coordination of their efforts in preparing the case against the Kaiser. In Britain, nothing further appears to have been done to pursue Hurst's proposal of an inter-allied committee. Indeed, in the months following the signing of the Treaty of Versailles, there is no indication of any consultation whatsoever by the British with their Allies about preparation for trial. Nor has evidence been found to suggest that France, Italy, or the United States ever took any similar initiatives. For example, the minutes of the Steering Committee set up by the American delegation to oversee implementation of the Treaty of Versailles never address the matter.[30] A copy of the

Hurst memorandum is found in the papers of James Brown Scott, indicating that the Americans were aware of the proposal for an inter-allied organisation to prepare the Kaiser's trial.[31]

When Clemenceau informed Maurice Hankey on 2 July 1919 that he was in agreement with holding the trial in England, might he also have assumed that the British took responsibility for the prosecution itself? This is implausible because the French had very definite concerns in the framing of the indictment. Just as the British were especially interested in issues like submarine warfare, the French were insistent upon addressing the atrocities committed in the parts of their country that were occupied. But also, like the British, they may have worried that in the debate about the origins of the war unpleasant secrets concerning their own conduct would emerge. Organising a trial was not only about ensuring that some matters were properly addressed, but also about guaranteeing that others were not. It may be going too far to assume that the French were completely idle. Important elements of their national archives disappeared during the Second World War, removed by the Germans and lost forever.

Maurice Hankey, the Cabinet Secretary, prepared a note on the trial of the Kaiser for the War Cabinet that is dated 29 July 1919. Hankey's view was that it was the duty of the Peace Conference, not the British Government, to obtain the surrender of Wilhelm from the Dutch. When that was done, Hankey said the British Government would then need to arrange transport of the Kaiser and his staff to England, and to deal with practical matters concerning his stay during the trial. Hankey said that Lloyd George had already entrusted the prosecution and preparation of the case to the Law Officers. He made no mention of Hurst's suggestion to establish an inter-allied body, in which France and the other Powers would participate. Hankey said that the procedure would be a matter for the special tribunal itself to decide. Also, the British judge would have to be selected.[32]

In mid-August 1919, the Attorney General, Gordon Hewart, convened a meeting at the House of Commons with the Solicitor General, Ernest Pollock, the Procurator General, John Mellor, and two senior barristers, Frederick Pollock and George Branson. The two Pollocks were cousins.[33] Raymond Wybrow Woods, a solicitor in the Procurator General's office, was assigned responsibility for preparing the case against the Kaiser. Woods was to cooperate with the two barristers, in accordance with English practice whereby solicitors prepare a case and then 'instruct' barristers to argue it in court.

Woods spent the next four months researching the charges against the Kaiser.

In mid-September, he wrote to the Foreign Office asking for relevant material in its possession. 'It is not, of course, possible to formulate precise charges until the evidence available has been examined', he said, but Woods had already compiled a list of matters that 'so far as can be judged at present, were premeditated crimes of policy sanctioned by the authorities responsible for the conduct of the War in Germany, as distinguished from incidental outrages committed by individual officers in the German Army'. This list included the invasion of Belgium and Luxembourg, the submarine campaign, terrorisation of civilians in occupied Belgium and France, and the use of poison gas. Woods asked to be provided with 'protests entered by the Foreign Office against breaches of the laws of War by Germany, together with the evidence on which the protests were based and accompanied by a reference to any correspondence which may have been issued in the form of White Papers'. Clearly, not only the Procurator General but also the Foreign Office knew that he was examining classic violations of the laws and customs of war. There was never any suggestion that these did not fit within the charge of offences 'against international morality and the sanctity of treaties'.

When he began his work, Woods appeared to be completely unfamiliar with what had already been done by the British Committee of Enquiry and the Commission on Responsibilities. Only in November 1919, more than two months into his work, did Woods acknowledge receiving a copy of the report of the Commission on Responsibilities, sent to him by Cecil Hurst of the Foreign Office.[34] It is quite astonishing that Hurst, who had first insisted that plans be made for the trial in late June 1919, had only then bothered to provide Woods with such an essential document. But since Woods actually worked for the Solicitor General, who had himself been a member of the Commission, there should have been no need to go to the Foreign Office in order to get the report. Woods also spent several weeks trying to locate 'de Lapradelle's pamphlet on the responsibility of the Kaiser', unaware that the report of Larnaude and de Lapradelle was not only part of the official documents of the Commission on Responsibilities,[35] it had also been distributed to all delegations at the Peace Conference on Clemenceau's instructions. When he asked Sir John Macdonnell to help him locate a copy, Woods said he thought it might have been published in 'one of the French reviews of international law'.[36] He eventually obtained a French-language version of the report and by mid-October arranged for its translation into English.[37] Woods

didn't know that there was already an English translation in the published record of the Commission.

Woods wrote to Hugh Bellot at the International Law Association
asking for documents, particularly the material provided to the Attorney
General's Committee of Enquiry.[38] He also corresponded with several of the
major publishing houses, including the presses of Oxford and Cambridge
Universities, Heinemann, Cassell, and Hodder & Stoughton. Hutchinson &
Co. provided him with advance proofs of the English version of the two-
volume *My War Memories 1914–1918* by General Ludendorff.[39]

As he collected this material, Woods prepared bundles for the two barristers to read. In early September, he sent them Louis Renault's *First
Violations of International Law by Germany*, Charles Oman's *The Outbreak
of the War 1914–1918*, Walter Dodd's *Modern Constitutions*, Lawrence Lowell's
The Governments of France, Italy and Germany, the first and second interim
reports of the Attorney General's Committee of Enquiry, and the report
of the Bryce Commission, published in 1915.[40] More materials were sent a
few days later, including *The Law of Nations and the War* by Pearce Higgins,
a collection of wartime speeches by Bethmann-Hollweg, and *Who Are the
Huns: The Law of Nations and Its Breakers*, by Ernst Müller. Woods understood that the Müller volume was German propaganda, but he thought it
would be useful in anticipating defence arguments at the trial. Both Pollock
and Branson answered Woods promptly, indicating that they were carefully
studying the material. Pollock said that rather than deal with translations,
he would prefer originals of the French and English materials, if practicable. When he spotted a typographic error in the proof of the Bethmann-
Hollweg book, *Revelations on the World War*, Woods helpfully notified the
publisher, Thornton Butterworth.[41]

The problem was not so much identifying war crimes as linking them to
Kaiser Wilhelm. Frederick Pollock wrote to Woods on 21 September:

> As previously advised I feel great doubt whether the ex-Kaiser can be made
> liable for German military atrocities in detail. He had no executive com-
> mand and there is nothing to show that he was personally consulted as to the
> policy of terrorism. That policy flowed from the damnable doctrine of *Kriegs
> räson und militarische Notwendigkeit* which Wilhelm II certainly did not invent.
> Subsequent approbation would hardly serve even if it could be proved and
> I don't see any proof: I should rather think that he believed, as the German
> public did, the story told by his own officers, and thought the Allies' charges
> were fictions.

Submarine warfare was an exception, Pollock thought, because it could not be undertaken without imperial orders. He pointed out that the navy was 'absolutely German', whereas the armies were organised by the component States and were only under overall command from Berlin. Pollock said he could not find in any of 'the German apologetic literature' attempts to justify the torpedoing of neutral merchant vessels without any warning. The issue was simply ignored, he said. 'The contention that merchantmen may not defend themselves (as in Capt. Fryatt's case) is absolutely novel and unfounded.' Pollock also pointed to the 'clear crimes' of Wilhelm involving the origin of the war. He referred to the German Emperor's determination to force a European war. 'The French Yellow Book clinches this.' Pollock also highlighted the breach of Belgian neutrality, 'a matter of high policy he can't get out of ... The case of Luxembourg is similar'.[42]

A skilled trial advocate, Pollock seems to have been the first to speculate on how Wilhelm might defend himself:

> What would I do if I were Wilhelm's counsel? We ought all to put that question to ourselves. I should advise him to follow Charles I's example—protest against the jurisdiction and the Court and say nothing more. But if he decided to plead then:
>   1. Admit nothing, claim all the rights of a prisoner in an English criminal court, require strict proof of all material facts.
>   2. Make all possible dilatory exceptions.
>   3. Rely on the usual German arguments only as a last resource, and then not as being absolutely correct (which might only exasperate the Court) but as being plausible enough from a German point of view to convince a reasonable German in Wilhelm II's position. I would make the trial last for the rest of William's life or till the world was bored with it, or at need ride for a scene in Court that would more or less discredit the tribunal even if it did my client no direct good.

Like the others, Pollock was not at all unsettled by the mysterious charge set out in Article 227 of a 'supreme offence against international morality and the sanctity of treaties'. He did not ask whether either classic war crimes or the unleashing of aggressive war actually fit within the four corners of the phrase concocted by President Wilson. Pollock was probably not even aware of the fact that the initial text adopted by the Council of Four declared the charge against Wilhelm was 'not to be described as a violation of criminal law'. Objections to the legality of the charge had already been raised in many quarters, including by Honduras in the plenary Peace Conference. Moreover, the Commission on Responsibilities had rejected the notion that the Kaiser could be prosecuted for starting the war, largely at the instigation of the British and the arguments of Pollock's cousin, Ernest Pollock, the Solicitor General. Frederick Pollock might well have given some thought as to how such arguments could be answered.[43]

Woods took an entirely different view of the situation, preferring to put the emphasis on the violations of the laws and customs of war and holding to the view, earlier advanced by the British delegates in the Commission on Responsibilities, rejecting prosecution for launching the war. In his reply to Pollock, he said the focus had been on 'crimes of policy as distinguished from incidental outrages committed by individual officers in the German Army'. More importantly, he expressed concern that focusing upon the charge of 'provoking and waging an unjust and aggressive war' could 'attain such dimensions and prove do inconclusive as to divert attention from those matters which are more readily susceptible of proof'.[44] The same day, Woods reported to Sir John Mellor enclosing a copy of the letter from Pollock. Woods said he had doubts about the wisdom of engaging in a general discussion about responsibility for the war. 'No doubt Sir Frederick Pollock is quite right in his view that the dominant factor in German politics was the determination to provoke war at an early date, but I am inclined to think that to embark upon this subject will raise a discussion to which there will be no end.'[45]

Woods found a kindred spirit in the Foreign Office. James W. Headlam Morley, then the deputy director of political intelligence and a veteran of the British delegation at the Paris Peace Conference, was already on record opposing prosecution based upon aggressive war. In a memorandum he had circulated in December 1918, Headlam Morley argued about the practical problems, not the legal issues, which were not within his expertise. He was concerned that any inquiry about responsibility for the origins of the war, especially in the adversarial context of a criminal trial, might ricochet onto the British Government. Germany alone could not be blamed for the arms race that preceded the outbreak of the conflict.[46]

In mid-October, Woods invited himself to the Foreign Office for a chat with Headlam Morley. There was nothing surreptitious about it. Woods officially informed colleagues in the Foreign Office of the meeting in a letter intended to flag his unease about prosecuting responsibility for the war itself. He said his concern was 'whether any general charge should be made of waging an aggressive and unjust war'. He anticipated that the Germans would lay stress on Russian meddling in the Balkans, with the support of Great

Britain and France, so as to encourage Serbia and form 'a solid Balkan front against the Central Powers'.[47]

In his report on the meeting with Woods, Headlam Morley questioned whether Article 227 of the Treaty of Versailles actually applied to responsibility for starting the war. He said he had been told that 'it was decided at Paris that the Emperor was to be tried only on the charge of the violation of Belgian neutrality and on the conduct of the war, and not on the charge of the responsibility for the war'. That was an approximation of what the Commission on Responsibilities had concluded, but not necessarily the view of the Council of Four, which had authored Article 227. Headlam Morley thought the words 'supreme offence against international morality' could be interpreted so as to include the Kaiser's responsibility for the war, 'but in interpreting the Treaty, the lawyers of course might be guided by any authoritative pronouncement about the intention which has been made. Is there any such pronouncement?' he asked.

Headlam Morley said that if requested, 'I shall strongly advise against including the charge for bringing about the war on general grounds'.[48] He warned against assuming the Kaiser would be convicted if charged with responsibility for starting the war. He thought there was no doubt that the cause of the world war was 'a system' of which the Emperor was the head. 'If, however, he is to be charged not only with the violation of Belgian neutrality, but also with the responsibility for the war, we must remember that there would have to be shown personal responsibility', said Headlam Morley. He said the world expected that Wilhelm could be proved guilty of having premeditated and deliberately brought about the war.[49]

Norman could offer Headlam Morley no useful insight into the intentions of those who had drafted Article 227. He referred to the notes and minutes of the meetings of the Council of Four, which would have been accessible to senior officials in the Foreign Office, but they provide no useful answers.[50] This correspondence attracted the attention of the Foreign Minister, George Curzon, who thought Headlam Morley was meddling in matters that did not concern him. On 25 October, Curzon minuted: 'This matter is entirely in the hands of Sir E. Pollock and I should have thought the proper course was to refer it to him and not to Mr Headlam Morley who, so far as I know, has no special authority to pronounce or advise in regard to it.'[51] There is a subsequent minute on the file, from Norman, that only confirms the reigning confusion:

We had understood that Sir E. Pollock was concerned only with the preparation of the lists of persons to be tried for breaches of the laws of war and the charges against those persons, and not with the trial of the ex-Emperor. Be that as it may, it seems strange that the Procurator General, who seems to have been entrusted with the task of drawing up the brief against the Emperor, should ask information of Mr Headlam Morley and not of Sir E. Pollock himself (if he is concerned or of the Prime Minister or Sir M. Hankey).[52]

As he was finalising his memorandum on the case against the Kaiser, Woods became more positive about prosecuting Wilhelm for starting the war. It may be that he had received a stern message from his superior, Ernest Pollock, or an indirect reprimand from Curzon. Whatever the impetus, the turning point in Woods's own assessment was the release, in late November 1919, of what were called the 'Kautsky papers'. Woods referred to these materials as 'the most important work we have yet obtained bearing, as it does, directly upon the responsibility of William II for the war'.[53]

At the time of the armistice, the German Social Democrat Karl Kautsky was commissioned by the Popular Government of Germany to assemble a documentary collection relating to the outbreak of the war using the files of the Foreign Office. Kautsky finished his work, with the help of his wife, Luise Kautsky-Ronsperger, in May 1919. Later in the year, the Ministerial Cabinet requested Count Max Montgelas and Professor Walther Schücking to prepare the material, consisting of more than a thousand documents, for publication. The four volumes appeared in November 1919. Substantial excerpts of the Kautsky papers appeared in The Times on 29 November.[54] Woods insisted, but in vain, that the Kautsky papers be translated into English by the Foreign Office. 'As you are aware these documents are so important that it is impossible for the Law Officers to advise whether a general charge should be made until they have the documents before them', he wrote in mid-January 1920.[55] A full translation into English was produced by the Carnegie Foundation in 1924 and published by Oxford University Press.

The Kautsky papers consist of internal correspondence of the German Foreign Ministry embellished by handwritten marginal notes of the Kaiser himself. These provide a portrait of a belligerent, opinionated, and tetchy autocrat who was directly engaged in German foreign policy. This was the first hard evidence of the Kaiser's personal role in the incitement of war. For example, on 30 June 1914, two days after the assassination in Sarajevo, Germany's Ambassador at Vienna, Heinrich von Tschirschky, wrote to the Imperial Chancellor: 'I frequently hear expressed here, even among serious people, the wish that *at last a final and fundamental reckoning should be had with the Serbs*. The Serbs should first be presented with a number of demands, and in case they should not accept these, energetic measures should be taken.' Von Tschirschky added: '*I take opportunity of every such occasion to advise quietly but very impressively and seriously against too hasty steps.*' The Kaiser's minute in the margins expressed irritation with the German Ambassador's pacific efforts: 'Who authorised him to act that way? That is very stupid ... Let Tschirschky be good enough to drop this nonsense! The Serbs must be disposed of, *and* that right *soon!*'[56] When the German minister to Belgrade wrote that Serbia had 'absolutely unexpected' the 'energetic tone and the detailed demands of the Austrian note', the Kaiser wrote: 'How hollow the whole so-called Serbian power is proving itself to be; thus it is seen to be with all the Slav nations! Just tread hard on the heels of that rabble!'[57]

The Woods Memorandum

Woods delivered an advance proof of his 300-page report, entitled 'The Arraignment of William II of Hohenzollern, Memorandum on the Responsibility of William II of Hohenzollern for Acts Committed in Breach of the Laws of War', to the Attorney General on 1 December 1919.[58] A few days later, he sent the report to the two barristers.[59] Not quite half of the volume is devoted to responsibility for 'waging an unjust and aggressive war', followed by a relatively short section on the violation of treaties. The rest of the report discusses breaches of the laws and customs of war, both on land and at sea, including the persecution of civilians in occupied France and Belgium, the executions of Captain Fryatt and Edith Cavell, submarine warfare, and the sinking of the *RMS Lusitania*.

With respect to violations of the laws and customs of war, the memorandum proposes prosecution for 'premeditated crimes of policy, sanctioned by the authorities', as distinct from 'incidental outrages committed by individual officers'. It says it would 'be difficult to fix responsibility upon William II for individual crimes, and to attempt to do so might be unduly to strain the doctrine of supreme responsibility, thereby prejudicing the case where the responsibility can be shewn [sic] to be actual and personal'.[60] Furthermore, emphasis in selecting charges should be placed on matters where his liability could be demonstrated to be 'direct and personal' rather than relying upon 'technical' points, such as responsibility under the constitution and 'technical responsibility for breaches of international law, however flagrant'.[61]

In analysing the case for the charge of provoking and waging an unjust and aggressive war, the memorandum begins with a general discussion of German foreign policy over the decade prior to the war, followed by an account of the events of July 1914, particularly the final five days before the outbreak of the conflict. Woods reviewed the German arguments, relying extensively on the war memoir published by the former Chancellor, Bethmann-Hollweg. Woods concluded that there could be little doubt that 'not later than the year 1913, a definitive determination had been reached by the authorities responsible for the Government of Germany to wage, and if necessary to provoke a war whenever a favourable opportunity presented itself, and in any event not later than 1914'.[62]

Referring to the Kautsky papers, Woods wrote that 'the information which it contains is a matter which requires careful consideration, involving as it does, not only questions of the sufficiency and effect of the evidence, but also questions of the practicability of presenting such a charge before the Tribunal, and restricting the reply to reasonable limits'.[63] But he had not abandoned his scepticism about charging the Kaiser with launching an aggressive war. Woods appeared to entertain a theory that the real culprits in provoking the war were the Russians. He concluded this part of the memorandum by recommending that attention be paid to the views of Headlam Morley, whose pessimism about the viability of a charge of provoking the war was already well known. 'It is hoped that he will furnish a critical memorandum which will, no doubt, be of great assistance to the Law Officers in coming to a decision upon the difficult question of making a general charge, which would open a discussion upon such debatable topics'.[64]

The memorandum turns to the issue of violation of the neutrality of Belgium and Luxembourg, a matter ostensibly contemplated in Article 227 by the phrase 'the sanctity of treaties'. Here, facts of the case were relatively straightforward, with any German plea or answer likely to be based on something resembling a doctrine of necessity. It was clear that the real reason for invading Belgium and Luxembourg was not an alleged threat of French attack through Belgium, but rather the strategic advantage to Germany in attacking France where its border was least fortified. No tribunal would treat seriously such an excuse. Woods turned, but only briefly, to the personal liability of the Kaiser for the violation of the neutrality treaties. He cited a German reply to a request from the British that Belgian neutrality be respected. The British

Ambassador reported that the German Secretary of State had told him no such assurance could be provided until the Emperor and the Chancellor had been consulted. Woods briefly addressed the rather feeble attempts of German jurists to justify the invasion, citing Müller, who claimed that when Bethmann-Hollweg made his notorious admission in the Reichstag, he 'was not speaking precisely as a jurist or as a professor of international law, but as a politician'.[65] Under the German Constitution, the Emperor was responsible for the conduct of foreign relations, and in the final days of July and first days of August, he had played a very active part. 'It is to be presumed that the declaration of war on Belgium was issued with his concurrence and in his name and that as head of the German Army the invasion of Belgium received his sanction and approval', the memorandum concludes.[66] Similar findings apply with respect to Luxembourg.

The remainder of the Woods memorandum deals with violations of the laws and customs of war. First, the deportation of the civilian population of Belgium and France, and forced labour is addressed. There was no doubt about the practice; the issue was the personal responsibility of Kaiser Wilhelm. According to Woods: 'It is tolerably clear that the practice of deporting the civilian populations from occupied territory was initiated by Hindenburg and Ludendorff.'[67] Both Woodrow Wilson and the King of Spain had formally protested the Belgian deportations, and Woods concluded that the Kaiser must have been informed. Belgian Cardinal Désiré-Joseph Mercier received word that if he were to make a request, the Emperor would halt the deportations. Wilhelm II replied to Mercier that the men would be returned to Belgium, although they would have to work for Germany there. Woods's conclusion was that it could not be shown that Wilhelm was directly responsible based upon documents that were then available. However, given the Kaiser's position, 'it appears to be a safe inference that they must have received his approval and sanction; that at any rate they were permitted by him to continue with full knowledge, and finally they were discontinued by his express order'.[68]

The memorandum considers the atrocities perpetrated in Belgium and France, relying here upon the Bryce Report of 1915. These include the murder of several priests, instances of 'loathsome debauchery' directed at French and Belgian women and girls,[69] pillage, and imposition of collective penalties. Woods wrote that it was 'not easy to say how far direct responsibility attaches to William II'. But, he added, the Emperor must be presumed to have approved of the German War Book, instructing German troops not to be 'dominated by humanitarian considerations, which degenerate into senti-mentality and flabby emotion'.[70] He also explained that the Kaiser's attitude towards the way in which the German army conducted the war in Belgium and France was manifested in his letter to the Emperor of Austria, where he said it was necessary 'to destroy by fire and sword, to massacre men, women, children and old men, and to leave standing neither a tree nor a house'.[71] Woods discussed the use of inhumane weapons, such as poison gas and 'liquid fire', explaining that the Hague Conventions on the laws and customs of war prohibit the use of arms, projectiles, and materials that cause unnecessary suffering. With respect to ill treatment of prisoners of war, the Woods memo-randum said there was no direct evidence of personal responsibility, 'but if, as appears to be the case, it was upon the express Orders of the High Command, he might as head of the German Army, be considered to have constitutional responsibility for these Orders'.[72]

Woods turned to the great excitement in English public opinion about the executions of Edith Cavell and Captain Fryatt. He had to acknowledge, however, that blaming the Kaiser was hardly straightforward, 'and unless he is to be made responsible on general grounds, the very facts which empha-sise the brutality of the executions may in the case of Edith Cavell at any rate tend to negative a personal order or knowledge on his part'.[73] Woods thought it not improbable that the speed with which the sentences were conducted may have been for the purpose of preventing an appeal for clemency to Kaiser Wilhelm. Woods described the execution of Edith Cavell in considerable detail, concluding that '[m]orally the crime was great, but whether it is one upon which a legal complaint can be founded against William II is another and more difficult matter'.[74] Captain Fryatt's case appeared to be an even clearer example of miscarriage of justice by German military courts. Fryatt had been acting in self-defence when his merchant vessel was attacked by a submarine. The memorandum speculated that disclosure of evidence by Germany, something to which Allied governments were entitled under the Treaty of Peace, 'would throw further light on William II's knowledge and approval of the action taken in these cases'.[75]

Submarine warfare is discussed, with special emphasis on the torpedoing of the *RMS Lusitania*. Woods said the fact that the Emperor, both in name and in fact, was 'the absolute head of affairs' constituted the 'keystone of the whole system of the administration of the German Government'. Admiral von Tirpitz is cited at length as authority for the pre-eminent role of Kaiser Wilhelm in the leadership of the German Navy. Woods wrote:

A perusal of the material available suggests that a satisfactory case can probably be made against William II of personal responsibility for Submarine
Warfare and of its incidents, including the sinking of the 'Lusitania' and of
Hospital Ships. Submarine warfare played so large a part in the war, and at one
time assumed such a menacing aspect to this country, that it will probably be
thought desirable to pursue this subject, with a view, if possible, to making it
the subject of a concrete charge against William II. The ruthless ferocity with
which Submarine warfare was waged, and the great number of lives of men,
women and children, sacrificed by reason of Germany's disregard of the long-
established rules of naval warfare, make a charge upon this heading specially
justified.

Woods wrote that a finding that submarine warfare was illegitimate and likely
to expose its perpetrators to serious penalties 'may in future wars, if such there
are to be, discourage belligerents who are unable to maintain a fleet at sea,
from engaging in this insidious form of attack which proved so difficult to
meet and constituted such a grave menace to the British Empire, and, therefore, to the Allied cause'.[76]

The Woods report is based on what today would be called 'open sources',
essentially documents already in the public domain, as well as memoirs by
some of the participants in the diplomatic activity surrounding the outbreak
of the World War. Indeed, it begins with the explanation that '[t]his memorandum is compiled from Books of Reference and sources of information
procurable in this Country'.[77] Only a few of these published sources were in
a language other than English, although there was a great deal of material in
other European languages that might have been consulted. Woods appears
to have had no investigators. He did not seek out secret or confidential materials. Witnesses or informers were not interviewed. There is a large file of
Woods's correspondence in the British National Archives as he prepared his
December 1919 memorandum, but nothing to indicate that he ever communicated with anybody beyond the borders of the sceptred isle. His report is
more like an early draft of a PhD thesis than a brief that a skilled lawyer could
use as the basis for a successful prosecution in a court of law.

The report is thin on the law as well as the facts. There is no attempt to
analyse the inscrutable expression, 'a supreme offense against international
morality and the sanctity of treaties'. The introduction says that its purpose
is not to consider the legal issues, which would 'ultimately require consideration', but rather to 'collate the evidence on questions of fact'.[78] But how
could Woods, or for that matter the most senior legal officials in the British
Government who authorised him to prepare the file, know what they were

looking for if they did not properly understand the charges against the Kaiser? Woods seems to have assumed that the enigmatic wording in Article 227 was no more than an innovative formulation of the original mandate given to the Commission on Responsibilities in January 1919, namely to establish responsibility for starting the war and to deal with crimes under international law committed during the war.

Describing as woefully inadequate the British preparations for the trial of the Kaiser would be an understatement. A useful comparison can be made with the work undertaken by the British, the Americans, the French, and the Soviets a quarter of a century later when, within a matter of three or four months, scores if not hundreds of lawyers and investigators built the case against the Nazi defendants at Nuremberg. Two possible conclusions present themselves. Firstly, the British, and the other Allied Powers, did not really take trial preparation seriously because they never believed the proceedings against the Kaiser would take place. Despite the promise of Article 227, from the moment it was adopted in June 1919 they tacitly assumed that the Dutch would not surrender Wilhelm II or that some other impediment would prevent the trial. Consequently, nothing more than half-hearted efforts were required. Compared to the other Allies, the perfunctory report delivered by Woods looks positively energetic. Secondly, and in the alternative, there may have been an assumption that were a trial to take place, it would be little more than theatrical, the judicial equivalent of a Potemkin village, a shambolic production before compliant judges where the outcome was predetermined. Whatever the explanation, when the time came to demand the Kaiser's surrender, there had been little progress in preparing the trial during the six months since signature of the Treaty of Versailles.

16

The Kaiser in Limbo

Concern about extradition or even a forcible intervention by the Allies in order to obtain custody of Wilhelm II diminished as the Peace Conference wound to a close. Word reached Amerongen from German diplomats that an official in the Dutch foreign ministry had said: 'If the Entente threatens violent measures, the Emperor will indeed take a bullet; if not, then his adjutant will do the job.'[1] An enterprising Japanese journalist, Bunshiro Suzuki, went to Amerongen to interview the Kaiser for the Tokyo *Asahi*. He was refused entrance to the castle by Dutch security forces. According to Suzuki, the correspondent of an American newspaper had been staying near the castle since the previous December in the hope of interviewing Wilhelm. The Japanese reporter was no more successful, although he once caught a glimpse of the Kaiser taking his morning walk: 'His hair was snow white and he wore a beard which was snow white. He has become rather thin, but there was something stately in his mien, even though he was wearing an ordinary suit. The ex-Kaiserin had become thin, her hair being white.'

Suzuki was told by Count Bentinck's oldest son of the Kaiser's daily routine. Normally, the ex-Emperor would rise at 8 am. After reading his letters, he would take breakfast. 'From 9.30 to 12.30 he goes out of the Castle and engages in wood-sawing, the ex-Kaiserin being always with him', Suzuki reported in the Japan *Gazette* of 9 June 1919.[2] The Kaiser's obsession with wood-cutting was notorious. There are films of him cutting small branches and logs with an axe, or sawing them. The Kaiser never used his left arm, which was perhaps 25 cm shorter than his right arm. His clothes were tailored to conceal this. Another report, from the commander of the Marechaussee charged with guarding the Kaiser, described his daily routine: 'In the morning—usually from 8 to 9—the ex-Kaiser takes a walk in the garden, after which he will have breakfast. Around 10 he comes back into the garden, and saws a lot, for which a small garden house and a so-called sawing place is built.'[3] Suzuki wrote in the Japan *Gazette*:

> After luncheon he takes a nap and then walks about the gardens. At dinner he is always attended by General von Gondard in military uniform, Count Bentinck, his two sons and a daughter, and five other attendants. After listening to music, the ex-Kaiser goes to bed. On Sundays, the ex-Kaiser attends the service in the Chapel of the Castle wearing all his decorations and uniform as former Emperor.[4]

Wilhelm's life at Amerongen, according to a British embassy dispatch in December 1919, was 'that of a favoured guest on a country estate, and he walks, shoots, cuts down trees and takes other forms of exercise in the grounds. He has lately shown himself more freely than he did at first in motor excursions, but he does not move far from the castle.' A German officer who visited Amerongen considered the Kaiser to be 'distressingly garrulous, to the point of showing a loss of mental faculties', but the British Ambassador said he was inclined to discount such accounts in the absence of further confirmation. Wilhelm was said to be in good health and spirits, and exceedingly voluble. A favourite subject, it seems, was his anger with the former Crown Prince, who was stuck in Wieringen. Count Godard Bentinck 'grumbles discreetly at the irksome and burdensome duties of hospitality which have been thrust upon him, but never leaves the side of his guest, and is believed to revel in the reflected lustre of a visitor whom he considered so distinguished', reported the British Ambassador. He added sarcastically that '"extinguished" would be a more suitable epithet.' The ex-Empress was described as 'dispirited and nervous', and very concerned about the threatened trial of her husband. 'She anxiously enquires of all who visit the castle whether they think that the Emperor with be extradited and tried', Graham reported to London in December 1919.[5]

The British *chargé d'affaires*, Arnold Robertson, initially expressed concern that Holland would become 'a centre of German monarchical and militarist intrigue'.[6] Rumours of German monarchist activity 'caused a certain uneasiness in Dutch official circles', although Robertson was inclined to regard the information as 'greatly exaggerated, at any rate in so far as William II and his eldest son are concerned'. One consequence was to provoke a shift in the position of the Dutch Socialists, who were less and less favourable to asylum for the Kaiser. The German Socialists, themselves nervous about the monarchists, influenced their Dutch counterparts. One of the Dutch leftists,

Pieter Jelles Troelstra, told the British Ambassador that '[i]nterests of Socialism are more important than the honour of Holland'.[7] The British envoy considered that although 'such speeches and articles may not influence attitude of Netherlands Government they show that a gradual change in public feeling is taking place on this question'. But Troelstra's views were unlikely to persuade the conservative Foreign Minister, who would attribute them to 'Bolshevik inspiration'.[8]

A *New York Times* article published in December 1919 was entitled 'Kaiser is Busy on His Defence'. It described how the Kautsky papers had delivered a 'knock-out blow' to the former Emperor, but offered no real indications that Wilhelm was preparing for trial.[9] Those in his entourage who wrote accounts of life at Amerongen, including his adjutant Sigurd von Ilsemann and Lady Norah Bentinck, never mention visits of lawyers with a view to preparing the defence. Instead, should the Dutch Government become inclined to co-operate in surrendering him to the Allies, the Kaiser's plan, according to his personal physician, was to 'slip back in total secrecy across the border'. Dr Haehner went on to say that the Kaiser's return 'would certainly lead to civil war ... Whether or not this would spell the end of the Kaiser was of no consequence, in such circumstances one's honour mattered more than one's life.'[10] Perhaps Haehner had forgotten that only a year earlier, when Germany's collapse seemed certain, Kaiser Wilhelm II had chosen life over honour.

There were reports that 'certain well-known German notabilities of the old regime, such as Baron von der Lanken and Prince Fürstenberg, have recently visited Amerongen and have had long interviews with the ex-Emperor'.[11] Yet the Dutch insisted that they were closely monitoring the Kaiser in order to prevent his involvement in political intrigue. A guard on duty at Amerongen prevented any visits to the Kaiser that had not been authorised by the local *burgemeester*, Rudolf Everhard Willem van Weede. The *burgemeester* did not allow any visits to the castle unless he had met the person and satisfied himself that the purpose was entirely innocent and non-political. According to a report from the British Ambassador, 'the total number of individuals who from first to last have been admitted to see the ex-Kaiser is extremely limited, and the *burgemeester* has personally vouched for the harmless character of every visit paid'. He described Van Weede as 'a naturally cautious man, who is profoundly impressed with the responsibility now incumbent on him'.[12]

Van Weede in turn kept the Dutch General Staff informed of the comings and goings at Amerongen. The British were informed by the Chief of the General Staff that 'anyone who imagined that plots could be occurring at Amerongen or at Wieringen evidently knew nothing of the precautions adopted by the Dutch authorities with the object of rendering such plots impossible'. The Dutch General said that after his country had 'unwillingly incurred the odium of affording an asylum to the ex-Emperor ... it was unlikely that he, who was responsible for all precautions taken, would run the risk of gravely aggravating that odium'. He said that if there was any royalist plot was underway in the Netherlands, it was not being hatched at Amerongen or Wieringen.[13]

There was serious flooding in the Netherlands in early 1920, threatening Amerongen.[14] The Dutch authorities considered moving the Kaiser temporarily to Zuylestein Castle, on higher ground, about a kilometre from the Bentinck estate. The Kaiserin's lady-in-waiting objected because the royal couple would have to endure the indignity of sharing a dressing room. The British Minister in The Hague said he had heard the wish freely expressed in Dutch circles that the floodwaters in Amerongen continue to rise. 'If, indeed, by some act of Providence, this self-invited and embarrassing guest could be "spurlos versenkt" ["sunk without a trace"], such a solution would be hailed with unmitigated relief', he wrote.[15]

In August 1919, Kaiser Wilhelm purchased a moated mansion in the town of Doorn, no more than 10 kilometres from Amerongen and a little closer to the city of Utrecht. A stately home with extensive grounds, Huis Doorn was owned by Ludolphine Marie Anne Labouchère, the Baroness van Heemstra. She claimed she did not know the identity of the purchaser until the last minute of the transaction. Otherwise, she said, she would have asked for a much higher price than the 1.55 million guilders that Wilhelm paid. Actor Audrey Hepburn was a Van Heemstra; her mother had spent much of her childhood at Huis Doorn. Another of the famous film star's ancestors actually befriended the Kaiser, going for long walks with him after he had settled in Doorn.

A Dutch estate agent organised the purchase. The Kaiser was concerned that the German Government might seize his assets and make the purchase impossible.[16] The Dutch Government insisted upon the suitability of supervised residence in Doorn. The British and the French thought it was much too close to the German border. Dutch authorities replied that it had been chosen for him and not by him, and that he had 'been shepherded into it by the Dutch Government, as they considered it a spot where he could be most safely and effectively supervised'.[17] The Dutch also claimed that the Kaiser had attempted to buy other places. They insisted that in two cases the deeds of sale were actually drawn up only to be vetoed by the government. What the criteria were and why the transactions were prevented is not clear. Moreover, given the subsequent insistence by the Dutch about applying the letter of the law, even to an uninvited alien like the Kaiser, the legal basis for preventing acquisition of property is also dubious. Once Doorn was selected, Queen Wilhelmina promised the Kaiser that he would be allowed to live there.[18] All of this suggests that as early as July and August 1919, the Dutch had assumed that the Kaiser would be a long-term resident, and that it was unlikely they would comply with the Allied demand in the final paragraph of Article 227 of the Treaty of Versailles.

Wilhelm apparently had not seen Huis Doorn before buying the place. On his first visit, before moving in, he was impressed by a Victorian carpet on the staircase. 'Gorgeous, just like at granny's', he exclaimed, referring to Queen Victoria.[19] Central heating and a lift were installed. The Dutch Government insisted that the entire estate be enclosed by fencing, at great cost, and gate houses were erected at the entrance.[20] The British Ambassador found the Kaiser's new home to be 'an unattractive place, small (it has only eleven bedrooms), and with grounds of about 120 acres, while it is much exposed to the public view—a drawback which is being remedied by new walls and plantations'.[21] The Kaiser was more positive. 'Busts, paintings and etchings of the Gr[eat] Elector, Frederick the Great, Grosspapa and Papa … along with pictures of the Prussian Army throughout its years of Glory' decorated the walls, he wrote proudly. A marble staircase was added to replace 'the fine old existing staircase'.[22] The extensive grounds provided plenty of timber for the former Emperor to pursue his favourite pastimes. The Kaiser did not move to Doorn until April 1920, after the Dutch had made clear to the Allies that there was no question of his surrender for trial. When he left Amerongen, he built a small hospital for the town as a souvenir of his visit and a sign of his appreciation. He entrusted its management to the Dutch branch of the Order of St John of Malta. There was also a romantic by-product of his stay at Amerongen Castle. His loyal aide, Sigurd van Ilsemann, married the daughter of Count Bentinck.[23]

European Royalty Mobilises

The Holy See offered the most visible opposition to trial of the Kaiser within the old order of Europe. Bishop Bonaventura Cerretti represented the Vatican at the Peace Conference where he lobbied delegates to treat Germany, and the Kaiser, with clemency.[24] On 25 June 1919, a few days before the Treaty of Versailles was signed, the semi-official newspaper of the Vatican, *Osservatore Romano*, published an article setting out arguments against prosecution of the Kaiser. At the same time, it launched a diplomatic offensive. Cardinal Pietro Gasparri, the Vatican's Secretary of State, wrote to the British Government, the only Allied Power in Paris with whom the Holy See then had diplomatic relations. Gasparri said that the Vatican was 'motivated by a sovereign and constant solicitude for the general welfare of peoples, and an ardent desire to put an end to the state of war from which, after so many years of bloodshed and ruin, countries were still suffering'. A tribunal composed of the States that were charging the Kaiser, regardless of the individuals who were appointed, would justly arouse suspicion, he contended. The proposed tribunal could not determine either the immediate or the remote causes of the conflict without considering the relevant diplomatic documents.

'Are the victorious powers willing to open the archives of their chancelleries?', asked Gasparri. 'And what guarantee will there be that no compromising documents have been destroyed or misplaced?' Noting that the Netherlands would be requested to extradite the Kaiser, Gasparri wrote:

> A great nation, like England or the United States, if placed in an analogous situation, would undoubtedly answer such a request by insisting that the right of asylum was sacred. This is probably what Holland, which has a deep sense of its own dignity, will answer. Will the victorious powers want to use force? It would be the solemn negation of a great principle proclaimed since the start of the war, namely that the rights of weaker peoples are no less sacred or worthy of respect than those of the strong.

Finally, the Cardinal warned that a refusal by the tribunal to convict would be a victory for the Kaiser. On the other hand, a conviction would have little value before public opinion, which Gasparri thought would tend to favour the Kaiser. 'In any case, the sentence cannot contain a penal sanction given that nothing is provided in any law or any code', he wrote.[25] The Foreign Office decided to leave the Vatican note unanswered.[26]

Following the signature of the Treaty of Versailles, Pope Benedict XV wrote to President Wilson questioning the value of prosecution, saying it could 'only render more bitter national hatred and postpone for a long time the pacification of souls for which all nations long'.[27] Wilson answered politely, promising to keep in mind the considerations of the Vatican.[28] According to a note in the Dutch archives, similar letters were sent to the governments of Italy and Britain.[29] The Kaiser was well informed about the Vatican's intervention on his behalf.[30] He did not greet this with enthusiasm. He subjected the Queen's representative in Utrecht, Van Lynden van Sandenburg, to a lengthy discourse on the relationship between Germany and the Holy See.[31]

The Vatican also intervened with the Dutch Government to indicate that extradition would displease Pope Benedict XV as well as most Allied Powers. The papal nuncio, Sebastiano Nicotra, met with Dutch Foreign Minister Van Karnebeek in early July 1919 to urge resistance to any demands for extradition. Van Karnebeek replied that no request had yet been received. Consequently, there was no need for the Dutch Government to take any action. Van Karnebeek told the Vatican emissary that he did not think the government would allow a request for extradition.[32] The Vatican also told the Dutch Government that if extradition or surrender was refused, 'civilised peoples would applaud the decision. The allies themselves would be pleased and would not insist. Confidentially, we are sure of this as far as Italy is concerned and an authorised source says the same thing for England.'[33]

The Vatican renewed its efforts on behalf of the Kaiser in January 1920 when Gasparri met Count de Salis, a British diplomat who was then Envoy Extraordinary and Minister Plenipotentiary to the Holy See. The same arguments were reprised, the Vatican insisting that prosecution would only incite animosity at a time when reconciliation was desirable. Moreover, the Vatican was also concerned that 'it would be well to avoid placing the Royal Family of England in a disagreeable position and at the same time shaking the throne not only of England but of every other monarchical State'.[34]

Victor Emmanuel III, the Italian King, also pursued a discreet campaign to spare the Kaiser, despite the fact that his own government had signed the Treaty of Versailles and was pledged to participate in the trial. The King of Italy told the British Ambassador in Rome, Rennell Rodd, of his displeasure with the plan to prosecute Wilhelm. 'He thought it would be a great mistake to make a martyr of him, and he could not understand by what tribunal he could be tried', Rodd reported to the Foreign Office. The

Italian King cited the efforts of the Pope and what he described as a campaign in the Kaiser's favour being pursued in the Catholic press. He warned that there was considerable opposition to the trial within Italy and said 'he had even heard that a good many votes might be recorded against the ratification of the Peace Treaty on account of the clauses providing for the trial of the ex-Emperor'.[35] A Dutch diplomat reported that the Italians had always viewed the German Kaiser as a good ally and were dismayed by the attempts to put him on trial.[36]

An Italian parliamentary commission mandated to study the Treaty of Versailles was very critical of Article 227. Observing that the crimes charged against Wilhelm were unknown in any existing criminal code, the Italian parliamentarians invoked the rule against retroactive prosecution, sometimes described as the principle of legality or by the Latin maxim *nullum crimen sine lege*. The commission concluded:

> The society of nations may establish for the future the criminal status of offenses against international morals or disregard of treaties, lay down the procedure for judging the culprit and provide for the penalty. But Count Hohenzollern's accusers cannot appoint judges; and it is impossible to ask Holland to extradite her guest for political crimes not within the purview of present treaties. The former emperor must be placed in a condition where he can do no further harm, but the eternal ideals which guarantee public and private law must be saved.[37]

A few days later, at a high-level meeting in Paris with Lloyd George, Clemenceau, and the Japanese envoy, Matsui, the Italian Prime Minister Tomasso Tittoni discussed the parliamentary commission. Tittoni reported that ratification of the Treaty of Versailles had been decided by twenty votes to three socialist votes. However, he said it was also agreed that the provisions dealing with trial of the Kaiser 'did not rest on a legal basis, because the crime had been defined after the event, and the tribunal had been designated by the persons who were charging the offence'.[38]

In July 1919, three German princes, Frederick Augustus, King of Saxony, William, Duke of Wurtemberg (formerly King of Wurtemberg), and Frederick, Duke of Baden, sent telegrams to King George V offering to substitute themselves for the Kaiser.[39] In November, they wrote again to King George V '[a]t the eleventh hour' about 'the monstrous proposal to demand the extradition of His Majesty'. They said that if trial were to take place,

> ... the world will behold the spectacle of an independent Monarch, overcome in honourable warfare by the superior forces of the Enemy, being arraigned,

against all the laws of War and of Nations, and against the traditions of Christian States, in a Court established by Enemy Powers, and possessing no jurisdiction whatsoever. In the name and on behalf of all German Princes who think and feel in common on this point, we turn to Your Majesty, whose House has a common origin with Ours, with the petition that Your Majesty will listen to our voice of warning.

They concluded: 'If Your Majesty, by allowing these proceedings, Yourself raise your hand against the Dignity of a great Ruler, who is your kinsman and was once your friend, every Government and every Throne, including that of Great Britain, will thereby be placed in jeopardy.'[40]

The letter reached the English King by a rather circuitous route, revealing a network of European royals organised to rescue one of their own. The trail begins with Friedrich Rosen, the German Ambassador in The Hague who had formerly been accredited to Madrid. Rosen exploited his personal relationship with the Spanish King, Alfonso XIII, who had made no secret of his sympathies for the Kaiser. At a Court dinner, King Alfonso expressed his outrage to the French Ambassador that kings were being treated differently from other people. He warned that prosecution would make a martyr of Wilhelm. The French Ambassador understood that the King's mother was pushing him to become 'the European champion of the unhappy monarchy'.[41] The British Ambassador, Esmé Howard, said he was inclined not to attribute much importance to the utterances of the Spanish King, 'who is of a spontaneous, impetuous, and generous character, and likes to champion those whom he believes to be in distress'.[42]

King Alfonso communicated with the King of Sweden, Gustav V, in the hopes that royal solidarity might calm English ardour for a trial. Gustav had been campaigning discreetly on behalf of Wilhelm and told the Dutch envoy in Stockholm that he was confident King George V was opposed to a trial.[43] The letter from the German princes arrived in England via the Swedish embassy, forwarded there by the Queen of Sweden. The Swedish Ambassador in London, Count Wrangel, delivered the letter to the Earl of Cromer who, as Lord Chamberlain of the Royal Household, was a senior aide to George V. Wrangel told Cromer that if Buckingham Palace would not accept the letter, his instructions were to stamp it and put it in the post, 'a course that he, not unnaturally, declined to contemplate'. Cromer delivered the letter personally to King George V. The King requested that the Foreign Office prepare a proper translation, return the original, and offer an opinion about how to respond.[44]

Charles Hardinge wrote to Lloyd George and Curzon proposing two alternatives, of which the first was a 'carefully prepared reply' and the second was to ignore the letter altogether. Hardinge said he preferred the former, 'in view of the status of the signatories and the substance of the letter, it should not be ignored'. He had taken the initiative to prepare a draft reply and to have it approved by the Legal Adviser.[45] Hardinge's draft reply repeated the terms of Article 227 of the Treaty of Versailles, referring to the pledge to vindicate solemn obligations of international morality. Whatever action might be taken by the Allies would, said the draft reply, 'be in accordance with the terms of the Treaty already concluded and ratified by the German Government'. Responding to a suggestion in the original letter ('We trust to the wisdom of Your Majesty, to prevent an act, the grave responsibility for which will be laid by history upon your shoulders'), the reply also said that 'the responsibility for the decision to proceed with the arraignment of the former German Emperor rests in common with all other responsibilities involved in the Treaty upon the Governments of all the Signatory Powers, and should not therefore be attributed to the Sovereign head of any Particular State'.[46]

King George reworded the final phrase so as to emphasise his own remoteness from any decision to prosecute Wilhelm:

> Your Majesty will no doubt appreciate that the responsibility for the decision to proceed with the arraignment of the former German Emperor can in no way be attributed to me personally, as the constitutional head of a sovereign State, but rests in common with all other responsibilities involved in the Treaty upon the Governments of all the Signatory Powers.[47]

He instructed the Foreign Office to prepare the reply 'in the usual way of Royal letters', as the German princes had done, without any beginning and with his signature at the end.[48] The letters were transmitted to the German princes through the British Embassy in Berlin.

'A Perceptible Hardening' of Dutch Opinion

Holland's Ambassador to London, Reneke de Marees van Swinderen, said that following adoption of the Treaty of Versailles, he had discussed the Kaiser issue with 'a number of highly placed Englishmen'. According to Van Swinderen, only one, George Curzon, considered that the Dutch Government would be justified in surrendering the Kaiser.[49] But who were the 'highly placed Englishmen'? The Royal Archives at Windsor Castle provide some evidence. In early July, Lord Rosebury wrote to the private secretary of King George V, Lord Stamfordham, to say that he had heard there was no chance the Dutch would surrender the Kaiser. 'This is good news,' he said.[50] F. G. Bowles wrote to Stamfordham saying the best solution might be for the Kaiser 'voluntarily to propose to go to some sufficiently distant and safe place, and to pledge himself to remain there until the Allied Powers would give him permission to leave it'.[51] An influential political operative, Lord Esher, referred to the 'idiotic Kaiser trial', and warned that there was incriminating evidence against the British and that they would do well to keep out of any judicial proceedings.[52] Even Curzon was wavering, although Van Swinderen might not have been aware of this. On 7 July 1919, Curzon wrote to Lloyd George to say he had always firmly supported trial of the Kaiser, and that he maintained his views, 'though perhaps less strongly than at the time when the subject was first raised'.[53]

When they met on 16 July 1919, Curzon asked Van Swinderen if the objections he had received from 'eminent personalities' concerned the trial as such or the trial in England, insisting that there was a big distinction between the two issues. Van Swinderen replied that they concerned both, but more particularly 'the policy of trial in any circumstances, which he now found was universally condemned'. Curzon pointed to the positive reception given the relevant articles in the Treaty of Peace, in Parliament, in the press, and in public opinion generally. Curzon acknowledged that there was debate about holding the trial in England, and that some had changed their minds about having a trial altogether. He reminded Van Swinderen that the treaty was signed not only by Britain, or for that matter by the five Great Powers, but by twenty-seven States. 'Was it to be believed that they had all been swept off their legs by a sentiment which had no real existence, and which was not supported by the public opinion of the States from which they came?', he asked.[54]

Van Swinderen turned to more practical matters, attempting to learn when the request for extradition might be made, and in what manner. Curzon told him that he did not think the Dutch should apply their legislation governing extradition. He did not view this as extradition, but rather as 'surrender in deference to the request of what was practically the entire civilised world, acting in accordance with the code of international morality and justice'.[55]

The Dutch Ambassador asked Curzon if there was any way the difficult situation could be avoided. 'I replied that he had himself suggested one at our last meeting, namely, that the Kaiser, without waiting for the action of the Dutch Government, should take the initiative by offering to surrender himself to the Allies', reported Curzon. Van Swinderen had his own novel suggestion. The Dutch Government could allow the Kaiser to 'retire to one of the Dutch colonies in a distant part of the world'. He asked Curzon if this might result in the demand for surrender being dropped, his disappearance to a remote exile being regarded 'as relieving the mind of Europe'. Curzon used words like 'evasion' and 'subterfuge' to describe such a manoeuvre. 'I am afraid that my conversation did not go far to relieve the anxieties of the Minister, nor, I imagine, to diminish the perplexities of the situation. But, as the Minister will probably repeat it to his government, I place it on record for what it may be worth.' Curzon's account of the meeting was circulated to the War Cabinet.[56] Van Swinderen reported that Curzon was not keen that the trial take place in London, but that he was adamant the Allies would proceed as soon as the treaty entered into force.[57]

The new British Minister in the Netherlands, Arnold Robertson, de-scribed the Dutch reaction to the signing of the Treaty of Versailles as '[d]isappointment, uneasiness and, to a large extent, ill-will towards the Allies in general and Great Britain in particular'. He said that the Dutch had not favoured a German victory, although they had expected it. They had hoped for a draw rather than a triumph for the Allies. 'They have an uneasy feeling that their neutrality throughout the war was apparently sympathetic towards the vanquished, and that they can lay no claim to the gratitude or even the respect of the victors.' Robertson said that the majority of the Dutch were unimpressed by 'the ideals for which the Allies fought'. Those who once were, he added, had become convinced that the Allies were hypocrites. He said few believed that Germany was responsible for the war. 'While most people admit that the Germans committed atrocities and violations of international law, many believe that the Allies also were far from guiltless', he wrote.[58]

Robertson wrote in early July 1919:

A considerable portion of public opinion in this country would disapprove of the surrender—not for any special reasons of sympathy with the Emperor and Crown Prince, but for reasons of national pride. The Socialists, for example, are, I understand, strongly opposed to the surrender. The Majority Socialists uphold the right of asylum for all alike, Emperor or peasant. The Communists consider that the victory of the Allies represents a victory of Imperialism and

Capitalism, and they do not hold the Emperor to be worse than anybody else. In Government circles very genuine difficulty is felt on grounds of international and of Dutch law.

Robertson warned the British Government of communications that might call forth 'a purely legal rejoinder, or which may contain statements which a country, that has thoroughly preserved what in its view was complete neutrality, might challenge or deny'.[59]

In early August 1919, Robertson reported 'a perceptible hardening' of Dutch opinion at both the official and the unofficial levels. He explained that this was partly due to a conviction, based upon letters and articles in the English press as well as reports from the Dutch Ambassador to London, that the Allies were not in agreement among themselves. The Dutch felt that 'considered public opinion in Great Britain is practically unanimous against the trial' with the exception of Prime Minister Lloyd George and Foreign Secretary Curzon. 'The general view appears to be that the Allies can produce no valid legal arguments which would convince the Dutch Government and public opinion, both now and in the future, that the Kaiser, who is in their opinion a political refugee in Dutch territory, should be handed over', he wrote. Robertson said the Dutch were comforted with the thought that they would be on safe ground legally. They would also 'mount a high horse of idealism', insisting it would not be consistent 'with their sense of honour, or with their self-respect, to hand over a refugee to his accusers merely because his surrender was demanded by a number of great States, a demand which would not be made if Holland were a formidable military Power'.[60]

In September, the Dutch press reported that a formal demand from the Allies to surrender the Kaiser was expected. According to the *Nieuwe Courant* of 20 September 1919, the inevitable Dutch refusal might not be entirely unwelcome. It said that although the Allied governments had made electoral commitments to hold a trial, 'an irregular procedure forcing the ex-Kaiser to appear as an accused might well have an effect different to that aimed at'. For this reason, 'the leading Statesmen of the Great Powers feel that they have reached an impasse from which a Dutch refusal would release them'.[61]

The Dutch showed concern that failure to cooperate on the Kaiser issue might encourage British support for Belgian claims to some Dutch territory as part of the post-war reconfiguration of Europe's borders. The Belgians were campaigning to be given a part of the province of Limburg, the southeastern appendage of the Netherlands that surrounds the city of Maastricht. Robertson reported that although the British were generally felt to support the Dutch case, 'it seems feared that we are veering round on account of German Emperor question. Dutch fears are of course likely to be played upon by Germans who are here in large numbers all over country and many of whom are taking houses for long terms at Hague and elsewhere.'[62] The Dutch Ambassador in London warned his government that the Allies might turn against the Netherlands in its dispute with Belgium if they did not surrender the Kaiser.[63]

Professor Joost Adriaan van Hamel, the Dutch academic and parliamentarian who had seen to his country's interests at the Peace Conference, and who would later serve as League of Nations High Commissioner for Danzig, contested the government's protection of the Kaiser. He was an advocate of the 'new justice' with an outlook similar to that of the French academics, Ferdinand Larnaude and Albert de Lapradelle, and the Greek Nikolaos Politis. With considerable foresight, he imagined a day when the Netherlands might cherish a reputation as a home for international justice. Its hospitality to Wilhelm would not help the nation's reputation in that area, he warned. On 18 October 1919, Van Hamel published an article in the *Amsterdammer* arguing against taking a position based upon 'the usual every day positive legal jurisprudence'. Van Hamel spoke of 'the tremendous change which has taken place in so many parts of the world'. He said 'common sense' made holding the ex-Kaiser responsible 'a question of justice which must be regarded according to the justice which has been born with us in this time'.

The Netherlands should not focus on the right of asylum or the fair trial guarantees, wrote Van Hamel. Rather, there should be only one overriding concern:

> It is this. Chroniclers of the future may not record 'that Holland, where Wilhelm von Hohenzollern was able to seek refuge after his Government had unchained war and trampled little Belgium under foot, and who fled after his country and army had suffered defeat, co-operated, for reasons of a juridical nature, to a situation by which the ex-Kaiser was able to evade being brought to account before a court of nations'.[64]

Van Hamel's prescient views were criticised in the Dutch press. The *Handelsblad* conceded that the 'new justice' to which Van Hamel had referred 'can be none other than the demand that whoever wages war contrary to right and treaty must no longer escape punishment, but must undergo just punishment for the greatest crime known to humanity'. It agreed the Dutch 'would be prepared to sacrifice some of the principles of the old system of punishments' in order to fulfil 'this new conception of justice', adding that 'premeditated war, unjust war may not be punishable by virtue of existing laws, but in the twentieth century everybody can and must know that a crime of that nature deserves the extreme penalty'. The *Handelsblad* said it was known that many of the Associated Powers opposed the trial 'in their hearts'. It said that because '[t]he wrong method has been chosen to make a just trial possible, people must therefore be content with the sentence that history will pronounce'.[65]

Het Weekblad van het Recht, the leading Dutch legal journal, cited the principle of non-retroactivity of criminal law that had been adopted at the time of the French Revolution. For Professor van Hamel, it said, 'that principle has lost its charm'. It described:

> ... a Court whereby judges, appointing their own accusers, will pronounce sentence according to rules fixed by themselves for crimes having no exact description, on the ground of unwritten, uncertain vague forms, with authority for arbitrary punishment. Here is a mighty historical and moral problem, which the *Entente* seek to solve, and morality will not be on the side of those who want a process of punishment contrary to all good and just forms.[66]

In mid-December, a Dutch-language version of the Kautsky papers was on display in all of the local bookshops. It had a small dust jacket with a portrait of Wilhelm and the words 'Wilhelm, Vredes Keizer?' ('Wilhelm, Kaiser of Peace?').[67] Kautsky's revelations prompted some shift in Dutch opinion towards cooperation with the Allies. Discussing the Kautsky papers, the *Handelsblad* described the Kaiser as 'very scared', 'furious', 'uneasy', and said the general feeling in the Netherlands was that 'he did everything to fan the flames and, if he did not foresee all, this merely shows that his great ambition was accompanied by a very moderate intellect'.[68] In a debate in the Second Chamber, on 9 December 1919, the leader of the Social Democratic Labour Party said that although he had previously felt sympathy for the Kaiser, the Kautsky papers put his presence in Holland in a different light. He felt that the Dutch were dealing with a man 'who had contributed in the most heedless manner, and guided by pernicious and obsolete views, to cause a world-wide calamity'.[69]

The apparent shift in Dutch attitudes did not go unnoticed outside the country. The British Prime Minister attributed this to the impact of the Kautsky documents upon public opinion. At the Anglo-French Conference in December 1919, he told Clemenceau that their publication had even turned socialists against the Kaiser, according to recent telegrams he had received from Holland. He said that the British Ambassador to the Netherlands had reported that 'the Kautsky revelations have given the *coup de grâce*' to any following or influence that the Kaiser might have possessed within the Netherlands. They had produced a 'profound impression', and provoked articles in the Dutch press whose tone was 'distinctly favourable to the extradition of the ex-Emperor, or, at any rate, to his expulsion from Holland'.[70]

'The principal reason that the Socialists fear the Kaiser is their fear he may become a centre of intrigue and of militarist reaction', observed Curzon.

'In that case, we had better press for his leaving Holland as soon as possible', said Lloyd George.

'Suppose we requested the Dutch to turn the Kaiser out of their territory, and the Dutch replied that they would be very pleased to do so as they had no concern with him, what would be the next step?' asked Curzon.

'If he crosses over to Germany, the present Government will hand him over to us. He would be much more likely to go to the United States', observed Lloyd George.

By this point, it had become clear that the United States would not ratify the Treaty of Versailles. Bonar Law questioned whether this would alter the right of the British and the French to insist on the Kaiser being surrendered. Gordon Hewart, the Attorney General, was also concerned about the absence of the Americans. Referring to the reference in Article 227 to a five-judge tribunal, with one judge being appointed by each of the Powers, Hewart asked whether the Germans might say: 'We will hand over the Kaiser to a tribunal constituted as above, but not to one where the United States is not represented.' Hewart had overlooked the fact that the Germans were not being asked to 'hand over the Kaiser'. But the point was a valid one, to the extent that German consent to Article 227 was a prerequisite for prosecution.

Lloyd George agreed that the absence of the Americans was 'a serious matter'. The same objection could be applied to the other German war criminals, and even to the reparations issue. He insisted that 'the defection of the United States does not alter circumstances'. Otherwise, he said, 'the whole thing might tumble to pieces. The Germans will say that they were influenced in signing the treaty by the fact that the Americans were associated with it'.

Philippe Berthelot reported on a recent official meeting with the chief German negotiator. 'Baron von Lersner said the non-association of the United States enabled the German Government to raise a legal question if they cared, but they did not propose to do this. He said he hoped the Allies would remember this and regard it as a proof of their good will.'

'Did they state this in writing?' asked Austen Chamberlain.

'No, they did not, but in another document they expressed the same sentiment', answered Berthelot.

'Yes, I think that is correct', said Chamberlain. 'It was expressed in somewhat the following form: "We hope that you will take this into account and give us credit for it when we surrender our criminals."'

'It is impossible for us to concede the point if the Germans raise it', insisted Lloyd George.

'Suppose the Kaiser is surrendered to us directly upon ratification of the treaty. What could the international tribunal do?', asked Balfour.

'A clause in the treaty lays it down that it should come into effect as soon as it is ratified by three Powers', said Hewart.

Lord Birkenhead confirmed this. 'The tribunal will have to quote this clause. It is desirable to proceed with the demand for the surrender of the Kaiser immediately the ratifications of the Treaty of Peace with Germany are exchanged.'[71]

That afternoon, the discussion returned briefly to the issue of the Kaiser. Lloyd George said that Lord Hugh Cecil, who was a Privy Councillor and Member of Parliament for Oxford University, had proposed that the Kaiser be interned in Dover Castle.[72] The meeting decided that Britain and France should make a formal request to the Dutch Government for the Kaiser 'immediately after the first procès-verbal of the ratification of the Treaty of Peace with Germany'.[73]

Clemenceau's travelling companion on the trip to England, General Jean Jules Henri Mordacq, had also been present at the Conference in London the previous December when Britain, France, and Italy agreed to put the Kaiser on trial. Mordacq thought the enthusiasm for a trial had cooled considerably in the course of the year. The English were still intent on bringing the Kaiser to justice, but 'with a calm and even an indifference that showed how, in twelve months, ideas had evolved'. Nevertheless, Mordacq said that: 'wherever I went, English public opinon was absolutely convinced that Wilhelm II would be brought to justice. How wrong they were.' While in London, Clemenceau had an audience with the King who departed from his usual reserve and discussed important political issues. According to Mordacq, King George V even made some discrete illusions to the appearance of Wilhelm II before the court. It seems this left Clemenceau with the impression that the English King might be trying to undermine the trial.[74]

In late 1919, Ronald Graham took over from Robertson as the British Minister in The Hague. 'To judge from discussions on the subject with the Dutchmen one meets', Graham reported to London, 'it might be imagined that any idea of extraditing the ex-Emperor is out of the question. The false analogy of the position of Prince Louis Napoleon when a refugee in England is frequently raised.' Graham was referring to the sanctuary provided to the French Emperor when the Second Empire collapsed in 1870. Napoleon III and his family, including Prince Louis Napoleon, moved to England. On the death of his father, Bonapartists proclaimed him Emperor Napoleon IV. Eager for battlefield experience, Louis Napoleon enlisted with British forces and was killed during the Zulu War of 1879.

Graham told the Foreign Office of 'a very widespread and strong impression that nobody outside Great Britain sincerely desires the ex-Emperor's extradition and trial, and that such few British statesmen as favour the idea only do so for the purpose of redeeming election pledges'. He thought that if a formal request were made pursuant to Article 227 of the Treaty of Versailles, a refusal by the Dutch Government 'will be in accordance with all expectation and will afford general relief. Justice, honour and the requirements of the Peace Treaty will have been satisfied'. Referring to a recent interview with Salomon Frederik van Oss, the editor of the *Haagsche Post*, Graham said: 'I gave him the other side of the picture, dwelling on the inconvenient, and even dangerous, position in which this country might be placed by having to provide a refuge for the ex-Emperor during an indefinite period.' Subsequently, Van Oss published a letter urging the expulsion of the ex-Emperor from Holland, supporting it with 'a strong editorial'. Graham believed that Van Oss was taken to task by Foreign Minister Van Karnebeek as a result. Graham thought 'a gradual change in public feeling is taking place'.[75]

The British Ambassador considered that the Dutch reaction would depend more upon the form of the request than on the legal arguments in support. 'Rightly or wrongly, the idea of delivering up a royal refugee, however guilty, to be tried by purely enemy judges and on enemy territory is repugnant to the Dutch sense of honour and fair play', he said. A 'direct summons' to hand over the Kaiser for trial in Great Britain or France was likely to be met with a direct refusal. This 'would be approved by the majority of the Dutch nation, if not by neutral opinion as a whole'. Graham thought that the result might be different if the request could be framed as one for Dutch support and cooperation for vindicating the sanctity of treaties, the rules of civilised warfare, and the prevention of catastrophic war, 'even if for so worthy a purpose old precedents have to be ignored and new ones created'.[76]

Six months had passed since the adoption of the Treaty of Versailles at the end of June 1919. There had been much speculation about how the Dutch would react to the request of surrender. The final act in a drama that had begun more than a year earlier, when first the War Cabinet and subsequently the leaders of the three European Allies had decided to put the Kaiser on trial, was about to be played out.

17

Demand for Surrender

In June 1919, the Allies agreed to postpone their request to the Dutch to surrender the Kaiser until the Treaty of Versailles entered into force. Pursuant to its final clause, the Treaty of Versailles would enter into force once it had been ratified by three of the Allied and Associated Powers and Germany. The instrument of ratification was deposited by Germany on 12 July 1919. However, the first *procès-verbal* of ratification was not prepared until 10 January 1920, by which time Britain, France, Italy, and Japan had all become parties. By this point, the United States had made clear that it would not ratify the treaty.

At one of its final meetings in June, the Council of Four assigned Robert Lansing to draft a letter to the Dutch requesting that they surrender the Kaiser. A text was debated and adopted, but its delivery was postponed until the entry into force of the treaty.[1] Had the Kaiser's surrender been demanded immediately upon signature of the Treaty of Versailles, the Dutch might have complied. But by January 1920, there was no longer the same unanimity, and ardour, that had prevailed among the five Powers. The Americans were not directly involved anymore, and the Japanese were indifferent, at best. The Italians were ambivalent. Clemenceau thought he had observed a change in mood in England, especially of the King, whom he had met the previous month on his visit to London. He described 'a certain indecision that some might go so far to qualify as a change in position', noting that the French ambassador to London had the same impression. Clemenceau's intuition was that the whole matter might be postponed indefinitely. The French Prime Minister, who was himself in his final weeks in office, insisted that it was necessary to put Holland 'up against the wall'.[2]

In January 1920, two new drafts of the note to the Dutch Government were prepared, one by the French Government[3] and the other, rather more

The Trial of the Kaiser. William A. Schabas. © William A. Schabas, 2018. Published 2018 by Oxford University Press.

succinct, by the Drafting Committee of the Supreme Council.[4] The British Lord Chancellor, Lord Birkenhead (formerly F. E. Smith), expressed a preference for the French version, although he said the differences in the texts were not considerable. According to Birkenhead, it was 'drawn up in judicial language and was particularly clear and precise. Speaking as a judge, the French draft makes a strong appeal to me.' The French text was adopted by the British, the French, and the Italians, with the addition of a paragraph from the Lansing draft of July 1919. They also decided that the note should be signed by 'the Powers' rather than use earlier formulations where the five countries were listed individually. This indirectly acknowledged the fact that the United States was no longer participating.[5]

On 16 January 1920, Clemenceau informed the Supreme Council that the note would be handed to the Dutch Minister at 6:30 in the evening. 'I myself have not known anything about this note', said the American representative, Hugh Wallace. 'This is a matter concerning the execution of a treaty which the United States has not yet ratified', replied Lloyd George. 'The Allies can inform Mr. Wallace of their decisions upon the subject; but it is difficult for them to ask to participate in the discussion.' The Japanese were also excluded from the drafting of the note, although they were invited to sign if they wished.[6]

The note constituted 'the official request to the Government of the Netherlands for the surrender to the Allies of William of Hohenzollern, ex-Emperor of Germany, in order that he may be put on trial'. It stated that had Wilhelm remained in Germany, his surrender by Germany would have been required under Article 228 of the Treaty of Versailles. It said the Dutch Government was aware 'of the unassailable reasons which imperatively demand that the premeditated violations of international treaties, as well as systematic disregard of the most sacred rules of international law, suffer, irrespective of persons, no matter of how high position, the penalties provided for by the Peace Congress'. Unlike Lansing's letter of June 1919, in which there were no details of the charges against the Kaiser beyond the phrases in Article 227, the note provided specifications about the allegations. After a brief reference to violation of neutrality, it recited a long list of breaches of the laws and customs of war: 'the barbarous and merciless hostage system', mass deportations, 'the carrying away of the young women of Lille, torn from their families and thrown defenceless into the most promiscuous environment', systematic devastation without military justification of entire territories,

unrestricted submarine warfare 'including the inhuman abandon of victims on the high seas', and 'innumerable acts committed by the German
authorities against non-combatants in contempt of the laws of war'. The
note implied that the Kaiser might not have ordered these atrocities, but
that he bore 'moral responsibility' to the extent that he permitted crimes
to be perpetrated. It did not allege responsibility for inciting or starting
the war.

'Holland would not be fulfilling her international obligations if she refused to join the other nations within the means at her disposal in carrying
out or at the very least in not hindering the punishment of the crimes committed', the note charged. It said the demand 'does not fall within the lines
of a public accusation of a fundamentally legal nature, but is an act of high
international policy, imposed by the conscience of the universe'. Accordingly,
the Netherlands, with its 'respect of Law and its Love of Justice', would not
attempt 'to help cover with her moral authority, violations of the essential
principles of the solidarity of nations, all equally interested in preventing the
return of a similar catastrophe'.[7]

The Allied demand 'occasioned a great flutter in Dutch Dovecotes and
there was much coming and going between various Ministries', according
to the British Ambassador, Ronald Graham.[8] Only three Dutch papers, the
Gazette d'Holland, Telegraaf, and *Vaderland* published the letter. Noting that
these appeared early in the day, the British Ambassador suspected the Dutch
Government had asked the press to suspend publication until the reply was
ready.[9] Graham said that the Secretary General of the Ministry of Foreign
Affairs, in communicating the news to the press, described the government as
being 'seriously embarrassed'.[10]

Graham anticipated that the Dutch would invoke the fact that the United
States had not ratified the treaty as impairing its validity. He thought that
many of the Dutch resented the Kaiser for having imposed such a difficult
situation upon their country. There was 'a widely expressed but somewhat
forlorn hope that he may himself come forward and take some course which
would extract them from it'.[11] Clemenceau's *aide de camp,* General Mordacq,
thought the letter had a great effect on the Dutch, although he recognised the
very strong influence of the 'German party'. Moreover, Mordacq suspected
intervention in support of the Kaiser traceable to his relatives in the English
royal family.[12]

Dutch Refusal

The Dutch replied to Clemenceau's message on 21 January 1920, rejecting the Allied request. Their position combined some legal argument with a broader appeal to notions of hospitality. The Dutch pointed out that unlike Germany, they were not a party to the Treaty of Versailles and consequently it imposed no legal obligations upon them. They recalled that they were in no way implicated in the origin of the war and that they had maintained, 'not without difficulty', their neutrality until the end of the conflict. The reply stated that the Dutch were in a totally different position from that of the other Powers with relation to the acts of the war. The Dutch Government said it 'energetically' opposed any suspicion 'as to its intent to cover the violations of the essential principles of the solidarity of nations by its sovereign rights or its moral authority, but it cannot recognise that it has an international obligation to become associated with the Powers in this act of high international policy'.

The letter went on to explain that were the League of Nations to establish a criminal court, 'by virtue of a statute previously enacted', the Netherlands would be free to adhere to the regime. However, at present it could not accept any obligations other than those 'imposed by the Laws of the Kingdom and the national traditions'. It said that, at present, neither Dutch laws, 'which are based on universally recognised principles of law', nor the traditions that had made the country 'a land of refuge for those vanquished in international conflicts', enabled the government to comply with the demands. 'Right and national honour, the respect of which is a sacred duty, oppose such action', it said.[13]

Ambassador Graham suspected the Dutch cabinet was divided, with the Minister for Foreign Affairs, backed by the Minister of Justice, opposed to surrender, and the Prime Minister 'more hesitating'. He thought the Dutch press had initially seemed to favour extradition, but 'official inspiration had led it to change its position'.[14] Graham wrote that the Dutch had been fortified by reports that the English leaders, with the exception of Lloyd George, were not keen on proceeding with a trial. Dutch public opinion did not seem to take the Allied demand very seriously. 'It is stated that Allied statesmen, though I have never been given a name, have written to this country imploring the Dutch Government to prevent the extradition of the ex-Emperor.'[15] A Dutch diplomat in London reported that '*milieux politiques ainsi que classes supérieures*' hope extradition will be refused, but '*masses populaires*' and the press support a trial.[16]

Graham begged London for 'some sign of strong British public opinion ... instead of strings of Press extracts approving Dutch attitude'.[17] Much of the English media remained silent on the issue, including the 'Northcliff press', an influential chain of sensationalist, populist, and sabre-rattling newspapers. The satirical magazine *Punch* ran a cartoon showing a Dutch peasant woman chatting with a caricatured Entente soldier replete with bicorne hat: 'So you say you'd like me to surrender the ex-Kaiser', she asks. 'Well ma'am, I didn't go as far as that. I only asked you for him.'[18] The London correspondent of the *Telegraaf* thought it had been a long time since a cartoon gave the situation so clearly, 'for there is a great difference between asking for the Kaiser and wanting to have him'.[19]

The Supreme Council of the Peace Conference was now reconfigured as the 'Conference of Ambassadors'. The Dutch note of 21 January was the first item on the agenda of the initial meeting of the Conference, held on 26 January 1920. Alexandre Millerand, who had replaced Georges Clemenceau as Prime Minister only a few days previously, hosted the session in his office. 'To me it seems obvious—and upon this point I should like to have the opinion of members of the Council—that the Dutch note cannot remain unanswered', began Millerand. The French Prime Minister said he had stressed the significance of 'international morality' in comments to the Dutch Minister. 'Yet even from the legal point of view, it is worth noting that Vattel, the authority on international law in his *Treatise on the Law of Nations*, indicates that any power which helps a hateful tyrant goes against its own duty. There is moreover a further consideration to establish: the demand for the extradition of the Kaiser might well be regarded under the circumstances in which it is made as the first act *de facto*, if not *de jure*, of the League of Nations, seeking to exercise an international jurisdiction in a matter involving crimes that have aroused the consciences of the civilised world', continued Millerand. The League of Nations had come into existence with the entry into force of the Treaty of Versailles. However, it took some time for it to become fully operational. Millerand thought it to be 'regrettable that these countries which, if I am not mistaken, have manifested the desire to enter into the League of Nations, do not lend a more friendly, helping hand in the first public act of the League'. Millerand expressed real irritation that 'the letter of the Dutch Government contains not one word in censure of the crimes with which we have to charge the Kaiser'.[20] The meeting agreed to draft a reply to the Dutch.

On 25 January, Ambassador Graham received a 'private letter' from Curzon, the Foreign Minister. The letter has not been found in the archives, but its contents can be gleaned from subsequent correspondence. Curzon informed him 'that the Allied demand was serious and unanimous, and was to be supported by every possible argument'. A 'private telegram' from Charles Hardinge, the Permanent Under-Secretary, followed a few days later. It too is without trace in the archives. Graham later insisted that the messages from London pushed him to be more aggressive and uncompromising than his own instincts directed.[21] On 28 January 1919, Hardinge conveyed instructions to Graham from Lloyd George that he should privately inform the Dutch Foreign Minister 'that the Kaiser question is not merely a question of Government policy, but one in which public opinion is very deeply interested'.[22] Lloyd George considered that public opinion demanded that 'the Kaiser should be tried and rendered incapable of again molesting the peace of the world'. The British Prime Minister wanted the Dutch Government to understand that by refusing the Allied demand, 'they are bound to come in conflict with a very strong, powerful and easily roused public opinion in England'.[23]

Graham dutifully conveyed the message to Van Karnebeek the next day. Once again, the Dutch Minister reminded Graham that the Netherlands had no obligations under the Treaty of Versailles. Van Karnebeek conceded that the tone of the Dutch press had been 'very foolish', but while he sought to calm the crisis he gave Graham nothing to suggest there could be any change in the official position. He warned that pressure would only strengthen Dutch resolve and further damage the relationship between the two countries, an observation that Graham found to be quite reasonable. According to Van Karnebeek, the refusal of surrender enjoyed the support of all segments of Dutch political life, 'even among the Communists'. Were the government to accede to the Allied demand, they would be unable to remain in office, he said. Van Karnebeek explained that extradition of a foreigner in the absence of a treaty would breach the Dutch Constitution, 'as all foreigners in Holland were assured of the same protection as were Dutch citizens'.[24] The Dutch Minister agreed that the Kaiser should not be allowed to foment unrest in Germany, but said that preventing this was something to be left to the Netherlands.[25]

Beyond gentle persuasion, what measures might be used, or at least threatened, to convince the Dutch Government to change its mind? The French report circulated by Clemenceau at the outset of the Peace Conference had invoked the spectre of exclusion from the League of Nations as well as 'methods recognised by present international law—rupture of diplomatic relations, a pacific blockade, economic boycott'.[26] At Lloyd George's request, the British Foreign Office prepared a memorandum setting out the options. These included disruption of diplomatic relations and withdrawal of the British mission, refusal to allow Dutch ships to enter British ports, refusal to give coal to Holland and to let Dutch ships use British coaling stations, and denying the Dutch access to their colonies by interrupting steamer services, postal, and telegraphic communication. Such a full or partial blockade, as the memorandum noted, would require the cooperation of Britain's allies as well as neutral powers. 'Presumably our Allies would co-operate with us', speculated the author of the note,[27] although this seems an unwarranted assumption. There was scepticism in the Foreign Office. One bureaucrat minuted: 'The interruption of our trade with Holland and the Dutch East Indies and of the trade between Holland and the Dutch East Indies would react most unfavourably on our present critical exchange position.' Another official commented that '[e]ven with all the weapons we possessed during the war—and which we possess no longer—we never succeeded in forcing the hands of the Dutch by means of economic pressure'. The official said this was due in part to 'the innate stubbornness of the Dutch' and in part to British dependence upon Dutch produce. He added that withdrawal of the British mission 'would probably leave the Dutch quite unmoved' and 'would only throw them more into the German orbit'.[28]

Pursuant to the Covenant of the League of Nations, several States, including the Netherlands, were invited to join the organisation. There was little doubt that the Dutch would accept within the two-month deadline they were given.[29] In his review of the history of the dispute, the Deputy Permanent Under-Secretary in the British Foreign Ministry, Eyre Crowe, observed that the Allied governments decided not to rescind the invitation to Holland to join the League 'presumably, because it must be doubtful whether under the terms of the covenant such invitation could legally be withheld'.[30]

The Conference of Ambassadors met on 3 February to consider the draft reply to the Dutch prepared by the French Delegation. The text did not address any of the legal objections, emphasising instead Holland's duties as a good international citizen. It expressed dismay at the absence, in the Dutch reply, of any word of disapproval of the crimes committed by the Emperor, crimes that violate 'the most elementary considerations of humanity and civilisation of which, in particular, so many Dutch nationals were innocent victims on the high seas', a reference to the German attacks on Dutch merchant vessels. Providing assistance in the punishment of such crimes was entirely consistent with the views of the seventeenth-century Dutch international lawyer Hugo Grotius, it said, citing the Latin phrase *puniendi aut dedendi aut certe amovendi*. It referred to 'reactionary manifestations that followed the Dutch refusal and the dangerous encouragement that was thereby given to those elements that were opposed to the delivery of fair and exemplary justice' to high officials. The draft said the Allies wished 'in a friendly way' to warn the Dutch that their attitude might 'weaken the precious reputation of impartiality enjoyed by the Dutch people, an attitude which might have a relationship with the economical and financial agreements recently concluded between Holland and Germany'.

The draft addressed a Dutch suggestion that a universal or global tribunal would be the appropriate place to judge the Kaiser. It said that 'they cannot wait for the creation of a global tribunal, with authority to try international crimes; it is precisely the judgment that is contemplated that will prepare the way for such a tribunal which will make the collective action of the universal conscience'. The League of Nations had not yet reached a stage in its development so that it could establish such a tribunal, the note said. 'Will not the refusal by the Dutch Government to surrender the former Emperor create a regrettable precedent that will tend to make ineffective the procedure of any international tribunal dealing with highly placed accused persons?'

There was an ominous reference to Dutch membership in the League of Nations. The Allies considered it 'a point of honour' that the invitation to the Netherlands not be rescinded. But the draft asked how it could be carried into effect if the country placed itself, 'from the very beginning, in opposition to the thought and action of the Allied Powers, which have invited Holland to be a co-member with them in the League of Nations'. Dutch indifference to housing the German imperial family so close to the German border would 'call into question and weaken the participation of Holland in the League of Nations, will risk compromising their loyal relations with the Allies'. Moreover, the country would thereby 'assume a direct responsibility both in the sheltering of a criminal from the claims of justice and in the monarchist propaganda against the democracies of Europe'.[31]

The Conference of Ambassadors agreed that it could go no further until the governments had given their instructions on the matter.[32] Hugh Wallace, the American Ambassador, told his Dutch counterpart after the meeting that the answer 'will be mildly worded but if Holland does not agree, I fear the next will be very drastic ... England is bent upon getting the Kaiser.'[33] In reality, England was bending.

A Napoleonic Solution Emerges

Graham wrote to Curzon on 30 January 1919 complaining that he was without instructions about how to proceed.[34] Perhaps he already sensed that British policy was in flux. For the past few days, discussions had been underway in London about abandoning the trial contemplated by Article 227 of the Treaty of Versailles and insisting, instead, that the Kaiser be interned in much the same manner as Napoleon more than a century earlier. At a meeting with Hardinge of the Foreign Office on 27 January, the Lord Chancellor, Birkenhead, said the Dutch reply to the Allies would have looked less like 'absolute defiance' if they had 'recognised the reasonableness of the Allies apprehensions by offering to hand him over for internment on some suitable spot and with such stipulations as might be proper on the subject of reasonable maintenance and treatment'. Hardinge believed some well-placed hints to the Dutch might lead them to propose exile as a solution. He thought the Falkland Islands would be appropriate.[35]

On 31 January, Hardinge instructed Graham to inform the Dutch that, due to English public opinion, continued refusal to surrender the Kaiser would 'inevitably provoke reprisals on their part which, in view of the traditional friendship between Great Britain and the Netherlands, no Government would regret more than that of His Majesty'. A second paragraph with the title 'Confidential' reminded Graham of the 'firm determination' of the British Government to demand the internment of the Kaiser 'under Allied control in some spot or island where he will be rendered incapable of molesting the peace of the world'. Hardinge said he would be glad to have Graham's views on such a proposal and whether he thought it was likely to be accepted.[36]

Graham requested more details about what was envisaged. He asked Hardinge to explain the meaning of 'banishment'. If it simply meant internment by the Allies, Graham thought it would not be considered any sort of concession by the Dutch. 'They would prefer a trial to internment without a trial, and they are perfectly aware that latter course would save Allies from embarrassment which they have no desire to spare them', he wrote.

Graham suggested that a 'spontaneous' initiative could come from the Dutch to intern the Kaiser themselves, with strict supervision of visits and correspondence. He might be held in the north of Holland, far from the German border, or in the Dutch West Indies, or in 'some distant locality possibly neutral, chosen by Allies, but with Dutch guard and supervision'. Graham thought that such a solution could probably be reached 'without pressure or menace'. He also sought Hardinge's reaction to another idea, whereby the Dutch would agree to trial or internment by the League of Nations.[37]

On 2 February 1920, Graham met with Van Karnebeek on a 'private and unofficial' basis. He warned the Dutch Foreign Minister of the 'very strong and unanimous feeling among the Allies on the question of the ex-Emperor, and of their determination to carry the matter through'. He said the views of the British Government, which he expected to deliver with 'a few days' time', would have 'unmistakable clarity and force' and 'could scarcely be anything but most unpalatable to the Netherlands Government'. The term 'reprisals' was used. Van Karnebeek thought it might involve opposition to Dutch membership in the League of Nations and even the withdrawal of diplomats from The Hague.[38] Describing the meeting with Graham to the Dutch Ambassador in London, Van Karnebeek said the British had threatened to break diplomatic relations, to deny the Dutch membership in the League of Nations, and to take 'mesures coërcitives'.[39]

Van Karnebeek protested to Graham that the shrill tone of the British message had shaken his faith 'in post-war ideals and, indeed, in the whole political future'. The Dutch Foreign Minister felt that '[i]f Holland had been a great Power, instead of a small one, no such menace would have been addressed to her'. Van Karnebeek spoke of 'national dignity and honour'. The greater the threat the stronger would be the Dutch resolve. In reply, Graham said that he could do nothing but urge compliance.[40] An alternative suggestion would have to come from the Netherlands. Slowly, at least according to Graham's account of the meeting, the idea of internment in a Dutch possession far from Europe was emerging.[41]

Graham discussed the communications he was receiving from London with his French colleague, Charles Benoist, a journalist and politician recently appointed as his country's Minister to The Hague. Graham was uneasy about acting alone and not in concert with other Allied diplomats. When Benoist reported this to Paris, the Quai d'Orsay told him that it could not join in any initiatives without an official request from London, but it confirmed its support of the rigid position being advocated by the British.[42] '[T]he instructions given to your colleague are consistent with our views. You may inform the Dutch Minister of Foreign Affairs of this, as well as your British colleague.'[43] On 3 February, Graham told Benoist that he had not yet made the official *démarche* with the Dutch Government. However, he reported that he had privately warned Van Karnebeek that this was coming. Benoist thought that Graham was trying to encourage the Dutch to come up with a counter-proposal, such as internment of the Kaiser in Java. He said that Graham read the telegram from the Foreign Office to him again. Benoist reported to Paris that the telegram spoke quite explicitly of reprisal, and of an attitude that could compromise good relations. He said it alluded to internment of the Kaiser 'under allied control'. This would be on 'an island that is not specified', chosen so that Wilhelm 'will never again be able to disrupt world peace'.[44]

Paul Cambon, the French Ambassador in London, complained to the Quai d'Orsay that the British had threatened reprisals against the Dutch without prior agreement with their allies. Cambon disagreed with the apparent endorsement of the British action in the instructions given to Ambassador Benoist in The Hague. Cambon was concerned that the French were only encouraging the British to act on their own. 'The question is more complicated than it appears to those in both London and Paris', he wrote. Cambon thought the issue had been presented incorrectly from the outset. He referred to legal experts who had insisted it was wrong to describe the matter as extradition. The Dutch were not parties to the Treaty of Versailles and had no obligation to surrender the Kaiser. Any cooperation on their part would be nothing more than an *acte de complaissance*. In any case, a breaking of diplomatic relations could only be counterproductive, he said. As for internment on a British island far from Europe, this was *de la pure imagination*, a *fantaisie*.[45] Cambon's intuitions proved to be quite perceptive.

A Draft Reply with Veiled Threats

On 6 February 1920, the Dutch Foreign Minister told Ambassador Graham that the Cabinet had considered the issue in light of their 'private conversation' earlier in the week.[46] There would be no change in the Dutch position on extradition, he said.[47] Meeting with Ambassador Benoist, Van Karnebeek said simply 'we cannot', to which the French envoy answered that the Allies

were in the same position. It was impossible for them to agree that implementation of a treaty of some 440 articles, covering a vast field of action, could
be set aside at the very outset.[48] But the Dutch were slowly starting to acknowledge 'legitimate concerns' of the Allies about the presence of Wilhelm
in their country, so close to the German border. Van Karnebeek characterised
Wilhelm as 'a broken and discredited man'. If the Allied governments would
place their confidence in the Dutch Government to ensure that the Kaiser
never posed a threat, it would show itself to be worthy of their trust. He told
Benoist that a non-European location was out of the question, but that the
Kaiser could be held at Doorn, in the castle he had purchased the previous
August.[49] Van Karnebeek said that he hoped the Kaiser would soon leave the
Netherlands, suggesting Chile or Peru as possibilities.[50] He told Graham 'that
a tone of menace used by Allied Governments in addressing Netherlands
Government would only render it more difficult for latter to go as far as they
could in meeting what they considered legitimate wishes of Allies [sic]'.[51]

Hardinge briefed the King's personal secretary on the new approach the
British Government was taking. Britain would drop its insistence on the trial
if the Dutch agreed that the Kaiser be domiciled 'in a place like the Falkland
Islands'. He would not be treated 'in a manner similar to that meted out to
Napoleon, but be permitted to live in comfort and more or less dignity with
his family if they wished to go with him'. Alternatively, the Dutch could
agree that Wilhelm be sent to one of their own colonies in the East Indies.
In that case, Britain would claim a right to supervise the situation so as to
ensure that conditions of internment were respected and that the Kaiser did
not escape.[52]

The change in the British position was formally presented to an Allied
Conference in London on 12 and 13 February. After a lengthy discussion of
the prosecution of German military and political leaders, Curzon returned to
the proposed reply to the Dutch. He described the draft prepared by Philippe
Berthelot as 'in effect a repetition of the request for the Kaiser's extradition
in strong terms'. Curzon said he was inclined to think that the Berthelot
draft 'did not put forward the aspect of the case as it appealed to the British
Government'. Curzon explained that '[s]o long as the Kaiser is within a few
miles of the German border, there is danger not only to Germany itself but
to all other countries, Holland included. In replying, the Allies might say that
they could not tolerate the Kaiser being left as a focus of intrigue in Holland.'
He said it was highly unlikely the Dutch would change their position on

extradition. The revised British proposal 'leaves them a loophole, whereby they might suggest his internment in Java or some such place', said Curzon.[53]

The following day, Curzon submitted a version of the French draft reply that he had reworked with Birkenhead and that better reflected the new British approach. Curzon said that 'if the Dutch would voluntarily intern the Kaiser in one of their overseas possessions, we should not insist on demanding his extradition ... He himself believed the Dutch would accept our suggestion as to the internment of the Kaiser overseas, and that this would solve the difficulty.'[54] Whereas the French draft had emphasised international justice and the responsibilities of the Dutch, given the atrocities allegedly perpetrated by the Kaiser, the British additions focused on the continuing threat posed by the Kaiser, an aspect that the French had essentially ignored.[55] In a sense, this reflected the classic debate about the purposes of criminal justice. Does it seek retribution and just punishment, as the French envisioned the matter, or prevention and security, as the British insisted?

Lloyd George was not entirely pleased with the conciliatory approach being urged by his Foreign Minister. To Curzon's proposal about internment, the Prime Minister answered enigmatically: 'Suppose we put the following to the Dutch Government: "What would have happened supposing Napoleon, instead of being captured and interned overseas, had managed to escape to Switzerland?"' Curzon said that in the draft it was 'hinted' that the Dutch might offer to intern the Kaiser in one of their distant colonies. He pointed out that the words 'however unacceptable' had been deliberately inserted.[56] Lloyd George said he had two suggestions. He wanted to include a few lines 'pointing out that over 10 million of the world's youth had been killed owing to the action of Germany in going to war, drawing attention to the devastation of formerly prosperous provinces of Allied countries, and laying stress upon the fact of the terrible destitution which still continues in the countries of Central Europe owing to the war, for which the Kaiser is held responsible'.[57]

This paragraph was the result:

> They cannot refrain from reminding the Government of the Netherlands that through the policy and acts of this man over ten million human beings, most of them in the flower of youth, have been killed in Europe, and three times that number have been mutilated of impaired in health; that thousands of square kilometres of territory alive with industry and happy homes have been utterly devastated; and that millions of people are at this moment suffering from bereavement and material losses, and bearing the burden of war debts exceeding

£30,000,000,000 incurred in defending their own freedom and that of the Netherlands and of the world. They would have expected some expression at least of condemnation of those crimes and of sympathy and understanding for those who have sustained such suffering in restoring law and liberty to Europe.[58]

Lloyd George also wanted a phrase warning the Dutch of the 'very serious situation' that they would face for failure to comply.[59] It was certainly a notch down from his earlier threats of blockade, sanctions, and exclusion from the League of Nations.

Yet another draft reply, this time prepared by Berthelot, was adopted at the final session of the Conference.[60] The redraft removed the reference to 'interning him and keeping him interned at a distance from the scene of his crimes'. In the final version, the text spoke of the failure of the Dutch to consider the possibility of effective measures of precaution, '*soit sur place, soit en maintenant l'ex-Empereur éloigné de la scene de ses crimes*'. Explicit reference to internment had been removed. Perhaps more significant, replacing this with the words *soit sur place* intimated that residence within Holland was not entirely ruled out.[61]

Soit sur place

The following day, Curzon instructed Ambassador Graham to deliver the note to the Dutch Government. 'While answering the Dutch contentions, and re-asserting the position of Allies, it affords to the Dutch Government the opportunity of making on its own account the suggestion of internment elsewhere', Curzon said. 'A place in Holland would not prove acceptable. Some remote Dutch colony will be required.'[62] Graham took due note of Curzon's position, observing that if this were really the view of the Allied Powers, they ought not to have used the phrase 'soit sur place'. '[T]hese words will be regarded as a direct invitation to formulate proposals for the safe internment of the ex-Emperor in Holland, and the Castle of Doorn is likely to be the spot proposed', he wrote to Curzon.[63]

The Allied note delivered by Ambassador Graham produced 'great irritation' in Dutch Government circles.[64] Foreign Minister Van Karnebeek prepared a reply in 'an equally strong and even in a disagreeable tone', comparable to that of the Allied note, answering each of the points one after the other. It concluded by stating that although the Netherlands did not perceive the Kaiser as a danger to peace, it was prepared to ensure that he would not become one. Preventing the Kaiser from political mischief was a matter for the Dutch Government alone, however. Van Karnebeek's reply was approved by the Queen, who was reported to have 'taken a strong personal interest' in the question. On 19 February, the reply was approved by the Cabinet, but hit a snag when it was shown to leaders of the parliamentary groups, who found it too severe. The parliamentarians insisted that the Dutch Government recognise the political danger posed by the Kaiser. At their insistence, the text was made more conciliatory.[65]

The Conference of Ambassadors returned to the issue on 24 February. 'I have just heard from The Hague that the Government of the Netherlands has taken very much amiss the tone of the last Allied note regarding the Kaiser', said Lloyd George. The Dutch seemed to have the impression that the demand came from Britain only, and that the other Powers were indifferent. Lloyd George said that if the other European States did not care whether the Kaiser remained in the Netherlands, 'they should say so, because it appears to me that the risks affect them more than they do my own country. If you share the view that the presence of the Kaiser in the Netherlands represents a danger to peace, then you should instruct your diplomats to exert pressure on the Dutch Government.'[66]

Curzon reviewed developments over recent weeks, saying he now expected the Dutch position would be internment of the Kaiser at Doorn. 'Speaking for myself, I hope that the Council will take the view that this should be resisted. The joint letter suggests that the Kaiser ought to be removed out of Europe. Possibly the Dutch will suggest Java, or Curaçao in the West Indies ... It matters little to us', Curzon continued, 'that the Kaiser be removed to the Malay Archipelago or to the West Indies. The principal thing is to checkmate the possibility of removing the Kaiser to Doorn. For this, very emphatic and strong action taken by all of the Powers is necessary.'[67]

It became evident that the French and the Italians did not share the British understanding of what was being asked of the Dutch. 'I must confess that I did not have the impression we had demanded internment in a colony', said Prime Minister Millerand.[68] Nitti of Italy agreed with Millerand: 'I am personally under the impression that when Holland was asked to give certain guarantees with respect to the Kaiser, our request could have been interpreted to mean that the Kaiser should be placed in a place further removed from the frontier.'[69] The Italians had already told the Dutch they would be satisfied as long as Wilhelm was compelled to reside at some distance from the border with Germany. They had even urged the Dutch to suggest this as a way of resolving the crisis.[70] Nitti now insisted that regardless of what their note had intended, 'the Allies will gain nothing and only place themselves in a difficult situation by insisting upon the removal of the Kaiser ... I have great admiration for the history of Great Britain, but I doubt whether she had been wise in sending Napoleon to Saint Helena. At the present moment, the Kaiser is not popular in Germany. His restoration appears to me to be a most improbable event. To persecute him would be to give him greater popularity that he would otherwise ever be likely to attain', said Nitti.[71]

Millerand proposed that the Allied governments tell the Dutch Government that 'the Kaiser should be sent to a far-off island as the best solution of the difficulty. But that suggestion should not be made a *sine qua non* condition.' He said that if the Dutch refused, then they must be made to understand that they were 'to take all necessary precautions to intern and guard the Kaiser'.[72] Lloyd George accepted this. 'If Monsieur Millerand's statement is the attitude taken by the Council, then the British Government will go along', he said. 'But let me add that we take a different view. This matter is not of sufficient consequence for there to be disagreement amongst us.'[73] The meeting agreed that the three Allied Powers would send identical notes to the Dutch. Berthelot prepared a draft for the meeting the following day. A committee consisting of Curzon, Scialoja, and Berthelot was to take the final decision on the text.[74]

In the afternoon of 26 February, the Ambassadors of Britain, France, and Italy called upon the Dutch Foreign Minister. Van Karnebeek asked for a written copy of their instructions. He was 'visibly impressed' when Graham provided a French version. He asked the ambassadors if it was a *mise-en-demeure*, that is, a kind of peremptory demand or ultimatum, but Graham denied this. He described the position as a 'friendly warning'. The three ambassadors repeated the message to the Prime Minister. Neither the Prime Minister nor the Foreign Minister offered any comment on the Allied *démarche*.[75] In a private meeting that followed, Van Karnebeek told Graham that his government 'would go as far as they possibly could to meet legitimate demands of Allies but they could not overstep limits set by Dutch Constitution'.[76] Van Karnebeek complained that the Allied note had been 'unnecessarily strong', objecting to the suggestion that by denying surrender of the Kaiser the Dutch were placing themselves outside of the international community.[77]

Graham lobbied for the British position with anyone who would listen to him. He met with the acting Permanent Under-Secretary in the Dutch Ministry of Foreign Affairs, Beerlaerts van Blokland, who made the analogy with a householder who has a dog that his neighbours consider to be dangerous. Even if the householder doesn't feel that way, he is bound to satisfy the neighbours that the dog is safely chained up and under proper control. Graham responded 'that the simile was scarcely flattering to the Royal exile', but what, he asked, if the dog had already bitten the neighbours and their children 'in the tenderest portions of their anatomy'? They were entitled not only to demand that the dog be chained up, but also that it be removed altogether from the neighbourhood. 'Chains were easy to break, and garden walls were low and easy to jump.'[78]

Graham and Van Karnebeek met at a reception on 4 March. Graham said that it would be acceptable if the Kaiser remained interned in the Netherlands. The only issue, he said, was that he had chosen his own place of residence. Van Karnebeek answered that Doorn had been chosen by the Dutch Government for want of a better alternative.[79]

East Indies, Curaçao, or Closer to Home

The Dutch replied on 2 March 1920, although the letter was only received three days later.[80] Van Karnebeek had told Benoist that the Dutch reply would satisfy the Allies.[81] The French Ambassador learned that it had been slightly toned down at the last minute.[82] Ambassador Van Swinderen delivered it personally to 10 Downing Street. Lloyd George refused to open the envelope, saying it would be discussed that afternoon in the Supreme Council. Lloyd George and Van Swinderen spoke at some length, debating fine points of Anglo-Dutch relations in the eighteenth century. When Van Swinderen said Wilhelm was 'much too old' to do any harm—Wilhelm was 60 at the time—Lloyd George answered that he still had able lieutenants 'in their prime'. To justify concerns about European security as long as the Kaiser remained in the Netherlands, Lloyd George recalled that an Irish national leader, Éamon de Valera, of Sinn Fein, had been imprisoned in England, but had managed to escape from Lincoln Gaol.[83]

The lengthy note, written in French, reprised the Dutch arguments, noting again that they were not parties to the Treaty of Versailles and had no obligations to surrender the former German Emperor. Both Curzon and Berthelot interpreted it as showing a willingness to make concessions. The French Minister thought the Dutch were prepared to take more robust measures of security and also to negotiate the place within the Netherlands where the Kaiser would be interned. They were deluding themselves. All that Van Karnebeek's letter said was that the government was '*conscient des devoirs qui lui impose la présence de l'ex-Empereur sur le territoire du Royaume, tant au point de vue de l'intérêt du pays même, qu'à celui de la sécurité internationale*'. It was aware of the duties imposed by the presence in Holland of the ex-Kaiser, in terms of both the country's self-interest and that of international security. Responding to earlier charges that the Dutch were indifferent to German atrocities, the note said that they were far from forgetting '*les actes contraires à l'humanité dont la guerre a donné le spectacle et contre lesquels il a protesté chaque fois que les nationaux néerlandais en ont été les innocentes victimes*'. The French and the British were angered that the Dutch failed to indicate who was guilty of the atrocities, thereby implying that all sides in the war bore some responsibility.[84]

The discussion concluded with a decision to send yet another note.[85] Ambassador Cambon was assigned to draft instructions to guide the ambassadors in The Hague. They were to have a 'conversation' with Van Karnebeek, indicating that the Allies were 'most painfully impressed by the passage in which the Dutch Government once again refrain from recognising the special character of the crimes committed by the Germans in the conduct of the war, and seem to postulate a common degree of responsibility and even of guilt'. Van Karnebeek was to be told that such an attitude 'cannot fail to produce a very unfortunate effect upon the sentiments of those countries whose peoples have endured such cruel and unparalleled outrages at the hands of Germany during the war'.

Cambon wrote that the Dutch note had failed to indicate where the Kaiser would be interned. 'If it is Doorn, this suggestion would be wholly unacceptable since Doorn would be exposed to the same risks as Amerongen, from which it is removed only a few miles, and is within a distance of fifty kilometres from the German frontier.' Cambon said that the Kaiser must be interned outside of Europe.[86]

The British seemed to have totally abandoned the idea of a trial of the Kaiser. The French, on the other hand, still hoped for justice to take its course. In early March, faced with Dutch intransigence on the surrender of the Kaiser, they briefly revived the notion of holding the trial *in absentia*[87] or convincing the Dutch to host the proceedings without it being necessary to expel Wilhelm from Holland.[88] Millerand had lost all patience. 'Do not take any personal initiative', he instructed his embassy in The Hague. 'For your personal information, I consider, and I have let this be known to the British Government, that the conversation with the Netherlands on this subject is a dead end and that that there is more to be lost than to be gained in continuing.'[89]

On 8 March, representatives of the three Allied governments, led by Graham, paid yet another visit to the Dutch Foreign Minister. Graham described the meeting as being 'of a very stiff character'. Van Karnebeek told the diplomats that the latest Allied initiative made it more difficult for his government to be accommodating. Van Karnebeek expressed surprise at the rapidity of the Allied reply to the Dutch note, describing it as '*du tic au tac*'. Sending the Kaiser to one of the Dutch colonies was out of the question. Referring to the Dutch East Indies, he mentioned the danger posed by the presence of the Kaiser in the midst of a population of 40 million Moslems. He made no attempt to hide Holland's very serious concerns about a pan-Islamic awakening, incited by the Germans, that could threaten its Asian empire.[90]

Graham and his colleagues believed that the Dutch might be induced to propose an alternative to Doorn, but within Holland.[91] Van Karnebeek insisted that the Allies ought to be satisfied with Dutch assurances that the Kaiser would not act improperly. Graham replied that there was no evidence they were willing or able to enforce such pledges. He pointed to the lack of censorship of the former Emperor's correspondence, the comings and goings of prominent German financial, political, and military personalities, and the regular visits from the German Ambassador to the Netherlands, Friedrich Rosen. Graham told Van Karnebeek that they were all aware, mainly from Dutch sources, 'of the strong wave of reaction and chauvinism which is passing over Germany at the present moment'. He referred to portraits of the Kaiser, as well as of Hindenburg and Ludendorff, being hung again in schools. 'Patriotic airs are being played, accompanied by patriotic demonstrations', he said.[92]

Graham thought the Dutch position could largely be explained by their assessment 'that our representations contain a large element of bluff'. Graham suspected that this view was encouraged by reports from the Dutch

Ambassador in London.⁹³ Eyre Crowe, who was then the Deputy Permanent Under-Secretary, minuted the message from Graham, observing that 'the difficulty of the situation lies just in the fact that the attitude of the allied governments does seem to partake of the element of bluff'. Crowe said that before delivering further lectures to Van Karnebeek, it would be helpful to determine whether the Allied governments really are serious, adding that the attitude taken by the Supreme Council made this quite doubtful. Crowe felt that if the Powers were ultimately going to back down, then 'we (the British government) are doing ourselves nothing but harm by taking a leading part in making demands and threats which we are not prepared to back'.⁹⁴

Van Karnebeek requested a meeting with Ambassador Graham, asking that it be 'private and confidential'.⁹⁵ Karnebeek had a similar *tête-à-tête* with Prévost, the French *chargé d'affaires*.⁹⁶ Graham reported to Curzon that Van Karnebeek had become 'more than conciliatory'. He and his colleagues, as well as the Queen, were concerned that the country was finding itself in 'antagonism' with the three great Allied Powers. Van Karnebeek harkened back to a statement of the Prime Minister in December 1918, shortly after the Kaiser's arrival, that anticipated a situation where 'foreign Governments may well wish to confer with the Netherland Government in order to assign to the ex-Emperor a permanent place of residence', and that this would be entirely acceptable to the extent it was 'compatible with the honour and dignity of the country'. The Dutch Foreign Minister complained to Graham that the clear invitation had never been taken up by the Allied Powers.⁹⁷

Van Karnebeek's point was disingenuous, because until the Dutch categorically refused to surrender the Kaiser, the issue of his temporary residence was not an issue. The Allies had presumed that he would be taken to England for trial and that whatever happened he was not going to make his way back to the Netherlands. Had the Allies raised the issue of the Kaiser's residence in the Netherlands prior to making their demand for his surrender, it would have implied a lack of resolve on their part to bring him to trial.

The Foreign Minister then set out the conditions that the Dutch would impose on the Kaiser. A Royal Decree would indicate 'a special place of abode within the Kingdom' for 'aliens dangerous to public tranquillity'. Van Karnebeek told Graham that over the past few days a government official had met with Wilhelm at Amerongen and obtained his written consent, not without some resistance, to censorship of his correspondence, and an undertaking to live in the country as a private person without involvement in politics of any kind. Van Karnebeek claimed that the Dutch Government 'had gone very far indeed, much further than they had originally intended to go, in order to be agreeable to the Allies'. He said the Queen had only consented with great reluctance to this course of action. When Graham questioned Van Karnebeek about the place of fixed residence, as this had not been made clear, the Dutch Foreign Minister said that the welfare of the ex-Empress had to be taken into consideration. He said the couple could not be separated, and that she was in very frail health and could not withstand a lengthy journey or residence in a hot climate. The options within the Netherlands were limited. The northern islands were not suitable because 'conditions of climate were severe and comforts were unobtainable'.[98]

Van Karnebeek indicated that the Kaiser's new home in Doorn had been designated by the government for security reasons. He said they had considered other alternatives, but found nothing appropriate. There was another problem, he said. The Kaiser was 'almost entirely destitute of resources', struggling to meet his monthly expenses at Amerongen. He had been selling paintings and jewellery in order to make ends meet. Graham had made his own inquiries, locating castles at Walcheren, Middelburg, and the island of Schouwen that might be suitable. He did not know whether they were on the market or if the Kaiser could afford them. It seems that neither Graham nor Van Karnebeek considered anything but castles. Graham appeared resigned to Doorn, although he made it clear to Van Karnebeek that his instructions were to insist on the 'Colonial Solution'. He told Curzon that if the Supreme Council could not accept Doorn, 'very strong pressure' would be required.[99]

Graham's acquiescence provoked mocking comments at the Foreign Office. 'Sr. R. Graham has now wobbled back to Doorn', minuted Curzon on the file. 'He himself suggested the Colonies and said deliberately that we could get that solution. Then he fell back on some other part of Holland than Doorn. Now he is all for Doorn. Next it will be Amerongen—and finally Berlin.' Hardinge wrote: 'It is all very uncomfortable, and we have lost prestige.'[100] Eyre Crowe thought Ambassador Graham to be extremely gullible. He dismissed 'the absurd contention' that the Dutch had been left in the dark about the intentions of the Allies until mid-January. The provisions of the treaty were well known. The issues had been debated in the Dutch newspapers. They had been regularly discussed at the diplomatic level.[101]

The Kapp Putsch

Since the end of the Second Reich, Germany had been ruled by what was called the Weimar Coalition, made up of social democrats, liberals, and more conservative Catholics. It was led by President Friedrich Ebert and Chancellor Gustav Bauer, both associated with the Social Democratic Party. Right-wing opposition to the coalition had gained some momentum by early 1920. When the government ordered certain military units to disband, there were signs of defiance. On 13 March 1920, an attempted *coup d'état* was led by elements of the armed forces. Wolfgang Kapp, a nationalist journalist, declared himself Chancellor after the government fled Berlin for Dresden. Some of the participants bore swastikas on their helmets. Adolf Hitler had been in touch with the coup plotters and was flown by the army to Berlin in order to join the putsch. Disguised with a fake beard, he claimed to be an accountant. The coup collapsed within a few days after the Weimar Coalition called for a general strike and it became apparent that there was little public support for the insurgents.

When he learned of the putsch, Curzon communicated with the British Minister in The Hague to point out how greatly this military *coup d'état*, which he described as 'monarchical', strengthened the case for removing the Kaiser from Europe. 'As long as he remains in Holland his presence is bound to be a constant focus of intrigue', wrote Curzon. 'Dutch Government themselves can no longer be insensible to this peril.' Curzon instructed Graham to warn the Dutch that 'we expect them to take special measures to guard against any possibility of the ex-Kaiser's escape and to prevent any communication with him from outside'.[102]

Speaking to the Supreme Council the next day, Curzon insisted that it was incumbent upon them to take special measures to guard against any possibility of the Kaiser's escape. When he finished his presentation, Curzon said the British Government had been given to understand that the Kaiser was financing the putsch.[103]

'Champagne tonight', Wilhelm told his adjutant.[104] But Wilhelm does not seem to have been involved in plotting the coup and was initially sceptical when he learned of it. He thought it 'over-hasty and badly planned', although he was soon 'hugely delighted at the turn of events', according to his personal physician, Alfred Haehner. The Kaiser did not appear surprised when the putsch failed. 'The people at home are all too weak', he said. 'All it really needs is a little shove and the government will go flying.'[105] Van Karnebeek told Graham that the gendarmerie at Amerongen had been increased by thirteen men and an officer as well as secret agents.[106]

On 17 March, Eyre Crowe circulated a lengthy memorandum on the Kaiser issue within the Foreign Office. Crowe seemed particularly concerned that by conceding on Doorn the Allies would suffer yet another defeat. '[T]he prestige of the Allies, already none too high, will suffer a fresh eclipse, and the Dutch will be encouraged to persevere in their traditional policy of snapping their fingers at the Allies', he wrote. But he asked what the Allies might be prepared to do in order to compel compliance. Denying membership in the League of Nations was no longer an option because the Dutch had already joined. He doubted that the Allies would want to close their embassies, questioning whether this would achieve the desired result in any event. 'The application of direct force may presumably be ruled out', he wrote.

Crowe was dismissive of arguments rejecting Doorn as the place of internment, noting that while they seemed based on its proximity to the German border, he thought that the real objection was that the Allies had already insisted that it was unsuitable. He was not impressed with the case put forward by the Dutch about the difficulties in identifying another location. He found the claim that they could not find a more appropriate place closer to the centre of the country to be difficult to believe. As for the financial issues, the argument that the Kaiser, having bought Doorn, could not afford another purchase was unconvincing. Moreover, 'it may well be replied that once the Dutch have acknowledged their duty to intern the ex-emperor, they cannot plead the element of cost as an excuse'. In conclusion, he said that to the extent the reason for continuing the dispute was Allied prestige, 'prudence demands the avoidance of a course which would make a third rebuff even more striking and ignominious'. Hardinge reacted by noting that this was 'a bad case of loss of prestige due to the exigencies of party politics at home'. Curzon thought this comment not to be fair, but minuted: 'I am greatly obliged to Sir E. Crowe for his memo.'[107]

Royal Decree of Internment

On 17 March 1920, the Dutch Government issued the Royal Decree formalising the Kaiser's residence in Holland:

We, Wilhelmina, &c., on the proposal of our Ministers of the Interior, of Justice and for Foreign Affairs, have determined to indicate as the area within which, with due observance of further provisions, the former German Emperor Wilhelm II will reside, that part of the Province of Utrecht to be defined by our aforesaid Ministers. Our aforesaid Ministers shall each, in so far as he is concerned, be entrusted with the execution of this decree.

The Hague, March 16, 1920.

Wilhelmina.

Signed also by the Ministers of
Interior, Justice and Foreign Affairs.[108]

Doorn was in the Province of Utrecht, the only Dutch province that had no border on either land or sea. At the same time, the Prime Minister wrote to the presidents of the First and Second Chambers of the Dutch Parliament explaining that '[t]he line of conduct pursued temporarily in respect of the residence of the former German Emperor Wilhelm II should assume a more definite form now that the Government have been unable to agree to his extradition'. The report to Parliament noted that the Kaiser had provided the government with an assurance 'that he will abstain from all political action and will consequently cause no political difficulties in the Netherlands'. The Kaiser's 'assurance' consisted of a written undertaking that he would remain within the Province of Utrecht and accept other controls upon his freedom of movement, as well as censorship of his correspondence.[109]

When Van Karnebeek gave Ambassador Graham the text of the Royal Decree, he said he hoped the British Ambassador appreciated how very far the Dutch Government had gone in order to satisfy the Allies. He explained that the Decree did not mention censorship, saying it was 'a measure to be imposed but not advertised, otherwise much of its value was destroyed'. Graham objected to the mention of Utrecht, as it seemed to mean Doorn, and he repeated that this was not acceptable to the Allies. Van Karnebeek said there was no mention of either Doorn or Amerongen, as he had promised, but that the legal advisers had insisted reference be made to a specific location. He said the location had been carefully chosen, with a railway on two sides and a river on a third side. The questionable suggestion was that this access would facilitate supervision, although it would also facilitate escape. Graham said the situation could be summed up as follows: 'Netherlands Government has been asked to deprive a refugee to Holland of privileges assured him by Dutch law. This they had been unable to do. But they fully realised duties, responsibilities and obligations they had incurred in the matter and would fulfil them in letter and in spirit.'[110]

Graham described the Royal Decree as having created a *fait accompli*. 'Stubborn obstinacy has always been a Dutch characteristic, and the Dutch have on this occasion not belied their reputation', he wrote to Curzon. But he also attributed a degree of good faith to the Netherlands. 'Rightly or wrongly, the Netherlands Government consider that, by keeping the ex-Emperor here in the past and, still more, by interning him for the future, they have rendered, and are rendering, a real service to the Allies and merit their gratitude', he wrote. Graham wrote a lengthy *post mortem*, explaining the result as a failure of diplomacy. He said he was convinced that despite Dutch repugnance at the idea of surrendering a political refugee, he believed a compromise could have been reached.[111]

Curzon told the Supreme Council that the Dutch Government had forced the hand of the Allies. The arrogance of the Dutch was already intolerable, and would be greatly increased, he said. But Curzon felt there could be no doubt that insistence on another place of internment would fail.[112] Berthelot prepared a draft note to be sent to the Dutch Government.[113] Although the text reflected 'delicacy and subtlety which one always associated with the French nation', Curzon thought it 'perhaps erred on the side of being too gentle'. He said 'something rather more stern' was required, and Berthelot did not disagree. Curzon proposed his own draft.[114] It took several days for the British and the French to agree upon the text of the note,[115] with Prime Minister Millerand intervening to insist that the tone be made more conciliatory.[116] The text was altered in accordance with Millerand's objections.[117] On 29 March 1920, it was presented by the Allied ambassadors in The Hague. Ronald Graham provided Prime Minister Ruijs de Beerenbrouck with the original English-language version, signed by Lloyd George, in a sealed envelope. The French-language text was read aloud. The Dutch head of government offered no comment.[118]

The negotiations 'died a natural death', wrote Charles Hardinge, the Permanent Under-Secretary. He had never been an enthusiast for trial of the Kaiser. Hardinge said '[t]he whole question from the beginning was a hollow sham'. He believed that 'anybody with sense' would have known the Dutch would refuse to extradite. 'Nevertheless, the Government lost a great deal of prestige in connection with this question …'.[119] Much later in the year, Lloyd George wrote to a Member of Parliament who complained that he was being heckled by voters about the failure to deliver on the electoral promise to bring the Kaiser to justice:

In view of the attitude thus taken up and adhered to by the Netherlands Government the surrender of the ex-Kaiser by diplomatic means could not be secured. You will agree that it was not contemplated in the promise given at the time of the election that we should proceed to the extremity of war with Holland in order to enforce the demand of the Allies for the surrender of the ex-Kaiser, and as the joint request and protest of all the Allies to the Netherlands did not avail to secure the desired end, the ex-Kaiser remains in Holland. It has proved impossible to complete the promise you refer to. No useful purpose would be served by a trial *in contumaciam*—that is, without the person incriminated being present, and without the possibility of carrying into effect the punishment awarded upon his arraignment—if he were found guilty.

The responsibility now rests with the Netherlands Government for his permanent safe custody, and perhaps the reflection has occurred to you, as it has to many, that if the ex-Kaiser had been found guilty by the Court, upon his arraignment before them, no greater or more enduring punishment would, or could, have been imposed than the action above recorded has secured.[120]

On 5 May 1921, the Supreme Council found Germany to be in default with respect to Article 227. What the nature of the default might be is a mystery because it was not Germany that had failed to surrender the Kaiser. On 11 May 1921, the German Government pledged to execute the unfulfilled portions of the treaty.[121]

The Kaiser remained in Doorn until the end of his life. Four days after the invasion of the Netherlands, in May 1940, German soldiers arrived at the Kaiser's castle with a letter from Hitler. Wilhelm was thrilled by the early Nazi victories. When the British Expeditionary Force was surrounded at Dunkirk, he gloated that '[t]he ordeal of Juda-England has begun'. He died on 4 June 1941, a few weeks before the German invasion of the Soviet Union. A Wehrmacht guard of honour and a military band were present for his funeral. Arthur Seyss-Inquart, who five years later would himself be convicted of crimes against humanity by the International Military Tribunal, in part for his ruthless conduct in Holland,[122] was Hitler's personal representative. He presented a huge wreath on behalf of the *führer*.[123]

Wilhelm's remains are in a mausoleum on the grounds of his home at Doorn. Every year on the anniversary of his death German monarchists pay tribute there. The Dutch Government confiscated the property after the Second World War, deeming it enemy property because Wilhelm had sent a telegram of congratulations to Hitler after the defeat of France and the

British withdrawal from Dunkirk. It is now a delightful museum, full of the Kaiser's folderol, including a collection of snuff boxes and cigarette cases, a library of works in English and German about the First World War and its aftermath, paintings of his beloved summer residence in Corfu, and a strange chair designed to replicate the saddle of a horse. The Kaiser believed he had his best thoughts sitting on horseback and sought to replicate the equestrian experience indoors.

18

Was He Guilty?

Inept diplomacy, misunderstanding, and royalist meddling all contributed to the failure to bring Kaiser Wilhelm II to justice. The British and the French, initially emboldened by their unanticipated victory over one of the world's greatest military powers, now found themselves humiliated by a small, neutral country. For the Dutch, it was a triumph of sovereignty, but one whose odour would become increasingly foul as the years passed. By the beginning of the twenty-first century, the city of The Hague was trumpeting itself as the 'capital of international justice'. It is the seat of several of the world's most important international tribunals, including the permanent International Criminal Court. Today, the Dutch constantly remind the world of their international law legacy, tracing it to one of the seminal figures of the discipline, Hugo Grotius. But they hardly behaved like the heirs of Grotius in 1919 and 1920.

When formulating their demand for extradition of the Kaiser in early 1920, the Allies suggested that the Dutch were under an obligation to surrender the Kaiser for trial. Replying to the Dutch refusal, the Supreme Council noted that the Dutch Government insisted upon viewing the question from the standpoint of its own duties. '*Il ne paraît pas considérer qu'il ait, en commun avec les nations civilisées, le devoir d'assurer la punition des crimes contre le droit et contre des principes de l'humanité, crimes dans lesquels Guillaume de Hohenzollern a assume, d'une manière indéniable, une lourde responsabilité*' ('It does not seem to consider that it has, together with the civilised nations, the duty to ensure punishment of crimes against the law and against the principles of humanity, crimes in which Wilhelm of Hohenzollern undeniably bears heavy responsibility'), read the note.[1]

A century after the first debates in November and December 1918, the international legal rules governing the surrender of those suspected of committing

The Trial of the Kaiser. William A. Schabas. © William A. Schabas, 2018. Published 2018 by Oxford University Press.

war crimes are only somewhat more robust. The 1948 Genocide Convention contains an obligation upon States Parties 'to grant extradition in accordance with their laws and treaties in force'.[2] The Geneva Conventions, adopted in 1949, also require States to investigate and prosecute serious war crimes, known as 'grave breaches', or alternatively 'hand such persons over for trial to another High Contracting Party concerned, provided such High Contracting Party has made out a prima facie case'.[3] A similar alternative obligation, known by the Latin phrase *aut dedere aut judicare*, that is, 'extradite or prosecute', appears in modern treaties such as the Convention Against Torture,[4] the Convention Against Enforced Disappearance,[5] and the draft convention on crimes against humanity of the International Law Commission.[6]

In 2015, the United Nations International Law Commission issued a report on the *aut dedere aut judicare* obligation following several years of study. It specifically considered whether the duty might exist in the absence of a binding treaty obligation. The Commission said that '[t]here was general disagreement with the conclusion that the customary nature of the obligation to extradite or prosecute could be inferred from the existence of customary rules proscribing specific international crimes'. At the same time, it insisted that these words 'should not be construed as implying that it has found that the obligation to extradite or prosecute has not become or is not yet crystallising into a rule of customary international law, be it general or regional'. The Commission observed that judges of the International Court of Justice had divergent views on the subject.[7] Perhaps, then, nearly a century after the Netherlands refused to surrender an individual to be tried for war crimes but also showed no inclination to hold a trial itself, it may be argued that this obligation now exists.

The Americans and the Dutch were not alone to blame for the failure to implement Article 227 of the Treaty of Versailles. Neither the British nor the French approached the challenge of the first international trial with either determination or professionalism. Within England, a significant element in the political class and the media and even in the Foreign Office was unenthusiastic about trying the Kaiser. Intervention by the King himself was rarely visible at the time and the archives do not add much to our understanding of his personal role. Still, there is enough to suggest that he did not welcome the prospect of a trial of his cousin, perhaps because of family ties. There was also a broader form of solidarity with a fellow monarch. Several personalities of Europe's old order, including royals in Spain, Italy, and Sweden, as well as the Pope, were at work behind the scenes to undermine the proposed trial.

Had the Kaiser been surrendered in January 1920, the Allies would have found themselves woefully unprepared. British lawyers had assembled a mediocre and inadequate brief. They were a step ahead of the French, who seem to have assumed they could improvise the whole business. The charges themselves were bewildering, leaving it uncertain whether and to what extent they included responsibility for starting the war and for violations of the laws and customs of war. The organisation and administration of such an international criminal proceeding was uncharted territory.

Alternatives to the rigid formula of Article 227 were certainly available. One option was trial *in absentia*, or what was at the time commonly described as *par contumacium*. Trial in the absence of the accused was then and still is not at all infrequent in continental legal systems. Even in common-law-based legal regimes, such proceedings are permitted under special circumstances, proving that there is no opposition as a matter of firm principle. For example, in most common-law jurisdictions a trial may continue in the absence of an accused person who has absconded. At the international level, *in absentia* trials are hardly unknown.[8] The Charter of the International Military Tribunal expressly authorised trial in the absence of a defendant.[9] The tribunal proceeded on this basis against one of the twenty-four accused, Martin Bormann.[10] Much more recently, the Special Tribunal for Lebanon, established by the United Nations Security Council to deal with a political assassination in 2005, has operated entirely in the absence of the accused. The defendants have all been represented by experienced counsel. Some of the accused may not even have been alive while the trial was underway.[11]

The idea that the Kaiser could be tried in his absence was mooted from time to time. The policy paper prepared in late 1918 by the French jurists, Ferdinand Larnaude and Albert Geouffre de Lapradelle, insisted that 'present or not present, the Emperor must be tried',[12] although it did not appear to favour *in absentia* trial because 'William II must be present to answer his charges'.[13] The British draft provisions of February 1919 also acknowledged the option, allowing that 'if the accused, having been duly cited, does not appear, the Court may proceed in his absence, and may give judgment upon the evidence at its disposal'. It required that the Court 'officially notify to the accused, so far as is practicable, the decision arrived at in his absence'.[14] When he met George Curzon immediately after the armistice, Georges Clemenceau indicated that he was favourable to the idea if the Kaiser could not be taken into custody.[15] Curzon did not seem opposed to the prospect when he reported to Lloyd George.[16] When the two quarrelled about where to hold the trial, in July 1919, Curzon returned to the idea of proceeding in the Kaiser's absence.[17] Replying to a question from Eyre Crowe of the Foreign Office, in October 1919, Clemenceau said *in absentia* trial would be a good way to address the problems with the Netherlands.[18] In early March 1920, the French Government revived this scenario.[19] Ambassador Cambon was instructed to submit the idea to the Supreme Council so that the United Kingdom would be forced to take a position, although it does not appear that he took any action on the matter.[20]

Another possibility was to hold the trial in the Netherlands itself. Lloyd George summarily dismissed the proposal when Curzon made the suggestion in July 1919.[21] In March 1920, writing in the *Telegraaf*, one of Holland's major newspapers, Carl Scharters proposed trying the Emperor before a 'moral tribunal' that would sit in The Hague, at the Peace Palace. Scharters's proposal involved equal numbers of judges from the Allied States, those of the Central Powers, and neutral countries. The tribunal would be empowered to pronounce a sentence, but not to impose a penalty. Once completed, the Emperor would then be confined to his castle at Doorn. Charles Benoist, the French Ambassador to The Hague, also toyed with the proposal that the Kaiser be tried in the Netherlands.[22] He thought the proceedings might be held in the Peace Palace, the monumental baroque edifice whose construction, financed by the Scottish-American businessman Andrew Carnegie, was only completed in 1913. The French *chargé d'affaires* in The Hague, Fernand Prévost, presented the proposal to his Foreign Minister, describing it as an 'ingenious' approach that addressed Dutch concerns while preserving the essence of Article 227.[23]

At several points, obstacles to the trial might simply have evaporated. On 10 November 1918, the Dutch could have refused entry to the Kaiser, sending him back to Belgium and, possibly, Allied custody. The shambolic kidnap attempt by Luke Lea and his cohorts could have succeeded. Difficult as it is to imagine, the spectacle of the fallen Prussian monarch being delivered by an American army staff car to a hotel in Paris is not outside the realm of possibility. Until the Dutch had formally granted the Kaiser asylum, his status remained uncertain. Developments within Germany such as the publication of the Kautsky papers and the Kapp Putsch eroded sympathy for him within the Netherlands. It would not have taken very much for public opinion to take a decisive turn.

The story of the Kaiser's flight to Holland and of Article 227 of the Treaty of Versailles provides its own fascination. But what of the trial itself? How might it have unfolded? Of what did the charges really consist? Would he have been convicted?[24]

The First International Criminal Court

The second paragraph of Article 227 provides for a 'special tribunal' to be composed of five judges, one from each of the following 'Powers': the United States of America, Great Britain, France, Italy, and Japan. But by the time the Treaty of Versailles entered into force, in January 1920, the United States Senate had refused ratification, a constitutional requirement. Lack of participation in the treaty would not necessarily disqualify an American judge, although it seems implausible that the United States would have cooperated in the appointment process given the position it had taken on the Versailles Treaty as a whole.

A tribunal with four judges rather than five presents a potential problem if there is a lack of unanimity. It is easier to resolve disputes with an odd number of judges than with an even number. Some international tribunals solve the problem by granting the presiding judge an extra vote in order to break a tie, known as a casting vote. While such a mechanism may not be objectionable in some types of dispute, it seems inappropriate in a criminal trial where questions of guilt or innocence are determined. The judges of the Article 227 special tribunal might even have decided that any verdict of guilt would require unanimity, as would be the rule with a lay jury. At Nuremberg, there were four judges, each appointed by the four occupying powers. They agreed without dissent on the guilt of most of the defendants. The Soviet judge, Iona Nikitchenko, disagreed with the three acquittals, the life sentence for Rudolf Hess, and the failure to declare certain organisations to be criminal.[25] Nuremberg confirms the viability of a tribunal with four judges rather than five.

None of the numerous practical or procedural issues were addressed in Article 227 of the treaty. While unsurprising that the Council of Four would have been concerned with such matters, it is astonishing that so little attention was given to these somewhat technical matters by government lawyers in the more than six months that elapsed between the signing of the treaty in June 1919 and its entry into force in January of 1920. There was a skirmish between Lloyd George, Curzon, and the King in July 1919 about the venue for the trial. It was never really resolved and no consensus was reached on where in England the proceedings would be held. The French and the British did not discuss how the tribunal would be funded, or the language of the proceedings. It seems to have been assumed that the procedural issues would be left largely to the judges. This is what was done at Nuremberg and also, much later, when the United Nations Security Council set up the ad hoc tribunals for the former Yugoslavia and Rwanda in the early 1990s.

Although the term 'international tribunal' is not employed in Article 227, it had been used in many of the debates to describe the court contemplated by the treaty. Were the 'special tribunal' actually established, it would undoubtedly be looked upon as the first genuinely international criminal tribunal. Established pursuant to an international convention to which a large number of countries had subscribed, and deciding offences described as breaches of international law, it would have been just as much an international court as the ones that sat in Nuremberg and Tokyo after the Second World War. Although the tribunal promised by Article 227 was never established, the provision is an important waymark in the development of international criminal justice. The reference in the Treaty of Versailles, and the debates and discussions that surrounded it, constitute the first real consideration of an international criminal court at the official level.

In an exchange with Woodrow Wilson, Lloyd George entertained the idea that the League of Nations might actually host the institution.[26] Perhaps Lloyd George thought emphasising the role of the League could help to sway Wilson, who was deeply attached to the project of international organisation. The French experts, Larnaude and de Lapradelle, thought it certain that the League of Nations would organise and create tribunals, but they believed it would take time and said 'it is not possible to postpone the immediate trial which the public conscience so insistently demands'.[27] In the November 1918 Imperial War Cabinet discussion, Curzon referred to 'a great act of initiation' that 'would really call the League of Nations in an effective manner into being', saying that this would be 'an act of justice taken by the world as a whole'.[28] The conclusions of the December 1918 London conference spoke of criminal justice for perpetrators of 'crimes against humanity and international right' as 'a very important security against future attempts to make war wrongfully or to violate international law' and as 'a necessary stage in the development of the authority of a League of Nations'.[29]

Essentially, this first initiative at international justice was being presented as a complement to the attempts to establish the League of Nations rather than as an integral part of the new international organisation. Twenty-six years later, a similar parallelism characterised the relationship between the United Nations and the International Military Tribunal that sat at Nuremberg. During the Second World War, there were proposals to establish a permanent international criminal court with the authority to try the Nazi war criminals. It was premised upon broad participation in the establishment of the tribunal, with prosecutors and judges chosen from among the member States, be they large or small. But this was rejected by the four 'Powers' in favour of a 'military tribunal' over which they exercised full control.[30]

Although in some ways less apparent in 1919 and 1920, it seems the same dynamics were at work. In addition to judges from the five 'Powers', the 'high tribunal' proposed by the Commission on Responsibilities would include members appointed by Belgium, Greece, Poland, Portugal, Romania, Serbia, and Czechoslovakia.[31] But the Council of Four virtually forgot about the smaller countries when it devised Article 227. Even more controversial was the participation of neutral countries. The 1918 memorandum by the French jurists discussed the problem at some length. It pointed in a positive and optimistic manner to the establishment of a permanent international criminal court by the League of Nations, but at the same time contended that there would be no place for neutral States in the trial of the Kaiser. 'Perhaps these neutrals would feel somewhat embarrassed, they who have done nothing for the great cause, to sit next to the representatives of the nations whose complete resources were, for four years, thrown into the terrible crucible of war', they wrote. In any event, 'the neutrals, by refraining from protesting against the violations of international law, the violation of Belgium's neutrality, the submarine warfare, have cut themselves off from all settlements concerning the war. They must not be admitted to "*the criminal liquidation*" of the conflict.'[32]

International Morality and the Sanctity of Treaties

The Kaiser was 'arraigned' for 'a supreme offence against international morality and the sanctity of treaties'. These are the words of the first paragraph of Article 227. The French version of the treaty speaks of an '*offense suprême contre la morale internationale et l'autorité sacrée des traités*'. The phrase was drafted one evening by Woodrow Wilson using language cribbed from a letter by Robert Lansing, who was opposed to trial and never intended for his words to form the basis of a criminal charge. The next day, Wilson's text was summarily endorsed, with almost no discussion or debate, by the other three leaders. Although Wilson's draft specified that the supreme offence was 'not to be described as a violation of criminal law',[33] these words were excised some weeks later at the demand of Lloyd George. The formulation is without precedent. It has never been invoked or applied subsequently before a court of law. Of what, exactly, did it consist?

Discussion about post-war prosecutions within the French and British Governments as well as at the international level during the sittings of the Commission on Responsibilities centred on three categories to define the nature of offences that might be punished. The first comprised the crime of starting the war, a notion that the Nuremberg Tribunal labelled 'crimes against peace' and that subsequently has been considered as 'the crime of aggression'. Crimes against peace were successfully prosecuted by the International Military Tribunal as well as by subsequent post-war courts applying international law.[34] The International Criminal Court has jurisdiction over the crime of aggression. It is defined in an amendment to the Rome Statute adopted in 2010. The provisions on the crime of aggression only became operational in 2018.

The second category was the violation of the neutrality of Belgium and Luxembourg. It seemed the most straightforward given Germany's admission that it had breached international law. The Kaiser was directly involved in the decision to invade the two countries. There were two theories about the legal basis for the charge. One relied upon the neutrality treaties themselves, which dated back many decades. But there were technical questions about their application to the conflict. The other was premised upon the notion that the inviolability of neutrality had become part of customary international law. Nevertheless, there was a big gap between determining that Germany had violated international law, regardless of whether the source was treaty or custom, and the conclusion that this was a punishable offence for which an individual Head of State could be prosecuted.

The Commission on Responsibilities described the breaches of neutrality as 'outrages upon the principles of the law of nations and upon international good faith', concluding 'they should be made the subject of a formal condemnation by the Conference'. It also said it was 'desirable that for the future penal sanctions should be provided for such grave outrages against the elementary principles of international law'.[35] Since then, massive attention has been given to the codification of international crimes, notably within United Nations bodies such as the International Law Commission and in the drafting of the Rome Statute of the International Criminal Court. It has not been seriously suggested that either violating the 'sanctity of treaties' or breaching neutrality should be made punishable. The Charter of the International Military Tribunal included 'war in violation of international treaties, agreements or assurances'[36] within the definition of crimes against peace, and the indictment contained an annex listing twenty-six treaties that Germany was alleged to have violated, including a few guaranteeing neutrality.[37] Most of this was ignored in the judgment, where waging of an aggressive war was determined without reference to violation of specific treaties.[38]

Violations of the laws and customs of war was the third of the categories. Many of the punishable acts had emerged over previous decades, even centuries. Examples familiar to the combatants in the First World War included the prohibition on expanding or 'dum-dum' bullets, condemned since the St Petersburg Declaration of 1868. The illegality of some conduct remained disputed, such as the use of poison gas, aerial bombardment, and submarine warfare. Because these were means and methods of warfare of recent invention, it was difficult to establish what the customs really were. The final report of the Commission on Responsibilities proposed a list of such violations of the laws and customs of war comprising several offences directed against civilian non-combatants, such as 'murders and massacres', 'systematic terrorism', 'putting hostages to death', 'torture of civilians' (but not, at least by implication, torture of combatants and spies), 'deliberate starvation of civilians', 'rape', and 'abduction of girls for the purposes of enforced prostitution'. The list of crimes committed on the battlefield against enemy combatants was more modest in length: 'use of deleterious and asphyxiating gasses', 'use of explosive or expanding bullets, and other inhuman appliances', 'directions to give no quarter', and 'misuse of flags of truce'. There was a general prohibition of ill-treatment of combatants who were wounded or who had become prisoners.[39] That German forces had committed some of these offences was beyond doubt. The challenge was linking the German Emperor to acts of individual combatants. Absent evidence that he had actually ordered atrocities, it was necessary to develop a theory of criminal liability based upon the fact that he was the supreme commander.

The Commission on Responsibilities recommended against prosecuting the Kaiser, or for that matter anyone else, for the offences of starting the war and breaching the neutrality of Belgium and Luxembourg. Instead, it

said that efforts should be directed at the less controversial and more certain category of 'laws and customs of war'. There was a major disagreement
with the Americans as to whether the Kaiser himself could be prosecuted
for such violations because of his status as Head of State. The majority of the
Commission favoured trying the Kaiser for violations of the laws and customs of war. It also advocated an extensive form of criminal liability by which
a person in authority, such as the German Emperor, could be deemed guilty
of the war crimes perpetrated by subordinates even if there was no evidence
that the accused had directed or ordered such acts. It was enough that he had
abstained from intervening to prevent or to punish such violations. With this,
too, the Americans were not in accord.

Articles 228, 229, and 230 of the Treaty of Versailles applied generally to
German military commanders, civilian officials, and combatants, contemplating trial before the military tribunals of the victors for 'acts in violation
of the laws and customs of war'. This was consistent with the American position in the Commission on Responsibilities. These provisions of the Treaty
of Versailles did not address the controversial issues of immunity for Heads of
State and liability for abstention or failure to intervene that had dogged the
Commission and that had, ultimately, been at the heart of its disputes. But the
language in Article 227 was different.

Presumably some of the vagueness of the term 'supreme offence against
international morality and the sanctity of treaties' would have received clarification in a more detailed formulation of the charges. Although not explicitly required by Article 227, the Kaiser had a right to know the substance of
the charges against him. The word 'arraignment' in Article 227 suggests the
formal statement of the charges at the outset of the trial. The judges of the
special tribunal would have expected more explanation, and the defendant
would have been entitled to this. At Nuremberg, the charges consisted of a
few succinct paragraphs, but the 'indictment' setting out the charges ran to
some sixty-five printed pages.[40] The judges of the special tribunal might well
have disagreed as to the scope of the charges and rejected some of the indictment at the beginning of the trial.

The meaning of a legal text, including one that defines an international
crime, is often understood with reference to the debates at the time of its
adoption. For example, some guidance about the extent of the crimes charged
at Nuremberg is provided by the record of the London Conference, where
the terms of Article VI of the Charter of the International Military Tribunal
were conceived. More recently, the provisions of the Rome Statute of the

International Criminal Court have been interpreted by judges with reference to the proceedings of the Rome Conference of 1998 where the text was adopted. However, the origins of Article 227 of the Treaty of Versailles are shrouded in mystery. It is impossible to discern what was meant by the American President when he drafted the text and by the four other leaders who endorsed it the following day. Probably if each of them had been asked to explain the meaning of Article 227, five quite different answers would have been provided. Lloyd George gave various explanations of the meaning of the provision that demonstrated his own confusion.

The Woods memorandum on prosecuting the Kaiser, prepared in late 1919, provides insight into how the British understood the scope of Article 227. It confirms the view of government lawyers that the charge in Article 227 of 'a supreme offence against international morality and the sanctity of treaties' encompassed all three of the categories, namely responsibility for starting the war, for breaching the neutrality of Belgium and Luxembourg, and for the atrocities and violations perpetrated during its course. The memorandum devoted much attention to liability for launching the war. For example, Woods thought that the Kautsky papers were of great importance. The Kautsky papers dealt with the Kaiser's involvement in Germany's decision to go to war. The memorandum also considered in detail the Kaiser's responsibility for violations of the laws and customs of war. Woods examined some of the isolated incidents that had outraged public opinion in England, such as the executions of Edith Cavell and of Captain Fryatt. He also considered submarine warfare and a range of other possible violations. Woods concluded that it was difficult to link the Kaiser to these crimes without an expansive approach to liability by which, essentially, the man in charge was guilty of everything perpetrated by those under his command. Whether or not such prosecution was viable is beside the point.[41]

The formal request to the Dutch for surrender of the Kaiser in January 1920 it the other important source in understanding the scope of Article 227. It refers to 'the cynical violation of the neutrality of Belgium and Luxembourg', including sexual and gender-based violence, submarine warfare, and mass deportations, but, significantly, does not contemplate responsibility for starting the war. The description of the charges in the Allied note is not without legal importance. The principle or doctrine of 'speciality' provides that the receiving State may only try a person on charges for which extradition has been authorised. It was well recognised in customary international law by the late nineteenth century.[42] Had the Netherlands decided to comply with the

Allied demand, the special tribunal might have considered itself to be bound by the terms of the note. The British and the French negotiators, for whom such details of international criminal law were probably unknown, do not appear to have ever given any thought to the issue of the content of the request for extradition and its legal consequences. They treated it as more of a rhetorical exercise rather than as a legally binding initiative.

Although Article 227 was never applied as such and therefore lacks an authoritative judicial interpretation, on several occasions it has been construed by judges and legal scholars as comprising a crime of waging an aggressive war. Writing in 1920, a French academic wrote that the charges included responsibility for initiating the war.[43] At Nuremberg, the judgment of the International Military Tribunal briefly referred to Article 227. It was cited in the context of a discussion of crimes against peace. The reference immediately followed this phrase: 'The prohibition of aggressive war demanded by the conscience of the world, finds its expression in the series of pacts and treaties to which the Tribunal has just referred.'[44] The clear implication is that Article 227 includes responsibility for launching an aggressive war. Writing at the same time, Professor Hersch Lauterpacht, one of the most distinguished international lawyers of the twentieth century, described Article 227 as 'solemn warning to any future aggressor'.[45]

The objection by the defence to all of these charges would be that they involved the retroactive application of criminal law. The rule against prosecuting someone for an act that was not recognised as a crime at the time of its commission dates at least as far back as the American and the French Revolutions. Article 1, Section 9, of the Constitution of the United States, ratified in 1788, prohibits the enactment of *ex post facto* legislation. Article VIII of the *Déclaration des droits de l'homme et du citoyen*, proclaimed by the French National Assembly on 26 August 1789, weeks after the storming of the Bastille, affirms the prohibition of prosecution for a crime that has not already been promulgated in a law. The charge that Article 227 of the Treaty of Versailles might violate this hallowed principle was repeated throughout the debates of the Commission on Responsibilities. Although it did not seem to trouble the leaders in the Council of Four, when the draft article was presented for approval to the plenary Peace Conference Honduras made a dramatic objection based upon the rule against retroactive prosecution. Its initiative may well have been instigated or encouraged by the United States.[46]

Even if there are merits to the charge of retroactivity, the initial question is whether judges of the special tribunal had any authority to address an objection made on this basis. The Constitutions of the United States and France may have been persuasive evidence of general principles of law, but they had no direct application to the interpretation of the Treaty of Versailles. When this issue arose at Nuremberg, the International Military Tribunal made it clear that it was without authority to rule on the legality of the crimes that it was charged with prosecuting. Nevertheless, the tribunal decided that it would address the substance of the claim that the prosecutions were retro-active in nature, 'in view of the great importance of the questions of law in-volved'.[47] Had there been a special tribunal in 1920 for the trial of the Kaiser, it might have taken the same course.

The Nuremberg defendants relied upon a brief prepared for them by Karl Schmitt, the notorious Nazi jurist. The contention that it was 'unjust to punish those who in defiance of treaties and assurances have attacked neighbouring states without warning' was 'obviously untrue', responded the judges at the International Military Tribunal. They explained that 'in such circumstances the attacker must know that he is doing wrong, and so far from it being unjust to punish him, it would be unjust if his wrong were allowed to go unpunished.[48]

When the judges at Nuremberg spoke of 'defiance of treaties', they were not referring to guarantees of neutrality, but rather to the prohibition of recourse to war as a means of settling international disputes, set out in the Kellogg-Briand Pact, ratified by Germany. But Kellogg-Briand was adopted in 1928 and could not therefore have been invoked before the special tribunal trying the Kaiser.

Undoubtedly, a hugely important legal development was taking place in the years from 1914 to 1945, as international law came to condemn the resort to force as a means of settling international disputes. This was all consolidated not only in the judgment of the International Military Tribunal, condemning several of the Nazi defendants for crimes against peace, but also in the pro-visions of the Charter of the United Nations. But at the beginning of this period, in July and August 1914, it was more difficult to contend that the use of force was prohibited by international law and, moreover, that it was a crime for which individual leaders could be prosecuted. When Austria attacked Serbia in late July 1914 because it failed to accept every condition in its ulti-matum, there was no sense that this was prohibited by international law. There were hopes that the dispute could be resolved by arbitration. It was never contended that Austria was legally required to resolve the dispute through judicial means and could not attack Serbia in order to achieve its ends.

It would have been more difficult for the Kaiser to invoke a principle of non-retroactivity with respect to violations of the laws and customs of war. A body of law governing the conduct of hostilities and the treatment of civilians, prisoners of war, and wounded combatants existed long before 1914. Issues about its scope arose because of the development of new methods of war, but these could generally be addressed by the application of recognised principles. For example, although poison gas had not previously been used in warfare, its illegality could be deduced from the prohibition of weapons that cause unnecessary suffering or superfluous harm affirmed in the St Petersburg Declaration of 1868. The various reports submitted to Sub-Commission I of the Commission on Responsibilities revealed a consensus on a broad range of acts that could be characterised as war crimes. For this reason, the list of war crimes proposed by the Commission in its Report has been viewed subsequently as authoritative.

Evidence for the Prosecution

Proceedings at an international criminal tribunal are typically divided into four phases: debate about preliminary issues such as jurisdiction; the presentation of evidence, with the prosecution calling evidence first, followed by the defence; submissions by the two sides based upon the conclusions to be drawn from the evidence; and the drafting and delivery of the judgment. Modern-day trials also have an appeals phase, recognising the requirement under international human rights law that anyone convicted of an offence is entitled to have the decision reviewed by another court.[49] But at Nuremberg, there was no appeal from the judgment. Article 227 of the Treaty of Versailles created a five-judge panel for the trial, but had no suggestion that a final judgment might be subject to appeal.

At Nuremberg, presentation of the case for the prosecution took about seventy-three days, beginning in the third week of November 1945 and concluding in early March 1946. Fewer than thirty-five witnesses were called to testify for the prosecution. Evidence from witnesses was also produced in the form of solemn declarations or affidavits, without them actually appearing in court. Although this may provide a guide to the length of the proceedings had the Kaiser been put on trial, it should be borne in mind that the International Military Tribunal dealt with twenty-two individual defendants, each of them represented by counsel. If the Nuremberg trial is any guide, the trial of the Kaiser would likely have been much shorter.

The case for the prosecution of the Kaiser before the special tribunal would probably have taken a month or two at most. The length of the proceedings would have depended upon the extent to which evidence of individual war crimes was submitted. That the acts themselves took place might well have been conceded by the Kaiser's defence lawyers. Their case with respect to violations of the laws and customs of war would hinge not so much on contesting the occurrence of various atrocities as arguing that the Kaiser himself played no role of any significance in their perpetration. As for starting the war and violating neutrality, the materials in the report of the Commission on Responsibilities and the British memorandum on prosecution point to evidence that was essentially documentary in nature and not subject to dispute as to its authenticity. The memoirs of various participants, especially those of the Central Powers, would also have been invoked. Whether live testimony by the authors of these works might have been required would have depended upon tactical decisions by the prosecutors and defence counsel. The Treaty of Versailles did not give them any power to summon witnesses or to compel production of evidence from within Germany.

The first challenge for the prosecution would be to demonstrate that Germany was responsible for starting the war, a matter that historians debate to this day. Of course, Germany had no connection with the assassination in Sarajevo, one of the Balkan provinces of the Austro-Hungarian Empire, on 28 June 1914. The act was quickly linked to Serbian extremists. Even the Austrian Emperor initially dismissed the tragic killings as 'the act of a little group of madmen'. But belligerent elements in both Austria and Germany quickly seized upon the incident to make claims on neighbouring Serbia. A 'decisive consultation' took place on 6 July in Potsdam, the home of the Kaiser. There, Germany and Austria agreed that the latter would send an ultimatum to Serbia with demands that could never be met. The ineluctable outcome was war with Serbia and, by ricochet, with its powerful ally, Russia.

Proving that the ultimatum was agreed at Potsdam posed no difficulty and would not be contested. But how would the prosecutor show that Germany and Austria were intent on war beyond suggesting a logical deduction from

the terms of the ultimatum? The key might be referring to acts and statements prior to 28 June 1914. There were a few anecdotal remarks by the
Kaiser and others suggesting a view that Europe was headed for a major
conflict. A succession of crises over the previous fifteen years or so manifested escalating tensions between Germany and the 'Entente Powers' composed of Britain, France, and Russia. And there had been a furious arms
race, with Germany constructing ever-larger battleships and other imposing
weaponry. But could not the same be said of Britain, France, and Russia?
The problem confronting the prosecution was that opening the door on
the history of European international relations over the decades preceding
Sarajevo might only muddy the waters. Moreover, defence counsel for the
Kaiser could have welcomed efforts by the prosecution to prove the development of aggressive intentions within Germany. It would invite an inquiry
into the conduct of the Allies, including the development of ever-more
powerful weapons. Wilhelm might well have made statements about the
inevitability of a European war, but able defence counsel would undoubtedly unearth similar statements by leading figures in England and France.
A prudent prosecutor might therefore opt to insist that the evidence be
confined to events subsequent to the assassination. But in speculating about
how the prosecution might build the case for the 'supreme offence against
international morality', misjudgement in framing the issues can certainly
not be ruled out.

Following the Potsdam conference and the delivery of the ultimatum to
Serbia, there was a period of a few weeks while the pot simmered. The Kaiser
went for a cruise of the Baltic on his yacht, while his Minister of War took
a vacation. This was hardly the course of a leader making plans for a great
conflict. It was alleged that this was a deliberate attempt to mislead, not something that would be easy to prove in the absence of informers from inside
the German regime. Over the final ten days of July, there was evidence of
German preparations for war. Certain classes of reserves were called to duty.
On 26 July, the German fleet was recalled from Norway. But by then, every
other Power was also getting ready for war.

The Austrian ultimatum set a deadline of 25 July. Four days later, Austria
began bombarding Belgrade and preparing for land invasion of Serbia. Britain,
France, and Russia made intense efforts to avert outright war, including proposals that the dispute be submitted to arbitration, possibly in The Hague in
the newly built Peace Palace. Germany's reluctance to contribute to this effort might be evidence of aggressive intent, but it was a conclusion that rested

on surmise. Conspiracy, and that is what was alleged, is notoriously difficult to prove without direct evidence from its participants. Today, electronic communications intercepts of various forms, sometimes from whistle-blowers within an organisation, facilitate proving conspiracies. Such material is selectively distributed by intelligence services. But there was nothing of the sort in 1914.

That Germany genuinely desired a war became increasingly apparent in the first days of August. Germany seemed to object to any wavering within Austria that might have prompted a peaceful resolution of the conflict. On 1 August, Wilhelm sent a telegram to his cousin, George V of England, stating: 'The troops on my frontier are, at this moment, being kept back by telegraphic and telephonic orders from crossing the French frontier.' The clear implication is that Germany had already issued mobilisation orders in some form, although it had not yet taken this step officially. In announcing that it was at war with France, on 3 August, Germany relied upon a false allegation that its territory had been bombarded by French airplanes.

Assuming that the prosecution could develop a convincing case that Germany had initiated the war, it remained to place the Kaiser within the conspiracy. The Emperor's irate and provocative handwritten annotations on Foreign Office correspondence, published in 1919 as the Kautsky papers, might help to make this part of the case. There was also the presumption, not at all unreasonable, that as the Emperor, he enjoyed supreme authority. Although his royal brethren in England, Belgium, Italy, Spain, and the Netherlands seemed to have increasingly secondary roles in government, the German Kaiser stood apart because of his great authority. Constitutional lawyers would be called by the prosecution to establish this.

Evidence of violation of the laws and customs of war would be easy to establish. Proving the Kaiser's role would be the difficult part. Instead of relying upon official documents from the archives of foreign ministries, most if not all of it uncontested, proof of war crimes could require testimony from individuals, many of them victims of violations of the laws and customs of war by German troops. At Nuremberg, the prosecution tended to avoid charges that relied upon such evidence and only a few victims were ever called to testify. Perhaps the prosecutor of the special tribunal would take the same course. The war crimes in the First World War tended to be isolated acts of individuals, the work of rogue soldiers rather than crimes of policy dictated from above in a brutal totalitarian infrastructure. Even the most celebrated cases, such as the infamous executions of Captain Fryatt and Edith Cavell, did not easily lend themselves to prosecution, as the British memorandum had concluded.

The exceptions would be war crimes committed on a large scale, where there was evidence that these had been ordered at the highest level. In 1921 and 1922, as part of their reluctant effort to implement Articles 228, 229, and 230 of the Treaty of Versailles, German courts undertook the prosecution of a U-boat commander, Karl Neumann, for sinking the *Dover Castle*, a hospital ship. The defendant established he was following orders from the Admiralty Staff when he fired his torpedoes.[50] The *RMS Lusitania* was the most notorious U-boat target, with more than 1,000 civilian victims. But the ship sank very quickly, in all likelihood because it was also transporting ammunition. One obstacle to establishing the Kaiser's liability for violations of the laws and customs of war was the somewhat decentralised structure of the German military. But unlike the land armies, whose affiliation was with the member States of the German federation, the navy fell directly under the authority of the central government in Berlin and, therefore, the Kaiser himself. Even with respect to submarine warfare, however, the prosecution was unlikely to be able to produce any direct evidence of the Kaiser's involvement.

The Commission on Responsibilities explored a theory of negligent liability. It often called this 'abstention', in that the leaders, including the Emperor, had failed to intervene to prevent such acts. To the extent that such violations could be shown to be widespread and systematic, rather than the work of undisciplined individuals, a prosecution for 'abstention' was in reality more like a claim that the only plausible explanation for such acts was the pursuit of official policy. Judges at the special tribunal might well have welcomed such an expansive theory of criminal responsibility. Decades later, what the members of the Commission often labelled 'abstention' provided the legal basis for a controversial conviction by an American military court of a Japanese general who had failed to stop his troops from sacking the Philippine capital, Manila, in the final days of the Second World War. Yamashita was sentenced to death and executed, his appeal denied by the United States Supreme Court despite two quite energetic dissenting opinions.[51] At the ad hoc tribunals for the former Yugoslavia and Rwanda, and the International Criminal Court, the doctrine, which is now labelled as 'command responsibility' or 'superior responsibility', was used as a secondary basis for findings of guilt on the relatively rare occasions when there was insufficient evidence that a commander actually ordered the perpetration of war crimes and other atrocities.[52] The Rome Statute of the International

Criminal Court offers a detailed codification of the concept, distinguishing between civilian superiors, for whom evidence of direct knowledge is required, and military commanders, who may be convicted if they 'should have known' of the plans or intentions of their subordinates.[53] Writers have often pointed to the post-Second World War trials as the beginning of this concept of liability for international crimes, but actually the debate appears to have its origins in the sessions of the Commission on Responsibilities.

The Defence

The second paragraph of Article 227 of the Treaty of Versailles declares that the special tribunal will ensure 'the guarantees essential to the right of defence'. Disputes would inevitably arise about the scope of such guarantees. A century later, they still do. Often, these involve complaints about the resources available to defence counsel, a matter of relevance to an indigent accused but of little concern to the Kaiser, who might have sold a painting or two in order to fund his defence. Perhaps the many hundreds of German women who offered to take his place in the dock would have devoted themselves to fund raising.

The Kaiser might have begun the proceedings with an objection to jurisdiction based upon his purported immunity as a Head of State. Judges of the special tribunal could have been tempted to expound upon the subject, but this would be unnecessary. Any such immunity belongs not to the individual, but to the State, which is free to waive any objection. When it signed and ratified the Treaty of Versailles, Germany accepted the legitimacy of a trial of its former Emperor.

Immunity is often confounded with the related but distinct defence of official capacity, whereby an individual contends that he or she was nothing more than an instrument of government or of the State. Modern-day international criminal tribunals prohibit such a defence, generally by means of an explicit provision in their statutes. The model is Article VII of the Charter of the International Military Tribunal,[54] famously interpreted in the final judgment: 'Crimes against international law are committed by men, not by abstract entities, and only by punishing individuals who commit such crimes can the provisions of international law be enforced.'[55] Ironically, the Kaiser might find himself arguing that his role in German Government was quite subordinate. When the Kautsky papers became public, he dismissed their significance as impulsive personal impressions that had no effect upon government policy.[56] Raising such a defence would be personally humiliating for the Kaiser, because it would be an admission of his own impotence, although it could open the door to acquittal. He might have been forced to choose between ego and survival.

It would take no particular creativity or insight from the Kaiser's lawyers to develop arguments about the retroactivity of the charges. Although the judges of the tribunal had no authority to rule on the legality of the charge, defence counsel might have argued that the judges could use the principle against retroactive crimes as a rule of interpretation. This would not constitute a direct challenge to the legality of Article 227, but rather a plea that it be understood in such a way as not to offend the non-retroactivity principle. For example, this argument could support the claim that Article 227 did not extend to responsibility for starting a war of aggression. In somewhat the same vein, although it is not quite the same argument, the Kaiser's defence could contend that the charges were defective because of their undoubted vagueness. However, it is unlikely that argument would advance the defence case very much. Judges would take the view that it was precisely their task to provide clarity and definition to an enigmatic provision.

The Kaiser might well answer charges relating to violations of the laws and customs of war by charging that the Allied armies were themselves guilty of illegal conduct. The British and the French had used poison gas and perhaps other inhumane weapons, and they engaged in war at sea and in the air using some of the same new technology as the Germans.[57] Known as the *tu quoque* defence, essentially 'you did it too', this is an argument doomed to failure at the legal level, yet immensely attractive in a trial where the accused insists upon the unfairness of the proceedings. At Nuremberg, the defendants produced a sworn statement from an American admiral claiming that his navy engaged in the same practices that the Germans were being accused of. Often invoked by critics of the trial, who mistakenly claim the tribunal ordered an acquittal on the charge, it is actually an example of the fundamental fairness of the proceedings. The judgment very carefully states that the sentence imposed upon Admiral Dönitz would not be 'assessed on the ground of his breaches of the international law of submarine warfare', thereby confirming that it was a crime, and implying that it was committed by the Allies as well.[58]

This chapter is entitled 'Was He Guilty?' Nothing about the charges and the evidence is simple or straightforward. Those who insist upon holding such a trial where issues of huge political and historical importance are discussed should never assume that the judgment will confirm their official narrative of the events. In debating whether to put the leading Nazis on trial, the British warned that the proceedings might be ridiculed as a 'put-up job'. Perhaps even more serious was the danger of what they described as 'turning the tables'. Public opinion might grow weary of the trial and even come to view the defendant as a victim. 'It is difficult to think that anybody would in the course of time look on Hitler as an injured man, but it is by no means unlikely that a long trial will result in a change of public feeling as to the justification of trying Hitler at all', they said.[59]

That Germany may bear responsibility for starting the First World War, that it violated international treaties by invading Belgium and Luxembourg, that members of its army and navy committed atrocities and other violations of the laws and customs of war, does not point to the inexorable conclusion that the Kaiser was guilty of international crimes. Analogies with future international trials are only useful to an extent. Not only was the crime against peace on firmer legal foundations in 1945, the evidence that Germany and Japan were the aggressors had a clarity that was lacking in 1914. While the armed forces of the Second Reich may well deserve condemnation for atrocities committed in the course of the First World War, they were of an order of magnitude that does not bear comparison with those of the Third Reich.

Punishment

In all of the debates about prosecuting the Kaiser, little consideration was ever given to the penalty he would suffer if convicted. Article 227 said it would be the duty of the tribunal 'to fix the punishment which it considers should be imposed'. The British draft statute of February 1919 stated that the tribunal would have the power to sentence a convicted person 'to such punishment as it shall think proper'. It also said that 'in fixing the punishment the Court may take into account extenuating circumstances'. Sub-Commission III proposed the following: 'When the accused is found by the tribunal to be guilty, the tribunal shall have the power to sentence him to any punishment which may be imposed for a like offence by any court in any country.'[60] Writing many years later, one of the members of the Council of Four when Article 227 was adopted, Vittorio Orlando, considered the failure to specify the penalty as a violation of basic principles. 'The judge in the case could have had the power to condemn the Kaiser to a penalty ranging from a one-franc fine up to death!', he observed.[61]

George Curzon said that when he discussed prosecution of the Kaiser with Clemenceau following the armistice, the subject of the penalty that might be imposed following conviction did not enter their minds. The goal of criminal proceedings would be to stigmatise the Kaiser 'as a universal outlaw so that there should be no land in which he could set his foot'.[62] Lloyd George campaigned in December 1919 on the slogan 'Hang the Kaiser', although he later said that he only meant the 'electoral gallows'.[63] Were the Kaiser tried in England, we can easily imagine King George V, his cousin, pleading for clemency and even ordering it. He was the King, after all, and blood is thicker than water. If the trial were held in Holland, the Dutch might have ruled out any possibility of execution as a possible outcome. Nobody had been executed in the Netherlands since 1870.

The preamble of the Rome Statute of the International Criminal Court says that putting an end to impunity will contribute to prevention. Only the most naïve could imagine that trial and conviction of the Kaiser might have deterred the terrible sequel to the Great War. Justice for the Kaiser could never provide a corrective for the injustice of Versailles. Obdurate and irascible, the Kaiser was not a man to be easily humbled. Perhaps then, even with a trial and a conviction, the Kaiser would have ended his days in Doorn, chastened not by the condemnation of historians, but by the obloquy of the first international criminal court, spending the final two decades of his life hosting fascist politicians from over the border, dreaming of royalist restoration, chopping wood, and ranting at the Jews.

As the Allies were swallowing their pride following the Dutch refusal to extradite the Kaiser or, at least, to intern him in a remote location, they were debating another bold step in international justice within the context of the treaty of peace with Turkey. In fulfilment of their pledge in May 1915 to bring to trial the perpetrators of the atrocities against the Armenians, they decided to depart from the model of the Treaty of Versailles with respect to penalties. A provision was added to the draft treaty requiring Turkey to hand over 'persons whose surrender may be required by the latter as being responsible for the massacres committed during the continuance of the state of war on territory which formed part of the Turkish Empire on August 1, 1914'. This became Article 230 of the Treaty of Sèvres. Ernest Pollock pointed out that the text applied only to massacres committed during the conflict. 'If it was desired to hold the power in reserve after the treaty was in force, in order to safeguard the Armenians against future atrocities, and to try the authors of them', the phrase would need to be changed.[64] His farsighted and progressive suggestion was not taken up. In any event, the Treaty of Sèvres never entered into force and trials for the Armenian genocide never took place. By this point in time, the League of Nations was already actively considering proposals for a permanent international criminal court. Its Advisory Committee of Jurists recommended establishment of a 'Court of International Criminal Justice'. The Third Committee of the League's General Assembly considered this to be 'premature', adding 'that it is best to entrust criminal cases to the ordinary tribunals as is at present the custom in international procedure'.[65]

This book began with the metaphor of the beaten path, attributed to Benjamin N. Cardozo, and eloquently expressed by the American prosecutor at the Nuremberg trial, Robert H. Jackson, as a way to explain legal development. Perhaps more than any other single individual, Jackson was the pioneer, the scout, who led the way down the figurative path. The International Military Tribunal was governed by its Charter, adopted at the conclusion of the London Conference in August 1945. Like Article 227 of the Treaty of Versailles, it was the creation of a few very powerful countries. Three of them, the United States, the United Kingdom, and France, participated in both exercises. But although it may have been drafted by only a small group of States, the Treaty of Versailles was signed and ratified by many. Besides Germany, France, Italy, the United Kingdom, and Japan, the Treaty of Versailles was ratified by twenty-two independent States. Although the United States never ratified the treaty, the reasons for its disagreements had nothing to do with Article 227, which it accepted. In its judgment of 30 September and 1 October 1946, the International Military Tribunal insisted that the Charter was not 'an arbitrary exercise of power on the part of the victorious nations', but rather 'the expression of international law existing at the time of its creation'. To that extent, the judges said, it was 'itself a contribution to international law'.[66] Perhaps the same can be said of Article 227 of the Treaty of Versailles, although with less enthusiasm and more reserve.

The riddles and the controversies that characterise the debates about international criminal justice at the end of the First World War all resonate today. Some have been largely resolved. Others remain controversial. In 1919, the crimes were defined in only embryonic form, whereas now there exist widely accepted texts. A century ago, an institutional home for international justice was contemplated, but never put into practice. The permanent International Criminal Court has been an important component of international organisation for more than a decade. Today, reports of atrocities invariably provoke calls that the perpetrators, and especially their leaders and commanders, be summoned to the bar of international justice. A complex and sophisticated legal framework provides the basis for prosecutions. Increasingly precise obligations deal with implementation.

Prior to the outbreak of the First World War, lawyers and policy-makers studied and discussed many important changes to the international legal order. Important standards had already been set out in the Hague Conventions of 1899 and 1907. Nowhere in these materials, however, do we find evidence suggesting that serious consideration was being given to the creation of an international criminal court. The idea emerged rather suddenly from the ferment of the war itself. The results were inconclusive and ultimately disappointing. Yet, to repeat Clemenceau's sage observation in the Council of Four when Article 227 was being considered, 'it was the beginning of something great'.[67]

Notes

PREFACE

1. M. Cherif Bassiouni, 'World War I: "The War to End All Wars" and the Birth of a Handicapped International Justice System' (2001–2002) 30 *Denver Journal of International Law and Policy* 244.
2. Harry M. Rhea, *The United States and the International Criminal Tribunals*, Antwerp: Intersentia, 2012.

CHAPTER I

1. Jackson's citation is not precise. Cardozo wrote that 'the power of precedent, when analysed, is the power of the beaten track': Benjamin Cardozo, *The Growth of the Law*, New Haven: Yale University Press, 1924, p. 62. Perhaps Cardozo was inspired by Oliver Wendell Holmes Jr, 'The Path of the Law' (1897) 10 *Harvard Law Review* 457.
2. 'Report to the President by Mr. Justice Jackson, October 7, 1946', in Robert H. Jackson, *Report of Robert H. Jackson, United States Representative to the International Conference on Military Trials*, Washington, DC: US Government Printing Office, 1949, pp. 432–40, at p. 437.
3. Covenant of the League of Nations, [1919] UKTS 4, Art. 22.
4. Treaty of Versailles, [1919] UKTS 4, Arts 227–30; Treaty of St Germain-en-Laye, [1919] UKTS 11, Arts 173–6; Treaty of Trianon, [1920] UKTS 10, Arts 157–60; Treaty of Neuilly-sur-Seine, [1919] UKTS 5, Arts 118–20; Treaty of Sèvres, 10 August 1920, Arts 226–30.
5. *R. v. Bow Street Metropolitan Stipendiary Magistrate, ex p. Pinochet Ugarte (No. 3)*, [2000] 1 AC 14.
6. *Arrest Warrant of 11 April 2000 (Democratic Republic of the Congo v. Belgium)*, Judgment, ICJ Reports 2002, p. 3, § 61.
7. Report of the International Law Commission, Sixty-ninth session (1 May–2 June and 3 July–4 August 2017), UN Doc. A/72/10, § 74.
8. *Prosecutor v. Bashir* (ICC-02/05-01/09), Corrigendum to the Decision Pursuant to Article 87(7) of the Rome Statute on the Failure by the Republic of Malawi to Comply with the Cooperation Requests Issued by the Court with Respect to the Arrest and Surrender of Omar Hassan Ahmad Al Bashir, 13 December 2011, § 23.

9. *Prosecutor v. Ruto et al.* (ICC-01/09-01/11), Reasons of Judge Eboe-Osuji, 5 April 2016, § 263.

10. *Prosecutor v. Bashir* (ICC-02/05-01/09), Decision on the Cooperation of the Democratic Republic of the Congo Regarding Omar Al Bashir's Arrest and Surrender to the Court, 9 April 2014, § 29.

11. *Prosecutor v. Bashir* (ICC-02/05-01/09), Minority Opinion of Judge Marc Perrin de Brichambaut, 6 July 2017, §§ 59–83.

12. Oona A. Hathaway and Scott J. Shapiro, *The Internationalists*, New York: Simon & Schuster, 2017.

13. General Treaty for the Renunciation of War as an Instrument of National Policy, (1928) 94 LNTS 57.

14. *France et al. v. Goering et al.*, Judgment, (1947) 1 IMT 171, at p. 186.

15. The crime of aggression, RC/Res.6.

16. Activation of the jurisdiction of the Court over the crime of aggression, ICC-ASP/16/Res.5.

17. Universal Declaration of Human Rights, GA Res. 217A (III), Art. 11(2).

18. Rome Statute of the International Criminal Court, (2002) 2187 UNTS 3, Art. 11.

19. *Kononov v. Latvia* [GC], No. 36376/04, ECHR 2010; *Kolk and Kislyiy v. Estonia* (dec.), Nos. 23052/04 and 24018/04, ECHR 2006-I.

20. *Vasiliauskas v. Lithuania* [GC], No. 35343/05, ECHR 2015; *Korbely v. Hungary* [GC], No. 9174/02, ECHR 2008.

CHAPTER 2

1. James Kendis and James Brockman, 'We're Going to Hang the Kaiser under the Nearest Linden Tree' [song lyrics], New York: Kendis-Brockman Music Co., 1917. See also Lothar Reinermann, 'Fleet Street and the Kaiser: British Public Opinion and Wilhelm II' (2008) 26 *German History* 469.

2. Annie Deperchin, 'The Laws of War', in Jay Winter (ed.), *The First World War*, Vol. I, Cambridge: Cambridge University Press, 2014, pp. 615–38, at pp. 629–30.

3. Goschen to Grey, 4 August 1914, TNA FO 371/2164/41041. See Isabel V. Hull, *A Scrap of Paper: Breaking and Making International Law During the Great War*, Ithaca, NY: Cornell University Press, 2014, pp. 16–50.

4. HC Deb. 3 August 1914 vol. 65 cc1822. See also T. G. Otte, *July Crisis, The World's Descent into War, July 1914*, Cambridge: Cambridge University Press, 2014, p. 495.

5. *Rapports sur la violation du droit des gens en Belgique*, Vol. I, Paris and Nancy: Berger-Levraut, 1916; *Violation of the Rights of Nations and of the Laws and Customs of War in Belgium, Reports of the Official Commission of the Belgian Government*, London: HMSO, 1915.

6. *Rapports et procès-verbaux d'enquête de la commission instituée en vue de constater les actes commis par l'ennemi en violation du droit des gens (Décret du 23 septembre 1914)*, Paris: Imprimerie nationale, 1915–1919. For detailed documentation on the inquiries, see Archives nationales (France), Pierrefitte-sur-Seine, AJ/4/32-40.

7. *Report of the Committee on Alleged German Outrages*, London: HMSO, 1915, p. 38.

8. John Horne and Alan Kramer, *German Atrocities, 1914: A History of Denial*, New Haven, CT and London: Yale University Press, 2001, pp. 232–7; John Horne and Alan Kramer, 'German "Atrocities" and Franco-German Opinion, 1914: The Evidence of German Soldiers' Diaries' (1994) 66 *Journal of Modern History* 1; Lothar Wieland, *Belgien, 1914: Die Frage des belgischen 'Franktireurkrieges' und due deutsche öffentliche Meinung von 1914 bis 1936*, Frankfurt: Peter Lang, 1984; Jeff Lipkes, *Rehearsals: The German Army in Belgium, 1914*, Leuven: Leuven University Press, 2007; Ruth Harris, 'The "Child of the Barbarian": Rape, Race and Nationalism in France during the First World War' (1993) 141 *Past & Present* 170; Isabel V. Hull, *A Scrap of Paper: Breaking and Making International Law During the Great War*, Ithaca, NY: Cornell University Press, 2014.

9. James Brown Scott, 'The Case of Captain Fryatt' (1916) 10 *American Journal of International Law* 865; James F. Willis, *Prologue to Nuremburg, The Politics and Diplomacy of Punishing War Criminals of the First World War*, Westport, CT and London: Greenwood Press, 1982, pp. 27–32.

10. Edgard Troimaux, 'Conseil de guerre, Deux pillards condamnés à mort', *Echo de Paris*, 5 October 1914, p. 2.

11. 'Affaire Vogelgesang' (1915) 42 *Journal du droit international* 54.

12. William Loubat, 'Des sanctions pénales du droit de la guerre', *Le Temps*, 28 April 1915, p. 1. Also, André Weiss, 'Des sanctions pénales du droit de la guerre', *Le Temps*, 2 May 1915, p. 1.

13. Convention relative to the Treatment of Prisoners of War, (1931) 118 LNTS 343, Arts 65–6.

14. James F. Willis, *Prologue to Nuremburg: The Politics and Diplomacy of Punishing War Criminals of the First World War*, Westport, CT and London: Greenwood Press, 1982, pp. 49–50.

15. Letter from Vice-President of the League to the Prime Minister, 24 March 1917, FMAE A/64, A-1025-3.

16. W. A. B., 'Hugh H. L. Bellot, D. C. L.' (1928) 14 *Transactions of the Grotius Society, Problems of Peace and War, Papers Read before the Society in the Year 1928* xi; J. H. Morgan, 'The Late Hugh Bellot, An Appreciation' (1928) 14 *Transactions of the Grotius Society, Problems of Peace and War, Papers Read before the Society in the Year 1928* xv.

17. Hugh H. L. Bellot, 'War Crimes: Their Prevention and Punishment' (1916) 2 *Problems of the War, The Grotius Society, Papers Read before the Society in the Year 1916* 31, at p. 51.

18. Projet de convention entre tous les pays alliés, projet de convention entre la France et la Grande Bretagne, August 1916, FMAE A/64, A-1025-3. See also 'Proposition de constitution d'une Haute Cour de justice des Alliés pour statuer sur les crimes et attentats des ennemis au cours de la guerre' (1917) 44 *Journal du droit international* 1121; Projet de Convention pour assurer le châtiment des crimes ennemis, 2 May 1917, FMAE A/64, A-1025-3.

19. 'Germany and the Laws of War', *Edinburgh Review*, October 1914, pp. 278–97.

20. F. Larnaude and A. de Lapradelle, 'Inquiry into the Penal Liabilities of the Emperor William II', in Commission on the Responsibility of the Authors of the War, Minutes of Meetings of the Commission, USNA 181.1201/16, pp. 4–18, at p. 5.

21. 'German Barbarities, Punishment after the War', *The Times*, 15 May 1915, p. 5.

22. 'Lusitania Outrage, Verdict of Wilful and Wholesale Murder', *The Irish Times*, 11 May 1915, p. 5; 'Jury's Striking Verdict', *The Times*, 11 May 1915, p. 9.

23. Hugh H. L. Bellot, 'War Crimes: Their Prevention and Punishment' (1916) 2 *Problems of the War, The Grotius Society, Papers Read before the Society in the Year 1916* 31, at p. 43.

24. ibid. p. 46.

25. Reparation for Acts of Devastation by German Army during withdrawal. Note by Mr Balfour covering note by French Ambassador, 11 September 1918, TNA CAB 24/64/25 (emphasis in the original).

26. Minutes of a Meeting of the War Cabinet, 10 Downing Street, 20 September 1918, 12 noon, TNA CAB 23/7/28.

27. Memorandum by the Secretary of State for Foreign Affairs, 8 October 1918, TNA CAB 24/66/31.

28. 'Communiqué du government français à la Presse, 5 October 1918' (1918) 45 *Journal du droit international* 1618; Jean Graven, 'La première tentative consecutive à la guerre mondiale de 1914–1918', in Julius Stone and Robert K. Woetzel (eds), *Towards a Feasible International Criminal Court*, Geneva: World Peace through Law Centre, 1970, pp. 96–103, at p. 97.

29. *Journal officiel de la République française*, 16 October 1918, *Sénat*, p. 706; (1918) 45 *Journal du droit international* 1623, at pp. 1628–9.

30. F. E. Smith and Gordon Hewart to Lloyd George, 30 September 1918, TNA CAB 24/66/56.

31. 'Sees Difficulties in President's Plan', *New York Times*, 12 January 1918, p. 3; William Camp, *The Glittering Prizes: A Biographical Study of F.E. Smith, First Earl of Birkenhead*, London: Macgibbon & Kee, 1960, pp. 108–9. The speech is reproduced in F. E. Smith, *The Speeches of Lord Birkenhead*, London: Cassell, 1929, pp. 93–115.

32. 'Punishment of Enemy Criminals', *The Times*, 19 September 1918, p. 3.

33. First Interim Report from the Committee of Enquiry into Breaches of the Laws of War, 13 January 1919, TNA CAB/24/111, p. 2.

34. 'The Attorney General's Address', in First Interim Report from the Committee of Enquiry into Breaches of the Laws of War, 13 January 1919, TNA CAB/24/111, pp. 6–11, at p. 7.

35. ibid. See also 'German Crimes, Responsibility and Punishment', *The Times*, 8 November 1918, p. 7.

36. Meeting of the War Cabinet and Imperial War Cabinet, 10 Downing Street, 5 November 1918, 12.30 P.M., TNA CAB/23/37/36, p. 3.

37. C. E. Caldwell, *Field Marshall Sir Henry Wilson: His Life and Diaries*, Vol. 2, London: Cassell, 1927, p. 149.

38. Seth P. Tillman, *Anglo-American Relations at the Paris Peace Conference of 1919*, Princeton: Princeton University Press, 1961, p. 63.

39. Vittorio Emanuele Orlando, 'On the Aborted Decision to Bring the German Emperor to Trial' (2007) 5 *Journal of International Criminal Justice* 1015, at p. 1025. Also, Vittorio Emanuele Orlando, *Memorie (1915–1919)*, Milan: Rizzoli, 1960; Vittorio Emanuele Orlando, *Scritti varii di diritto publicco e scienza politica*, Milan: Giuffrè, 1940, pp. 95ff; Vittorio Emanuele Orlando, *Raccolta di scritti di diritto pubblico in onore di Giovanni Vacchelli, Vita e pensiero*, Milan: Università Catolica del Sacro Cuore, 1938, pp. 337ff.

40. A. de Lapradelle and F. Larnaude, *Examen de la responsabilité pénale de l'Empereur Guillaume II d'Allemagne*, Paris: Imprimerie nationale, 1918; (1919) 46 *Journal du droit international* 131; Recueil des actes, pp. 10–28. An English-language version of the report is an annex to the minutes of the first meeting of the Commission on Responsibilities: F. Larnaude and A. de Lapradelle, 'Inquiry into the Penal Liabilities of the Emperor William II', in Commission on the Responsibility of the Authors of the War, Minutes of Meetings of the Commission, USNA 181.1201/16, pp. 4–18.

41. Meeting of the Imperial War Cabinet, 10 Downing Street, 20 November 1918, 12 noon, TNA CAB/23/37/37, p. 5.

42. ibid.

43. Leonard Mosley, *Curzon, The End of an Epoch*, London: Longmans, 1960, pp. 186–7.

44. Curzon to Lloyd George, 13 November 1918, LG F/11/9/23; David Lloyd George, *Memoirs of the Peace Conference*, New Haven, CT: Yale University Press, 1939, p. 55.

45. David Lloyd George, *Memoirs of the Peace Conference*, New Haven, CT: Yale University Press, 1939, p. 54.

46. Maurice Hankey, *The Supreme Control at the Paris Peace Conference 1919: A Commentary*, London: George Allen & Unwin, 1963, p. 13.

47. Winston S. Churchill, *Great Contemporaries*, London: Putnam, 1937, p. 288.

48. Winston S. Churchill, *The World Crisis: The Aftermath, 1918–1922*, Vol. IV, London: Bloomsbury, 2015, pp. 18–19. The quotation comes from Wilde's play *A Woman of No Importance*.

49. G. Bennett, *British Foreign Policy during the Curzon Period, 1919–24*, London: Springer, 1995, p. 1.

50. Meeting of the Imperial War Cabinet, 10 Downing Street, 20 November 1918, 12 noon, TNA CAB/23/37/37, p. 5. The précis of Curzon's remarks in the Cabinet Minutes finds slightly more ample development in Lloyd George's account: David Lloyd George, *Memoirs of the Peace Conference*, New Haven, CT: Yale University Press, 1939, pp. 56–7.

51. F. Larnaude and A. de Lapradelle, 'Inquiry into the Penal Liabilities of the Emperor William II', in Commission on the Responsibility of the Authors of the War, Minutes of Meetings of the Commission, USNA 181.1201/16, pp. 4–18, at p. 10.

52. Meeting of the Imperial War Cabinet, 10 Downing Street, 20 November 1918, 12 noon, TNA CAB/23/37/37, p. 5; David Lloyd George, *Memoirs of the Peace Conference*, New Haven, CT: Yale University Press, 1939, pp. 56–7.

53. ibid.

54. Meeting of the Imperial War Cabinet, 10 Downing Street, 20 November 1918, 12 noon, TNA CAB/23/37/37, p. 6; David Lloyd George, *Memoirs of the Peace Conference*, New Haven, CT: Yale University Press, 1939, p. 57.

55. Meeting of the Imperial War Cabinet, 10 Downing Street, 20 November 1918, 12 noon, TNA CAB/23/37/37, p. 6. See also Robert Borden, *Robert Laird Borden: His Memoirs*, London: Macmillan, 1938, p. 868.

56. Winston S. Churchill, 'The Truth about the Ex-Kaiser', *Colliers*, 25 October 1930, pp. 16, 42–6, at p. 45.

57. Meeting of the Imperial War Cabinet, 10 Downing Street, 20 November 1918, 12 noon, TNA CAB/23/37/37, p. 6.

58. Winston S. Churchill, *The World Crisis: The Aftermath, 1918–1922*, Vol. IV, London: Bloomsbury, 2015, p. 18.

59. Meeting of the Imperial War Cabinet, 10 Downing Street, 20 November 1918, 12 noon, TNA CAB/23/37/37, p. 6.

60. ibid., p. 7.

61. ibid.; David Lloyd George, *Memoirs of the Peace Conference*, New Haven, CT: Yale University Press, 1939, pp. 57–8.

CHAPTER 3

1. Christopher Clark, *Iron Kingdom: The Rise and Downfall of Prussia, 1600–1947*, Cambridge, MA: Belknap Press, 2006, pp. 612–19.

2. John C. G. Röhl, *Wilhelm II: Into the Abyss of War and Exile, 1900–1941*, Cambridge: Cambridge University Press, 2014, p. 1183.

3. ibid. p. 1226.

4. John C. G. Röhl, *The Kaiser and His Court: Wilhelm II and the Government of Germany*, Cambridge: Cambridge University Press, 1996, p. 14.

5. Virginia Cowles, *The Kaiser*, London: Collins, 1963, p. 404.

6. John Wheeler Bennett, *Hindenberg: The Wooden Titan*, London: Macmillan, 1936, p. 197.

7. Maurice Baumont, *The Fall of the Kaiser*, London: George Allen & Unwin, 1931, pp. 101–5.

8. John C. G. Röhl, *Wilhelm II: Into the Abyss of War and Exile, 1900–1941*, Cambridge: Cambridge University Press, 2014, p. 1187; Wolfram Pyta, *Hindenburg, Herrschaft zwischen Hohenzollern und Hitler*, Munich: Siedler, 2007, pp. 361–77.

9. Klaus W. Jonas, *The Life of Crown Prince William*, Pittsburgh, PA: University of Pittsburgh Press, 1961, p. 120. A somewhat different version of the letter appears in Charles F. Horne (ed.), *Source Records of the Great War*, Vol. VI, New York: National Alumni, 1923, p. 411.

10. Sigurd von Ilsemann, *Der Kaiser in Holland. Aufzeichnungen des letzten Flügeladjutanten Kaiser Wilhelms II*, Vol. 1: *Amerongen und Doorn, 1918–1923*, Munich: Biederstein, 1968, pp. 43–4.

11. Friedrich Rosen, *Aus Einem Diplomatischen Wanderleben*, Wiesbaden: Limes Verlag, 1959, p. 216. Also, Rosen to Ebert, 17 November 1918, BPNL 145, pp. 214–18.

12. Maurice van Vollenhoven, *Memoires, beschouwingen, belevenissen, reizen en anecdoten*, Amsterdam: Elsevier, 1946, pp. 404–5; Maurice van Vollenhoven, *Les Vraies Ambasssades*, Brussels: Elsevier, 1954, pp. 214–15; Van Vollenhoven to Van Karnebeek, 9 November 1918, BPNL 117, pp. 728–9; Balfour to Townley, 14 December 1918, TNA FO 371/3227.

13. Susan Townley, *'Indiscretions' of Lady Susan*, New York: D. Appleton & Co., 1922, pp. 285–9.

14. Wilson S. Churchill, *Great Contemporaries*, London: Putnam, 1937, p. 38.

15. Susan Townley, *'Indiscretions' of Lady Susan*, New York: D. Appleton & Co., 1922, pp. 285–9. See also the account that Henri Houben, the French honorary consul at Maastricht, provided to Charles Benoist: Charles Benoist, *Souvenirs de Charles Benoist, 1902–1933*, Vol. III, Paris: Plon, 1933, pp. 383–5.

16. Norah Bentinck, *The Kaiser in Exile*, New York: George Doran, 1921, pp. 1–2.

17. ibid. p. 15.

18. Philipp Scheidemann, *Memoiren eines Sozialdemokraten*, Vol. 2, Dresden: Reissner, 1928, p. 257.

19. Sally Marks, '"My Name Is Ozymandias": The Kaiser in Exile' (1983) 16(2) *Central European History* 122, at p. 123, fn. 3.

20. Nigel J. Ashton and Duco Hellema, 'Hanging the Kaiser: Anglo-Dutch Relations and the Fate of Wilhelm II, 1918–20' (2000) 11 *Diplomacy and Statecraft* 53, at pp. 55–6; Nigel J. Ashton and Duco Hellema, '"Hang the Kaiser!"; De Brits-Nederlandse betrekkingen en het lot van Ex-Keizer Wilhelm II, 1918–1920', in Duco Hellema, C. Wiebes, and B. Zeeman (eds), *Buitenlandse Zaken: Vierde Jaarboek voor de geschiedenis van de Nederlandse politiek*, The Hague: Sdu Uitgevers, 1998; Marc Frey, *Der Erste Weltkrieg und die Niederlande, Ein neutrales Land im politischen und wirtschaftlichen Kalkül der Kriegsgegner*, Berlin: Walter de Gruyter, 2009, p. 333; H. J. Scheffer, *November 1918: Journaal van een Revolutie die niet Doorging*, Amsterdam: De Bataafsche Leeuw, 1984, pp. 60–2; C. Smit, *Diplomatieke geschiedenis van Nederland: inzonderheid sedert de vestiging van het Koninkrijk*, The Hague: Martinus Nijhoff, 1950, pp. 332–3; W. Gutsche, *Ein Kaiser im Exil: Der Letzte Deutsche Kaiser Wilhelm II in Holland; Ein Kritische Biographie*, Marburg: Willibald Hirtzeroth, 1991, pp. 24–6.

21. Martin Kohlrausch, 'Meer dan eenden voederen, Nieuwe literatuur over keizer Wilhelm II en Nederland' (2017) 130 *Tijdschrift voor Geschiedenis* 625, at pp. 632–3.

22. Hubert P. van Tuyll van Serooskerken, *Small Countries in a Big Power World: The Belgian-Dutch Conflict at Versailles*, Leiden and Boston: Brill, 2017, p. 112.

23. Viktoria Luise, *The Kaiser's Daughter*, London: W. H. Allen, 1977, p. 137.

24. 'Guillaume hôte encombrant', *Le Petit Journal*, 23 November 1918, p. 1; De Stuers to Van Karnebeek, 30 November 1918, BPNL 117, pp. 769–70, at p. 769.

25. Van Karnebeek Diary, 3 December 1918, BPNL 117, pp. 771–4, at pp. 771–2.

26. *Tweede Kamer*, 33ste Vergadering, 10 December 1918, pp. 658–9. Also, Telegram, 20 December 1918, DNA 2.05.26 stuk 195. For an English translation, see Robertson to Balfour, 13 December 1918, TNA FO 371/3227. See also the answer to a question in the Senate by Van Karnebeek: *Eerste Kamer*, Vel. 8 (Verbeterblad.), p. 17.

27. Townley to Balfour, 12 December 1918, TNA FO 371/3227.

28. Van Karnebeek Diary, 3 December 1918, DNA 2.05.25 inventaris 54; Garrett to the Acting Secretary of State, 10 December 1918, FRUS PPC II, pp. 78–9.

29. Balfour to Townley, 14 December 1918, TNA FO 371/3227.

30. German Ex-Emperor, 24 December 1918, TNA FO 371/3227.

31. De Fleuriau to Balfour, 25 November 1918, TNA FO 371/3256.

32. Balfour to Townley, 28 November 1918, TNA FO 371/3256.

33. Fallon to Hymans, 28 December 1918, BPNL 146, pp. 1138–9.

34. Garrett to the Acting Secretary of State, 31 December 1918, FRUS PPC II, pp. 80–4, at p. 81.

35. *Tweede Kamer*, 34ste Vergadering, 11 December 1918, p. 685.

36. Nigel J. Ashton and Duco Hellema, 'Hanging the Kaiser: Anglo-Dutch Relations and the Fate of Wilhelm II, 1918–20' (2000) 11 *Diplomacy and Statecraft* 53, at p. 57.

37. De Stuers to Van Karnebeek, 21 December 1918, BPNL 117, pp. 815–18, at pp. 816–17.

38. De Stuers to Van Karnebeek, 26 December 1918, BPNL 117, pp. 833–4, at p. 834.

39. Gevers to Van Karnebeek, 30 October 1918, BPNL 117, pp. 708–10; Gevers to Van Karnebeek, 6 November 1918, BPNL 117, pp. 723–4.

40. 'Kaiser in Exile, Scenes on Arrival', *The Times*, 13 November 1918, p. 8.

41. ibid..

42. Townley to Balfour, 12 November 1918, TNA FO 371/3227.

43. Townley to Hardinge, 22 November 1918, TNA FO 371/3788.

44. Hardinge to Townley, 29 November 1918, TNA FO 371/3788. See also Fallon to Hymans, 4 January 1919, BPNL 146, pp. 1140–2.

45. Kenneth Rose, *King George V*, London: Macmillan, 1983, p. 231.

46. HC Deb. 19 February 1919 vol. 112 cc918–20.

47. Susan Townley, *'Indiscretions' of Lady Susan*, New York: D. Appleton & Co., 1922, pp. 281–5.

48. Townley to Balfour, 17 November 1918, TNA FO 371/3227.

49. Norah Bentinck, *The Kaiser in Exile*, New York: George Doran, 1921, p. 23.

50. Townley to Hardinge, 17 November 1918, TNA FO 371/3227.

51. Graham to Director of Military Intelligence, 23 April 1919, TNA FO 371/3227; John C. G. Röhl, *Wilhelm II: Into the Abyss of War and Exile, 1900–1941*, Cambridge: Cambridge University Press, 2014, pp. 1190–1; Sally Marks, '"My Name Is Ozymandias": The Kaiser in Exile' (1983) 16(2) *Central European History* 122, pp. 130–1. Also, Rumbold to Curzon, 1 September 1919, TNA FO 371/3794.

52. Correspondence respecting the Kaiser's royal train, DNA 2.04.78.

53. Garrett to the Acting Secretary of State, The Hague, 12 December 1918, FRUS PPC II, p. 80.

54. 'Kaiser's Serious Illness, Recovering from Influenza', *The Times*, 6 January 1919, p. 8. Also: 'The Kaiser's Illness', *The Times*, 28 December 1918, p. 5.

55. Garrett to Acting Secretary of State, 31 December 1918, USNA 763.72/12807; BPNL 46, pp. 923–7. The document is reproduced in FRUS PPC II, pp. 80–5, but without the paragraph about the psychological problems of the 'lonely guest at Amerongen'.

CHAPTER 4

1. 'Proceedings of the Committee', in First Interim Report from the Committee of Enquiry into Breaches of the Laws of War, 13 January 1919, TNA CAB/24/111, pp. 11–17, at p. 12.

2. The reference to the original French text is A. de Lapradelle and F. Larnaude, *Examen de la responsabilité pénale de l'Empereur Guillaume II*, Paris: Imprimerie nationale, 1918.

3. 'Memorandum on the Detention of Napoleon Buonaparte', in Second Interim Report from the Committee of Enquiry into Breaches of the Laws of War, 3 June 1919, TNA CAB/24/111, pp. 149–391, at pp. 363–91.

4. Hugh Bellot, 'The Detention of Napoleon Buonaparte' (1923) 23 *Law Quarterly Review* 170.

5. 'Reasons for Recommendations', in First Interim Report from the Committee of Enquiry into Breaches of the Laws of War, 13 January 1919, TNA CAB/24/111, pp. 18–32, § 46.

6. Gary Bass, *Stay the Hand of Vengeance: The Politics of War Crimes Tribunals*, Princeton, NJ: Princeton University Press, 2000, pp. 49–51.

7. Charles Vane (ed.), *Memoirs and Correspondence of Viscount Castlereagh*, 3rd series, Vol. II, London: William Shoburl, 1851, pp. 434–5.

8. Emmanuel Decaux, 'Le statut du Chef d'État déchu' (1980) 26 *Annuaire français de droit international* 101–39, at p. 106. Also, Gary Bass, *Stay the Hand of Vengeance*, Princeton, NJ: Princeton University Press, 2000, pp. 37–8.

9. T. D. Gill and Elise van Sliedregt, 'Guantánamo Bay: A Reflection on the Legal Status and Rights of "Unlawful Enemy Combatants"' (2005) 1 *Utrecht Law Review* 28.

10. Memorandum upon the Disposition of the Army of Buonaparte, 15 July 1815, TNA FO 92/21.

11. Hugh Bellot, 'The Detention of Napoleon Buonaparte' (1923) 23 *Law Quarterly Review* 170, at pp. 186–7.

12. An Act for the more effectually detaining in custody Napoleon Buonaparte, 53 Geo. III, Cap. XXII.

13. See below, pp. 274–6.

14. 'Germany and the Laws of War', *Edinburgh Review*, October 1914, pp. 278–97.

15. 'German Barbarities, Punishment after the War', *The Times*, 15 May 1915, p. 5.

16. Louis Renault, 'De l'application du droit pénal aux faits de guerre' (1915) 42 *Journal du Droit International* 313, at pp. 335–7.

17. (1918) 45 *Journal du droit international* 1619.

18. 'Une consultation juridique sur l'extradition de Guillaume II', *La Croix*, 23 November 1918, p. 4. See also Vincent Laniol, 'Ferdinand Larnaude, un « délégué technique » à la conférence de la Paix de 1919 entre expertise et « culture de guerre »' (2012) 149 *Relations internationales* 43.

19. Proceedings of the Opening Session of the Conference of Paris, 18 January 1919, USNA 180.0201/1. Also, Criminal Liability of Emperor Wilhelm II, TNA FO 608/247/2.

20. F. Larnaude and A. de Lapradelle, 'Inquiry into the Penal Liabilities of the Emperor William II', in Commission on the Responsibility of the Authors of the War, Minutes of Meetings of the Commission, USNA 181.1201/16, pp. 4–18.

21. A. de Lapradelle and F. Larnaude, *Examen de la responsabilité pénale de l'Empereur Guillaume II*, Paris: Imprimerie nationale, 1918.

22. A. de Lapradelle and F. Larnaude, 'Examen de la responsabilité pénale de l'Empereur Guillaume II d'Allemagne' (1919) 46 *Journal du droit international* 131.

23. See, e.g., 'Guglielmo II al Tribunale della Società della Nazione?', *La Stampa*, 21 January 1919, p. 1; 'Fix Atrocities on Kaiser', *New York Times*, 21 January 1918, p. 1; 'Kaiser's Responsibility, French Jurists' Report', *The Times*, 20 January 1919, p. 10.

24. 'The Attorney General's Address', in First Interim Report from the Committee of Enquiry into Breaches of the Laws of War, 13 January 1919, TNA CAB/24/111, pp. 6–11, at p. 7. See also 'German Crimes, Responsibility and Punishment', *The Times*, 8 November 1918, p. 7.

25. 'Proceedings of the Committee', in First Interim Report from the Committee of Enquiry into Breaches of the Laws of War, 13 January 1919, TNA CAB/24/111, pp. 11–17, at p. 12.

26. Pollock to Holmes, 30 January 1919, in Mark de Wolfe Howe (ed.), *Holmes-Pollock Letters: The Correspondence of Mr Justice Holmes and Sir Frederick Pollock, 1874–1932*, Vol. II, Cambridge, MA: Belknap Press, 1961, pp. 4–5.

27. 'Report of Special Sub-Committee on Law', in First Interim Report from the Committee of Enquiry into Breaches of the Laws of War, 13 January 1919, TNA CAB/24/111, pp. 95–9.

28. 'Proceedings of the Committee', in First Interim Report from the Committee of Enquiry into Breaches of the Laws of War, 13 January 1919, TNA CAB/24/111, pp. 11–17, at p. 13.

29. 'Interim Recommendations of the Committee', in First Interim Report from the Committee of Enquiry into Breaches of the Laws of War, 13 January 1919, TNA CAB/24/111, pp. 13–17.

30. ibid. p. 17.

31. 'Reasons for Recommendations', in First Interim Report from the Committee of Enquiry into Breaches of the Laws of War, 13 January 1919, TNA CAB/24/111, pp. 18–32, §§ 45–9.

32. 'Report of Special Sub-Committee on Law', in First Interim Report from the Committee of Enquiry into Breaches of the Laws of War, 13 January 1919, TNA CAB/24/111, pp. 95–9, at p. 95.

33. 'Reasons for Recommendations', in First Interim Report from the Committee of Enquiry into Breaches of the Laws of War, 13 January 1919, TNA CAB/24/111, pp. 18–32, at p. 30.

34. 'Report of Special Sub-Committee on Law', in First Interim Report from the Committee of Enquiry into Breaches of the Laws of War, 13 January 1919, TNA CAB/24/111, pp. 95–9, at p. 98.

35. F. Larnaude and A. de Lapradelle, 'Inquiry into the Penal Liabilities of the Emperor William II', in Commission on the Responsibility of the Authors of the War, Minutes of Meetings of the Commission, USNA 181.1201/16, pp. 4–18, at p. 5.

36. 'Report of Special Sub-Committee on Law', in First Interim Report from the Committee of Enquiry into Breaches of the Laws of War, 13 January 1919, TNA CAB/24/111, pp. 95–9, at p. 98.

37. F. Larnaude and A. de Lapradelle, 'Inquiry into the Penal Liabilities of the Emperor William II', in Commission on the Responsibility of the Authors of the War, Minutes of Meetings of the Commission, USNA 181.1201/16, pp. 4–18, at p. 7.

38. ibid. p. 9.

39. *France et al. v. Goering et al.*, Motion adopted by all Defense Counsel, 19 November 1945, (1947) 1 IMT 168.

40. *France et al. v. Goering et al.*, Judgment, (1947) 1 IMT 171, at p. 219. See also Oona A. Hathaway and Scott J. Shapiro, *The Internationalists*, New York: Simon & Schuster, 2017.

41. F. Larnaude and A. de Lapradelle, 'Inquiry into the Penal Liabilities of the Emperor William II', in Commission on the Responsibility of the Authors of the War, Minutes of Meetings of the Commission, USNA 181.1201/16, pp. 4–18, at p. 10.

42. ibid.

43. ibid. p. 16.

44. 'Report of Special Sub-Committee on Law', in First Interim Report from the Committee of Enquiry into Breaches of the Laws of War, 13 January 1919, TNA CAB/24/111, pp. 95–9, at pp. 96–7.

45. 'Reasons for Recommendations', First Interim Report from the Committee of Enquiry into Breaches of the Laws of War, 13 January 1919, TNA CAB/24/111, pp. 18–32, § 45.

46. 'Report of Special Sub-Committee on Law', in First Interim Report from the Committee of Enquiry into Breaches of the Laws of War, 13 January 1919, TNA CAB/24/111, pp. 95–9, at p. 97.

47. ibid.

48. James Wycliffe Headlam, *The History of Twelve Days, July 24th to August 4th, 1914*, London: T. Fisher Unwin, 1915.

49. Memorandum by Mr Headlam Morley, 12 December 1918, TNA FO 371/3227.
50. F. Larnaude and A. de Lapradelle, 'Inquiry into the Penal Liabilities of the Emperor William II', in Commission on the Responsibility of the Authors of the War, Minutes of Meetings of the Commission, USNA 181.1201/16, pp. 4–18, at p. 11.
51. ibid. p. 14.
52. ibid. p. 16.
53. ibid.
54. ibid. p. 8.
55. First Interim Report from the Committee of Enquiry into Breaches of the Laws of War, 13 January 1919, TNA CAB/24/111, p. 31.
56. John Macdonnell, 'Note on Immunity of Sovereigns', in First Interim Report from the Committee of Enquiry into Breaches of the Laws of War, 13 January 1919, TNA CAB/24/111, pp. 32–5, at p. 35. See also J. H. Morgan, 'The Plea of Superior Orders', in First Interim Report from the Committee of Enquiry into Breaches of the Laws of War, 13 January 1919, TNA CAB/24/111, pp. 36–53, at pp. 48–51.
57. David Hunter Miller and James Brown Scott, 'Observations on the Responsibility of the Authors of the War and for Crimes Committed in the War' in David Hunter Miller, *My Diary at the Conference of Paris, with Documents,* Vol. III, [New York]: Printed for the author, 1924, pp. 456–7. George A. Finch prepared a much lengthier opinion on some of the legal issues, but he did not address the immunity question. See George Finch, 'Memorandum Regarding the Responsibility of the Authors of the War and for Crimes Committed in the War', in David Hunter Miller, *My Diary at the Conference of Paris,* Vol. III, pp. 458–506; Memorandum regarding the Responsibility of the Authors of the War and for the Crimes Committed in the War, Scott Papers, Box 30.3b. Some American academics were more favourable to prosecution: Quincy Wright, 'The Legal Liability of the Kaiser' (1919) 13 *American Political Science Review* 120; Richard Floyd Clarke, 'In the Matter of the Position of William Hohenzollern, Kaiser of Germany: Under International Law', TNA, FO 371/3227, discussed in Kirsten Sellars, 'Trying the Kaiser: The Origins of International Criminal Law', in Morten Bergsmo, Cheah Wui Ling, and Yi Ping (eds), *Historical Origins of International Criminal Law,* Vol. 1, Brussels: Torkel Opsahl Academic EPublisher, 2014, pp. 195–212, at pp. 202–5. On the American approach generally, see Binoy Kampmark, 'Sacred Sovereigns and Punishable War Crimes: The Ambivalence of the Wilson Administration towards a Trial of Kaiser Wilhelm' (2007) 53 *Australian Journal of Politics and History* 519.
58. *Arrest Warrant of 11 April 2000 (Democratic Republic of the Congo v. Belgium),* Judgment, ICJ Reports 2002, p. 3, § 61.
59. F. Larnaude and A. de Lapradelle, 'Inquiry into the Penal Liabilities of the Emperor William II', in Commission on the Responsibility of the Authors of the War, Minutes of Meetings of the Commission, USNA 181.1201/16, pp. 4–18, at p. 6.

60. 'Reasons for Recommendations', First Interim Report from the Committee of Enquiry into Breaches of the Laws of War, 13 January 1919, TNA CAB/24/111, pp. 18–32, § 20.

61. F. Larnaude and A. de Lapradelle, 'Inquiry into the Penal Liabilities of the Emperor William II', in Commission on the Responsibility of the Authors of the War, Minutes of Meetings of the Commission, USNA 181.1201/16, pp. 4–18, at p. 9.

62. 'Report of Special Sub-Committee on Law', in First Interim Report from the Committee of Enquiry into Breaches of the Laws of War, 13 January 1919, TNA CAB/24/111, pp. 95–9, at p. 96.

63. 'Reasons for Recommendations', First Interim Report from the Committee of Enquiry into Breaches of the Laws of War, 13 January 1919, TNA CAB/24/111, pp. 18–32, § 32.

64. George A. Finch, 'Memorandum Regarding the Responsibility of the Authors of the War and for Crimes Committed in the War' in David Hunter Miller, *My Diary at the Conference of Paris, with Documents*, Vol. III, [New York]: Printed for the author, 1924, pp. 458–506, at pp. 505–6.

65. 'Report of Special Sub-Committee on Law', in First Interim Report from the Committee of Enquiry into Breaches of the Laws of War, 13 January 1919, TNA CAB/24/111, pp. 95–9, at p. 96. See also 'Reasons for Recommendations', First Interim Report from the Committee of Enquiry into Breaches of the Laws of War, 13 January 1919, TNA CAB/24/111, pp. 18–32, § 34.

66. 'Interim Recommendations of the Committee', in First Interim Report from the Committee of Enquiry into Breaches of the Laws of War, 13 January 1919, TNA CAB/24/111, pp. 13–17, at pp. 14–15.

67. F. Larnaude and A. de Lapradelle, 'Inquiry into the Penal Liabilities of the Emperor William II', in Commission on the Responsibility of the Authors of the War, Minutes of Meetings of the Commission, USNA 181.1201/16, pp. 4–18, at p. 16.

68. ibid. p. 15.

69. ibid.

70. 'Interim Recommendations of the Committee', in First Interim Report from the Committee of Enquiry into Breaches of the Laws of War, 13 January 1919, TNA CAB/24/111, pp. 13–17, at p. 15.

71. 'Report of Special Sub-Committee on Law', in First Interim Report from the Committee of Enquiry into Breaches of the Laws of War, 13 January 1919, TNA CAB/24/111, pp. 95–9, at p. 99.

72. 'Interim Recommendations of the Committee', in First Interim Report from the Committee of Enquiry into Breaches of the Laws of War, 13 January 1919, TNA CAB/24/111, pp. 13–17, at p. 16.

73. ibid.

74. F. Larnaude and A. de Lapradelle, 'Inquiry into the Penal Liabilities of the Emperor William II', in Commission on the Responsibility of the Authors of

the War, Minutes of Meetings of the Commission, USNA 181.1201/16, pp. 4–18, at p. 16.

75. ibid. p. 18. With respect to the legality of an extradition request, see also the opinion of Professor H. Barthélemy, 'Guillaume II peut être extradé', *Le Matin*, 26 November 1918.

CHAPTER 5

1. Meeting of the Imperial War Cabinet, 10 Downing Street, 28 November 1918, 11.45 am, TNA CAB 23/39, p. 2.

2. David Lloyd George, *Memoirs of the Peace Conference*, Vol. I, New Haven, CT, Yale University Press, 1939, p. 65.

3. Lansing to Wilson, 7 February 1920, WWP 64, pp. 381–2.

4. Meeting of the Imperial War Cabinet, 10 Downing Street, 28 November 1918, 11.45 am, TNA CAB 23/39, pp. 2–4, 8–11; RA PS/PSO/GV/CQ/1560/1; LG F/147/7/2.

5. See above, p. 43.

6. Robert Borden, *Robert Laird Borden: His Memoirs*, London: Macmillan, 1938, p. 872.

7. William Camp, *The Glittering Prizes, A Biographical Study of F.E. Smith, First Earl of Birkenhead*, London: Macgibbon & Kee, 1960, p. 122.

8. Meeting of the Imperial War Cabinet, 10 Downing Street, 28 November 1918, 11.45 am, TNA CAB 23/39, p. 4.

9. 'Report of Special Sub-Committee on Law', in First Interim Report from the Committee of Enquiry into Breaches of the Laws of War, 13 January 1919, TNA CAB/24/111, pp. 95–9.

10. Meeting of the Imperial War Cabinet, 10 Downing Street, 28 November 1918, 11.45 am, TNA CAB 23/39, p. 10.

11. 'Prime Minister on German Crimes', *The Times*, 30 November 1918, p. 6.

12. David Lloyd George, *Memoirs of the Peace Conference*, Vol. I, New Haven, CT: Yale University Press, 1939, pp. 80–1.

13. The Special Representative (House) to the Secretary of State, 25 November 1918, FRUS PPC I, p. 333.

14. Colonel E. M. House to the Secretary of State, 30 November 1918, FRUS PPC I, pp. 333–4; House Diary, 30 November 1918, cited in Keith L. Nelson, *Victors Divided: America and the Allies in Germany, 1918–1923*, Berkeley, CA: University of California Press, 1975, p. 290.

15. Vittorio Emanuele Orlando, 'On the Aborted Decision to Bring the German Emperor to Trial' (2007) 5 *Journal of International Criminal Justice* 1015, at p. 1024.

16. Henri Mordacq, *Le Ministère Clemenceau, Journal d'un témoin*, Vol. III, Paris: Plon, 1931, pp. 26–7.

17. Notes of an Allied Conversation held in the Cabinet Room, 10 Downing Street, 2 December 1918, 11 am, TNA CAB 28/5 (IC 98), p. 5.

18. ibid.

19. ibid. A few days later, Sonnino expressed similar views to the French Ambassador in Rome: Barrere to Pichon, 8 December 1918, FMAE A/64, A-1025-4.

20. ibid. p. 6.

21. ibid.

22. ibid.

23. ibid. p. 7.

24. ibid.

25. ibid.

26. ibid. See also David Lloyd George, *Memoirs of the Peace Conference*, Vol. I, New Haven, CT: Yale University Press, 1939, pp. 80–1.

27. ibid. p. 6.

28. Conclusions of an Allied Conversation at 10 Downing Street, 2 December 1918, at 11 am, TNA CAB 28/5 (IC 98(a)).

29. Notes of an Allied Conversation held in the Cabinet Room, 10 Downing Street, 2 December 1918, 4 pm, TNA CAB 28/5 (IC 99), pp. 3–4. For the draft, see Notes of an Allied Conversation held in the Cabinet Room, 10 Downing Street, 2 December 1918, 11 am, Annex, TNA CAB 28/5 (IC 98(a)).

30. Meeting of the Imperial War Cabinet, 10 Downing Street, 2 December 1918, at 10.30 am, TNA CAB 23/42, p. 2.

31. ibid. See also Robert Borden, *Robert Laird Borden: His Memoirs*, London: Macmillan, 1938, p. 874.

32. ibid. pp. 2–3.

33. See Notes of an Allied Conversation held in the Cabinet Room, 10 Downing Street, 2 December 1918, at 4 pm, TNA CAB 28/5 (IC 99), p. 3.

34. Meeting of the Imperial War Cabinet, 10 Downing Street, 2 December 1918, at 10.30 am, TNA CAB 23/42, p. 3.

35. ibid.

36. ibid. pp. 3–4.

37. ibid. p. 4.

38. ibid.

39. Notes of an Allied Conversation held in the Cabinet Room, 10 Downing Street, 3 December 1918, at 11.15 am, TNA CAB 23/42, TNA CAB 28/5 (IC 100), p. 2.

40. Telegram to Col. House, 2 December 1918, LG/F/147/7/3/a; Foreign Office to Barclay and Bayley, 2 December 1918, TNA FO 371/3227; TNA FO 608/247/2.

41. Grahame to Balfour, 3 December 1918, TNA FO 371/3227; TNA FO 608/247/2.

42. Acting Secretary of State to Secretary of State, FRUS PPC I, 7 December 1918, pp. 340–2, at p. 341.

43. David Lloyd George, *Memoirs of the Peace Conference*, Vol. I, New Haven, CT: Yale University Press, 1939, p. 86.

44. Barclay to Balfour, 4 December 1918, TNA FO 371/3227; TNA FO 608/247/2.

45. The Counselor for the Department of State (Polk) to the Assistant Secretary of State (Phillips), 6 December 1918, FRUS PPC II, p. 78.

46. James F. Willis, *Prologue to Nuremburg: The Politics and Diplomacy of Punishing War Criminals of the First World War*, Westport, CT and London: Greenwood Press, 1982, p. 47.

CHAPTER 6

1. H. W. V. Temperley (ed.), *A History of the Peace Conference of Paris*, Vol. I, London: Henry Frowde and Hodder & Stoughton, 1920, pp. 148–53.

2. Hubert P. Van Tuyll, *The Netherlands and World War I: Espionage, Diplomacy and Survival*, The Hague: Brill, 2001; Maartje M. Abbenhuis, *The Art of Staying Neutral: The Netherlands in the First World War, 1914–1918*, Amsterdam: University of Amsterdam Press, 2006.

3. Michael Bothe, 'Neutrality, Concept and General Rules', in Rüdiger Wolfrum (ed.), *The Max Planck Encyclopedia of Public International Law*, Vol. VII, Oxford: Oxford University Press, 2012, pp. 617–34.

4. Hague Convention (V) Respecting the Rights and Duties of Neutral Powers and Persons in Case of War on Land, (1907) 3 Martens NRG, 3rd ser. 713, 205 Parry's Consol. TS 299, Art. 1.

5. ibid. Art. 20. For a list of all States Parties to the Convention, see James Brown Scott (ed.), *The Hague Conventions and Declarations of 1899 and 1907*, New York: Oxford University Press, 1915, pp. 139–40.

6. Townley to Van Karnebeek, 10 November 1918, BPNL 117, p. 729.

7. Townley to Van Karnebeek, 11 November 1918, BPNL 117, p. 730.

8. Letter from French Embassy in London, 17 November 1918, TNA FO 371/3227. Also, Annual Report on the Netherlands for the Year 1919, TNA FO 371/3838.

9. Minutes of Cabinet Meeting, 11 November 1918, BPNL 117, p. 729.

10. *Tweede Kamer*, 21ste Vergadering, 14 November 1918, p. 396.

11. *Tweede Kamer*, 22ste Vergadering, 15 November 1918, pp. 400–1.

12. ibid. pp. 410–11.

13. *Tweede Kamer*, 23ste Vergadering, 19 November 1918, p. 438. See also Townley to Balfour, 21 November 1918, TNA FO 371/3256.

14. *Tweede Kamer*, 24ste Vergadering, 20 November 1918, pp. 453–5.

15. ibid. p. 468.

16. Townley to Balfour, 21 November 1918, TNA FO 371/3256 (emphasis in the original).

17. Van Karnebeek to Cremer, 21 November 1918, FRUS PPC II, pp. 76–7.

18. Van Lijnden van Sandenburg to Van Karnebeek, 28 November 1918, BPNL 117, pp. 763–5, at p. 763.

19. Sally Marks, '"My Name Is Ozymandias": The Kaiser in Exile' (1983) 16(2) *Central European History* 122, p. 132, n. 35.

20. Rosen to Van Karnebeek, 26 November 1918, BPNL 117, p. 761.

21. *Tweede Kamer*, 33ste Vergadering, 10 December 1918, p. 658; The Minister in the Netherlands (Garrett) to the Secretary of State, 30 November 1918, FRUS PPC II, p. 77; Robertson to Balfour, 13 December 1918, TNA FO 371/3227.

22. *Tweede Kamer*, 31ste Vergadering, 5 December 1918, p. 619.

23. Ernst Heldring Diary, 3 December 1918, BPNL 117, pp. 774–6, at p. 775.

24. Friedrich Rosen, *Aus Einem Diplomatischen Wanderleben*, Wiesbaden: Limes Verlag, 1959, p. 249.

25. Sally Marks, "'My Name Is Ozymandias": The Kaiser in Exile' (1983) 16(2) *Central European History* 122, p. 133.

26. ibid. p. 134.

27. Townley to Balfour, 30 November 1918, TNA FO 371/3256.

28. Queen Wilhelmina to King George V, 26 December 1918, TNA FO 371/3256.

29. King George V to Queen Wilhelmina, BPNL 117, p. 907. A draft of the letter in the British Archives dated 17 January 1919 is worded slightly differently: '... features in the situation, which would render a visit on my part to the Netherlands at the present time open to very serious misinterpretation both in your country and in mine; (and it might be added in the world at large)', TNA FO 371/3256. See also Fallon to Hymans, 2 December 1918, BPNL 146, p. 1123; Garrett to Lansing, 7 January 1919, TNA 862.001 W64/57, BPNL 146, pp. 927–30.

30. Loder, Struyken, and Bres to Van Karnebeek, 9 December 1918, DNA 2.05.25 inventaris 144, BPNL 146, pp. 1195–1203.

31. *Tweede Kamer*, 33ste Vergadering, 10 December 1918, pp. 658–9. For the English translation, see Robertson to Balfour, 13 December 1918, TNA FO 371/3227.

32. *Tweede Kamer*, 34ste Vergadering, 11 December 1918, p. 679.

33. ibid. p. 686.

34. *Tweede Kamer*, 35ste Vergadering, 12 December 1918, p. 704.

35. *Tweede Kamer*, 34ste Vergadering, 11 December 1918, p. 685.

36. Townley to Balfour, 11 December 1918, TNA FO 371/3227; TNA FO 608/247/2.

37. Graham to Curzon, 12 March 1920, DBFP IX, p. 706. See below, p. 285.

38. Garrett to the Acting Secretary of State, 31 December 1918, FRUS PPC II, pp. 80–4, at p. 82.

39. Garrett to the Commission to Negotiate Peace, 8 January 1919, FRUS PPC II, pp. 84–5.

40. Garrett to the Acting Secretary of State, 10 December 1918, FRUS PPC II, pp. 78–9.

41. Garrett to the Acting Secretary of State, 31 December 1918, FRUS PPC II, pp. 80–4, at p. 81.

42. ibid. p. 83.

CHAPTER 7

1. *France et al. v. Goering et al.*, Judgment, (1947) 1 IMT 171, at pp. 250, 252, 265.

2. *A-G Israel v. Eichmann*, (1968) 36 ILR 5 (District Court, Jerusalem), paras 40, 41, 44, 50. There is also an interlocutory decision on the issue: Shabtai Rosenne (ed.), *6,000,000 Accusers, The Opening of the Eichmann Trial*, Jerusalem: Jerusalem Post, 1961, pp. 303–5.

3. *Prosecutor v. Nikolić* (IT-94-2-PT), Decision on Defence Motion Challenging the Exercise of Jurisdiction by the Tribunal, 9 October 2002, § 84; *Prosecutor v. Nikolić* (IT-94-2-AR73), Decision on Interlocutory Appeal Concerning Legality of Arrest, 5 June 2003, § 23.

4. Brian McAllister Linn, *The US Army and Counterinsurgency in the Philippines*, Chapel Hill, NC and London: University of North Carolina Press, 1989, p. 75.

5. Luke Lea and William T. Alderson, 'The Attempt to Capture the Kaiser' (1961) 20 *Tennessee Historical Quarterly* 222, at pp. 223–4; Luke Lea, 'Kaiser Story', p. 1, Lea Papers, Box 45.2A; Luke Lea, 'The Kaiser Story', TSLA D570.9.L3. See also Sworn testimony of Luke Lea, 26 January 1919, § 19, Lea Papers, Box 40.9.

6. Luke Lea and William T. Alderson, 'The Attempt to Capture the Kaiser' (1961) 20 *Tennessee Historical Quarterly* 222, at p. 233.

7. Jack H. McCall Jr, '"Amazingly Indiscreet": The Plot to Capture Wilhelm II' (2009) 73 *Journal of Military History* 449, at p. 451.

8. Leonard Schlup, 'Pugnacious Progressive: Senator Luke Lea as a Political Leader from Tennessee in the Wilson Era' (1984) 21 *International Review of History and Political Science* 52; Mary Tidwell, *Luke Lea of Tennessee*, Bowling Green, OH: Bowling Green State University Popular Press, 1993.

9. Robert Lewis Taylor, 'Profiles, Borough Defender—II', *The New Yorker*, 12 July 1941, p. 20.

10. Luke Lea Diary, 24 December 1918, p. 145, Lea Papers, Box 26.5.

11. ibid.

12. ibid. pp. 145–6.

13. Luke Lea and William T. Alderson, 'The Attempt to Capture the Kaiser' (1961) 20 *Tennessee Historical Quarterly* 222, at p. 225.

14. Sworn testimony of Luke Lea, 26 January 1919, § 5, Lea Papers, Box 40.9; Report on investigation, 17 February 1919, Lea Papers, Box 40.9.

15. Robert Lewis Taylor, 'Profiles, Borough Defender—II', *The New Yorker*, 12 July 1941, p. 21.

16. Luke Lea, 'Kaiser Story', TSA DS 70.9.L.3, p. 16; Luke Lea and William T. Alderson, 'The Attempt to Capture the Kaiser' (1961) 20 *Tennessee Historical Quarterly* 222, at pp. 226–7.

17. *Papers Relating to the Foreign Relations of the United States 1919, The Lansing Papers 1914–1920*, Vol. I, Washington, DC: US Government Printing Office, 1940, pp. 48–67.

18. Sworn testimony of Luke Lea, 26 January 1919, paras 12–15, Lea Papers, Box 40.9.

19. Allan Nevins (ed.), *The Letters and Journal of Brand Whitlock*, New York and London: Appleton Century, 1936, ch. 12.

20. Report on investigation, 17 February 1919, Lea Papers, Box 40.9.

21. Luke Lea and William T. Alderson, 'The Attempt to Capture the Kaiser' (1961) 20 *Tennessee Historical Quarterly* 222, at pp. 228–9.

22. The text of the original *laissez-passer* with an English translation are in the Tennessee State Archives as an attachment to Henderson to Hibbs, 12 August 1949, Lea Papers, Box 40.9. For an English translation, see Luke Lea and William

T. Alderson, 'The Attempt to Capture the Kaiser' (1961) 20 *Tennessee Historical Quarterly* 222, at pp. 228–9.

23. Luke Lea and William T. Alderson, 'The Attempt to Capture the Kaiser' (1961) 20 *Tennessee Historical Quarterly* 222, at p. 230.

24. Luke Lea, 'Kaiser Story', p. 31, Lea Papers, Box 45.2A. Also, Luke Lea and William T. Alderson, 'The Attempt to Capture the Kaiser' (1961) 20 *Tennessee Historical Quarterly* 222, at p. 232.

25. Luke Lea, 'Kaiser Story', p. 32, Lea Papers, Box 45.2A.

26. Edwards to Garrett, 9 January 1919, USNA 811.221/58.

27. Luke Lea and William T. Alderson, 'The Attempt to Capture the Kaiser' (1961) 20 *Tennessee Historical Quarterly* 222, at p. 235.

28. Luke Lea, 'Kaiser Story', pp. 34–5, Lea Papers, Box 45.2A.

29. Sworn testimony of Luke Lea, 26 January 1919, § 17, Lea Papers, Box 40.9.

30. Edwards to Garrett, 9 January 1919, USNA 811.221/58.

31. Luke Lea, 'Kaiser Story', pp. 35–6, Lea Papers, Box 45.2A.

32. Garrett to Acting Secretary of State, 10 January 1919, USNA 811.221/54 Telegram, FRUS PPC II, p. 85.

33. Luke Lea, 'Kaiser Story', p. 38, Lea Papers, Box 45.2A; Luke Lea and William T. Alderson, 'The Attempt to Capture the Kaiser' (1961) 20 *Tennessee Historical Quarterly* 222, at p. 239.

34. Luke Lea, 'Kaiser Story', p. 39, Lea Papers, Box 45.2A.

35. Edwards to Garrett, 9 January 1919, USNA 811.221/58.

36. Luke Lea, 'Kaiser Story', p. 4, Lea Papers, Box 45.2A.

37. Sworn testimony of Luke Lea, 26 January 1919, § 17, Lea Papers, Box 40.9.

38. Robert Lewis Taylor, 'Profiles, Borough Defender—II', *The New Yorker*, 12 July 1941, p. 20, at p. 21.

39. Luke Lea, 'Kaiser Story', pp. 41–2, Lea Papers, Box 45.2A.

40. Edwards to Garrett, 9 January 1919, USNA 811.221/58.

41. Sigurd von Ilsemann, *Der Kaiser in Holland. Aufzeichnungen des letzten Flügeladjutanten Kaiser Wilhelms II*, Vol. 1: *Amerongen und Doorn, 1918–1923*, p. 86.

42. Edwards to Garrett, 9 January 1919, USNA 811.221/58.

43. Garrett to Acting Secretary of State, 10 January 1919, FRUS PPC II, p. 85.

44. Allan Nevins (ed.), *The Letters and Journal of Brand Whitlock*, New York and London: Appleton Century, 1936, ch. 12.

45. Whitlock to Garrett, 7 January 1919, 811.221/58; USNA Garrett to Acting Secretary of State, 10 January 1919, USNA 811.221/54; Telegram, FRUS PPC II, p. 85.

46. Garrett to Acting Secretary of State, 10 January 1919, USNA 811.221/54; Telegram, FRUS PPC II, p. 85.

47. Edwards to Garrett, 9 January 1919, USNA 811.221/58.

48. Garrett to Acting Secretary of State, 10 January 1919, USNA 811.221/54; Telegram, FRUS PPC II, p. 85. See also Edwards to Garrett, 9 January 1919, USNA 811.221/58.

49. ibid.

50. Sworn testimony of Luke Lea, 26 January 1919, §§ 8–9, 43, Lea Papers, Box 40.9.
51. ibid.
52. ibid. § 10, Lea Papers, Box 40.9.
53. Sworn testimony of Luke Lea, 26 January 1919, §§ 59–60, Lea Papers, Box 40.9.
54. Luke Lea, 'Kaiser Story', pp. 65–6, Lea Papers, Box 45.2A.
55. Bethel to Pershing, 12 February 1919, § 2, Lea Papers, Box 40.9.
56. ibid. § 5.
57. O'Brian to Lea, 17 February 1919, Lea Papers, Box 40.9.
58. 'Won't Act in Lea Case', *New York Times*, 1 April 1919, p. 2.
59. Luke Lea, 'Kaiser Story', p. 13, Lea Papers, Box 45.2A.

CHAPTER 8

1. Margaret MacMillan, *Paris 1919: Six Months That Changed the World*, New York: Random House, 2001, p. xxv.
2. William A. Schabas, 'International Prosecution of Sexual and Gender-Based Crimes Perpetrated During the First World War', in Martin Böse, Michael Bohlander, André Klip, and Otto Lagodny (eds), *Festschrift for Wolfgang Schomburg*, Leiden: Brill, 2018, pp. 395–410.
3. Treaty between the Principal Allied and Associated Powers and Poland, (1919) 112 BSP 232. See also: Treaty between the Principal Allied and Associated Powers and the Serb-Croat-Slovene State, (1919) TS 17, Art. 2; Treaty between the Principal Allied and Associated Powers and Czecho-Slovakia, (1919) TS 20, Art. 2; Treaty between the Principal Allied and Associated Powers and Roumania, (1920) TS 6, Art. 2.
4. Universal Declaration of Human Rights, GA Res. 217A (III), Art. 2.
5. Naoko Shimazu, *Japan, Race and Equality: The Racial Equality Proposal of 1919*, London: Routledge, 2009; Paul Gordon Lauren, *The Evolution of Human Rights: Visions Seen*, Philadelphia, PA: University of Pennsylvania, 1998, pp. 268–75; Margaret McMillan, *Paris 1919: Six Months That Changed the World*, New York: Random House, 2001, pp. 302–21.
6. Lloyd George to Balfour, 20 August 1919, DBFP VI, pp. 174–5.
7. M. Cherif Bassiouni, 'World War I: "The War to End All Wars" and the Birth of a Handicapped International Justice System' (2001–2002) 30 *Denver Journal of International Law and Policy* 244; Gary Bass, *Stay the Hand of Vengeance: The Politics of War Crimes Tribunals*, Princeton: Princeton University Press, 2000, pp. 58–105; Joseph Rikhof, 'The Istanbul and Leipzig Trials: Myth or Reality?', in Morten Bergsmo, Cheah Wui Ling, and Yi Ping (eds), *Historical Origins of International Criminal Law*, Vol. 1, Brussels: Torkel Opsahl Academic EPublisher, 2014, pp. 259–96; Wolfgang Form, 'Law as Farce: On the Miscarriage of Justice at the German Leipzig Trials: The Llandovery Castle Case', in Morten Bergsmo, Cheah Wui Ling, and Yi Ping (eds), *Historical Origins of International Criminal Law*, Vol. 1, Brussels: Torkel Opsahl Academic EPublisher, 2014, pp. 299–322; Matthias Neuner, 'When Justice Is Left to the Losers: The Leipzig War Crimes

Trials', in Morten Bergsmo, Cheah Wui Ling, and Yi Ping (eds), *Historical Origins of International Criminal Law*, Vol. 1, Brussels: Torkel Opsahl Academic EPublisher, 2014, pp. 333–78; Jürgen Mattäus, 'The Lessons of Leipzig: Punishing German War Criminals after the First World War', in Patricia Heberer and Jürgen Mattäus (eds), *Atrocities on Trial: Historical Perspectives on the Politics of Prosecuting War Crimes*, Lincoln, NE: University of Nebraska Press, 2008, pp. 3–23; Mark Lewis, *The Birth of the New Justice: The Internationalisation of Crime and Punishment*, Oxford: Oxford University Press, 2014; James F. Willis, *Prologue to Nuremburg: The Politics and Diplomacy of Punishing War Criminals of the First World War*, Westport, CT and London: Greenwood Press, 1982; Gerd Henkel, *Die Leipziger Prozesse: Deutsche Kriegsverbrechen und ihre strafrechtliche Verfolgung nach dem Ersten Weltkrieg*, Hamburg: Hamburger Institute, 2003; United Nations War Crimes Commission, *History of the United Nations War Crimes Commission and the Development of the Laws of War*, London: HMSO, 1948, pp. 46–51; Gerd Henkel, *The Leipzig Trials: German War Crimes and Their Legal Consequences after 1921*, Dordrecht: Republic of Letters, 2014; Claud Mullins, *The Leipzig Trials: An Account of the War Criminals' Trials and a Study of German Mentality*, London: Witherby, 1921.

8. Secretary's Notes of a Conversation held in M. Pichon's Rooms at the Quai d'Orsay, 12 January 1919, 4 pm, USNA 180.03101/2.

9. Plan of the Preliminary Conversations between the Allied Ministers, 5 January 1919, USNA 180.03101/2. See also Plan of Preliminary Conversation between Allied Ministers, as of 13 January 1919, TNA FO 608/161.

10. Conversation held in M. Pichon's Rooms at the Quai d'Orsay, 17 January 1919, 3 pm, USNA 180.03101/9.

11. David Lloyd George, *Memoirs of the Peace Conference*, Vol. I, New Haven, CT: Yale University Press, 1939, p. 94; Conversation held in M. Pichon's Rooms at the Quai d'Orsay, 17 January 1919, 3 pm, USNA 180.03101/9.

12. Preliminary Peace Conference, Protocol No. 1, 18 January 1919, USNA 180.0201/1; TNA CAB 29/23.

13. Preliminary Peace Conference, Protocol No. 1, 18 January 1919, USNA 180.0201/1, p. 9. Clemenceau's remarks in the shorthand notes of the session are more laconic: TNA CAB 29/23, p. 17.

14. Preliminary Peace Conference, Protocol No. 1, 25 January 1919, USNA 180.0201/2, Annex II.

15. Bureau of the Conference, Minutes, Excerpt, 25 January 1919, USNA 181.12/1; USNA 181.12/2.

16. On the work of the Commission, see: Mark Lewis, *The Birth of the New Justice: The Internationalisation of Crime and Punishment, 1919–1950*, Oxford: Oxford University Press, 2014, pp. 27–63; James F. Willis, *Prologue to Nuremberg*, Westport, CT: Greenwood Press, 1982, pp. 65–97; United Nations War Crimes Commission, *History of the United Nations War Crimes Commission and the Development of the Laws of War*, London: HMSO, 1948, pp. 32–40; H. M. Rhea, 'The Commission on the Responsibility of the Authors of the War and on Enforcement of Penalties

and Its Contribution to International Criminal Justice After World War II' (2014) 25 *Criminal Law Forum* 147.

17. Bureau of the Conference, Minutes, Excerpt, 25 January 1919, USNA 181.12/1; USNA 181.12/2.

18. Sally Marks, *Innocent Abroad: Belgium at the Paris Peace Conference of 1919*, Chapel Hill, NC: University of North Carolina Press, 1981, pp. 106–7.

19. Preliminary Peace Conference, Protocol No. 1, 25 January 1919, USNA 180.0201/2; Translation of French stenographic report of speeches delivered in French at the session of the Peace Conference of 25 January 1919, USNA 180.0201/2.

20. Conference of Powers with Special Interests, Minutes, Excerpt, 27 January 1919, USNA 181.12/4.

21. F. R. Coudert, 'An Appreciation of James Brown Scott' (1943) 37 *American Journal of International Law* 559.

22. Georges Clemenceau, *Grandeurs et misères d'une victoire*, Paris: Plon, 1930, p. 116.

23. Rudolph Binion, *Defeated Leaders: The Political Fate of Caillaux, Jouvenel, and Tardieu*, New York: Columbia University Press, 1960.

24. Sally Marks, 'Edouard Rolin-Jaequemyns', in Warren F. Kuehl (ed.), *Biographical Dictionary of Internationalists*, Westport, CT: Greenwood Press, 1983, pp. 624–5; 'Baron Edouard Rolin-Jaequemyns' (1937) 18 *British Yearbook of International Law* 156.

25. L. A. Sicilianos and T. Skouteris, 'Editorial Note' (2012) 23 *European Journal of International Law* 215; R. Holsti, 'Nicolas Politis, 1872–1942' (1942) 36 *American Journal of International Law* 475; William A. Schabas, 'Nikolaos Politis and the Earliest Negotiation to Establish an International Criminal Court', in Jean-Paul Jacqué, Florence Benoît-Rohmer, Panagiotis Grigoriou, and Maria Daniella Marouda (eds), *Liber Amicorum Stelios Perrakis*, Athens: I. Sideris, 2017, pp. 167–77.

26. Second Meeting of the Commission on Responsibilities, 7 February 1919, Minutes: USNA 181.1201/16, pp. 19–25, at p. 22; USNA 181.1201/2 (M 820, Roll 140, 641–62), p. 13; USNA 181.1201/2 (M 820, Roll 140, 663–84, Part 2), p. 2; USNA 181.1201/2 (M 820, Roll 140, 712–33), p. 13; Recueil des actes, pp. 31–7, at p. 33; Paix de Versailles, pp. 16–29, at p. 23; USNA 181.1201/2 (M 820, Roll 140, 734–59, Part 2 French), p. 2.

27. Conférence de la Paix 1919–1920, *Recueil des actes de la Conférence, Partie IV B (2), Commission des responsabilités des auteurs de la guerre et sanctions*, Paris: Imprimerie nationale, 1922.

28. Commission on the Responsibility of the Authors of the War, Minutes of Meetings of the Commission, USNA 181.1201/16. A copy of the same document is in the Yale University Library (Frank L. Polk Papers, Group No. 656, Series No. III, Box No. 30).

29. TNA FO 678/245. The transcript of the first and second meetings of the plenary Commission, and of several of the sessions of the Sub-Commissions, have not been found in the British National Archives, although the covering letter from the Secretariat indicates that these were made and sent to the British Government.

30. Albert Geouffre de Lapradelle (ed.), *La Paix de Versailles: Responsabilité des auteurs de la guerre et des sanctions*, Vol. III, Paris: Éditions internationales, 1930.

31. A notable example is Tardieu's opening speech at the first meeting of the Commission: First Meeting of the Commission on Responsibilities, 3 February 1919, Minutes: USNA 181.1201/1 (M 820, Roll 140, 415–25), p. 2; USNA 181.1201/1 (M 820, Roll 140, 439–41), p. 1; USNA 181.1201/1 (M 820, Roll 140, 491–3), p. 1.

32. First Meeting of the Commission on Responsibilities, 3 February 1919, Minutes: Recueil des actes, pp. 5–9, at p. 5, USNA 181.1201/1 (M 820, Roll 140, 376–84), p. 4; USNA 181.1201/1 (M 820, Roll 140, 460–75), p. 2; USNA 181.1201/1 (M 820, Roll 140, 518–39 French), p. 1; USNA 181.1201/1 (M 820, Roll 140, 597–605 Italian), p. 3.

33. First Meeting of the Commission on Responsibilities, 3 February 1919, Minutes: USNA 181.1201/1 (M 820, Roll 140, 376–84), p. 6; USNA 181.1201/1 (M 820, Roll 140, 415–25), pp. 2–3; USNA 181.1201/1 (M 820, Roll 140, 439–41), p. 2; USNA 181.1201/1 (M 820, Roll 140, 460–75), p. 4; USNA 181.1201/1 (M 820, Roll 140, 491–3), p. 2; Recueil des actes, pp. 5–9, at p. 7; USNA 181.1201/1 (M 820, Roll 140, 518–39 French), pp. 5–7; Paix de Versailles, pp. 9–15, at pp. 9–10; USNA 181.1201/1 (M 820, Roll 140, 597–605 Italian), pp. 4–5.

34. Plan of the Organisation of the Sub-Commissions of the Commission of Responsibilities, Annex I to Minutes of Second Meeting, USNA 181.1201/16, p. 26; USNA 181.12/6; Recueil des actes, p. 38.

35. Plan of the Organisation of the Sub-Commissions of the Commission of Responsibilities, Annex I to Minutes of Second Meeting, Art. IV, USNA 181.1201/16, pp. 25–6; USNA 181.12/6; Recueil des actes, p. 38.

36. Joint First Meeting of Sub-Commissions II and III, 14 February 1919, Minutes: USNA 181.12201/1 (M 820, Roll 143, 333–45); TNA FO 608/246; USNA 181.12201/1 (M 820, Roll 143, 346–50); USNA 181.12201/1 (M 820, Roll 143, 356–72 French); USNA 181.12201/1 (M 820, Roll 143, 373–94 French); Recueil des actes, pp. 302–5.

37. Pollock to Lloyd George, 7 February 1919, LG F/27/1/1; Hanworth Papers, Ms Eng. Hist. C 943.1-211. See also Pollock to Balfour, 8 February 1919, Hanworth Papers, Ms Eng. Hist. C 943.1-211.

38. Pollock to Lloyd George, 7 February 1919, LG F/27/1/1; Hanworth Papers, Ms Eng. Hist. C 943.1-211.

39. Ian Malcolm, Note on Punishment for War Offences, 18 February 1919, Hanworth Papers, Ms Eng. Hist. C 943.1-211.

40. Fourth Meeting of Sub-Commission III, 25 February 1919, Minutes: USNA 181.12301/4 (M 820, Roll 144, 3–22), TNA FO 608/246, pp. 2–3; USNA 181.12301/4 (M 820, Roll 144, 28–32), p. 1; USNA 181.12301/4 (M 820, Roll 144, 33–55 French), p. 3; Recueil des actes, pp. 338–42, at p. 339; Paix de Versailles, pp. 312–24, at p. 313.

41. Margaret MacMillan, *Paris 1919: Six Months That Changed the World*, New York: Random House, 2001, p. 55.

42. Hankey to Lloyd George, 1 March 1919, LG F/23/4/28.

43. Fifth Meeting of Sub-Commission III, 4 March 1919, Minutes: TNA FO 608/ 246; USNA 181.12301/5 (M 820, Roll 144, 63–83), p. 16; USNA 181.12301/5 (M 820, Roll 144, 84–103), pp. 16–17; USNA 181.12301/5 (M 820, Roll 144, 104–12), p. 7; USNA 181.12301/5 (M 820, Roll 144, 113–39 French), p. 25; Recueil des actes, pp. 350–6, at p. 356.

44. Minutes of the Meetings of the Commissioners Plenipotentiary, 5 March 1919, USNA 184.00101/28, FRUS PPC XI, pp. 93–4.

45. Lansing to Polk, 14 March 1919, Lansing Papers, Princeton (File VII, Personal Correspondence, 1916–1919), cited in James F. Willis, *Prologue to Nuremburg: The Politics and Diplomacy of Punishing War Criminals of the First World War*, Westport, CT and London: Greenwood Press, 1982, p. 70.

46. Robert Lansing, *The Peace Negotiations: A Personal Narrative*, Boston and New York: Houghton Mifflin, 1921, p. 3.

47. Draft Report of the Commission, USNA 181.1201/16, pp. 83–96; Recueil des actes, pp. 119–37; Paix de Versailles, pp. 385–409.

48. 'Les responsabilités', *Le Temps*, 27 February 1919, p. 1.

49. 'La commission des responsabilités', *Le Temps*, 14 March 1919, p. 4.

50. Charles A. Selden, 'Ex-Kaiser's Fate Divides Delegates', *New York Times*, 12 March 1919, p. 1.

51. Fifth Meeting of the Commission on Responsibilities, 14 March 1919, Minutes: USNA 181.1201/16, pp. 62–6, at p. 62; Recueil des actes, pp. 90–6, at pp. 90–1; USNA 181.1201/5 (M820, Roll 141, 264–81), pp. 2–3; USNA 181.1201/5 (M820, Roll 141, 282–92), pp. 2–3; USNA 181.1201/5 (M820, Roll 141, 314–22), p. 2.

52. Meeting of the Supreme War Council, Quai d'Orsay, Paris, 12 March 1919, 3.00 pm, USNA 180.03101/57, p. 1; FRUS PPC IV, pp. 331–45, at pp. 331–3.

53. Meeting of the Supreme War Council, Quai d'Orsay, Paris, 12 March 1919, 3.00 pm, USNA 180.03101/57, p. 3; FRUS PPC IV, pp. 331–45, at pp. 331–3.

54. ibid.

55. Fourth Meeting of the Commission on Responsibilities, 13 March 1919, Minutes: USNA 181.1201/16, pp. 57–61, at p. 60; USNA 181.1201/4 (M 820, Roll 141, 156–76), pp. 14–15; USNA 181.1201/4 (M 820, Roll 141, 199–209), p. 6; Recueil des actes, pp. 82–9, at p. 87; Paix de Versailles, pp. 339–52, at p. 348; USNA 181.1201/4 (M 820, Roll 141, 213–41 French), pp. 19–20; USNA 181.1201/4 (M 820, Roll 141, 242–55 French), pp. 10–11. Stenographic notes: TNA FO 678/245, pp. 294–321, at pp. 312–13.

56. Hankey to Lloyd George, 13 March 1919, LG F/23/4/30.

57. Lloyd George to Hankey, 13 March 1919, LG F/23/4/31.

58. ibid.

59. Sixth Meeting of the Commission on Responsibilities, 15 March 1919, Minutes: USNA 181.1201/16, pp. 67–8, at p. 67; USNA 181.1201/6 (M 820, Roll 141, 368–75), p. 2; USNA 181.1201/6 (M 820, Roll 141, 376–9), p. 2; Recueil des actes, pp. 97–9, at p. 97; Paix de Versailles, pp. 364–8, at pp. 364–5; USNA

181.1201/6 (M 820, Roll 141, 388–95 French), pp. 1–2. Stenographic notes: TNA FO 678/245, pp. 347–53, at pp. 347–9.

60. Sixth Meeting of the Commission on Responsibilities, 15 March 1919, Minutes: USNA 181.1201/6 (M 820, Roll 141, 368–75), p. 3; USNA 181.1201/6 (M 820, Roll 141, 376–9), p. 2; USNA 181.1201/6 (M 820, Roll 141, 388–95 French), p. 3.

61. Seventh Meeting of the Commission on Responsibilities, 17 March 1919, Minutes: USNA 181.1201/7 (M 820, Roll 141, 403–23), pp. 2–3; USNA 181.1201/7 (M 820, Roll 141, 464–92 French), p. 3; Paix de Versailles, pp. 369–83, at pp. 370–1; Recueil des actes, pp. 100–7, at p. 101. Stenographic notes: TNA FO 678/245, pp. 355–82, at p. 358.

62. Seventh Meeting of the Commission on Responsibilities, 17 March 1919, Minutes: USNA 181.1201/7 (M 820, Roll 141, 403–23), p. 3; Paix de Versailles, pp. 369–83, at p. 371; USNA 181.1201/7 (M 820, Roll 141, 464–92 French), p. 4. Stenographic notes: TNA FO 678/245, pp. 355–82, at p. 358.

63. Seventh Meeting of the Commission on Responsibilities, 17 March 1919, Minutes: USNA 181.1201/7 (M 820, Roll 141, 403–23), pp. 4–5; USNA 181.1201/16, pp. 69–74, at p. 70; Paix de Versailles, pp. 369–83, at pp. 371–2; USNA 181.1201/7 (M 820, Roll 141, 464–92 French), pp. 6–7. Stenographic notes: TNA FO 678/245, pp. 355–82, at pp. 360–1.

64. Seventh Meeting of the Commission on Responsibilities, 17 March 1919, Minutes: USNA 181.1201/7 (M 820, Roll 141, 403–23), p. 11; Paix de Versailles, pp. 369–83, at p. 376; USNA 181.1201/7 (M 820, Roll 141, 464–92 French), pp. 17–18. Stenographic notes: TNA FO 678/245, pp. 355–82, at pp. 369–70.

65. Report of the Commission on Responsibilities, USNA 181.1201/16, pp. 112–76; (1920) 14 *American Journal of International Law* 95; *Violations of the Laws and Customs of War*, Oxford: Clarendon Press, 1919; Recueil des actes, pp. 162–234; Paix de Versailles, pp. 453–556; USNA 181.1202/7 (Italian).

66. Report of the Commission on Responsibilities, USNA 181.1201/16, pp. 115–76, at p. 162.

67. Meeting of the Council of Four, 2 April 1919, 4 pm, Mantoux I, pp. 120–4, at p. 121; Deliberations I, pp. 115–24, at p. 119.

68. Report of the Commission on Responsibilities, USNA 181.1201/16, pp. 115–76, at p. 162.

69. ibid. p. 173.

70. ibid.

71. Pollock to Lloyd George, 29 March 1919, LG F/27/1/2.

72. Draft Report of the Commission, USNA 181.1201/16, pp. 83–96, at pp. 95–6.

73. Tenth Meeting of the Commission on Responsibilities, 27 March 1919, Minutes: USNA 181.1201/16, pp. 103–8, at pp. 103–4; Recueil des actes, pp. 148–54, at p. 149. Stenographic notes: TNA FO 678/245, pp. 463–95, at pp. 464–5.

74. See the reference to *travaux préparatoires* in the Vienna Convention on the Law of Treaties, (1980) 1155 UNTS 331, Art. 32.

75. Robert H. Jackson, *Report of Robert H. Jackson, United States Representative to the International Conference on Military Trials*, Washington, DC: US Government Printing Office, 1949.

76. Virginia Morris and Michael Scharf, *An Insider's Guide to the International Criminal for the Former Yugoslavia*, Irvington-on-Hudson, NY: Transnational Publishers, 1995.

77. For references, see William A. Schabas, *The International Criminal Court: A Commentary on the Rome Statute*, 2nd edn, Oxford: Oxford University Press, 2016.

78. Jackson Nyamunya Maogoto, 'The 1919 Paris Peace Conference and the Allied Commission: Challenging Sovereignty through Supranational Criminal Jurisdiction', in Morten Bergsmo, Cheah Wui Ling, and Yi Ping (eds), *Historical Origins of International Criminal Law*, Vol. 1, Brussels: Torkel Opsahl Academic EPublisher, 2014, pp. 171–94.

79. *Prosecutor v. Ruto et al.* (ICC-01/09-01/11), Reasons of Judge Eboe-Osuji, 5 April 2016, §§ 246–56; *Prosecutor v. Bashir* (ICC-02/05-01/09), Corrigendum to the Decision Pursuant to Article 87(7) of the Rome Statute on the Failure by the Republic of Malawi to Comply with the Cooperation Requests Issued by the Court with Respect to the Arrest and Surrender of Omar Hassan Ahmad Al Bashir, 13 December 2011, § 23. See also 'The Role of International Judicial Bodies in Administering the Rule of Law', Address by Luis Moreno-Ocampo, 30 May 2009, p. 3.

80. Question of International Criminal Jurisdiction, Report by Ricardo J. Alfaro, Special Rapporteur, UN Doc. A/CN.4/15, § 8.

CHAPTER 9

1. M. Cherif Bassiouni, *Introduction to International Criminal Law*, Ardsley, NY: Transnational, 2003, p. 109.

2. Antonio Cassese, *International Criminal Law*, 2nd edn, Oxford: Oxford University Press, 2008, pp. 11–13.

3. M. Cherif Bassiouni, *Introduction to International Criminal Law*, Ardsley, NY: Transnational, 2003, p. 122.

4. The historiography on responsibility for the start of the war is massive (see, e.g., Jean-Jacques Becker and Gerd Krumeich, '1914: Outbreak', in Jay Winter (ed.), *The First World War*, Vol. I, Cambridge: Cambridge University Press, 2014, pp. 39–64), but does not need to be discussed in this study. Here, the concern is not with the actual facts or their interpretation, but rather with what was known and how this was understood by those who organised the prosecutions at the time.

5. For copies of the various coloured books, see *The Times Documentary History of the War*, Vol. I: *Diplomatic*, Part 1 and Vol. II: *Diplomatic*, Part 2, London: The Times Publishing, 1917.

6. Report Presented to the Preliminary Peace Conference by the Commission on the Responsibility of the Authors of the War and on Enforcement of Penalties, USNA 181.1201/16, pp. 112–76, at pp. 115–21; Recueil des actes, pp. 161–234, at

pp. 162–70; USNA 181.1202/7 (Italian), pp. 5–14; (1920) 14 *American Journal of International Law* 95; *Violations of the Laws and Customs of War*, Oxford: Clarendon Press, 1919, pp. 4–16.

7. Memorandum of reservations presented by the Representatives of the United States, 4 April 1919, USNA 181.1201/16, pp. 162–74, at p. 165.

8. James Brown Scott, 'The Trial of the Kaiser', in Edward M. House and Charles Seymour (eds), *What Really Happened at Paris*, London: Hodder & Stoughton, 1921, pp. 231–58.

9. Memorandum of the French Delegation, 17 February 1919, USNA 181.12101/1 (M 820, Roll 143, 56–81); USNA 181.12101/4 (M 820, Roll 143, 218–27); USNA 181.1201/16, pp. 46–9; Paix de Versailles, pp. 37–54; Paix de Versailles, pp. 40–54. Complementary Memorandum of the Hellenic Delegation, 5 March 1919, USNA 181.12101/4 (M 820, Roll 143, 275–6); Paix de Versailles, pp. 167–70. Memorandum of the Serb Delegation, 5 March 1919, USNA 181.12101/4 (M 820, Roll 143, 261–89); USNA 181.1201/16, p. 50; Paix de Versailles, pp. 185–203.

10. First Meeting of Sub-Commission I, 17 February 1919, Minutes: USNA 181.12101/2 (M 820, Roll 143, 17–33); USNA 181.12101/2 (M 820, Roll 143, 34–49); USNA 181.12101/1 (M 820, Roll 143, 50–4 British Secretary's Notes); USNA 181.12101/2 (M 820, Roll 143, 436–50 French); Recueil des Actes, pp. 283–6; Paix de Versailles, pp. 235–41. Stenographic notes: TNA FO 608/246, pp. 331–44. Second Meeting of Sub-Commission I, 19 February 1919, Minutes, USNA 181.12101/2 (M 820, Roll 143, 82–91); USNA 181.12101/2 (M 820, Roll 143, 92–7); USNA 181.12101/2 (M 820, Roll 143, 112–28 French); Recueil des Actes, pp. 287–90; Paix de Versailles, IV, pp. 242–9. Stenographic notes: TNA FO 608/246, pp. 345–59. Third Meeting of Sub-Commission I, 24 February 1919, Minutes: TNA FO 608/246; USNA 181.12101/3 (M 820, Roll 143, 133–48); USNA 181.12101/3 (M 820, Roll 143, 149–59); USNA 181.12101/3 (M 820, Roll 143, 161–74 French); Recueil des Actes, pp. 293–7; Paix de Versailles, IV, pp. 250–6. Stenographic notes: TNA FO 608/246, pp. 360–73.

11. Interim Report of Sub-Commission I, USNA 181.12101/4 (M 820, Roll 143, 184–7), TNA FO 608/246; USNA 181.12102/2 (M 820, Roll 143, 302–5); USNA 181.12101/4 (M 820, Roll 143, 208–12 French); USNA 181.12102/2 (M 820, Roll 143, 306–8 French).

12. Coleman Phillipson, *International Law and the Great War*, London: T. Fisher Unwin, 1915.

13. Report of Sub-Commission I on Criminal Acts, USNA 181.1201/16, pp. 39–45, at p. 39.

14. ibid. p. 41.

15. ibid. pp. 41–4.

16. ibid. pp. 39–45; USNA 181.12102/2 (M 820, Roll 143, 309–14 French); Recueil des actes, pp. 59–66.

17. Fourth Meeting of Sub-Commission I, 5 March 1919, Minutes: USNA 181.12101/4 (M 820, Roll 143, 184–7), TNA FO 608/246; USNA 181.12101/

4 (M 820, Roll 143, 181–3); USNA 181.12101/4 (M 820, Roll 143, 188–95 French); Recueil des Actes, pp. 298–9. Stenographic notes: TNA FO 608/246, pp. 374–81.

18. Note on the Report of the Sub-Commission on the Responsibility for the War, 19 March 1919, TNA FO 608/246.

19. Third Meeting of the Commission on Responsibilities, Minutes, 12 March 1919, USNA 181.1201/16, pp. 35–9, at p. 35; USNA 181.1201/3 (M 820, Roll 141, 5–24), p. 2; USNA 181.1201/3 (M 820, Roll 141, 25–32), p. 2; USNA 181.1201/3 (M 820, Roll 141, 33–57), p. 4; USNA 181.1201/3 (M 820, Roll 141, 58–69 French), p. 2; USNA 181.1201/3 (M 820, Roll 141, 70–91 French), p. 3; Recueil des actes, pp. 52–8, at p. 53.

20. Draft Report of the Commission, USNA 181.1201/16, pp. 83–96, at pp. 83–4.

21. ibid.

22. Eighth Meeting of the Commission on Responsibilities, 24 March 1919, Minutes: USNA 181.1201/16, pp. 76–82, at pp. 77–8; USNA 181.1201/8 (M 820, Roll 141, 555–60 French), p. 5; USNA 181.1201/8 (M 820, Roll 141, 566–99 French), p. 7; USNA 181.1201/8 (M 820, Roll 141, 600–15 French), p. 4; Paix de Versailles, pp. 413–22, at p. 415; Recueil des actes, pp. 109–18, at p. 111. Stenographic notes: TNA FO 608/245, pp. 383–421, at p. 390.

23. Eighth Meeting of the Commission on Responsibilities, Minutes, 24 March 1919, USNA 181.1201/16, pp. 76–82, at p. 78; USNA 181.1201/8 (M 820, Roll 141, 500–23), p. 5; USNA 181.1201/8 (M 820, Roll 141, 524–54), pp. 6–7; USNA 181.1201/8 (M 820, Roll 141, 566–99 French), pp. 12–13; USNA 181.1201/8 (M 820, Roll 141, 600–15 French), p. 5; Recueil des actes, pp. 109–18, at p. 112; Paix de Versailles, pp. 413–22, at p. 416. Stenographic notes: TNA FO 608/245, pp. 383–421, at pp. 395–6.

24. Eighth Meeting of the Commission on Responsibilities, Minutes, 24 March 1919, USNA 181.1201/16, pp. 76–82, at p. 78; USNA 181.1201/8 (M 820, Roll 141, 524–54), pp. 7–8; USNA 181.1201/8 (M 820, Roll 141, 566–99 French), pp. 13–14; USNA 181.1201/8 (M 820, Roll 141, 600–15 French), p. 6; Paix de Versailles, pp. 413–22, at p. 417; Recueil des actes, pp. 109–18, at p. 112. Stenographic notes: TNA FO 608/245, pp. 383–421, at p. 397.

25. Draft Report of the Commission, USNA 181.1201/16, pp. 83–96, at pp. 86–7.

26. Eighth Meeting of the Commission on Responsibilities, Minutes, 24 March 1919, USNA 181.1201/16, pp. 76–82, at p. 79; USNA 181.1201/8 (M 820, Roll 141, 500–23), p. 9; USNA 181.1201/8 (M 820, Roll 141, 600–15 French), p. 7; USNA 181.1201/8 (M 820, Roll 141, 566–99 French), pp. 16–17; Paix de Versailles, pp. 413–22, at p. 417; Recueil des actes, pp. 109–18, at p. 113. Stenographic notes: TNA FO 608/245, pp. 383–421, at pp. 399–400.

27. Eighth Meeting of the Commission on Responsibilities, Minutes, 24 March 1919, USNA 181.1201/8 (M 820, Roll 141, 500–23), p. 10; USNA 181.1201/8 (M 820, Roll 141, 566–99 French), p. 17. Stenographic notes: TNA FO 608/245, pp. 383–421, at p. 400.

28. Kaiser Wilhelm II visited Jerusalem in 1898. See John C. G. Röhl, *Wilhelm II: The Kaiser's Personal Monarchy, 1888–1900*, Cambridge: Cambridge University Press, 2004, pp. 952–4.

29. Eighth Meeting of the Commission on Responsibilities, Minutes, 24 March 1919, USNA 181.1201/8 (M 820, Roll 141, 500–23), p. 10; USNA 181.1201/8 (M 820, Roll 141, 600–15 French), p. 8; USNA 181.1201/8 (M 820, Roll 141, 566–99 French), p. 18; Paix de Versailles, pp. 413–22, at p. 418. Stenographic notes: TNA FO 608/245, pp. 383–421, at p. 401.

30. Memorandum submitted by the British delegates, 13 February 1919, USNA 181.1201/16, pp. 27–33, at p. 28; Scott Papers, Box 30.3a, pp. 2–3; Recueil des actes, pp. 41–50, at p. 42.

31. Memorandum of the French Delegation, 17 February 1919, USNA 181.12101/1 (M 820, Roll 143, 56–81); USNA 181.12101/4 (M 820, Roll 143, 218–27); USNA 181.1201/16, pp. 46–9; Paix de Versailles, pp. 40–54.

32. Second Meeting of Sub-Commission II, 17 February 1919, Minutes: USNA 181.12201/2 (M 820, Roll 143, 412–33), TNA FO 608/246, p. 2; Recueil des actes, pp. 306–12, at p. 306; Paix de Versailles, pp. 263–77, at p. 263. Stenographic notes: TNA FO 608/246, pp. 113–42, at pp. 113–14.

33. Second Meeting of Sub-Commission II, 17 February 1919, Minutes: USNA 181.12201/2 (M 820, Roll 143, 412–33); Recueil des actes, pp. 306–12, at pp. 306–7; Paix de Versailles, pp. 263–77, at pp. 263–4. Stenographic notes: TNA FO 608/246, pp. 113–42, at pp. 114–15.

34. Second Meeting of Sub-Commission II, 17 February 1919, Minutes: USNA 181.12201/2 (M 820, Roll 143, 412–33); Paix de Versailles, pp. 263–77, at p. 266. Stenographic notes: TNA FO 608/246, pp. 113–42, at p. 118.

35. Second Meeting of Sub-Commission II, 17 February 1919, Minutes: USNA 181.12201/2 (M 820, Roll 143, 412–33); Paix de Versailles, pp. 263–77, at p. 266. Stenographic notes: TNA FO 608/246, pp. 113–42, at p. 119.

36. Second Meeting of Sub-Commission II, 17 February 1919, Minutes: USNA 181.12201/2 (M 820, Roll 143, 412–33); Recueil des actes, pp. 306–12, at p. 308; Paix de Versailles, pp. 263–77, at p. 275. Stenographic notes: TNA FO 608/246, pp. 113–42, at pp. 137–8.

37. Second Meeting of Sub-Commission II, 17 February 1919, Minutes: USNA 181.12201/2 (M 820, Roll 143, 412–33), p. 11.

38. Notes on Meeting of Sub-Committee [sic] on Responsibilities for the War, USNA 181.12201/2.

39. Report of Sub-Commission II, USNA 181.1201/16, pp. 45–6; TNA FO 608/246; Recueil des actes, pp. 67–9.

40. Third Meeting of the Commission on Responsibilities, Minutes, 12 March 1919, USNA 181.1201/16, pp. 35–9, at p. 36; TNA FO 608/245, pp. 274–93, p. 276; Recueil des actes, pp. 52–8, at p. 53.

41. Draft Report of the Commission, USNA 181.1201/16, pp. 83–96, at p. 91.

42. Report of the Commission on Responsibilities, USNA 181.1201/16, pp. 115–76, at pp. 124–5.

43. Ninth Meeting of the Commission on Responsibilities, 25 March 1919, Minutes: USNA 181.1201/16, pp. 97–102, at p. 100; USNA 181.1201/9 (M 820, Roll 141, 714–47 French), p. 20. Stenographic notes: TNA FO 608/245, pp. 422–62, at p. 439.

44. Ninth Meeting of the Commission on Responsibilities, 25 March 1919, Minutes: USNA 181.1201/16, pp. 97–102, at p. 100; USNA 181.1201/9 (M 820, Roll 141, 647–75), p. 12; USNA 181.1201/9 (M 820, Roll 141, 676–704), p. 13; USNA 181.1201/9 (M 820, Roll 141, 714–47 French), p. 21 *bis*. Stenographic notes: TNA FO 608/245, pp. 422–62, at pp. 439–40.

45. Ninth Meeting of the Commission on Responsibilities, 25 March 1919, Minutes: USNA 181.1201/16, pp. 97–102, at p. 100; USNA 181.1201/9 (M 820, Roll 141, 647–75), p. 13; USNA 181.1201/9 (M 820, Roll 141, 676–704), p. 14; USNA 181.1201/9 (M 820, Roll 141, 714–47 French), p. 21 *bis*. Stenographic notes: TNA FO 608/245, pp. 422–62, at p. 441.

46. ibid.

47. Draft Report of the Commission, USNA 181.1201/16, pp. 83–96, at pp. 87–9.

48. Eighth Meeting of the Commission on Responsibilities, 24 March 1919, Minutes: USNA 181.1201/16, pp. 76–82, at p. 81; USNA 181.1201/8 (M 820, Roll 141, 500–23), pp. 19–20; USNA 181.1201/8 (M 820, Roll 141, 600–15 French), pp. 12–13; USNA 181.1201/8 (M 820, Roll 141, 566–99 French), pp. 16–17; Paix de Versailles, pp. 413–22, at p. 420; Recueil des actes, pp. 109–18, at p. 116.

49. Memorandum submitted by the Serbian delegate, 18 February 1919, USNA 181.1201/16, p. 50; Recueil des actes, p. 291.

50. Report of Sub-Commission I on Criminal Acts, USNA 181.1201/16, pp. 39–45, at p. 40.

51. ibid. pp. 44–5.

52. Annie Deperchin, 'The Laws of War', in Jay Winter (ed.), *The First World War*, Vol. I, Cambridge: Cambridge University Press, 2014, pp. 615–38, at pp. 629–30; T. G. Otte, *July Crisis: The World's Descent into War, July 1914*, Cambridge: Cambridge University Press, 2014, p. 501; 'Germany and the Neutrality of Belgium' (1914) 8 *American Journal of International Law* 877, at p. 880; 'Why Germany Made War', *The Times*, 11 August 1914, p. 5.

53. Hague Convention (V) Respecting the Rights and Duties of Neutral Powers and Persons in Case of War on Land, (1907) 3 Martens NRG, 3rd ser. 713, 205 Parry's Consol. TS 299.

54. Eighth Meeting of the Commission on Responsibilities, 24 March 1919, Minutes: USNA 181.1201/16, pp. 76–82, at p. 80; USNA 181.1201/8 (M 820, Roll 141, 500–23), p. 15; USNA 181.1201/8 (M 820, Roll 141, 600–15 French), p. 10; USNA 181.1201/8 (M 820, Roll 141, 566–99 French), p. 26; Paix de Versailles, pp. 413–22, at p. 419; Recueil des actes, pp. 109–18, at p. 115. Stenographic notes: TNA FO 608/245, pp. 383–421, at p. 409. In Sub-Commission III, Lansing made the same point with respect to the

Hague Conventions on the laws and customs of war: Third Meeting of Sub-Commission III, 21 February 1919, Minutes: USNA 181/12301/3 (M 820, Roll 143, 715–26), TNA FO 608/246, pp. 8–9; USNA 181/12301/3 (M 820, Roll 143, 732–46), p. 11; USNA 181/12301/3 (M 820, Roll 143, 747–51), p. 5; USNA 181/12301/3 (M 820, Roll 143, 756–66), p. 9; USNA 181/12301/3 (M 820, Roll 143, 771–90 French), pp. 15–16; Recueil des actes, pp. 331–4, at p. 333; Paix de Versailles, pp. 307–11, at p. 309. Stenographic notes: TNA FO 608/246, pp. 520–39, at p. 536.

55. Hague Convention (V) Respecting the Rights and Duties of Neutral Powers and Persons in Case of War on Land, (*1907*) 3 Martens NRG, 3rd ser. 713, 205 Parry's Consol. TS 299, Art. 20.

56. Eighth Meeting of the Commission on Responsibilities, 24 March 1919, Minutes: USNA 181.1201/16, pp. 76–82, at p. 81; USNA 181.1201/8 (M 820, Roll 141, 500–23), p. 17; USNA 181.1201/8 (M 820, Roll 141, 600–15 French), p. 12; USNA 181.1201/8 (M 820, Roll 141, 566–99 French), p. 24; Paix de Versailles, pp. 413–22, at p. 420; Recueil des actes, pp. 109–18, at p. 116. Stenographic notes: TNA FO 608/245, pp. 383–421, at p. 411.

57. Eighth Meeting of the Commission on Responsibilities, 24 March 1919, Minutes: USNA 181.1201/16, pp. 76–82, at p. 80; USNA 181.1201/8 (M 820, Roll 141, 500–23), pp. 14–16; USNA 181.1201/8 (M 820, Roll 141, 600–15 French), p. 10; USNA 181.1201/8 (M 820, Roll 141, 566–99 French), p. 24; Paix de Versailles, pp. 413–22, at p. 419; Recueil des actes, pp. 109–18, at p. 115. Stenographic notes: TNA FO 608/245, pp. 383–421, at p. 409.

58. Report of the Commission on Responsibilities, USNA 181.1201/16, pp. 115–76, at p. 121.

59. Eighth Meeting of the Commission on Responsibilities, 24 March 1919, Minutes: USNA 181.1201/16, pp. 76–82, at p. 80; USNA 181.1201/8 (M 820, Roll 141, 500–23), p. 14; USNA 181.1201/8 (M 820, Roll 141, 600–15 French), p. 9; USNA 181.1201/8 (M 820, Roll 141, 566–99 French), pp. 16–17; Paix de Versailles, pp. 413–22, at p. 419; Recueil des actes, pp. 109–18, at p. 115. Stenographic notes: TNA FO 608/245, pp. 383–421, at p. 407.

60. Eighth Meeting of the Commission on Responsibilities, 24 March 1919, Minutes: USNA 181.1201/16, pp. 76–82, at p. 80; USNA 181.1201/8 (M 820, Roll 141, 500–23), p. 14; USNA 181.1201/8 (M 820, Roll 141, 600–15 French), p. 9; USNA 181.1201/8 (M 820, Roll 141, 566–99 French), pp. 16–17; Paix de Versailles, pp. 413–22, at pp. 418–19; Recueil des actes, pp. 109–18, at pp. 114–15. Stenographic notes: TNA FO 608/245, pp. 383–421, at p. 407.

61. Eighth Meeting of the Commission on Responsibilities, 24 March 1919, Minutes: USNA 181.1201/16, pp. 76–82, at pp. 80–1; USNA 181.1201/8 (M 820, Roll 141, 500–23), pp. 16–17; USNA 181.1201/8 (M 820, Roll 141, 600–15 French), p. 11; USNA 181.1201/8 (M 820, Roll 141, 566–99 French), pp. 16–17; Paix de Versailles, pp. 413–22, at p. 420; Recueil des actes, pp. 109–18, at p. 116. Stenographic notes: TNA FO 608/245, pp. 383–421, at p. 410.

62. Memorandum submitted by the British delegates, 13 February 1919, USNA 181.1201/16, pp. 27–33, at p. 28; Scott Papers, Box 30.3a, pp. 2–3; Recueil des actes, pp. 41–50, at p. 45.

63. ibid.

64. Memorandum of British Solicitor General, 17 February 1919, USNA 181.12201/2 (M 820, Roll 143, 434–5); Recueil des actes, pp. 313–14.

65. Second Meeting of Sub-Commission II, 17 February 1919, Minutes: USNA 181.12201/2 (M 820, Roll 143, 412–33), p. 16; Recueil des actes, pp. 306–12, at pp. 308–9; Paix de Versailles, pp. 263–77, at pp. 271–2. Stenographic notes: TNA FO 608/246, pp. 113–42, at pp. 130–1.

66. Second Meeting of Sub-Commission II, 17 February 1919, Minutes: USNA 181.12201/2 (M 820, Roll 143, 412–33), p. 16; Recueil des actes, pp. 306–12, at p. 310; Paix de Versailles, pp. 263–77, at pp. 272–3. Stenographic notes: TNA FO 608/246, pp. 113–42, at p. 132.

67. Second Meeting of Sub-Commission II, 17 February 1919, Minutes: USNA 181.12201/2 (M 820, Roll 143, 412–33), p. 18; Recueil des actes, pp. 306–12, at p. 310; Paix de Versailles, pp. 263–77, at p. 273. Stenographic notes: TNA FO 608/246, pp. 113–42, at p. 133.

68. Second Meeting of Sub-Commission II, 17 February 1919, Minutes: USNA 181.12201/2 (M 820, Roll 143, 412–33), p. 20; Paix de Versailles, pp. 263–77, at p. 275. Stenographic notes: TNA FO 608/246, pp. 113–42, at pp. 134–5.

69. Revised British memorandum, 20 February 1919, Recueil des actes, p. 318. Also, Third Meeting of Sub-Commission II, 20 February 1919, Minutes: USNA 181.12201/3 (M 820, Roll 143, 450–70), pp. 7–8; USNA 181.12201/3 (M 820, Roll 143, 471–98 French), p. 3; Paix de Versailles, pp. 278–91, at pp. 278–9. Stenographic notes: TNA FO 608/246, pp. 143–70, at p. 145.

70. Third Meeting of Sub-Commission II, 20 February 1919, Minutes: USNA 181.12201/3 (M 820, Roll 143, 450–70), p. 12; USNA 181.12201/3 (M 820, Roll 143, 471–98 French), p. 13; Recueil des actes, pp. 315–17, at p. 316; Paix de Versailles, pp. 278–91, at p. 284. Stenographic notes: TNA FO 608/246, pp. 143–70, at p. 156.

71. See above, p. 132.

72. Third Meeting of Sub-Commission II, 20 February 1919, Minutes: USNA 181.12201/3 (M 820, Roll 143, 450–70), p. 20; USNA 181.12201/3 (M 820, Roll 143, 471–98 French), p. 26; Recueil des actes, pp. 315–17, at p. 317; Paix de Versailles, pp. 278–91, at p. 290. Stenographic notes: TNA FO 608/246, pp. 143–70, at p. 170.

73. Pollock to Balfour, 26 February 1919, LG F/89/2/34, Hanworth Papers, Ms Eng. Hist. C 943.1-211.

74. Kerr to Lloyd George, 28 February 1919, LG F/89/2/34.

75. Kerr to Lloyd George, 1 March 1919, LG F/87/3/36.

76. Fourth Meeting of Sub-Commission II, 6 March 1919, Minutes: USNA 181.12201/4 (M 820, Roll 143, 499–519), p. 2; FO 608/246, p. 2.

77. Fourth Meeting of Sub-Commission II, 6 March 1919, Minutes: USNA 181.12201/4 (M 820, Roll 143, 499–519), p. 4; FO 608/246, p. 2.
78. Fourth Meeting of Sub-Commission II, 6 March 1919, Minutes: USNA 181.12201/4 (M 820, Roll 143, 499–519), pp. 5–6. Stenographic notes: TNA FO 608/246, pp. 171–203, at pp. 179–80.
79. Report of Sub-Commission II, USNA 181.1201/16, pp. 45–6, at p. 46.
80. Third Meeting of the Commission on Responsibilities, Minutes, 12 March 1919, USNA 181.1201/16, pp. 35–9, at p. 36; USNA 181.1201/3 (M 820, Roll 141, 5–24), p. 4; USNA 181.1201/3 (M 820, Roll 141, 25–32), p. 4; TNA FO 608/245, pp. 274–93, pp. 276–7; Recueil des actes, pp. 52–8, at p. 53. Stenographic notes: TNA FO 608/245, pp. 274–93, at pp. 276–7.
81. Third Meeting of the Commission on Responsibilities, Minutes, 12 March 1919, USNA 181.1201/16, pp. 35–9, at p. 36; USNA 181.1201/3 (M 820, Roll 141, 5–24), p. 5; USNA 181.1201/3 (M 820, Roll 141, 25–32), p. 8; TNA FO 608/245, pp. 274–93, p. 279; Recueil des actes, pp. 52–8, at p. 54. Stenographic notes: TNA FO 608/245, pp. 274–93, at p. 279.
82. Ninth Meeting of the Commission on Responsibilities, 25 March 1919, Minutes: USNA 181.1201/16, pp. 97–102, at p. 100; USNA 181.1201/9 (M 820, Roll 141, 647–75), pp. 14–15; USNA 181.1201/9 (M 820, Roll 141, 676–704), p. 15; USNA 181.1201/9 (M 820, Roll 141, 714–47 French), pp. 22–3. Stenographic notes: TNA FO 608/245, pp. 422–62, at p. 441.
83. Draft Report of the Commission, USNA 181.1201/16, pp. 83–96, at p. 92.
84. Ninth Meeting of the Commission on Responsibilities, 25 March 1919, Minutes: USNA 181.1201/16, pp. 97–102, at p. 100; USNA 181.1201/9 (M 820, Roll 141, 647–75), p. 15; USNA 181.1201/9 (M 820, Roll 141, 676–704), p. 15; USNA 181.1201/9 (M 820, Roll 141, 714–47 French), p. 23. Stenographic notes: TNA FO 608/245, pp. 422–62, at p. 441.
85. Ninth Meeting of the Commission on Responsibilities, 25 March 1919, Minutes: USNA 181.1201/16, pp. 97–102, at p. 100; USNA 181.1201/9 (M 820, Roll 141, 647–75), p. 17; USNA 181.1201/9 (M 820, Roll 141, 676–704), pp. 17–18; USNA 181.1201/9 (M 820, Roll 141, 714–47 French), p. 23. Stenographic notes: TNA FO 608/245, pp. 422–62, at p. 444.
86. Ninth Meeting of the Commission on Responsibilities, 25 March 1919, Minutes: USNA 181.1201/16, pp. 97–102, at p. 100; USNA 181.1201/9 (M 820, Roll 141, 647–75), p. 18; USNA 181.1201/9 (M 820, Roll 141, 676–704), p. 19.
87. Report of the Commission on Responsibilities, USNA 181.1201/16, pp. 115–76, at p. 125.
88. Agreement for the Prosecution and Punishment of Major War Criminals of the European Axis, and Establishing the Charter of the International Military Tribunal (IMT), Annex, (1951) 82 UNTS 279, Art. 6(a).
89. *France et al. v. Goering et al.*, Judgment, (1947) 1 IMT 171, at p. 186.
90. Rome Statute of the International Criminal Court, (2002) 2187 UNTS 3, Art. 5(1).

91. The crime of aggression, RC/Res.6.
92. Activation of the jurisdiction of the Court over the crime of aggression, ICC-ASP/16/Res.5.

CHAPTER 10

1. See, e.g., 'Draft convention on the laws and customs of war', in *Correspondence respecting to the Proposed conference at Brussels on the Rules of Military Warfare*, Parliamentary Papers, Miscellaneous No. 1, 1874.
2. *Enquête dans les Balkans, Rapport présenté aux Directeurs de la Dotation par les Membres de la Commission d'enquête*, Paris: Dotation Carnegie, 1914, pp. 201–231.
3. Preliminary Peace Conference, Protocol No. 1, 25 January 1919, USNA 180.0201/2, Annex II.
4. Plan of the Organisation of the Sub-Commissions of the Commission of Responsibilities, Annex I to Minutes of Second Meeting, USNA 181.1201/16, p. 26; USNA 181.12/6; Recueil des actes, p. 38.
5. *Report of the Committee on Alleged German Outrages*, London: HMSO, 1915, p. 38.
6. *Rapports et procès-verbaux d'enquête de la commission instituée en vue de constater les actes commis par l'ennemi en violation du droit des gens (Décret du 23 septembre 1914)*, Paris: Imprimerie nationale, 1915–1919.
7. Report of the Commission on Responsibilities, USNA 181.1201/16, pp. 115–76, at pp. 122–3.
8. Report of the Commission on Responsibilities, USNA 181.1201/16, pp. 115–76, at p. 130.
9. ibid.
10. ibid.
11. ibid.
12. ibid. p. 135.
13. ibid. p. 154.
14. *Dithmar and Boldt ('Llandovery Castle')*, (1922) 16 *American Journal of International Law* 708, (1921) 2 *International Law Reports* 437.
15. Report of the Commission on Responsibilities, USNA 181.1201/16, pp. 115–76, at p. 149.
16. ibid. p. 155.
17. ibid. p. 157.
18. ibid. p. 122.
19. Penalties for the Crimes of the War—Statement of Principles set forth by the Belgian Delegate, 21 February 1919, USNA 181.12301/3 (M 820, Roll 143, 727–8); TNA FO 608/246, USNA 181/12301/3 (M 820, Roll 143, 747–51), p. 2; USNA 181.12301/3 (M 820, Roll 143, 767–8); Recueil des actes, p. 337.
20. Second Meeting of Sub-Commission III, 18 February 1919, Minutes: USNA 181/12301/3 (M 820, Roll 143, 649–62), TNA FO 608/246, p. 3; USNA 181/12301/3 (M 820, Roll 143, 664–9), p. 2; USNA 181/12301/3 (M 820, Roll 143, 670–82), p. 3; USNA 181/12301/3 (M 820, Roll 143, 683–97), p. 3; USNA 181/

12301/3 (M 820, Roll 143, 698–714 French), pp. 3–4; Recueil des Actes, pp. 326–30, at p. 327; Paix de Versailles, pp. 295–302, at p. 296. Stenographic notes: TNA FO 608/246, pp. 503–519, at pp. 504–5.

21. Third Meeting of Sub-Commission III, 21 February 1919, Minutes: USNA 181/12301/3 (M 820, Roll 143, 715–26), p. 8 (emphasis in the original); USNA 181/12301/3 (M 820, Roll 143, 732–46), pp. 28–9; TNA FO 608/246, USNA 181/12301/3 (M 820, Roll 143, 747–51), p. 4; USNA 181/12301/3 (M 820, Roll 143, 756–66), p. 8; USNA 181/12301/3 (M 820, Roll 143, 771–90 French), pp. 14–15; Recueil des actes, pp. 331–4, at p. 333; Paix de Versailles, pp. 307–11, at p. 309. Stenographic notes: TNA FO 608/246, pp. 520–39, at p. 534.

22. United Nations Commission for the Investigation of War Crimes, Report of the Sub-Committee, 26 November 1943, FNA 382AP/68; 'Transmission of Particulars of War Crimes to the Secretariat of the United Nations War Crimes Commission, 13 December 1943', NAC RG-25, Vol. 3033, 4060-40C, Part Two; René Cassin, 'Note of Violations of the Laws and Customs of War Perpetrated by the Germans Since September 1939', in London International Assembly, *Reports on Punishment of War Crimes*, London, 1943, pp. 48–55, at pp. 50–1; United Nations War Crimes Commission, *History of the United Nations War Crimes Commission and the Development of the Laws of War*, London: HMSO, 1948, pp. 34–5. See also: Information concerning human rights arising from trials of war criminals, UN Doc. E/CN.4/W.19, pp. 8–9.

23. *United States v. Alstötter et al.*, (1951) 3 TWC 954 (US Military Commission), pp. 1057, 1181; *Klinge*, (1948) LRTWC 1 (Eidsivating Lagmannsrett and Supreme Court of Norway), p. 12.

24. 'Trial of Edward Schoengrath et al', (1948) 11 LRTWC 83 (British Military Tribunal), at pp. 93–4.

25. 'Proceedings of the Committee', in First Interim Report from the Committee of Enquiry into Breaches of the Laws of War, 13 January 1919, TNA CAB/24/111, pp. 11–17, at p. 17; 'Report of Special Sub-Committee on Law', in First Interim Report from the Committee of Enquiry into Breaches of the Laws of War, 13 January 1919, TNA CAB/24/111, pp. 95–9, at p. 98.

26. Memorandum submitted by the British delegates, 13 February 1919, USNA 181.1201/16, pp. 27–33; Scott Papers, Box 30.3a; Recueil des actes, pp. 313–15.

27. Memorandum by the Solicitor General for England, 21 February 1919, USNA 181/12301/3 (M 820, Roll 143, 729–31); USNA 181/12301/3 (M 820, Roll 143, 752–4); Recueil des actes, pp. 335–7.

28. Note sommaire au sujet des faits criminals qui ont amené la guerre mondiale, qui en ont accompagné le début et qui ont été commis au cours des hostilités, Recueil des actes, 29 January 1919, pp. 370–81. There is an English version of this document in the US National Archives with the annotation 'translation rather rough': USNA 181.12101/1.

29. Liste des crimes contre le droit des gens, 24 February 1919, Recueil des actes, pp. 343–5.

30. Acts Committed by German Submarines Contrary to the Law of Nations, USNA 181.12101/3 (M 820, Roll 143, 769–70); Recueil des actes, p. 297.

31. Note sommaire au sujet des infractions au droit des gens commis à l'égard de la Belgique par l'armée et les autorités allemandes (1914–1918), Recueil des actes, pp. 382–409.

32. Memorandum submitted by the Italian delegation, 24 February 1919, USNA 181.12101/3, Recueil des actes, pp. 410–12.

33. Rapport de la Commission interalliée sur les violations des Conventions de la Haye et du droit international en général commises de 1915 à 1918 par les Bulgares en Serbie occupée, 24 February 1919, Receuil des actes, pp. 413–30.

34. Note sur les crimes commis par les Bulgares, les Turcs et les Allemands contre les populations hélleniques, 25 February 1919, Recueil des actes, pp. 431–71.

35. Liste des navires japonais coulés par des sous-marins ennemis sans avertissement et sans précaution pour la sécurité des équipages et des passagers, Recueil des actes, pp. 515–16.

36. Third Meeting of Sub-Commission III, 21 February 1919, Minutes: USNA 181/12301/3 (M 820, Roll 143, 715–26), p. 6; USNA 181/12301/3 (M 820, Roll 143, 732–46), p. 7; USNA 181/12301/3 (M 820, Roll 143, 756–66), p. 6; USNA 181/12301/3 (M 820, Roll 143, 771–90 French), p. 11; Paix de Versailles, pp. 307–11, at pp. 307–8. Stenographic notes: TNA FO 608/246, pp. 520–39, at pp. 530–1.

37. Note sommaire sur les exactions commises, contrairement au droit des gens en Pologne par les armées ennemies de 1914 à 1918, 5 March 1919, Recueil des actes, pp. 474–8. See also: Rapport (extraits) adressé par le Président de la ville de Varsovie au sujet des dommages causés à la ville de Varsovie par l'occupation allemande, 19 December 1918, Recueil des actes, p. 479; Rapport de la Commission gouvernementale des prisonniers de guerre, Varsovie, à la délégation polonaise à la Conférence de la pais, 4 February 1919, Recueil des actes, pp. 480–2.

38. Convention for the Amelioration of the Condition of the Wounded and Sick in Armies in the Field, (1907) 15 UKTS 15.

39. Declaration Renouncing the Use, in Time of War, of Explosive Projectiles Under 400 Grammes Weight, in D. Schindler and J. Toman (eds), The Laws of Armed Conflicts, The Hague: Martinus Nijhoff, 1988, p. 102.

40. Declaration concerning expanding bullets, The Hague, 29 July 1899, in James Brown Scott (ed.), The Hague Conventions and Declarations of 1899 and 1907, New York: Oxford University Press, 1915, p. 227.

41. Memorandum by the Solicitor General for England, 21 February 1919, USNA 181/12301/3 (M 820, Roll 143, 729–31); USNA 181/12301/3 (M 820, Roll 143, 752–4); Recueil des actes, pp. 335–7.

42. Hague Convention (IX) relative to Bombardment by Naval Forces in Time of War, (1907) 3 Martens NRG, 3rd ser. 604, TS 542.

43. Hague Convention (X) relative to Adaptation to Maritime War of the Principles of the Geneva Convention, (1910) 3 Martens NRG, 3rd ser. 630, TS 543.

44. Memorandum on the Principles which should determine Inhuman and Improper Acts of War, 26 February 1919, USNA 181.1201/16, p. 55.

45. House Diary, 24 July 1915, cited in James F. Willis, *Prologue to Nuremburg: The Politics and Diplomacy of Punishing War Criminals of the First World War*, Westport, CT and London: Greenwood Press, 1982, p. 41.

46. *Papers Relating to the Foreign Relations of the United States 1919, The Lansing Papers 1914–1920*, Vol. I, Washington, DC: US Government Printing Office, 1940, pp. 29–47.

47. Report of Sub-Commission III on the Laws and Customs of War, USNA 181.1201/16, pp. 50–4, at p. 53.

48. Report of the Commission on Responsibilities, USNA 181.1201/16, pp. 115–76, at pp. 173–4.

49. Report of Sub-Commission I on Criminal Acts, USNA 181.1201/16, pp. 39–45, at pp. 40–1.

50. ibid.

51. Report of Sub-Commission III on the Laws and Customs of War, USNA 181.1201/16, pp. 50–4, at pp. 50–1.

52. Report of Sub-Commission III on the Laws and Customs of War, USNA 181.1201/16, pp. 50–4, at p. 51; Recueil des actes, pp. 74–80, at p. 75. See also the references by Rolin-Jaequemyns, Third Meeting of Sub-Commission III, 21 February 1919, Minutes: USNA 181/12301/3 (M 820, Roll 143, 715–26), p. 7 (emphasis in the original); USNA 181/12301/3 (M 820, Roll 143, 732–46), p. 10; USNA 181/12301/3 (M 820, Roll 143, 756–66), pp. 7–8, and in Memorandum by the Solicitor General for England, 21 February 1919, USNA 181/12301/3 (M 820, Roll 143, 729–31); USNA 181/12301/3 (M 820, Roll 143, 752–4); Recueil des actes, pp. 335–7.

53. Draft Report of the Commission, USNA 181.1201/16, pp. 83–96, at pp. 89–90.

54. Ninth Meeting of the Commission on Responsibilities, 25 March 1919, Minutes: USNA 181.1201/16, pp. 97–102, at p. 98; USNA 181.1201/9 (M 820, Roll 141, 647–75), p. 5; USNA 181.1201/9 (M 820, Roll 141, 676–704), pp. 6–7; TNA FO 608/245, pp. 422–62, at p. 7; USNA 181.1201/9 (M 820, Roll 141, 714–47 French), p. 7. Stenographic notes: TNA FO 608/245, pp. 422–62, at p. 7. See also Larnaude's comments in Meeting of Sub-Commission III, 4 March 1919, Minutes: TNA FO 608/246, pp. 7–8; USNA 181.12301/5 (M 820, Roll 144, 63–83), pp. 7–8; USNA 181.12301/5 (M 820, Roll 144, 84–103), pp. 8–9; USNA 181.12301/5 (M 820, Roll 144, 113–39 French), p. 12; Recueil des actes, pp. 350–6, at pp. 352–3.

55. Draft Report of the Commission, USNA 181.1201/16, pp. 83–96, at p. 89.

56. Report of the Commission on Responsibilities, USNA 181.1201/16, pp. 115–76, at p. 122.

57. ibid., pp. 124 and 125.

58. Memorandum submitted by the British delegates, 13 February 1919, USNA 181.1201/16, pp. 27–33, at p. 30; Scott Papers, Box 30.3a; Recueil des actes,

pp. 41–50. Also, Memorandum of the British Delegation, 14 February 1919, USNA 181.1201/16, p. 34; USNA 181.12201/1.

59. 'Interim Recommendations of the Committee', in First Interim Report from the Committee of Enquiry into Breaches of the Laws of War, 13 January 1919, TNA CAB/24/111, pp. 13–17, at p. 13.

60. Report of Sub-Commission I on Criminal Acts, USNA 181.1201/16, pp. 39–45, at p. 39.

61. Rapport par la première sous-commission (actes criminels), Receuil des actes, pp. 59–62, at p. 59.

62. Report of Sub-Commission I on Criminal Acts, USNA 181.1201/16, pp. 39–45, at p. 40.

63. Rapport par la première sous-commission (actes criminels), Receuil des actes, pp. 59–62, at p. 60.

64. Report of Sub-Commission I on Criminal Acts, USNA 181.1201/16, pp. 39–45, at p. 41.

65. Rapport par la première sous-commission (actes criminels), Receuil des actes, pp. 59–62, at p. 62.

66. Report of Sub-Commission III on the Laws and Customs of War, USNA 181.1201/16, pp. 50–4, at p. 51.

67. Second Meeting of Sub-Commission III, 18 February 1919, Minutes: USNA 181/12301/3 (M 820, Roll 143, 649–62), p. 10; USNA 181/12301/3 (M 820, Roll 143, 664–9), p. 5; USNA 181/12301/3 (M 820, Roll 143, 670–82), pp. 10–11; USNA 181/12301/3 (M 820, Roll 143, 683–97), pp. 10–11; USNA 181/12301/3 (M 820, Roll 143, 698–714 French), p. 13; Recueil des actes, pp. 326–30, at p. 329; Paix de Versailles, pp. 295–302, at p. 300. Stenographic notes: TNA FO 608/246, pp. 503–19, at p. 515.

68. Draft Report of the Commission, USNA 181.1201/16, pp. 83–96, at p. 89.

69. Rapport (projet) de la Commission, Recueil des actes, pp. 119–37, at p. 127.

70. Draft Report of the Commission, USNA 181.1201/16, pp. 83–96, at p. 91.

71. Rapport (projet) de la Commission, Recueil des actes, pp. 119–37, at p. 130.

72. Eighth Meeting of the Commission on Responsibilities, 24 March 1919, Minutes: USNA 181.1201/16, pp. 76–82, at p. 81; USNA 181.1201/8 (M 820, Roll 141, 500–23), p. 20. Stenographic notes: TNA FO 608/245, pp. 383–421, at p. 415. The various sets of minutes and stenographic notes differ about what was actually said.

73. Eighth Meeting of the Commission on Responsibilities, 24 March 1919, Minutes: USNA 181.1201/8 (M 820, Roll 141, 500–23), p. 20.

74. Eighth Meeting of the Commission on Responsibilities, 24 March 1919, Stenographic notes: TNA FO 608/245, pp. 383–421, at p. 415.

75. Eighth Meeting of the Commission on Responsibilities, 24 March 1919, Minutes: USNA 181.1201/16, pp. 76–82, at p. 81.

76. Eighth Meeting of the Commission on Responsibilities, 24 March 1919, Minutes: USNA 181.1201/8 (M 820, Roll 141, 500–23), p. 20.

77. Eighth Meeting of the Commission on Responsibilities, 24 March 1919, Minutes: USNA 181.1201/16, pp. 76–82, at pp. 81–2; USNA 181.1201/8 (M 820, Roll 141, 500–23), pp. 21–3; USNA 181.1201/8 (M 820, Roll 141, 524–54), pp. 25–8; USNA 181.1201/8 (M 820, Roll 141, 566–99 French), pp. 32–6; USNA 181.1201/8 (M 820, Roll 141, 600–15 French), p. 14; Recueil des actes, pp. 109–18, at p. 117; Paix de Versailles, pp. 413–22, at p. 421. Stenographic notes: TNA FO 608/245, pp. 383–421, at pp. 416–20.

78. Memorandum on the Principles which should determine Inhuman and Improper Acts of War, 26 February 1919, USNA 181.1201/16, p. 55.

79. Eighth Meeting of the Commission on Responsibilities, 24 March 1919, Minutes: USNA 181.1201/16, pp. 76–82, at p. 82; USNA 181.1201/8 (M 820, Roll 141, 500–23), pp. 21–3; USNA 181.1201/8 (M 820, Roll 141, 524–54), pp. 28–9; USNA 181.1201/8 (M 820, Roll 141, 566–99 French), pp. 35–6; USNA 181.1201/8 (M 820, Roll 141, 600–15 French), p. 15; Recueil des actes, pp. 109–18, at p. 118; Paix de Versailles, pp. 413–22, at pp. 421–2. Stenographic notes: TNA FO 608/245, pp. 383–421, at pp. 416–20.

80. Eighth Meeting of the Commission on Responsibilities, 24 March 1919, Minutes: USNA 181.1201/16, pp. 76–82, at p. 82; USNA 181.1201/8 (M 820, Roll 141, 500–23), pp. 23–4; USNA 181.1201/8 (M 820, Roll 141, 524–54), pp. 29–30; USNA 181.1201/8 (M 820, Roll 141, 566–99 French), pp. 36–7; USNA 181.1201/8 (M 820, Roll 141, 600–15 French), p. 15; Recueil des actes, pp. 109–18, at p. 118; Paix de Versailles, pp. 413–22, at p. 422. Stenographic notes: TNA FO 608/245, pp. 383–421, at pp. 416–20.

81. Eighth Meeting of the Commission on Responsibilities, 24 March 1919, Minutes: USNA 181.1201/16, pp. 76–82, at p. 82; USNA 181.1201/8 (M 820, Roll 141, 500–23), pp. 21–3; USNA 181.1201/8 (M 820, Roll 141, 524–54), pp. 31–2; USNA 181.1201/8 (M 820, Roll 141, 566–99 French), pp. 37–8; USNA 181.1201/8 (M 820, Roll 141, 600–15 French), p. 15; Recueil des actes, pp. 109–18, at p. 118; Paix de Versailles, pp. 413–22, at p. 422. Stenographic notes: TNA FO 608/245, pp. 383–421, at pp. 416–20.

82. Eighth Meeting of the Commission on Responsibilities, 24 March 1919, Minutes: USNA 181.1201/16, pp. 76–82, at p. 82; USNA 181.1201/8 (M 820, Roll 141, 500–23), pp. 21–3; USNA 181.1201/8 (M 820, Roll 141, 524–54), p. 31; USNA 181.1201/8 (M 820, Roll 141, 566–99 French), p. 38; USNA 181.1201/8 (M 820, Roll 141, 600–15 French), p. 16; Recueil des actes, pp. 109–18, at p. 118; Paix de Versailles, pp. 413–22, at p. 422. Stenographic notes: TNA FO 608/245, pp. 383–421, at pp. 416–20.

83. Ninth Meeting of the Commission on Responsibilities, 25 March 1919, Minutes: USNA 181.1201/16, pp. 97–102, at p. 99; USNA 181.1201/9 (M 820, Roll 141, 647–75), p. 11; USNA 181.1201/9 (M 820, Roll 141, 676–704), p. 12; USNA 181.1201/9 (M 820, Roll 141, 714–47 French), p. 18; Recueil des actes, pp. 138–47, at pp. 141–2. Stenographic notes: TNA FO 608/245, pp. 422–62, at p. 437.

84. Report of the Commission on Responsibilities, USNA 181.1201/16, pp. 115–76, at p. 165.

85. ibid. p. 171.

86. Correspondence between the War Crimes Commission and HM Government in London Regarding the Punishment of Crimes Committed on Religious, Racial or Political Grounds, UNWCC Doc. C.78, 15 February 1945, NAC RG-25,Vol. 3033, 4060-40C, Part Four.

87. Minutes of Conference Session of 23 July 1945, in Robert H. Jackson, *Report of Robert H. Jackson, United States Representative to the International Conference on Military Trials*, Washington, DC: US Government Printing Office, 1949, pp. 328–47, at p. 331.

88. Philippe Sands, *East West Street*, London: Weidenfield & Nicolson, 2016, pp. 110–11.

89. *Prosecutor v. Tadić* (IT-94-1-AR72), Decision on the Defence Motion for Interlocutory Appeal on Jurisdiction, 2 October 1995, § 140.

90. United Nations War Crimes Commission, *History of the United Nations War Crimes Commission and the Development of the Laws of War*, London: HMSO, 1948, p. 36. For a more modern formulation of the same idea in the work of the United Nations International Law Commission, see First report on crimes against humanity, by Sean D. Murphy, Special Rapporteur, UN Doc. A/CN.4/680, § 30.

91. Meeting of the Imperial War Cabinet, 10 Downing Street, 20 November 1918, 12 noon, TNA CAB/23/37/37, p. 6. See also Robert Borden, *Robert Laird Borden: His Memoirs*, London: Macmillan, 1938, p. 868.

92. Meeting of the Imperial War Cabinet, 10 Downing Street, 20 November 1918, 12 noon, TNA CAB 23/37, p. 7; David Lloyd George, *Memoirs of the Peace Conference*, New Haven, CT: Yale University Press, 1939, pp. 57–8.

93. 'Report of Special Sub-Committee on Law', in First Interim Report from the Committee of Enquiry into Breaches of the Laws of War, 13 January 1919, TNA CAB/24/111, pp. 95–9, at pp. 96–7.

94. 'Prime Minister on German Crimes', *The Times*, 30 November 1918, p. 6.

95. Notes of an Allied Conversation held in the Cabinet Room, 10 Downing Street, 2 December 1918, 4 pm, TNA CAB 28/5 (IC 99), pp. 3–4. For the draft, see Notes of an Allied Conversation held in the Cabinet Room, 10 Downing Street, 2 December 1918, 11 am, Annex, TNA CAB 28/5 (IC 98(a)).

96. Bertie to Delcassé, 19 May 1915, TNA FO 146/1574, FMAE Guerre, 1914–1918, Turquie, Vol. 887, 105–6.

97. Bertie to Grey, 19 May 1915, TNA FO 371/2488; Delcassé to Bertie, 20 May 1915, FMAE Guerre, 1914–1918, Turquie, Vol. 887, 117; Bertie to Delcassé, 21 May 1915, FMAE Guerre, 1914–1918, Turquie, Vol. 887, 121–2.

98. Bertie to Grey, 24 May 1915, TNA FO 371/2488.

99. Press Release, 23 May 1915, TNA FO 146/4471; 'Allies Stern Warning to Turkey', *The Times*, 25 May 1915.

100. Sharp to Secretary of State, 28 May 1915, FRUS 1915 Supplement, The World War, p. 981; Morgenthau to Secretary of State, 18 June 1915, FRUS 1915 Supplement, The World War, p. 982.

101. Second Meeting of the Commission on Responsibilities, 7 February 1919, Minutes: USNA 181.1201/16, pp. 19–25, at p. 19; USNA 181.1201/2 (M 820, Roll 140, 641–62), p. 2; USNA 181.1201/2 (M 820, Roll 140, 712–33), p. 3; Recueil des actes, pp. 31–7, at p. 31; Paix de Versailles, pp. 16–29, at p. 17.

102. Draft Synopsis of Treaty of Peace with Turkey, DBFP VII, pp. 125–8, at p. 127.

103. Notes of an Allied Conference, 10 Downing Street, 21 February 1920, 5 pm, DBFP VII, pp. 189–94, at p. 191.

104. Cambon to Lloyd George, 11 March 1920, TNA CAB 24/101; Hankey to Chairman, Drafting Committee of the Peace Conference, 30 March 1920, TNA CAB 24/101.

105. London Conference Minutes, 19 July 1945, in Robert H. Jackson, *Report of Robert H. Jackson, United States Representative to the International Conference on Military Trials*, Washington, DC: US Government Printing Office, 1949, pp. 295–309, at p. 297.

106. ibid. p. 299.

107. David Scheffer, *All the Missing Souls: A Personal History of the War Crimes Tribunals*, Princeton, NJ: Princeton University Press, 2012.

CHAPTER 11

1. See above, pp. 12–13.

2. Meeting of the Imperial War Cabinet, 10 Downing Street, 20 November 1918, 12 noon, TNA CAB/23/37/37, p. 5.

3. F. Larnaude and A. de Lapradelle, 'Inquiry into the Penal Liabilities of the Emperor William II', in Commission on the Responsibility of the Authors of the War, Minutes of Meetings of the Commission, USNA 181.1201/16, pp. 4–18, at p. 10.

4. ibid. p. 9.

5. Meeting of Sub-Commission III, 4 March 1919, Minutes: TNA FO 608/246, p. 4; USNA 181.12301/5 (M 820, Roll 144, 63–83), p. 4; USNA 181.12301/5 (M 820, Roll 144, 84–103), p. 5; USNA 181.12301/5 (M 820, Roll 144, 104–12), p. 3; USNA 181.12301/5 (M 820, Roll 144, 113–39 French), p. 5.

6. Preliminary Peace Conference, Protocol No. 1, 25 January 1919, USNA 180.0201/2, Annex II.

7. Memorandum of the American Delegation, 10 February 1919, USNA 181.1201/16, pp. 33–4; USNA 181.12201/1; TNA FO 608/246.

8. George A. Finch, 'Memorandum Regarding the Responsibility of the Authors of the War and for Crimes Committed in the War', in David Hunter Miller, *My Diary at the Conference of Paris, with Documents*, Vol. III, [New York]: Printed for the author, 1924, pp. 458–506, at pp. 505–6.

9. Meeting of Sub-Commission III, 4 March 1919, Minutes: TNA FO 608/246, pp. 2–3; USNA 181.12301/5 (M 820, Roll 144, 63–83), pp. 2–3; USNA 181.12301/5 (M 820, Roll 144, 84–103), pp. 3–4; USNA 181.12301/5 (M 820, Roll 144, 104–12), pp. 1–2; USNA 181.12301/5 (M 820, Roll 144, 113–39 French), pp. 1–2; Recueil des actes, pp. 350–6, at pp. 350–2.

10. Second Meeting of the Commission on Responsibilities, 7 February 1919, Minutes: USNA 181.1201/16, pp. 19–25, at pp. 23–4; USNA 181.1201/2 (M 820, Roll 140,641–62), pp. 17–21; USNA 181.1201/2 (M 820, Roll 140,663–84, Part 2), pp. 3–7; Recueil des actes, pp. 31–7, at pp. 35–7; Paix de Versailles, pp. 16–29, at pp. 25–9; USNA 181.1201/2 (M 820, Roll 140,734–59, Part 2 French), pp. 10–12.

11. Memorandum presented by the Solicitor General of England, 7 February 1919, TNA FO 608/246; USNA 185.118.22; USNA 181.1201/16, pp. 26–7, at p. 27; Recueil des actes, p. 40.

12. Joint First Meeting of Sub-Commissions II and III, 14 February 1919, Minutes: USNA 181.12201/1 (M 820, Roll 143,333–45), p. 3; USNA 181.12201/1 (M 820, Roll 143,346–50), pp. 2–3; USNA 181.12201/1 (M 820, Roll 143,356–72 French), pp. 11–12; USNA 181.12201/1 (M 820, Roll 143, 373–94 French), pp. 6–7; Recueil des actes, pp. 302–5, p. 303. Stenographic notes: TNA FO 608/246, p. 3.

13. See above, pp. 127–8.

14. Meeting of Sub-Commission III, 4 March 1919, Minutes: TNA FO 608/246, p. 1; USNA 181.12301/5 (M 820, Roll 144,63–83), p. 1; USNA 181.12301/5 (M 820, Roll 144,84–103), p. 2; USNA 181.12301/5 (M 820, Roll 144, 104–12), p. 3; USNA 181.12301/5 (M 820, Roll 144, 113–39 French), p. 2; Recueil des actes, pp. 350–6, at p. 350.

15. Memorandum submitted by the British delegates, 13 February 1919, USNA 181.1201/16, pp. 27–33, at p. 30; Scott Papers, Box 30.3a, p. 11; Recueil des actes, pp. 41–50, at p. 47.

16. Draft report of Sub-Commission III, 4 March 1919, USNA 181.12302/2.

17. Meeting of Sub-Commission III, 4 March 1919, Minutes: TNA FO 608/246, p. 17; USNA 181.12301/5 (M 820, Roll 144, 63–83), p. 17; USNA 181.12301/6 (M 820, Roll 144, 165–86), pp. 15–16; USNA 181.12301/6 (M 820, Roll 144, 187–96), p. 6; USNA 181.12301/5 (M 820, Roll 144, 197–220 French), p. 17; Recueil des actes, pp. 359–66, at pp. 357–8.

18. Meeting of Sub-Commission III, 4 March 1919, Minutes: TNA FO 608/246, pp. 11–19; USNA 181.12301/5 (M 820, Roll 144, 63–83), pp. 11–19; USNA 181.12301/5 (M 820, Roll 144, 84–103), pp. 12–18; USNA 181.12301/5 (M 820, Roll 144, 104–12), pp. 6–8; USNA 181.12301/5 (M 820, Roll 144, 113–39 French), pp. 17–27; Recueil des actes, pp. 350–6, at pp. 354–6.

19. Swiss Minister 3 April, Responsibility for the War, TNA FO 608/247/17.

20. Third Meeting of the Commission on Responsibilities, 12 March 1919, Minutes: USNA 181.1201/16, pp. 35–9, at pp. 37–8; USNA 181.1201/3 (M 820, Roll 141, 5–24), pp. 7–10; USNA 181.1201/3 (M 820, Roll 141, 25–32), pp. 5–6; USNA 181.1201/3 (M 820, Roll 141, 33–57), pp. 11–14; USNA 181.1201/3 (M 820, Roll 141, 58–69 French), pp. 6–9; USNA 181.1201/3 (M 820, Roll 141, 70–91 French), pp. 7–10; Recueil des actes, pp. 52–8, at pp. 55–6. Stenographic notes: TNA FO 678/245, pp. 274–93, at pp. 280–3.

21. Third Meeting of the Commission on Responsibilities, 12 March 1919, Minutes: USNA 181.1201/16, pp. 35–9, at pp. 38–9; USNA 181.1201/3 (M 820,

Roll 141, 5–24), pp. 10–24; USNA 181.1201/3 (M 820, Roll 141, 25–32), pp. 6–9; USNA 181.1201/3 (M 820, Roll 141, 33–57), pp. 14–24; USNA 181.1201/3 (M 820, Roll 141, 58–69 French), pp. 9–13; USNA 181.1201/3 (M 820, Roll 141, 70–91 French), pp. 11–21; Recueil des actes, pp. 52–8, at pp. 56–8. Stenographic notes: TNA FO 678/245, pp. 274–93, at pp. 283–93.

22. Fourth Meeting of the Commission on Responsibilities, 13 March 1919, Minutes: USNA 181.1201/16, pp. 57–61, at pp. 57–8; USNA 181.1201/4 (M 820, Roll 141, 156–76), pp. 1–2; USNA 181.1201/4 (M 820, Roll 141, 199–209), pp. 1–2; Recueil des actes, pp. 82–9, at p. 83; Paix de Versailles, pp. 339–52, at p. 340; USNA 181.1201/4 (M 820, Roll 141, 213–41 French), pp. 3–4; USNA 181.1201/4 (M 820, Roll 141, 242–55 French), pp. 2–3. Stenographic notes: TNA FO 678/245, pp. 294–321, at pp. 296–7.

23. Fourth Meeting of the Commission on Responsibilities, 13 March 1919, Minutes: USNA 181.1201/16, pp. 57–61, at p. 58; USNA 181.1201/4 (M 820, Roll 141, 156–76), pp. 3–4; USNA 181.1201/4 (M 820, Roll 141, 199–209), pp. 2–3; Recueil des actes, pp. 82–9, at p. 84; Paix de Versailles, pp. 339–52, at p. 341; USNA 181.1201/4 (M 820, Roll 141, 213–41 French), pp. 6–7; USNA 181.1201/4 (M 820, Roll 141, 242–55 French), p. 4. Stenographic notes: TNA FO 678/245, pp. 294–321, at pp. 299–300.

24. Fourth Meeting of the Commission on Responsibilities, 13 March 1919, Minutes: USNA 181.1201/16, pp. 57–61, at p. 58; USNA 181.1201/4 (M 820, Roll 141, 156–76), pp. 5–6; USNA 181.1201/4 (M 820, Roll 141, 199–209), p. 203; Recueil des actes, pp. 82–9, at p. 84; Paix de Versailles, pp. 339–52, at p. 342; USNA 181.1201/4 (M 820, Roll 141, 213–41 French), pp. 7–8; USNA 181.1201/4 (M 820, Roll 141, 242–55 French), pp. 4–5. Stenographic notes: TNA FO 678/245, pp. 294–321, at pp. 300–1.

25. Draft Report of the Commission, USNA 181.1201/16, pp. 83–96, at pp. 92–4.

26. Ninth Meeting of the Commission on Responsibilities, 25 March 1919, Minutes: USNA 181.1201/16, pp. 97–102, at p. 101; USNA 181.1201/9 (M 820, Roll 141, 647–75), pp. 21–2; USNA 181.1201/9 (M 820, Roll 141, 676–704), pp. 22–4; Receuil des actes, pp. 138–47, at p. 145; Paix de Versailles, pp. 423–31, at pp. 429–30; USNA 181.1201/9 (M 820, Roll 141, 714–47 French), pp. 31–4. Stenographic notes: TNA FO 608/245, pp. 422–62, at pp. 452–5.

27. Report of the Commission on Responsibilities, USNA 181.1201/16, pp. 115–76, at pp. 126–7.

28. Memorandum of reservations presented by the Representatives of the United States, 4 April 1919, USNA 181.1201/16, pp. 162–74.

29. Report of the Commission on Responsibilities, USNA 181.1201/16, pp. 115–76, at p. 123.

30. James Brown Scott, 'The Trial of the Kaiser', in Edward M. House and Charles Seymour (eds), *What Really Happened at Paris?*, London: Hodder & Stoughton, 1921, pp. 231–58, at p. 238.

31. F. Larnaude and A. de Lapradelle, 'Inquiry into the Penal Liabilities of the Emperor William II', in Commission on the Responsibility of the Authors of

the War, Minutes of Meetings of the Commission, USNA 181.1201/16, pp. 4–18, at pp. 8–10.

32. First Interim Report from the Committee of Enquiry into Breaches of the Laws of War, 13 January 1919, TNA CAB/24/111, p. 31.

33. Memorandum submitted by the British delegates, 13 February 1919, USNA 181.1201/16, pp. 27–33, at p. 28; Scott Papers, Box 30.3a, pp. 2–3; Recueil des actes, pp. 41–50, at p. 42.

34. Memorandum submitted by the British delegates, 13 February 1919, USNA 181.1201/16, pp. 27–33, at p. 29; Scott Papers, Box 30.3a, pp. 5–6; Recueil des actes, pp. 41–50, at p. 44.

35. Third Meeting of the Commission on Responsibilities, Minutes, 12 March 1919, USNA 181.1201/16, pp. 35–9, at p. 37; USNA 181.1201/3 (M 820, Roll 141, 5–24), p. 9; USNA 181.1201/3 (M 820, Roll 141, 25–32), p. 6; USNA 181.1201/3 (M 820, Roll 141, 33–57), p. 13; TNA FO 678/245, pp. 274–93, at p. 283; USNA 181.1201/3 (M 820, Roll 141, 58–69 French), p. 8; USNA 181.1201/3 (M 820, Roll 141, 70–91 French), pp. 10–11; Recueil des actes, pp. 52–8, at p. 56.

36. Third Meeting of the Commission on Responsibilities, Minutes, 12 March 1919, USNA 181.1201/16, pp. 35–9, at p. 38; USNA 181.1201/3 (M 820, Roll 141, 5–24), pp. 10–12; USNA 181.1201/3 (M 820, Roll 141, 25–32), pp. 6–7; USNA 181.1201/3 (M 820, Roll 141, 33–57), pp. 13–17; TNA FO 678/245, pp. 274–93, at pp. 284–6; USNA 181.1201/3 (M 820, Roll 141, 58–69 French), pp. 9–10; USNA 181.1201/3 (M 820, Roll 141, 70–91 French), pp. 11–13; Recueil des actes, pp. 52–8, at p. 56.

37. See Geoffrey Robertson, *The Tyrannicide Brief*, London: Vintage, 2006.

38. Third Meeting of the Commission on Responsibilities, Minutes, 12 March 1919, USNA 181.1201/16, pp. 35–9, at p. 38; USNA 181.1201/3 (M 820, Roll 141, 5–24), pp. 12–14; USNA 181.1201/3 (M 820, Roll 141, 25–32), p. 7; USNA 181.1201/3 (M 820, Roll 141, 33–57), pp. 17–19; TNA FO 678/245, pp. 274–93, at pp. 286–7; USNA 181.1201/3 (M 820, Roll 141, 58–69 French), pp. 10–11; USNA 181.1201/3 (M 820, Roll 141, 70–91 French), pp. 13–14; Recueil des actes, pp. 52–8, at p. 57.

39. Report of Sub-Commission III on the Laws and Customs of War, USNA 181.1201/16, pp. 50–4, at p. 53.

40. Emphasis in the original.

41. Third Meeting of the Commission on Responsibilities, Minutes, 12 March 1919, USNA 181.1201/16, pp. 35–9, at pp. 38–9; USNA 181.1201/3 (M 820, Roll 141, 5–24), pp. 13–14 (emphasis in the original); USNA 181.1201/3 (M 820, Roll 141, 25–32), pp. 8–9; USNA 181.1201/3 (M 820, Roll 141, 33–57), pp. 19–24; TNA FO 678/245, pp. 274–93, at pp. 287–92; USNA 181.1201/3 (M 820, Roll 141, 58–69 French), pp. 11–13; USNA 181.1201/3 (M 820, Roll 141, 70–91 French), pp. 14–20; Recueil des actes, pp. 52–8, at pp. 57–8.

42. Fourth Meeting of the Commission on Responsibilities, Minutes, 13 March 1919, USNA 181.1201/16, pp. 57–61, at pp. 58–9; USNA 181.1201/4 (M 820, Roll 141, 156–76), pp. 7–10; USNA 181.1201/4 (M 820, Roll 141, 177–98), pp. 6–10;

USNA 181.1201/4 (M 820, Roll 141, 199–209), p. 5; Recueil des actes, pp. 82–9, at p. 84–6; Paix de Versailles, pp. 339–52, at pp. 342–4; TNA FO 678/245, pp. 294–321, at pp. 302–8; USNA 181.1201/4 (M 820, Roll 141, 213–41 French), pp. 9–15; USNA 181.1201/4 (M 820, Roll 141, 242–55 French), pp. 5–8.

43. Fourth Meeting of the Commission on Responsibilities, Minutes, 13 March 1919, USNA 181.1201/4 (M 820, Roll 141, 199–209), p. 6; Paix de Versailles, pp. 339–52, at p. 348; TNA FO 678/245, pp. 294–321, at p. 316; USNA 181.1201/4 (M 820, Roll 141, 213–41 French), pp. 23–4; Paix de Versailles, pp. 339–52, at p. 350.

44. Fifth Meeting of the Commission on Responsibilities, 14 March 1919, Minutes: USNA 181.1201/16, pp. 62–6, at p. 64; Recueil des actes, pp. 90–6, at p. 93; USNA 181.1201/5 (M820, Roll 141, 264–81), p. 10; USNA 181.1201/5 (M820, Roll 141, 314–22), p. 5.

45. Fifth Meeting of the Commission on Responsibilities, 14 March 1919, Minutes: USNA 181.1201/16, pp. 62–6, at p. 65; Recueil des actes, pp. 90–6, at p. 95; USNA 181.1201/5 (M820, Roll 141, 264–81), p. 13; USNA 181.1201/5 (M820, Roll 141, 282–92), p. 7; USNA 181.1201/5 (M820, Roll 141, 314–22), p. 7.

46. Seventh Meeting of the Commission on Responsibilities, 17 March 1919, Minutes: USNA 181.1201/16, pp. 69–74, at p. 70; USNA 181.1201/7 (M 820, Roll 141, 403–23), pp. 3–4; USNA 181.1201/7 (M 820, Roll 141, 425–36), p. 3; Recueil des actes, pp. 100–7, at p. 101; Paix de Versailles, pp. 369–83, at p. 371; USNA 181.1201/7 (M 820, Roll 141, 464–92 French), pp. 5–6. Stenographic notes: TNA FO 678/245, pp. 355–82, at pp. 5–6.

47. Seventh Meeting of the Commission on Responsibilities, 17 March 1919, Minutes: USNA 181.1201/16, pp. 69–74, at p. 71; USNA 181.1201/7 (M 820, Roll 141, 403–23), pp. 8–9; USNA 181.1201/7 (M 820, Roll 141, 425–36), pp. 5–6; Recueil des actes, pp. 100–7, at p. 103; Paix de Versailles, pp. 369–83, at p. 374; USNA 181.1201/7 (M 820, Roll 141, 464–92 French), p. 11. Stenographic notes: TNA FO 678/245, pp. 355–82, at pp. 365–6.

48. Draft Report of the Commission, USNA 181.1201/16, pp. 83–96, at p. 93.

49. ibid. p. 91.

50. Eighth Meeting of the Commission on Responsibilities, 24 March 1919, Minutes: USNA 181.1201/16, pp. 76–82, at pp. 77–8; TNA FO 608/245, pp. 383–421, at p. 390; USNA 181.1201/8 (M 820, Roll 141, 555–60 French), p. 5; USNA 181.1201/8 (M 820, Roll 141, 566–99 French), p. 7; USNA 181.1201/8 (M 820, Roll 141, 600–15 French), p. 4; Paix de Versailles, pp. 413–22, at p. 415; Recueil des actes, pp. 109–18, at p. 111.

51. Ninth Meeting of the Commission on Responsibilities, 25 March 1919, Minutes: USNA 181.1201/16, pp. 97–102, at p. 101; USNA 181.1201/9 (M 820, Roll 141, 647–75), p. 26; USNA 181.1201/9 (M 820, Roll 141, 676–704), p. 27.

52. Ninth Meeting of the Commission on Responsibilities, 25 March 1919, Minutes: USNA 181.1201/16, pp. 97–102, at pp. 98–9; USNA 181.1201/9 (M 820, Roll 141, 647–75), pp. 5–10; USNA 181.1201/9 (M 820, Roll 141, 676–704), pp. 2–5; USNA 181.1201/9 (M 820, Roll 141, 714–47 French), pp. 8–14. Stenographic notes: TNA FO 608/245, pp. 422–62, at pp. 428–36.

53. Redraft of Chapter III of the Report, USNA 181.1201/16, pp. 107–8; Receuil des actes, pp. 155–6.

54. Tenth Meeting of the Commission on Responsibilities, 27 March 1919, Minutes: USNA 181.1201/16, pp. 103–8, at p. 105; USNA 181.1201/10 (M820, Roll 141, 774–94), p. 10; USNA 181.1201/10 (M820, Roll 141, 795–823), p. 12; USNA 181.1201/10 (M820, Roll 141, 824–57 French), p. 16. Stenographic notes: TNA FO 678/245, pp. 463–95, at pp. 477.

55. A. de Lapradelle and F. Larnaude, 'Inquiry into the Penal Liabilities of the Emperor William II', USNA 181.1201/16, pp. 4–18.

56. Memorandum submitted by the British delegates, 13 February 1919, USNA 181.1201/16, pp. 27–33, at p. 29; Recueil des actes, pp. 41–50, at p. 44.

57. Report of the Commission on Responsibilities, USNA 181.1201/16, pp. 112–76, at p. 126.

58. Draft Report of Sub-Commission III, USNA 181/12302/2, p. 8.

59. Second draft Report of Sub-Commission III, 8 March 1919, USNA 181.12302/3.

60. Meeting of Sub-Commission III, 8 March 1919, USNA 181.12301/6 (M 820, Roll 144, 140–64), pp. 11–12; TNA FO 608/246, pp. 11–12; USNA 181.12301/6 (M 820, Roll 144, 165–86), p. 8; USNA 181.12301/6 (M 820, Roll 144, 197–220 French), p. 8; Recueil des actes, pp. 359–66, at pp. 364–5.

61. Meeting of Sub-Commission III, 8 March 1919, USNA 181.12301/6 (M 820, Roll 144, 140–64), pp. 11–12; TNA FO 608/246, pp. 11–12; USNA 181.12301/6 (M 820, Roll 144, 165–86), pp. 2–3; USNA 181.12301/6 (M 820, Roll 144, 187–96), p. 2; USNA 181.12301/6 (M 820, Roll 144, 197–220 French), p. 4; Recueil des actes, pp. 359–66, at p. 360.

62. Meeting of Sub-Commission III, 8 March 1919, USNA 181.12301/6 (M 820, Roll 144, 140–64), pp. 11–12; TNA FO 608/246, pp. 11–12; USNA 181.12301/6 (M 820, Roll 144, 165–86), p. 4; USNA 181.12301/6 (M 820, Roll 144, 187–96), p. 3; USNA 181.12301/6 (M 820, Roll 144, 197–220 French), p. 5; Recueil des actes, pp. 359–66, at pp. 360–1.

63. Meeting of Sub-Commission III, 8 March 1919, USNA 181.12301/6 (M 820, Roll 144, 140–64), pp. 11–12; TNA FO 608/246, pp. 11–12; USNA 181.12301/6 (M 820, Roll 144, 165–86), p. 5; USNA 181.12301/6 (M 820, Roll 144, 187–96), p. 3; USNA 181.12301/6 (M 820, Roll 144, 197–220 French), pp. 5–6; Recueil des actes, pp. 359–66, at p. 361.

64. Meeting of Sub-Commission III, 8 March 1919, USNA 181.12301/6 (M 820, Roll 144, 140–64), pp. 11–12; TNA FO 608/246, pp. 11–12; USNA 181.12301/6 (M 820, Roll 144, 165–86), pp. 6–7; USNA 181.12301/6 (M 820, Roll 144, 187–96), pp. 3–4; USNA 181.12301/6 (M 820, Roll 144, 197–220 French), pp. 7–8; Recueil des actes, pp. 359–66, at p. 362.

65. Meeting of Sub-Commission III, 8 March 1919, USNA 181.12301/6 (M 820, Roll 144, 140–64), pp. 11–12; TNA FO 608/246, pp. 11–12; USNA 181.12301/6 (M 820, Roll 144, 165–86), p. 10; USNA 181.12301/6 (M 820, Roll 144, 197–220 French), p. 12; Recueil des actes, pp. 359–66, at p. 363.

66. Meeting of Sub-Commission III, 8 March 1919, USNA 181.12301/6 (M 820, Roll 144, 140–64), pp. 11–12; TNA FO 608/246, pp. 11–12; USNA 181.12301/6 (M 820, Roll 144, 165–86), pp. 11–12; USNA 181.12301/6 (M 820, Roll 144, 187–96), p. 4; USNA 181.12301/6 (M 820, Roll 144, 197–220 French), pp. 12–13; Recueil des actes, pp. 359–66, at p. 363.

67. Meeting of Sub-Commission III, 8 March 1919, USNA 181.12301/6 (M 820, Roll 144, 187–96), p. 4; TNA FO 608/246, p. 4; USNA 181.12301/6 (M 820, Roll 144, 197–220 French), p. 12; Recueil des actes, pp. 359–66, at p. 363.

68. Third Meeting of the Commission on Responsibilities, Minutes, 12 March 1919, USNA 181.1201/16, pp. 35–9, at pp. 36–7; USNA 181.1201/3 (M 820, Roll 141, 5–24), p. 57; USNA 181.1201/3 (M 820, Roll 141, 25–32), p. 3; USNA 181.1201/3 (M 820, Roll 141, 33–57), pp. 8–10; USNA 181.1201/3 (M 820, Roll 141, 58–69 French), p. 5; USNA 181.1201/3 (M 820, Roll 141, 70–91 French), pp. 6–7; Recueil des actes, pp. 52–8, at p. 54.

69. Fourth Meeting of the Commission on Responsibilities, Minutes, 13 March 1919, USNA 181.1201/16, pp. 57–61, at p. 59; USNA 181.1201/4 (M 820, Roll 141, 156–76), p. 10; USNA 181.1201/4 (M 820, Roll 141, 199–209), p. 5; Recueil des actes, pp. 82–9, at p. 86.

70. Fourth Meeting of the Commission on Responsibilities, Minutes, 13 March 1919, USNA 181.1201/16, pp. 57–61, at p. 60; USNA 181.1201/4 (M 820, Roll 141, 156–76), pp. 18–19; USNA 181.1201/4 (M 820, Roll 141, 199–209), p. 9; Recueil des actes, pp. 82–9, at p. 88; Paix de Versailles, pp. 339–52, at pp. 350–1; TNA FO 678/245, pp. 294–321, at pp. 317–18; USNA 181.1201/4 (M 820, Roll 141, 213–41 French), p. 24.

71. Fifth Meeting of the Commission on Responsibilities, 14 March 1919, Minutes: USNA 181.1201/16, pp. 62–6, at pp. 65–6; Recueil des actes, pp. 90–6, at p. 96; USNA 181.1201/5 (M820, Roll 141, 264–81), p. 16; USNA 181.1201/5 (M820, Roll 141, 282–92), p. 9; USNA 181.1201/5 (M820, Roll 141, 314–22), p. 8.

72. Draft Report of the Commission, USNA 181.1201/16, pp. 83–96, at p. 93.

73. Ninth Meeting of the Commission on Responsibilities, 25 March 1919, Minutes: USNA 181.1201/16, pp. 97–102, at p. 101; USNA 181.1201/9 (M 820, Roll 141, 647–75), p. 20; USNA 181.1201/9 (M 820, Roll 141, 676–704), pp. 20–1. Stenographic notes: TNA FO 608/245, pp. 422–62, at pp. 450–1.

74. Memorandum of reservations presented by the Representatives of the United States, 4 April 1919, USNA 181.1201/16, pp. 162–74.

CHAPTER 12

1. Paul Mantoux, *Les délibérations du conseil des quatre (24 mars–28 juin 1919)*, Paris: Centre national de la recherche scientifique, 1955. Citations to the proceedings that appear in the pages that follow are based principally upon the French-language notes of Mantoux. I have avoided strictly literal translation into English given that Mantoux's text is itself a translation from English into French, with the exception of remarks by Orlando and, possibly, by Clemenceau,

who used both languages. I felt that a degree of licence was desirable given the likelihood that some of what Wilson and Lloyd George said was inevitably lost in translation by Mantoux. This explains slight differences between the English citations in this book and the published English translation of the deliberations, which tends to be exceedingly literal and sometimes rather awkward.

2. Paul Mantoux, *Paris Peace Conference 1919, Proceedings of the Council of Four (March 24–April 18)*, Geneva: Droz, 1964; Arthur Link (ed.), *The Deliberations of the Council of Four (March 24–June 28, 1919), Notes of the Official Interpreter, Paul Mantoux*, Princeton, NJ: Princeton University Press, 1992.

3. Charles Hardinge, *Old Diplomacy*, London: John Murray, 1947, pp. 231–2.

4. Luigi Aldrovandi Marescotti, *Guerra diplomatica; ricordi e frammenti di diario (1914–1919)*, Milan: Mondadori, 1936; Luigi Aldrovandi Marescotti, *Nuovi ricordi e frammenti di diario*, Milan: Mondadori, 1938; Luigi Aldrovandi Marescotti, *Guerre diplomatique, 1914–1919*, Paris: Gallimard, 1939; Luigi Aldrovandi Marescotti, *Der Krieg der Diplomaten; Erinnerungen und Tagebuchauszüge, 1914–1919*, Munich: Paul Hugendubel, 1940.

5. Wilson probably had in mind Andrew Marvell's 'An Horation Ode upon Cromwell's Return from Ireland'.

6. Meeting of the Council of Four, 1 April 1919, Mantoux I, pp. 109–14, at p. 114; Deliberations I, pp. 110–11; WWP 56, p. 510.

7. Meeting of the Council of Four, 2 April 1919, 4 pm, Mantoux I, pp. 120–4; WWP 56, pp. 525–34; Deliberations I, pp. 115–24.

8. Grayson to Tumulty, 10 April 1919, WWP 57, p. 235.

9. Grayson Diary, 5 April 1919, WWP 57, p. 3; House Diary, 7 April 1919, WWP 57, p. 71.

10. ibid.

11. Edwin A. Weinstein, *Woodrow Wilson: A Medical and Psychological Biography*, Princeton, NJ: Princeton University Press, 1981, p. 342.

12. ibid. p. 344.

13. Lansing to Wilson, 4 April 1919, USNA 181.1202/7.

14. Robert Lansing, *The Peace Negotiations: A Personal Narrative*, Boston and New York: Houghton Mifflin, 1921, p. 47.

15. ibid. pp. 41–2.

16. Benham Diary, 8 April 1919, WWP 57, p. 141.

17. ibid.

18. Baker Diary, 19 May 1919, WWP 59, p. 285.

19. Lansing to Wilson, 8 April 1919, USNA 181.1202/7.

20. House Diary, 7 April 1919, WWP 57, p. 72.

21. Grayson Diary, WWP 57, p. 98.

22. *Dithmar and Boldt ('Llandovery Castle')*, (1922) 16 *American Journal of International Law* 708, (1921) 2 *International Law Reports* 437.

23. Meeting of the Council of Four, 8 April 1919, 3 pm, Mantoux I, pp. 184–92; WWP 57, pp. 121–30; Deliberations I, pp. 187–95.

24. House Diary, 8 April 1919, WWP 57, pp. 139–40, at p. 140.

25. Outline Suggested with regard to Responsibility and Punishment, LG F/147/8/9. A slightly different version of the text appears in Mantoux's notes of a Meeting of the Council of Four, 9 April 1919, 11 am, WWP 57, pp. 149–55, at pp. 149–50:

> Holland will be requested to deliver the ex-Kaiser to the Allied and Associated Powers, in order to be tried by a special tribunal. This tribunal will be composed of five judges designated respectively by the five following powers: the United States of America, Great Britain, France, Italy, and Japan. The crime for which it is proposed to bring the ex-Kaiser to trial will not be defined as a violation of the criminal law, but as a supreme offense against international morality and the sanctity of treaties. The penalty to be pronounced is left to the discretion of the court, which must follow the highest principles of international morality with a view to vindicating the solemn obligations of international agreements and the inviolability of international morality.

    Mantoux was the translator. The explanation for the variations may be that this was a translation into English of his original French version (Mantoux I, pp. 195–202, at p. 195), which was itself a translation from English.
26. Grayson Diary, 9 April 1919, WWP 57, p. 145.
27. Meeting of the Council of Four, 9 April 1919, 11 am, Mantoux I, pp. 195–202, at p. 196; WWP 57, pp. 149–55, at p. 150; Deliberations I, pp. 197–203, at p. 198. Hankey took official minutes of the 11 am meeting, but they record nothing of the discussion concerning war crimes and the Kaiser: FRUS PPC V, pp. 59–61.
28. Grayson Diary, 9 April 1919, WWP 57, p. 146.
29. Outline Suggested with regard to Responsibility and Punishment, LG F/147/8/9.
30. Hankey to Dutasta, 10 April 1919, TNA FO 608/247/12.
31. Grayson Diary, 9 April 1919, WWP 57, p. 146.
32. Wilson to Lansing, 9 April 1919, USNA 185.118/59; WWP 57, pp. 149, 631.
33. Lansing to Wilson, 10 April 1919, USNA 185.118/59.
34. ibid.
35. Meeting of the Council of Four and the Council of Foreign Ministers, 16 April 1919, 4 pm, Mantoux I, pp. 265–9, at p. 269; WWP 57, pp. 400–5, at p. 405; Deliberations I, pp. 265–9, at p. 269; FRUS PPC IV, p. 482.
36. Paul Hymans, *Mémoires*, Brussels: Université libre de Bruxelles, 1958, p. 479.
37. Meeting of the Council of Four and the Council of Foreign Ministers, 16 April 1919, 4 pm, Mantoux I, pp. 265–9, at p. 269; WWP 57, pp. 400–5, at p. 405; Deliberations I, pp. 265–9, at p. 269; FRUS PPC IV, p. 482.
38. Notes of a Meeting of the Dominion Prime Ministers, 11 April 1919, 9 am, TNA CAB 29/28.
39. Massey to Lloyd George, 24 April 1919, LG F/36/4/9.

CHAPTER 13

1. Draft clauses prepared by the Drafting Committee, FRUS PPC V, pp. 401–2.
2. 'Responsabilités et sanctions', *Le Temps*, 29 April 1919, p. 4; 'Arraignment of the Kaiser', *The Times*, 30 April 1919, p. 12.

3. Minutes of a Meeting of the British Empire Delegation, 28 April 1919 at 11 am, in M. Dockrill (ed.), *British Documents on Foreign Affairs, Series I, The Paris Peace Conference of 1919, British Empire Delegation Minutes, March–June 1919, Reports of Peace Conference Commissions*, Vol. IV, [Frederick, MD]: University Publications of America, 1989 pp. 55–7.

4. Borden to White, with Enclosure, 3 May 1919, WWP 58, pp. 415–16.

5. Meeting of the Council of Four, 1 May 1919, 11 am, FRUS PPC V, pp. 389–402; USNA 180.03401/135; WWP 58, pp. 277–96.

6. Arthur S. Link (ed.), *The Papers of Woodrow Wilson, April 23–May 9, 1919*, Vol. 58, Princeton, NJ: Princeton University Press, 1988, p. 278, fn. 3 (editorial footnote, presumably by Arthur S. Link).

7. James Brown Scott, 'The Trial of the Kaiser', in Edward M. House and Charles Seymour (eds), *What Really Happened at Paris?*, London: Hodder & Stoughton, 1921, pp. 231–58, at pp. 245–6.

8. ibid. p. 237.

9. Meeting of the Council of Four, 14 May 1919, 11.00 am (12.15 pm according to Hankey's minutes), Mantoux II, pp. 64–72, at pp. 70–1; Deliberations II, pp. 60–9, at p. 67; WWP 59, pp. 130–9, at p. 131; FRUS PPC V, pp. 605–13, at p. 605.

10. FRUS PPC V, pp. 401–2.

11. Robert Lansing, *The Big Four, and Others of the Peace Conference*, New York: Houghton Mifflin, 1921, p. 20.

12. USNA 180.0201/6, pp. 50–1; FRUS PPC III, pp. 388–90. For the French version of the declaration of Honduras: Conférence de Paix 1919–1920, *Recueil des Actes de la Conférence, Partie III*, Paris: Imprimerie Nationale, 1922, pp. 190–1; the declaration is annexed, at pp. 388–90.

13. Plenary Session, 6 May 1919, USNA 180.0201/6; FRUS PPC III, pp. 333–88, at p. 334.

14. Bonilla to Stabler, 3 May 1919, USNA 185.118/68.

15. H. W. V. Temperley (ed.), *A History of the Peace Conference of Paris*, Vol. II, London: Henry Frowde and Hodder & Stoughton, p. 1.

16. 'Address of Count Brockdorff-Rantzau of May 7, 1919', in *German White Book Concerning the Responsibility of the Authors of the War*, New York: Oxford University Press, 1924, pp. 3–5.

17. Note of Count Brockdorff-Rantzau, 13 May 1919, USNA 185.118/82.

18. Klotz to Clemenceau, 19 May 1919, WWP 59, p. 275; USNA 180.03401/19.

19. Draft letter, approved by Klotz, Scott, Lord Sumner, M. Crespi and M. Sakutaro Tachi, to be submitted to the Council of Four, WWP 59, pp. 275–6; USNA 180.03401/19.

20. Meeting of the Council of Four, 20 May 1919, 11 am, WWP 59, pp. 297–309, at p. 298; USNA 180/03401/20; FRUS PPC V, pp. 732–8, at p. 733. For the letter itself, see FRUS PPC V, pp. 743–4; 'Note of Clemenceau of May 20, 1919', in *German White Book Concerning the Responsibility of the Authors of the War*, New York: Oxford University Press, 1924, p. 7.

21. Meeting of the Council of Four, 12 June 1919, 4 pm, FRUS PPC VI, pp. 348–56, at p. 350.

22. Translation of Note from Herr Brockdorff-Rantzau, 24 May 1919, WWP 59, pp. 488–502, at p. 492; USNA 180.03401/32.

23. Observations on the Report of the Commission of the Allied and Associated Governments as to the Responsibility of the Authors of the War, 27 May 1919, TNA FO 371/4271; FRUS PPC VI, pp. 781–901; *German White Book Concerning the Responsibility of the Authors of the War*, New York: Oxford University Press, 1924. An original German version is in the United States Archives: USNA 185.118/120.

24. Memorandum Submitted to the Council of Principal Allied and Associated Powers by the Committee on Responsibilities in order to justify the articles of Conditions of Peace, CP 62, Appendix VIII, USNA 180.03401/62 and USNA 185.118/89; Memorandum présenté au Conseil des principales puissances alliées et associées par le Comité des responsabilités pour justifier les articles des conditions de paix, Scott Papers, Box 23.35b.

25. Meeting of the Council of Four, 12 June 1919, 11 am, Mantoux II, pp. 390–4; Deliberations II, pp. 401–5; WWP 60, pp. 436–62; FRUS PPC VI, pp. 324–47; USNA 180.03401/61.

26. Draft letter, USNA 180.03401/61; FRUS PPC VI, pp. 330–4; WWP 60, pp. 460–2.

27. Meeting of the Council of Four, 12 June 1919, 11 am, Mantoux II, pp. 390–4; Deliberations II, pp. 401–5; WWP 60, pp. 436–62; FRUS PPC VI, 324–47; USNA 180.03401/61.

28. Meeting of the Council of Four, 12 June 1919, 4 pm, Mantoux II, pp. 395–401, at p. 396; FRUS PPC VI, pp. 348–56; USNA 180.03401/62.

29. Reply of the Allied and Associated Powers to the Observations of the German Delegation on the Conditions of Peace, FRUS PPC XIII, pp. 544–5; Scott Papers, Box 24.6; H. W. V. Temperley (ed.), *A History of the Peace Conference of Paris*, Vol. II, London: Henry Frowde and Hodder & Stoughton, 1920, pp. 304–6 (excerpts).

30. Robert Lansing, *Some Legal Questions of the Peace Conference*, Washington, DC: Government Printing Office, 1919, p. 18.

31. Meeting of the Council of Four, 23 June 1919, 11 am, FRUS PPC VI, pp. 617–22, at pp. 617–20; WWP 61, pp. 82–8; USNA 180.03401/83; Mantoux II, pp. 482–90, at pp. 482–5; Deliberations II, pp. 520–7, at pp. 520–3.

32. Meeting of the Council of Four, 22 June 1919, 7.20 pm (7.15 pm according to Hankey's minutes), FRUS PPC VI, p. 607; WWP 61, p. 70; Mantoux II, pp. 478–80; Deliberations II, pp. 512–14.

33. Translation of German note, 22 June 1919, FRUS PPC VI, pp. 609–11; WWP 61, pp. 72–6; Deliberations II, pp. 515–18.

34. Grayson Diary, 22 June 1919, WWP 61, p. 69.

35. Meeting of the Council of Four, 22 June 1919, 7.20 pm (7.15 pm according to Hankey's minutes), FRUS PPC VI, p. 607; WWP 61, p. 70; Mantoux II, pp. 478–80; Deliberations II, pp. 512–14.

36. Meeting of the Principal Allied and Associated Powers, 22 June 1919, 9.00 pm, FRUS PPC VI, p. 607. For the full text of the reply, see Reply to German note of 22nd June 1919, WWP 61, pp. 76–7; USNA 180.03401/81; FRUS PPC VI, pp. 612–13.
37. Meeting of the Council of Four, 23 June 1919, 9 am, WWP 61, pp. 79–81; FRUS PPC VI, pp. 613–15; Mantoux II, p. 481; Deliberations II, pp. 519–20.
38. Meeting of the Council of Four, 23 June 1919, 4 pm, Mantoux II, pp. 491–6, at p. 491; Deliberations II, pp. 528–33, at p. 528.
39. Meeting of the Council of Four, 23 June 1919, 4 pm, Mantoux II, pp. 491–6, at p. 496; Deliberations II, pp. 528–33, at p. 533.
40. Meeting of the Council of Four, 23 June 1919, 5 pm, FRUS PPC VI, pp. 641–4, at p. 644; WWP 61, pp. 99–104, at p. 104; USNA 180.03401/86. For the note, FRUS PPC VI, p. 644.

CHAPTER 14

1. Meeting of the Imperial War Cabinet, 10 Downing Street, 28 November 1918, 11.45 am, TNA CAB 23/39, pp. 2–4, 8–11. Also, 'Our Attitude Towards the Ex-Kaiser', Extract from Minutes of a Meeting of the Imperial War Cabinet, 10 Downing Street, 28 November 1918, 11:45 am, RA PS/PSO/GV/CQ/1560/1; LG F/147/7/2.
2. Memorandum from Dr J. A. van Hamel, 6 May 1919, USNA 185/118/71; Scott Papers, Box 30.8b.
3. Curzon to Townley, 19 June 1919, TNA FO 608/144/3; TNA FO 371/4271.
4. Meeting of the Council of Four, 25 June 1919, 4 pm, FRUS PPC VI, pp. 669–78, at pp. 670–1; Mantoux II, pp. 511–21, at pp. 518–19; Deliberations II, pp. 546–57, at pp. 554–5.
5. Draft of communication to the Government of the Netherlands, WWP 61, pp. 200–1; FRUS PPC VI, pp. 705–6; USNA 180.03401/93.
6. Lansing to Wilson, 26 June 1919, WWP 61, p. 199; FRUS PPC VI, pp. 704–5.
7. Meeting of the Council of Five, 26 June 1919, 11 am, FRUS PPC VI, pp. 697–704, at p. 699; Mantoux II, pp. 522–9, at p. 524; Deliberations II, pp. 557–64, at p. 558. Also, Hankey to Dutasta, 27 June 1919, USNA 185.118/118.
8. Hankey to Berthelot, 27 June 1919, FMAE A/64, A-1025-4.
9. British Military Mission, 27 June 1919, TNA FO 608/144/3.
10. Curzon to Balfour, 27 June 1919, TNA FO 608/144/3.
11. Cypher telegram to Townley, 26 June 1919, TNA FO 608/144/3.
12. Townley to Curzon, 29 June 1919, TNA FO 371/4271.
13. Meeting of the Council of Five, 26 June 1919, 11 am, FRUS PPC VI, pp. 697–704, at p. 700; Mantoux II, pp. 522–9, at p. 523; Deliberations II, pp. 557–64, at pp. 558–60.
14. Hankey to Dutasta, 28 June 1919, USNA 185.118/124, including 'Altered Paragraph in Note as Handed to Dutch Government by French Minister'. Also

Meeting of the Council of Four, 28 June 1919, at 11 am, FRUS PPC VI, pp. 740–3, at p. 740.

15. Telegram to the Dutch Government, 26 June 1919, LG F/147/7/3; USNA 180.03401/95; USNA 185.118/117; USNA 185.118/119, FRUS PPC VI, p. 722. For the first draft of the telegram, see FRUS PPC VI, pp. 714–15. See also: Balfour to Townley, 1 July 1919, DBFP V, pp. 8–9.

16. Meeting of the Council of Four, 26 June 1919, at 4 pm, USNA 180.03401/93; FRUS PPC VI, pp. 710–14, at p. 710; TNA FO 371/4271; Mantoux II, pp. 530–40, at p. 535; Deliberations II, pp. 565–75, at pp. 569–70.

17. Robertson to Curzon, 1 July 1919, DBFP V, pp. 9–10. See also Prevost to Berthelot, 1 July 1919, FMAE A/64, A-1025-4.

18. Curzon to Balfour, 9 July 1919, DBFP V, pp. 21–2.

19. Robertson to Curzon, 1 July 1919, DBFP V, pp. 9–10; TNA FO 371/4271.

20. Prevost to Berthelot, 8 July 1919, FMAE A/64, A-1025-4; Robertson to Balfour, 10 July 1919, DBFP V, pp. 22–2.

21. Van Sandenburg to Van Karnebeek, 5 July 1919, BPNL 156, pp. 15–17; Sigurd von Ilsemann, *Der Kaiser in Holland, Aufzeichnungen des letzten Flügeladjutanten Kaiser Wilhelms II*, Vol. 1: *Amerongen und Doorn, 1918–1923*, Munich: Biederstein, 1968, p. 111.

22. Wilhelm Hohenzollern, *The Kaiser's Memoirs*, New York and London: Harper & Brothers, 1922, pp. 292–302.

23. Bethmann-Hollweg to Clemenceau, 25 June 1919, WWP 61, p. 340; TNA FO 371/4271; FRUS PPC VI, pp. 756–7.

24. Maurice Hankey, *The Supreme Control at the Paris Peace Conference 1919: A Commentary*, London: George Allen & Unwin, 1963, p. 190.

25. Meeting of the Council of Four, 28 June 1919, 4.15 pm (5.00 pm according to Hankey's minutes), Mantoux II, pp. 562–7, at pp. 562–3; Deliberations II, pp. 598–603, at pp. 598–9; WWP 61, pp. 334–41, at pp. 334–5; FRUS PPC VI, pp. 751–6, at pp. 751–2. Also, Hankey to Dutasta, 28 June 1919, USNA 185.118/125.

26. Hankey to Dutasta, 26 June 1919, TNA FO 147/1/12.

27. Memorandum, 4 July 1919, USNA 185.118/129.

28. Draft of Reply to the letter of Herr von Bethmann-Hollweg drawn up by the Committee on Responsibilities, in its Session of July 15, 1919, Scott Papers, Box 23.35b; TNA FO 371/4271; FMAE A/64, A-1025-4.

29. Meeting of the Heads of Delegations of the Five Great Powers, Quai d'Orsay, Paris, 29 July 1919, 3.30 pm, FRUS PPC VII, pp. 369–80, at p. 378.

30. Von Wieterscheim to Lloyd George, August 1919, TNA FO 371/4271; Von Wieterscheim to Clemenceau, August 1919, FMAE A/64, A-1025-4.

31. Von Lersner to Clemenceau, 5 August 1919, TNA FO 371/4271.

32. 'Ex Kaiser's Sons Offer to Suffer in His Stead', *New York Times*, 5 July 1919, p. 1.

33. Crown Prince to King, 9 February 1920 (translation), RA PS/PSO/GV/CQ/1560/1/39.

CHAPTER 15

1. Mantoux II, pp. 511–21, at p. 513.
2. Meeting of the Council of Four, 25 June 1919, 4 pm, USNA 180.03401/92; FRUS PPC VI, pp. 669–78, at pp. 670–1; Mantoux II, pp. 511–21, at pp. 512–13; Deliberations II, pp. 546–57, at pp. 554–5.
3. Meeting of the Council of Four, 26 June 1919, at 11 am, USNA 180.03401/93; FRUS PPC VI, pp. 697–704, at p. 701; Deliberations II, pp. 557–64, at pp. 558–60.
4. Memorandum on telephone call from Hankey to Buckingham Palace, 5 July 1919, 2.15 pm, RA PS/PSO/GV/CQ/1560/1/9.
5. Parliamentary Debates, House of Commons, 3 July 1919, Vol. 117, cc1216–17.
6. 'The Ex-Kaiser to be Tried in London', *Daily Mail*, 4 July 1919, p. 5.
7. 'Dutch to Give Up Kaiser for Trial', *New York Times*, 5 July 1919, p. 1.
8. Richard V. Oulahan, 'Premier Surprised Americans', *New York Times*, 4 July 1919, p. 1.
9. War Cabinet minute, 23 July 1919, TNA FO 371/4271.
10. Kenneth Rose, *King George V*, London: Macmillan, 1983, p. 229.
11. Harold Nicolson, *King George the Fifth: His Life and Reign*, London: Constable, 1952, p. 337.
12. Stephen Roskill, *Hankey: Man of Secrets*, Vol. II: *1919–1931*, London: Collins, 1972, p. 99.
13. Letter from Stamfordham to J. T. Davies (at 10 Downing Street), 7 July 1919, RA PS/PSO/GV/CQ/1560/1/10.
14. Hankey to Stamfordham, 8 July 1919, RA PS/PSO/GV/CQ/1560/1/13.
15. Stamfordham to Hankey, 11 July 1919, RA PS/PSO/GV/CQ/1560/1/16 (emphasis in the original).
16. Hankey to Stamfordham, 11 July 1919, RA PS/PSO/GV/CQ/1560/1/17.
17. Bishop of Chelmsford (Rev. JE Watts-Ditchfield) to Stamfordham, 10 July 1919, RA PS/PSO/GV/CQ/1560/1/14.
18. Bowles to Stamfordham, 11 July 1919, RA PS/PSO/GV/CQ/1560/1/17.
19. Leonard Mosley, *Curzon: The End of an Epoch*, London: Longmans, 1960, p. 188.
20. Alan Sharp, *David Lloyd George*, London: Haus Publishing, 2008, pp. 178–179.
21. Curzon to Lloyd George, 7 July 1919, LG F/12/1/21.
22. Curzon to Stamfordham, 8 July 1919, RA PS/PSO/GV/CQ/1560/1/11.
23. Curzon to Lloyd George, 7 July 1919, LG F/12/1/21.
24. Lloyd George to Curzon, 8 July 1919, LG F/12/1/22.
25. Curzon to Lloyd George, 9 July 1919, LG F/12/11/23.
26. War Cabinet 598, 23 July 1919, TNA FO 372/4271.
27. William Camp, *The Glittering Prizes: A Biographical Study of F. E. Smith, First Earl of Birkenhead*, London: Macgibbon & Kee, 1960, p. 122.
28. Kapt.-Leut. Waldemar Kolle, Minute to file by Hurst, 30 June 1919, TNA FO 608/247/13.
29. Memorandum, C. B. Hurst, 12 July 1919, TNA FO 608/146/3.

30. Minutes of the Steering Committee of the American Delegation, FRUS PPC XI, pp. 453–79.

31. Memorandum, C. B. Hurst, 12 July 1919, Scott Papers, Box 23.35b.

32. War Cabinet, The Trial of the Kaiser, Note by the Secretary, 29 July 1919, RA PS/PSO/GV/CQ/1560/1/20; TNA CAB/24/85.

33. Hewart to Pollock, 15 August 1919, TNA TS 26/3.

34. Hurst to Woods, 12 November 1919, TNA TS 26/2; TNA FO 608/146/3; Woods to Hurst, 13 November 1919, TNA TS 26/3; TNA FO 608/146/3.

35. Woods to Malkin, 9 September 1919, TNA TS/3/43; Constant to Woods, 17 September 1919, TNA TS/3/43; Woods to Constant, 19 September 1919, TNA TS/3/43.

36. Woods to Macdonnell, 20 September 1919, TNA TS/3/43.

37. Woods to Branson, 16 October 1919, TNA TS/3/43.

38. Mellor to Bellot, 20 August 1919, TNA TS 26/3.

39. Woods to Hutchison & Co., 20 August 1919, TNA TS 26/3.

40. Woods to Branson, 5 September 1919, TNA TS 26/3; Woods to Pollock, 9 September 1919, TNA TS 26/3.

41. Woods to Butterworth, 29 October 1919, TNA TS 26/3. And for the courteous reply: Butterworth to Woods, 30 October 1919, TNA TS 26/3.

42. Frederick Pollock to Woods, 19 September 1919, TNA TS/3/43.

43. ibid.

44. Woods to Frederick Pollock, 22 September 1919, TNA TS/3/43.

45. Woods to Mellor, 22 September 1919, TNA TS/3/43.

46. Memorandum by Mr Headlam Morley, 14 December 1918, TNA FO 371/3227; TNA FO/608/247.

47. Woods to Under-Secretary of State, 23 October 1919, TNA TS/3/43.

48. Headlam Morley to Norman, 22 October 1919, TNA FO 608/147/1/12.

49. ibid.

50. Norman to Headlam Morley, 22 October 1919, TNA FO 608/147/1/12.

51. Minute of Curzon, 25 October 1919, TNA FO 608/147/1/12.

52. Minute of Norman, 25 October 1919, TNA FO 608/147/1/12.

53. Woods to Branson, 3 December 1919, TNA TS 3/43.

54. 'July 5, 1914. The Potsdam War Conspiracy. New Wilhlemstrasse Documents. Kautsky's Survey', The Times, 29 November 1919, p. 13.

55. Woods to Mellor, 16 January 1920, TNA TS 26/2.

56. 'The Ambassador at Vienna to the Imperial Chancellor, Vienna, June 30, 1914', in Max Montgelas and Walter Schücking (eds), Outbreak of the World War: German Documents Collected by Karl Kautsky, New York: Oxford University Press, 1924, p. 61 (emphasis in the original).

57. 'The Minister at Belgrade to the Foreign Office, Belgrade, July 24, 1914', in Max Montgelas and Walter Schücking (eds), Outbreak of the World War: German Documents Collected by Karl Kautsky, New York: Oxford University Press, 1924, p. 186.

58. Woods to Ernest Pollock, 5 December 1919, TNA TS 3/43.

59. Woods to Frederick Pollock, 11 December 1919, TNA TS 3/43; Woods to Branson, 11 December 1919, TNA TS 3/43.

60. Article 227 of the Treaty of Peace, The Arraignment of William II of Hohenzollern, Memorandum on the Responsibility of William II of Hohenzollern for Acts Committed in Breach of the Laws of War, TNA TS 26/1, p. 12.

61. ibid. p. 15.

62. ibid. p. 42.

63. ibid. p. 147.

64. ibid. p. 150.

65. ibid. p. 157, citing Ernst Müller-Meiningen, *Who Are the Huns? The Law of Nations and Its Breakers*, Berlin: Georg Reimer, 1915, p. 6.

66. ibid. p. 173.

67. ibid. p. 192.

68. ibid. pp. 196–7.

69. ibid. p. 201.

70. ibid. p. 211.

71. ibid. p. 213.

72. ibid. pp. 227–8.

73. ibid. p. 230.

74. ibid. p. 239.

75. ibid. p. 247.

76. ibid. p. 297.

77. ibid. p. 1.

78. ibid. p. 11.

CHAPTER 16

1. Sigurd von Ilsemann, *Der Kaiser in Holland, Aufzeichnungen des letzten Flügeladjutanten Kaiser Wilhelms II*, Vol. 1: *Amerongen und Doorn, 1918–1923*, Munich: Biederstein, 1968, p. 108.

2. Bunshiro Suzuki, 'Ex-Kaiser Turned Pale', *Japan Gazette*, 9 June 1919; Bunshiro Suzuki, 'How "Little Willie" Loves Japan', *Japan Gazette*, 10 June 1919.

3. Van Houten to Inspector of the Marechaussee, 29 March 1920, DNA 2.13.44 inventaris 139.

4. Bunshiro Suzuki, 'Ex-Kaiser Turned Pale', *Japan Gazette*, 9 June 1919; Bunshiro Suzuki, 'How "Little Willie" Loves Japan', *Japan Gazette*, 10 June 1919.

5. Graham to Curzon, 17 December 1919, DBFP V, pp. 924–9; TNA FO 371/4272; RA PS/PSO/GV/CQ/1560/1/22.

6. Robertson to Curzon, 20 August 1919, DBFP V, p. 230.

7. Graham to Curzon, 11 December 1919, TNA FO 371/4272.

8. Graham to Curzon, 17 December 1919, DBFP V, pp. 924–9, at p. 925; RA PS/PSO/GV/CQ/1560/1/22; TNA FO 371/4272.

9. Edwin L. James, 'Ex-Kaiser Is Busy on His Defence', *New York Times*, 27 December 1919, p. 1.

10. John C. G. Röhl, *Wilhelm II: Into the Abyss of War and Exile 1900–1941*, Cambridge: Cambridge University Press, 2014, p. 1197, citing Haehner's diary in the Stadarchiv Cologne.

11. Graham to Curzon, 17 December 1919, DBFP V, pp. 924–9, at p. 925; RA PS/ PSO/GV/CQ/1560/1/22; TNA FO 371/4272.

12. Graham to Curzon, 17 December 1919, DBFP V, pp. 924–9, at p. 926; TNA FO 371/4272.

13. ibid.

14. 'Ex-Kaiser Threatened by Floods', *The Times*, 5 January 1920, p. 12.

15. Graham to Curzon, 30 January 1920, LG F/57/3/9; DBFP IX, pp. 621–4.

16. Sigurd von Ilsemann, *Der Kaiser in Holland, Aufzeichnungen des letzten Flügeladjutanten Kaiser Wilhelms II*, Vol. 1: *Amerongen und Doorn, 1918–1923*, Munich: Biederstein, 1968, p. 113.

17. Graham to Curzon, 12 March 1920, DBFP IX, pp. 706–10.

18. Graham to Curzon, 20 March 1920, DBFP IX, pp. 718–20.

19. Graham to Curzon, 17 May 1920, LG F/12/3/34.

20. ibid.

21. ibid.

22. John C. G., Röhl, *Wilhelm II: Into the Abyss of War and Exile 1900–1941*, Cambridge: Cambridge University Press, 2014, p. 1192, citing Willibald Gutsche, *Ein Kaiser im Exil: Der letzte deutsche Kaiser Wilhelm II in Holland. Eine kritische Biographie*, Marburg: Hitzeroth, 1991, p. 202.

23. Benoist to Cambon, 3 February 1920, FMAE A/64, A-1025-4; 'Ex-Kaiser Presents Hospital to Amerongen; His Aide Weds Countess Elizabeth Bentinck', *New York Times*, 24 September 1920.

24. John Pollard, *The Papacy in an Age of Totalitarianism*, Oxford: Oxford University Press, 2014, p. 79; S. A. Stehlin, 'The Emergence of a New Vatican Diplomacy During the Great War and Its Aftermath, 1914–1929', in P. C. Kent and John Pollard (eds), *Papal Diplomacy in the Modern Age*, Westport, CT: Praeger, 1991, pp. 75–86.

25. Gasparri to Gaisford, 23 June 1919, TNA FO 371/4271.

26. Balfour to Curzon, 22 July 1919, TNA FO 371/4271.

27. Cossio to Wilson, Enclosure, 1 July 1919, WWP 62, pp. 26–7.

28. Wilson to Benedict XV, 15 August 1919, WWP 62, pp. 26–7.

29. Van Karnebeek to The Queen, 18 July 1919, BPNL 156, pp. 48–9, at p. 48; Gasparri to Balfour, 4 July 1919, DBFP V, p. 17; TNA FO 608/147/1/12.

30. Van Lynden van Sandenburg recording, 2 August 1918, BPNL 156, p. 188.

31. Van Lynden van Sandenburg to Van Karnebeek, 29 July 1919, BPNL pp. 186–8, at p. 187.

32. Van Karnebeek Diary, 15 July 1919, DNA 2.05.25 inventaris 54; BPNL 156, p. 28.

33. Van Karnebeek to The Queen, 18 July 1919, BPNL 156, pp. 48–9, at p. 49.

34. De Salis to Curzon, 26 January 1920, DBFP IX, pp. 619–20; TNA FO 371/4272.

35. Rodd to 'George', 18 August 1919, LG F/56/2/35.

36. Van Panhuys to Van Karnebeek, 9 September 1919, BBBNA 156, pp. 171–2, at p. 171.

37. Cited in Simeon E. Baldwin, 'The Proposed Trial of the Former Kaiser' (1919) 29 *Yale Law Journal* 75, at p. 81.

38. Notes of a Meeting of the Heads of Delegations of the Five Great Powers, 15 September 1919, FRUS PPC VIII, p. 214.

39. The Ex-Emperor of Germany, TNA FO 371/4271.

40. The translation in the Royal Archives is slightly different: Saxony, Wurtemberg and Baden to George V, 7, 22 and 26 November 1919, RA PS/PSO/GV/CQ/1560/1/25.

41. Bard to Foreign Ministry, 21 January 1920, FMAE A/64, A-1025-4; Royen to Van Karnebeek, 7 December 1919, BPNL 156, pp. 333–4.

42. Howard to Curzon, 31 January 1920, DBFP IX, pp. 624–6.

43. Sweerts de Landan Wyborgh to Van Karnebeek, 5 December 1919, BPNL 156, pp. 332–3.

44. Cromer to Hardinge, 16 January 1919, RA PS/PSO/GV/CQ/1560/1/27.

45. Hardinge to Lloyd George and Curzon, 17 January 1920, RA PS/PSO/GV/CQ/1560/1/30.

46. Hardinge to Lloyd George, 17 January 1920, LG F/12/3/2.

47. Draft reply, approved by King, 24 January 1920, RA PS/PSO/GV/CQ/1560/1/35; LG F/12/3/2.

48. Cromer to Hardinge, 25 January 1919, RA PS/PSO/GV/CQ/1560/1/36. See also Harold Nicolson, *King George the Fifth: His Life and Reign*, London: Constable, 1952, pp. 337–8.

49. Curzon to Balfour, 9 July 1919, DBFP V, pp. 21–2.

50. Lord Rosebury to Stamfordham, 10 July 1919, RA PS/PSO/GV/CQ/1560/1/15.

51. Bowles to Stamfordham, 11 July 1919, RA PS/PSO/GV/CQ/1560/1/17.

52. Esher to Stamfordham, 8 July 1919, RA PS/PSO/GV/CQ/1560/1/12.

53. Curzon to Lloyd George, 7 July 1919, LG F/12/1/21.

54. Curzon to Robertson, 17 July 1919, TNA FO 608/144/3; TNA FO 371/4271; DBFP V, pp. 35–9.

55. ibid.

56. ibid.

57. Van Swinderen to Van Karnebeek, 31 July 1919, BPNL 156, pp. 68–9, at p. 68; Van Karnebeek to The Queen, 18 July 1919, BPNL 156, pp. 48–9, at p. 48.

58. Robertson to Curzon, 3 July 1919, DBFP V, pp. 14–15.

59. Robertson to Curzon, 3 July 1919, DBFP V, pp. 10–11; TNA FO 371/4271.

60. Robertson to Curzon, 1 August 1919, DBFP V, pp. 83–5; TNA FO 371/4271.

61. Robertson to Curzon, 19 September 1919, TNA FO 371/4271.

62. Robertson to Curzon, 8 August 1919, DBFP V, p. 178.

63. Robertson to Curzon, 24 September 1919, DBFP V, p. 571; TNA FO 371/4271.

64. J. A. van Hamel, 'The Trial of the Ex-Kaiser', *Amsterdammer*, 18 October 1919. English translation annexed to Robertson to Curzon, 21 October 1919, TNA FO 371/4271.

65. 'The Ex-Kaiser', *Handelsblad*, 25 October 1919, English translation in Graham to Curzon, 29 October 1919, TNA FO 371/4271

66. 'A Dangerous Advice', *Het Weekblad van het Recht*, 25 October 1919, English translation in Graham to Curzon, 29 October 1919, TNA FO 371/4271.

67. Graham to Curzon, 19 December 1919, FO 371/4272.

68. Translation from the *Handelsblad* evening edition, 19 December 1919, TNA TS 26/2. See also Kirsten Sellars, 'The First World War, Wilhelm II and Article 227: The Origin of the Idea of "Aggression" in International Criminal Law', in Claus Kreß and Stefan Barriga (eds), *The Crime of Aggression: A Commentary*, Cambridge: Cambridge University Press, 2017, pp. 21–48, at p. 44; and Kirsten Sellars, 'Trying the Kaiser: The Origins of International Criminal Law', in Morten Bergsmo, Cheah Wui Ling, and Yi Ping (eds), *Historical Origins of International Criminal Law*, Vol. 1, Brussels: Torkel Opsahl Academic EPublisher, 2014, pp. 195–212.

69. Graham to Curzon, 11 December 1919, TNA FO 371/4272.

70. Notes of an Anglo-French Conference, 10 Downing Street, 13 December 1919, 11 am, DBFP II, pp. 753–65, at pp. 758–60.

71. ibid.

72. Notes of an Anglo-French Conference, 10 Downing Street, 13 December 1919, 3.30 pm, DBFP II, pp. 772–5, at p. 774.

73. Conferences of the Allied and Associated Powers and of the British and French Governments, 10 Downing Street, 11, 12 and 13 December, Text of Resolutions, DBFP II, pp. 782–4, at p. 783; Curzon to Graham, 16 December 1919, TNA FO 371/4272.

74. Henri Mordacq, *Le Ministère Clemenceau, Journal d'un témoin*, Vol. IV, Paris: Plon, 1931, pp. 227–9, 292–300.

75. Graham to Curzon, 11 December 1919, TNA FP 371/4272.

76. Graham to Curzon, 17 December 1919, DBFP V, pp. 924–9; TNA FO 371/4272; RA PS/PSO/GV/CQ/1560/1/22. See also Graham's account in his Annual Report to the Foreign Office: TNA FO 371/3848, pp. 4–5.

CHAPTER 17

1. See above, pp. 215–16.

2. Henri Mordacq, *Le Ministère Clemenceau, Journal d'un témoin*, Vol. IV, Paris: Plon, 1931, pp. 292–3.

3. Draft of the French Delegation, 12 January 1920, DBFP II, pp. 889–90. For the handwritten first draft, see FMAE A/64, A-1025-4.

4. Draft Note to the Netherlands prepared by Drafting Committee, 10 January 1920, DBFP II, p. 890.

5. Meeting of the Heads of Delegations of the British, French, and Italian Governments, Quai d'Orsay, 15 January 1920, 3 pm, DBFP II, pp. 884–9, at pp. 884–6.

6. Notes of a Meeting of the Supreme Council, 16 January 1920, 4 pm, DBFP II, pp. 910–12; USNA 180.03801/7; FRUS PPC IX, pp. 883–6.

7. Draft Note to the Queen of Holland demanding the Delivery of the Kaiser for Trial, 15 January 1920, DBFP II, pp. 912–13; FMAE A/64, A-1025-4; USNA 180.03801/7; FRUS PPC IX, pp. 887–8; Derby to Curzon, 24 January 1920, TNA FO 371/4272. The note was published: 'Demand for the Ex-Kaiser, Allied Note to Holland', *The Times*, 19 January 1920, p. 12.

8. Graham to Curzon, 19 January 1920, DBFP IX, pp. 611–12; TNA FO 371/4272.

9. Graham to Hardinge, 20 January 1920, DBFP IX, p. 612; TNA FO 371/4272. Also, Benoist to Foreign Ministry, 19 January 1920, FMAE A/64, A-1025-4.

10. Graham to Hardinge, 23 January 1920, DBFP IX, p. 613; Benoist to Foreign Ministry, 20 January 1920, FMAE A/64, A-1025-4.

11. Graham to Curzon, 19 January 1920, DBFP IX, pp. 611–12; TNA FO 371/4272.

12. Henri Mordacq, *Le Ministère Clemenceau, Journal d'un témoin*, Vol. IV, Paris: Plon, 1931, p. 293.

13. Note from the Dutch Government relative to the delivery of the ex-Emperor of Germany, 24 January 1920, Appendix A, USNA 180.03301/1; FMAE A/64, A-1025-4; *Mededeelingen van den Minister Buitenlandsche Zaken aan de Staten-Generaal Juni 1919–April 1920*, pp. 12–13; BPNL 156, pp. 391–2; Derby to Curzon, 24 January 1920, TNA FO 371/4272. The note was published: 'The Kaiser, Extradition Refused', *The Times*, 24 January 1920, p. 12. For drafts of the note, see Heemskerk to Van Karnebeek, 15 January 1919, BPNL 156, pp. 384–5; also BPNL 156, pp. 392–5.

14. Graham to Hardinge, 23 January 1920, DBFP IX, p. 613; TNA FO 371/4272; Graham to Hardinge, 24 January 1920, DBFP IX, p. 613; TNA FO 371/4272.

15. Graham to Curzon, 30 January 1920, LG F/57/3/9; DBFP IX, pp. 621–4.

16. Michiels van Verduynen to Van Karnebeek, 19 January 1920, BPNL 156, p. 389.

17. Graham to Hardinge, 1 February 1920, DBFP IX, pp. 627–8.

18. 'Wanted', *Punch, or the London Charivari*, 21 January 1920.

19. 'The Ex-Kaiser, Drama or Comedy?', *Telegraaf*, 28 January 1920.

20. Notes of a meeting held in Mr Millerand's room, 26 January 1920, 10.30 am, USNA 180.03301/1; Derby to Curzon, 26 January 1920, DBFP IX, p. 617.

21. Graham to Curzon, 20 March 1920, DBFP IX, pp. 718–26, at p. 720.

22. For Hardinge's account of the episode, see Charles Hardinge, *Old Diplomacy*, London: John Murray, 1947, pp. 247–8.

23. Hardinge to Graham, 28 January 1920, DBFP IX, p. 620; TNA FO 371/4272.

24. Graham to Curzon, 30 January 1920, LG F/57/3/9; DBFP IX, pp. 621–4.

25. Van Karnebeek Diary, 29 January 1920, DNA 2.05.25 inventaris 54; BPNL 156, pp. 417–81.

26. F. Larnaude and A. de Lapradelle, 'Inquiry into the Penal Liabilities of the Emperor William II', in Commission on the Responsibility of the Authors of the War, Minutes of Meetings of the Commission, USNA 181.1201/16, pp. 4–18, at p. 17.

27. Refusal of the Netherlands Government to Surrender the Ex-Kaiser, Possible Reprisals, DBFP IX, pp. 628–30; TNA FO 371/4272.

28. ibid.

29. B. de Jong van Beek en Donk, 'Switzerland, Holland, and the League of Nations' (1920) 82 *The Advocate of Peace* 22, at pp. 24–5. See also: Robertson to Curzon, 25 September 1919, DBFP V, pp. 571–2; Graham to Curzon, 16 December 1919, DBFP V, p. 924.

30. Memorandum by Sir E. Crowe, Internment of the Ex-Emperor, 17 March 1920, DBFP IX, pp. 713–16.

31. Draft of Reply to Holland (Extradition of the Ex-Emperor), Note of the French Delegation, Annex A, USNA 180.03301/4; Projet de réponse à la Hollande (Extradition de l'ex-Empereur), DBFP IX, pp. 635–7; FMAE A/64, A-1025-4.

32. Meeting of the Conference of Ambassadors at the Quai d'Orsay, 3 February 1920, 11.30 am, USNA 180.03301/4; Derby to Curzon, 3 February 1920, DBFP IX, pp, 634–5.

33. Loudon to Van Karnebeek, 3 February 1920, BPNL 156, p. 432.

34. Graham to Curzon, 30 January 1920, LG F/57/3/9; DBFP IX, pp. 621–4.

35. Birkenhead to Lloyd George, 27 January 1920, LG F/4/7/14.

36. Hardinge to Graham, 31 January 1920, DBFP IX, p. 624; TNA FO 371/4272.

37. Graham to Hardinge, 1 February 1920, DBFP IX, pp. 627–8; TNA FO 371/4272.

38. Graham to Curzon, 4 February 1920, DBFP IX, pp. 646–8; Van Karnebeek Diary, 2 February 1920, DNA 2.05.25 inventaris 54, BPNL 156, pp. 423–4.

39. Van Karnebeek to London, 5 February 1920, BPNL 156, p. 434 (internal Dutch diplomatic correspondence was often in French).

40. Graham to Curzon, 4 February 1920, DBFP IX, pp. 646–8; Van Karnebeek Diary, 2 February 1920, DNA 2.05.25 inventaris 54.

41. Graham to Curzon, 4 February 1920, DBFP IX, pp. 646–8.

42. Benoist to Millerand, 2 February 1920, FMAE A/64, A-1025-4.

43. Millerand to Benoist, undated, FMAE A/64, A-1025-4.

44. Benoist to Millerand, 3 February 1920, FMAE A/64, A-1025-4. See also: Charles Benoist, *Souvenirs de Charles Benoist, 1902–1933*, Vol. III, Paris: Plon, 1933, pp. 388–90.

45. Cambon to Millerand, 3 February 1920, FMAE A/64, A-1025-4.

46. See Cabinet minutes, 5 February 1920, BPNL 156, p. 433.

47. Graham to Curzon, 6 February 1920, DBFP IX, pp. 662–3.

48. Benoist to Millerand, 7 February 1920, FMAE A/64, A-1025-4; Charles Benoist, *Souvenirs de Charles Benoist, 1902–1933*, Vol. III, Paris: Plon, 1933, pp. 392–3.

49. Benoist to Millerand, 7 February 1920, FMAE A/64, A-1025-4.

50. Graham to Curzon, 6 February 1920, DBFP IX, pp. 662–3.

51. Graham to Curzon, 7 February 1920, DBFP IX, p. 671.

52. Stamfordham to King George V, 4 February 1920, RA PS/PSO/GV/CQ/1560/1/38.

53. Notes of an Allied Conference, 10 Downing Street, 12 February 1920, 3.30 pm, DBFP VII, pp. 12–21, at p. 21.

54. Notes of an Allied Conference, 10 Downing Street, 13 February 1920, 11.30 am, DBFP VII, pp. 22–8, at p. 24.

55. Projet de réponse à la Hollande, 13 February 1920, DBFP VII, pp. 29–31.

56. Notes of an Allied Conference, 10 Downing Street, 13 February 1920, 11.30 am, DBFP VII, pp. 22–8, at p. 25.

57. ibid.

58. ibid., p. 26.

59. ibid.

60. Notes of an Allied Conference, 10 Downing Street, 13 February 1920, 4.00 pm, DBFP VII, pp. 31–41, at p. 37; Notes of an Allied Conference, 10 Downing Street, 14 February 1920, 10.30 am, DBFP VII, pp. 42–51, at p. 42.

61. Texte de la réponse à la Hollande (Extradition de l'ex-Empereur), FMAE A/64, A-1025-4; BPNL 156, pp. 490–2. The note was published: 'Ex-Kaiser Still Intriguing, Allies' Advice to Holland', The Times, 17 February 1920, p. 18.

62. Curzon to Graham, 14 February 1920, DBFP IX, pp. 681–2.

63. Graham to Curzon, 16 February 1920, DBFP IX, pp. 682–4.

64. Graham to Curzon, 23 February 1920, DBFP IX, pp. 685–6.

65. ibid.

66. Notes of an Allied Conference, 10 Downing Street, 24 February 1920, 11.00 am, DBFP VII, pp. 217–28, at p. 220.

67. ibid. pp. 220–1.

68. ibid. pp. 221–2.

69. ibid. pp. 222–3.

70. Louden to Van Karnebeek, 19 January 1920, BPNL 156, p. 389. Also, Van Karnebeek to Van Royen, 5 February 1920, BPNL 156, p. 434; Van Royen to Van Karnebeek, 11 February 1920, BPNL 156, p. 453.

71. Notes of an Allied Conference, 10 Downing Street, 24 February 1920, 11.00 am, DBFP VII, pp. 217–28, at p. 223.

72. ibid.

73. ibid. p. 225.

74. Notes of an Allied Conference, 10 Downing Street, 25 February 1920, 11.30 am, DBFP VII, pp. 238–49, at p. 249.

75. Graham to Curzon, 27 February 1920, DBFP IX, pp. 690–1.

76. Graham to Curzon, 26 February 1920, DBFP IX, pp. 688–9; Benoist to Millerand, 26 February 1920, FMAE A/64, A-1025-4; Charles Benoist, Souvenirs de Charles Benoist, 1902–1933, Vol. III, Paris: Plon, 1933, pp. 396–7.

77. Graham to Curzon, 27 February 1920, DBFP IX, pp. 690–1.

78. ibid.

79. Van Karnebeek Diary, 4 March 1920, DNA 2.05.25 inventaris 54; BPNL 156, p. 487.

80. Van Karnebeek to Lloyd George, 2 March 1920, BPNL 156, pp. 493–4.

81. Benoist to Millerand, 5 March 1920, FMAE A/64, A-1025-4.

82. ibid.

83. Notes of an Allied Conference, 10 Downing Street, 5 March 1920, 3.00 pm, DBFP VII, pp. 423–30, at p. 425. See also: Van Swinderen to Van Karnebeek, 5 March 1920, BPNL 156, pp. 488–90.

84. ibid. p. 426.

85. ibid. p. 428.

86. Telegram to His Britannic Majesty's representative at The Hague, 6 March 1920, FMAE A/64, A-1025-4.

87. Millerand to Cambon, 6 March 1920, FMAE A/64, A-1025-4.

88. Prévost to Millerand, 8 March 1920, FMAE A/64, A-1025-4.

89. Millerand to Prévost, 10 March 1920, FMAE A/64, A-1025-4.

90. Prevost to Millerand, 9 March 1920, FMAE A/64, A-1025-4.

91. Graham to Curzon, 8 March 1920, DBFP IX, p. 700; Graham to Curzon, 9 March 1920, DBFP IX, pp. 700–1 and 702–4; Prevost to Millerand, 8 March 1920, FMAE A/64, A-1025-4; Prévost to Millerand, 9 March 1920, FMAE A/64, A-1025-4.

92. Graham to Curzon, 9 March 1920, DBFP IX, pp. 702–4.

93. ibid. pp. 700–1.

94. ibid.

95. Graham to Curzon, 12 March 1920, DBFP IX, pp. 706–10, at p. 706.

96. Prévost to Millerand, 13 March 1920, FMAE A/64, A-1025-4.

97. Graham to Curzon, 12 March 1920, DBFP IX, pp. 706–10, at p. 706.

98. ibid. pp. 706–10.

99. ibid.

100. ibid.

101. Minute by Crowe, Graham to Curzon, 20 March 1920, DBFP IX, p. 719.

102. Curzon to Graham, 14 March 1920, DBFP IX, p. 711.

103. Notes of an Allied Conference, 10 Downing Street, 15 March 1920, 12 noon, DBFP VII, pp. 492–506, at p. 493.

104. Sigurd von Ilsemann, *Der Kaiser in Holland, Aufzeichnungen des letzten Flügeladjutanten Kaiser Wilhelms II*, Vol. 1: *Amerongen und Doorn, 1918–1923*, Munich: Biederstein, 1968, p. 149.

105. John C. G. Röhl, *Wilhelm II: Into the Abyss of War and Exile 1900–1941*, Cambridge: Cambridge University Press, 2014, p. 1223, citing Haehner's diary in the Stadarchiv Cologne.

106. Graham to Curzon, 15 March 1920, DBFP IX, pp. 711–12.

107. Memorandum by Sir E. Crowe, Internment of the Ex-Emperor, 17 March 1920, DBFP IX, pp. 713–16.

108. Telegram en clair from Sir R. Graham, 17 March 1920, DBFP VII, p. 552.

109. ibid.

110. Graham to Curzon, 17 March 1920, DBFP IX, p. 716.

111. Graham to Curzon, 20 March 1920, DBFP IX, pp. 718–20.

112. Notes of an Allied Conference, 10 Downing Street, 18 March 1920, 4 pm, DBFP VII, pp. 542–51, at pp. 549–50. Also, Berthelot to Millerand, 19 March 1920, FMAE A/64, A-1025-4.

113. Draft Reply to the Dutch Note with Regard to the Extradition of the Ex-Emperor, DBFP VII, pp. 600–1; Annexe 1, Projet de réponse à la note hollandaise, FMAE A/64, A-1025-4.

114. Annexe 2—Projet de Lord Curzon, FMAE A/64, A-1025-4.

115. Notes of a Conference of Ambassadors and Foreign Ministers, London, 23 March 1920, 4 pm, DBFP VII, pp. 591–3; Notes of a Conference of Ambassadors and Foreign Ministers, London, 24 March 1920, 4 pm, DBFP VII, pp. 606–16; Reply to the Dutch Government, as approved by the Conference of Ambassadors and Foreign Ministers, 24 March 1920, DBFP VII, pp. 616–17; Texte du projet de réponse au Gouvernement hollandaise, relative au séjour de l'ex-empereur sur le territoire des Pays-Bas, FMAE A/64, A-1025-4; Notes of a Conference of Ambassadors and Foreign Ministers, London, 26 March 1920, 3.30 pm, DBFP VII, pp. 650–8.

116. Millerand to Berthelot, 25 March 1920, FMAE A/64, A-1025-4.

117. Lloyd George to PM of the Netherlands, 24 March 1920, LG F/147/7/4.

118. Curzon to French Ambassador in London, 25 March 1920, DBFP IX, pp. 727–8; Curzon to Graham, 26 March 1920, DBFP IX, p. 728; Graham to Curzon, 29 March 1920, DBFP IX, p. 728; Benoist to Millerand, 30 March 1920, FMAE A/64, A-1025-4.

119. Charles Hardinge, *Old Diplomacy*, London: John Murray, 1947, p. 248.

120. 'Trial of the Ex-Kaiser, Mr Lloyd George and His Election Pledge', *The Times*, 5 November 1920, p. 5.

121. Treaty of Versailles: Annotations of the Text, FRUS PPC XIII, pp. 55–754, at p. 376.

122. *France et al. v. Goering et al.*, Judgment, (1947) 1 IMT 171, at pp. 329–30.

123. John C. G. Röhl, *Wilhelm II: Into the Abyss of War and Exile 1900–1941*, Cambridge: Cambridge University Press, 2014, pp. 1263–7.

CHAPTER 18

1. Texte de la réponse à la Hollande (Extradition de l'Ex-Empereur), FMAE A/64, A-1025-4; BPNL 156, pp. 490–2. The note was published: 'Ex-Kaiser Still Intriguing, Allies' Advice to Holland', *The Times*, 17 February 1920, p. 18.

2. Convention on the Prevention and Punishment of the Crime of Genocide, (1951) 78 UNTS 277, Art. 7.

3. Geneva Convention for the Amelioration of the Condition of the Wounded and Sick in Armed Forces in the Field, (1950) 75 UNTS 31, Art. 49; Geneva Convention for the Amelioration of the Condition of Wounded, Sick and Shipwrecked Members of Armed Forces at Sea, (1950) 75 UNTS 85, Art. 50; Geneva Convention Relative to the Treatment of Prisoners of War, (1950) 75 UNTS 135, Art. 129; Geneva Convention Relative to the Protection of Civilian Persons in Times of War, (1950) 75 UNTS 287, Art. 146.

4. Convention Against Torture and Other Cruel, Inhuman or Degrading Treatment or Punishment, (1987) 1465 UNTS 85, Art. 7. See also *Questions relating to the Obligation to Prosecute or Extradite (Belgium v. Senegal)*, Judgment, ICJ Reports 2012, p. 422.

5. International Convention for the Protection of All Persons from Enforced Disappearance, (2010) 2716 UNTS 3, Art. 11.

6. Report of the International Law Commission, Sixty-eighth session (2 May–10 June and 4 July–12 August 2016), UN Doc. A/71/10, pp. 273–6.

7. Report of the International Law Commission, Sixty-sixth session (5 May–6 June and 7 July–8 August 2014), UN Doc. A/69/10, pp. 160–1.

8. Mohamed Hadi Zakerhossein and Anne-Marie de Brouwer, 'Diverse Approaches to Total and Partial *in Absentia* Trials by International Criminal Tribunals' (2015) 26 *Criminal Law Forum* 186.

9. Agreement for the Prosecution and Punishment of Major War Criminals of the European Axis, and Establishing the Charter of the International Military Tribunal (IMT), Annex, (1951) 82 UNTS 279, Art. 12.

10. *France et al. v. Goering et al.*, Judgment, (1947) 1 IMT 171, at p. 338. See also: Preliminary Hearing, Saturday, 17 November 1945, (1947) 1 IMT 26; Order of the Tribunal Regarding Notice to Defendant Bormann, (1947) 1 IMT 102–3; Certificates of Compliance with Orders of the Tribunal Regarding Notice to Members of Groups and Organisations and to Defendant Bormann, (1947) 1 IMT 104–6.

11. *Prosecutor v. Ayyash et al.* (STL-11-01/I/TC), Decision to Hold Trial *in Absentia*, 1 February 2012; *Prosecutor v. Ayyash et al.* (STL-11-01/I/TC), Decision on Reconsideration of the *in Absentia* Decision, 11 July 2012; *Prosecutor v. Ayyash et al.* (STL-11-01/PT/AC/AR126.1), Decision on Defence Appeals Against Trial Chamber's Decision on Reconsideration of the Trial *in Absentia*, 1 November 2012.

12. F. Larnaude and A. de Lapradelle, 'Inquiry into the Penal Liabilities of the Emperor William II', in Commission on the Responsibility of the Authors of the War, Minutes of Meetings of the Commission, USNA 181.1201/16, pp. 4–18, at p. 18.

13. ibid. p. 16.

14. Memorandum submitted by the British delegates, 13 February 1919, USNA 181.1201/16, pp. 27–33, at p. 28, at p. 32.

15. Meeting of the Imperial War Cabinet, 10 Downing Street, 20 November 1918, 12 noon, TNA CAB/23/37/37, p. 5. The précis of Curzon's remarks in the Cabinet Minutes finds slightly more ample development in Lloyd George's account: David Lloyd George, *Memoirs of the Peace Conference*, New Haven, CT: Yale University Press, 1939, pp. 56–7.

16. Leonard Mosley, *Curzon: The End of an Epoch*, London: Longmans, 1960, pp. 186–7.

17. Notes of an Allied Conference, 10 Downing Street, 11–12 February 1920, 3.30 pm, DBFP VII, pp. 12–21, at p. 13.

18. Crowe to Curzon, 3 October 1919, TNA FO 608/146/3; TNA FO 371/4271; DBFP V, pp. 609–10.

19. Millerand to Cambon, 6 March 1920, FMAE A/64, A-1025-4; Cambon to Millerand, 7 March 1920, FMAE A/64, A-1025-4; Cambon to Millerand, 9 March 1920, FMAE A/64, A-1025-4. See also: Cambon to Millerand, 10 March 1920, FMAE A/64, A-1025-4.

20. Millerand to Cambon, 9 March 1920, FMAE A/64, A-1025-4.

21. Curzon to Lloyd George, 7 July 1919, LG F/12/1/21; Lloyd George to Curzon, 8 July 1919, LG F/12/1/22.

22. Charles Benoist, *Souvenirs de Charles Benoist, 1902–1933*, Vol. III, Paris: Plon, 1933, p. 393.

23. Prévost to Millerand, 8 March 1920, FMAE A/64, A-1025-4.

24. Other writers have speculated on the conduct of a trial of the Emperor. See Paul Mevis and Jan M. Reijntjes, 'Hang the Kaiser! But for What, and Would It Be Justice?' (2014) 2 *Erasmus Law Review* 98; Hans Andriessen, Paul Mevis, and Willem Sinninghe Samsté (eds), *Het proces tegen Wilhelm II*, Tielt: Lannoo, 2016. There is also a book on the subject, written in the late 1930s by a Nazi sympathiser: George Sylvester Viereck, *The Kaiser on Trial*, Richmond, VA: Greystone Press, 1937.

25. *France et al. v. Goering et al.*, Dissenting Opinion of the Soviet Judge, (1947) 1 IMT 342.

26. Meeting of the Council of Four, 2 April 1919, 4 pm, Mantoux I, pp. 120–4, at p. 122; Deliberations I, pp. 115–24, at p. 120; WWP 56, pp. 525–34, at p. 532.

27. F. Larnaude and A. de Lapradelle, 'Inquiry into the Penal Liabilities of the Emperor William II', in Commission on the Responsibility of the Authors of the War, Minutes of Meetings of the Commission, USNA 181.1201/16, pp. 4–18, at p. 14.

28. Meeting of the Imperial War Cabinet, 10 Downing Street, 20 November 1918, 12 noon, TNA CAB 23/37/37, p. 5.

29. Notes of an Allied Conversation held in the Cabinet Room, 10 Downing Street, 2 December 1918, 4 pm, TNA CAB 28/5 (IC 99), pp. 3–4.

30. William A. Schabas, 'The United Nations War Crimes Commission's Proposal for an International Criminal Court' (2014) 25 *Criminal Law Forum* 171.

31. Report of the Commission on Responsibilities, USNA 181.1201/16, pp. 115–76, at p. 126.

32. F. Larnaude and A. de Lapradelle, 'Inquiry into the Penal Liabilities of the Emperor William II', in Commission on the Responsibility of the Authors of the War, Minutes of Meetings of the Commission, USNA 181.1201/16, pp. 4–18, at p. 15 (emphasis in the original).

33. Outline Suggested with regard to Responsibility and Punishment, LG F/147/8/9.

34. *United States v. Von Leeb et al.*, Judgment, (1949) 11 TWC 462; *United States v. Von Weizsaecker et al.*, Judgment, (1949) 14 TWC 308.

35. Report of the Commission on Responsibilities, USNA 181.1201/16, pp. 115–76, at p. 125.

36. Agreement for the Prosecution and Punishment of Major War Criminals of the European Axis, and Establishing the Charter of the International Military Tribunal (IMT), Annex, (1951) 82 UNTS 279, Art. VI(a).

37. *France et al. v. Goering et al.*, Indictment, (1947) 1 IMT 27, at pp. 84–92.

38. *France et al. v. Goering et al.*, Judgment, (1947) 1 IMT 171, at pp. 216–18.

39. See above, pp. 141, 144–6.

40. *France et al. v. Goering et al.*, Indictment, (1947) 1 IMT 27.

41. Article 227 of the Treaty of Peace, The Arraignment of William II of Hohenzollern, Memorandum on the Responsibility of William II of Hohenzollern for Acts Committed in Breach of the Laws of War, TNA TS 26/1.

42. For example, *United States v. Rauscher*, 119 US 407, 416–17 (1886).

43. Eugene Dreyfus, 'L'extradition de l'ex Empereur d'Allemagne Guillaume II, Point de vue allemand' (1920) *Revue du droit international* 132, at p. 143.

44. *France et al. v. Goering et al.*, Judgment, (1947) 1 IMT 171, at p. 222.

45. Hersch Lauterpacht, 'Draft Nuremberg Speeches' (2012) 1 *Cambridge Journal of International and Comparative Law* 45, at p. 55.

46. USNA 180.0201/6, pp. 50–1; FRUS PPC III, pp. 388–90; Conférence de Paix 1919–1920, *Recueil des Actes de la Conférence, Partie III*, Paris: Imprimerie Nationale, 1922, pp. 388–90.

47. *France et al. v. Goering et al.*, Judgment, (1947) 1 IMT 171, at p. 219.

48. ibid.

49. International Covenant on Civil and Political Rights, (1976) 999 UNTS 171, Art. 14(5).

50. *Empire v. Karl Neumann ('Dover Castle')*, (1922) 16 *American Journal of International Law* 704.

51. *In re. Yamashita*, 327 US 1; 66 SCt 340; 90 LEd 499; 'Trial of General Tomoyuki Yamashita', (1948) 4 LRTWC 1.

52. *Prosecutor v. Delalić et al.* (IT-96-21-T), Judgment, 16 November 1998; *Prosecutor v. Delalić et al.* (IT-96-21-A), Judgment, 20 February 2001; Guénaël Mettraux, *The Law of Command Responsibility*, Oxford: Oxford University Press, 2009.

53. Rome Statute of the International Criminal Court, (2002) 2187 UNTS 3, Art. 28.

54. Agreement for the Prosecution and Punishment of Major War Criminals of the European Axis, and Establishing the Charter of the International Military Tribunal (IMT), Annex, (1951) 82 UNTS 279.

55. *France et al. v. Goering et al.*, Judgment, (1947) 1 IMT 171, at p. 223.

56. *Handelsblad*, 29 December 1919, TNA TS 26/2; TNA FO 371/4272.

57. Isabel V. Hull, *A Scrap of Paper: Breaking and Making International Law During the Great War*, Ithaca, NY: Cornell University Press, 2014, pp. 322–5.

58. *France et al. v. Goering et al.*, Judgment, (1947) 1 IMT 171, at p. 313.

59. Aide-mémoire from the United Kingdom, 23 April 1945, in Robert H. Jackson, *Report of Robert H. Jackson, United States Representative to the International Conference on Military Trials*, Washington, DC: US Government Printing Office, 1949, pp. 18–20.

60. Report of Sub-Commission III on the Laws and Customs of War, USNA 181.1201/16, pp. 50–4, at p. 53.

61. Vittorio Emanuele Orlando, 'On the Aborted Decision to Bring the German Emperor to Trial' (2007) 5 *Journal of International Criminal Justice* 1015, at p. 1018.

62. Meeting of the Imperial War Cabinet, 10 Downing Street, 20 November 1918, 12 noon, TNA CAB 23/37/37, p. 5.

63. Alexandre Ribot, *Journal d'Alexandre Ribot et correspondances inédites, 1914–22*, Paris: Plon, 1936, p. 294.

64. Notes of a Conference of Ambassadors and Foreign Ministers, London, 23 March 1920, 4 pm, DBFP VII, pp. 591–8, at p. 594.

65. Historical Survey of the Question of International Criminal Jurisdiction—Memorandum submitted by the Secretary-General, UN Doc. A/CN.4/7/Rev.1, pp. 10–12.

66. *France et al. v. Goering et al.*, Judgment, (1947) 1 IMT 171, at p. 461.

67. Meeting of the Council of Four, 2 April 1919, 4 pm, Mantoux I, pp. 120–4, at p. 124; Deliberations I, pp. 115–24; WWP 56, pp. 525–34.

Bibliography

Abbreviations

BPNL	C. Smit (ed.), *Beschieden betreffende de buitenlandse politiek van Nederland, 1814–1919: Derde Periode, 1899–1919,* The Hague: Martinus Nijhoff, 1964–1974 and J. Woltring (ed.), *Documenten betreffende de buitenlandse politiek van Nederland 1919–1945: Periode A, 1918–1930,* The Hague: Martinus Nijhoff, 1976
DBFP	E. L. Woodward and Rohan Butler (eds), *Documents on British Foreign Policy,* First series, London: Her Majesty's Stationery Office, 1947–1960
Deliberations	Arthur Link (ed.), *The Deliberations of the Council of Four (March 24–June 28, 1919), Notes of the Official Interpreter, Paul Mantoux,* Princeton, NJ: Princeton University Press, 1992
DNA	Dutch National Archives
FMAE	Archives of the French Foreign Ministry
FNA	French National Archives
FRUS PPC	*Papers Relating to the Foreign Relations of the United States 1919, Paris Peace Conference,* Washington, DC: US Government Printing Office, 1942–1947
Hanworth Papers	Hanworth Papers (Bodleian Library, University of Oxford)
IMT	International Military Tribunal
LG	Lloyd George Papers (Parliamentary Archives)
LNTS	League of Nations Treaty Series
Lea Papers	Luke Lea Papers (Tennessee State Library and Archives)
LRTWC	Law Reports of the Trials of the War Criminals
Mantoux	Paul Mantoux, *Les délibérations du conseil des quatre (24 mars–28 juin 1919),* Paris: Centre national de la recherche scientifique, 1955
NAC	National Archives of Canada
Paix de Versailles	Alfred Geouffre de Lapradelle (ed.), *La Paix de Versailles, Responsabilité des auteurs de la guerre et des sanctions,* Vol. III, Paris: Éditions internationales, 1930
RA	Royal Archives (Windsor Castle)
Recueil des actes	Conférence de la Paix 1919–1920, *Recueil des actes de la Conférence, Partie IV B (2), Commission des responsabilités des auteurs de la guerre et sanctions,* Paris: Imprimerie nationale, 1922

Scott Papers	James Brown Scott Papers (Georgetown University)
TNA	The National Archives (United Kingdom)
TSLA	Tennessee State Library and Archives
TWC	Trials of the War Criminals
UNWCC	United Nations War Crimes Commission
UNTS	United Nations Treaty Series
USNA	United States National Archives
WWP	Arthur S. Link (ed.), *The Papers of Woodrow Wilson*, Princeton, NJ: Princeton University Press, 1987–1989

UNPUBLISHED SOURCES

Archivio centrale dello Stato (Rome)
    Vittorio Emanuele Orlando Papers
Bodleian Library, University of Oxford
    Hanworth Papers
    Curzon Papers
Georgetown University Library
    James Brown Scott Papers
Ministère des Affaires étrangères, Paris
    Guerre (1914–1918), Turquie
    Pays-Bas (1918–1929)
    Série A Paix (1914–1920)
Nationaal Archief (The Hague)
    Correspondence respecting the Kaiser's royal train (2.04.78)
    Van Karnebeek Diary (2.05.25 inventaris 54)
    Legal opinion—Loder, Struyken and Bres to Van Karnebeek
        (2.05.25 inventaris 144)
National Archives (College Park, MD)
    Records of the American Commission to Negotiate Peace (RG 256)
National Archives (Kew Gardens, London)
    Cabinet Papers (CAB 23, 24, 28, 29)
    Treasury Solicitors (TS 3, 26)
    Foreign Office (FO 371, 608)
Parliamentary Archives (House of Lords)
    Lloyd George Papers
Royal Archives (Windsor Castle)
    George V Papers
Tennessee State Archives
    Luke Lea Papers
    Thomas Perkins Henderson Papers
Yale University Library
    Frank L. Polk Papers

PUBLISHED DOCUMENTARY COLLECTIONS

France

Conférence de la Paix 1919–1920, *Recueil des actes de la Conférence, Partie IV B (2), Commission des responsabilités des auteurs de la guerre et sanctions*, Paris: Imprimerie nationale, 1922.

Lapradelle, Albert Geouffre de (ed.), *La Paix de Versailles, Responsabilité des auteurs de la guerre et des sanctions*, Paris: Éditions internationales, 1930.

Germany

German White Book Concerning the Responsibility of the Authors of the War, New York: Oxford University Press, 1924.

The Netherlands

Smit, C. (ed.), *Beschieden betreffende de buitenlandse politiek van Nederland, 1814–1919: Derde Periode, 1899–1919*, The Hague: Martinus Nijhoff, 1964–1974.

Woltring, J. (ed.), *Documenten betreffende de buitenlandse politiek van Nederland 1919–1945: Periode A, 1918–1930*, The Hague: Martinus Nijhoff, 1976.

United Kingdom

Dockrill, M. (ed.), *British Documents on Foreign Affairs, Series I, The Paris Peace Conference of 1919, British Empire Delegation Minutes, March–June 1919, Reports of Peace Conference Commissions*, Vol. IV, Frederick, MD: University Publications of America, 1989.

Woodward, E. L. and Rohan Butler (eds), *Documents on British Foreign Policy*, First series, London: Her Majesty's Stationery Office, 1947–1960.

United States

Link, Arthur S. (ed.), *The Papers of Woodrow Wilson*, Princeton, NJ: Princeton University Press, 1987–1989.

Papers Relating to the Foreign Relations of the United States, 1919, Paris Peace Conference, Washington, DC: US Government Printing Office, 1942–1947.

Papers Relating to the Foreign Relations of the United States, 1915, The World War, Washington, DC: US Government Printing Office, 1928.

Papers Relating to the Foreign Relations of the United States, Robert Lansing Papers, 1914–1919, Washington, DC: US Government Printing Office, 1940.

BOOKS AND JOURNAL ARTICLES

'Affaire Vogelgesang' (1915) 42 *Journal du droit international* 54.

'Baron Edouard Rolin-Jaequemyns' (1937) 18 *British Yearbook of International Law* 156.

'Germany and the Neutrality of Belgium' (1914) 8 *American Journal of International Law* 877.

Abbenhuis, Maartje M., *The Art of Staying Neutral: The Netherlands in the First World War, 1914–1918*, Amsterdam: University of Amsterdam Press, 2006.

Afflerbach, Holger (ed.), *Kaiser Wilhelm II. als Oberster Kriegsherr im Ersten Weltkrieg. Quellen aus der militärischen Umgebung des Kaisers. 1914–1918*, Munich: Oldenbourg, 2005.

Andriessen, Hans, Paul Mevis, and Willem Sinninghe Samsté (eds), *Het proces tegen Wilhelm II*, Tielt: Lannoo, 2016.

Ashton, Nigel J. and Duco Hellema, "'Hang the Kaiser!"; De Brits-Nederlandse betrekkingen en het lot van ex-Keizer Wilhelm II, 1918–1920', in Duco Hellema, C. Wiebes, and B. Zeeman (eds), *Buitenlandse Zaken: Vierde Jaarboek voor de geschiedenis van de Nederlandse politiek*, The Hague: Sdu Uitgevers, 1998.

Ashton, Nigel J. and Duco Hellema, 'Hanging the Kaiser: Anglo-Dutch Relations and the Fate of Wilhelm II, 1918–20' (2000) 11(2) *Diplomacy and Statecraft* 53.

Baldwin, Simeon E., 'The Proposed Trial of the Former Kaiser' (1919) 29 *Yale Law Journal* 75.

Bass, Gary, *Stay the Hand of Vengeance: The Politics of War Crimes Tribunals*, Princeton, NJ: Princeton University Press, 2000.

Bassiouni, M. Cherif, 'World War I: "The War to End All Wars" and the Birth of a Handicapped International Justice System' (2001–2002) 30 *Denver Journal of International Law and Policy* 244.

Bassiouni, M. Cherif, *Introduction to International Criminal Law*, Ardsley, NY: Transnational, 2003.

Baumont, Maurice, *The Fall of the Kaiser*, London: Allen & Unwin, 1931.

Becker, Jean-Jacques and Gerd Krumeich, '1914: Outbreak', in Jay Winter (ed.), *The First World War*, Vol. I, Cambridge: Cambridge University Press, 2014, pp. 39–64.

Bellot, Hugh H. L., 'War Crimes: Their Prevention and Punishment' (1916) 2 *Problems of the War: The Grotius Society, Papers Read before the Society in the Year 1916* 31.

Bellot, Hugh H. L., 'The Detention of Napoleon Buonaparte' (1923) 23 *Law Quarterly Review* 170.

Bennett, G., *British Foreign Policy during the Curzon Period, 1919–24*, London: Springer, 1995.

Bennett, John Wheeler, *Hindenberg: The Wooden Titan*, London: Macmillan, 1936.

Benoist, Charles, *Souvenirs de Charles Benoist, 1902–1933*, Vol. III, Paris: Plon, 1933.

Bentinck, Norah, *The Kaiser in Exile*, New York: George Doran, 1921.

Binion, Rudolph, *Defeated Leaders: The Political Fate of Caillaux, Jouvenel, and Tardieu*, New York: Columbia University Press, 1960.

Borden, Robert, *Robert Laird Borden: His Memoirs*, London: Macmillan, 1938.

Bothe, Michael, 'Neutrality, Concept and General Rules', in Rüdiger Wolfrum (ed.), *The Max Planck Encyclopedia of Public International Law*, Vol. VII, Oxford: Oxford University Press, 2012, pp. 617–34.

Caldwell, C. E., *Field Marshall Sir Henry Wilson: His Life and Diaries*, Vol. 2, London: Cassell, 1927.

Camp, William, *The Glittering Prizes, A Biographical Study of F. E. Smith, First Earl of Birkenhead*, London: Macgibbon & Kee, 1960.

Cardozo, Benjamin, *The Nature of the Judicial Process*, New Haven, CT: Yale University Press, 1921.

Cardozo, Benjamin, *The Growth of the Law*, New Haven, CT: Yale University Press, 1924.

Cassese, Antonio, *International Criminal Law*, 2nd edn, Oxford: Oxford University Press, 2008.

Churchill, Winston S., 'The Truth about the Ex-Kaiser', *Colliers*, 25 October 1930, pp. 16, 42–6.

Churchill, Winston S., *Great Contemporaries*, London: Putnam, 1937.

Churchill, Winston S., *The World Crisis: The Aftermath, 1918–1922*, Vol. IV, London: Bloomsbury, 2015.

Clark, Christopher, *Iron Kingdom: The Rise and Downfall of Prussia, 1600–1947*, Cambridge: Belknap Press, 2006.

Clark, Christopher, *Kaiser Wilhelm II: A Life in Power*, London: Penguin, 2009.

Clemenceau, Georges, *Grandeurs et misères d'une victoire*, Paris: Plon, 1930.

Coudert, F. R., 'An Appeciation of James Brown Scott' (1943) 37 *American Journal of International Law* 559.

Cowles, Virginia, *The Kaiser*, London: Collins, 1963.

Decaux, Emmanuel, 'Le statut du Chef d'État déchu' (1980) 26 *Annuaire français de droit international* 101.

Deperchin, Annie, 'The Laws of War', in Jay Winter (ed.), *The First World War*, Vol. I, Cambridge: Cambridge University Press, 2014, pp. 615–38.

Dreyfus, Eugene, 'L'extradition de l'ex Empereur d'Allemagne Guillaume II, Point de vue allemand' (1920) *Revue du droit international* 132.

Dumas, J., *Les sanctions pénales des crimes allemands*, Paris: Librairie A. Rousseau, 1916.

Form, Wolfgang, 'Law as Farce: On the Miscarriage of Justice at the German Leipzig Trials: The Llandovery Castle Case', in Morten Bergsmo, Cheah Wui Ling, and Yi Ping (eds), *Historical Origins of International Criminal Law*, Vol. 1, Brussels: Torkel Opsahl Academic EPublisher, 2014, pp. 299–322.

Frey, Marc, *Der Erste Weltkrieg und die Niederlande, Ein neutrales Land im politischen und wirtschaftlichen Kalkül der Kriegsgegner*, Berlin: Walter, 2009.

Garner, James W., *International Law and the World War*, London: Longmans Green, 1920.

Garner, James W., 'Punishment of Offenders against the Laws and Customs of War' (1920) 14 *American Journal of International Law* 70.

George, David Lloyd, *Memoirs of the Peace Conference*, New Haven, CT: Yale University Press, 1939.

Gill, T. D. and Elise van Sliedregt, 'Guantánamo Bay: A Reflection on the Legal Status and Rights of "Unlawful Enemy Combatants"' (2005) 1 *Utrecht Law Review* 28.

Graven, Jean, 'La première tentative consecutive à la guerre mondiate de 1914–1918', in Julius Stone and Robert K. Woetzel (eds), *Towards a Feasible International Criminal Court*, Geneva: World Peace through Law Centre, 1970, pp. 96–103.

Gutsche, W., *Ein Kaiser im Exil: Der Letzte Deutsche Kaiser Wilhelm II in Holland; Ein Kritische Biographie*, Marburg: Willibald Hirtzeroth, 1991.

Hankey, Maurice, *The Supreme Control at the Paris Peace Conference 1919: A Commentary*, London: Allen & Unwin, 1963.

Hardinge, Charles, *Old Diplomacy*, London: John Murray, 1947.

Harris, Ruth, 'The "Child of the Barbarian": Rape, Race and Nationalism in France during the First World War' (1993) 141 *Past & Present* 170.

Hathaway, Oona A. and Scott J. Shapiro, *The Internationalists*, New York: Simon & Schuster, 2017.

Headlam, James Wycliffe, *The History of Twelve Days: July 24th to August 4th, 1914*, London: T. Fisher Unwin, 1915.

Henkel, Gerd, *Die Leipziger Prozesse: Deutsche Kriegsverbrechen und ihre strafrechtliche Verfolgung nach dem Ersten Weltkrieg*, Hamburg: Hamburger Institute, 2003.

Henkel, Gerd, *The Leipzig Trials: German War Crimes and Their Legal Consequences after 1921*, Dordrecht: Republic of Letters, 2014.

Hohenzollern, Luise Viktoria, *The Kaiser's Daughter*, London: W. H. Allen, 1977.

Hohenzollern, Wilhelm, *The Kaiser's Memoirs*, New York and London: Harper and Brothers, 1922.

Holmes, Oliver Wendell, Jr, 'The Path of the Law' (1897) 10 *Harvard Law Review* 457.

Holsti, R., 'Nicolas Politis, 1872–1942' (1942) 36 *American Journal of International Law* 475.

Horne, Charles F. (ed.), *Source Records of the Great War*, Vol. VI, [New York]: National Alumni, 1923.

Horne, John and Alan Kramer, 'German "Atrocities" and Franco-German Opinion, 1914: The Evidence of German Soldiers' Diaries' (1994) 66 *Journal of Modern History* 1.

Horne, John and Alan Kramer, *German Atrocities, 1914: A History of Denial*, New Haven, CT and London: Yale University Press, 2001.

Howe, Mark DeWolfe (ed.), *Holmes–Pollock Letters, The Correspondence of Mr Justice Holmes and Sir Frederick Pollock, 1874–1932*, Vol. II, Cambridge, MA: Belknap Press, 1961.

Hull, Isabel V., *A Scrap of Paper: Breaking and Making International Law During the Great War*, Ithaca, NY: Cornell University Press, 2014.

Hymans, Paul, *Mémoires*, Brussels: Université libre de Bruxelles, 1958.

Ilsemann, Sigurd von, *Der Kaiser in Holland, Aufzeichnungen des letzten Flügeladjutanten Kaiser Wilhelms II*, Vol. 1 : *Amerongen und Doorn, 1918–1923*, Munich: Biederstein, 1968.

Ilsemann, Sigurd von, *Der Kaiser in Nederland, I, Aantekeningen van de laatste vleugeladjudant van keizer Wilhelm II uit Amerongen en Doorn 1918–1923*, Baarn: Hollandia, 1968.

Ilsemann, Sigurd von, *Wilhelm II in Nederland 1918–1941, Dagboekfragmenten bezorgd door Jacco Pekelder en Wendy Landewé*, Soesterberg: Aspekt, 2014.

Jackson, Robert H., *Report of Robert H. Jackson, United States Representative to the International Conference on Military Trials*, Washington, DC: US Government Printing Office, 1949.

Jonas, Klaus W., *The Life of Crown Prince William*, Pittsburgh, PA: University of Pittsburgh Press, 1961.

Jong van Beek en Donk, B. de, 'Switzerland, Holland, and the League of Nations' (1920) 82(1) *The Advocate of Peace* 22.

Kampmark, Binoy, 'Sacred Sovereigns and Punishable War Crimes: The Ambivalence of the Wilson Administration towards a Trial of Kaiser Wilhelm' (2007) 53 *Australian Journal of Politics and History* 519.

Kohlrausch, Martin, *Der Monarch im Skandal. Die Logik der Massenmedien und die Transformation der wilhelminischen Monarchie*, Berlin: Akademie, 2005.

Kohlrausch, Martin, 'Meer dan eenden voederen, Nieuwe literatuur over keizer Wilhelm II en Nederland' (2017) 130 *Tijdschrift voor Geschiedenis* 625.

Lansing, Robert, *The Big Four, and Others of the Peace Conference*, New York: Houghton Mifflin, 1921.

Lansing, Robert, *The Peace Negotiations: A Personal Narrative*, Boston and New York: Houghton Mifflin, 1921.

Lapradelle, Albert Geouffre de and Ferdinand Larnaude, *Examen de la responsabilité pénale de l'Empereur Guillaume II d'Allemagne*, Paris: Imprimerie nationale, 1918.

Lapradelle, Albert Geouffre de and Ferdinand Larnaude, 'Examen de la responsabilité pénale de l'Empereur Guillaume II d'Allemagne' (1919) 46 *Journal du droit international* 131.

Lauren, Paul Gordon, *The Evolution of Human Rights: Visions Seen*, Philadelphia, PA: University of Pennsylvania, 1998.

Lauterpacht, Hersch, 'Draft Nuremberg Speeches' (2012) 1 *Cambridge Journal of International and Comparative Law* 45.

Lea, Luke and William T. Alderson, 'The Attempt to Capture the Kaiser' (1961) 20 *Tennessee Historical Quarterly* 222.

Lewis, Mark, *The Birth of the New Justice: The Internationalisation of Crime and Punishment*, Oxford: Oxford University Press, 2014.

Link, Arthur (ed.), *The Deliberations of the Council of Four (March 24–June 28, 1919), Notes of the Official Interpreter, Paul Mantoux*, Princeton, NJ: Princeton University Press, 1992.

Linn, Brian McAllister, *The US Army and Counterinsurgency in the Philippines*, Chapel Hill, NC and London: University of North Carolina Press, 1989.

Lipkes, Jeff, *Rehearsals: The German Army in Belgium, 1914*, Leuven: Leuven University Press, 2007.

Lombardi, Giorgio, 'Il Trattato di Pace di Versailles ed il mancato processo al Kaiser', in P. Ungari and M. P. Pietrosanti Malintoppi (eds), *Verso un Tribunale permanente internazionale sui crimini contro l'umanità. Precedenti storici e prospettive di istituzion*, Rome: Euroma La Goliardica, 1998, pp. 31–4.

London International Assembly, *Reports on Punishment of War Crimes*, London, 1943.

Ludwig, Emil, *Kaiser Wilhelm II*, London and New York: G. P. Putnam's Sons, 1926.

MacMillan, Margaret, *Paris 1919: Six Months That Changed the World*, New York: Random House, 2001.

Mantoux, Paul, *Les délibérations du conseil des quatre (24 mars–28 juin 1919)*, Paris: Centre national de la recherche scientifique, 1955.

Mantoux, Paul, *Paris Peace Conference 1919: Proceedings of the Council of Four (March 24–April 18)*, Geneva: Droz, 1964.

Maogoto, Jackson Nyamunya, 'The 1919 Paris Peace Conference and the Allied Commission: Challenging Sovereignty through Supranational Criminal Jurisdiction', in Morten Bergsmo, Cheah Wui Ling, and Yi Ping (eds), *Historical Origins of International Criminal Law*, Vol. 1, Brussels: Torkel Opsahl Academic EPublisher, 2014, pp. 171–94.

Marescotti, Luigi Aldrovandi, *Guerra diplomatica; ricordi e frammenti di diario (1914–1919)*, Milan: Mondadori, 1936.

Marescotti, Luigi Aldrovandi, *Nuovi ricordi e frammenti di diario*, Milan: Mondadori, 1938.

Marescotti, Luigi Aldrovandi, *Guerre diplomatique, 1914–1919*, Paris: Gallimard, 1939.

Marescotti, Luigi Aldrovandi, *Der Krieg der Diplomaten; Erinnerungen und Tagebuchauszüge, 1914–1919*, Munich: Paul Hugendubel, 1940.

Marks, Sally, *Innocent Abroad: Belgium at the Paris Peace Conference of 1919*, Chapel Hill, NC: University of North Carolina Press, 1981.

Marks, Sally, 'Edouard Rolin-Jaequemyns', in Warren F. Kuehl (ed.), *Biographical Dictionary of Internationalists*, Westport, CT: Greenwood Press, 1983, pp. 624–5.

Marks, Sally, '"My Name Is Ozymandias": The Kaiser in Exile' (1983) 16(2) *Central European History* 122.

Mattäus, Jürgen, 'The Lessons of Leipzig: Punishing German War Criminals after the First World War', in Patricia Heberer and Jürgen Mattäus (eds), *Atrocities on Trial: Historical Perspectives on the Politics of Prosecuting War Crimes*, Lincoln, NE: University of Nebraska Press, 2008, pp. 3–23.

McCall, Jack H., Jr, '"Amazingly Indiscreet": The Plot to Capture Wilhelm II' (2009) 73 *Journal of Military History* 449.

Mettraux, Guénaël, *The Law of Command Responsibility*, Oxford: Oxford University Press, 2009.

Mevis, Paul and Jan M. Reijntjes, 'Hang the Kaiser! But for What, and Would It Be Justice?' (2014) 2 *Erasmus Law Review* 98.

Miller, David Hunter, *My Diary at the Conference of Paris, with Documents*, Vol. III, [New York]: Printed for the author, 1924.

Montgelas, Max and Walter Schücking (eds), *Outbreak of the World War: German Documents Collected by Karl Kautsky*, New York: Oxford University Press, 1924.

Mordacq, Henri, *Le Ministère Clemenceau, Journal d'un témoin*, Paris: Plon, 1931.

Morgan, J. H., 'The Late Hugh Bellot, An Appreciation' (1928) 14 *Transactions of the Grotius Society, Problems of Peace and War, Papers Read before the Society in the Year 1928* xv.

Morris, Virginia and Michael Scharf, *An Insider's Guide to the International Criminal for the former Yugoslavia*, Irvington-on-Hudson, NY: Transnational Publishers, 1995.

Mosley, Leonard, *Curzon: The End of an Epoch*, London: Longmans, 1960.

Müller-Meiningen, Ernst, *Who are the Huns? The Law of Nations and Its Breakers*, Berlin: Georg Reimer, 1915.

Mullins, Claud, *The Leipzig Trials: An Account of the War Criminals' Trials and a Study of German Mentality*, London: Witherby, 1921.

Nelson, Keith L., *Victors Divided: America and the Allies in Germany, 1918–1923*, Berkeley, CA: University of California Press, 1975.

Neuner, Matthias, 'When Justice Is Left to the Losers: The Leipzig War Crimes Trials', in Morten Bergsmo, Cheah Wui Ling, and Yi Ping (eds), *Historical Origins of International Criminal Law*, Vol. 1, Brussels: Torkel Opsahl Academic EPublisher, 2014, pp. 333–78.

Nevins, Allan (ed.), *The Letters and Journal of Brand Whitlock*, New York and London: Appleton Century, 1936.

Nicolson, Harold, *King George the Fifth: His Life and Reign*, London: Constable, 1952.

Orlando, Vittorio Emanuele, *Raccolta di scritti di diritto pubblico in onore di Giovanni Vacchelli, Vita e pensiero*, Milan: Università Catolica del Sacro Cuore, 1938.

Orlando, Vittorio Emanuele, *Scritti varii di diritto publicco e scienza politica*, Milan: Giuffrè, 1940.

Orlando, Vittorio Emanuele, *Memorie (1915–1919)*, Milan: Rizzoli, 1960.

Orlando, Vittorio Emanuele, 'On the Aborted Decision to Bring the German Emperor to Trial' (2007) 5 *Journal of International Criminal Justice* 1015.

Otte, T. G., *July Crisis: The World's Descent into War, July 1914*, Cambridge: Cambridge University Press, 2014.

Phillipson, Coleman, *International Law and the Great War*, London: T. Fisher Unwin, 1915.

Pic, P., 'Violation systématique des lois de la guerre par les Austro-Allemands; Les sanctions nécessaires' (1916) 23 *Revue générale du droit international public* 243.

Pollard, John, *The Papacy in an Age of Totalitarianism*, Oxford: Oxford University Press, 2014.

Pollock, Frederick, *For my Grandson: Remembrances of an Ancient Victorian*, London: John Murray, 1933.

Pyta, Wolfram, *Hindenburg, Herrschaft zwischen Hohenzollern und Hitler*, Munich: Siedler, 2007.

Reinermann, Lothar, 'Fleet Street and the Kaiser: British Public Opinion and Wilhelm II' (2008) 26 *German History* 469.

Renault, Louis, 'De l'application du droit pénal aux faits de guerre' (1915) 42 *Journal du droit international* 313.

Rhea, Harry M., *The United States and the International Criminal Tribunals*, Antwerp: Intersentia, 2012.

Rhea, Harry M., 'The Commission on the Responsibility of the Authors of the War and on Enforcement of Penalties and Its Contribution to International Criminal Justice after World War II' (2014) 25 *Criminal Law Forum* 147.

Ribot, Alexandre, *Journal d'Alexandre Ribot et correspondances inédites, 1914–22*, Paris: Plon, 1936.

Rikhof, Joseph, 'The Istanbul and Leipzig Trials: Myth or Reality?', in Morten Bergsmo, Cheah Wui Ling, and Yi Ping (eds), *Historical Origins of International Criminal Law*, Vol. 1, Brussels: Torkel Opsahl Academic EPublisher, 2014, pp. 259–96.

Robertson, Geoffrey, *The Tyrannicide Brief*, London: Vintage, 2006.

Röhl, John C. G., *The Kaiser and his Court: Wilhelm II and the Government of Germany*, Cambridge: Cambridge University Press, 1996.

Röhl, John C. G., *Wilhelm II: The Kaiser's Personal Monarchy, 1888–1900*, Cambridge: Cambridge University Press, 2004.

Röhl, John C. G., *Wilhelm II: Into the Abyss of War and Exile 1900–1941*, Cambridge: Cambridge University Press, 2014.

Rose, Kenneth, *King George V*, London: Macmillan, 1983.

Rosen, Friedrich, *Aus Einem Diplomatischen Wanderleben*, Wiesbaden: Limes Verlag, 1959.

Roskill, Stephen, *Hankey: Man of Secrets*, Vol. II: *1919–1931*, London: Collins, 1972.

Sands, Philippe, *East West Street*, London: Weidenfield & Nicolson, 2016.

Schabas, William A., 'The United Nations War Crimes Commission's Proposal for an International Criminal Court' (2014) 25 *Criminal Law Forum* 171.

Schabas, William A., *The International Criminal Court: A Commentary on the Rome Statute*, 2nd edn, Oxford: Oxford University Press, 2016.

Schabas, William A., 'Nikolaos Politis and the Earliest Negotiation to Establish an International Criminal Court', in Jean-Paul Jacqué, Florence Benoît-Rohmer, Panagiotis Grigoriou, and Maria Daniella Marouda (eds), *Liber Amicorum Stelios Perrakis*, Athens: I. Sideris, 2017, pp. 167–77.

Schabas, William A., 'International Prosecution of Sexual and Gender-Based Crimes Perpetrated During the First World War', in Martin Böse, Michael Bohlander, André Klip, and Otto Lagodny (eds), *Festschrift for Wolfgang Schomburg*, Leiden: Brill, 2018, pp. 395–410.

Scheffer, David, *All the Missing Souls: A Personal History of the War Crimes Tribunals*, Princeton, NJ: Princeton University Press, 2012.

Scheffer, H. J., *November 1918: Journaal van een Revolutie die niet Doorging*, Amsterdam: De Bataafsche Leeuw, 1984.

Scheidemann, Philipp, *Memoiren eines Sozialdemokraten*, Vol. 2, Dresden: Reissner, 1928.

Schindler, D. and J. Toman (eds), *The Laws of Armed Conflicts*, The Hague: Martinus Nijhoff, 1988.

Schlup, Leonard, 'Pugnacious Progressive: Senator Luke Lea as a Political Leader from Tennessee in the Wilson Era' (1984) 21 *International Review of History and Political Science* 52.

Schuursma, Rolf, 'Het beste van het interbellum: Herman Adriaan van Karnebeek (1918–1927)', in Duco Hellema, Bert Zeeman, and Bert van der Zwan (eds), *De Nederlandse ministers van Buitenlandse Zaken in de twintigste eeuw*, Utrecht: Sdu, 1999, pp. 82–97.

Scott, James Brown, 'The Case of Captain Fryatt' (1916) 10 *American Journal of International Law* 865.

Scott, James Brown, 'The Trial of the Kaiser', in Edward M. House and Charles Seymour (eds), *What Really Happened at Paris*, London: Hodder & Stoughton, 1921.

Sellars, Kirsten, 'Delegitimizing Aggression: First Steps and False Starts after the First World War' (2012) 10 *Journal of International Criminal Justice* 10.

Sellars, Kirsten, 'Trying the Kaiser: The Origins of International Criminal Law', in Morten Bergsmo, Cheah Wui Ling, and Yi Ping (eds), *Historical Origins of International Criminal Law*, Vol. 1, Brussels: Torkel Opsahl Academic EPublisher, 2014, pp. 195–212.

Sellars, Kirsten, 'The First World War, Wilhelm II and Article 227: The Origin of the Idea of "Aggression" in International Criminal Law', in Claus Kreß and Stefan Barriga (eds), *The Crime of Aggression: A Commentary*, Cambridge: Cambridge University Press, 2017.

Sharp, Alan, *David Lloyd George*, London: Haus Publishing, 2008.

Shimazum, Naoko, *Japan, Race and Equality: The Racial Equality Proposal of 1919*, London: Routledge, 2009.

Sicilianos, L. A. and T. Skouteris, 'Editorial Note' (2012) 23 *European Journal of International Law* 215.

Sluis, Rolf ter, *De 'Keizer-Quaestie', Nederland en de vlucht van Wilhelm II, november 1918–maart 1920*, Doorn: Foundation Simon Vestdijk, 1996.

Smit, C., *Diplomatieke geschiedenis van Nederland: inzonderheid sedert de vestiging van het Koninkrijk*, The Hague: Martinus Nijhoff, 1950.

Smith, F. E., *The Speeches of Lord Birkenhead*, London: Cassell, 1929.

Stehlin, S. A., 'The Emergence of a New Vatican Diplomacy during the Great War and Its Aftermath, 1914–1929', in P. C. Kent and John Pollard (eds), *Papal Diplomacy in the Modern Age*, Westport, CT: Praeger, 1991.

Temperley, H. W. V. (ed.), *A History of the Peace Conference of Paris*, Vol. I, London: Henry Frowde and Hodder & Stoughton, 1920.

Tidwell, Mary, *Luke Lea of Tennessee*, Bowling Green, OH: Bowling Green State University Popular Press, 1993.

Tillman, Seth P., *Anglo-American Relations at the Paris Peace Conference of 1919*, Princeton, NJ: Princeton University Press, 1961.

Townley, Susan, *'Indiscretions' of Lady Susan*, New York: D. Appleton & Co., 1922.

Tuyll van Serooskerken, Hubert P. van, *The Netherlands and World War I: Espionage, Diplomacy and Survival*, The Hague: Brill, 2001.

Tuyll van Serooskerken, Hubert P. van, *Small Countries in a Big Power World: The Belgian–Dutch Conflict at Versailles, 1919*, The Hague: Brill, 2017.

United Nations War Crimes Commission, *History of the United Nations War Crimes Commission and the Development of the Laws of War*, London: HMSO, 1948.

Vane, Charles (ed.), *Memoirs and Correspondence of Viscount Castlereagh*, 3rd series, Vol. II, London: William Shoburl, 1851.

Viereck, George Sylvester, *The Kaiser on Trial*, Richmond, VA: Greystone Press, 1937.

Vollenhoven, Maurice van, *Memoires, beschouwingen, belevenissen, reizen en anecdoten*, Amsterdam: Elsevier, 1946.

Vollenhoven, Maurice van, *Les Vraies ambassades. Considérations sur la vie. Souvenirs d'un diplomate*, Brussels: Elsevier, 1954.

W. A. B., 'Hugh H. L. Bellot, D. C. L.' (1928) 14 *Transactions of the Grotius Society, Problems of Peace and War, Papers Read before the Society in the Year 1928* xi.

Weinstein, Edwin A., *Woodrow Wilson: A Medical and Psychological Biography*, Princeton, NJ: Princeton University Press, 1981.

Wieland, Lothar, *Belgien, 1914: Die Frage des belgischen 'Franktireurkrieges' und due deutsche öffentliche Meinung von 1914 bis 1936*, Frankfurt: Peter Lang, 1984.

Willis, James F., *Prologue to Nuremburg: The Politics and Diplomacy of Punishing War Criminals of the First World War*, Westport, CT and London: Greenwood Press, 1982.

Wright, Quincy, 'The Legal Liability of the Kaiser' (1919) 13 *American Political Science Review* 120.

Zakerhossein, Mohamed Hadi and Anne-Marie de Brouwer, 'Diverse Approaches to Total and Partial *in Absentia* Trials by International Criminal Tribunals' (2015) 26 *Criminal Law Forum* 186.

Index